For Alma, Christiane   Eva, Marga and Samuel

inside the **visible**

impulse of the **possible**

Cecilia Vicuña, 1994

Womanliness therefore could be assumed and worn as a mask, both to hide the possession of masculinity and to avert the reprisals expected if she was found to possess it—much as a thief will turn out his pockets and ask to be searched to prove that he has not the stolen goods. The reader may now ask how I define womanliness or where I draw the line between genuine womanliness and the "masquerade." My suggestion is not, however, that there is any such difference; whether radical or superficial, they are the same thing.

—Joan Rivière, 1929

I would call "feminine" the moment of rupture and negativity which conditions the newness of any practice.

—Julia Kristeva, 1974

The matrix is a feminine unconscious space of simultaneous co-emergence and co-fading of the I and the stranger that is neither fused nor rejected. Links between several joint partial subjects co-emerging in differentiation in rapports-without-relating, and connections with their hybrid objects, produce/interlace "woman" that is not confined to the contours of the one-body with its inside versus outside polarity, and indicate a sexual difference based on webbing of links and not on essence or negation.

—Bracha Lichtenberg Ettinger, 1995

CLAUDE CAHUN, *Self-Portrait*, 1932. Gelatin silver print.
10 x 7.7 cm. Collection of John Wakeham, Jersey.

INSIDE THE VISIBLE

an elliptical traverse of 20th century art

in, of, and from the feminine

curated and edited by M. Catherine de Zegher

The Institute of Contemporary Art, Boston
The Kanaal Art Foundation, Kortrijk, Flanders

The MIT Press
Cambridge, Massachusetts, and London, England

This catalogue is published on the occasion of the exhibition *Inside the Visible,* subtitled *Begin the Beguine in Flanders* that was initiated at the Béguinage of Saint-Elizabeth, Kortrijk (Flanders, Belgium) and organized by the Kanaal Art Foundation from April 16, 1994 to May 28, 1995. The exhibition has been granted the honorary title of "Cultural Ambassador of Flanders" by the Flemish Government in 1994-95.

ICa

Inside the Visible was further elaborated and organized by The Institute of Contemporary Art, Boston. It was exhibited at the ICA from January 30 to May 12, 1996.

Through the generosity of:

CULTURAL AMBASSADOR OF FLANDERS

Milena Kalinovska

We hoped! The verdict? . . . only tears,
each one cut off from everyone,
rudely cut off, tripped up, thrown down,
blood siphoned from the heart. Dead stone,
she walks still, sways . . . alone.
—Anna Akhmatova, "The Requiem," 1940

I am beginning with an excerpt from a poem by the Russian poet Anna Akhmatova, dedicated to the millions of victims of Stalinist persecution, in order to give a voice to silenced witnesses. Akhmatova is known to have broken with literary conventions. Intensely feminine and historically rooted, she gave an unwavering poetic expression to an anguish that her nation suffered during terrible times. Anna Akhmatova personifies both the social dimension and the artistic qualities that characterize the artists of *Inside the Visible*. Exploring concepts of sexual and racial "otherness," Catherine de Zegher's selection reflects these artists' breadth of concerns and manner of working, showing the intensity of vision that they have contributed to the art of the twentieth century. Purposely, de Zegher has looked at three distinct periods, the 1930s–40s, 1960s–70s, and 1990s, politically and socially intense times when women artists responded with true imagination that distinctly marked the art they produced.

It has been exhilarating for The ICA to participate in organizing *Inside the Visible*, which has grown out of a series of twelve individual process-oriented exhibitions organized by the Kanaal Art Foundation at the Béguinage of Kortrijk, a medieval secular convent in a small town in Flanders, Belgium. Developing the notion of "women's work" from a specific social and historical site where women lived apart from mainstream society, this exhibition considers how women develop an intrinsically direct visceral and evocative language. This language approximates and translates the experience of working outside of codified patriarchal culture. Using this site as a starting point for understanding artwork created by women in the twentieth century is one of the innovative challenges that informed the process of this exhibition.

On the occasion of "Expanding Internationalism: A Conference on International Exhibitions," held in May 1990 in Venice, a number of curators, critics, and writers from different parts of the world gathered to ask themselves questions such as: what are the new models of exhibitions? What would reengage artists and the public in a true understanding of the process of making art? What kind of impact should this have on the process of making exhibitions? One of the key conclusions was the need to respond with each exhibition to the place in which the exhibition originates. The truly focused international exhibition takes into account the diversity of situations and is sensitive to the contradictory history of cultural exchanges.

Cross-cultural exchange, in the case of the present exhibition, has aimed for a fusion of the work from the past to that of the present in an institution which, while 60 years old, has been dedicated to current thought. Never shying away from controversy or hard questioning, The ICA cherishes independence and promotes exhibitions that attempt to open doors to new understandings of our culture. The experience of women artists, existing outside of the mainstream in the twentieth century, calls for our attention and reevaluation. *Inside the Visible* began as a project outside of established forms, making creative use of a historically pertinent site, and was guided by a desire to make a difference to the cultural scene well beyond the site where it was originally conceived. This exhibition is a tribute to the implicit passages from the local to the global, from the specificity of each woman's work to their prominent role in art of this century.

I would like to commend the Flemish Community in Belgium for so generously sponsoring and encouraging this entire process, which has culminated in a major international exhibition presented in the United States. Our gratitude goes to the Minister President of the Government of Flanders, Luc Van den Brande; former Minister of Culture Hugo Weckx; Minister of Culture Luc Martens; Minister of Justice of the Federal Government of Belgium, Stefaan De Clerck; Federal Minister of Employment and Equal Opportunity Policy, Miet Smet; Federal Minister of Finances, Philippe Maystadt; Maria De Smet; Diane Verstraeten; Chris Rogiers; Jan Vermassen; Philippe Capiau; Bart Hendrickx; Françoise Maertens; Jenny Van Gelder; the Province of West Flanders; the City and the Public Center for Social Welfare of Kortrijk; and the National Lottery of Belgium.

It has indeed been an honor and a pleasure to work with Catherine de Zegher, Director of the Kanaal Art Foundation and Visiting Curator of The ICA, and to share in her process of thinking. Including over 120 historical and contemporary works of art from collections worldwide and resting on a basis of complex scholarly thinking and writing, *Inside the Visible* is a project extremely ambitious in scope. I would like to express my heartfelt gratitude to all who have made this exhibition possible: an extraordinary group of artists and writers; Catherine David, who, along with Branka Bogdanov, selected a series of films from the 1920s to the present, including works by: Germaine Dulac, Agnes Varda, Maya Deren, Marguerite Duras, Chantal Akerman, Sara Driver, Sue Friedrich, Helma Sanders-Brahms, Trinh Minh-ha, Jane Campion, Mona Hatoum, Kira Muratova, Barbara Loden, Peng Xio Lien, Yvonne Rainer, Ulrike Ottinger, and Franciska Lambrechts; Clara Wainwright, community artist who has collaborated with four area women's shelters and The ICA DocentTeens on a quiltmaking project, "Women and Shelter"; again, Branka Bogdanov for her innovative use of video to bring the perspectives of artists and scholars into view for our audiences; Laura Brown, for coordinating with artists Cecilia Vicuña and Gail Burton to present a poetry series that forms an integral layer of this exhibition; the numerous lending museums, galleries, and individuals; our generous funders; The ICA Exhibitions Committee, Board of Trustees, and members.

The staff of The ICA was particularly responsive to the demands of this challenging project, and I am extremely grateful to them all. It is through the in-depth research and tireless efforts of Marcella Beccaria that the loans were secured and the exhibition developed into completeness. Her commitment to this project was extraordinary. My thanks to Pat Kramer, whose tenacity and resourcefulness helped The ICA to cultivate new funding and community partners around this project. The thorough understanding and skillful grantwriting of Susan

Weiss also enabled us to undertake this project financially. The various aspects of this remarkable publication were coordinated with sensitivity and rigor by Kristen Lubben, an intern whose initiative and dedication are exemplary. My deep thanks to Tim Obetz for his care regarding the installation and design concerns that mark any truly complex exhibition; and to Lia Gangitano for her leading support of these efforts throughout the process of Inside the Visible. The curatorial department was assisted by exceptional interns who generously volunteered their time and knowledge: Carmen Sofia Asteinza, Jessica Dandona, Chris Hadrick, Lara Neubauer, Maria Ritz, and Jason Zalk. Also for their continued support, ICA staff members: Chris McCarthy, the installation crew, gallery staff, and DocentTeens.

My thanks to the President of the Kanaal Art Foundation, Francis De Beir, to the Board of Directors, and to the staff, particularly Arlette Libeer, for diligently working together with us. It is a pleasure to collaborate with architect Paul Robbrecht, whose specially designed juxtapositions of works in the exhibition have kept in mind the importance of the continual reinvention of the aesthetic experience. We welcome his insights into our space.

Catherine de Zegher would also like to express her gratitude to all of the artists, writers, and advisors for contributing so generously to the development of this project. Her warm thanks go to Jean Fisher and Catherine David for their valuable advice from the earliest phases of this project; Benjamin Buchloh for accompanying her along with keen criticism and everlasting encouragement; Bracha Lichtenberg Ettinger and Griselda Pollock for their insightful comments and continued support; Avis Newman, Cecilia Vicuña, and Anna Maria Maiolino for their instructive observations; Louise Bourgeois, Nancy Spero, Martha Rosler, Mona Hatoum, Ellen Gallagher, Lili Dujourie, Lynn Silverman, Ann Veronica Janssens, and Joëlle Tuerlinckx for their enthusiastic involvement; Paul De Vylder, Lawrence Rinder, Sônia Salzstein, Guy Brett, Yve-Alain Bois, Ernst van Alphen, Miwon Kwon, Margaret Sundell, Rina Carvajal, Sally Stein, Serge Guilbaut, Laurie Monahan, and Judith Mastai for their commitment to this project; and Philippe De Jaegere for his undiminished concern and patient generosity.

As a cross-cultural project, the catalogue of Inside the Visible has been an extremely demanding and, ultimately, rewarding experience. Our profound thanks to our collaborators at The MIT Press, without whose efforts and talents this publication would not have been achieved: Roger Conover, Daniele Levine, Matthew Abbate and Michael Sims. Lois Nesbitt had the immense task of editing the English manuscript, which she achieved with finely honed precision and unrelenting comprehension. Also our thanks are directed to all the translators for their sensitive exactitude. Luc Derycke provided an innovative design that accords well with the open-endedness of the book. The lithography was realized through the kind support of Stephan De Jaegere.

This exhibition and its programs have been made possible by the generous support of AT&T; Bank of Boston; the Boston Council for the Arts & Humanities; Arthur F. Blanchard Trust/Boston Safe Deposit and Trust Company, Trustee; Catherine and Paul Buttenwieser; Patricia Phelps de Cisneros; Sunny DuPree, Esq.; Charles Engelhard Foundation; Government of Flanders, Cultural Ambassadorship of Flanders; General Cinema/Neiman Marcus Publication Fund; Kapor Family Foundation; Barbara Fish Lee; Massachusetts Cultural Council; Ministério das Relações Exteriores e Ministério da Cultura do Brasil; National Endowment for the Arts, a federal agency; Bessie Pappas Charitable Foundation; Nathaniel Saltonstall Arts Fund; David Harold Stoneman Fund; Very Special Arts Massachusetts; Andy Warhol Foundation for the Visual Arts; Helene Wilson; and ICA patrons and members. They are also supported by the British Council and Goethe Institut, Boston.

In-kind support has been provided by Sabena Airlines, Phoenix Media Communications Group, Sonesta International Hotels Corporation, and TANK.

Milena Kalinovska

Various individuals and institutions have supported our research efforts during the course of this project, and I would like to express our gratitude to: Jerry Gorovoy; Wendy Williams, Diana Bulman, Robert Miller Gallery; Pamela Clapp; Adrien Ostier; Louise Downie, Jersey Museums Services; Suzanne Pagé, Gérard Audinet, Musée d'Art Moderne de la Ville de Paris; Zabriskie Gallery, New York; Leslie Tonkonow, New York; Rick Wester; Maïder Poustis, Berggruen & Cie; John Wakeham; Kate Bush, Institute of Contemporary Arts, London; J. J. Lee, Andrew Hunter, Vancouver Art Gallery; Matthew Teitelbaum, Art Gallery of Ontario; Lula Wanderley; Denise Mattar, Museu de Arte Moderna do Rio de Janeiro; Luciano Figueiredo, Projeto Hélio Oiticica; James Randeau, Andrea Miller-Keller, Wadsworth Atheneum, Hartford, Connecticut; Mario Diacono; Marjorie Jacobson; Americas Society, New York; Jay Joplin, White Cube, London; Corinne Diserens; Barry Rosen; Jackie Haliday, Gimpel Fils, London; Janice Slater, Scottisch National Gallery of Modern Art, Edinburgh; Claudia Gabriele Philipp, Museum für Kunst und Gewerbe, Hamburg; Glenn Lowry; Museum of Modern Art, New York; Rainer Schoch, Germanisches National Museum, Nürnberg; Kunst und Ausstellungshalle der Bundesrepublik Deutschland, Bonn; Freya Mülhaupt, Berlinische Galerie, Berlin; Maria Morzuch, Jaromir Jedlinski, Muzeum Sztuki, Lodz, Poland; Ikkan Art International, inc., New York; Catherine Docter, San Francisco; Barbara Haskell, Adam Weinberg, Whitney Museum of American Art, New York; Cécile Panzieri, Mary Sabbatino, Galerie Lelong, New York; Andrea Accornero; Guido Accornero; Paolo Accornero; Luciana Virando; Salone del Libro, Turin; Giancarlo and Giuliana Ellena Salzano; Corrado Levi; Caterina Riconda and Ruben Levi; Carla Monzini Garabelli; Riccardo Passoni, Sig. ra Gennuso; Galleria d'Arte Moderna e Contemporanea, Turin; Rodney Hill, Jay Gorney Modern Art, New York; Judith Belinfante, Stephan Hartog, Jewish Historical Museum, Amsterdam; Susan Fisher Sterling, National Museum of Women in the Arts, Washington D.C.; Per Hovdenakk, Henie-Onstad Kunstsenter, Hovikodden; Ada Schendel Bento; Sergio Fadel; Museu de Arte Contemporanea, São Paulo; Richard Akagawa; Elizabeth Finch, The Drawing Center, New York; Shari Zolla; Elizabeth Thompson; Christina Horeau, Galerie René Blouin, Montreal; Johannes Wasmuth; Walburga Krupp, Stiftung Hans Arp und Sophie Taeuber-Arp, Rolandseck; Tania Grunert; Argos Distribution, Brussels; Jean-François Jaeger, Galerie Jeanne Bucher, Paris; Guy Weelen; Galerie Alice Pauli, Lausanne; Denise Cadé Gallery, New York; Maria Balderama; Micheline Szwajcer Gallery, Antwerp; Scott Catto, P.P.O.W., New York; Leo Castelli Gallery, New York; Kunstsammlung Nordrhein Westfalen, Düsseldorf; Bill O'Connor, US Art International, Boston; and Frank Eulaers and Keith Brumberg, Maertens Art Transport, Brussels.

List of Lenders to the exhibition

Andrea Accornero, Turin
Paolo Accornero, Turin
Ada Schendel Bento, São Paulo
Guy Brett, London
Christine Buci-Glucksmann, Paris
Richard Castellane, Esq., Hubbardsville, New York
Gilberto Chateaubriand, Rio de Janeiro
Family of Lygia Clark, Rio de Janeiro
Frances and Thomas Dittmer, New York
Charlene Engelhard, Boston
Sergio Fadel, Rio de Janeiro
Fundação Calouste Gulbenkian, Centro de Arte Moderna José de Azeredo Perdigão, Lisbon
Fundación Gego, Caracas
Galerie Jeanne Bucher, Paris
Galerie Lelong, New York
Galleria Civica d'Arte Moderna e Contemporanea, Turin
Anna Garis, Turin
Galerie Berinson, Berlin
Germanisches Nationalmuseum, Nürnberg
Gimpel Fils, London
Jay Gorney Modern Art, New York
Konrad Gromholt, Hovikodden (Norway)
Pat Hearn Gallery, New York
Henie-Onstad Art Center, Hovikodden (Norway)
The Israel Museum, Jerusalem
Jewish Historical Museum, Amsterdam
Kanaal Art Foundation, Kortrijk (Belgium)
Helen Kornblum, St. Louis, Missouri
Lisson Gallery, London
Estate of Ana Mendieta
David Medalla, London
Robert Miller Gallery, New York
Museu de Arte Moderna do Rio de Janeiro
Muzeum Sztuki, Lodz (Poland)
Louise R. Noum, Des Moines, Iowa
Patricia Phelps de Cisneros, Caracas
P.P.O.W., New York
Private Collection, Des Moines, Iowa
Private Collection, New York
Private Collection, Paris
Private Collections, Turin
Sackner Archive of Concrete and Visual Poetry, Miami Beach, Florida
Giuliana Ellena Salzano, Turin
Private Collection, Edinburgh
Stiftung Hans Arp und Sophie Taeuber-Arp, e.V., Rolandseck (Germany)
Richard and Roselyne Swig, San Francisco
Jack Tilton Gallery, New York
Leslie Tonkonow, New York
University Art Museum, University of California at Berkeley
Vancouver Art Gallery, Emily Carr Trust
Wadsworth Atheneum, Hartford, Connecticut
The Whitney Museum of American Art, New York
Betty and George Woodman, New York
Donald Young Gallery, Seattle

We gratefully acknowledge those lenders who have participated after the date of publication and regret that their names cannot be mentioned here.

Edited by M. Catherine de Zegher
Designed by Luc Derycke
Lithography by Scancolor, Kortrijk (Belgium)
This book was printed and bound by Snoeck-Ducaju & Zoon, Ghent (Belgium).

Library of Congress Cataloging-in-Publication Data

Inside the visible : an elliptical traverse of twentieth century art in, of, and from the feminine / edited by M. Catherine de Zegher.
            p.   cm.
        Exhibition: Institute of Contemporary Art in Boston, Jan. 30–May 12, 1996.
        Includes bibliographical references.
        ISBN 0-262-54081-9 (pbk. : alk. paper)
        1. Women artists—Exhibitions. 2. Art, Modern—20th century—Exhibitions.
I. Zegher, M. Catherine de. II. Institute of Contemporary Art (Boston, Mass.)
N8354.I58 1996
704´.042´090407474461—dc20   95-47948
                                                                CIP

Contents

I. Parts of/for

1930s-40s

1960-70s

1990s

Contents

II. The Blank in the Page

III. The Weaving of Water and Words

IV. Enjambment: "La donna è mobile"

ETYMONS

---

not so   PN

DA DI ME   **ZAZZ**

OMA DO RE TÉ   **O MA QU**

ZI MATA DURA   **RRO RRO**

DI O. Q DURA   **RU K**

TI MA TOITURA   **ASHM ZT**

DI ZRATATITOILA   **PLGE**

                                  ZR KRN NMTOTO

LA LA LAR·R·RITA

LAR·R·RITA   **NM E SHCHU**

LAR·R·RITA   **KM NE SCU**

I love you

    mi o do ré mi   mi o
      "marmelade"

ADON LACROIX.

Introduction

Inside the Visible

M. Catherine de Zegher

T wo sound poems by the Belgian poet Adon Lacroix elliptically address artistic experience
that is folded into visibility, as into dough, shaping the exhibition *Inside the Visible*. The
first, "Visual Words, Sounds Seen, Thoughts Felt, Feelings Thought" (1917), favors haptic (as
distinguished from optical) space without establishing an opposition between the tactile and
the retinal. The poem reflects Lacroix's concern with the primacy of the idea in art but also
with the gesture, as she describes the participation of the audience in the creative act.[1] While
this poem introduces the notion of con-fusion and co-emergence (which will be discussed
below), the second poem, "Etymons" (1919),[2] through one rhythmic line of its multilingual
puns, triggers the notion of "eclipse." Both considerations, drawing on disciplines from phenomenology and psychoanalysis to art history and sociology, proved crucial in conceiving
Inside the Visible. Some details about Lacroix's life in the United States may clarify the association of ideas. In May 1914 Lacroix married the several years younger Emmanuel Radnitsky
(later known as Man Ray). She introduced him to her realm of language (Belgian and French
poetry and art), translating and reading to him the works of literary adventurers such as
Mallarmé, Rimbaud, and Lautréamont. Later Lacroix became the interpreter between Man
Ray and Marcel Duchamp, since Man Ray's French and Duchamp's English were only a few
steps beyond rudimentary.[3]

Reading her phonetic poem "Etymons," it occurred to me that the fifth line in the first
column, "DI O.Q DURA," and the third line in the second column, "O MA QU," significantly resemble in sound and in sign one of Duchamp's most famous works, *L.H.O.O.Q.*, dated
1919. Lacroix's poem (evidently composed some time before it was published, together with
work by Duchamp, in March 1919) is sufficiently close in date to Duchamp's "rectified"[4]
reproduction of the *Mona Lisa* to presume a connection. Although this remains an educated
guess, it seems to me that Lacroix's sentence probably figured as an *idée reçue*, or another
available readymade for Duchamp and the "master's" narrative. His "mistress's" voice disappeared a few years later, when Lacroix officially divorced Man Ray after a long and painful
process involving disputes over finances. Consequently, she no longer belonged to "the
group." More important than proving that Duchamp used Lacroix's dadaist poem is the role of
the woman as muse—as readymade[5]—appropriated and erased. The former approach only
raises inexpedient questions of originality, filiation, and belatedness (who was first?), while
the latter introduces the critical reading of woman as sign or as *objet trouvé*, the coming-into-
language and articulation of " beginnings," and the underlying mechanisms of "in/visibility" at
issue in the exhibition.

If the above speculation is true, Duchamp's attitude might be more sexist (or misogynist) than a first reading of the phonetic punning of the title *L.H.O.O.Q.* ("Elle a chaud au cul"— "She has a hot bottom") suggests: the woman as a deceiver, *a-muse*, and a seducer. However, as Jon Thompson demonstrates, Duchamp is too complex to admit such a one-sided formulation of gender and sexual difference: "The title, replete with its subversive erotic meanings, together with the drawn addition of masculine facial hair, serves to complete a complex, cyclical process of double-inversion, from female into male and back into female once again. In linguistic terms the title turns the whole arrangement into the very model of the 'demi-tour.'"[6] Thompson continues: "In as far as it is intended to restore or to 'rectify,' to return the object to its original identity in some way, it is motion toward the neutral, toward, if you like, the primal state of the mythic androgyne. . . . This point of neutrality, as well as a location for transformation, is also a locus of reconciliation." It is the "hinge" that, for Duchamp, determines the sum total of relationships (Jean-François Lyotard). The either/or is simply not applicable. The principle of opposition, mainly exemplified by an oscillation between male and female parts in his work, thus inaugurating a recurrent pattern of mutual confirmation in which the recognition of difference is endlessly delayed, is in this sense only realizable in a fluid, ongoing engagement. "Difference is a form of transaction: it is of the very essence of the 'Infra-thin' that difference exists not in things, but in the space between them. The idea of observable, fixed, masculine and feminine characteristics is thus the product of a curtailment of exchange out of which there arises an illusion of difference."[7]

Difference is far more entangled and complex than we like to admit. Taking this into account, I have attempted to develop an exhibition concept that bypasses the artificiality of "oppositional thinking" while acknowledging the work of deconstructionism, feminism, and poststructuralism, which has been instrumental in revealing the operations that tend to marginalize certain kinds of artistic production while centralizing others. Unfolding as an open-ended process, this exhibition is prompted by observation of multiple convergences in aesthetic practices both in time (over different periods of the twentieth century) and in space (in different parts of the world). The curatorial procedure may be likened to an excavation of material traces and fragmentary histories, which would be recombined into new stratigraphies or configurations to produce new meanings and insights of reality. Several recurrent cycles, rather than a linear survey with its investment in artistic originality and genealogies, structure the exhibition. This suggests a hybrid form of modernism not bound "to the progressive and decisive character of avant-gardism: the play of reference, deference and difference."[8] Clustering in three periods, the selection of works exploring reiterative material processes echoes recurrent social-political-economic situations: around the 1930s–40s, 1960s–70s, and 1990s. This conception disregards mainstream formations and includes women artists of different backgrounds and of diverse artistic practices. Moreover, as the work crosses different temporal and spatial zones, finding new audiences each with its own symbolic worldview, it undergoes shifts in significance. The exhibition thus addresses the specificity of the encounter between work and viewer and the continual reinvention of the aesthetic experience.

As a manifestation of culture, art both reflects changing sociopolitical and economic circumstances and expresses a singular thought, yet it is not reducible to either. Despite the recurrence of similar crises throughout the twentieth century, such as the periodic rise of state repression, nationalism, and xenophobia, different times demand different resolutions. Nonetheless, at times of crisis, there seems to be an urge to deconstruct existing representational codes, to search for "new beginnings," in order to imagine the world anew. At any time, there exist different perceptions of the same reality, or material expressions of coexisting and often conflicting realities. That which does not fit has too often been dismissed, delayed, or rendered invisible by the privileged terms of hegemonic elites whose existence is nevertheless predicated on this eclipse of difference. One aim of this exhibition is to break down such polarities, allowing the perturbing, the dissenting, the dangerous, the repressed to reemerge and to ask if it is possible to think "difference" without naming it and subsuming it under reductive and totalizing systems of thought (naming the Other: that is, identifying, classifying, separating, and fixing alterity). Is it possible to deracialize and degender difference and think it in positive, nonreifying terms?[9] To seek work in which "sameness" and "difference" are in a perpetual state of mutual negotiation where one neither swallows nor ejects the other?[10]

This shifting experience and thought are embodied in the exhibited works by an absence of fixity that attends to the ambiguous, the permuting, the composite, the flexible, the ephemeral. We may draw an analogy between this attitude of negotiating alterity and Derrida's play of the supplement or trace—that which both adds to and substitutes for an imaginary "origin": a perpetual reinscription that resists hierarchies and fixed positions. In this sense, the notions of interdependency (Derrida) and co-emergence (Lichtenberg Ettinger) are basic to the selection of works and the development of the exhibition. *Inside the Visible* attempts to echo the potential of the selected works, revealing content through its formal iconographical process rather than imposing a form on a predetermined semantic content. The image that comes to mind is a web, a network of traces formed not from any a priori image but through the working processes themselves. Umberto Eco would call it "open work," one that is "in-formed" but does not display a readily available content, thereby allowing the viewer the freedom to imagine several possible realities. If art is to do more than replicate established signs and mediated realities, then it must continuously place in circulation the "not-yet-commodified" language. According to Jean Fisher, "If we talk about the context of art, it must also be in its specificity and mutability, not only in terms of the conditions of its making (the perspectives of the artist) but also of its reception (its relation with a diversity of viewers). It is here that the affectivity of a work of art (its potential to act and to be acted upon) is reducible neither to essence, as in the modernist tradition, nor to sociopolitical forces, a tendency in some postmodernist discourses."[11]

Certain art practices separated themselves from the rise of repressive totalitarian systems[12]—in prewar Europe during the 1930s and 1940s; after 1968 in Europe and North and South America (during the dictatorships); and in the 1990s, with racism and conservatism increasing everywhere. These practices, on which my selection draws, often feature similar material processes that address alterity. Instead of responding with traditional models and reaffirming obsolete conventions of pictorial representation, some "internationally less known" (women) artists have articulated independent voices. Contributing next to the restrictive main axis of modernism, they have addressed questions of distribution and audience, of participation and the "feminine." Psychoanalysis and feminist art practice/theory enable us today to see and to focus on what is in eclipse, or what does not align with what is considered important at the moment or has different qualities of perceptibility. Through repoliticizing the body, the ceaseless play of unraveling (hidden) traps of language, and challenging the triumphant gaze, some women artists have participated for decades in the development of issues essential to the art of the 1990s.

A major topic in contemporary art and feminist art theory is the problematic of the gaze and its relation to the phallic. The exhibition examines another possibility of seeing than the gaze as analyzed and recognized by phallocentric theories. This exploration is not new, however; it is at stake in the legacies of twentieth-century art, as the works produced by diverse women artists represented here make clear. What is new is its symbolization through theorizing and naming—as the "matrixial gaze," by Bracha Lichtenberg Ettinger[13]—which makes it legible in the works of art. This radically extends and reshapes our understanding of some artistic practices, but also of their temporary eclipse. Following Lichtenberg Ettinger's painting and psychoanalytical theory, Griselda Pollock states that modalities based on the rejection/assimilation (self/other, love/hate, aggression/identification) paradigm apply to how paintings are viewed as much as to how societies treat immigrants. "What is not us, strange and unknown, be that woman for man, the other for the white European, the painting for the viewer is positioned under this phallic logic as either one of the two terms: to be assimilated and if that is not possible to be cast off as completely other."[14]

Lichtenberg Ettinger, using her psychoanalytic experience combined with a feminist anxiety about the unacknowledged elements of feminine specificity in that discourse, argues for "a shift of the phallic" by introducing the "matrix." She draws on the image—even at this time of paranoia about essentialism—of the intrauterine meeting in the late stages of pregnancy as a model for human situations and processes in which the *non-I* is not an intruder but a partner in difference. Matrix is thus, to summarize Lichtenberg Ettinger's ideas,

> an unconscious space of simultaneous emergence and fading of the *I* and the unknown *non-I*; matrix is a shared borderspace in which *differentiation-in-co-emergence* and *distance-in-proximity* are continuously rehoned and reorganized by metramorphosis created by—and further creating—*relations-without-relating* on the thresholds of being and absence, memory and oblivion, subject and object, me and the stranger, I and non-I. The metramorphic consciousness has no center, it constantly slides to the borderline, to the margins. Its gaze escapes the margins and returns to the margins. Through this process the limits, borderlines, and thresholds conceived are continually transgressed or dissolved, thus allowing the creation of new ones.[15]

Furthermore, Pollock argues,

> If we allow ourselves to introduce into culture another symbolic signifier to stand beside the phallus (signifier of difference and division in terms of absence and loss orchestrating these either/or models), could we not be on the way to allowing the invisible feminine bodily specificity to enter and realign aspects of our consciousness and unconsciousness? This will surely extend as do all these metaphors of sexual difference to other Others— issues of race, immigration, diaspora, genocide are tangled at the moment around the lack of means to signify other possible relations between different subjects—*I* and *non-I*. The matrix as symbol is about that encounter in difference which tries neither to master, nor assimilate, nor reject, nor alienate. It is a symbol of the coexistence in one space of two bodies, two subjectivities whose encounter at this moment is not an either/or. . . . This feminist theoretization is not an alternative in opposition to the phallus; rather, the opening up of the symbolic field to extended possibilities which, in a nonphallic logic, do not need to displace the other in order to be.[16]

Julia Kristeva's notion of semiotic analysis has provided us "necessary tools for systematic description of how images or languages or other sign systems produce meanings and positions for the consumption of meanings," or, in other words, has provided "new ways to understand the role of cultural activities in the making of meanings, but more importantly in the making of social subjects."[17] Some thus treat the work of art less as an object and more as a process that "creates" the subject, art as "a social practice, as a totality of many relations and determinations, i.e., pressures and limits."[18] Not only is art a part of social production; it is itself productive. Consequently, art is a crucial forum for the contestation of social arrangements. In this view art is not static and fetishized but above all dynamic: constitutive rather than constituted. If in order to become a fully social being the individual must become a fully competent user of language, and if language constructs both individualities, or subjects, and also the (social) link between them, the necessity for symbolizing and naming the feminine becomes clear.

By submitting the complex structure of visual language to critical analysis, hereby also drawing on ideas that emerge in art making, the exhibition further explores the sexual and the racial Other, which are deeply embedded in the collective cultural imagination. Paralleling this working method, where art is producer of theory and not only given to theory, the exhibition's concept was developed *after* the works. It seemed to me that, using a variety of visual forms and media, women artists have drawn attention to the margins and to latent interests operative in social strategies insisting on cultural and psychic limitations. Nevertheless, while feminist art history engages in a politics of knowledge and focuses on historical forms of explanation of women's artistic production (and omission), the women artists whose work is shown here appear to recognize that working within and not outside patriarchal discourse with what is on hand—a kind of bricolage—erodes established meanings and naturalized differences and destabilizes fixed gender and racial categories. Their need to deconstruct existing representational codes is a search for "beginnings"[19] in the sense described by Edward Said: "Beginning is making or producing difference; but difference which is the result of combining the already-familiar with the fertile novelty of human work in language. Beginning is basically an activity which ultimately implies return and repetition rather than simple linear accomplishment; beginning and beginning-again are historical whereas origins are divine; a beginning not only creates but is its own method because it has intention."[20]

Built upon associations of ideas, gathering and juxtaposing a wide range of works, the exhibition's method of selection and display evolves from this notion of "beginning," in the sense that its four sections are arranged as a series of investigations of some aspects of this concept. In turn, each section draws from three periods (around 1930s–40s, 1960s–70s, 1990s); together they constitute a frame with interconnections. The cyclic development or reinvention of artistic procedures shifting meanings, not the auratic original "as a moment of irretrievable plenitude and truth," motivates the project. The model of repetition—Freudian to begin with—has been discussed within the field of art in several essays by Benjamin Buchloh[21] and later by Hal Foster,[22] who endorses the Freudian notion of "deferred action" (*Nachträglichkeit*) as developed by Lacan. Avoiding mechanistic speculations about priority, influence, and imitation—which too often disavow or repress marginalized art practices—this approach considers simultaneous "rediscoveries" and repetitions of (avant-garde) paradigms by investigating the actual conditions of reception—the audience's disposition and demands, cultural legitimation, institutional mediation between demand and legitimation—and transformation. This clarification is developed within the discursive practice, without recourse to transcendental categories of causality and determination.[23] To expand this (post)structuralist approach to a larger group of artists at the periphery of the Western European and North American mainstream,[24] the exhibition presents aesthetic objects that emerge from these discursive formations and at first seem structurally, formally, and materially analogous to mainstream examples but that address "differences" and "delays" across other cultural space-times.

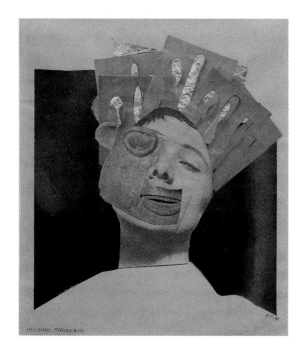

HANNAH HÖCH,
*Indische Tänzerin: Aus einem
ethnographischen Museum
(Indian Female Dancer: From an
Ethnographic Museum),*
1930. Photomontage. 10 1/8 x 8
7/8 in. The Museum of Modern
Art, New York,
Frances Keech Fund.

For extended periods in the twentieth century, pictorial strategies ranging from the ready-made and the photograph (sharing essential features), to collage and assemblage, to geometric abstraction, to the grid and constructed sculpture (all formally intricately connected), which sought to dislodge all transcendental modes of thinking and seeing, were often excluded from the general reception process, even more so when these practices challenged *other* ideological conventions of coding and of meaning in art.[25] *Inside the Visible*, which gradually unfolds in time and in space over each of the four sections, deliberately includes a variety of aesthetic strategies that go beyond the dichotomy of "original" and "readymade."[26] The exhibition points not only to the erasure of historical memory and exclusion of different sexual, racial, class, and ethnic subjectivities but also to the crucial role of women artists in gaining partial recognition of ignored subjectivities via identity politics and multicultural models.

As the title *Parts of/for* indicates, the first section regards women artists as active contributors to the vital enterprise of twentieth-century art. The term *parts for* addresses the actions assigned to woman as performer in the theater of/or life,[27] and *parts of* refers to the fragmentation and dismembering of the fetishized and above all silenced woman as sign. Triangulated by the common terms of sexuality, meaning, and language, the passive and abject image of woman subjected to the mastering gaze became itself the primary object for women in their manufacturing of sexual but also racial difference (often through self-portraiture). Even though the 1970s generated much feminist cultural activity, it was earlier, from the late 1920s through the 1940s, that artists such as Hannah Höch (Germany), Claude Cahun (France/U.K.), Louise Bourgeois (France/U.S.), and Carol Rama (Italy) articulated the problematics of bodies reduced to pieces, partial objects. Their reconciliation of existing visual and textual material (collage/montage) with their own specific formal languages (photography, painting, sculpture) both asserts and undermines sexual and racial difference. One way to be legible and comprehensible is to copy and overdo Western male discourse. An art practice that "doubles the mimicry back on itself, miming the miming, to the point where it becomes a strategy" produces a reverse discourse.[28]

In these works, aesthetic negotiation of the subject mirrors back to the viewer an imaginary bodily unity—as other and as cultural other—exposed, shattered, and collaged in pieces reiterating a fantasy of a chaotic body, fluid and fragmentary, both producer and consumer of desire and drives. According to Lacan, the ego fears most the return of this prior stage when the body was still in pieces and reacts aggressively against the chaotic world within and without, against that *stranger*, against all others who seem to represent this chaos and strangeness for us (women, Jews, black people, homosexuals, immigrants). Even if Lacan does not specify his theory of the subject as historical, Hal Foster—following Klaus Theweleit—believes that such a "traumatized, armored, and aggressive subject is not just any being across history and culture: it is a theory of the modern subject as fascistic subject."[29] To disarmor and challenge this holistic/fascistic subject these artists—Höch, Cahun, Bourgeois, and Carol Rama—in prewar Europe celebrated exactly the "dark" forces that most frightened it: sexuality, *jouissance*, the unconscious, surrendering it to fragmentation. They proceeded by painting (Carol Rama's *Marta, I Scopini*, etc.), drawing, or sculpting (Bourgeois's early wood sculptures) abject subject matter (the domestic, dirt, hair, excrement) deemed inappropriate by a conservative culture, or by montaging (often feminine) body parts with androgynous parts (Cahun's *Aveux non avenus*) or ethnographic fragments representing body parts (Höch's *From an Ethnographic Museum*). However, mocking the ideal of plenitude, with its illusion of homogenization (difference subsumed by wholeness), these works criticized political issues of the representation of race, class, and gender while diverging in an ironic way from the then-current (expressionist, even surrealist) use of primitivism and its pendant of patriarchal "primitivization" as the main instrument of authority through which gender, race, and class

are constituted.[30] "Oscillation is therefore important in Höch's montages—prompting a disjunctive shift between one allegorical reading and another, allowing different types of identification and distance."[31] Bourgeois's early wood sculptures differ from the "primitive" in that they issue from a personal identification of "relationships between one and others" in the others' absence.

Somewhere between displaying individualism and anti-individualism, the work of these artists raises questions about the body as commodity, institutional display, industrial obsession, and machinic fragmentation, but also about colonialism, world war, and military mutilation. In traumatic relation to such military-industrial events, the modern subject becomes armored against otherness within and without.[32] In the 1960s and 1970s, when the death of the subject was pronounced and when structuralism recoded all cultural activity as a language, some women artists, claiming their *selves* alive, again drew attention to these questions. Martha Rosler (U.S.), miming the fear of the shattered body by overdoing it in her collage series *Bringing the War Home* (1967–72) at the time of U.S. military involvement in Vietnam and in her video *Vital Statistics of a Citizen Simply Obtained* (1977), dispersed the fixed subject and disrupted its structures. In the obsessive and aggregate projection of the phallus (another body part and symbol of power) onto household objects, Yayoi Kusama (Japan) defied oppressive forces and male power by bringing it *inside* and by possessing it symbolically herself. Inversely, the Cuban artist Ana Mendieta brought the/her body outdoors and performed in various locations for the *Silueta, Fetish*, and *Rupestrian Sculptures* (1973–80). Despite the self-consciousness of this act, her earth/body works were often reduced to a primitivist interpretation of the "earth mother and the female will." But it was precisely through a process of self-othering, "a self-primitivizing," that Mendieta as a Third World woman artist turned our exoticizing gaze back onto us by literally affirming and tracing her silhouette, her absence. By insisting on recognition of the structuring principles of primi-

tivism—with its attributes of the threatening, the irrational, the repressed, the dangerous—these artists introduced explanations of how marginalization from public language is determined. At the same time, this has led paradoxically to a reinforced exclusion of their work from the "mainstream."

Predictably, the challenge to disrupt the dominant signifying continuity, to disturb identity, system, and order, and to problematize representational authority was taken up by a number of women artists and black artists. "What does not respect borders, positions, rules. The in-between, the ambiguous, the composite" has been described by Julia Kristeva as *abjection*. This theory draws on two key elements: a blurring of boundaries between self and other, which relates to psychoanalytic ideas of the "visceral unconscious" and the "bodily ego" and the notion of "base materialism" introduced by Georges Bataille, which challenges dominant concepts of the mind/body dualism and social taboos through investigation of degraded elements.[33] Although the concept of abjection has always been latent, it has been a central theoretical impulse in art of the 1990s. However, while in most current practices the abject entails a restriction of subjectivity to sexuality, gender, and ethnicity and dismantles historical reflection, some artists have developed a dialectic between the mnemonic dimension and politics of cultural representation, between human-made/technological reality and that imposed

CARRIE MAE WEEMS,
Untitled (Kitchen Table Series: Woman with friends),
1990.
Triptych, three silver prints.
27 1/4 x 27 1/4 in.
Courtesy of the artist and P.P.O.W. Gallery, New York.
Photo: John Marcy.

by nature. In this sense, always suggesting a becoming and transforming, the video installations of Jana Sterbak (Czechoslovakia/Canada) (e.g., *Declaration*, 1993; *Condition*, 1995,
realized in collaboration with the Belgian video artist Ana Torfs) and her "useless prosthesis-
like" sculptures have since the late 1970s pointed to the absurdity of our sociopolitical institutions and their inability to confront psychological reality. At the same time, these works
refuse the reduction described in Sterbak's quote from her countryman Milan Kundera's *Les
testaments trahis*: "I have always deeply, violently detested those who try to find an *attitude*
(political, philosophical, religious, etc.) in a work of art, instead of seeking therein an *intention to know*, understand or grasp some aspect or other of reality."

Around the intersection of (loaded) history, representation, and subjectivity, two artists,
from very different backgrounds, have made photodiptychs and -triptychs staging the self
through a series of "masquerades" in *tableaux vivants*: figurative in the *Untitled (Kitchen Table
Series)* (1990) of Carrie Mae Weems (U.S.), literal in the *Untitled (Portraits)* (1990–93) of
Nadine Tasseel (Belgium). In a spare studio setup of domestic ordinariness—a kitchen table
and overhead lamp—Weems articulates relationships in contemporary culture, moving
beyond the colonizing gaze of the deep-rooted stereotype toward an understanding of and
empathy for African Americans as "people first." Including herself as the female protagonist
acting in a fictional narrative, she breaks away from the more obvious and oppositional issues
of black-white relations to confront the contradictions within "black on black" involvements.[34]
Tasseel does not allow outdated patriarchal and painterly assumptions from (Flemish and
European) art history to overrule her own story. Against a decor of neo-Gothic Leatherette,
Tasseel's literal linking of the nude model with "womanliness assumed and worn as a mask"
(Joan Rivière)—masks made by cutting out images of women from Flemish primitives to
Italian mannerists—is rendered ironic by her photographic use of allegorical displacement.[35]

Parts of/for introduces an invisible feminine dimension of plurality and difference, on the one
hand by recognizing the enunciations of our feminist predecessors and on the other hand by
acknowledging the importance of their dissent from the phallic norms of fixed identity and
fixed boundaries. That a radical poetics of alterity is not feminine through mere transference
of some gendered essence becomes even more evident in the second section of the exhibition: *The Blank in the Page*. The works selected risk "incoherence" through their acceptance
that the act of marking the blank surface may constitute a refiguring or coming-into-language
from a space of uncertainty. As much as language is a vehicle to define the self, and thus a
means of empowerment, it also deidentifies the self since strangeness/otherness of the self
occurs as soon as it is constructed, outside the self, as soon as it is symbolized. Drawing or
writing: the tracing of the blank sheet is the beginning act of symbolizing the self and its reality. The exhibition explores the meanings and expressions privileged in drawing as "beginnings." This act is not to be interpreted as the sign of a transcendent subject but as a continuous redefining of existence, open to remappings and negotiations with alterity, seeking the
limits of the self and the knowable. Here the emphasis lies in spatiality and its metaphoric
implications: "transgression of borderlines," multidirectional mediation of alterity, of territory,
and so on.

In *Leben? oder Theater? Ein Singspiel (Life? or Theater? An Operetta*, 1940–42) by
Charlotte Salomon (Germany/France), the lyrics and images of her 784 painted pages cannot
be considered as mutually exclusive, with the words explaining the represented story and the
images illustrating the narrated events. Instead the handwriting and watercolors blur and distort in their interaction. In the beginning, the texts written on semitransparent tracing paper

veil the image, but inscription increasingly takes over the pictures toward the end of her *script*, as Salomon finished her book, surrendered, and sometime later died in Auschwitz at the age of twenty-six. Almost literally through her work, her *(song)play* of signs, she could be alive, following Kristeva, who would even say "that signs are what produce a body" and symbolic production has the power to constitute *soma*.[36] Facing the possibility of death (during girlhood in a house of suicides, schooling in a fascist state, and years in exile) Salomon told a chronicle of growth, an autobiography without an "I," where right from the question marks in the title she handed the main task to viewers: Unravel this story. See if it's true.[37]

Also reflected in a series of gouaches is Salomon's critical attitude toward the holistic notions of painting and its masterpieces. Although modernism challenged the premodern mode of a unique subject in a centralized composition and developed the postmodern notion of a contingent subject, modernism, and especially the project of abstraction—in its attempts at universality and nonhierarchical relationships—has banned drawing as the performance of the artist's masterful skills. It seems appropriate today to reconsider the transformation of "graphic gesture into mere facture" and to revalidate the act of drawing as "direct graphic notation" in all its different spatial aspects of the knowable.[38] Most striking therefore is the work of Hanne Darboven (Germany) from the 1970s through the 1990s. Oscillating between serial obsession and archival intention, here language is written or drawn in its most rational and formal way, responding to the modernist model, where the artist's physical competence in execution is abandoned and where endless and anonymous repetition and permutation are celebrated. But instead of abolishing drawing as the trace of individual inscription, the result of Darboven's persistent writing is delirious and carries the irrational in her installations. The serial nature of her archival work suggests that language as a system of symbolization conceals the fact that there is no ultimate order.

Conversely, the lengthy scrolls and friezes (*Stalks, Codex Artaud, Torture of Women* from the 1970s) of Nancy Spero (U.S.)—in the "apparent artlessness of arrangement, its calculated confusion of human and hybrid, male and female, mythic and modern, gesture and print, its modesty of material and process and its unexpected monumentality, the grandeur of its themes (abjection and *jouissance*), the elegance and diversity of its borrowings"—pull insistently yet ambivalently "toward *la peinture féminine* as some sort of parallel to the claims of French feminists such as Hélène Cixous to *l'écriture féminine*: which means to a form of writing marked by the pulsions of a female sexual body, and effecting various kinds of displacement on the western phallogocentric tradition of writing and the subject. . . . They scavenge. They offer stories about stories, images of other images, and they revel in parody, quotation and repetition."[39] But within this long, drawn-out sequence of sentence elements, significant blanks remain, stimulating the productivity of reading/looking itself, and with it the possibility of transformation. Furthermore, "the flexibility of drawing and collage becomes a metaphor for the malleable subject, traversed by conflicting and 'bisexual' (active and passive) desires."[40]

Since the exhibition favors "drawing," it seems appropriate to give a technical definition of drawing, which is to extend the gesture of making a picture, sketch or plan with a pencil, pen and ink, charcoal, or crayon into the gesture of accomplishing all kinds of prints (lithography, intaglio, etching, aquatint), montage/collage, and even some forms of painting (gouache, etc.), photography (a drawing with light), and sculpture (a drawing in space, a drawing in earth). The notion of flexibility and open-endedness in the selected works pervades the exhibition of those works. This attitude toward display is already imbricated in how Mira Schendel (Switzerland/Brazil) was installing her *Objetos graficos (Graphic Objects)* in

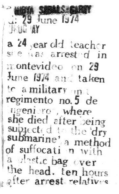

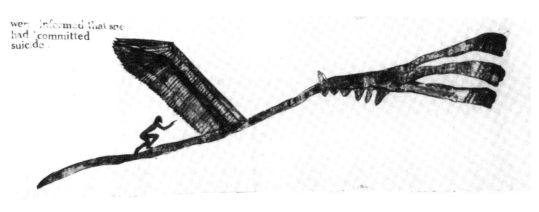

were informed that she
had committed
suicide.

a 24 year old teacher
she was arrested in
montevideo on 29
June 1974 and taken
to a military unit
regimento no. 5 de
ugeniero, where
she died after being
subjected to the 'dry
submarine' a method
of suffocation with
a plastic bag over
the head. ten hours
after arrest relatives

NANCY SPERO,
Torture of Women,
1976. Detail.
Handprinting,
painted collage on
paper.
20 in. x 1.25 ft.
(14 panels)
Collection
National Gallery
of Art, Ottawa.

Brazil in the 1960s and 1970s. Suspended in space, her repetitive marks, lines, scratches, and industrial and handwritten letters transferred onto thin translucent paper and mounted between transparent acrylic plates constitute a labyrinthine *ambience* for the reader, who, incited to circulate, can discern the work's opacity and transparency, front and back sides, casual and schematic content from an everyday experience of reality. "The blank paper in Schendel's work is the scene of disorientation, of indeterminacy—and of freedom: of possibility rather than necessity."[41]

These works tell us that neither perceptual vision nor skill is privileged, but rather a process appealing simultaneously to different senses and a development of nonrepresentational methods questioning the process of symbolization that produces a material thing. They not only favor tactility and sensuality but share a sensitivity for music in language (most explicit in the music scores of Salomon's *Operetta* and Darboven's *Symphonie Partituren*).[42] Consisting of photographic panels with automatic writing and an audiotape with recordings of simple, repetitive rhythms, Susan Hiller's (U.S./U.K.) *Élan* (1982) likewise offers multiple angles of entry: and often it is the rough sound. Both the improvised chanting and the "illuminated" script are wordless and indecipherable, although Hiller's voice, bereft of words, communicates, and her handmade marks convey meaning, albeit without revealing a literal content.[43] "Hiller's calligraphic script reclaims the earlier Surrealists' 'automatic writing' whose significance was lost in its aesthetic mutation into the reified gestural mark of late modernism. If this came to signify a creative self, by contrast, her performative gesture speaks of the creative process."[44]

Drawing on the impenetrable silences between words and images, the work of Lili Dujourie (Belgium) and Avis Newman (U.K.)—literally without sound—paradoxically resonates a human longing, a straining toward an indefinite objective, a coming-into-being: the otherness of language. For both artists, the illusionary antagonism of veiling and unveiling in Western pictorialism questions painting as a vehicle of self-definition. Dujourie's sculptures and videos from the early seventies deal with "the present hidden from view, the invisible because offstage." *American Imperialism* (1972), consisting of a steel sheet leaning against a monochromatically painted wall with the part of the wall behind the sheet unpainted, not only critiques an international aesthetic politics (minimalism) issuing from a hegemonic culture but also denounces each superficiality in the observation process. Her work can never be grasped from a single point of view and calls forth that which escapes the fixed (male) gaze, staging the other's appearance as a desired image. Her soundless videos in particular produce meaning through the rhythmic sensuality of bodily movements that underscore the instability of one's identity in language. Performing behind and in front of the camera, that voyeuristic instrument, Dujourie *acts* on and off the set. In the series *Hommage à* (1972–73) the "painter's model" remains mute, but we catch "the vibrations of the many voices of desire as it flows through the body that is also the body of the other" crawling over the bed, moving around, walking away out of sight, shooting the film, coming back, doubting.

In her painting installations from the late 1980s–90s, such as the *Backlight Series*, Newman "addresses the fear that attends any creative act, alluding directly to the Mallarméan fear of the blank page and to its equivalent in painting: the empty canvas. . . . In fact, the canvas is not empty, nor the page blank; there is no virgin territory. It is the awareness of all that the canvas itself represents that holds the artist back. 'Making your own mark', therefore, implies a denial of, or an act of 'transgression' against, previous practice— her own and others'—which is invariably accompanied by a sense of loss."[45] In both Newman's and Dujourie's work "the ordered naturalism of the Renaissance tradition is sub-verted by a sensitive understanding of the doubt inherent in Mannerist or Baroque illusion-ism and theatricality. In certain respects, Mannerism's dismantling of the Renaissance uni-verse of harmony and certitude parallels our current interrogation of Modernity: there is a recognition that the desire for an integrated subject of knowledge predicated on the absence of an other cannot be sustained where reality is felt to be otherwise."[46]

The material process of Newman's work—its veilings and unveilings, its tracings and retracings—by no means infers a search for transcendental origins, for "there is nothing that is not already a written trace." Jean Fisher argues that "rather, we might speak of retracing the borders between the unrepresentable lived body and the fictions with which it is surrounded, a leading back to the psychic truth of the present." In a very different perspective on "traces" of history, Bracha Lichtenberg Ettinger (Israel/France) produces her paintings from the 1990s, such as *Matrixial Borderlines* and *Autistworks*, by processing photocopies of exhumed documents (about exile, deportation, and the Holocaust) and items from her family album and from psychoanalytical reviews that are reproduced, veiled, manipulated, altered, or touched up with ink and paint, until the residual traces of the "originals" fuse with the new traces in this dissolution.[47] Effacing the effacement and any immediate reference, working between the inscription and the support, between appearance and disappearance, Lichtenberg Ettinger turns the gaze to that which cannot be looked at, "in an art of the palimpsest." Like Walter Benjamin and Edmond Jabès, these artists consider memory a source of transformative energy.

The interweaving of language, alterity, and space are further explored in the third section, *The Weaving of Water and Words*,[48] pivoting on works from the 1960s by Gego (Germany/Venezuela) and Agnes Martin (Canada/U.S.). Although they work in what has been referred to as the abstract sublime, their oeuvres are also informed by a relationship to nature—its ecstasy and immensity of space—and an interest in the weaving grid. How does this work (and furthermore the work of each artist in this section) relate to the sub-lime—or traumatic—other (of nature)? How does the viewer assume its grid formation? I will address these questions in terms of "the smooth and the striated" and/or of "the nomad and the sedentary space" as conceived by Gilles Deleuze and Félix Guattari.[49] A careful phenome-nological reading of Martin's paintings reveals "sequences of illusions of textures that change as viewing distance changes."[50] From an earlier materiality of the woven canvas, gesso, pen-ciled or painted grids and bands, "the paintings go atmospheric," or, rather, they feel like mist. Similarly, the accumulative system of joining wire cables in Gego's kinesthetic structures

Reticulárea (*ambientación*) and *Dibujos sin papel* go "cosmic" and engage the entering viewer in a process of bodily extension. Through the beholder's movements, the regular grid tracings—on canvas by Martin and in space by Gego (she calls her wire sculptures "drawings without paper")[51]—seem to dissolve or dematerialize. Here the striated space is not simply opposed to or different from the smooth space: the two only exist in mixture and in passages from one to another. In this sense, and conversely to one's expectation about the striated in fabric, Cecilia Vicuña's (Chile/U.S.) weavings from the 1970s–90s seem to belong to the smooth space, where variation and development of form are continuous and unlimited, where the lines go in all directions, where "the stop follows from the trajectory."[52] In nature or in the city, interior or exterior, Vicuña's work, its linkages, signals, and orientations change according to temporary vegetation, occupation, and precipitation.[53]

These works examine the flattened, geometrized, ordered grid as means of crowding out the dimensions of the real and of mastering the three-dimensional space in an instrumental, clear, or "objectivist optical" way. The fabric of the grid, the very weft of the object, dissolves, shifts, or fractures, leaving the subject-viewer without the unitary vantage that provides a sense of security and of control. "To liberate space from the tyranny of logic is also to free the eroticized body." Grasping at cityscapes, the destabilizing, distorted grid in the paintings (1930–90) of Maria Helena Vieira da Silva (Portugal/Brazil/France) dismembers (Renaissance) central perspective and proposes "an ungraspable (baroque) spatiality in its construction of a multitude of fragmentary glimpses."[54] Simultaneously she problematizes the fragility of the utopian modern city, of the sedentary space of measures and properties. Hers is haptic rather than optical perception, the unwillingness to procure the eye a precise focus, a unique locus from which to observe the world.

The refusal to allow the reader a scene for commanding the other or aggrandizing the self is also crucial in Theresa Hak Kyung Cha's (Korea/U.S.) videos, particularly *Passages Paysages* (1978), and Lynn Silverman's (U.S./U.K.) landscape photographs of the desert (*Horizons*, 1979) and of the sky (*1:1*, 1992) but also of tables with lamps and cords. Furthermore, the critical analysis of video and film by Cha and of photography by Silverman gives rise to work where "there is neither horizon nor background nor perspective nor limit nor outline or form nor center." It remains impossible to grasp the whole work without its parts or the parts without the whole: there is no intermediary distance, or all distance is intermediary. "The smooth always possesses a greater power of deterritorialization than the striated." It is a nomad space occupied by intensities: a space of exile, a space of voyage too. It is not the measurable quantity of movement that is important, nor something only in the mind, but "the mode of spatialization, the manner of being in space, of being for space." However reluctantly, I am designating this space as the space of the "feminine." Immediately I must add that this refers to the theory of matrixial borderspace and its metramorphic encounters, rather than to the metaphor of land and the female body and its masculinist exploration. Too often this reading of an overtly sexualized symbolic has been applied to the landscape painting (also from the thirties) of Emily Carr (Canada). More relevant, and in contradistinction to a narcissistic romantic convention, her work oriented toward land and territory—the space of the First Nations people—engages the fear of "the abject other" and the awe for "the sublime other" to question the objectifying gaze of aesthetic convention and its desire to master (and thence to internalize and obliterate) the other.

Since Carr's time, an awareness of our attitudes toward alterity has become prominent in visual art. Again drawing on the grid and its obsessive structure of repetition while subverting its logic of organization, the works of Mona Hatoum (Lebanon/U.K.), Ellen Gallagher (U.S.), and Nathalie Hervieux (France) embody relations to the world where the "threatening" differ-ence is negotiated. Consisting solely of Hatoum's own hair, her installation *Recollection* (1995) at the Béguinage of Saint Elizabeth in Kortrijk (Belgium) depicts this intermediary process by distance in proximity, by (human) absence in presence. Recollecting these unregarded traces of beauty and life but also of abjection, violence, war, and death, she uses her hair strands as "ready-made graphic lines," refusing to lie straight and containing their own energy and ten-sility.[55] When carefully walking into the space, where single knotted hairs hang from the ceil-ing, curl in little "dust" bowls over the floor, and are woven into a small "relic" attached to a table, the beholder (whose face is slightly brushed by these strands of hair) senses invisibility in existence. Even so, Gallagher's canvases from the 1990s covered with sheets of paper, mostly taken from children's penmanship copybooks, provide both a texture, "guiding lines," and an asymmetrical grid for marking, for beginning, for writing, for telling a story that was supposed to have no history, no inscription. In close vision, scattered over the paintings, chains of little eyes and mouths with thick lips appear as bodily and socially inferential pic-tograms issuing from pre-1960s consumergenic stereotyping iconography of black people. The imagery comes from the racially charged, popularized nineteenth-century American reception of the African body.[56] The absent body, the sentient body, remains subject and object in the serial photograph sequences of Hervieux. Fixing painting in time, placing time in space, at the core of the photographic system, her self-images are in flux, becoming more than being.

One common property of the works in the exhibition is their allusion to ideas that do not have material substance but are made material in the work itself; this work makes palpable the conceptual engagement with "beginnings." In the final section, *Enjambment: "La donna è mobile,"*[57] this becomes most intelligible. The works are a simultaneity of body, eye, hand, thought, and action and also of past, present, future. Art as not simply visual but as an inte-gration of many effects of the embodied mind, incorporating rhythm, light, sound, smell, and spatiality, enables an encounter in which art's material presence resonates with the body and its reminiscences.[58] Most works do not privilege the retinal but destabilize the gaze either by favoring peripheral vision or by evoking other physical sensations. The dispersal of the bodily in space references nonexclusive senses: the scopic in the touch, the tactile in the eye. But the bodily regards also the art object, which is part of the projections of one's own body: it expresses the operations of the body, the physical act of making/viewing the work. The exhibi-tion questions the *location of the body*, but whose body? Which body—whole or not? In this sense the triangle that inspires the exhibition structure is that of maker, art object, and beholder not as fixed entities with determinable positions but as inherently unstable energies in a fluctuating relation both unique (insofar as the work interacts with a consciousness, with its own individuated history) and contingent (insofar as each individual encounter shifts the meaning of the work). This means that, depending on the context, work, maker, and beholder exist potentially in a state of transformation.

In the mid-1930s Katarzyna Kobro (USSR/Poland) poignantly articulated the constant development of form and shaping of space in her essay "Functionalism"[59] and also in her works *Space Compositions*. Fundamental for her was art seen as a totality of existence and as a search for an "open rhythm" pertaining to both the social and the individual aspects of daily life. Kobro's early spatial deliberations based on a dynamic point of view are geometric con-structions; later she progressively opened up the work to the surrounding space: a *unistic* sculpture aims at a spatial unity. "The general assumption of Unism is the unity of a work of art with the place in which it arises, or with the natural conditions that had already existed before the work of art was made," or, "A unity of what has arisen with what has been prior to the work of art is the main postulate of Unism."[60] The element of action implied in Kobro's work remained essential. "The device which gives uniformity to a piece of sculpture without isolating it, is the spatio-temporal calculated rhythm. By rhythm we mean a regular sequence of shapes in space. . . . This rhythm of shapes can grow in any direction; it can add new extensions to existing ones, not contained by the work."[61] Kobro and Strzeminski further argue that "sculpture is not a wholly plastic phenomenon, for it assumes the coexistence of space and time within itself. These are the two elements that are united in the concept of motion, which is a synthetic, spatio-temporal concept." According to them, "Optics are insufficient; only a rhythm which is a result of spatial changes occurring in time can be the unifying factor," and since "time is only potentially inherent within a single plane," it seems that "the element of time becomes significant only when the eyes are set in motion." Time thus "in a work of three-dimensional art, appears in an open manner as a result of the beholding motion around the work of art." They conclude that "the main task is: to build up a transition from individual shapes which are purely spatial and nontemporal, through the potential rhythm, up to the rhythm of the whole work of art or to the overt rhythm which unites the whole work into a single spatio-temporal unity." Kobro's (utopian) investigations were abandoned in 1939 at the beginning of World War II. After Hitler's seizure of power in Poland most of Kobro's sculptures were destroyed as *entartete Kunst* (degenerate art).

The *abstract* or *concrete* work of Sophie Taeuber-Arp (Switzerland/France) from the 1930s, and later in the 1960s–70s the *neoconcrete* work of Lygia Clark (Brazil) and the work of Eva Hesse (Germany/U.S.), seek to integrate life seamlessly into art. Organic in mood and largely geometric in form, Taeuber's textile designs and wood reliefs (sometimes entirely built within a circle), as well as her series of line drawings, often appear animated by their own inner energy, adopting variable positions and merging with the surrounding space. In this sense it has been argued that the choreographic element, this transmutation of the rhythmic pattern of dance into two dimensions, has been of fundamental importance for Taeuber in

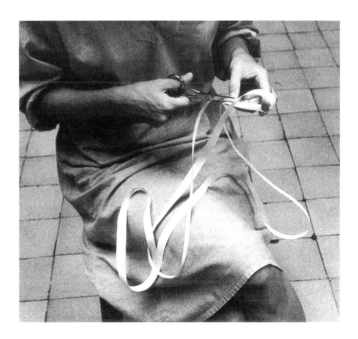

Lygia Clark,
Caminhando (Going),
1964.
Photo: Beto Felicio.

obtaining an *unregelmässig-Regelmässigkeit*.[62] Belonging to the neoconcrete group in Brazil, Lygia Clark felt the need to break away from the universalist claims of geometric abstraction while maintaining a nonfigurative, geometric vocabulary and the social concerns of constructivism. Affirming the values of modernity and eschewing "regionalist realism," she restated the problem of subjectivity in a Brazilian context, a country that had suffered from colonialism and even more from neocolonial dependence.

According to Guy Brett, "Clark's individual and collective 'propositions' using plastic, sacking, stones, air, string, sand, water, etc., are not 'representations' but cells, nucleuses, or energy-centers. The object itself is secondary, appropriated, incomplete, existing only to initiate dialogue, and to indicate 'environmental and social wholes'. Literally, in many cases, they cannot exist without human support."[63] Downplaying the *object* in favor of the spectator's bodily action, Clark considers her *Bichos* (*Beasts*, 1960) as "living organisms, essentially active works": "a total, existential integration is established between it and you," and "what occurs is a kind of embrace between two living entities." Eventually, her words about her *Caminhando* (*Going*, 1964)[64] suggest fusing opposites, a continuum, an interdependence in movement, a matrixial space: "If I use a Möbius strip for this experiment, it's because it breaks with our spatial habits: right/left; front/back, etc. It forces us to experience a limitless time and a continuous space."[65] The bodily aspect in her work also undoubtedly references the effects of a nonparticipatory attitude to the world: the abuse of the body (torture of slaves in the nineteenth century and of political prisoners in the twentieth). Again, most manifest in Clark's work is the action of time and of spatialization, "the fact that the work is *always in the present, always in the process of beginning ove*r, of beginning the impulse that gave birth to it over again—whose origin and evolution it contains simultaneously" (*Neoconcretist Manifesto*).

This nonexistence of the object also appears in Eva Hesse's fragile sculptures from the sixties made of perishable materials. For some time Hesse had studied circles, squares, rectangles, and triangles, timeless operations, unspoiled and outside history, which entertained the utopian hope of building a new social order, but building ahistorically rather than in a continuation of history. However, according to William Wilson, "Hesse studied her relation to rectangles as a model of her relations to rules. The rules of the rectangle are not her rules: the rules which govern geometric shapes are immaterial, are deduced or derived from some transcendental plane outside and above history." Hers are the "home-made, hand-made approximate rectangles" with disregarded materials serving unpredictable purposes. Wilson continues: "Born into a Nazi Germany of 1936 that was ensphering itself, requiring uniform adaptation to its stylizations of thought and feeling, providing no margins for gypsies, Jews, homosexuals, handicapped people, and others unable to conform to an ideal, Eva Hesse and her family were excluded as useless misfits. She chose not to forget, and not to take revenge on history for not being pure and perfect. That is to say that she does not try to construct with timeless ahistorical principles, but to re-construct from within the unforgettable historical events."[66] Anxiety, culpability, the sense of loss, of instability (of eventual disappearance) and exile, of disillusion are constitutive of her work and its transparency of procedure, and not the result of a specific construction. Victor Azoulay refers to her *denazification* of language.

Gesture as actualization, performance of language/title that gives form, the object as trace, pure materialization of gesture: Hesse's sculptures (*Ingeminate*, 1965; *Repetition*, 1967; *Addendum*, 1967) as well as those of Anna Maria Maiolino (*Nineteen I, This, Other, That, There Are Nine, Coiled, Segmented*, 1991–93) articulate the singular connections among language, body/gesture, and work in an uninterrupted flow of enchained repetitions. The desire of the hand. Work grounded in the visceral and related to the *informe*: "an attack on form that lies within form, and not outside it." Inside the visible. The performing hand. *The doing hand.* Maiolino's (Italy/Venezuela/Brazil) most recent "sculpture-objects" insist on the essence of daily/domestic gestures and their repetitiveness. The obsessive manufacture of little balls or cylindrical rolls (*Codicillis*, 1993) from molded clay results in simple shapes that suggest an oscillation between what enters and what leaves the orifices of the body. If repetition is an attempt to perpetuate sameness, then her enunciation and enumeration emphasize that in sameness lies difference. Repeated in the making is the uniqueness of each movement: the interplay between intention and creation, the act and the material. "Each little ball is like no other." Hers is a liberating commitment to the generating process and not to the end product. "Intimate in my work is the repetition of the gesture: the form asserts and annuls itself dynamically, forcing the action of another gesture in the unending search for an identification. Thus, it will always be: 'One, None, One Hundred Thousand' (Pirandello)."

Also generated at the juncture of infinite time and the instant are the recent "suppositions of form" of Joëlle Tuerlinckx (Belgium). Experimenting with pieces of paper, paper balls, confetti, and colored plasticine placed mostly on the floor, and also with s(light) projections on the wall, she describes the results as "substantiated conjectures relative to form, more precisely, tangible thought." Instead of courting the exhibition space, Tuerlinckx's work

> seems withdrawn, to the point that it appears to be a renouncement of any attempt to take possession of the space. Her work seeks minimal presence. Boundaries are mocked to the extent that one experiences the work more as tenuous, shifting energy than as a series of striking shapes. She focuses on the moment immediately prior to the forms being fixed. Tuerlinckx's exhibitions can be typified as thought experiments wherein destructive and constructive impulses redeem each other simultaneously . . . lacerated old structural images giving rise to a fragmentary new order.[67]

Speaking of the possibilities inherent in her working method, she explains: "When I draw a line on a piece of paper I can't delay the moment in order to make each point the result of a well-defined choice. Using materials like plasticine or pieces of confetti placed next to one another halts the evolution of a form because it crystallizes within a decelerated time frame, like film where the choice occurs twenty-four times a second." Hierarchies between artistic and domestic domain, event and nonevent, assertion and uncertainty fall away, while the work emphasizes the nonspectacle and visual primacy is questioned by "the choreographies that steer a visitor's movements."[68]

New possibilities for connections in the shared (exhibition) space between the work, the maker, and the beholder also figure in the 1970s photographs of Francesca Woodman (U.S.) and in the 1990s sculptural installations of Ann Veronica Janssens (Belgium). In distinct ways both artists' work assumes a liminal space hovering between appearance and disappearance, opacity and transparency, center and margins, inside and outside. In this exhibition, caught in the figures of ellipsis and repetition, Woodman's photographs can be considered as an open end in a cyclic move referring back to the self-portraits represented in the first section, while Janssens's sculptural proposals relate to the spatial experience at issue in the earlier work of Katarzyna Kobro in the fourth section. Grounded in a comparable engagement with social reality and surrounding space, Janssens takes the "abandonment of the dualistic conception of sculpture and space" even further, to the extent that the visual is audible is tactile is haptic is visual is . . . in a continuous permutation of perceptual conditions. These concerns are magnificently articulated in her contribution to the exhibition at the historical site of the

JOËLLE TUERLINCKX,
Installation view at
Musée des Beaux-Arts,
Charleroi (Belgium),
1994.

béguinage in Kortrijk. While the space of the old building remained closed to visitors, once in a while a series of deafening sounds like terrifying thunderclaps or cannon shots resonated from inside and made the walls, including the tinkling windows, tremble on their foundations. On the verge of implosion, the building seemed to become a huge, rectangular, resonating Pandora's box containing the turbulent forces *within* human relationships. Tenaciously researching sculpture, Janssens made here a monument of loss, but also a monument of promise since without such literal "commemorative volume" it avoids "the logic of the monument"[69] and concerns the space of our experience.

To conclude, I want to stress that the four sections of the exhibition may be structurally useful, but mainly they constitute a complex whole elucidating crossovers among all of these very different works. To narrate a story one has to make it linear, but, in fact, this upsets the story. Only beginnings can disrupt linearity. Through this elliptical exhibition display the beholder can identify other connections and unaccustomed juxtapositions. Released from the demand to "say" things, language can waver into the realm of "nothingness," leaving the reader with fragmentary evocations instead of the overly explicit rhetoric of public speech. History is in one place and presence in another. The story is always partial, merely a fragment. An exhibition as an event should be transitory; it should be neither an answer nor a fixed statement but rather a spectrum of activities that offers different perspectives, a set of relationships, a discussion, a dialogue without canon. The most appropriate way to realize such a display, and one capable of generating amazement, seems to me in the manner of a *Wunderkammer*. The *Wunderkammer* is a private collection of objects assembled according to personal perception, desire, and reminiscence, not according to the "objective" system of classification used in contemporary museums. The *Wunderkammer*, a personalized collage of reality, though reflective of mainstream, authoritarian systems of communication, is also a locus of puzzlement. *Inside the Visible* is conceived within this space of amazement shared by the artwork, the maker, and the beholder—in what may be called a "participatory relation." Here art is considered "as resisting fixed categorizations and as a site of plural poetics and singular jouissance."

It may seem paradoxical to argue against the separation of the world into exact oppositions and then confirm the binary system by selecting work on the basis of gender. However, this decision should be considered as an effort to show, in the absence of a rewriting of "history," the partiality of its structures and codes, and to display the art of women because their roles as active agents of culture have too often been minimized, delayed, or ignored. Certainly, such a historical perspective seeks not to redeem forgotten art pioneers from darkness but rather to consider the repressed subjects folded into an established art history. In an act of transformation the exhibition tries to cover art (history) made by women artists during the twentieth century to unveil an invisible area of knowledge and expose those power relations in which language is manipulated to "naturalize" and immobilize sociopolitically constructed categories of otherness. Similarly, as Judith Butler suggests, calling each totalizing concept into question, "Feminist critique ought also to understand how the category of 'women,' the subject of feminism, is produced and restrained by the very structures of power through which emancipation is sought."

Furthermore, the exhibition evokes "nomadic" movement, not only literally that of cyclic rhythm but more importantly that of the state of exile, fragmentation, and uncertainty. Although the topic of exile is far too complex to elaborate here, exile often occurs when what is privileged leaves no space for difference. It seems no mere coincidence that many of the exhibiting artists were either marginalized by their societies—including, of course, the art world—or exiled for political reasons. The nomadic beguine movement at the end of the

FRANCESCA WOODMAN,
Providence, 1975–76.
Black and white
photograph.
8 x 10 in.
Courtesy of Betty and
George Woodman.

twelfth century in Flanders exemplifies this recurring state of exclusion from language and women's rebellion against it.[70] This instance, drawn from my own Belgian background in a leap back in time, determined the practical locus of development for *Inside the Visible*.

The beguine movement occurred just as the struggle for human rights began to topple the feudal system: freedom of trade, communal franchises, and, as a consequence, a certain personal religious independence became realities. Many women no longer wanted to live under the constraints of existing social structures and chose an apostolic life in spiritual freedom, exempt from men, institutions, and possessions. Sometimes unable to join religious orders for lack of sufficient dowry or noble origin but also because they refused any restriction or latency, these women adopted a semireligious life, devoting themselves to asceticism, prayer, writing, welfare, and lacework, but without pronouncing perpetual vows. During the thirteenth and fourteenth centuries, as the beguine movement spread from Flanders along and beyond the Rhine in Germany and in northeastern France, the majority of these "unruly" women, begging for their living and wandering from one place to another, began to gather into free communities called *béguinages*.

The originality and power of the beguines lie in the perfect amalgamation of their doctrine with their spiritual experience. The contrast between the then-current (male) scholastic doctrine and theirs is a contrast between a doctrine that remains fettered to the intellect and one that is applied to life itself. This latter doctrine allows one to rise to a higher kind of knowledge, not merely theoretical but constitutive of being. Although the literary aspect of the beguines' writings is important, their main achievement lies in their efforts to reform the Church at a time when it was undermined by schisms, sclerosis, simony, and intellectual aridity, and to install new forms of life. Novelty, liberty, and poverty are their supreme leitmotivs. But the institutional Church, unable to control the proliferation of the beguine movement and its spiritual aspiration for innovation, tried to protect itself by means of the Inquisition and various interdictions.[71] The beguines were suspected by the clergy, first because they were neither cloistered nor bound by perpetual vows nor had an official status, and second because they played an incontestable part in the revolution that was to allow the laity to become acquainted with the sacred texts and with theological knowledge, no longer exclusively through sermons and prayer books but, thanks to translations and writings, in the vernacular. The prose and poetry of the beguines, whether simple or learned, has nothing in common with the rhetoric of medieval Latin authors.[72]

Since the *béguinage* is, in a certain way, a space of the "subversive stitch," it seemed a particularly appropriate place to initiate an exhibition about language practices of women in the twentieth century. In the ancient Béguinage of Saint Elizabeth in Kortrijk (Belgium), *Inside the Visible* evolved out of *Begin the Beguine in Flanders*, a series of one-person, process-oriented shows of work by contemporary artists. This provided the opportunity to discuss at length with the artists the upcoming group exhibition, including their projects and their instructive observations. At that moment, the local, Flemish *béguinage* reveals a translational quality, assisting in the "realignment" of memory and the present and in the repetitive field that addresses language. The site seemed to require the reinscription of global relations, though there is no a priori causality between singular events that are contingent. Following Homi Bhabha, we can ask if it is possible to be committed to the specificity of event yet linked to a transhistorical memory. As a response, it is important to open up an intervening space, a space of translation. This exhibition and catalogue constitute such a space: here is an attempt to maintain the singularity of each event and person while articulating "a problem in the representation or signification of the historical 'time' of the global or the transnational as it is experienced today."[73]

Assuming the equivalent importance of a discourse of artistic specificity and one of cultural globalism, the catalogue was conceived accordingly. General essays at the beginning of

NANCY SPERO,
Codex Artaud XXII,
1972. Detail.
Painting and typewriter,
collage on paper,
24 x 114 in.
Photo: David
Reynolds.

the book introduce the subject matter of the exhibition from different points of view; these are followed by essays describing the work of each artist. In this way the artworks resist being reduced to puzzle pieces pasted into some curatorial design. At the same time this working method allows gender to be considered not as constituted coherently in different historical contexts but as intersected by racial, class, ethnic, sexual, and regional modalities of discursively constituted identities.[74] "Some texts may not be models of explanatory clarity as their purpose is to allow into formal language insights into those domains against which language is established. Thus there is of necessity a lot of wordplay, punning, neologism, apparent paradox, all of which, when read poetically, allow glimpses into the meanings that alone can convey the processes of the psyche and allow the effects of the text to work on you," comments Griselda Pollock. In a correlative attempt, these artworks and texts interrogate language for its transmission of our experiences and for its ability to modify our perceptions of reality and our understanding of each other. Developed through poetics rather than polemics, the exhibition is certainly not a definitive survey but an unpredictable assemblage of positions permitting multiple convergences and divergences while asking for an open play and transformation of meaning.

NOTES:

1. Neil Baldwin, *Man Ray, American Artist* (New York: Da Capo Press, 1988), 61. "In the preface to the exhibition catalogue for Man Ray's second show at the Daniel Gallery (December 1916–January 1917) Adon Lacroix wrote to promote 'the idea' in all art, 'including the picture painted . . . the substance itself; color; and from the color—the subject—ideas and matter are one in painting.'"
2. "Etymons" was published in the first and only issue of *TNT* (New York, March 1919) with contributions by Henry S. Reynolds, Adolf Wolff, Walter Arensberg, Man Ray, Philippe Soupault, Marcel Duchamp, and Charles Sheeler.
3. Baldwin, *Man Ray*, 35–46.
4. Jon B. Thompson, "In the Groves of Philadelphia—A Female Hanging," in *Tema Celeste* (1993): 41–49: "Duchamp himself described a 'rectified' readymade as a pre-factured object, recontexted by an act of inscription. It would seem to imply some form of correction, or a restoration of the object to a previously more total, less deviant condition."
5. Although the equation of woman and readymade might seem exaggerated or inadequate, I would like to mention that, according to Jon B. Thompson, "there is ample evidence to support the view that Duchamp—despite its having originated in the gentlemen's room—saw the urinal as essentially feminine in character, even as the very essence of womanhood. . . . Furthermore, given the evidence overall, it would seem reasonable to suppose that his original attribution was a fully worked out part of the game plan. In other words, that his reference to the 'woman from Philadelphia' was intended as a tautological description of the urinal itself: that the work that Duchamp called *Fountain* was none other than the 'woman from Philadelphia' in person."
6. Thompson, "In the Groves of Philadelphia," 44–45.
7. Ibid., 48. This notion of difference relates to the theory of the "matrix," to be discussed below.
8. Griselda Pollock, *Avant-garde Gambits 1888–1893: Gender and the Color of Art History* (New York: Thames and Hudson, 1993).
9. Jean Fisher, "Hors d'Oeuvres," in *The Raw and the Cooked* (Madrid: Museo Nacional Centro de Arte Reina Sophia, 1994).
10. Bracha Lichtenberg Ettinger, "Matrix and Metramorphosis," in *Differences: A Journal of Feminist Cultural Studies* 4, no. 3 (1992).
11. Fisher, "Hors d'Oeuvres."
12. In "Figures of Authority, Ciphers of Regression," *October* 16 (1981) Benjamin H. D. Buchloh remarks that, concerning "regressive art," not a single woman can be counted among either the German neoexpressionists or the Italian painters of *arte cifra*.
13. Lichtenberg Ettinger, "Matrix and Metramorphosis"; *Matrix. Halala Lapsus* (Oxford: Museum of Modern Art, 1993); "The Becoming Threshold of Matrixial Borderlines," in *Traveller's Tales* (London: Routledge, 1994); "The Almost-Missed Encounters as Eroticized Aerials of the Psyche," *Third Text* 28/29 (1994); and *The Matrixial Gaze* (Leeds: University of Leeds, Feminist Arts and Histories Network, 1995).
14. Griselda Pollock, "Oeuvres Autistes," *Versus* 3 (1994): 14–18.
15. Summarized from various discussions by Lichtenberg Ettinger.

16. Ibid., 14–18.

17. Griselda Pollock, *Vision and Difference* (London: Routledge, 1988), 1–17.

18. Ibid., 7.

19. The concept of "beginning" is one root of the title *Inside the Visible: Begin the Beguine in Flanders*, used as the exhibition project gradually unfolded over a year (April 1994–April 1995) at the Kortrijk *béguinage* in preparation for the ICA exhibition in Boston.

20. Edward W. Said, *Beginnings: Intention and Method* (New York: Columbia University Press, 1985).

21. Most poignantly in Benjamin H. D. Buchloh, "The Primary Colors for the Second Time: A Paradigm Repetition of the Neo-Avant-Garde," *October* 37 (1986): 41–52.

22. Hal Foster, "Postmodernism in Parallax," *October* 63 (1993): 3–20; and "What's Neo about the Neo-Avant-Garde?" *October* 70 (1994): 5–32.

23. Buchloh, "The Primary Colors for the Second Time," 43.

24. In "What's Neo about the Neo-Avant-Garde?" Hal Foster claims that "in postwar art the problem of repetition is primarily the problem of the neo-avant-garde, a loose grouping of North American and Western European artists of the 1950s and 1960s."

25. Benjamin H. D. Buchloh, "Ready Made, Objet Trouvé, Idée Reçue," in *Dissent: The Issue of Modern Art in Boston* (Boston: Institute of Contemporary Art, 1986).

26. Lichtenberg Ettinger, "The Almost-Missed Encounters as Eroticized Aerials of the Psyche."

27. I also want to refer here to the title of Charlotte Salomon's work *Leben? oder Theater? (Life? or Theater?)*.

28. Lisa Tickner, "Nancy Spero: Images of Women and *la peinture féminine*," in *Nancy Spero*, exhib. cat. (London: Institute of Contemporary Art, 1987), 16, quoting from Toril Moi, *New French Feminisms and Sexual/Textual Politics* (London: Methuen, 1985), 140, on Irigaray's textual strategies.

29. Hal Foster, "Postmodernism in Parallax," *October* 63 (1993): 3–20; on this subject see Klaus Theweleit, *Männerphantasien* (Frankfurt: Verlag Roter Stern, 1977). Published in English as *Male Fantasies* (Minneapolis: University of Minnesota Press, 1982).

30. See also Maud Lavin, *Cut with the Kitchen Knife: The Weimar Photomontages of Hannah Höch* (New Haven: Yale University Press, 1993), 159–84; and Desa Philippi, "The Conjuncture of Race and Gender in Anthropology and Art History: A Critical Study of Nancy Spero's Work," *Third Text* 1 (Autumn 1987): 34.

31. Lavin, *Cut with the Kitchen Knife*, 167.

32. Foster, "Postmodernism in Parallax," 8.

33. Jack Ben-Levi, Craig Houser, Leslie C. Jones, and Simon Taylor, *Abject Art: Repulsion and Desire in American Art* (New York: Whitney Museum of American Art, 1993), 7.

34. Susan Fisher Sterling, "Signifying: Photographs and Texts in the Work of Carrie Mae Weems," exhib. cat. (Washington, D.C.: National Museum of Women in the Arts, 1994), 18–36. She notes: "Unlike such artists as Lorna Simpson or Cindy Sherman, who resist debasement of women via language or film by never revealing themselves fully to the camera, Weems leaps over this convention of Postmodernism to assert her photographic persona's integrity, tying it directly to her own as photographer and creator. Weems thereby enables her female character to gaze directly back at the viewer as an equal, taking full possession of her sexuality and sense of self in the process."

35. During the 1970s May Wilson worked in almost the reverse way: in her "ridiculous portraits" the artist pasted her own face onto postcard images of Victorian ladies and classical nudes, in order to parody and thus deconstruct patriarchal notions of the ideal woman (Ben-Levi et al., *Abject Art*, 51–52).

36. John Lechte, "Art, Love, and Melancholy in the Work of Julia Kristeva," in *Abjection, Melancholia and Love*, ed. John Fletcher and Andrew Benjamin (London: Routledge, 1990), 24–41; Perry Meisel, "Interview with Julia Kristeva," trans. Margaret Waller, *Partisan Review* 51 (Winter 1984): 131–32.

37. Mary Lowenthal Felstiner, *To Paint Her Life: Charlotte Salomon in the Nazi Era* (New York: Harper Collins, 1994).

38. Benjamin H. D. Buchloh, "Pandora's Painting: From Abstract Fallacies to Heroic Travesties," in *Gerhard Richter*, exhib. cat. (New York: Marian Goodman Gallery, 1993).

39. Tickner, "Nancy Spero," 5–8.

40. Ibid., 11–12.

41. Guy Brett, "A Radical Leap," in *Art in Latin America: The Modern Era, 1820–1980* (London: The Hayward Gallery, 1989), 275–76.

42. Hanne Darboven in the exhibition catalogue of the Kunsthalle, Basel, 1991: *Epiloog ABC Symphonie—opus 37* (1986/89) and *Symphonie Fin de Siècle—opus 27* (1989/90).

43. For a detailed description of *Élan* see also: Lynne Cook, "Susan Hiller," in *The British Show*, exhib. cat. (British Council Tour of Australia, 1985–88), 71–74.

44. Jean Fisher, "Susan Hiller: *Élan* and Other Evocations," in this volume.

45. Patricia Bickers, "Avis Newman: Vicious Circle," in *Vicious Circle*, exhib. cat. (Dublin: Douglas Hyde Gallery, and Amsterdam: De Appel Foundation, 1993).

46. Ibid., 6.

47. Rosi Huhn, "Das Problem der Entsorgung in Kunst und Kultur als Passage zum 'positiven Barbarentum,'" in

Werkverzeichnis: Zeichnungen, Frottagen, Fundstücke, Textfragmente aus der europäischen Literatur und Benjamins "Passagen-Werk" (Mainz: Verlag Hermann Schmidt, 1992).

48. The title derives from that of Cecilia Vicuña's book *Unravelling Words and the Weaving of Water*, trans. Eliot Weinberger and Suzanne Jill Levine (Minnesota: Graywolf Press, 1992).

49. Gilles Deleuze and Félix Guattari, *A Thousand Plateaus: Capitalism and Schizophrenia*, trans. Brian Massumi (Minneapolis: University of Minnesota Press, 1987), 474–500.

50. See Rosalind E. Krauss, "The /cloud/," in this volume.

51. Gego also made beautiful drawings and watercolors on paper.

52. Deleuze and Guattari, *A Thousand Plateaus*.

53. See my essay "Cecilia Vicuña's *Ouvrage*: Knot a Not, Notes as Knots," in this volume.

54. See Serge Guilbault, "The Taming of the Saccadic Eye: The Work of Vieira da Silva in Paris," in this volume.

55. Guy Brett on the work of Mona Hatoum in a lecture at the Tate Gallery, London, 1995.

56. Mario Diacono, "Ellen Gallagher: Crypto-graphing the History-sized Body," exhibition leaflet (Boston, 1994). See also James Weldon Johnson, *Autobiography of an Ex-coloured Man*, 1912.

57. The title of an aria from Verdi's *Rigoletto.*

58. Fisher, "Hors d'Oeuvres."

59. Katarzyna Kobro, "Functionalism," in *Forma* 4 (January 1936) (translated in *Tre pionérer for polsk avant-garde: Lladyslaw Strzemski, Katarzy Kobro, Henryk Stazewski med et appendix om Franciska Clausen*, exhib. cat. [Fys Kunstmuseum, Sweden, 1995]). She also worked with and wrote in collaboration with her husband, Wladyslaw Strzeminski.

60. Katarzyna Kobro, Wladyslaw Strzeminski, *Composition of Space: Calculations of Space-Time Rhythm* (a.r. Library, 1931); translated in ibid.

61. Ibid.

62. Carolyn Lanchner, *Sophie Taeuber-Arp*, exhib. cat. (New York: Museum of Modern Art, 1981).

63. Guy Brett, "Lygia Clark: The Borderline between Art and Life," *Third Text* 1 (Autumn 1987): 65–94.

64. In *October* 69 (Summer 1994), Yve-Alain Bois describes her *Caminhando*: "You make a Möbius strip out of paper. Using scissors, poke a hole in the middle of the band and start cutting lengthwise; when you have worked your way back to the point of your original cut (which would have the effect of separating the strip into two), avoid it and choose another place to divide the strip, then go on, each time choosing right or left, until you cannot divide the strip again. Everything flows from the inescapable, ineffaceable moment of this choice: the unfolding is this moment, all or almost nothing. Once the 'trail' of the Trailing is followed, all that remains is a heap of paper spagetti to be thrown in the trash."

65. Lygia Clark, "Nostalgia of the Body," *October* 69 (Summer 1994).

66. William Wilson in a letter to the author (1995); see also his essay "Eva Hesse: On the Threshold of Illusions" in this volume.

67. Mark Kremer, "A Sweet Iconoclasm: The Work of Joëlle Tuerlinckx," *Witte de With Cahier* 3 (Rotterdam, 1995).

68. Ibid.

69. Rosalind E. Krauss, "Sculpture in the Expanded Field," in *The Originality of the Avant-Garde and Other Modernist Myths* (Cambridge, Mass.: MIT Press, 1985).

70. At one point, following a collaboration on the exhibition "America: Bride of the Sun: 500 Years of Latin America and Low Countries," Paul Vandenbroeck and I thought of curating two parallel exhibitions about art by women articulating independent rather than "fringe" voices: one concerning the medieval *béguinages*, the other twentieth-century art. Both exhibitions could, and now do, exist separately, and the twentieth-century exhibition, *Inside the Visible*, evolved out of a *beguinage* in Flanders. For more information on the beguines and *béguinages*, see Emilie Zum Brunn and Georgette Epiney-Burgard, *Women Mystics in Medieval Europe* (New York: Paragon House, 1989); and Paul Vandenbroeck, *Hooglied. De Beeldwereld van Religieuze Vrouwen in de Zuidelijke Nederlanden, vanaf de 13e eeuw*, exhib. cat. (Brussels: Paleis voor Schone Kunsten, 1994). My discussion of the beguines is based on their descriptions.

71. Marguerite Porete (in 1310) and many other beguines were burned alive by the Inquisition.

72. Zum Brunn and Epiney-Burgard: "For example, it is in Beatrice of Nazareth's little book, *The Seven Manners of Love*, that we meet for the first time the expression *without a why*, which was taken up again by Hadewijch of Antwerp, Marguerite Porete, and Catherine of Genoa, and which finally became famous with Eckhart."

73. Homi K. Bhabha, "Unsatisfied: Notes on Vernacular Cosmopolitan," lecture at Cascais Biennial, Portugal, 1995.

74. Judith Butler, *Gender Trouble: Feminism and the Subversion of Identity* (New York: Routledge, 1990).

All things
are too small
to hold me,
I am so vast

In the Infinite
I reach
for the Uncreated

I have
touched it,
it undoes me
wider than wide

Everything else
is too narrow

You know this well,
you who are also there

Hadewijch II, 13th century

The Echoes of Enchantment

Jean Fisher

> He who already knows cannot go beyond a known horizon.
> —Georges Bataille, *Inner Experience*

A constellation of anxieties pervades the beginning of this writing about *creative process*—indeed, makes beginning nearly impossible, insofar as several strands of thought are deeply entangled in my mind, and no one emerges with any clarity. I am sure about one thing only, which is the need to approach a certain body of visual art as a way of saying and a way of hearing that, however much it may conform to the formalized languages of Western art, somehow contains a resonance oblique and elusive to the net of words by which we might seek to ensnare it. The air that it pervades is charged with sense yet inscribed with the impossibility of sedimenting into any satisfactory meaning. We are at the threshold where language falters. What is presented is not a representation of any nameable thing but a poetics, in the ancient sense of *poiesis*: a movement of coming-into-thought, of the process of making, of creating.

How might this murmur, this obliqueness, be spoken? Language is the material without which there is no thought. We structure knowledge of the world, the self, and others through language, the "voice of the dead" that comes to us fully formed from the "outside," but language also divides us from ourselves and our bodies: that which names "I" and "you" is inherently metaphorical; it stands in for the absent object, always displaced, never where it is said to be. Body and language, or existence and thought, form a troubling dichotomy—perhaps *the* dichotomy around which most others circulate or which they allegorize, but one that may open up the imaginative space of art.

I emphasize *saying* and *hearing* here to distract the gaze and diminish the privilege given to vision in order to create a space for the body. To regard a work as a surface or a semiotic organization of signs offering readily recoverable meaning is, with Zeuxis, to fail to see that there is "nothing" behind the painted veil but one's own desire for there to be "something." It also creates a distance from the work's actual, material presence, ignoring other sensations that may, synesthetically, contribute to its affectivity: the vibrations of rhythm and spatiality, scale and volume, touch and smell, lightness, stillness, silence. Finally, this approach fixes on the form of the "object," whereas I am more enchanted by the enigma of making—the dynamic relation between the work, the maker, and the viewer who is also a remaker. Making is understood here as an act of saying, and viewing as an act of hearing; the one necessarily presupposing the other, whose very lack of coincidence marks the distance between them.

"Maker," "work," "viewer"—these may be thought *not* as fixed entities but as relatively unstable energies in a fluctuating field. This field is recognizable insofar as the participants are both consumers and users of a shared language; unique insofar as each participant comes with his/her own speech or language of desire informed by an individuated psychosocial history; and contingent since each encounter produces shifts in the work's meaning beyond that intended by the maker.

To speak, however, is no guarantee that one will be heard. As consumers and users of available systems of language, visual and verbal, we are all caught in a vast machinery of inherited meanings whose very place in the hierarchies of power assures their authority and within which not all speech acts are accorded legitimation. Where the demand of the institutional sets up irreconcilable contradictions in relation to the particular, tension inevitably arises between an "own" or vernacular speech, which seeks to express a reality as lived and its role in the formation of individual or local identities, and institutionalized language, which seeks to homogenize reality and identity within a prescribed ideological framework.

In relation to this nexus of power, I am not at all invisible, nor am I speechless; but the authorizing powers of society are willfully blind and deaf. Or, to be more precise, it is not a case of my/our invisibility but of an excessive visibility of a certain order, thrown into relief by the grid of distinctions and effects through which Western authority, in its panoptic gaze, differentiates itself from its nominated others, seeks even to separate us from one another. The exterior—what is given to be seen—becomes the alibi for a whole set of assumptions about imagined inner, innate characteristics. "I" am caught in a disequilibrium between what I feel to be my existence in the world and what is said about my place within it. I remain uneasy, beside myself. The situation is, then, rather of a suffocating inadequacy of the place in which I am bound to speak or, more precisely, of the network of relations in which I am located and in which the question "To whom can I speak?" becomes increasingly pressing.

The thoughts that compel this narrative circulate around a space of contemplation; it is also a place, a town within a town, once self-sufficient within itself—the *béguinage* in Kortrijk (Belgium), where the initiative for this exhibition originated. It is one of many such places built for a community of women, pious and celibate but not strictly affiliated with the religious orders, that arose in Flanders early in the thirteenth century.[1] The origins of the *béguinages* remain obscure, but they were associated with a religious movement among women in the region, whose force had dissipated by the end of the seventeenth century,[2] when it was probably suppressed by the disciplinary forces that came into play with the rationalist and capitalist restructuring of the social and physical body. During the movement's heyday, the women produced an extensive body of writings known as "mystical," the earliest and best known among them perhaps those of Hadewijch of Antwerp.

These voices reverberate down the centuries on the wings of mystery and enchantment; poetic and elliptical, oscillating between the excesses of a defiled body and the ecstasies of the erotico-spiritual garden of delights, they speak of an experience largely unknown to us, trapped in the folds of rationalist accounts of history, to be appropriated by those hagiographies of saints that serve the agendas of the Church or, more recently, by the discourses of psychoanalysis, which in many ways they prefigure. Yet something of these voices catches our breath: a recognition of sorts, not of the mystical experience itself but of what may have given rise to it—a need to express an own sense and understanding of the world for which the dominant uses and forms of language remain unbearably inadequate.

Cecilia Vicuña,
Hilumbres Allqa.
Installation at
the Béguinage of
Kortrijk (Belgium).
Courtesy Kanaal
Art Foundation,
Kortrijk.

I realize that in raising such notions as the "mystical" I risk plunging this text into a territory scarred by the disbelief and accusations of imprecision of thought by which rationalism once enclosed it. But rather than evade the subject, we need to take on board the passion that subtends mystical thought and detheologize and repoliticize it. We must untangle it from the confessional and a certain politics to which it was subject and regard it as a way of experiencing and saying quintessentially human since it bears directly upon our relation to language. Mystic speech, as has often been said of art, "speaks for itself" (although, contrary to belief, this does not mean that the image or object presents an easily recoverable meaning: the "itself" is by no means transparent!). The term has no determinable signified; as Michel de Certeau points out, it "speaks of language itself not things."[3] For similar reasons, Georges Bataille sought to rename the mystical "inner experience."[4] However, despite—or perhaps because of—the indignities and distortions to which the word *mystic* has been subjected, I feel compelled to keep it: to let its irritant presence circulate as a reminder of its groundedness in an act of *dissent*. Mystic speech presents a way of saying and hearing that presses against the normative uses of language and the sense of subjectivity itself.

It is, of course, precisely because of the failure of language that the mystic experience itself cannot be written; it is externalized first and foremost through vocalization and a "theatricalization" of the body, affects that are *ecstatic* insofar as they are interpreted as "possessions" originating from a place "without," from an Other who speaks to and through "me," my body—the hearing of voices, delirious speech, visions, trance or catalepsis, putrescence, and the appearance of stigmata. Thus, the writings, poems, songs, and autobiographies are either transcriptions of affects or the sufferer's attempt to give meaningful account of the experience's trajectory. There is, here, a double aestheticization: an imaging through the body, followed by some form of textual representation.

That the languages of both the body and the writings are articulated through the symbolism of religious discourse seems inevitable, given that the limit of one's horizon of understanding is the available knowledge of the world, which was at that time circumscribed by Christian theology. Perhaps more significant is with what, of this body of available knowledge, the women of the *béguinages* chose to identify: the *vita activa* of Martha, the *vita speculativa* of Mary, the stigmatization of Mary Magdalene, and the Passion of Christ, through whose imitation the body and spirit would be likewise resurrected, transformed, in a state of unmediated union, or oneness of the soul, with the Other: God as Love. It is a trajectory and state fraught with paradoxes and the unknown and hence not attainable through "reason." Reason is discredited and rejected here: mystic speech is "unreasonable."[5]

A recognition constantly resurfaces: "I is an other." The mystic is not "at home" in his or her relations with the world. At one level, this dis-ease is a *reproach* or critique of the place assigned to this subject by a symbolic order perceived as "corrupt" and by which the sufferer has been corrupted (in the sense of *falsified*). Captive to the imaginary, the mystic's identity is caught up in the undifferentiated sea of an insatiable desire of an other whose ideal object this self-castigating, guilty, and unworthy self strives, impossibly, to be. Should, then, the *travail* not be to find the means of sublimating this desire through naming the symbolic referent, thereby effecting a distance between self and other that would enable an individuated self to emerge? Yet since knowledge in the nameable world is deemed untrustworthy, or corrupting of the body, the only feasible referent is that without name or body which is absolutely other and distant: "God." Hence, paradoxically, the path taken leads not to the individuated self but to a transformation that is also an intimation of its dissolution into nothingness. The desire of "God" produces ecstasy, which impregnates the unbreachable distance between the self and its object of desire. For Teresa d'Avila, ecstasy "becomes language . . . [which] finds its conjugation in bodily zones. . . . Her ecstasy is completely inscribed. The body becomes the place of writing and the inscription of desire . . . the zone in which the language of desire, just because it never finds the other as object, can perpetuate itself."[6]

The path of the unsayable reaches the threshold of the unknowable. The revelation—in our own time—is that the impossible-real object, that which stands for the desire of the other and calls the subject into being, occupies a place of emptiness, disguising the "nothing" that the subject is. Here, then, is the "truth"—the "something"—revealed by the painted veil. It is an intuition of a failure in representation, the betrayal of the subject by the fiction that is the symbolic order of language. As such, it signals a "surplus," a zone of resistance to subjectivation capable nonetheless of reimagining the self and releasing the pulsations of desire into the vibrations of the song, of another writing, that is the ceaseless tracing of this unknown, unrepresentability.

Thus, in speaking of Teresa d'Avila's *El libro de la vida*, Elisabetta Rasy describes how

[Teresa] relates two autobiographies painfully parallel, the story of her illness and the history of her speech to speak the body, to speak God—symmetrical utopias, impossible totality . . . between these two autobiographies there is a real void: a no-man's-land in which man and woman are exiled, where difference is annulled but at the same time suffocates and accentuates beyond any norm where the transgression one inhabits consumes the law. This also for the woman is the place of writing that has neither subject nor object that is not writing itself.[7]

In seeking a place from which to speak, to signify and recreate the self, "place" becomes the act of signifying itself. This self-dispossession stands in opposition to the West's privileging of a self structured through the acquisition of material knowledge. As Paul Vandenbroeck points out, for the mystics it was "not an intellectual appropriation (still less a material one) but an 'annihilation' or 'destitution': a dismantling of desires, passions, knowledge, the emotions. They had, however, analyzed their psyches to their very depths: and what they rejected was not through ignorance but through knowledge. And the latter was in its turn annihilated in order to be cured in the original sense of the term: to become again whole, intact without distinction, without difference and without the differend."[8] To answer the question, "Why did women choose the ascetic life of the *béguinages*?," we have to ask in turn, "For those so inclined, how else could they pursue their desire to understand the nature of existence?" Certainly not in the domestic sphere; nor in the universities governed by the Church, from which they were, of course, barred. It is as if only the most condensed places—the circumscribed routines of the *béguinage*, the pages of the book—could free the space of the imagination. And who knows how far reading was done under cover of what was more "proper" to women's pursuits: music, embroidery, tapestry, and lace-making? In such collaborations between mind and hand, the passage of thought and the pulsions of desire become the rhythm and harmony of the song, the very warp and weft of the fabric.

Another voice preoccupies me, not mystical but no less poignant: that of Sor Juana Inés de la Cruz (1648–1697), which emerged from a century of sociopolitical and religious turmoil at the threshold of the Enlightenment. Born in Mexico City, when Mexico was still the *virreinato*, Nueva España, this illegitimate child of Spanish parentage developed a passion for learning as a child in her grandfather's library.[9] At sixteen, beautiful, talented, and knowledgeable, she was taken under the protection of the court. Yet within four years she elected to enter the convent, where she was to spend the rest of her life. Here she pursued her studies, accumulating books and musical and scientific instruments; composing songs; writing and publishing love poetry, religious commentaries, and plays; and holding debates with visiting intelligentsia—until the Inquisition, no longer able to tolerate such worldliness (or the power that it conferred), began disciplinary measures against her. She eventually capitulated, abandoning writing and her books to attend victims of the plague which was then ravishing Mexico City and from which she was to die two years later.

More surely than we can ascertain for the women of the *béguinages*, Juana Inés's turn away from the conventions of secular life appears to have been prompted by a passionate intellectual curiosity (Octavio Paz describes her as a thief of knowledge, "neutralizing her sexuality beneath the nun's habit"), and like the mystics she expressed this through a poetics both ascetic and sensual, devoted to Love as a spiritual passion that transcended gender. Juana Inés was, however, far more grounded in material reality, in natural rather than supernatural phenomena, expressing, according to Paz, a narcissism that we would identify with the romanticism that opened onto our "modern" sensibility. Her writings are heterogeneous and synthetic, shifting between the languages of classical culture, the popular speech of the *criollos* and *mestizo* populations, and the *nahuatl* of the Mexicans, reflecting the syncretic culture emerging in colonial Mexico of which she was one of the first and greatest poets. She was, moreover, a passionate advocate of education for women, identifying with Isis, the Egyptian universal mother but also the inventor of writing; and as writing is a symbol of Mind in the nun's Neoplatonic hermeticism, so Mind is on the side of the feminine. In Juana Inés, desire for the infinite follows the metonymical path of the seducer, like that described for Don Giovanni:[10] the desire of the other transcribed into an obsessive accumulation of knowledge in which writing measures the impossible distance from the other even as it ceaselessly attempts to fill the void.

Two ways of saying, of reflecting on the limits of knowledge, the mystic and the intellectual, emerged from a place of impossibility, from the will to say the unutterable. Two "heresies": on the one hand, the mystic union with God that effectively eliminates the mediating authority of the symbolic order, and on the other the woman of letters whose transgression is to take the place of the law; both efficiently suppressed for the following two and a half centuries. Yet there is more behind these acts of saying than the pulsions of a singular desire. In more recent accounts of the mystics—the men as well as the women—the dis-ease is as much societal as individual: their world is one of sociopolitical turmoil in which they, typically, come from the ranks of the newly disenfranchised. Many of the *béguines*, especially the itinerant mendicants, were part of the new rural poor created by the proto-capitalism of the Middle Ages.[11] Teresa d'Avila, writing in the sixteenth century, belonged to a *hidalguía* (aristocracy) that had lost its status and holdings.[12] Sor Juana, disenfranchised by the circumstances of her birth, lived through the unrest of a colony in search of a unified identity, its coherence threatened from both without and within—a New World vigor resentful of the political and economic control of Spain while in constant fear of uprisings by the conquered Mexicans. In these voices, exiled from both the past and a certain future, one glimpses a fretful response to a social body perceived as disintegrating or corrupted, plunged, like themselves, into a real for which there is not yet a containable discourse. Hence, as de Certeau argues, mysticism is the companion of *dissent*.[13]

Any speech act is limited by the horizon of possibility of existing knowledge and yet, as an expression of an individuated psychosocial history, is a potential erasure of, or challenge to, those limits, capable of opening a space to "unauthorized" realities. Psychosocial conflict and the eruption of the real into consciousness are universal human experiences, although their intensity, objects, and interpretations must be conditioned by the depth of that horizon, by the particularities of what a society deems permissible to speak and what, in turn, it strives to conceal as the unsayable. Our own circumstances, therefore, are not such that we should expect ordinarily to find them expressed in the language of religious faith. The mystic trajectory may however find an analogy with the creative process since it too attempts to speak against the grain of inherited assumptions about existence. By way of example I want to mention the work of two artists who connect rather directly, albeit in very different ways, to mystic speech: Yves Klein and Susan Hiller.

That Klein's work connects to the mystic tradition was made explicit by the artist himself in his *Leap into the Void* and perhaps also by the blue body imprints of his female models, which "embody" the metaphysical union of flesh with the infinite. Among the commentaries on Klein's work, little of which addresses this aspect, Maurizio Calvesi tells us that

> all of his researches comprise none other than an organic utopian philosophy. A true attempt to construct his own universe, or better, in his own words, "a new humanism," whose origins and key lie in esoteric religion and the alchemical mystery of theosophy. Klein's philosophy was never simply the result of research but of a sudden drunkenness or rapture, which changed his behavior and work and, in the last analysis, his life. It has the appearance of Saint Paul struck by lightning on the road to Damascus.[14]

Klein, a devout Catholic, spent time occasionally at the convent of Santa Rita da Cascia, the Protector of Desperate and Hopeless Causes. In 1979, seventeen years after Klein's death, a painter employed by the convent to restore the basilica asked the nuns if they had a spare piece of gold leaf. Not knowing then its aesthetic significance, the nuns presented a casket containing gold ingots and colored pigments that turned out to be an ex-voto given by Klein to the convent. In a separate compartment of the box was a handwritten, seven-part dedication to Santa Rita that, in its intoxicated garrulousness, oscillating between the base and the elevated, the finite and the infinite, echoes the language of desire:

> —The BLUE, the GOLD, the PINK, the IMMATERIAL, the VOID, the architecture of the air, the urban planning of the air, the air-conditioning of the great geographical spaces for a return to a human life in nature, in the Paradisiac state of legend. These three fine gold ingots are the product of the sale of the 4 ZONES OF IMMATERIAL PAINTING SENSIBILITY.
> —Under the earthly care of Santa Rita da Cascia: the Pictorial Sensibility, the monochromes, the I.K.B.s, the sponge sculptures, the immaterial, the static anthropometrical imprints, positive, negative and in movement, the shrouds, the Fountains of Fire, of Water and Fire,—the architecture of the air, the urbanism of the air, the air-conditioning of geographic spaces thus transformed into constant Gardens of Eden rediscovered on the surface of our globe—the Void.
> —Santa Rita da Cascia, Saint of impossible and desperate causes, thanks be to you for all the powerful, decisive and marvelous help which you have granted me so far—I thank you with all my heart. Even if I am personally not worthy to receive it grant me your aid again and always in my heart and protect everything that I have created so that, despite my unworthiness, it will always be of great beauty.[15]

Klein's simple but elegant presentation of the sheer vibrancy of color and light through the raw materiality of pigment and gold is one of the clearest attempts in art to evoke that transformative immateriality, that fugitive moment of lightness and ecstasy, to which mystic speech so often refers.

One evening, while staying in the village of Loupien, near Sète (France), Susan Hiller picked up a blue pencil and began to make random marks on a blank sheet of drawing paper. Lost for seven years, the pages of script reappeared in 1979, and from them the artist made *Sisters of Menon*, first as a set of framed and annotated panels arranged in a cruciform (1979), and later as a book (1983). *Sisters of Menon* was the beginning of the artist's involvement in "automatic writing," practiced by psychic mediums to "get in touch" with the "dead" and by the surrealists to get in touch with unconscious processes. Hiller's involvement in "automatic writing" has little to do with "magic" or revelations of modernism's autonomous creative self and more with processes of creative thought, which the work of art "reembodies." In *Sisters* the script appears alphabetic, although the opacity of its "message" resists any "reasoned" interpretation. Alien to the artist's characteristic work, the script appears with all the rhythm of an incantation or song:

> who is this one
> I am this one
> Menon is
> Menon is this one
> you are this one
> last night we were 3 sisters now we are 4 sisters
> you are the sister of Menon
> we are 3 sisters
> we live on the air in the water
> Menon
> we three sisters are your sister
> this is the
> nothing that we are
> the riddle is the sister of the zero

What is the "riddle" that is answered, albeit in cryptic form, even as it is posed? "Menon" resonates with auditory puns, anagrams, and metonymies: nomen, no men, me non, *mais non*, no name, one, and no one . . . subjectivity framed as a paradox, an affirmative-negative: I am . . . we are . . . nothing. In a self-effacing movement, the one who writes is not only the "I am," named "Menon," of the utterance; it is heterogeneous, it multiplies, it lacks gravity or boundedness ("we live on the air in the water"). "I" moves in the rhythmic, limitless time-space of the other, but the "nothing" that "I/we/you are" is not simply nothing: it is the place from which writing comes into being. As with the mystic narrative, the will to substantiate the movement of desire is not metaphorical. As Achille Bonito Oliva has pointed out, "Art is a metonymical practice of desire, a progressive shift of a poisoned vision."[16] This is not to say that "writing" or the image of art bears any easily determinable relation to the repressed signifier; since the emergence of the latter is subject to resistance, it must be refracted and disguised through a relay of substitutes bound into a discursive field, substitutes that, nonetheless, will always bear the traces of its "presence."

Art sustained primarily by the experience of the maker (who struggles with the very impossibility of language, or representation, to produce a meaningful account of the self's existence in its world, in contradistinction to visual production, which is content, however artfully, to establish meanings or to reaffirm existing ones) suffers, like mystic speech, from a problem of legitimation. As de Certeau says of the mystic text: "Deprived of the legitimacy that would be given it by a social status (hierarchical, professional, etc.), the author presents himself in the name of what speaks within him: the Real. . . . But he still has to show that he is indeed in the very place from which he is presumed to speak. He must, by his text itself, make what founds his text believable."[17] Autobiographical writing in itself does not guarantee escape from the determinations of the symbolic order that would reveal an "authentic" self. It is not

Susan Hiller, *Sisters of Menon*, 1972 (scripts), 1979 (commentaries).
Detail. Bleu pencil on A4 paper. Collection of the artist.

a question of authenticity. Insofar as the unconscious (conventionally understood as that most intimate to the self) is, by Freud's definition, profoundly social in its formation, identity *is* the image of the other. One is always inscribed by the other. The disparity between the image of the self constructed through inherited discourses and its own sense of existence exposes an inherent indeterminacy of language, something like an excess of signifiers in the semantic field unable to fix or stabilize identity. Through this field of multiple possibilities, infused with "sense" but absent of meaning, where the phantasms of unconscious desire interface with the pressures of conscious thought, the self ceaselessly dialogues with itself to find coherence. Also in the field of the imagination the self finds the potential for transformation: if there is no "authentic" self, then what is already inscribed can always be reinscribed, differently. Here, perhaps, lie the workings of the creative process.

The language of desire of both aesthetic and mystic practice, in order to be heard, must found a place from which to speak, find a way of using language even though it may place it in crisis. A fiction is established. Like Alfred Hitchcock's "MacGuffin," it has no meaning outside the significance given it by the protagonists, but it functions as the *pretext* that sets the narrative in motion. In Teresa's *Morados* the fiction is the crystal castle; like the *béguinage*—or its closed garden of delights—it is a multifaceted complex of dwellings or spaces, each of which has its own sensuous bodily affects (sound, smell, taste, texture), which the author minutely catalogues with evident pleasure. Through the castle Teresa speaks to the community of sisters, demonstrating to them the writing of desire.

In visual art the fiction is the "veil," which again means "nothing" in itself since, surely, it conceals nothing more than its own fictionality. Its value for the perceiver lies in its power to activate and organize the movement of desire: our desire to know what is behind it engenders imaginative thought and knowledge. Hence, knowledge is discovered not in the object but in the search, and the search can only be predicated on an a priori belief that there is something "lost" to be found. What might this be if not the sense of a "lost" unity of the self? Yet if the language of art seeks to imagine unity, it can only discover its impossibility, becoming, in effect, an "affirmation of alterity."[18]

The veil of art emerges through a compelling materiality, a spatial dynamics of the work of thought on matter, already a transcription of a transcription of the movement of desire that struggles to move outward from the self to the other (in this sense, art is social). But the resonance that emanates from this echo of an image in the interstices of the language of art is that neither of the maker nor of the viewer but of a third: a scene, like the crystal castle, for "communication." Within this ineffable space I am, in turn, captivated by an *immediate*, unmediated affectivity. This is why the artwork cannot be apprehended in reproduction. It is a space that is sensuous, thick with sense, with an indeterminacy that can invoke several possible meanings. Unable to map myself as a coherent self within the work's multiple coordinates, I am set adrift in uncertainty. Words fail me, and I am struck dumb. I "lose" myself; time appears suspended, and I am discharged into the no-time of a free-floating reminiscence.

Is this the ecstasy of which the mystics wrote? Perhaps, but I have no way of knowing. In any case, in this moment I am caught up in the sonorous tones of the infinite: something felt or heard, but not seen. In this moment my body is reappropriated, reinscribed by the language of desire. It surrenders, with a sense of lightness and release, or a diabolical laughter, to an alterity in which the play of desire is freed from the constraints of the everyday to pursue the other as object, which it can never find. Art's scene of communication alludes to this irreconcilable distance between self and other. It "communicates" the pathos of incommunicability, an interiority that is an infinite exteriority. However, in this scene the realization of the unknowable frees language into the energy fields of fantasy and imagination, where we intimate new intuitions of hitherto unthought realities. This, perhaps, is the nature of its enchantment.

> Ecstasy is, it seems, communication, which is opposed to the "turning in on oneself" of which I have spoken. . . . But we reach ecstasy by a contestation of knowledge. Were I to stop at ecstasy and grasp it, in the end I would define it. But nothing resists the contestation of knowledge and I have seen at the end that the idea of communication itself leaves naked—not knowing anything. . . . I remain in intolerable non-knowledge, which has no other way out than ecstasy.[19]

NOTES:

1. For information on the *béguinages* I am indebted to the scholarly and elegant essay by Paul Vandenbroeck, "Tu m'effleures, moi qui suis intouchable," in *Le jardin clos de l'âme. L'imaginaire des religieuses dans les Pays-Bas du Sud, depuis le 13e siècle*, exhib. cat. (Brussels: Société des Expositions, Palais des Beaux-Arts de Bruxelles, 1994), 13–153.
2. The Kortrijk *béguinage* functioned until fairly recently, although there is now only one *béguine* still in residence.
3. Michel de Certeau, *The Mystic Fable*, vol. 1: *The Sixteenth and Seventeenth Centuries*, trans. Michael B. Smith (Chicago: University of Chicago Press, 1992), 145.
4. Georges Bataille, *Inner Experience*, trans. Leslie Anne Boldt (Albany: State University of New York Press, 1988), 3.
5. In our own secular time, attempts to understand the mystic experience have drawn on Freud's symptomatology of conversion hysteria. Here psychic conflict is represented in somatic symptoms as a consequence of the ego's inability to symbolize the thing that challenges its coherence and from which flight is impossible. Vandenbroeck, however, points out that the mystic trajectory is a self-analysis toward the "cure."
6. Achille Bonito Oliva, "L'assedio dello specchio," in *Passo dello strabismo sulle arti* (Milan: Feltrinelli, 1978), 20.
7. Elisabetta Rasy, *La lingua della nutrice* (Rome: Edizioni delle donne, 1978), 126 (translation by Stella Santacatterina).
8. Vandenbroeck, "Tu m'effleures," 124 (my translation). We might add that this parallels certain aspects of the psychoanalytic "cure," where the knowledge apprehended on a conscious level is a deception that obscures the "truth" that the unconscious, through the body and its symptoms, strives to make audible. The task of analysis is first to listen to bodily experience, which is never metaphorical but real.
9. Octavio Paz, *Sor Juana Inés de la Cruz o Las trampas de la fe* (Barcelona: Seix Barral Biblioteca Breve, 1982; English edition: *Sor Juana or the Traps of Faith* [Cambridge: Harvard University Press, 1988]).
10. Bonito Oliva, "L'assedio dello specchio," 15–24.
11. Vandenbroeck, "Tu m'effleures," 16.
12. Michel de Certeau, "Mystic Speech," in *Heterologies: Discourses on the Other*, trans. Brian Massumi (Minneapolis: University of Minnesota Press, 1986), 84.
13. Ibid., 85.
14. Maurizio Calvesi, "Klein's Utopia," *Arte e Creazione* (January/February 1968) (translation by Stella Santacatterina).
15. Yves Klein, extract of inscription in the ex-voto to Santa Rita da Cascia, reproduced in Pierre Restany, *Yves Klein e la mistica di Santa Rita da Cascia* (Milan: Editoriale Domus and Monastero S. Rita da Cascia, 1981).
16. Achille Bonito Oliva, "Organo/Obliquo," in *Passo dello Strabismo*, 7.
17. Michel de Certeau, "The Institution of Speech," in *The Mystic Fable*, 180.
18. Achille Bonito Oliva, "Il comportamento mancato. Il senso di colpa, la morte, il suicidio," in *Passo dello Strabismo*, 35.
19. Bataille, *Inner Experience*, 12.

NADINE TASSEEL,
Untitled, 1992.
Black and white photograph.
30 x 40 cm.
Courtesy of the artist.

Allegory as Art of Interfacing
(A Failed Fable, an Iconographical Incident, and an Anachronistic Symposium)

Paul De Vylder

By learning to understand language as "form," we have banished objects to the realm of chaos. Unrestrained by and free from the rules of language, objects turn into shadows of themselves, they become mè onta: actual nonentities, appearances of an unnameable materiality. Only the pure form, the nous, hovers as the highest fundamental principle or even as extreme a priori over the chaotic waters of matter or substance.

This gathering of philosophemes, from Anaxagoras and Aristotle to Kant and Saussure, is a useful concoction to link the ambivalent status of language to the Pelasgic myth of origin (as narrated here by Robert Graves):

> In the beginning, Eurynome, the Goddess of All Things, rose naked from Chaos, but found nothing substantial for her feet to rest upon, and therefore divided the sea from the sky, dancing lonely upon its waves. She danced towards the south, and the wind set in motion behind her seemed something new and apart with which to begin a work of creation. Wheeling about, she caught hold of this north wind, rubbed it between her hands, and behold! the great serpent Orphion. Eurynome danced to warm herself, wildly and more wildly, until Orphion, grown lustful, coiled about those divine limbs and was moved to couple with her. Now, the North Wind, who is also called Boreas, fertilizes; which is why mares often turn their hind-quarters to the wind and breed foals without aid of a stallion. So Eurynome was likewise got with child.[1]

Graves accompanies this story with the following clarification:

> In this archaic religious system there were, as yet, neither gods nor priests, but only a universal goddess and her priestesses, women being the dominant sex and man her frightened victim. Fatherhood was not honored, conception being attributed to the wind, the eating of beans, or the accidental swallowing of an insect; inheritance was matrilineal and snakes were regarded as incarnations of the dead. Eurynome ("wide wandering") was the goddess's title as the visible moon; her Sumerian name was Iahu ("exalted dove"), a title which later passed to Jehovah as the Creator. It was as a dove that Marduk symbolically sliced her in two at the Babylonian Spring Festival, when he inaugurated the new world order.[2]

Whoever writes chaotic texts needn't apologize afterward; one can't avert chaos with verbal incantations. Whoever tries to handle chaos doesn't even need good intentions: if chaos is a discursive strategy, speaking is panic and its strategic importance futile. Chaos can't be controlled or dominated; it reemerges wherever it thinks fit, and texts marked by its stamp can't be rearranged into usable textures. If so, chaotic texts have to be patched together until they fit around the instrument of language. Only then, one discovers, one can no longer abide language as instrument and barely as instrumentarium (a whole room full of bells and whistles, crowbars and tweezers). What chaotic texts tell us can't be conveyed, neither beforehand nor afterward, unless one is willing to haul up all the bells and whistles and crowbars and tweezers and start the cacophony from the beginning. One avoids chaotic texts, one thwarts them, and if they can not be avoided or thwarted, they are embalmed like literary cadavers; we refuse to have any other choice.

And yet—and this is a "yet" we have been waiting for—chaos is our sole defense against the constriction by language, against the constricting of language, against the string, the thread, the rope that is language, against the rope that strangles us while connecting us, not slowly and without our noticing it, but a priori and with everyone's cooperation.

And yet—and this is a "yet" that no one expects here—chaos is no outsider, no outside of language, no extralinguistic lifesaver; chaos is the correlate of language-as-thread, of language-as-texture: language-as-thread only exists because of language-as-chaos. We take cover under the heading "Truth" in order to ignore as much as possible this Janus character of language, while the lot of us are using formulas like "the return of the repressed" as if they were sacred mantras.

Hence this text on allegory, on speech saying something different from what it says, speech vacillating between what it says and what it makes us understand, speech that can only speak because it masks what it has to say, speech oscillating. Hence this vacillating, oscillating language of male voices in a catalogue about artworks by women. Hence also why the underside of logos is expressed by being designated by feminism as the controller of logos. Hence also the refusal to schematize and to put woman on the side of "chaos" and man on the side of "order." Hence the challenging of "the phallus as copula," the challenging of the symbolic order as phallocracy, not through an assertive argumentation by woman as iconoclast but by fragments of speech by man as waverer. Hence this oscillating text on the oscillation of language, hence this vacillating text in the network of text as intertext, hence the interfacing, the switching and the incomplete speaking, the speaking without finishing or finish.

"The veil is the core of the secret" says one of those text fragments; "the veil is the secret of language" I pose here as guiding principle. Proceeding from this provisional speaking, it is almost necessary to dedicate this text to Claude Cahun, Hannah Höch, Nadine Tasseel, and . . . .

The Fable

Once we have overcome the simplism that the work of art is a text having itself as subject, we arrive in a zone riddled with romantic echoes. Hidden behind and transformed by reflection theories, symbolic adages resound that, in undiluted form, would be merely irritating. Let me name three.

The most erudite form is a theory of reflection in which the work of art is a kind of monodic focus on, or concentrate of, the dominant discourse or types of discourses. In advertising form it appears as a quality label attributed to some kind of cultural object that, like a sponge, is supposed to collect in itself the essence of a worldview, an ideology, a *Zeitgeist* (this far too skinny ghost haunting the ages). One can also distinguish an idiotic form, not because the other forms are that sharp-witted but because this form distinguishes itself purely by its idiotic pretenses: the artwork is here the singular appearance by which reality "shows itself," "makes an appearance," "appears" (or the other way round), as a kind of phenomenological Yellow Pages possessing the gift of didactically representing "loss of reality" to the poor in spirit.

I lump this and similar stories together as the fable of the micro- and macrocosm because the work of art is understood here as a kind of portable version of a totalizing and thus even less surveyable whole. Condensed in this way, the fable is a useful approach to a similar phantasm: the information microcosm/macrocosm.

> It is well known how the simple presence of the television changes the rest of the habitat into a kind of archaic envelope, a vestige of human relations whose very survival remains perplexing. As soon as this scene is no longer haunted by its actors and their fantasies, as soon as behavior is crystallized on certain screens and operational terminals, what's left appears only as a large useless body, deserted and condemned. The real itself appears as a large useless body.[3]

That I here use a quote from Baudrillard is no attempt to suddenly give a semiotic turn to my argument; it is the start of the introduction of a formal problem of metalabile[4] textual production that I will call *interfacing*.

Within the discourse of Baudrillard this quote is characteristic of a number of diversionary tactics and movements around the concept of "illusion." "Hyperreality," "simulation," "simulacra," "strategy," and "seduction" are key words with which he occupies positions that he himself ultimately recognizes as "schizophrenic." That "schizo" is both the subject of his text and the object of his speech: "It is the end of interiority and intimacy, the overexposure and transparence of the world which traverses [the schizo] without obstacle. He can no longer produce the limits of his own being, can no longer play nor stage himself, can no longer produce himself as mirror. He is now only pure screen, switching center for all the networks of influence."[5] The network is shown here as a kind of Total-Simulation-Machine, a drawing of a state of things in which we witness the schizophrenic overflowing of mythos and logos: the image of the world as "net" or as "network," of the gods as masters of the "strings, nets, and snares," of the cosmic spider "weaving" the world,[6] is one of the most widespread and archaic metaphors of the ambiguity of the world as totality.[7] "The images of string, of rope, of snare, of texture are ambivalent: they express both a privileged situation (being linked to God, to be in a relation to the cosmic *Urgrund*) and a pitiful and tragic situation (being condemned, chained, predestinated, etc.)."[8] What makes Baudrillard's version of this cosmic cobweb interesting is not so much the paradoxical provocation of an ambiguous but merry nightmare as the totalizing turn that he gives to the notion of "interface":

> The famous Japanese car that talks to you, that "spontaneously" informs you of its general state and even of your general state, possibly refusing to function if you are not functioning well, the car as deliberating consultant and partner in the general negotiations of a lifestyle, something—or someone: at this point there is no longer any difference—with which you are connected. The fundamental issue becomes the communication with the car itself, a perpetual test of the subject's presence with his own objects, an uninterrupted interface.[9]

In Baudrillard the interface, as intermediary instance between the different extensions of a network, becomes the metaphorical place or fault line where the consumption of (hyper)reality suddenly changes to the production of "reality." This is exactly the point where the (image)text reacts against experience as behavior of consumption. In that sense this (image)text is not the reflection, not the concentration or the crystallization of reality but its *counterpart*.

Hence the hilarious nature of my microcosm/macrocosm fable: in the idiotic fable another fable is hidden, the fable of the interface as *fatum*, as inevitable, narcissistic coupling of an absent subject to an absent reality.

In the metalabile oscillations of the image as rebus, the interface is not the contact area between different codes of simulation, it is the switching edge: the area in the network where the different (fragmented) codes stimulate or inhibit each other.

Described in this way the rebus interface can be compared to a *synapse*: the place in the nervous system where, in addition to the transmission of the impulse, the integration of information takes place. Remarkable about this analogy is that it is exactly by means of simulation models that the relation between electronic networks and neural switches can be studied or, expressed more formally, that the integration of information can be represented as a complex process in which "threshold functions," "inhibition values," and "excitation values" are balanced against each other.[10]

The bend that I made, by way of Baudrillard, to get from the evocation of postmodernity as polymorphous theater of information to the formal polymorphy of the rebus discourse, was thus necessary: against the reading of the interface as totalizing metaphor, I pose another metaphor, that of interface as synapse. Interfacing in this way becomes the nonlinear switching algebra of the network that must still be characterized as its rhetorical manifestation: *allegory*.

The Incident

1848: the exaltation after the stormy February revolution must have been so general that even a proponent of "l'art pour l'art" like Théophile Gautier forgot his principles and burst out enthusiastically: "The old icons don't mean a thing any more. We have to create anew a whole symbolism that corresponds to the ideas and aspirations of our time, theologically, politically and allegorically."[11] The enthusiasm concerned a *Concours des figures symboliques de la République* which the early Second Republic had called almost immediately and made public in the *Moniteur* of March 18, 1848.[12] A pleiad of artists responded to this call to design an allegorical figure representing the Republic: 696 artists in total, represented by 451 paintings, 173 sculptures, and 72 medallions.[13]

In spite of the general enthusiasm for this project, the result was, to say the least, disappointing: "What an exhibition! Present were pink, green, yellow Republics; Republics surrounded by the attributes of '89: broken chains, equilateral triangles, fasces, tables of the law; Republics in silk dresses, in dressing gowns, in floral dresses, or as national guards."[14] The regained Republican fervor indeed contrasted rather strongly with the meager loans, adaptations, combinations, and recombinations from Ripa's *Iconologia* and his more recent French followers like Gravelot, Cochin, and J. B. Huet.[15] This contrast is, in "explanatory" form, illustrated on the bottom of the frame of Hippolyte Flandrin's entry: "The Republic takes as her base and throne the altar of Fraternity on which she sacrifices all hatred, represented by a snake. She brings peace to the world, and with her right hand presents it its symbol; in her left hand she holds the French flag, the flagpole fortified by a fasces, emblem of union. The Republic is white and pure, it is a virgin without a blemish! Her throne is posed on the globe, her wings are stretched, indicating the grandeur of her future."[16] Flandrin's work was awarded first place, but except for the illustrative value of the quote, the fortunes of this work have no relevance here. The participation of Honoré Daumier on the other hand is remarkable; even more remarkably, he was, together with the Ingrist Flandrin, one of the twenty laureates.[17]

The result of this selection was that Daumier, together with the other laureates, could make a monumental version of his design paid for by the state. And here the allegorical boat capsized completely: Daumier's design was, much more than an unhappy compromise, a monstrous hybrid. His *Republic* looks like a swollen version of *Charity* from volume 1 of Gravelot and Cochin's *Iconologie par figures*, a nursing matron showing more affinity with his porridge-eating plebeians[18] than with the whitewashed figures that had become typical of such allegories.

In the middle of the nineteenth century the humanistic *ut pictura poesis* tradition had degenerated so much to the "Prosperity" and "Progress," "Industry" and "Justice" ghosts on the fronts of bank buildings and museums, on commemorative signs and medallions, on trade union flags and pavilions of world exhibitions, that Daumier never could inflate his Republic as Magna Mater to the required monumental dimensions without drifting from the hybrid into the grotesque. He never finished the definitive version and drew his own "realistic" conclusions: "The devil take those allegories without head or tail."[19]

This story about Daumier and the *Concours des figures symboliques de la République* could be a vignette of the condition of allegory around 1850 (if it went underground in the history of figurative arts, it has reemerged now, in postmodern form); but there is more to this story: for it was Courbet who stimulated Daumier to venture into this allegorical labyrinth. *Why* we don't know. We only know that Courbet himself toyed with the idea of participating in the contest but finally withdrew and left the fight for realism to his sole friend. Less than seven years later, in 1855, Courbet showed his famous *L'atelier du peintre, allégorie réelle*, to which title he added "determining a phase of seven years of my artistic life."[20]

That this gigantic work is an allegory cannot be disputed in any meaningful way. The work has been thoroughly dealt with iconographically, or if one prefers iconologically, in all kinds of articles and monographs.[21] The painting can "literally" be read as a rather theatrical representation of the studio of Courbet; on closer examination this theater seems to be rather empathically staged: it is a "turning stage" on which the world of Arts and Letters (the right-hand side) and the representatives of the social classes (the left side: "the world of trivial life") meet around the central and starkly illuminated image of Nature. In that sense the painting is a realistic bringing up to date of humanist allegories like *Apollo and the Muses*, *The Studio of Apelles*, and even the *Porta Virtutis*. In its turn the bringing up to date is also a programmatic piece of work: "painted art theory" in the terms used by Matthias Winner,[22] and it can thus also be read as an homage to art, to realism, and to the artist Courbet himself.

The combination of this egocentric homage to controversial figures like Apollonie Sabatier, P.-J. Proudhon, A. Bruyas, V. Cuenot, M. Buchon, Champfleury, and Baudelaire suggests that underneath the artistic allegory hides a political masquerade: the figures of "the world of trivial life" staging a (for the politically self-conscious Courbet not unusual) *charade* in which Achille Fould, Louis Veuillot, Lazare Carnot, Garibaldi, Alexander Herzen, and Napoléon III can be recognized.[23] Finally, if "atelier" equals "Masonic workshop," a Masonic reading is possible in which the red mannequin and the standing (female) nude model, as figurations of the two pillars Jachin and Boaz ("sun and moon," "king and queen"), accompany

59

the alchemical child: the Rebis, a reading[24] further elaborated in the dossier that Hélène Toussaint edited for the catalogue of the great Courbet exhibition of 1977.

Courbet's *Atelier* is thus the second part in my questioning of the disappearance and reemergence of allegorical discourse: this painting is certainly an allegory, but it is also a realistic representation that not only admits allegoresis[25] but stimulates it; but what does "allégorie réelle" mean? Courbet always played the role of provocateur with gusto; his haughty behavior, his affectedly coarse and brutal way of speaking, his bizarre mixture of anarchist and socialist insubordination, and, more specifically, his antiacademic and aggressive iconoclasm often led his combination "allegorical/real" to be dismissed as a grandiloquent variant of the paradox: as paradoxism.

If this is the case, then Courbet's *Atelier* is nothing more than a detour, a perhaps intriguing focus on the complexity of "the disappearance of allegory," but a detour nevertheless. But there is more at stake than the mere fine-tuning of an art historical problem: the question is not to what degree a "real allegory" is a terminological provocation or a programmatic irony, but how to get a view over a field (*champ énonciatif*) in which an allegory can or cannot be represented as "real." This question can be approached step by step, from Courbet/Proudhon and realism through Friedrich Creuzer and romantic symbolism, to Marsilio Ficino and Pico della Mirandola and humanistic Neoplatonism. It doesn't require much imagination to make from this gathering a meeting and, why not, a banquet.

The Symposium

The symposium starts with a diatribe by Proudhon, who, even though he finds the *Atelier* of his friend Courbet far too arrogant, sketches a picture of the programmatic discourse at the origin of the painting:

> For, finally, your gods, your saints, your great men, all of these historical characters, fairylike, dramatic, allegorical, romantic, and chivalrous, all of those, closer to reality, that figure in your landscapes, your seascapes, your genre paintings, what is all that, except imagination, nightmare, or even more: avowal of impotence? You speak of invention, creation, liberty! and you have never been anything else but a follower of mythologists, theosophists, poets, novelists, fabulists, historiographers, as if art only existed to illustrate revelation, epic, comedy, or history.[26]

At first the rejection of the whole pandemonium of gods and nymphs, of troubadours and crusaders seems to be Proudhon's breaking point. But all of those phantoms are only black sheep easily pointed to and, in 1865, even more easily ridiculed. The actual aggression is directed against "imagination," a term used by Proudhon to belittle everything that he considers to be an antipode of reality. In that sense he is neither cross nor prophetic: from David on, the cry for Reality and Nature as all-encompassing slogan gets louder, and up to the twentieth century we can see how, in all kinds of critical articles and art historical writings, the opposition perception/imagination is crudely elevated to a criterion of modernity (in painting).

The confused entanglement woven by the juxtaposition of (sensory) reality and imagination, from Aristotelian mimesis to Kantian apperception and hypotyposis,[27] here only forms the background for Proudhon's aggressive dichotomy. For if we are not fooled by his frontal attack on what he calls "impotent idealism," we notice that, almost hidden by the verbal assault, the nerve of his discourse twitches on the smallest possible spot: the word *illustrate*.

Realism can and may be anything, if only it is not "illustrative." Reality and realism are to be coupled together by a link that can only be aped and parodied by all of the imaginary and imaginative figures so openly despised by Proudhon. But all of those ghostly figures are nothing but the polychrome decor behind which hides an aesthetic upstart—a relatively friendly term compared with what Walter Benjamin calls a "usurper": "For more than a hundred years the philosophy of art has been dominated by a usurper, who has come to power in the confusion of romanticism. The love of the romantic aestheticians for the glittering and ultimately noncommittal insight of the absolute has introduced even in the simplest of art theoretical debates a concept of symbol that has nothing in common with the real one except for the term."[28] Here it becomes clear why Proudhon so carefully covered up the concept of "symbol," on which is founded the hyperbolic coupling of image to reality: what Benjamin in his *Origin of German Tragic Drama* calls the *Entstellung* carried out by romanticism from theology to aesthetics[29] shows up in Proudhon, in reverse fashion, as negation (*Verneinung*) by means of the term *theosophy*.

Hence he wants to divert all attention, unsuccessfully, from the appearance or the form to the "idea" (the "ideal," the "imaginary"): "For this misuse takes place wherever in the work of art the 'appearance' of an 'idea' is taken as a 'symbol.' The unity of sensory and transcendental objects, the paradox of the theological symbol, is distorted into a relation of appearance and being."[30] Here enters Friedrich Creuzer, the third participant in our symposium, with an exposition of the distinction between symbol and allegory: "This [allegorical representation] means solely a general concept, or an idea, different from itself; the other the sensualized, embodied idea itself. There a usurpation takes place. . . . Here that concept itself has descended into this corporeal world, and in the Symbol we see it as itself and without mediation."[31] Although Creuzer establishes in his work a wayward connection between allegory and symbol, from the comparison above it becomes apparent how strongly his concept of symbol fits in with the "distorted theology" of romantic aesthetics as propagated by Schlegel, Goethe, and Schelling.[32] The quasi-divine, "unmediated" power of the symbol, discovered by Creuzer in the classics, is also discovered in dialectical form by Hegel:

> For what characterizes the symbol in Hegel's usage is precisely the quality he calls "inadequacy." The symbol is a groping adumbration of something inexpressible. The monstrosity of Indian and Egyptian divinities with their animal forms and their inorganic features are for Hegel the hallmark of this inadequacy. He contrasts this symbolic art which, to him, stands only in the forecourt of the temple of art with the art of the Greeks which for him, as for Winckelmann, reveals the essence of art as such. Here meaning and sensuous appearance, "the inward and the outward . . . are no longer distinct . . . The manifesting and the manifested is resolved into a concrete unity."[33]

Benedetto Croce, although he even more drastically reduced the relation between allegory and symbol ("allegory is art aping science"),[34] baldly indicated the breeding ground of this romantic symbolism: "Platonism or, more accurately, neo-Platonism was revived by the creator of the history of figurative art, Winckelmann."[35] The affiliations in this Neoplatonic undercurrent are more numerous and complex than even Croce suspected—the unraveling of it, spurred on by the Warburg Institute, was still to come—but the connection that he made between romantic aesthetics and Neoplatonism was correct. Creuzer demonstrates this connection: "Here reigns the unspeakable, which, while looking to express itself, finally lets its earthly form explode, as a weak cask, through the infinite power of its being. Hereby, however, the clarity of contemplation itself is destroyed, and there remains only a speechless astonishment."[36] This is pure cabala: the interweaving among Creuzer's mystic concept of symbol, cabala, and (Neoplatonic) gnosis is now demonstrated by our fourth speaker, Markos, a Valentinian Gnostic from the second century: "When at the beginning the fatherless father, who is neither man nor woman, wanted to make his unspeakable being speakable and his invisible being visible, he opened his mouth and produced a word that resembled him. Because it came to him, it showed him what it was, in that it appeared as figure of the invisible."[37] In this symposium the Markos text documents the connection between the Neoplatonic gnosis and the eldest forms of the Schi'ur Koma (the cabalist contemplation of the divine being) and at the same time provides an archaic mirror image of the romantic concept of symbol that Benjamin, from his first intervention on, suspected of being a "theological usurper."

Between this gnosis/cabala interference, eighteenth-century illuminism, and romantic symbolism, by way of Paracelsus, Jacob Boehme, and Angelus Silesius, a historical fabric of relations can be indicated that may be called the magical-alchemical filiation.[38] That this filiation was noticed by contemporaries becomes apparent from the effect of a number of lectures on Schelling by Jacob Burckhardt: "Schelling is a gnostic. . . . I thought that at any moment some monstrous Asian god would waddle in on twelve legs and raise twelve arms in order to take off six hats from his six heads."[39] Opposite this magical-alchemical filiation a second line can be drawn between the Neoplatonic humanism of the Renaissance and the "borderline between physis and meaning" of the baroque: "While in the symbol with the explanation of decline the transfigured appearance of nature reveals itself fleetingly in the light of revelation, in Allegory the *facies hippocratica* of history appears as fossilized original landscape before the eyes of the spectator."[40] I call this the allegorical filiation and immediately give the floor to Pico della Mirandola, who discloses his own *champ énonciatif*: "In Porphyry you will enjoy the copiousness of matter and the multiformity of religion; in Iamblichus you will revere an occult philosophy and strange foreign mysteries (barbarorum mysteria) . . . not to mention Proclus, who abounds in Asiatic richness, and those stemming from him, Hermias, Damascius, Olympiodorus . . . in all of whom there ever gleams . . . 'the Divine,' which is the distinctive mark of the Platonists."[41]

The common background of Dionysus the Areopagite, Plotinus, Proclus, Iamblichus is not only literally mentioned by the humanists of the Renaissance in their writings; it is just as recognizable in the programmatic representations and cycles of their allegories.[42] Even the exuberant syncretism that links the Church Fathers to the cabala and Pythagoras to Augustine forms part of a rhetorical discourse[43] more game than moralization: "The enjoyment Pico derived from occult authors was vicarious and poetical; they exercised his imagination in the employment of outlandish metaphors. It never occurred to him, as it did to less speculative minds, that the turgid lore of the dialectical magi might be put to more nefarious use than amplifying the Platonic 'mystères littéraires.' Black magic, in the sense that it appealed to Agrippa of Nettesheim, he rejected as a vile superstition."[44]

Occultum: the word is dropped here in all of its ambiguity. What for the magical-alchemical filiation was the key notion for a secret and forbidden deciphering of the "unspeakable," the secret of the "immanence," is here, in the allegorical filiation, the go-ahead for an inexhaustible game of hardly visible, but hence fascinating, links: "Hinc appelata mysteria: nec mysteria quae non occulta."[45]

This inexhaustible game of veil behind veil, this *serio ludere* of the humanists has more to do with the *orthoos mainesthai* (correct rage) that Plato in his *Sophist* considered a ritual "purification of the soul"[46] than with the bourgeois-romantic interpretation of mystery as an "embodiment of being in appearance."

That the humanists of the Renaissance distorted the mysteries of the classics by reading them as hieroglyphs, or more, that they distorted the hieroglyphs by explaining them as mystery writings is, in the light of Benjamin's reading of history as a "fossilized original landscape," to be understood starting from the superior detachment of allegory in opposition to the mystifying promises of the romantic concept of symbol: "In Benjamin this is conceived in such a way . . . that somewhere there were historical fundamental phenomena that were originally present but have decayed and are coded into the allegorical, and thus return in the allegorical as what is literal [das Buchstabenhafte]."[47] Images that are characters and characters that are images can be read, in this context, as the moving signs or *grammata* of a (Freudian) rebus. We now also discover that such a staging had already been indicated in the allegorical veils read by the humanists in what was for them an antique dream language: "The obscurity of expression, the mystery surrounding the so concealed idea, is for them the most beautiful ornament, a powerful cause of attraction . . . *Vela faciunt honorem secreti.*"[48] "The veil is the core of the mystery": the oscillating language of allegory cannot be opposed more clearly to the romantic pretensions of the "unmediated" symbol. Is not the link thus made between what I would call the mise-en-scène of the rebus and what Roland Barthes insists on calling the text/plurality?

> The codes of representation explode today in favor of a multiple space of which the model can no longer be painting (the picture as "tableau") but would rather be theater (the theatrical scene), as has been announced, or at least desired, by Mallarmé. And then: if literature and painting cease to be taken as a hierarchical reflection, the one being the rearview mirror of the other, why then consider them any longer as objects at the same time solidary and separated, in short: categorized? Why not annul their differences (which are purely substantial)? Why not renounce the plurality of "arts," in order to better promote that of "texts"?[49]

Our symposium draws to an end; only the eighteenth-century Abbé Pluche still has to utter a complaint: "Since a painting is only intended to show what one does not tell me, it is ridiculous that an effort is needed to understand it. . . . And usually, when I succeed in guessing the intention of these mysterious characters, I find that what one tells me is hardly worth the expense of that effort."[50] Here "allegory" is mixed up with a rhetorical figure, "allegorism."[51] Moreover, the pious abbé considers the painted enigmas that his colleagues, the Jesuits, propagated for didactic and other reasons, as a civilized but superfluous pastime:

> The enigmas which we are considering here had no such pretentions: they derive not from the oracle of Minos or the hieroglyphs of Egypt, and contain not even the moral wisdom of the precepts of Pythagoras: their classical precedents are the after-dinner amusements of which we read in Aulus Gellius and Athenaeus, the riddles propounded by the Greeks around the banqueting table, when the wine had been flowing, and when the answer which found most favour was that which provided entertainment rather than instruction, and displayed wit rather than wisdom.[52]

Is this voluntary or involuntary confusion of concepts not already an announcement of Benjamin's romantic "usurper"? Or is Jesuitism involved, an attempt to dispose of humanist allegories as nothing more than an "exercise & divertissement de l'esprit"?

Neither the conceptual confusion nor the belittling to *divertissement* is, however, a match for the bewildering and playful labyrinth of allegory itself. Posed in this way, allegory is a game to the extent that it is an aporia, and an aporia to the extent that it articulates the aporia.[53] Or, in Barthes's terms, "the problem is to *maintain* the enigma in the initial void of its response."[54]

Translated from the Flemish by Marc Holthof

NOTES:
1. Robert Graves, *The Greek Myths* (Harmondsworth, 1960), 1:27.
2. Ibid., 1:28.
3. Jean Baudrillard, "The Ecstasy of Communication," in Hal Foster, ed., *Postmodern Culture* (London, 1983), 129.
4. The term *metalability* does not exist, but as neologism it does form a useful counterpart or pendant of *metastability*. Just as a metastabile condition can, from a small margin of stability, be disturbed until it transforms into a condition of greater or definitive stability, so a metalabile condition would show only a small margin of lability in which it continued to oscillate at the border of total lability.
5. Baudrillard, "The Ecstasy of Communication," 133.
6. See Mircea Eliade, *Images et symboles* (Paris, 1952), passim; and "Cordes et Marionettes," in *Méphistophélès et l'androgyne* (Paris, 1962), 200–37.
7. For an elaboration of this metaphor of network as cybernetic myth, see P. De Vylder, "Het Hilton-Systeem," in *Nox C, Chloroform* (1993), 131–47.
8. Eliade, *Méphistophélès et l'androgyne*, 221.
9. Baudrillard, "The Ecstasy of Communication," 127.
10. See, for example, C. E. Shannon and J. McCarthy., eds., *Automata Studies*, Annals of Mathematics Studies 34 (Princeton, 1956).
11. Théophile Gautier, in *La Presse*, April 21, 1848, as cited in M. Spencer, *The Art Criticism of Théophile Gautier* (Geneva, 1969), 44.
12. See A. Boime, "The Second Republic's Contest for the Figure of the Republic," *Art Bulletin* 53 (1971): 68–83.
13. Ibid., 72.
14. (Probably) Champfleury in *Le Pamphlet*, September 3, 1848, as cied in idem, *Le réalisme: Textes choisis et présentés par G. et J. LaCambre* (Paris, 1973), 209.
15. Gravelot and Cochin, *Iconologie par figures*, 4 vols. (Paris, 1789–91); J. B. Huet, *Le trésor des artistes et des amateurs d'art, ou le guide des peintres, dessinateurs, graveurs, architectes, décorateurs, etc., dans le choix des sujets allégoriques ou emblématiques qu'ils ont à employer dans leurs compositions*, 3 vols. (Paris, 1810).
16. As cited in Boime, "The Second Republic's Contest," 81.
17. See B. Lemann, "Daumier and the Republic," *Gazette des Beaux-Arts* 6, no. 27 (1945): 105–20; and T. J. Clark, *The Absolute Bourgeois: Artists and Politics in France, 1848–1851* (London, 1973), especially "The Art of the Republic," 31–71.
18. I refer here to a drawing by Daumier from ca. 1850: *La Soupe,* wash drawing, 40 x 28 cm, Paris, Musée du Louvre.
19. Honoré Daumier as cited in T. de Banville, *Mes souvenirs* (Paris, 1883), 166.
20. Gustave Courbet, *L'atelier du peintre . . .,* 1854–55, oil on canvas, 359 x 598 cm, Paris, Musée du Louvre.
21. To mention the most important: R. Huyghe, G. Bazin, and H. Adhemar, *Courbet, L'atelier du peintre, Allégorie réelle*, 1855 (Paris, 1944); B. Nicholson, *Courbet: The Studio of the Painter* (London, 1973); H. Toussaint, "Le dossier de 'L'atelier' de Courbet," in *Gustave Courbet*, exhib. cat. (Paris, Grand Palais, 1977–78), 241–77.
22. M. Winner, "Gemalte Kunsttheorie. Zu Gustave Courbets 'Allégorie réelle' unter der Tradition," *Jahrbuch der Berliner Museen* 4 (1962): 151–85.
23. See on this Toussaint, "Le dossier," 251–58.
24. Ibid., 261–63.
25. "Allegoresis" is here understood, contrary to "allegory" (the allegorical text/image-text of allegorical discourse), as an allegorical reading or as a specific type of commentary, on the model of "exegesis" or traditional text or image explanation.
26. P.-J. Proudhon, *Du principe de l'art et de sa destination sociale* (Paris, 1865), 200.
27. For a treatment of this problematic in Kant and his contemporaries, see M. Podro, *The Manifold in Perception: Theories of Art from Kant to Hildebrand* (Oxford, 1972).
28. Walter Benjamin, *Ursprung des deutschen Trauerspiels* (Frankfurt, 1978), 138.
29. Ibid., 138–39.

30. Ibid., 138.

31. Friedrich Creuzer, *Symbolik und Mythologie der alten Völker* (1819), as cited in ibid., 143.

32. See Tzvetan Todorov, "Symbole et allégorie," in *Théories du symbole* (Paris, 1977), 235–60.

33. E. H. Gombrich, "Icones Symbolicae," in *Symbolic Images* (London, 1972), 188.

34. Benedetto Croce, *Aesthetic* (Boston, 1978; original Italian edition, 1901): "There is no double bottom to art, but one only; in art all is symbolical, because all is ideal. But if the symbol be conceived as separable—if the symbol can be on one side, and on the other the thing symbolized, we fall back again into the intellectualist error: the so called symbol is the exposition of an abstract concept, an allegory; it is science, or art aping science" (34).

35. Ibid., 262.

36. Creuzer, as cited in Benjamin, *Ursprung*, 143.

37. Markos, as cited in G. Scholem, *Von der mythischen Gewalt der Gottheit* (Frankfurt, 1977), 18.

38. See A. Viatte, *Les sources occultes du romantisme*, 2 vols. (Paris, 1965).

39. Jacob Burckhardt, as cited in E. Wind, *Pagan Mysteries in the Renaissance* (Harmondsworth, 1967), 23.

40. Benjamin, *Ursprung*, 145.

41. Giovanni Pico della Mirandola, *De hominis dignitate*, as cited in Wind, *Pagan Mysteries*, 8.

42. See the already cited works by Wind and Gombrich, which, besides original contributions concerning the iconography of such works, contain many bibliographical references.

43. "These books [of the cabala] I procured at no small expense, and read them with the greatest attention and indefatigable labours. In them I found—God is my witness—not so much of the Jewish as the Christian religion. Here was the mystery of the Trinity, here the incarnation of the Word, here the divinity of the Messiah. . . . On those matters which pertain to philosophy you would think you were hearing Pythagoras and Plato, whose theories are so akin to the Christian faith that our Augustine gave infinite thanks to God because the books of the Platonists had come into his hands." (Pico della Mirandola, as cited in Wind, *Pagan Mysteries*, 20–21.)

44. Ibid., 8.

45. Pico della Mirandola, as cited in ibid., 11 ("Hence they are called mysteries: because there are no mysteries that are not hidden").

46. "The cleansing of the soul, the welcoming of death, the power to enter into communion with the beyond, the ability to 'rage correctly' (orthoos mainesthai), these benefits which Plato recognised were commonly provided by the mystical initiations were to be obtained through his philosophy by rational exercise, by a training in the art of dialectic whose aim it was to purge the soul of error" (ibid., 3).

47. Theodor W. Adorno, "Die Idee der Naturgeschichte," in *Philosophische Frühschriften* (Frankfurt, 1973), 359.

48. H. L. Marrou, *Saint Augustin et la fin de la culture antique*, as cited in Wind, *Pagan Mysteries*, 10 ("The veils form the greatness of the mystery").

49. Roland Barthes, S/Z (Paris, 1970), 62.

50. Abbé Pluche (1748), as cited in Gombrich, "Icones Symbolicae," 123.

51. "Allegorism, imitation of allegory, consists in a prolonged and continuous metaphor, which, while being extended to the whole proposition, only provokes one sole and unique meaning, as if offering to the mind one sole and unique object" (P. Fontanier, *Les Figures du Discours* (Paris, 1970; first edition, 1821–30), 116.

52. J. Montagu, "The Painted Enigma and French Seventeenth-Century Art," *Journal of the Warburg and Courtauld Institutes* 31 (1968): 309.

53. "'The Social Contract' [by Rousseau] . . . is structured like an aporia: it persists in performing what it has shown to be impossible to do. As such, we can call it an allegory" (Paul De Man, *Allegories of Reading*, as cited in Craig Owens, "The Allegorical Impulse," in Brian Wallis, ed., *Art after Modernism* [New York, 1964], 228).

54. Barthes, S/Z, 81.

NANCY SPERO, *Sheelag Na-gig at Home*, 1995.
Courtesy of the artist. Photo: David Reynolds.

Inscriptions in the Feminine

Griselda Pollock

I n 1971 Bridget Riley said that women artists needed feminism—"this hysteria"—like they
needed a hole in the head. The statement appeared in *Art and Sexual Politics*, one of the
earliest publications to confront this topic.[1] In the climate of a still hegemonic modernism, to
conjoin the terms *art, sex,* and *politics* was a transgression. In the 1990s, it remains theoretically and critically perplexing yet unquestionably necessary.

I

On the field of cultural contest in the early 1970s, two historic paradigms met head-on: modernism and feminism. Despite institutionalized modernism's considerable attractions for the
many women artists who embraced its aesthetic liberties, the movement had performed the
"liberal lie": in pursuit of universal truths, absolute values, and aesthetic purity, gender and all
other forms of social positioning were deemed irrelevant. Yet they remained not only determinant but structural, valorizing only certain meanings and identities as significantly modern.
For Clement Greenberg, a critic who played a powerful role in defining the central achievements of modernism, gender, like class or race, was part of the baggage of ideological conflict
in modern societies that must be expunged if ambitious art was to perform its heroic act of
self-preservation within capitalism and against fascism.[2] For women, however, burdened by
the oppressive weight of gender created in the preceding century, modernism's apparent
autonomy beckoned, promising a realm of new freedoms.

   For nineteenth-century bourgeois cultures, gender was a central column upholding social
hierarchies. Denied access to social and political subjecthood, defined as legal minors and
economic dependents, condemned to intellectual pauperism, women were, however, allowed
a confined sphere of "feminine" influence and moral authority exclusively in the home. This
domesticated female mission was nonetheless allowed limited ideological endorsement
through a specifically *feminine* art and literature. The difficulty was that the price of access to
this feminine art was total subjection to the prevailing definition of what it was to be
"Woman"—a classed as well as racializing trope.[3] *Overfeminization* resulted from this historical development in which the "empire of gender saturated the entirety of one's being."[4]
All women became but another face of the singular abstraction Woman.

Modernism, which emerged just as women were politically challenging the bourgeois state for the right to self-representation (at the level of culture as much as of politics),[5] seemed to offer an antidote to this generalizing sexualization through its apparent aesthetic autonomy from the social and its prizing of unique—ungendered—individuality. To be an artist under the modernist dispensation promised women a way to be more than mere "women artists" or lady painters. The woman question engaged all of society in a profound debate about enunciations of femininity, which were defined in relation to other key terms: nature or history, the home or the social, timeless entity or changing possibility.[6] Modernism, identified with progress and the possibility of social transformation and with the invention of new identities in opposition to notions of tradition, eternal verity, and the decrees of nature, seemed to offer a space for women to reinvent themselves as "new women," identified with freedom, progress, and radical change—these figuring an escape from overfeminization.

But it was a lie. Modernism simply inverted the problem and produced for women a radical *underfeminization* without altering masculine hegemony. In a founding text of revived feminism, published in 1973, Carol Duncan identified early twentieth-century modernism not merely as overtly masculinist—in its continuing preoccupation with white men's experience—but as assertively *virile*—socially as well as iconographically obsessed with male heterosexuality as the defining trope of artistic creativity.[7] Across Europe in avant-garde centers, male artists depicted the site of modern artistic production, the studio, as the scene of a dramatic encounter between male creator and his sexual object, woman, the product of which uneven exchange was a virile modern art written on the bodies of working women. *His* freedom was articulated as sexual, as were the wellsprings of this modern creativity. The emergent mythologies of the modern artist produced a specifically gendered concept of the autogenetic artist—the artist who creates himself—which was initially staged through the cultural murder of the Mother and of the maternal feminine and through the construction of a masculine subjectivity in relation to the tropes of a degraded, prostituted, or lesbian sexuality. From Degas, Toulouse-Lautrec, and Rouault through to the definitive icon of early modernism (centrally positioned in the Museum of Modern Art's narrative space), Picasso's *Demoiselles d'Avignon* (1907), this trope of masculine creativity shaped in dramatic encounter with a primal sexuality—figured through an abject or monstrous female body—forms a major genealogy of modern art.[8] Julia Kristeva writes: "This is why one of the most accurate representations of creation, that is, of [modern] artistic practice, is the series of paintings by Willem de Kooning entitled *Woman*: savage, explosive, funny inaccessible creatures in spite of the fact they have been massacred by the artist."[9] Carol Duncan, writing with her coauthor Alan Wallach, analyzes the narrative enshrined in the Museum of Modern Art that runs from *Demoiselles* to *Woman I* as the performance of a virile, sexually assertive masculine psychodrama encountering and mastering the monstrous or fertile feminine.[10]

Such a history presented specific dilemmas for modernist women artists. In what terms could femininity and creativity be articulated in these modernist spaces and narratives of artistic innovation? How could women artists reclaim their image, their bodies as signs of a different embodiment of cultural agency? Could the body of woman also be the body of creative intellect and sexuality?[11] An artist like Paula Modersohn Becker, engaged by what she found in Paris on visits between 1900 and 1907, attempted to combine the tropes of untrammeled creativity (nature, the body, paradise, the wild) and female generativity in her self-portrait of 1906, but the iconic load buckled under its contradictory, or rather culturally unauthorized, connotations.

During the 1920s and 1930s, drawn to the surrealist investigation of sexuality and the unconscious, women artists were confounded by the governing fantasies of a masculine heterosexual psyche in which woman as muse, *femme-enfant*, or goddess obstructed any acknowledged articulation of an autonomous feminine subjectivity.[12] From the thirties to the fifties women were attracted to the spaces and practices of a more abstract modernism, with its as yet unwritten scripts and its distance from the ideological overload of figurative representation then articulating so crudely the male/female dichotomies. Yet even here women found themselves caught in another deadly paradox. To gain access to more of their humanity, they would be permitted none to their femininity. Any traces of a gendered perspective or aesthetic sensibility would immediately suspend their claims to being considered serious artists, while, of course, any art that cannot call upon the full range of the producer's material and social experience will feel incomplete, inauthentic, like a masquerade.[13] Ambitious modernist women negotiated this contradiction in constant fear that their modernist credentials would be compromised by the contamination of gender, which official modernist critics never failed to discern and, detecting, to use to support the continuing hierarchy in which art by men was seen as unmarked, ungendered, universal in its revelations about the human condition while art made by women was always deemed to lack breadth, remaining partial, local, gender-based, and impossible to consider as art pure and simple; it was still, and always, *women's* art. That meant not really art at all. That is why Bridget Riley and her generation viewed feminism and its embrace of an avowed woman's perspective with the gravest of suspicions.[14] Femininity, not feminism, is what reveals a "hole" in the "head"—a female body in place of a modernist rationality or cerebral unconscious.

Women's art was, therefore, *other*, and that otherness offered nothing but the signs of what it lacked vis-à-vis what the masculinist modernist institution found in the art of men. Georgia O'Keeffe's flowers are sexual and feminine, whereas Monet's or Van Gogh's are triumphs of pure color and responses to nature.[15] These contradictions never stopped the women producing in any of the moments or movements of twentieth-century modernism and beyond, but they have progressively ensured the invisibility of women artists in the consolidated narratives and celebratory exhibitions that canonized an institutional and later an academic history of modern art. *Inside the Visible* challenges that invisibility by proposing to excavate a feminist genealogy of twentieth-century artists who are women, creating other chains of association and dialogues across time and space that frame and examine the contradictions of sexual difference and cultural positioning. This reveals a consistent history of artistic practices by women that can now cross this threshold of institutional blindness, creating unexpected links and conversations across this century's artistic moments at the margins as much as in the centers. This is possible because in excavating an erased past we reenvision the prehistory of the present: the modernist moment that is the lost condition of our postmodern situation. The premise of that historical project lies in a theoretical revolution that enables us now to *see* artists and work that had been made invisible, illegible, irrelevant. The feminist questioning of the present permits us to decipher the past and thus realign that present through a historically enriched understanding of the interrupted continuities of women's struggles in the modern era. It has taken more than twenty years of continuous theoretical work to imagine other ways to read (for) our histories and thus to situate our presents as something more profound than mere passing novelty or political fashion. The contradictions at the heart of official modernism were retrospectively revealed in the 1970s when a specifically *feminist* discourse emerged to challenge the liberal lie with *a repoliticization of the question of gender*: art and sexual politics.

The repoliticization of gender is a historically new set of theorizations of sexual difference. The aim is to work beyond the opposition—to use a *tactical* insistence on sexual difference in order *strategically* to rupture the power systems that operate upon this explicit, sometimes latent, use of gender as an axis of hierarchy and power. The aim is to seek ways in which the difference of the feminine might function not merely as an alternative but as the dialectical spring to release us from the binary trap represented by sex/gender. This involves its own creative paradox: to seek articulations of the specifically feminine whose effects upon the totality of culture will be to displace homogeneity in favor of a radical heterogeneity. "Gender"—the division of the world into fixed oppositions anthropomorphically figured as man and woman—erases many other forms of difference: issues of sexuality and cultural diversity. The "feminine" serves to name its own political constituency and also, beyond the visible forms of gender, to signal a radical alterity in relation to a culture that dominates in the name of Man. Displacing the reign of gender that we have inherited will open doors to critical confrontations with all forms of xenophobia: fears of difference, of the stranger, of the other.[16]

II

> But feminist criticism is also likely to be complicitous with the institution,
> and the work of recognising how that may be,
> is the place where feminist criticism can move from opposition to critique, and thus to change.
> —Gayatri Spivak, "Imperialism and Sexual Difference"[17]

Feminist criticism challenges the liberal lie—the modernist unconscious of gender—by reasserting the importance of gender in making and analyzing art. Feminism was at first *oppositional*, celebrating the signs of women's gender identities and proclivities in a simple reversal of the modernist erasure. An alternative tradition, a neglected history of women artists, was excavated and new organizations and campaigns established to promote and exhibit contemporary art by women. There can be no denying the immense tactical importance of feminism's explosion onto the art scene since the early 1970s. Lucy Lippard has written eloquently of what it meant as a critic to come to a feminist awareness of modernism's blinkered view of art without a sex.[18] In 1980 Lippard claimed that "feminism's greatest contribution to the future of art has probably been precisely its *lack* of contribution to modernism." Offering a socially concerned alternative, threading female experience into the fabric of mainstream art through autobiography, narrative, and collage, feminism aimed not to add a new style, or shift the formal trajectory of art. "The goal of feminism is to change the character of art."[19] The politicization of gender, for Lippard, participated in a broader project to reconnect artistic practices to communities and social purposes radically opposed to the institutionalized elitism of canonized modernist culture.[20]

In a project as complex as that facing contemporary feminism no strategies are without value and significance, and I do not intend to fall into the usual traps of creating theoretical orthodoxy. I want to advance another perspective on the problematic of reading the visual arts made by women from an engaged feminist commitment. I draw on a particular set of resources, references, politics, and theories that form one corner of the patchwork of the long-term project that feminism represents in the histories of modernity and in the futures that we are now making.[21]

I want to outline a parallel trajectory that, taking its cue from Gayatri Spivak, represents the *critical* position, reexamining both the liberal lie and oppositional feminism in a dialectic in which reversal is not the tactic. Intervention is the organizing idea in practices that accept that there is no outside to use as a resource against a dominant inside; there is no elsewhere beyond the spaces of discourse, although unrecognized, unspoken elements appear within that discourse once its own contradictions are deconstructed from the internal alterity of a feminist position. Feminist strategies such as pivoting the center, reading against the grain, taking the view from elsewhere that is in fact right here, and seeing with a *matrixial* gaze take us from the certainties of men and women, the logics of sameness (women aiming to be assimilated to the dominant norms of power and social effectivity through economic and social equality with privileged men) and of difference (women asserting their irreducible otherness in opposition to the dominant culture and society through the specificities of their bodies, language, psyches, or maternally defined culture). The construct gender (or "sex" in the many languages that do not have this term) has been shifted by feminism in its perverse alliances with other streams of intellectual and political challenge to Western bourgeois modernity. Feminism has flourished in the poststructuralist universe of textuality, positionality, subjectivity, process, play, and difference. For many this reads as a betrayal of the politics that seem so much more palpable in the discourse and practice of oppositional feminism. Rather politics is critically reframed in another form of the move to challenge the character of existing discursive and institutional definitions of art and, as importantly, of artist by situating politics at the level of representation, cultural institution, signs, and their subjects.

The dominant mode of consumption and criticism of twentieth-century art is curatorial. The histories of modern art were primarily shaped by the museum, and its categories continue to define what is studied and how it is studied in colleges, universities, and art publications. Preservation and cataloguing promote divisions between and hierarchies of painting, sculpture, drawing, printmaking, collage, photomontage, photography, film, design, and so forth. These produce segregated histories. Cataloguing is by artist, and thus authorship defines the field. This authorship reflects the partnerships among the museum, the academy, and the market by representing the artist in the bourgeois form of creative, autonomous, proprietary, and self-possessing subject whose authorizing signature becomes the value-determining brand name of a marketable commodity that is culturally consumed and remembered in that personally packaged form.[22] Finally, periodization classifies these authored, media-defined practices into chapters in the narrative of modern art *-isms*—made concrete in museum displays and chronicled in published surveys.

The dominance of this curatorial model poses specific problems for any artistic practices that do not easily conform to those modes that already presuppose their content—modes tailored to selective practices and their related myths of artistic identity that the museum anticipates and then confirms as a continuing history of great male individuals grouped into a teleology of innovative movements. Practices and identities other than these cannot be placed in this model that presents itself merely as the mirror of a spontaneously produced, self-canonizing culture. Oppositional criticism leaves this structure in place while inadvertently confirming that what is outside its remit is outsider art, even when the published aim is assimilation.

Thus, feminism has needed to develop forms of analysis that can confront the difference of women as *other* than what is *other* to this masculine order while exposing the sexual politics of dominant discourses and institutions. Attempts to write histories of the last twenty years have yielded too easily to the curatorial model, turning politics and debates into camps and positions: essentialism versus (de)constructionism, politics versus theory, painting versus scripto-visual media, American versus European. These are dangerous disfigurements and forms of internal alienation that we cannot afford.

I want to do a little archaeology into the moment of feminism's confrontation with modernism and its unconscious in order to offer a particular, provisional, but I hope productive contribution to what must remain an expanded and complex field of possibilities all motivated by the need to confront the dilemmas and horrors of late twentieth-century societies with a feminist commitment. Feminism must begin to consider its own histories without murdering its mothers or falling into the postmodern trap of neotribalism.

III

Certain contemporary thinkers, as is well known, consider that modernity is the characterised as the first epoch in human history in which human beings attempt to live without religion. In its present form, is not feminism in the process of becoming one? Or is it, on the contrary and as avant-garde feminists hope, that having started with the idea of difference, feminism will be able to break free of its belief in Woman, Her power, Her writing, so as to channel this demand for difference into each and every element of the female whole, and finally, to bring out the singularity of each woman, and beyond this, her multiplicities, her plural languages, beyond the horizon, beyond sight, beyond faith itself.
—Julia Kristeva, "Women's Time"[23]

In 1977 the artist Mary Kelly gave a paper at a conference entitled "Art and Sexual Politics." As an intervention in the developing discourse of feminist criticism, the paper alerted its readers to the curatorial model: "First of all, I'd like to make a distinction between 'feminist practice' and 'the feminist problematic' in art (problematic in the sense that a concept cannot be isolated from the general theoretical or ideological framework in which it is used). For one aspect of 'the problematic' is the absence of a notion of 'practice' in the way it is currently being phrased: i.e., 'What *is* feminist art?' This provokes moralistic answers like 'It is this, and not this.'"[24]

Drawing on Louis Althusser's radical redefinition of "the ideological" as a "nonunitary complex of social practices and systems of representation which have political consequences," Kelly shifted from the terrain of art discourse, that is, artists expressing themselves, which feminism had taken over, to validate *women* as artists expressing their *women-selves* to produce a "feminist art." The adjective *feminist* designates neither the author and her intentions, nor the active reference to the gender experience of the artist or her art's content, nor a new curatorial -*ism*. Rather it attaches here to interventions on the bases of their *effects* in rupturing existing regimes of power and ideological meaning, sexual and other forms of social difference.[25]

Althusser's theory of ideology is premised on an intervention into Marxism by another revolutionary force in twentieth-century thought: psychoanalysis. There is no ideology without a subject, claimed Althusser, making subjectivity a necessary element in social theories of power. *Critical* feminism can be defined precisely through its long-term and conflicted engagement with the notion of the subject and available theorizations of subjectivity.[26] Kelly's "Sexual Politics," written while she was making the *The Post Partum Document* (1975–83), symptomatically refers to its moment of production in London in the mid-1970s.[27] Out of that critical, political, and theoretical juncture she developed a way of theorizing woman as artist through the simultaneous formation of the subject in ideology, language, and sexual difference.

Poststructural psychoanalysis here supplied feminism with a path through the thickets and riddles of women's dilemmas under patriarchy: How are we made into the masculine and feminine creatures of this regime ruled by the father? What happens to the mother in this order? What excess is created by the submission to the law of castration? What aspects of that excess, difference, cannot be articulated in its phallic signifying systems, and how can we access what the culture represses and renders unconscious or unsignified? How can we read the traces of feminine otherness that lack signifiers in a phallocentric system but that press upon the feminine subject in fantasy, dream, hysteria, hallucination, and even madness? Could a psychoanalytically tuned theory of reading allow us to recover feminine meanings deposited in artistic practices that hitherto fell below the threshold of intelligibility and visibility?

Kelly drew on a Freudian theory of narcissism and its related concept of identification to suggest ways to decipher the traces of this complex in the art currently being made by feminists. Underlying her analysis are two related ideas. The body—so often a key referent in feminist politics—is understood as a fantastic image of the imaginary ego, itself composed of identifications. This mocks any idea of a fixed identity or one based in a physical, anatomically defined body. Yet it does not deny the importance of a specifically feminine corporeality created through the impact of the maternal imago, voice, physical presence, and form and through later experiences of sexualities and reproduction. Equally, subjectivity is imagined as a perpetual flow of fantastic identifications that traverse empirically given genders or categories. Thus certain classic binary oppositions are instantly displaced: inside (the body) and outside (the world, society), imaginary and real, fantastic and empirical, individual and social, natural and cultural. In the Freudian theoretical frame, the notion of gender and its underpinning in any concept of nature or an actual, singular, anatomical body becomes impossible while the impact of the uneven and asymmetrical processes of sexual and social differentiation and related fantasies are paramount. Representation is not treated as the externalization of what is inside a coherent and discrete subject but defined as an imprecise domain permeating the purely imaginary boundaries of self and other, inside and out, private and public, body and object, and so forth. The work of art ceases to be a fetishized object, the deposit of a coherent, autonomous subject/author. It is theorized as a text, a site of a working through culturally as well as personally freighted materials. Art practice, in addition to the meanings that the artist actively calculates and manufactures, registers traces of the processes of subjectivity that are always both conscious and unconscious at the level of a productive semiosis—a production of meaning via signs in which the culture of reception, the reader, is as vital as the process of producing.

Kelly addressed a number of practices currently characteristic of an avowed feminist art movement. Far from offering iconographic or overtly political interpretations of individual pieces, she read the works *symptomatically* for unconscious investment as a way of indexing fantasies and desires of socially and culturally specific feminine subjectivities. She identified four tendencies based on Freud's theories of narcissism: female culture (mother art)—identification with the woman who feeds you; female anatomy (body art)—identification with herself; feminine experience (ego art)—identification with an image of what she would like to be; and feminine discourse (other art), which articulates intersubjective relationships that constitute her as a feminine subject, not object. This approach refused, therefore, to read into artwork known habits of women (central cores, typical colors, favored themes); indeed, to analyze art by interpreting symptoms at the level of psychic structures is a journey of discovery. The feminine (woman) is in many ways as unknown to those of us shaped within its terms as it was to the analytical community that turned off the lights of interested knowledge. Kelly read for what she called "feminine inscriptions."

> In summary, I think that feminine narcissism is an essential component of the feminist problematic in so far as it includes a symptomatic reading of our visual inscriptions, a reading based on absences as much as on presences; that such a reading suggests the way in which heterogeneous signifying processes underlie and often erupt into signifying practice; that because of the coincidence of language and patriarchy the "feminine" is (metaphorically) set on the side of the heterogeneous, the unnameable, the unsaid; and that in so far as the feminine is said, articulated in language, it is profoundly subversive.[28]

The phrase, "inscriptions in the feminine," has an archaeological ring to it. As if deciphering an ancient culture whose language is lost while its strange monuments remain to puzzle and provoke our curiosity, we must assume that we do not yet know what is being traced upon the surfaces of culture by artists speaking in, from, or of the feminine. A feminist reading for the inscriptions of the feminine means listening for the traces of a subjectivity formed in the feminine within and in conflict with a phallocentric system. Beyond that, it implies figuring out what working from that place, however unconsciously, might be *producing*, as yet unarticulated, unrepresented, unsignified, unrecognized.

The feminine is both the repressed of patriarchal culture and its excess, beyond yet inside its limits, that which will radically alter the system by emerging into signification. Woman has already been posed as a riddle and an enigma by Freud himself in his lectures on femininity.[29] I do not mean to compound that myth of feminine indecipherability. I am arguing that there exist other, feminine, heterogeneous meanings whose outlines we trace in current regimes of sense merely as otherness. In a phallocentric culture such meanings are denied a scheme of signs to acknowledge them in the Symbolic, and so they do not appear to make sense—or they are treated merely as signs confirming the stereotype of feminine difference, lack, insufficiency. Yet at some level this feminine other is always being used by masculine culture as its material support, a resource, a negated excess critical to the arrangements of the current symbolic order and its hierarchies. We need not invent a whole new language to speak the always already known feminine that this culture has repressed like an ice block in its deep freeze. Rather, the model of excavation and decipherment offers a way to explode the simultaneous abuse of women's inscriptions in culture as the negative cipher of masculine dominance and the negation of this alterity through cultural inattention to its specificities.

I am reminded here of Isak Dinesen's short story "The Blank Page." In a convent high in the hills above fields blue with flax seeded from the Holy Land, nuns spin and weave linen for the nuptial beds of royalty and nobility. Treasured in the same convent are small cuttings from these noble beds, bearing the stains of virginity-proving blood, each framed and mounted with its dynastic armorial bearings and a name. A procession of elderly, mantilla-clad women makes regular pilgrimage to this "museum" of "women's art" to read upon each blooded page stories of marriages, intrigues, children, alliances, the rise and fall of famous houses. One canvas merits special notice, attracts more gazes, incites the most profound contemplation. "The frame is as fine as any, and as proudly carries the golden plate with the royal crown. But on this plate no name is inscribed and the linen within the frame is snow-white from corner to corner—a blank page."[30]

Susan Gubar has used this story as a metaphor for women modernists' complex relation to creativity and its sexed bodies.[31] She sees the royal princesses framed within the narratives of patriarchal society: bodies used and claimed as objects of kinship exchange. The blood is both the sign of that exchange and the trace of women's only way into culture: bleeding into art, painting with their bodies. Within such a gallery, that which does not enter signification "in blood" via such circuits of woman as object appears blank. Yet by the unswerving loyalty to that truth women are moved to greatest contemplation of another story—one that might be traced upon an only apparently uninscribed surface, one that might be projected upon its open screen. The story does not celebrate silence as a female cultural virtue: it brilliantly creates a double image, hinged both to the blankness ascribed to female dissidence in a phallocentric text and to the possibility of meanings "otherwise" that press upon its heterogeneous surface.[32] The multifaceted image of the blank page complements the theme "inside the visible." It marks the spot where women's cultures appear unreadable according to the dominant narratives of art, art history, modernity, and modernism, while to a different eye that seeks beyond the visible for the index to other meanings, lives, traces of other configurations of the subject and the body, the surface is rich in possibilities for those desiring to decipher inscriptions of the feminine as dissidence, difference, and heterogeneity.

Here arguments proposed by Luce Irigaray and Hélène Cixous speak eloquently of our need to imagine new signifiers, to generate the signifying system that would allow a feminine imaginary and a feminine symbolic to be an effective part of the culture that at present leaves women in exile, in dereliction, in the wilderness of the enforced blanked-out page.[33] While both writers have been assumed to be positing a feminine essence in the body of women from which these new metaphors would stem, I hear them calling for new semiotic relations between the corporeality of the subject and the filters or signs through which meanings that might articulate otherwise what feminine subjects now are forced to experience hysterically or psychotically because there are no metaphors to accommodate their own psychic, fantastic, and sexual lives. Such positions accept the body as an irreducible materiality for experience always semiotically mediated, unconsciously imagined, lived, experienced through the defiles of significations, from the most archaic pictograms up through fantasy to fully symbolic, linguistic thought.[34] The problematic is, as Bracha Lichtenberg Ettinger argues, at the level of the filters, the signifiers, the symbols, which do not fully exist for feminine otherness within a system exclusively signified by the phallus.[35] The feminist problematic might be thought of as the inventing of such semiotic resources in order that our corporeal drives and the fantasies through which they are experienced might be signifiable for us, to us, and to our thereby radically altered culture.

At present, women's culture suffers unbearably from too much "reading in." Critics appear confident in their interpretations of artwork by women: it means this; she is saying that; it is feminist because she shows this . . . Apparently, we already know what women are, feel, experience as women. The work remains tied in a loop of current ideological constructions of femininities. This denies the radical unknownness of the unconscious and the depth and profundity of the alterity to which patriarchal cultures condemn those it calls "woman." Thus the feminine ceases to function as a radical rupture of patriarchy, and we produce an idealized femininity based on the identification with the good mother to the exclusion of female aggression and other sadistic impulses or the ambivalence at the heart of all subjectivity.[36]

This exhibition realizes what it has taken, historically, theoretically, aesthetically, to create the spaces within which marginalized work that addresses the effaced codes of feminine difference and feminine inscription in culture from socially, sexually, and culturally oppressed and liminal spaces can be brought into intelligibility. The exhibition proposes a different way of reading the history via periodizations that mimic historic shifts in social alignments, fascism, the cold war, and postmodernity, all revealed to have crucial subtexts related to the histories of sexual difference. In the conjunction of work on a specifically feminist problematic in the present and a revisioned prehistory of that moment, the radical shift from curatorial and modernist narrative is achieved; work by contemporary artists sharing this project in turn becomes legible and affective.

Across that field we can work less as historians than as archaeologists—reading the discarded, ignored, or recently recovered monuments of women's revolutionary poetics for the inscriptions in the feminine that articulate their own moments—politically, socially, sexually, semiotically—yet also constitute a chapter in a longer *durée*, a different temporality of the feminine within phallocentric cultures of which we are witnessing but the latest chapter.

In "Women's Time," Julia Kristeva suggests that women are caught in varying time systems: the historical challenge for emancipation reflected a desire to become a part of linear, historical time associated with the bourgeois nation-state and its political identities. This was the time of political campaigns for equality and participation, of the desire to escape absolute difference and join the same, the one, the masculine. Distinct from that expression is the embrace of feminine difference, which operates within the rhythms and cycles of female sexuality and the archaic organizations of reproduction: the time of body and sex. To this moment belongs the French writing of Cixous and the publishing house *des femmes*. This second feminism, associated with psychoanalysis and literature, the time of the unconscious, is no less historical: it operates on the longer temporality of the institution of sexual difference, the time of reproduction, which differs from the epochs that Marx theorized as the modes of production in which nations and classes operate. In a dialectical resolution of this opposition, Kristeva calls for a third *space*, rather than time: naming the women's movement a signifying space that must both accept the symbolic law—sacrifice of something of our materiality to language in order to be a signifying, nonpsychotic subject in social history—and transcend anthropomorphism: that is, representation of sacrifice and difference only in the figures of man and woman. Gender contains us within its fictions, and it needs to be disrupted. This does not imply some futuristic androgyny that will erase sexual specificity. It sets us on a path to imagine ourselves outside of sexual dimorphism. It is in this sense that the feminine can function of and for itself, and also as the dissidence that disturbs the rule of phallocentrism, radically realigning culture and its relations of difference.

Much of the historical work exhibited in this show is both interesting and difficult to decipher because it operates on this edge, dispersing identity, inventing more bodies and masks, hybridizing the genders, in a radical poetics of difference that is feminine not through depositing some gendered essence but through rupturing the phallic norms of fixed gender, fixed identity, fixed sexualities, fixed boundaries. Hannah Höch's photomontages from the exotic wonderland of mass-produced media culture produce a constant stream of shocks and disturbances where hybrids do not relax into fixed meanings. Claude Cahun's collaboration with Suzanne Malherbes produced a series of haunting images of the Jewish, lesbian, surrealist artist, multiplying the inventive possibilities of feminine imaginary beings through the poetics of photomontage, collage, and photographic fantasy and the dissipation of self-portraiture. No simple, reassuring positivity haunts these images: shocking, confusing, interrogative, perverse, they mark the site of feminine inscription as challenge to the certainties of the contemporary feminist movement as much as of the dominant culture.

IV

Matrix is an unconscious space of simultaneous emergence and fading of the *I* and the unknown *non-I*
which is neither fused, nor rejected. Matrix is based on feminine/ore-natal interrelations and exhibits
shared borderspace in which I call *differentiation-in-co-emergence* and *distance-in proximity* are continuously rehoned and reorganized by metramorphosis created by—and further creating—*relations without
relating* on the borders of absence and presence, object and subject, me and the stranger.
—Bracha Lichtenberg Ettinger[37]

Significant as are Kristeva's theses for a radical feminist signifying practice, she remains
bound within an imaginary that only partially conceives how to disrupt the law of subjectivity
ruled by the phallus. Bracha Lichtenberg Ettinger, painter, psychoanalyst, and feminist theorist, further develops feminist theorization of subjectivity and representation in ways sugges-
tive for visual inscriptions by women artists.

Feminism has been waging a war on the myths, legends, texts, and canons of what it
names patriarchal culture. Using poststructuralist theory, such a culture is defined as phallocentric, not only ruled by the name of the father but semantically organized around the privileged signifier, the Phallus, in whose sovereign and single image being and meaning are said
to be exclusively constituted by oppositions: love/hate, one/Other, presence/absence, incorpo-
ration/rejection. Even feminist attempts to critique phallocentrism have found themselves
caught in its conceptual confines, defined relative to dominant phallic binarism.

Lichtenberg Ettinger, through an artistic practice dealing with heavily freighted materials
that bear the wounds and scars of Europe's horrendous tragedy carved upon her own familial
text, began to intimate another dimension of this feminist project to see through what structures the phallic system to something that is not phallic but resides with it, at times an alternative, at times a supplement, always a relief, sub- rather than presymbolic.[38] She names this
stratum of subjectivization—this level at which subjectivity is forged and we become subjects—*matrixial*. The matrix is linked to "the feminine," but by this concept neither a biological nor an anatomical description is intended. The matrix refers to the subjectivities associated with invisible feminine sexual specificity raised to the level of a symbol—that is, it is a filter for archaic sensations and the most archaic form of meaning, the pictogram, which relates
to a moment when the earliest processes of subjectivization occur between at least two partial
subjectivities. This matrixial possibility can be discerned in texts, signifiers, legends, paintings, ourselves, and for the artist its recognition and theorization arose out of daily reflection
on the very processes of her own absorption in and obligation to the traces of historical subjectivities erased in the horrors of fascist modernity yet daily companions in the continuing
"besideness" of the survivors' child.

Certain psychoanalytical perspectives and processes may offer the way to understand and
"work through" a phenomenon that, because the history that it memorializes was so horrifi-
cally deviant, must be grasped as rupturing the temporal finiteness that the word *history* typically conveys. This happened, but it is not in the past. We therefore live in a moment both
"after history" yet continuously "beside"[39] history, which may correspond to what Freud
uncovered in his archaeology of the split subject. The human subject is not the end product
of a narrative development called maturation but a discontinuous layering and sedimentation
of always active elements that filter through from archaic moments and strata via the unconscious to form a continuous consciousness of "beside," to use the artist's vocabulary, rather
than of "under." In this perspective, painting may be, as Lichtenberg Ettinger describes it,

symbologenic. It may generate not an image of the trauma but a symbol that allows the fore-cluded the relief of signification, a pathway into language.

Many of the artist's works are possessed by an image and a process of working with it that reveal what I call "after painting" in the "after history." The use of found photographs links this project with the Duchampian tradition of the readymade. Lichtenberg Ettinger's use of the readymade launches us into a radically different sphere beyond the conceptually informed feminist art moment of the 1970s–80s, passing through psychoanalysis to the unconscious and fantasy via the touch of painting, a less frequent site of feminist intervention. Distinct from the highly motivated and often hard-hitting confrontation between art practice and the popular cultures here ap- or depropriated, this project keeps to the margins and thresholds where another process of meaning is glimpsed: what the artist calls *metramorphosis*.

> Metramorphosis is the process of change in borderlines and thresholds between being and absence, memory and oblivion, I and non-I, a process of transgression and fading away. The metramorphic consciousness has no center, cannot hold a fixed gaze—or, if it has a center, constantly slides to the borderline, to the margins. Its gaze escapes the margins and returns to the margins. Through this process the limits, borderlines, and thresholds conceived are continually transgressed or dissolved, thus allowing the creation of new ones.[40]

A great deal of feminist theorization and artistic practice has identified the gaze as a key issue.[41] In necessarily deconstructing the politics of vision by defining the gaze within a phallic regime of sexual difference, feminists have equally been trapped within a scopic regime that can only imagine the gaze in terms of mastery and sadism or as, in psychoanalytical terms, a phallic *objet a*, the lost object defined by castration (i.e., separation, rejection, hate).[42] Lichtenberg Ettinger's method permits a glimpse of another kind of vanishing point—a matrixial gaze, beyond appearance—not locked into this logic of subject/object, presence/absence, see/seer, same (self)/different (other).[43]

> The matrixial gaze emerges by a simultaneous reversal of with-in and with-out (and does not represent the eternal inside), by a transgression of borderlinks manifested in the contact with-in/-out an art work by a transcendence of the subject-object interval which is not a fusion, since it is based on a-priori shareability in difference.
> In the matrixial aesthetic experience, relations without relating transform the unknown Other into a still unknown partial-subject within an encounter. The subject's relations with the Other do not turn it into a known object, swallowed or fused, rejected or abjected. The non-I as subject changes me while the I changes it; all the participants are receiving and investing libido with-in and with-out the joint process of change itself—the metramorphosis, with-in and with-out their common borderspace.[44]

Metramorphosis gives us access to another kind of sense-making and a route for the feminine to filter into the symbolic, into meaning. This feminine is thus not specular, and can only be murdered by being trapped in a phallic gaze.

Strategies of representation in the visual arts, from painting to photography and film, have been institutionalized to lure our gaze and suture our desire to that to which the culture wishes to fix us. Feminist interventions in the visual of arts have, therefore, of necessity had to negotiate the gaze, desire, suture, and spectatorship. For a period during the 1970s, this produced a "negative aesthetics" among certain feminists, a radical distanciation from any aspect of the spectacle and visual pleasure, a distrust of the visual image, of the iconicity especially of women. The necessary work of ground clearing has been done, and those artists associated most strongly with such moves, such as Mary Kelly and Laura Mulvey, have themselves reclaimed the territories of desire in the field of vision. Lichtenberg Ettinger's place in this feminist genealogy emerges via the conjugation of feminist interventions in the politics of representation and sexual difference with modernity's genocidal horror. She argues that one level of the image is that which is beyond appearance: thus loss, *objet a*, nonsymbolized fragments of the body, and traces of the archaic maternal body—"that aspect or element which is severed from the subject and cannot become a visible object on the level of specular imaginary recognition. *Objet a* is the invisible par excellence, it is a remnant of the signified which cannot appear in representation"[45]—may in art achieve a borderline visibility. Because of the connections between woman in phallocentric culture and *objet a*, woman and Other, this beyond appearance connects to the feminine, and this borderline visibility that an excess in art achieves may be a means to access it and theorize it—not just for women but as a means of realigning all subjects in relation to elements of the unconscious that have not been allowed to filter into the symbolic, which yet insist through what Freud called the experience of the "uncanny."[46]

In the post-Holocaust era, Europe and America are once again breeding its fascisms and racisms, targeted now on other Others. In such a phallic structure, any group can find itself victimized as the Other that must be destroyed or repressed. There can be a future but only through creative alliance, through covenant, through what the artist calls a coemergence in difference. But the philosophical and political legacies of modernity provide neither a social nor a psychic model for such unfamiliar proximities and covenantal differences. In the apparently unlikely spaces of feminist artistic practice in all of its difference from crude notions of art versus society, theory versus practice, we find an understanding of subjectivity that provides such a nonphallic and nonfascist model for relations between subjectivities. Neither in its relation to feminism nor to the issues of racism and postcolonial practice does the matrix offer cozy plurality or compromised coexistence. The matrix is one of the most challenging new theorizations to emerge, allied with the ethical philosophy of Emmanuel Levinas and the anti-Oedipal psychoanalysis of Deleuze and Guattari in arguing that the very forms of our current thinking imprison us in models of subjectivity that sustain and prolong social horrors that threaten our survival and have already compromised our humanity.

Lichtenberg Ettinger theorizes a way to imagine the Symbolic expanded to contain more than one symbol—more than one "signifier of signifiers" for subjectivity. Neither replacing nor merely supplementing the phallus, itself *the* signifier for subjectivity based on the opposition of on/off, absence/presence, and all related binaries of assimilation versus rejection, she proposes the matrix, a symbol of coexisting and coemerging part-subjectivities that holds special promise for women, for whom this aspect has particular and profound resonance in allowing elements of their feminine but invisible bodily specificity and the fantasies to which it gives rise to filter into signification. But the matrix, while a distinctly feminine symbol theoretically premised on the idea of the coterminous existence of two mutually affecting part-subjectivities that cohabit one imaginary space in late pregnancy, is, like the phallus, in effect a neutral symbol. It is, therefore, as relevant for the realignment of masculine subjectivity that also shares in the stratum of subjectivity on this matrixial, borderline space of the several that predates and thus preconditions the moment of the One—that is, the point from which orthodox psychoanalysis dates the commencement of subjectivity.

79

Intra-uterine fantasies in adults and children point to a primary recognition of an out-side to the *me*, which is composed of the inside of an-other. . . . In my view, these are traces of *joint* recordings of experience related to feminine invisible bodily specificity and to late prenatal conditions, emanating from joint bodily contacts and joint psychic *borderspace*. I have hypothesized that a certain awareness of a borderspace shared with an intimate stranger and a joint *co-emergence in difference* is a feminine dimension in subjectivity. Such awareness alternates with that of being *one*, either separate or fused. The matrixial awareness accompanies us from the dawn of life and is traced in the psy-che by archaic modes of experience-organisation in terms of adjustments and retunings of sensorial impressions. Affected time-space-body instances induce psychic events and traces corresponding to an archaic level, and the concepts of connectivity and the sub-symbolic suggest a way of conceptualizing the organisation of the matrixial stratum of subjectivisation.[47]

The matrix speaks to what we already intimate, to hallucinated memories of a shared bor-derspace that Freud himself acknowledged in his work on the "womb fantasies" that are part of the uncanny.[48] But such intimations are foreclosed—denied a signifier—by a culture that does not allow us to speak of this realm of subjectivity so relevant to feminine desire. Even raising it here makes me anticipate accusations of essentialism, regression, fundamentalism. Yet what can be more obvious than the possible impact of the curious, indeed uncanny, moment of the mature infant both storing up sensory impressions of the other with which it cohabited and registering the impact of that other's fantasies as she carried and fantasized about an unknown other within the most interior spaces of her body and the most intimate places of her own psychic life, reviving in turn her own archaic memories?

Matrix can also be referred to our experiences in the presence of art as viewers. As view-ers we, *I*, experience the space of the artwork as a *non-I*, but not simply as an object for assignment to an appropriately mastered curatorial or art historical category. Affectively, art offers us a moving encounter with an uncanny other, or with a screen across which seeps something already familiar, curious, intriguing, disturbing—a shock, a moment of grace. Thus this specific theorization of the matrix as a symbol of the invisible feminine specificity ensures that we begin to rethink the experiences of artistic activity through the prism of a feminine pressure on the Symbolic, the feminine as a continuous shadow on the phallic order, a sub-symbolic dimension that certain art forms and certain theories reach out to, offering signifiers for a momentary glimpse and an uncanny touch.

Art practices function precisely as a politics in the field of the Symbolic: the place of meanings and identities, fantasies and negations. The femininity of which I speak is neither that of the confidently overknown and overfeminized Victorian discourse on women, nor that of the disdained stereotypes that haunted the underfeminized moment of high modernism. We can imagine now why nineteenth-century women were able to be culturally active insofar as Victorian society publicly promoted a cultural space for the difference of femininity. It pro-vided, however impoverished, the representational support for the tentative and difficult articulation in culture of something excessive to that culture's dominant concerns. We may be able, therefore, to learn from a differently conceived archaeology of other moments in the his-tories of femininity—this is quite different from studying "women and impressionism" or "women in modernism." The field of history and culture is then configured not by art, artist, movement, or style but by the politics and semiotics of sexual difference, the complex rela-tions between social and symbolic definitions of the subject, gender, class, and race, between lived identities and articulated and represented ones, between sexuality in the field of vision ✓ and on the plane of social practice. Feminism can in no way simply inhabit the discursive structures of art history. It refashions the objects that are art history's or art criticism's domain according to a radically different theorization of art as inscription across the imaginary and symbolic field of the subject in semiotic sociality.

In alliance with the theories of the sign and of semiosis, artistic practice is defined not as the site of expression of the individual subject present to itself and outside language or the ideologically determined meaning of the socially determined subject. In a 1973 essay "The System and the Speaking Subject," Julia Kristeva identified these both as ultimately totalitarian themes and proposed the subject theorized by psychoanalysis as the necessary term to prevent semiotics from slipping into a formalism that would make it once again a servant of the oppressive patriarchal triad of state, church, and family. Artistic practice is named a signifying productivity whose resources are the subject—defined as subjectivity-on-trial, a constantly unstable intersection between individual and social histories, individually inflected and socially circulated signs. Aesthetic practices are sites of a special variability and dissonance in this relation whose norm is an ordering of meaning, a fixing of signs both predicated upon and constantly renovated by forces excessive to it, processes of its own becoming. Such theories must pass, however, through the prism of difference where we can attend to both the specificities of the feminine and the role of the feminine to stand for all that might be Other to a monolithic phallocentrism. Lichtenberg Ettinger's suggestion that there may be more than one symbol (the one being the phallus that forces us to think of sex as the One and its Other, and thus in fact always and only as the One) opens up art criticism to ask: What is involved in a nonphallic, matrixial reading of an artistic text? What would be a matrixial exhibition? The matrix reveals the sexual difference at work in our forms of knowledge, interpretation, and curatorship and once acknowledged will change the politics of selection, viewing, and response.

Shoshana Felman's autobiography, *What Does a Woman Want? Reading and Sexual Difference*, equally questions the very premises on which feminist theories of art and reading are founded. She argues for an inversion: instead of imagining the feminist as being a resistant or oppositional reader of cultural signs, she suggests that we only *become* feminist when we read for the resistance of the text, its transgressions of patriarchal assumptions and prescriptions.[49] She calls this "the feminine resistance of the text."

This relates to a further recognition of the necessity for questioning our own assumptions. Feminists have drawn heavily on a discourse of the personal, using women's experience as a counterforce to official knowledge. Yet getting personal is not unproblematic. ✓ Felman argues that we cannot trust ourselves, for as subjects we work with implantations and borrowed ideas. She writes: "I will suggest that *none of us, as women, has as yet, precisely, an autobiography*. Trained to see ourselves as objects and to be positioned as the Other, estranged to ourselves, we have a story that cannot by definition be self-present to us, a story, that, in other words, is not a story, but *must become* a story. . . . And it cannot become a story except through the *bond of reading*, that is through the *story of the Other* (the story read by other women, the story told by other women, the story of women told by others) insofar as this story of the Other, as our own autobiography, *has as yet precisely to be owned*."[50] Neither getting personal nor being a resistant reader will get us this ownership. Felman concludes: "I will propose that we might be able to engender, or to access our story only indirectly—by conjugating literature, theory and autobiography together through the act of reading and by reading, thus, into the texts of culture, at once our sexual difference and our autobiography as missing."[51]

Inscriptions in the feminine require decipherment as much by their producers, for the artist is also one of the first readers, as by their producers on the cultural field, readers/critics. Without readers or viewers, who then "own" (i.e., recognize) the work, the work in a profound sense never exists. This has been the fate of women's cultural history because of art history's virtually complete erasure of women artists from its text. Unread, they are unable to be sites for the production of meaning. But their meaning is not locked safe within the paintings simply waiting for someone to reveal it. The meaning exists only in that conjugation with the literature, or the visual culture, with the theory, that is, the means of understand it and turn it into knowledge, and the subjects who will seek in these texts access to a story radically unknown to themselves that is yet, in some way, the missing story of themselves. As Lichtenberg Ettinger puts it:

> The work of art does not illustrate or establish theory; theory can only partly cover—uncover—the work of art. Sometimes the work of art produces seeds of theory from which, upon elaboration, art slips away. These seeds should be sown somewhere else. The most graceful moments in the covenant between art and theory can occur when theoretical elements, only indirectly or partly intended for particular works of art, and visual elements that refuse theory, collide. In doing so they transform the borderline between the two domains so that art is momentarily touched by theory while theory takes on a new meaning.[52]

Feminist analysis of the visual arts is not a mirror of what is already produced and confined by its formal mode of existence. It must be motivated by this desire to find oneself—but not in the sense of a existential or authentic being, woman. To decipher femininity is to explore difference as much more than *the* difference as currently defined by existing social modes of gender. As Lacan said, there is as yet no signifier for what the sexual difference of women might be. Lichtenberg Ettinger glosses Lacan's statements about woman, that the feminine is repressed for women and that she can no more reach to what the phallic symbol places in the space of the Other, the thing, the hole in real—or whatever formulation tries to capture in language this profound paradox: "The woman doesn't exist and doesn't signify anything."[53] But feminist theory makes a difference: radically unknown it may be, but femininity is not unknowable, and artistic practices may be one revolutionary semiotic site where that difference could be, has been, is being inscribed, where that Other, as Lichtenberg Ettinger has argued, seeps across a threshold to achieve a borderline visibility and create matrixial affects when we let our present subjectivities be altered by the transforming encounter.

Femininity stands for the resistance in the text to existing stories and knowledges, to the negative face of sexual difference in a culture that either presumes to know what woman is (and wants) or utterly denies its relevance or interest. In this sense femininity or "woman" means both something specifically about women—as yet unspecified—and something about the limits of phallocentric culture as a whole that is unable to deal with difference in any form. Woman in the psychoanalytical model is both the sign of a division into gender and the sign of the limits of a discourse premised on sexual difference as the model for all difference: rendering social, cultural, and racial diversity and divergence always merely signs of lack, negativity, or a threatening otherness that must at all costs be suppressed. Thus the art made by women may in effect not be about Woman but about that space of difference, dissidence, diversity, and rupture. No simple positivity awaits us—but an invitation to read for the feminine against the grain of cultural modes that render it blankness. Yet for all that, we paradoxically must hold on to its specific pertinence and affective richness—and anxiety—for those of us formed in this feminine with all of its pleasures and negativities.

The idea of inscriptions *in the feminine* and *of the feminine* also evokes the ghostly trace of that mythic finger that carved the law for the Jewish people on tablets of stone—one of the most compelling images of the relation between marking, human identity, and symbolic law. Feminists have more often turned to that most misogynist of cultures, the Greek, to find a metaphor for women's place in relation to the law or the polis—the Sphinx, who did not as far as we know carve her message but spoke her riddle outside the city gates. In a feminist displacement of the Oedipus myth of masculine desire and rivalry from the origins of Western culture by turning attention to the murder of the mother in the Clytemnestra myth, Marianne Hirsch cites Muriel Ruykeser's feminist poem about the Oedipus story.[54] Ruykeser reminds us that the Sphinx's question about what walks on four legs, then two, then three might actually have had the answer: woman, and not as Oedipus narcissistically gave it, man—at which the Sphinx rightly cast herself off her pillar and said, "Oh God, patriarchy, I'm not staying around for that. They'll only make a monster of me."

Indeed they did—monstrosity or silent iconicity have been the Sphinx's and our feminine legacy in Greco-Christian cultures ever since. Using inscription in reference to Mosaic tablets bypasses that image of origin and exclusion to replace it with the idea of the text animated by those living out its rules of being human and repeatedly interpreting its textual possibilities. Inscription, for all it connotes writing over imaging, has become a determinant feature of work by women, where tracing—through line as drawing, through light on photosensitive plates and paper, through electronically generated text, handwritten stories, electric wires, through movement in the space of performance—is so major a feature. It also invokes Hélène Cixous's call for *écriture féminine* (writing the body)—both ideas concerned with the invention of not only a language for feminine desire and corporeality but an alphabet measured to its drives and pleasures. The work of Nancy Spero has been cited in reference to such an ambition—a work that inscribes an invented alphabet composed of images of the joyous, self-laboring bodies of women playing on scrolls that unroll through space. Insofar as art in general can be defined as a graphic activity, a marking by hand and body, whether we are talking about classic forms of drawing and painting or newer modes of performance and other radical uses of bodies and things traced in and tracing space, it is easier to grasp the presence of the body, and the body not as originary sight, a given entity, but as a complex semiotic fantasy, a letter even. Talking of inscription does not privilege work that uses words or mimics text. It does not favor conceptual work over painterliness nor intellectual over other modes of practice. It suggests that the whole of culture be conceived as text, but where text is, in Cixous's phrase, also a *sext*.[55]

This model moves us away from the problems of defining art as feminist or assuming that art by a woman is woman's art—which some may endorse and others dread. Endorsement comes from our complicity with the way in which the institution of art as a whole plays to the fantasies of an ideal ego—what Sarah Kofman in her brilliant reading of Freud's theories of art shows to be a desire for a narcissistic masculine ideal projected onto both the artist and the realm of art as its perpetual site of discovery.[56] Feminists are as subject to the desire for and fantasy of a great figure who will provide this narcissistic ideal, and feminist art history contains plenty of examples of this writing in the mode of heroine worship. We inevitably reinvent and search for the good mother to deal with our rivalry as well as our loss. Here lies this difference between *opposition* that merely provides an alternative within the field of gender, so that "women" become in fact a supplement reinforcing its regime, and *critique*, which tries to define what the institution is and how we can work against being complicit with it. Which means self-analysis. That is the model that I discern in Felman, who argues that the analysis of texts that address our subjectivity and its lived histories is, in fact, a writing of the self—but critically, analytically. In that sense the model of the analytical discourse and space has been used in several contexts recently to suggest a relation of the viewer/reader to the artwork in the space of exhibition. Displacing the phallic paradigm of curatorial mastery, the exhibition becomes both a place to stage the co-presence of several artists whose work the dominant narratives have made invisible or aberrant. "Feminist" is the epithet neither for an artist nor for a curator. It marks both a problematic and a political desire. For the desiring viewer, it is an analytical space, wherein the question "What am I?" is addressed neither to a master nor to a bureaucrat, and not by a hysteric.[57]

A final twist brings us to the theories that inform this exhibition: the matrix and its semiotic figure: metramorphosis. The matrix poses a stratum of subjectivity and subjectivization that is not so much presymbolic on a putative time line of subject development but subsymbolic. It awaits and is realized in the generation of symbols or signifiers that reach that threshold and hold its pulse for a moment of elusive visibility. Once meaning passes across it, the signs become once again part of a phallic signifying system, metonyms or metaphors, associations or substitutions, and hence phallic signifiers based on presence, absence, and replacement. There is indeed something uncanny. Freud imagined the uncanny as linked to fearful moments, particularly to castration anxiety. But, as Lichtenberg Ettinger points out, he also counted womb fantasies among the uncanny things that once seemed familiar, but were never fearful, and later have an aura of strangeness.[58] Lichtenberg Ettinger argues that these latter archaic traces may not necessarily be fearful—and that they do not necessarily involve this either/or, presence /absence. There may be, in post-Lacanian language, a matrixial *objet a*, a marker of a loss but one not condemned, as in the phallic system, to be the point of possible breakdown of the subject. This is important insofar as there is a collusion between *objet a*, woman, thing, and a hole in signification—like the darkness upon which meaning, man, writes *him*-self. The darkness is the condition of lightness having form. The matrix allows us to theorize a different passageway, for what is inside yet beyond the visible, to the field of visibility, which I have also called the field of intelligibility and inscription. "Matrix is not about the Woman but about a feminine dimension of plurality and difference of the several in a joint subjectivity via metramorphosis." There is always going to be some loss of archaic fragments of the body sensations—*objets a*—in both phallic and matrixial paradigms. "But metramorphosis does not relate to the circulation of these lacks in the same way as metaphors and metonyms do in the phallic system." Thus,

> Within the matrixial network, what is lost to the one can be inscribed as traces in the other, and metramorphosis can allow passages of these traces from the *non-I* to *I* and back again in an enlarged stratum of subjectivization. . . . As both are parts of the same stratum, sharing and shared by the same borderlines, traces belonging to *I* as well as *Non-I* and traces recorded in the joint space can be redistributed. The borderline between what one has and what one has lost and between the Other and the Thing therefore become thresholds, on the edges of subjectivity.[59]

I am fully aware that this level of theorization and this language seems downright difficult let alone both obscure and remote from the affirmations of feminist identity or celebrations of female creativity that have so enriched the feminist community and culture in general. Why is such a way of thinking through the feminist problematic necessary? I would suggest that we need to treat art a lot more seriously and realize what artists may be doing for us, how art produces a dimension for our political revolution rather then merely reflecting or representing what we want to know at the so-called cultural or entertainment end of our movement. The old avant-garde ideas of working at the limits of the accepted and the known bred a heroic image of imperial pioneering. What I propose is politically remote from such postures, but it shares that dissident concern with a borderline and a sense of the political in going beyond the known aesthetically—hence necessitating a radically new way of theorizing that tries to comprehend what is being done and who is doing it. Through Kristeva's inspirations we can argue for the necessity of a continuing commitment to a revolution that can not only accommodate women but be made by the dissidence of the feminine, providing a framework in which art, politics, and sex conjoin. Through Lichtenberg Ettinger's radical theorization of matrix and its process, metramorphosis, we can understand art as a practice both in and on, shifting the current symbolic; politics, as the radical transformation of the borderlines of meaning and subjectivity; sex, as the unfixing rather than final designating marker of difference and loss; and sexual difference, as one of *the* questions of the last quarter of this modernist century.

Thus after modernism, we pose feminism. That is, I present what I have outlined as critical feminism, as the place where theory, art/literature, and autobiography are conjugated. Here, struggling with the complexity of subjectivity and its inscriptions, articulated with the riddles of sexual difference and the politics of feminine alterity, we might decipher the inscriptions of the feminine, of what is uncannily familiar, and even a graceful solace, a *jouissance* that can be touched at the matrixial threshold where art, working "in and of the feminine"—inscribing the resistance of the feminine—opens for us to glimpse "a beyond that is inside the visible."

NOTES:

1. Thomas B. Hess and Elizabeth C. Baker, *Art and Sexual Politics* (London: Collier MacMillan, 1973), 83.

2. Clement Greenberg, "Avant-Garde and Kitsch" (1939), reprinted in *Art and Culture* (Boston: Beacon Press, 1961).

3. To be otherwise was to be expelled from the category. "A woman of genius does not exist; when she does, she is a man," Bettina van Hutton, as quoted in Octave Uzanne, *The Modern Woman* (1912).

4. Denise Riley, *Am I That Name? Feminism, and the Category of "Women" in History* (London: MacMillan, 1988), 14.

5. Lisa Tickner, *The Spectacle of Women* (London: Chatto and Windus, 1987) is the most profound and important study of the role of representation and the enunciations of femininity in culture and politics in the historic confrontation between women and the bourgeois state.

6. See Tickner, "Representation," in *The Spectacle of Women*, on how suffrage campaigners used Darwinism to promote the notion of women's character adapting to historical change; and see Riley, "Does Sex Have a History?" in *Am I That Name?* for how the term *woman* evolves in correlation with concepts of the social, both being spheres of male control and intervention, the other from which man appears to stand apart.

7. Carol Duncan, "Virility and Male Domination in Early Twentieth Century Vanguard Painting" (1973), in *Aesthetics and Power* (1992). Duncan points to the widespread trope of the male artist in the studio with the sexually displayed naked model as a new kind of ideological icon of virile sexual freedom that becomes synonymous with artistic creativity and is styled through the use of non-European aesthetics misnamed to serve European sexual fantasies as "primitive."

8. Griselda Pollock, "Fathers of Modern Art: Mothers of Invention," *Differences* 3, no. 4 (Fall 1992).

9. Julia Kristeva, "A New Kind of Intellectual—The Dissident," in *The Kristeva Reader*, ed. Toril Moi (Oxford: Basil Blackwell, 1987), 297.

10. Carol Duncan and Alan Wallach, "Ritual and Ordeal on 53rd Street," *Studio International*, 1977.

11. For a brilliant analysis of this problematic see Claudine Mitchell, "Intellectuality and Sexuality: Camille Claudel, Fin de Siecle Sculptress," *Art History* 12, no. 4 (1989): 419–47.

12. Gloria Orenstein, "Women of Surrealism," *Feminist Art Journal*, no. 2 (1973); Whitney Chadwick, *Women Artists and the Surrealist Movement* (London: Thames and Hudson, 1991).

13. This point was made by Virginia Woolf writing of the difficulty for her artistic foremothers, like Charlotte Brontë, who was obliged to travesty herself in the heavy prose style and masculine sentence structure of Victorian novel writers. See Woolf, *A Room of One's Own* (London: Harmondsworth, 1928 and 1945), 69–74.

14. If I had any remaining doubts about this claim, they were dispelled when requesting photographs for a book of essays about women in the visual arts in the twentieth century from a renowned artist who is a woman. She wished not to be included in a book as she refused to be considered a "woman artist," even though I was careful not to use the term, which in my own work I have repeatedly shown to be a negating category.

15. The exhibition "Georgia O'Keeffe American and Modern," at its London venue in 1993, was greeted by a barrage of violent criticism in which a male art-critical establishment crawled over the surfaces of her paintings to reassure themselves that she wasn't any good at it so that they would not have to confront the complex articulation of modernism, Americanism, and a singular woman's perspective and sensibility on life, beauty, nature, belonging, displacement, and desire.

16. I am indebted to Adrian Piper for her work on xenophobia, which she also presented at the first conference of the Feminist Arts and Histories Network in Leeds, September 1993.

17. Gayatri Spivak, "Imperialism and Sexual Difference," *Oxford Literary Review* 8, nos. 1–2 (1986): 225.

18. Lucy Lippard, "Changing since Changes," introduction to *From the Center* (New York: Basic Books, 1977).

19. Lucy Lippard, "Sweeping Exchanges: The Contribution of Feminism to the Art of the 1970s," *Art Journal*, Fall/Winter 1980, 362.

20. To change the character of art is not to retreat from either art or society. This is the significance of the models outlined above. They do not shrink from social reality no matter how painful, nor do they shrink from the role that art must play as fantasy, dream, imagination. They contribute most to the avant-garde by slowing it down. They locate a network of minor roads that simply covers more territory than the so-called freeways. These roads are not, however, dead ends. They simply pass more people's houses. And they are more likely to be invited in. Ibid., 365.

21. A world that treats issues as fashions has prematurely declared that we live in a postfeminist age. This is to mistake the temporality and character of the project, which is neither religious (feminism as new belief system) nor melodramatic (woman as victim). The campaigns for the vote in the West took almost a hundred years, and they were premised on a history of feminism that reaches back into the Middle Ages. The project of the new wave is as dense, complex, and ambitious as any that women have undertaken radically to redefine the nature of sociality and human identity. It will take long years of patient analysis, research, and continuing activism. In the brief twenty-five years of this phase of women's long contest for their specific humanity, much has been achieved in an intellectual, cultural, and political revolution and much remains. Patience and the long view are required while we look to art made by women in the present and to that which at last we are beginning to be able to see and read from the past to be a major part of our research into the riddles that women constantly confront.

22. Mary Kelly, "Reviewing Modernist Criticism," *Screen* 22, no. 3 (1981): 44–45.

23. Kristeva, "Women's Time," in *The Kristeva Reader*, 208.

24. Mary Kelly, "Sexual Politics" (1977), reprinted in R. Parker and Griselda Pollock, *Framing Feminism: Art and the Women's Movement 1970–1985* (London: Pandora, 1987, 1995).

25. For a fuller discussion of these points see Griselda Pollock, "Feminism and Modernism," in Parker and Pollock, *Framing Feminism*.

26. What is dismissively called theory is precisely a development that parallels while running its own unique course the crisis of social theory in later twentieth-century capitalist and socialist societies: it concerns agency, social determination, and the role of the unconscious in both ideological bondage and resistance. The term *subjectivity* and its related phrase, *sexual difference*, mark the necessity to expand social analysis beyond the boundaries of historical materialism and structural functionalism.

27. This was shortly after Juliet Mitchell's *Psychoanalysis and Feminism* was published in 1974; after the first Patriarchy Conference in 1975, where Lacanian ideas were proposed by Cora Kaplan and Elizabeth Cowie; after *Screen* magazine made a historic turn to psychoanalysis with the publication in 1975 of Laura Mulvey's "Visual Pleasure and Narrative Cinema" and Stephen Heath's Lacanian film analyses; after Laura Mulvey and Peter Wollen had made *Riddles of the Sphinx* (1976), where they asked about the politics of the unconscious in a film form that clearly borrowed much from Freud's theories of the dream and Mary Kelly's retheorization and documentation of maternal femininity.

28. Kelly, "Sexual Politics," 73.

29. Sigmund Freud, "Femininity," in *New Introductory Lectures on Psychoanalysis*, Penguin Freud Library, vol. 2 (Harmondsworth: Penguin Books, 1973), 145–69.

30. Isak Dinesen [Karen Blixen], "The Blank Page," in *Last Tales* (1957) (London: Penguin Books, 1986), 104.

31. Susan Gubar, "'The Blank Page' and Issues of Female Creativity," in *New Feminist Criticism* ed. Elaine Showalter (London: Virago Press, 1986), 292–313.

32. Here lies an early prefiguration of both John Cage's music of silence and Robert Rauschenberg's white paintings.

33. Hélène Cixous, "The Laugh of the Medusa," in *New French Feminisms*, ed. Elaine Marks and Isabelle de Courtivron (Brighton: Harvester Press, 1981); Margaret Whitford, *Luce Irigaray: Philosophy in the Feminine* (London: Routledge, 1991).

34. This reading of Cixous and Irigaray is enriched by the theories of Bracha Lichtenberg Ettinger, artist in this exhibition and major feminist theorist. I am indebted here to her "Metramorphic Borderlinks and Matrixial Borderspace in Subjectivity as Encounter," in *Rethinking Borders*, ed. John Welchman (New York: Macmillan, 1995).

35. Bracha Lichtenberg Ettinger, "Matrix and Metramorphosis," *Differences* 4, no. 3 (1992): 176–210.

36. The peace movements and those that link women with ecology and nature are undoubtedly profound and powerful moments of feminist contestation. Premised on an identification with the great and good mother, they, however, exclude difficult aspects of feminine aggression, competitiveness, violence, and anger, which nonetheless erupt to fracture women's organizations, leaving the traces (some would say scars) of the more ambivalent and complex psychic pressures that constitute all subjectivities. Indeed, as Julia Kristeva has argued, violated subjects can become the possessed agents of the violence inflicted upon them. Women creators cannot be theorized without also acknowledging women terrorists (Kristeva, "Women's Time," 203).

37. Lichtenberg Ettinger, "Metramorphic Borderlinks and Matrixial Borderspace."

38. For a longer analysis of the artist's work see Griselda Pollock, "After the Reapers: Gleaning the Feminine and a Future in the Work of Bracha Lichtenberg Ettinger," in *Generations and Geographies in the Visual Arts: Feminist Readings*, ed. Griselda Pollock (London: Routledge, 1996).

39. All through her *Matrix. Halal(a)—Lapsus: Notes on Painting 1985–1992* (Oxford: Museum of Modern Art, 1993), Lichtenberg Ettinger is tracing "places of beside."

40. Lichtenberg Ettinger, "Matrix and Metramorphosis," 201.

41. These derive from Laura Mulvey's key formulation about cinema spectatorship, "Visual Pleasure and the Narrative Cinema," *Screen* 16, no. 3 (1975).

42. "The gaze is a model of a 'pure' *objet a*. When *beyond appearance* we search for a 'lacking something,' separated, fragmented and lost, this lacking something is not *any* 'no-thing.' It is a *particular nothing* ." Lichtenberg Ettinger argues that within Lacanian psychoanalysis, this lacking something is always assimilated to the "symbolic value of the lacking Phallus." Her explorations in artistic practice and psychoanalysis led her to propose, via a reading of Freud's "The Uncanny," another symbolic value and signifier for loss based on fantasies of uterine life: the matrix. See Lichtenberg Ettinger, *The Matrixial Gaze* (Leeds: University of Leeds, Feminist Arts and Histories Network, 1995).

43. For the full theoretical explanation of this gaze see Lichtenberg Ettinger, *The Matrixial Gaze*.

44. Ibid., 43.

45. Bracha Lichtenberg Ettinger, "Woman-Other-Thing: A Matrixial Touch," in *Bracha Lichtenberg Ettinger: Matrix Borderlines* (Oxford: Museum of Modern Art, 1993), 17.

46. See Bracha Lichtenberg Ettinger, *The Matrixial Gaze*, for her analysis of Freud's "The Uncanny" and her attention to his recognition of one source of the uncanny in "womb fantasies," i.e., fantasies about that intimate relation to the maternal body.

47. Bracha Lichtenberg Ettinger, "The Becoming Thresholds of Matrixial Borderlines," in *Travellers' Tales*, ed. George Robertson et al. (London: Routledge, 1994), 41.

48. For a full discussion of this see Lichtenberg Ettinger, *The Matrixial Gaze*.

49. Shoshana Felman, *What Does a Woman Want? Reading and Sexual Difference* (Baltimore: Johns Hopkins University Press, 1993).

50. Ibid, 14.

51. Ibid.

52. Lichtenberg Ettinger, "Woman-Other-Thing: A Matrixial Touch," 11.

53. As quoted in Jsacques Lacan, *Encore* (1972–73), 69; quoted in Lichtenberg Ettinger, "Woman-Other-Thing: A Matrixial Touch," 15.

54. Ruykeser's poem is called "Myth" and is discussed by Marianne Hirsch in *The Mother Daughter Plot: Narrative, Psychoanalysis and Feminism* (Bloomington: Indiana University Press, 1989), 1–2.

55. Cixous, "The Laugh of the Medusa," 255.

56. Sarah Kofman, *The Childhood of Art* (New York: Columbia University Press, 1988).

57. This is a reference to Parveen Adams's use of Lacan's four discourses (master, bureaucratic, hysteric, and analyst) as exempla of the subject's relation to knowledge and lack. Adams suggests that some feminist exhibitions produce an effect comparable to the analytical scenario: "The spectator watches, if not her own history, then a history from which she can identify herself. The elements come from something like her history, from something in respect of which she has a history. The stories are not so much quotations as a selection of signifiers, where selection is always an interpretation. . . . For an interpretation always involves discomfort, the recognition that something is at stake, something other than we thought we said." (Parveen Adams, "The Art of Analysis: Mary Kelly's Interim," *October*, no.58 [Fall 1991], 92.) Another, less tragic view of the analytical theater, drawing on Kristeva's work, can be found in Louise Parsons, "Revolutionary Poetics: A Kristevan Reading of Sally Potter's *The Golddiggers*," Ph.D. theses, University of Leeds, 1994.

58. The fullest explanation of Freud's theory of the uncanny and the feminine is given in Lichtenberg Ettinger, *The Matrixial Gaze*.

59. Ibid., 18.

BRACHA LICHTENBERG ETTINGER,
Matrixial Borderline,
1990-91. Detail.
India ink, pencil,
pastel, photocopy
on paper and Plexiglas.
Four panels with
twenty-five elements,
160 x 35 cm.
Photo: Yoram Lehmann.
Courtesy of the artist.

The With-In-Visible Screen

Bracha Lichtenberg Ettinger

Introduction by Griselda Pollock

Bracha Lichtenberg Ettinger, an artist in this exhibition, is also a major feminist theorist in the field of psychoanalysis. Continuing feminism's provocation of psychoanalysis to confront its own blind spot—femininity—the artist as theorist found in her reflections on her daily painting practice in the studio the seeds of a radical retheorization of the place/space of the feminine in subjectivity. It has long been agreed that the feminine is "outside" current phallic constructions of subjectivity while remaining its historic precondition, a structured repression. Thus the feminine has been sought in the pre-Oedipal moments of the subject. Yet many have argued that the feminine must also play a part in the Symbolic order—it must be spoken, signified, and belong in the field of desire—if women are not to reconfirm the phallic negation of the feminine as "Other," "Thing," "beyond," "not-all," and all other locutions invented by masculine theorists. Lichtenberg Ettinger's theory of the matrix suggests another pathway through current feminist debates within a psychoanalytically informed theory of sexual difference.

The matrix is a symbol, just as the phallus is in the work of Jacques Lacan. Here a symbol is never a symbol of something; it has no intrinsic meaning, for it is a signifier. A symbol is a term in a system by means of which meaning is produced through the play of differences at the level of the signifiers. Matrix, as a symbol, is a means in symbolic language to allow into signification, into the realm of discursive meaning, a stratum from human subjectivization framed by the invisible specificity of the feminine body. It is not the symbol of that invisible specificity of the feminine body; it is a means of its being signified for a subject, a subject being the effect of certain psychological formations, and the entry into the use of symbols, language. A symbol is, therefore, a form; its content or referents derive from archaic and imaginary registers of meaning and affects governed by what analysts call pictograms (basic meaning forms like presence/absence, love/hate) and by phantasy. None of these resources is premised on pure perceptual or given realities. All subjects, men as much as women, may carry, within these psychic registers, affects and traces of the contact with the invisible specificity of the feminine body from the most archaic moments when they were but proto- or partial subjects. The matrix as symbol hypothesizes affects persisting from this stratum of subject formation that concern a relational borderline between mutually unknown and unknowable entities, which Lichtenberg Ettinger names "I" and "non-I."

The artist uses the image, and I stress the metaphoric load of the imagined coexistence of mother and unborn child in the latest stages of pregnancy, both to conceive an archaic experience of several unknown partial subjects coemerging and coeffecting and to generate a symbol for a form of intersubjective encounter radically different from the predominant (phallic) model. The phallic model opposes One and Other in ways that infiltrate and inform many contemporary theories and practices (sexism, racism, homophobia), all characterized by an either/or polarity in which difference implies threat and is dealt with only via phantasies of assimilation or absolute rejection. Matrix suggests that while this model is significant for certain facets of subject formation, there may be other paradigms, such as that of the several that came before the decisive moment of the One versus its (constituting) Other. Through the concept of the matrix, we can move beyond the metaphorics of phallocentric language in which the feminine can only be imagined as Other, as difference as a term for the excluded or the threatening, or again as something that threatens to reabsorb the subject into her originary oneness. Such phantasies, so often premised on the attribution of meaning to the visible signs of feminine corporeality (I am thinking of Freud's theories of castration based on the boy's fright at the sight of female genitals without a penis), are associated with ideas of the dangerous castrated and castrating woman and with the engulfing monstrous, swamping mother as a nonsubjective void synonymous with death. They infiltrate Western culture from its most esteemed works to its most commercially popular, from the Medusa to Ripley and her Aliens.

Lichtenberg Ettinger's hypothesis relies on three assumptions central to psychoanalytic thought. First, our psyche is produced. But, becoming a subject, she emphasizes, relates to traces of links with female body and woman's phantasy. The birthed infant is acculturated by social systems—inscribed in laws and customs of which the key one is language—and is thereby made into a social, speaking, sexed subject at the level of the unconscious psyche. For psychoanalysis, however, the starting point is usually birth. Because of the baby's extreme physical immaturity at birth, its needs for survival are predicated upon a complex of interactions in which given neurological responses are overtaken by the necessity to relate and to interact with human subjects. Hence need becomes demand; in the ever-lurking danger that demand may not be satisfied, desire is born. Humans acquire subjectivity in this troubled space of loss and dependencies that induce phantasy, influence imaginary demands, and produce desire. The debates are about how we are subjectivized—in relation to what forces, conditions, possibilities, and, as importantly, what signifiers and symbols.

Second, this process implies a fundamental and constitutive fissure between what we might call the Real—an inchoate corporeality into which we are born and of which remain some possible but always unknowable traces (Lacan called these objets petit a)—the Imaginary—a way of making sense of the world and our corporeally mediated experience of it characterized by phantasy—and the Symbolic—the sense given to the world and our places within it by a public, social system of signs that enable communication of meaning between subject members of the social order. Signification is a good thing in the theory of the matrix, which is not nostalgic for the chaos of the prelinguistic or the possible psychosis of those who cannot find themselves in language. In this theory, the direction from the Real to the Symbolic is emphasized, for it is not only symbolic signification that is at stake, but also desire.

The problem, for feminists at least, is that if the Symbolic order is patriarchal, and theorized as only imaginable through the prism of one kind of signification, let us call it phallic, then a lot of phantasy and traces of archaic sensations and impressions will not only be excluded but, in technical terms, foreclosed. These elements that have no signifiers to allow them to become part of sense, meaning, language, culture, consciousness and self-understanding, deal with things that relate to things that are not phallic—let us call this the feminine. We will then find ourselves living in a skewed world, even though we may sometimes have hallucinations or uncanny sensations of some other way of putting things together.

Traditionally psychoanalysis theorizes the journey toward being a subject as becoming possible only when the infant intimates—however archaically and certainly not in thoughts or words—its separateness from the mother (who stands for the whole world of sensation and life). This intimation of separateness comes about through an aggressive act, for instance biting the nipple, which until that moment might only have been experienced as part of a physical continuum with the infant. The discovery that it is not one with it, and that food, comfort, etc. are not under its control, generates an impulse either to incorporate the nipple, the breast, the food, the mother, or to reject it absolutely in a moment of aggressive, destructive hatred. This is the basis for the aggression that seems to attend this model of subjectivity. Such a model of separation is called phallic, which means a way of making sense of the world based on binary oppositions: presence/absence, on/off, love/hate, incorporation/rejection, and so forth.

But there may be other pathway and other relations that allow the other to affect the subject across a borderline of irreducible difference. Lichtenberg Ettinger's third assumption is that another kind of difference, not at all orchestrated by the phallus, produces another field of desire. There is a model for this—a tricky one in the present climate. The model is that of advanced pregnancy, when an almost born infant exists, unknown and at this time unknowable, to an Other with whom it lies in the most intimate proximity; the pictogram for this would be distance in proximity. There is no doubt that the mother-subject is affected by the presence of this non-I, this other that is not a full subject confronting her but a partial subject sharing a joint space of affectivity—relations without relating. Might the infant not retain some sensations, patterned on its body from this physical intimacy with a noisy, throbbing, warm, rocking physicality where there are also muted sound and spoken rhythms? Without becoming essentialist, it is possible to imagine a moment of the coexistence of the several, each unknown to the other, neither rejected nor assimilated, yet mutually affecting, subjectivizing at different levels and in different registers. Such a possibility, however, where subjectivity is created via alternations and links between partial subjects and objects, is unimaginable and unspeakable in a culture in which the only theory of the Symbolic we have equates the Symbolic exclusively with the phallic and allows no other pathways into it or other dimensions to account for relations between subjects, forcing those who already intimate such apprehensions to believe themselves mad or hysterical.

Bracha Lichtenberg Ettinger hypothesizes just such another dimension. She calls it the feminine and names the symbol by means of which such sensations and affects, "memories" and phantasies, might be altered to filter through to our Symbolic level of understanding—and social change—the matrix. The artist-psychoanalyst situates her interests not in the pre-Oedipal as presymbolic domain, but in what she calls the subsymbolic—a stratum of subjectivity not at all orchestrated in relation to the phallus, though it exists side by side with the phallic stratum. The subsymbolic that interweaves into the Symbolic network carries pre-Oedipal as well as prenatal inscriptions. This theory thus proposes to give symbolic form to the contribution to human subjectivity and to processes of subjectivization produced in relation or made by the invisible specificity of the feminine body as it enters into archaic sensations, phantasies, and finally culture through aesthetic affects and effects. Neither the particular contents of phantasies concerning what happens in the last months of infant post-maturity in the womb nor the current scientific-biological theories about it are the issues here. Women's rights over their bodies are not questioned either. But if we allow ourselves to introduce into culture another symbolic signifier to stand beside the phallus (a supplementary signifier to that of difference as absence and loss that orchestrates the either/or modes), could we not be on the way to allowing the invisible feminine bodily specificity that has been an element of the most archaic experiences of us all—men and women—to enter and realign aspects of our consciousnesses and unconsciousnesses?

This will surely be valuable for women, who as subjects in the feminine under phallic law have been cast as irredeemably Other. It will surely extend, as do all metaphors of sexual differ- ence, to other Others—impinging on issues of race, immigration, and genocide that are tangled around the lack of means to signify other possible relations between different subjects. That space for difference as a creative moment of almost encounter in place of the phallic demarcation of difference as a line of division gives this practice and this theory its particular resonance. Thus, Lichtenberg Ettinger elaborated a theory of difference, in which difference isn't based on essen- tialism, but on a webbing of links and relations.

The psychoanalytically theorized concept of the matrix, however, comes out of art. This theo- rization has many facets and radically realigns the way we think about the process of making and seeing painting, at the same time as it offers a radical contribution to the theorization of feminin- ity, not as the Other of masculinity as it must remain in an exclusively phallic model of the sub- ject. While women will necessarily have a privileged relation to the matrix because of their rela- tions to the maternal moment (whether or not they have children themselves), the matrix exceeds the invisible feminine bodily specificity that it symbolizes to allow into the Symbolic elements of subjective encounters that will prove to be critically important at the level of all political and ethical reflection on our relations to the other, the stranger, the unknown, difference.

Memory which concerns us, even if it is not ours, but is, how to say it! beside ours, and which deter- mines us almost as much as our history.
—Georges Perec, *Je suis né*

Neither he nor I are *pure gaze* on *pure being*.
—Maurice Merleau-Ponty, *Le visible et l'invisible*

Weaving the Feminine into Culture by Matrixial Diggings in/of Art

Discussing art in the psychoanalytical context is inseparable, to my mind, from debating sexu- al difference, since we enter the function of art by way of the libido and through extensions of the psyche closest to the edges of corpo-*reality*. "The woman," as Jacques Lacan puts it, "does not exist and does not signify anything."[1] She is Other/Thing-as-absence, but this may be so—I put forward a reservation—from the phallic angle only. From this point of view, art leans on the ruins of "woman"-as-absence, and marking a feminine in art thus becomes auto- matically phallic too. I will here articulate a feminine aspect in/for/from art *neither* via a model of male "castration" and paternal prohibition *nor* as pure bodily experience. From the prism that I have called *matrixial,* to the extent that "woman" diffracts, she also digs channels of meaning and sketches an area of difference with sublimational outlets and ethical values paradoxical in the phallic paradigm.

Germs of ideas that thrived in my paintings and in my "notes"[2] dealing with making art were textured into psychoanalytic theory in a seizure where "the [art]works, and then reflec- tions on these works by [the artist] himself converge with the path of research on phantasy."[3] Theory does not exhaust painting; painting does not melt into theory. Painting produces theo- ry and kernels that can transform it; theory does not alter painting in process; it can draw stalks out of it and translate them into its own language. While painting produces theory, theory casts light on painting in a backward projection. Yet sometimes theory seeps in and anticipates approximations of what will become a future painting—an instigation that will retroactively be revealed. Theoretical articulation of painting further differentiates the Real.[4] The touch in painting changes the thought and goes elsewhere; the thought alters and returns to the touch. Painting and theory illuminate each other asymmetrically when adjacent, but their temporalities are different. There also exists an interrange between painting and theory that belongs to the field of art, as an interrange exists between the Real of the psychic id, the act of painting, and the Symbolic. For me, painting and theory are not different aspects that attest to the *same* thing but differentiated levels of working. As one moves with-in-ter the two, further ideas on/of poetic processes and aesthetic objects emerge.

The concepts of *matrixial* gaze and screen, with the aid of which I propose to explore artwork and processes of art making, enable us to conceive of and perceive links connecting artist, viewer, and artwork. I term *metramorphosis*[5] specific routes of passability and transmissibility, transitivity, temporary conductivity and transference between various psychic strata, between subject and several other subjects, and between subjects and composite, hybrid objects—routes through which "woman" that is not the preserve of women alone is inscribed in a subsymbolic web, knitted just-in-to the edges of the symbolic universe that cannot appropriate her by its preestablished signifiers.

The matrix refers, to begin with, to a phantasy of nonprohibited prebirth incest of the subject-to-be with what I call the *archaic-becoming-m/Other-to-be,* which informs an aesthetic field of coemergence and cofading with the neither fused nor rejected, unrecognized other.[6] In Freud's discussion of the aesthetic experience of the uncanny,[7] the phantasy of the maternal womb is included within the male "castration" prototype, while in Lacan's considerations[8] it is excluded by this inclusion and disappears. I suggest that a sex difference linked to female bodily specificity produces for man and woman an-other "subject"-ive and "object"-ive sphere. Mapping the matrixial stratum into a connectionist field,[9] I will try to elaborate an intersubjective web of relations linking the gaze and the screen shared by artwork and phantasy with woman, where "woman" is confined neither to one-body nor to either-sex boundaries.

The "feminine archaic origin" that shed a light on the matrix doesn't indicate any limitation on woman's rights over her body, quite the contrary![10]

What stems from art returns into art, but transformed. Art meanwhile transmutes as well.

In order to forge the matrixial gaze and screen, a nonlinear sieve of several threads had to be interlaced in the present essay. Some threads dropped halfway will be gathered later.

The Angle of the Phallus

We must make a detour along the paths of psychoanalytical theory to arrive at matrixial aesthetic/poïetic principles. Art is linked to a cluster of notions revolving around the mental object as absent or detached from the corpo-real event, a lacking object that Lacan termed *objet a.* If this cluster is entirely phallic, then so is art within psychoanalytic theory. But if it has nonphallic aspects and we conceive of a matrixial *objet a* that participates in an unconscious and subjectivizing larger Symbolic, informed by the Other that is not conceived of as "the treasure of the signifiers" alone, we may further develop aesthetic ideas in psychoanalysis without them being automatically appropriated by, even produced for, a phallic paradigm.

For Freud, male's bodily specificity—the penis—is regarded as the *only* sex difference for *both* sexes; the sexuality of girls is fundamentally male, and the libido has only one essence. "Little girls" are "little boys"; "The sexuality of little girls is of a wholly *masculine* character . . . libido is invariably and necessarily of a *masculine* nature."[11] To that Freud later adds[12] that only the "activity" and "passivity" meanings are essential as significations of masculine and feminine, while the sociological and biological ones are secondary. Following that, "maleness exists, but not femaleness. The antithesis here is between having a male genital and being castrated. Not until development has reached completion at puberty does the sexual polarity coincide with male and female; maleness combines subject, activity, and possession of the penis; femaleness takes over object and passivity."[13] Progressively, the libido moves from being considered masculine into being phallic-male, and its psychic inscription corresponds to a "castration" model that polarizes those who possess the penis and those who don't into subjects and objects: "This phase, which already deserves to be described as genital . . . is differentiated from the final organization of sexual maturity in *one essential respect.* For it *knows* only one kind of genital: *the male one.* For that reason I have named it the *'phallic' stage of organization.* . . . For both sexes, only one genital, namely the *male* one, comes into account. What is present, therefore, is not a primacy of the genitals, but a *primacy of the phallus.*"[14]

Lacan's famous statement that "the woman does not exist and does not signify anything" echoes Freud's remark on the prepubertial, mainly pre-Oedipal nonexistence of femaleness, but a shift occurs: *her* "lack" in the Real inscribes "nothing" in a Symbolic to which imaginary representation is considered subjected. The phallus mainly stands for a symbolic principle: it is a "signifier of signifiers" of absence *and* of difference—or of difference conceived *as* absence. But it is also the only imaginary representation of sex difference, and "castration" is the only passageway to symbolic significance where oppositions and exclusions resonate. The penis, like any other pregenital part object, is subjugated in the Oedipus complex to retroactive applications of symbolic castration. In that sense, boys undergo the same process as girls: both must renounce the attachment to bodily organs qua part objects and repress their pre-Oedipal mothers. "Man" confronts the question of *having*/not-having the phallus, and "woman" of *being*/not-being a phallic object of desire for men. The incest taboo established by the paternal Law separates son and pre-Oedipal mother and produces desire *as* repressed and infinitely displaced. Desire, as well as the subject, both phallic and patterned upon the boy's repression of the maternal body, are supposed to account for desire and subject in general. Boys give up what they "have" in the imaginary, while girls are supposed to renounce *what they do not have . . .* and *be* it through masquerade. "It is in order to be the phallus, that is, the signifier of the desire of the Other, that the woman will reject an essential part of her femininity, notably all its attributes, through masquerade,"[15] that is, a "woman" assumes a mask through which the original threatening object of desire becomes unrecognizable, and she desirable. Or else, she is a shameful and envious castrated incomplete creature and/or a horrible figure of transgression of the paternal taboo, castrating and personifying the threat of psychosis, all intended by the expression "essential part of her femininity" for whose denial "masquerade" stands in. Joan Rivière's masquerade is trapped inside the phallic vicious circle, since "womanliness" is created, for her, through a distance from "femininity" opened by the phallus. Conceived of as a denial of women's inferiority in relation to male sex difference, the concept of masquerade in fact constructs femininity precisely as castration. Masquerade, this "compulsive ogling and coquetting," is undifferentiated from "genuine womanliness," that is, all females are equal as castrated/castrating behind a mask; with "the mask of womanliness being peeled away . . . she was revealed either as castrated (lifeless, incapable of pleasure) or as wishing to castrate."[16] From the angle of the phallus, "masqueraded" as/or "genuine," woman becomes a subject by virtue of her participation in what I view as the *inside-the-phallus subjectivizing dimension* by sacrificing some enigmatic femininity and camouflaging her "castration."

Phantasmatic Trace of Traumatic Trace

The phallic arena is based on the mechanism of castration; hence its subjectivization is characterized by cuts from bodily events (Real) by means of the signifier (Symbolic), in order to leave the inhuman behind and enter the specifically human. These incisions create some psychic wild residues: the *objet (petit) a.* In the course of these cuts, the subject itself emerges: when language dims the archaic modes of experience and when discourse, which conducts and presents the laws and orders of language and society, nests in their place and restructures the archaic processes and events as no longer accessible. The *objet a* is a trace of the pre-Oedipal partial drive's engagements with the archaic part object and the pre-Oedipal mother qua object or real Other (which I call *m/Other*). Even though unabsorbed by the Symbolic and imageless, the *objet a* is sliced in consonance with the display of significance determined by the signifier and is therefore still a phallic inscription of "bodily samplings."[17] The gaze is such a trace in the psychic field of vision (scopic), concealed—and revealed—through the phantasy's screen. Lacan related to this trace as "extimate": an inaccessible, intimate exteriority that dwells inside the non-conscious self but outside its "subject"-ive realm. The *objet a* indexes that something enjoyable or painful has happened in the domain of the Real, in relation to the Thing. "What is closest to us is the intolerable imminence of *jouissance*."[18] The gaze is already a garbage of what is closest to us and springs from contact with the corpo-real Thing. We may understand the gaze as a phantasmatic trace of a traumatic trace. From the angle of the Symbolic and the Imaginary, this residue remains forever a hole, a "cause of the desire"[19] that does not satisfy desire. From the angle of the Real, the gaze wakes up and perishes in accordance with trails molded by libidinal energy channeled via partial drives; therefore the gaze indexes a "surplus-of-enjoying/paining" (*plus-de-jouir*).

Following Maurice Merleau-Ponty while establishing a difference from or even opposing him,[20] Lacan states that the gaze is prior to and split from the eyes of the seer, that my existence as a visible being looked at from all directions in "the spectacle of the world" is prior to and split from my existence as a seeing being. The gaze turns us into a picture to be looked at in phantasy in which we do not appear to ourselves—except as a *stain* in the picture, or as a screen between the gaze and the picture, or as a stain on the screen. With *my* gaze I do not meet *the* gaze that my soul longs to see, but only a gaze imagined by me in the field of the Other. I meet only substitutes; there is no contact with the relic my desire longs for, since it was created as a cut from the sensing, feeling, paining, and enjoying me who participates in real events and as a hole in my self, who thinks by way of the chains of the signifier. This gaze, so absent, a hole, can even be conceived of as a retroactive product of a *cause* throughout symbolic articulation. When I try to focus on the gaze, it vanishes "in so far as the gaze *qua objet a* may come to symbolize this central lack expressed in the phenomenon of castration."[21] Erecting the lack as castration means that the subject emerges in place of the gaze, that the gaze turns me into a visible object while its visibility and my visibility by it are severed from me as a conscious seeing subject. In art, in accordance with Freud's idea of the uncanny, the gaze—says Lacan—"is presented to us only in the form of a strange contingency, symbolic of what we find on the horizon, as the thrust of our experience, namely, the lack that constitutes castration anxiety."[22]

An uncanny strangeness is tied to the Other's gaze. Does indeed *only* castration anxiety, which stems from a phallic theoretical model suited—as Freud confessed[23]—for male sexuality *only* (and presented as the measure of sexuality in general, that is, of female sexuality as well) lie behind this aesthetic experience that arises in our meeting with an artwork?

Although, for Lacan, all mutuality between the gazed-at / the seer (as subject) that is also visible (as object), that is, me, and the *gaze* of the Other is illusionary, and any encounter is a miss, he nevertheless indicates, following Merleau-Ponty, a nameless substance of *Voyure* and a point of contact—a *tychic* point[24]—at which the invisible gaze and the visible gazed-at have met in the Real before the emergence of the subject as split. The lost tychic point is liable to shimmer out from a screen between the gaze and the picture, and through it the subject too is *present* in the picture—as a stain.

Veil of Separation—Veil of Contact

The relations between the subject of desire, the gaze that recedes but induces desire, the visual art object that is outside the subject (artist, viewer) yet is made by subjects, and the picture engraved in the eye of the subject as an impression get complicated when between the gaze outside and a picture inside lies an entity both permeable *and* opaque: a screen. "The gaze . . . is always this which prevents me, at each point, from being a screen," but "if I am anything in the picture, it is always in the form of the screen, which earlier I called the stain, the spot."[25] The screen, then, is both a mediating entity through which I enter the picture as a stain and also, in contrast, something I am prevented from entering into—because of the gaze. This paradox alludes to two possibilities with regard to the screen: (1) the screen of phantasy as Lacan usually conceptualizes it—in the lap of the phallus, in harmony with the castration mechanism and in relation to a radical, alienated, and alienating Other—is a separating veil between the gaze and the desiring subject; (2) the screen, in an interpretation closer to Merleau-Ponty's, may be a veil of contact-mediation where the gaze and the gazed-at subject meet and touch, where we may characterize the gaze as symbiotic. But Lacan develops only the dimension of fissure and rift and rejects the symbiosis, since "his" Other is radically separated from the subject and produces the gazed-at as disjointed and alienated from the gaze.

In Lacan the gaze is phallic, for desire takes shape even in the domain of vision through primary ruptures from part objects in the form of "self-mutilation."[26] The Oedipus complex that retroactively organizes the totality of the pre-Oedipal libidinal partial dimension is reduced to castration (not without echoing the libido, conceived as masculine by Freud), presented as the exclusive process of passage that separates events from the Real while creating the subject as divided. "The *objet a*, if taken only in Lacan's sense, is a container of the effect [and] the signification of castration,"[27] and since sexuality "exercises its proper activity through the mediation—paradoxical as that may seem—of the partial drives,"[28] all three (the gaze as the lacking object that causes desire and is analogous to the "woman" as a real m/Other-Thing, the desiring subject who emerges in its place and induces a "woman"-object, and sexuality) are shaped in Freudian and Lacanian theory by phallus/castration, though for each author this pair has a different meaning. Since the visual artist doesn't organize fields of representations or optical-geometric perspectives but buries/inserts/produces his/her desire in painting (in sculpture, etc.), the artist initiates a dialogue with a gaze connected to sexuality beyond appearance, beyond the visible, beyond that perceived by the senses. The viewer can glean something of the hidden gaze if s/he refrains from any conscious attempt to capture it, if s/he "lays down the arms"—to use Lacan's expression—at the painting's threshold and gives in.

Since the "beyond appearance" is constructed to echo the pair phallus/castration, the gaze appears in art as incarnation of the "phallic ghost."[29] And although Lacan himself remarked in the seventies that this model is conceived "in a male way only,"[30] he didn't posit another possibility for the inscription of the gaze via art in culture. Not only the subject but out-of-the-subject psychic entities like *jouissance* and *objet a* still dwell in the realm of the phallus—as its inside, outside, or extimate. From the outset the phallus governs, as Jacques-Alain Miller remarks, all three spheres of the psyche: it is symbolic; it is imaginary, it is even between the Symbolic and the Imaginary; and it has a correlate in the male Real—the penis. "A single and same marker dominates the whole register concerning the relationship of the sexuated. . . . All is reduced to this signifier: the phallus."[31] The phallus governs all three spheres of the psyche—but also structures their "holes" as well! From where can we then start again? Lacan asks himself this question and replies: we should start again from the woman qua "not-all."[32]

Jouissance of the Edge

Desire also is exclusively phallic according to this model. "Castration is even the only liberator of desire that may be conceived of," but we are nevertheless aware of an additional sexuality: "*Jouissance behind castration* . . . the unthinkable *jouissance* [that] is the *jouissance* of the subject before the mark of the signifier . . . would be inconceivable without feminine sexuality."[33] Something of the erotic antennae of the psyche transmits to, and receives from the Other through phantasy—I suggest—echoes of archaic partial relations and feminine *jouissance* of before-as-beside the phallic era, which are neither fabricated nor entirely appropriated by the current Symbolic. Such echoes are invested as a gaze and embedded in painting *beyond* the visible as *in-side* that is *be-side* it. In the feminine, as we shall see, the gaze may have a borderline in-visibility and is not forever cut or totally lost for/from visibility.

Sexual *jouissance*, partial drives and libido, the Thing and the feminine beyond-the-phallus are summoned together here to elucidate the emergence of another gaze in art. To these, the enigmatic term *sinthôme*[34] will be added. The experience of the *uncanny*, that Freud brings up as fundamental in the relation between viewer and artwork, is based on the gaze's approaching consciousness: "The libido . . . can only be participant of the hole, which moreover goes for all other modes through which the body and the Real are presented. . . . [It is] through this that I'm trying to get back to the function of art. . . . And when I say that art can go so far as to arrive at the symptom, this is what I will try to substantiate."[35] "One sublimates, [Freud] tells us, with impulses. . . . Where do these impulses come from? From sexuality's horizon . . . their [fulfilled] *jouissance* is linked to sexuality. [But] about sexuality we know nothing. . . . The enigma can be put this way: as *jouissance* of the edge, how could it be measured by an equivalence to sexual *jouissance* ?" The *edge structure* of the archaic partial drive associates with what will gradually crystallize as feminine in a configuration that holds together Woman-Other-Thing. "The relationship of sublimation to *jouissance,* in so far as it is *sexual jouissance,* can only be explained by that [anatomy] . . . the *objet a* is that which tickles *das Ding* [the Thing] from the inside. . . . That is what makes up the essential merit of what we call the work of art."[36]

My psychoanalytic perspective does not intend to cast a biological shadow on art. Artworks do not lean on "naturally" given part objects, but the "artistic machine," as Deleuze puts it, produces "fragments without totality, cut-up particles, vessels without communication, partitioned scenes" analogous to part objects. The artistic machine also produces resonances and effects deriving from resonance "that life cannot realize" that are linked to Eros and "machines for forced movement" linked to Thanatos.[37] *Art is not an effect of the lost object; painting is not produced by a preexisting gaze, but produces it.* In this sense we will return to the archaic object, the partial becoming-subject and woman-m/Other-to-be and their encounter in the context of creating/producing and viewing art via the matrixial borderspace.

"There Is No Sexual Rapport"

Mainly logical and topological but also aesthetic-poetic considerations led Lacan, rarely, in his very late seminars,[38] to imply enigmatically a psychic zone in which feminine sexual rapport might occur. A supplementary femininity, hardly disengaged from psychosis, is drawn out of thinking about art, while Lacan otherwise returns incessantly to the formula "there is no sexual rapport," that is, no link to the experience of woman, no contact with feminine-Other in sexual relations based on the phallic model of male *jouissance* in both sexes, and mainly, no ways to report on a sexual rapport that would be feminine-Other if/where it does occur, since it is not inscribed in the Symbolic.

Phallic sexual *jouissance* in men and women relates to an organ of the subject or to the other-as-an-object that represents an organ, and not to the other as an-other-*subject*; it is therefore "an obstacle to sexual rapport."[39] Describing *jouissance* by means of the signifier qua castration "has the value of a sexual nonrapport."[40] The signifier kills the libidinal event, and so sexuality can't be inscribed *as* rapport. However, a different *jouissance* that is not obstacle but fulfillment resists this "death" even though language "sanctions"[41] it. The feminine *jouissance* that is unthinkably known but is not inscribed in the *unconscious structured like a language* aspires to release itself in the scopic field as *an-other gaze* that would shape *an-other* desire, but as long as *all* desire is formulated as a symbolic castration of *jouissance*'s continuity, all *jouissance* is "reduced to the phallic signifier"[42] that prevents its passability into culture.

The Hybrid Sub-Unconscious[43]

Through making art and reflecting on it, is it possible to formulate theoretical paths that are not a tear or a cut and that do not collapse onto the royal way of the phallus?

From with-in this process out, feminine passageways can be articulated as threads within a connectionist psychic web of *severality.*

Lacan in his late theory describes the intrapsychic spheres as rings, linked to each other by a Borromean knot, a kind of braid where the stem of the Real is inseparable from the stems of the Imaginary and the Symbolic. Here, the Real itself already stores some kind of knowledge that can be articulated, "something that is written and should be read in deciphering it." "She [a "woman"] manages to succeed at sexual union. Only this union is the union . . . of each of these three strands. The sexual union . . . is internal to its weave. And that is where she plays her part, in really showing us what a knot is."[44] A "disharmonious"[45] unconscious deals with knowledge that is independent of the signifier, more imminent to us than phantasy. If knowledge gathered in the Real is not a bulk of data awaiting decoding by signifiers but an "invention" that comes to pass in any "first encounter with sexual rapport" then, I would suggest, a metramorphic process of intersection and interchange embraces and discharges unthought subknowledge from the knotted Real into meaningful coinscription in artwork where it is written for the first time, and from there, onto a hybrid sub-unconscious weave in which are traced: encounter that is a covenant, a sexual rapport and its feminine-Other-desire, and intrapsychic knots that join into interpsychic borderlinks. Inventions are inseparable from their inscription as sub-unconscious, joint, and conductible *co-meanings of co-emergence*.

Does a woman-*knot* only *demonstrate* in real ex-sistence or is something of *her* extricated toward the subject?

Experiencing feminine *jouissance* is not sufficient. Conceptualizing a nonphallic feminine difference is possible only inasmuch as whatever of it that evades preestablished discourse can still trace itself, be written, have a meaning, become thinkable. Only if traces of the feminine difference and of the failure of the phallus make intelligible sense may we advance a nonphallic subjective dimension. *The paradigm itself should rotate* if we claim that traces of the feminine-beyond-the-phallus and its rapport can be culturally reported. In the shift from the individual's knot to a matrixial web of borderlinks, a feminine *jouissance between trauma and phantasy* engraves subknowledge *between phantasy and desire* in an enlarged subjectivity.

A Becoming-archaic-m/Other-to-be and Nonprohibited Prebirth Incest

The premise of intersubjectivity, a cornerstone in the ethics of Emmanuel Levinas, is forsaken by Lacan in the wake of a theoretical inversion. For the early Lacan of the fifties, this premise is condensed in the formula "the subject's desire is the desire of the Other": relations toward significant others take place in terms of the symbolic satisfaction brought about by recognition of the subject stemming from the Other and reaching the subject through discourse. The passage through others occurs only in as much as the Other vehicled by them is represented by signifiers and represents society, culture, history, Law.

Why evoke the intersubjective experience in the field of the very late Lacanian theory? What difference it will make for a feminine-Other-desire?

Where, theoretically speaking, could an encounter occur between the Other's desire and the trauma of the *I*?

In the classical Lacanian theory, the desire of the subject, not its phantasy, reflects the desire of the Other—not its phantasy; trauma is individual, and phantasy is in correlation to *jouissance assumed* in the realm of the Other. In what sense may one formulate the desire of the Other in direct and positive relation to the *jouissance* of the subject, when desire is a concept that "kills" *jouissance* and the Other is an alienated network of the signifiers' chains?

Where would the subject's trauma and phantasy meet with the phantasy of the Other? What would the term *phantasy of the Other* mean?

An-*other* Other, different from "the treasure of the signifier" is assumed here for these ideas to flourish.

The first hint that something strange, deviating from the phallus and bound to intersubjective relations, might take place in the field of symbolic desire can, I believe, be traced in this exceptional expression: "phantasy as the desire of the other,"[46] which in Lacan's early theory sounds like a slip of the tongue.[47] I connect this expression to a possible linkage of the subject's trauma and phantasy (axis of the Real) to the Other's desire (axis of the Symbolic). The real Other toward whose desire the subject aspires in his phantasy is the mythic m/Other; but also, I add, the woman as archaic-m/Other-to-be in whose phantasy and desire the subject, even before s/he was born, was already playing a part. The *jouissance* that spurs on the level of prebirth incest, and the links between the trauma and phantasy of the becoming-subject (*I*), male or female, and the trauma, phantasy, and desire of the "woman" as becoming-archaic-m/Other-to-be (*non-I*), both of them in their status of partial subjects *and* part objects for each other—"grains" of *I* and *non-I* and not yet "mother" and "infant"—constitute a cluster of feminine rapport. And this rapport (which for psychoanalytic theory is sexual in the partial dimension) is inscribed to make sense.

An im-pure object co-responds to a diffracted subjectivity, to a matrixial covenant of severality. And since "the *jouissance*, [which] does not wait for phallic organization to enter into play, will take on aspects of *revelation* that it will keep forever,"[48] it founds beyond appearance an-other gaze on a *with-in-visible borderscreen*, which enchants us as beauty, confers secrets, and fascinates us as sublime even when it incarnates the horrible. The matrixial gaze apprehended in sublimation that relates to *"jouissance* of the edge" as feminine creates/exposes the matrixial screen itself, from which it also disengages and to which it also returns, inside which are hidden both *I*(s) and *non-I*(s) in a semisealed and semipermeable conglomerate web. The encounter with-in the matrixial veil in the screen of phantasy attests that traces are interwoven: that something that diverges from the *non-I* engraves traces in the *I* and something that abandons the *I* is still attaining the *non-I* somewhere, somehow, and that the object itself is assembled as hybrid and remains an incompatible composite that neither assimilates and fuses with its components nor rejects and disjoins them.

An Erotic Encounter of Grains

The incestuous in/out-side rapport between subject-to-be and archaic-m/Other-to-be, connected to female corporeal invisible specificity where this incest takes place, is the basis in the Real for a matrixial stratum. This basis should not mislead us into seeking the matrixial encounter in biological nature, just as the phallic structure does not stand for, though is related to, the corpo-real male sexual organ. In the phallus, her sex difference based on a "lack" of male's organ in the Real inscribes "nothing" in the Symbolic and inspires imaginary horror of castration. In the matrix, her sex difference in terms of female bodily specificity inscribes a paradoxical sphere on the Symbolic's margins. The trauma and phantasy of prebirth incest arise in link with feminine-Other-desire. The archaic incest with-in/out may go under a process I term matrixial *fading-by-transformation* as well as under phallic *foreclusion*. When female bodily specificity is taken into account as a *different* sex difference that informs subjectivity, jointness (rather than being/not-being, presence/absence) and conductible border-links between subjects and objects (rather than rapture and castration, having/not-having), as well as transmissibility and shareability of assembled, hybrid objects, not only disturb the phallic interior (intrapsychic) and exterior (cultural and social) scene but also in-form a *beside* (not opposed)—intersubjective to begin with (but intrapsychic as well)—alternative scene and enlarge the Symbolic beyond the phallic scope. Fading-by-transformation involved in metramorphic passages onto becoming-Symbolic is an outcome of change and transmission, fragmentation and severalization, dispersal and resharing of the *already* joint and plural-several (and not plural-infinite) elements of the feminine sphere.

"There are subjective positions that are wider than those of the subject of the signifier; that's what one studies with the phantasy,"[49] for phantasy is not subordinated to the retroactive action of the chains of the signifier. If the *I* is a subject plus *jouissance*, then libidinal energy is not entirely lost in the process of symbolization. The subject emerging in relation to the Other qua network of signifiers *replaces* the traces; the *I*, in contrast, and likewise (by means of the same parameters) the *non-I*, includes them. Extimate relations enable us to locate the gaze in the *non-I* as well, as a kind of in-(me)side out-side(me), and to deposit in a wider-Other erotic traces that are inscribed in the Psyche but not by distinct signifiers. In the matrixial borderspace, the relation between *jouissance* and gaze designates the difference of each subject-in-jointness; reciprocal inversion of inside and outside does not designate symbiosis. I suggest that with each inversion of inside-outside and with each exchange between the matrixial several "grains" information is added. Hence the conductible metramorphosis and the redistributed hybrid gaze carry heterogeneity.

"Does an erotic gaze leave traces there where it has just been inscribed, at the level of the other, that is, in someone else?"

"The subject is the one who erases the trace by transforming it into gaze, slit, fleeting perception; it is through this that he encounters what it is of the other who has left a trace; he passed by here, he is beyond."[50]

The phantasmatic matrixial web of *I/non-I* includes traces of whoever was there, as an inscribed subknowledge that is not just traces of "nothing" but also of what is beyond and yet inter-with-in me. Inasmuch as the matrixial stratum emerges first of all in the experience related to the womb as inside *or* outside *me* and as outside *and* inside *us*, it spreads out between trauma and phantasy of each becoming-subject together with the trauma and phantasy of its specific becoming-m/Other-to-be. This stratum is bounded through singular feminine/prenatal encounters as inscriptions with-in-dialogue with the desire of an *assembled* woman-Other. The desire of the woman as subject within such singular series of encounters is already a *webbed* desire, further composited but not fused or mingled with the Name of the Father. *Her*-desire is both phallic and matrixial. An exclusively phallic desire in such a meeting, which would have designated the reduction of the libido as masculine (only) to the signifier at the price of the destruction of supplementary feminine eroticism, would only have deepened the misunderstanding into which each subject is born: "Otto Rank came close to this when he spoke of the trauma of birth. There is no other trauma: Man is born misunderstood. . . . That is what it has transmitted to you by 'giving you life.'. . . There is no other trauma of birth than that of being born desired. Desired, or not—it's all the same since it comes through the by/speak-being (parl'être)."[51]

Feminine-Other-Desire

In the matrixial borderspace neither motherhood nor mother/child relations is the issue but a "before" as beside that relates to inscriptions of/from female corporeal specificity that is not yet processed in psychoanalysis. It is too dangerous. It is a chief *silenced* hole in the phallic paradigm. Already Freud took steps against it, for it hurts male sexuality and narcissism.[52] If Freud develops the narrative of the archaic father and names the taboo of incest structured by/for it in the Oedipus complex as prohibition of the son's passion toward the pre-Oedipal mother, which conditions repression and structures desire as its infinite displacement, there is no similar structure, prohibition or repression, concerning matrixial incest. Indeed it can't be forbidden—it occurs to give life. Yet for its high psychotic potentiality[53] in the phallic paradigm it was not merely excluded from the Symbolic (from which it could then return to produce desire) but silenced and marginalized as unthought of. Whatever of it escaped this destiny serves patriarchy: the desire to have children in heterosexually regulated units of society. This aspect was elaborated and subjugated to the general phallic model while the silenced matrixial desire of *linking with the unknown* and *bounding with unknown others in the process of becoming and transforming* puts patriarchy, on the contrary, in danger. The feminine other sex difference was sacrificed, I believe, to protect male narcissism in the name of both sexes, to preserve the phallic psychic integrity of subjects of both sexes, and to reflect/maintain/reproduce/transmit its structure.

For the "woman," I suggest, both the exclusion of the matrixial incestual rapport *and* this rapport itself coexist on levels of trauma, phantasy, and desire. The matrixial difference is actually—but not in principle—absent from the Symbolic in its actual definition. The desire of the *non-I* as a by/speak-being creates in misunderstanding the inheritance transmitted to the coemerging *I*. The *non-I*'s desire, I suggest, includes traces of the *partially* foreclosed incest in search of ways to become known. "The desire to know meets obstacles. In order to embody the obstacle I have invented the knot."[54] Lacan's knots account enigmatically for feminine desire in the still—and up until the end—phallic paradigm of his late theory. However, with the idea of the "knot" it is already evident that the possibility of describing supplementary femininity within the phallus has been exhausted. In the shift from this impasse to the matrixial paradigm, metramorphosis, not knot, accounts for feminine rapport, *jouissance*, and desire in the subject.

A Phallus-Bypassing Subknowledge

The enigma of feminine/(late)-prenatal encounter that affects originary repression and archaic pictograms, a silent reality before as beside the signifier and outside the signified, is neither foreclosed nor repressed but faded-by-transformation for "woman." Something of it is delivered into sub-unconscious margins via matrixial covenant(s) that art assembles. Yet we must beware of understanding that the archaic m/Other-to-be linked to the Thing and undergoing fading-by-transformation is simply the ancient mother, just as the "origin"-al father is not the actual father in the past. Even Melanie Klein assumes in the place of the Thing the mythic body of the mother, Lacan argues. Thus, raising the "woman" to the level of the Thing in art via sublimation does not, even in the matrixial field, designate a regressive return to the womb. Rather, something is contrived in the relation to the mute/vanished Thing: elusive and transient "deviant" creatures, which the signifier cannot tame because they are out of its zone. If the Thing, site of primordial extimacy outside the field of representation, is absent and "alien"[55] in the phallus, in the matrix it is neither totally absent nor entirely alienated. Something escapes into culture and something in culture nourishes the feminine with a bypassing-phallus subknowledge. Something is created that is not impossible to "isolate as a function," to "distill as a process," to "embody in an entity," "by removing a moment of its fluidity and deposing it elsewhere." There is a "montage" "based on the confusion between the mark and its place (the mark as it designates itself; the mark as it designates its place), or again, between entities of a different order." There is a neutral intrapsychic *matrice* deduced from the phallus, "an essential (constitutive) lack, a hole in the universe of speech" (Miller), in relation to which "we talk, we write, we live in the too early/too late."[56] There is also an androgynous intrapsychic figure-matrice (Lyotard).[57] There is also a hybrid assemblage, a feminine intra- *and* interpsychic matrixial trace. If we transfer the elusive matrice from the intra-subjective field of the Nothing and the All, the One and the Infinite in which J. A. Miller describes it qua lack, to an intersubjective matrixial field of severality where it is in-between presence and absence, and if we neutralize it of its extimate neutrality and feminize it as a *beyond-passage* to-with-in the phantasy of the *I* and *non-I*, it becomes possible to perceive traces of real events as participating in processes and functions of conductibility and transformation. When the neuter, sexless figure-matrice turns into a feminine matrixial trace, the interior extimate zone is not only a neuter place in which events occur on the corporeal borders and dissolve into grooves, leaving psychic traces in their place but also a simultaneous, unexpected creation of an *encounter*. Place, event, and their grooves in several grains coemerge with-in-to a shared space. Foreclosed according to the phallic model from the Symbolic, the matrixial Thing creates cracks in sublimation, which in psychoanalysis has been considered exclusively phallic, resulting from the Oedipus complex and favoring male subjects. The matrix infiltrates through non-Oedipal feminine-covenantal sublimation and is sown in art.

Metramorphic Borderlinks in Subsymbolic Sieve

Judith Butler, commenting on Mary Douglas's *Purity and Danger*, argues that though Douglas shows how social taboos, imposed through binary distinctions like those of within and without institute and maintain the boundaries of the body in identity as male and female, she can't point toward an alternative configuration of culture beyond the binary frame. Butler quotes: "Ideas about separating, purifying, demarcating and punishing transgressions have as their main function to impose system on an inherently untidy experience" while "any kind of unregulated permeability constitutes a site of pollution and endangerment." With Kristeva's "abject" "the alien is effectively established through (this) expulsion"; consolidation of "inner" and "outer," "pure" and "defiled" both maintain social regulation and control and establish the Other as rejected and repulsive. Not only Law and Order, but also Creation, is founded in the phallic paradigm that underlines social conventions, on the marking of a frontier between pure and impure[58] in order to overcome the "abyss" that becomes its Other, its inaccessible side. Janine Chasseguet-Smirgel presents the castrating separation as a universal principle of order and not as related to social conventions or ideology. The breach of separation between subject and object is presented as perversion.[59] Where indeed such a transgression in the phallic paradigm does stand for a collapse of the difference between desire, phantasm, and event while castration establishes the difference between event and representation, in the matrixial paradigm differentiation-in-transgression stands for a creative principle that does not correspond to the phallic Law and Order and *does not replace* them either. For the matrix, creation is before-as-beside the univocal line of birth/Creation-as-castration; it is in the im-pure zone of *neither* day *nor* night, of *both* light *and* darkness. The problem, as Butlers argues, is not only how to deconstruct prohibition sanctions that regulate "man" and "woman," "me" and "Other" into fixed identities and constitute phallic Law and desire, but mainly how to achieve "an openness to resignification and recontextualization" of sexuality;[60] the problem is how to describe/invent another process of meaning donation/revelation/production.

In the matrixial stratum of subjectivization, several *I* and *non-I* "grains" that reciprocally don't cognize each other discern one another, connect with each other by conductible borderlinks through exchanging affects and pathic information and share hybrid objects and a borderspace of primary differentiation. Difference from a feminine angle diffracts—a sexual difference based on webbing of links and not on essence. Traces of encounter-events are distilled into a web that interlaces in intersubjectivity; something *between* the "grains" reports and transfers itself. Differentiation and difference in coemergence are attuned by metramorphoses that create—and that are created with-in—rapport-without-relating in permutations of distance-in-proximity along borderlinks transiting between presence and loss, subject and object, the foreigner and myself. Here, *I*'s phantasy relates to *non-I*'s desire, the phantasy of the *non-I* relates to her archaic-m/Other-to-be's desire, and so on. Libidinal *jouissance* has not totally evaporated from the matrixial desire. A subsymbolic sieve inscribes its *besidedness* in relation to the phallic one.

The feminine participates in the in-formation of the subject via transformation-by-transgression toward differentiated-in-jointness others. The matrix is a dynamic borderspace of active/passive coemergence with-in and with-out the unrecognized other that inscribes joint existential ontogenesis, a becoming-memory in relation to a feminine-Other desire. We may describe the matrixial borderspace after Francisco Varela's autopoïesis[61] as a space of *co-poïesis*. Metramorphosis knits with the rotation of its involuntary trails the matrixial scope itself. The effects of the erratic actions of this creative potentiality are inscribed in singular encounters between *I*(s) and *non-I*(s). Some of the *non-I*'s foreignness will never yield to the mastery of my phallic recognition, yet we are the witnesses of others-becoming-ours; we share with our strangers an-other space.

"Not All" between Center and Nothingness, With-in-ter a Foreigner

"There is no sexual rapport except for neighboring generations; namely, parents on the one hand, and children on the other. That's what the interdiction of incest wards off. I talk about sexual rapport."[62] Sexual rapport, then, relates both to interdicted pre-Oedipal incest (with the mother) warded off by psychoanalysis and to feminine supplementary sexuality. And what about the prenatal incest?

To the phallus, which relates at the beginning to male sex-difference, the entire space of sublimation was connected. Does the matrix too have a sublimational outlet?

Not in the phallic paradigm. This one encloses the matrix with no possibility of sublimation of its creative principle from "woman" for women. But, as I have elaborated elsewhere,[63] Freud's aesthetic experience of the uncanny hides "intra-uterine life" or "womb" phantasies,[64] and, inasmuch as there is *sinthôme*, something of the feminine rapport rises to the surface as a gaze, by means of metramorphosis, just as something of the horror of castration emerges through the phallic gaze. In the aesthetic matrixial experience, sexual rapport and no-sexual-rapport coexist.

> It is inasmuch as there is "sinthôme" that there is no sexual equivalence, which is to say there is rapport. Where there is rapport, it is inasmuch as there is sinthôme, which is to say . . . it is by sinthôme that the other sex is sustained. . . . The sinthôme, is precisely speaking the sex I don't belong to, which is to say a woman. . . . The sinthôme's direct link, it is this something which must be situated in its doings with the Real . . . of the unconscious. . . . It is the sinthôme we must deal with in the very rapport Freud maintained was natural—which doesn't mean a thing: the sexual rapport. All that subsists of the sexual rapport is that geometry which we alluded to in relation to the glove. That is all that remains for the human space as a basis for the rapport.[65]

If we return to the gaze in order to examine it in light of Lacan's late theory, it seems to me that the status of the phallic—and even rarely its opposite, symbiotic—gazes and screens should be reviewed. The artwork attests that something of the matrixial layer may infiltrate beyond anxiety to the poïetic and the aesthetic object, and from them onward, just until the margins of ethical questions. Locating femininity in psychoanalysis by means of the *objet a* as a phallic foreign body involves the "woman" with the ethical issue of locating the stranger as a "virus" that should disappear. In the phallic paradigm, each imaginary other to which the *I* relates, and hence also the exile, is a parasite destined for annihilation either by assimilation or by banishment. In the matrix, the stranger, neither cut out from the system nor assimilated to it, *cannot* be articulated as a parasite; along our metramorphosis, the others and I share a destiny in which each of us is partial and relative "between being and nothingness." Even in the process of dissolving, each temporary, unpredictable, and unique covenant will still twinkle and rediffuse traces during transformations. In the matrixial space, foreignness and femininity stand for a continual negotiation without exhausting recognition, without claiming full understanding, without even expecting love and harmony, without definite resolution.

Matrixial Covenant

If in Lacan's late theory the "woman" is Other even when she is a *between center and nothing*, in the matrix she is not a radical Other but a border-Other, a *becoming in-ter-with the Other*, an *im-pure becoming*[66]-*between in jointness*,

> the *between* involved in sexual rapport but displaced and precisely *Other-imposed*. . . . What I advanced today concerns *only* the woman. And it is she who, in this figure of the Other, gives us an illustration within our reach to be, as a poet has written, "between center and absence,"[67] between the meaning she takes from what I've called the *at-least-one*, between the center as *pure existence* or *jouis-presence* and absence . . . which I could not write but to define as "Not-all," *that which is not included in the phallic function*, yet which is not its negation . . . absence which is no less *jouissance* then being *jouis-absence*.[68]

Between what kind of "center" and "nothing," do the partial subjects coemerge?

In the phallic paradigm, the archaic "nothing" is the focus of silence on the elusive feminine rapport, the foreclusion of intrauterine incest. The archaic "center" is precisely the focus of its *jouissance* as *presence*. Beyond the originary feminine/prenatal real stage, if "man" is *either* at the center of such a rapport—and then also inside psychosis, *or* cut away from it and in the arms of the law that edifices *desire* as masculine, for "woman" there are *between*-instants that are not either/or between oppositions that the phallus represents but and-and or neither/nor, paradoxical in terms of the phallic dimension. An and-and is linked with sexual rapport.[69] "Woman" in the matrix is not confined to the contours of the one-body with its inside versus outside polarity. The matrixial gaze that emerges/hides in the painting and the with-*in*(ter)-*visible* screen that is a veil extended from the in-outer screen of painting to the out-inner screen of phantasy in which *I* and *non-I* perceive/conduct/produce grains of our- and other-selves as a web that lurks in wait for splints of the gaze, testify that something of this impossible positions of and-and and in-ter-with-the Other is exposed in art and is accessible for abstraction in the sphere of ethics and for further conceptualization. Something of it, but not-All. The phallic-Symbolic can't appropriate it entirely, but the psychoanalytic field of the Symbolic itself is transformed by the matrix to stand for the beyond-the-phallus as well through artwork and writing-art.

In the matrixial stratum of subjectivity, the connection between phantasy and desire allows heterogeneity, while in the phallic plane phantasy and desire exclude each other. The matrix intertwines the woman as *between* subject and object and *between* center and nothingness on the axis of heterogeneous severality, while the phallus posits her as *either* a subject in the masculine format *or* an object patterned upon masculine desire. The *beyond the phallus* domain sketched by Lacan from within the phallic perspective still detains the woman on the axis of One and Infinite, with its same and oppositions, all and nothing—as its surplus, residue, Other, while the matrixial viewpoint is a priori that of the several. The matrixial desire is an aspiration and an inspiration from a feminine *jouissance* toward the edges of a wider Symbolic. The feminine conductible difference re(a)sonates and penetrates into the transsubjective field that potentially transgresses even generations. A "memory which concerns us, even if it is not ours, but is, how to say it! beside ours, and which determines us almost as much as our history" is thus "inscribed in our possible."[70]

Inscription from inside the Shell

A matrixial covenant zooms in in contingency and fades out by asymmetrical with-in-ter metramorphosis. The series of encounters between the coemerging *I* and *non-I* via conductible links on the phantasy/phantasy level and on the phantasy/desire level, and the connections between the *I* and *non-I* and their shared hybrid *objet(s) a,* beyond time, like such a series of conjunctions beyond place, shape a unique borderspace that gives birth to co-meanings of I-with/for-Other from "within the shell."[71] Just as the woman beyond the phallus is several *and* in between, so too the matrixial gaze is diffracted with-in-ter the screen. Between-beyond visual artworks, specific erotic aerials of singular almost-missed encounters approach visibility.

The matrixial desire thrives not from a phantasy about sharing but from a border share-ability in phantasy and in trauma that re(a)sonates onto feminine-Other-desire. Thus, in the matrixial field, we have to recycle—after shaking up and renovating—and add to the sur-plus-of-*jouissance* residues contrived from transgressivity that explore and retreat, severalize and compose. Traces of rapport-without-relating are scattered in an asymmetrical and non-equivalent way to in-form a covenant-in-differentiation based on re-co-naissance—re-joint-birth—as a kind of unthought subknowledge that re(a)sonates the meaning of heterogeneity, or heterogeneity as comeaning, to the threshold of culture and dig in it a nonphallic border-space by means of webbing.

Self-Dehiscence through Fission

Lacan's paradoxical screen extends mostly by phallic strings but rarely also by symbiotic cables hidden inside the phallus, while the matrixial screen offers a different, third possibility. According to Lacan, the painter lays down his own post-Oedipal phallic gaze in order to meet the object of the gaze of the Other, as the unexpected viewer—we can continue along the same line—will do too, in order to traverse the poïetic and aesthetic object. The painter's touch seizes a prior inner touch that resembles the one that participates in regression but, in contrast to it, creates—as in psychological time-reversal—a stimulus toward which the touch arises as a response. The gaze that had touched the Thing inside its shell is behind the bor-derline of this move. The gaze attracts, menaces, or amazes the artist on the border of the Irreal. Face to face with the terrible and fascinating power of the gaze on the horizon line, still saturated with ashes of originary *jouissance*, consciousness can only hinder the touch and sum it up by offering images and symbols for the imageless and symbolless.

The Thing touched from the inside of the shell by archaic gaze—where is it located?

The Thing is the psychoanalytic analogue of Merleau-Ponty's "flesh [*chair*] of the world." Presubjective and preobjective, it precedes the separation into subject and object and the differentiation between self and world. It embodies in*corp*oration of the outside in the inside and of the inside in the outside. From the inhuman, intersections are formed between sensing and sensed, touching and touched, seeing and seen, invisible and visible. The visible—preobject—is imprinted in the process of the emergence of the subject, and the seer—presubject—participates in determining the emergence of the object.[72] The "sensible's pulp" is this junction of inside and outside in "profound, thick contact,"[73] a double incorporation and reversibility. The indivisibility of seeing that Lacan calls *Voyure* is a dimension in a general indivisibility register that contains intersections. "As soon as this strange system of exchanges is given, all problems of painting are present" says Merleau-Ponty. "The drawing and the painting . . . are the inside of the outside and the outside of the inside, which is rendered possible by the duplicity of sensing."[74] This form of existence in the world, in which sensed and sensing intercoil and scroll, retreats with the separation from the flesh /Thing that occurs as a kind of dehiscence through fission. The self-splitting-apart from the inside of the shell gives birth to the bifurcation of subject and object, seer and seen, invisible and visible. In Lacan's teaching, because of the privilege of the castrating function, it is not the Thing that bifurcates; rather, the alienated Other constitutes the subject *in place of* events since discourse, anchored in language that is prior to the subject, acts from the Other's realm for severance and split. If Merleau-Ponty's dehiscence attests to a continual outgrowth that leaves a symbiosis—yet in which inside and outside are not confused—slowly behind, Lacan's "castration" announces alienation on the ruins of symbiosis.

The gaze is, thus, a relic of a split from an aggregate that knitted presubject and preobject together with a partial drive. The phallic gaze is the invisible as the inside of the visible's shell stripped of its libidinal charge, which from dawning represents an outside captivated within. And just as the fabric and its lining are not perceived from the same point of view, there is a schism between my eye and the gaze of the Other,[75] embodied by the screen of phantasy. Something of the gaze is cast upon the screen of phantasy when the subject is suspended, and if something of me appears on the screen, then it appears as a stain from which the gaze has dropped away. Since we understand the screen not as optical but as libidinal phenomenon, and since projection on the screen is not of an empirical object but of a gaze/cause-of-desire that is a leftover of ancient split and a surplus of bygone *jouissance*, we may also suggest a matrixial productive-conductive projection of a gaze with-in(ter)-to the screen; a gaze that is not yet *and* no more a "nothing," neither is it a whole, spread inter-with-in several elements, producing and transforming the qualities of the screen itself.

The Im-pure Hollowed Gaze

Since seeing is an "action at a distance,"[76] the field of vision facilitates the fissure between visible and invisible and provides a convenient format for a model of gaze as phallic and lacking. The field of tangibility provides a convenient format for a symbiotic gaze, hinted in Lacan by the "screen of mediation," as what had existed before the fissure. In the touch,[77] contact and separation are not opposed to each other; the touch allows us to emphasize transformations of proximity-in-distance. For the matrixial gaze, the reversibility[78] of the visible and the tangible seems pregnant with possibilities as a basis of transitivity between the several. If in the model of the symbiotic gaze and screen—that Lacan suggests and rejects—the reversibility evoked by Merleau-Ponty is emphasized by Lacan as nondifferentiation, the matrixial gaze with-in-side the artwork beyond appearance is inspired by the reversibility's other aspects: fission and segregation not as split and separation but as partialization and fragmentation, exchange, intersection, and synergy leading to transgression and transitivity.

In the borderspace of fading out and zooming in, not only the presubject and the preobject intersect and imprint poïetic archaic traces upon each other and in a connectionist web from the outset, but also the preother, the archaic *non-I*, the other grain-partner(s) in the field of coemergence. The matrixial stratum draws a phenomenological field of I with/for *some* other(s), and we may understand the gaze that Lacan analyzes after Sartre as *in rare moments* matrixial, when it does not concern "the organ of sight" but is the flash of apprehending "the existence of others" as "looking at me" qua "locus of relation."[79] In this sense, the gaze may transgress the portrayal of the animosity of the Other and represent instants of difference without alienation. The matrixial gaze germinates in a zone in which "neither he nor I are *pure gaze* on *pure being*."[80] The oscillation of borderlinks sifts a hollowed gaze as an im-pure gaze: not defiled as opposed to pure but inter-with the pure and the defiled/impure.[81]

To Emerge In-to-gather-with Painting

In art theory, the gaze serves to analyze artworks from the perspective of their being objects that contain something of the *jouissance* and the desire of the subject who produces them or looks at them, like human artifacts submitted as tribute to the Other, or like objects in the status of subjects, or even like "subjective objects,"[82] which have undergone sublimation from archaic layers. Both the post- and the pre-Oedipal phallic gazes that repose upon the partial drive in the scopic zone expel the feminine from art and offer themselves in its place or *herself* as their object. The matrixial gaze reinstates the feminine to its nomadic space as a link with-in-ter several subjects and *between* subject and object, as a composite object for fragmented and several subjectivity, and as an in-between entity/process/phenomenon of transmissible and conductible mediation. Thus, three kinds of gaze (the dividing and splitting phallic gaze, the touching symbiotic gaze, and the hollowed matrixial gaze), more than articulating seeing and touching, articulate the structure of the subject as incorporating femininity in symbiosis or foreclosing the feminine as a total Other—in the phallus, or as widening its frontiers to contain "woman" with-in-difference as a becoming-inter-Other—in the matrix; they clarify the status of the woman as either a subject or an object—in the phallus—or as an incompatible interlace of the two—in the matrix—and about the mutable relations between the visible and the invisible that art reflects *and* produces. Through painting, the matrixial gaze "tells" us not only that there is a feminine existence outside the phallus—in the Real—but also that there is a sublimation of the hidden feminine toward a sublime that ex-sists (to use Lacan's expression: existing as standing outside the site of) the body.

We can recapitulate the matrixial gaze in terms of *objet a* or *a-links*. A matrixial gaze emerges with-in and with-out oscillations onto the screen. The borderlink is an *enjoy-sense* (*jouis-sens*) that is not just experience but inscription without prescription. Fragments of unfamiliar others turn into grains—part objects or partial subjects—that continue being unfamiliar with-in-the encounter. The fluidity of the experience is inscribed in metramorphosis as an asymmetrical reciprocal relation that creates erotic antennae, shared but possessing different re(a)sonating minimal sense for each partial subject. These aerials register what returns from the Other as traces and transmit a centerless or multi-(several, not infinite)-centered gaze.

Through metramorphosis, grains are entwined in severality with no central control. The artwork is created in a process that is passive in part and active in part, since no particular separate grain will have the control over the gaze, nor will any of them suffer its absolute loss. The matrixial gaze is a cause-of-desire that resides in the elusiveness of successive rapports and transformations. Each partial subject is cosensitive and a witness: "Let us be one for the other a system . . . sensitive one to the other, in which one knows the other, not only in that which he endures on his behalf, but more generally *as a witness*."[83] Some-thing of the Thing partly perishes in its diffraction among the several; something that had dissolved in one passes to some others; elements of one matrixial web also pass to other matrixial webs, since each grain is a partner in several webs.

Through metramorphosis, the artist and the viewer coemerge in various unique ways in-to-gather-with the work. My painting and the one I look at convey the rays of the phallic gaze, the extensions of the symbiotic one, and the aerials of the matrixial gaze. The phallic gaze excites us while threatening to annihilate us in its emergence to the screen; the symbiotic gaze invites us to submerge inside it while threatening to annihilate us together with the screen. The matrixial gaze thrills us while fragmenting, scattering, and joining grains together and turning us into participatory witnesses; it enchants and horrifies us while attenuating us into particles participating in a drama wider than of our individual selves. It is extricated with the unknown, and it threatens to partially extract its presence via dispersion and diffraction, whether we wish it or not.

Tracing a Web in a Screen

Several elements are sprayed on the screen not as a stain but as a web. The matrixial gaze is not a meeting missed as a result of castration but an almost-missed encounter between the erotic antennae that extend from with-in and with-out ourselves toward an emerging feminine-Other desire. The matrixial gaze creates in the course of its inscription—and inscribes while emerging—the singularity of each encounter, designated for another transgression later on. Metramorphic means of transport conduct traces of "events without witnesses"[84] and convey them on to witnesses who were not there, to witnesses without events.

So, what is your witnessing worth?

For the matrixial gaze, it makes no difference if the materials of artwork come from with-in, as source/origin, or from with-out, as readymade. Source/origin and found/readymade, two opposite poles in the phallus, lose their opposition in the matrix.[85] Here you can't smooth over the difference between the two, but also you can't elaborate or lose the one at the expense of the other. If you can't contrast them, how will you share (in-)them as yet *different* dimensions of the same work?

In the encounter with the matrixial gaze you can sometimes, in a momentary revelation, register your own part in the trauma and the phantasy of the other, and then—then—you cannot chose the moment to terminate the covenant, and to what extent, and how, and if at all, since the phallus can't master the matrix.

Left with the enigmatic burden of awareness of the other's trauma, what will you do?

And the shared screen?

The with-in-visible matrixial screen is a web into which subjectivity is woven in different ways in art—by trauma, by phantasy, by desire. It is in between us, it is a veil spread between joint traumas, fractions of phantasy from out into the inside, and aspects of painting in-to the outside. On the screen's interlaced threshold, a feminine gaze diffracts. How would transformation and transmission, fragmentation and severalization, dispersal and sharing of the *already* joint and several be discovered, beyond appearance, beyond that is inside the visible, in-side the with-in-visible screen?

Bracha Lichtenberg Ettinger

Someones Were There

Traces, sprayed and aspired toward matrixial desire, are transferred to the edges of painting. And nothing guides us how to transform a symptom into a *sinthôme*, how to join in the poïetic process and the aestetic experience, and why, and if at all. Neither in the phallic screen, nor in the matrixial. Once there, the artwork casts some of its shadow on the cultural field, entices or impels it to expand its frontiers sooner or later and to embrace some of its traces; it gives birth to concepts, but once you turn back to the artwork with concepts aroused by/from it, it further transforms and takes up seducing and luring from another site. Contrary to the symptom, an artwork is not replaced by the Symbolic. Contrary to *jouissance*, artwork does not exhaust its erotic potential.

The gaze alleges that *something was there* and that the event had passed, and also that *someones were there* and these *someones have already changed*. The voyage from *jouissance* through the gaze to the subject in terms of castration designates a phallic sublimational zone that acts and signifies in a retroactive gear even the limits of the *tyche*. The strayings of the feminine *jouissance* onto subjectivity and the dispersal of its residues in art wrap a matrixial sublimational zone in veils of anticipation. In order to overcome the limitation of the cleft produced by the pair phantasy/desire, and in order to come closer to the unconscious sub-knowledge of the Real, we may speak, with Miller, of "the *passions* of the *a*."[86]

Producing/Transferring, Looking/Conducting, and Transmitting

In the matrixial field, the two classical "deportees" from the Symbolic—the feminine and the pre-natal, which have been allowed to join together mainly in psychosis and in mysticism—inaugurate border accessibility, require a share in the aesthetic experience, and claim specific processes of subjectivization and sublimation. They also assert particular modes of distillation from ontogenesis to comeaning and partial integration into culture, as well as ethical ramifications and filtration to the symbolic.

When Freud's psychotic patient gets dressed with femininity to such an extent that he incorporates in his Real a "woman," he is delirious and his oeuvre is psychosis. The incarnation of his femininity stands in direct relation to the foreclosure of the feminine from the phallic-symbolic system. And when a woman incarnates a "woman" without masquerade, is she psychotic?

Femininity, in Freud's conception, is femininity in or for men, and men reflect the feminine for women. When the artist, James Joyce (for Lacan) or Leonardo (for Freud), materializes/realizes "woman," his creation is a poetic writing or a painting. He exposes/creates a symbolic relation the like of which has hitherto not been known. And when a woman artist orients questions on/of/from the feminine toward an Other-woman and realizes/incarnates "woman" in writing or in painting?

Matrixial *écriture*[87] within artistic texture is singular; it is to be rescued covenant after covenant. Something of the enjoy-meaning of the gaze is inscribed while at the same time the revelation of the subject-with-in-for-others on the matrixial with-in-visible screen resonates the almost-missed encounter of *I* and *non-I* with the gaze.

The matrixial screen that is inter-with-in joint phantasy is at the same time also inter-with-out shared painting in its expansion with-in-visibility, with-in(ter) producing/transferring; looking/conducting and transmitting, beyond time and place. The matrixial screen in art hides the traces of the gaze and also exposes them, as a sanctuary would its relics. The matrixial screen and its gaze, which create and record variations in a singular hybrid assemblage, are

110

revelation and apparition that resonate into artwork the intensification and the fading away of the modalities and qualities and of its fraction with-in the feminine difference. They also produce new gazes, new (*a*) links and *objet(s) a*. In the encounter with-in-out art, something is likely to metramorphose the borders of the Symbolic into thresholds. Whatever of it, which, to be apprehended, links the joint several subjects and the hybrid objects in rapports-without-relating in distance-in-proximity and with-in coemergence-in-differentiation, will not be appropriated by the phallus, yet will make sense. Will it stay *with-in-visible*?

NOTES:

Translations from Jacques-Alain Miller, Maurice Merleau-Ponty, and Jacques Lacan are by Joseph Simas in collaboration with Bracha Lichtenberg Ettinger, unless otherwise indicated. I would like to thank Richard Flantz for his help in translating some passages of my essay that were originally written in Hebrew.

1. Jacques Lacan, *Le séminaire de Jacques Lacan, Livre XX : Encore,* ed. Jacques-Alain Miller (Paris: Seuil, 1975).
2. See Bracha Lichtenberg Ettinger, *Matrix. Halal(a)—Lapsus: Notes on Painting 1985–1992,* trans. Joseph Simas (Oxford: Museum of Modern Art, 1993).
3. Jacques Lacan, "L'identification," unpublished seminar, June 1962.
4. The Real, in Lacanian psychoanalysis, is the psychic realm closest to corporeal experience. The "Real," the "archaic," and even the "id" do not mean "nature" or "body" in psychoanalysis.
5. See Bracha Lichtenberg Ettinger, "Matrix and Metramorphosis," *Differences* 3, no. 4 (1992), originally presented at Hamburg University, June 19, 1991; and "Metramorphic Borderlinks and Matrixial Borderspace," in *Rethinking Borders,* ed. John Welchman (London: Macmillan, 1995), originally presented at the Tate Gallery, London, April 2, 1993.
6. The matrix here is not an interior passive receptacle, a general neutral origin, or a cultural general grid.
7. Sigmund Freud, "The 'Uncanny'" (1919), *The Standard Edition of the Complete Psychological Works of Sigmund Freud,* trans. James Strachey (London: Hogarth Press, 1955), 17:248–49, 244.
8. Jacques Lacan, *Le séminaire de Jacques Lacan, Livre XI : Les quatre concepts fondamentaux de la psychanalyse,* ed. Jacques-Alain Miller (Paris: Seuil, 1973). In English as *The Four Fundamental Concepts of Psycho-Analysis,* trans. Alan Sheridan (New York: Norton, 1981).
9. On subsymbolic elements and connectivity, see Paul Smolensky, "On the Proper Treatment of Connectionism," *Behavioral and Brain Sciences* 11 (1988): 1–74.
10. I refer to the very late stages of pregnancy in which the subject-to-be, which is not yet subject, is already "postmature" (Winnicott); we assume that phantasy life has already begun and significance can, therefore, be retroactively attributed to it. (As for early stages of pregnancy, we can speak of a matrixial object but not of subject nor even of partial subject.) As a concept the matrix supports women's full response-ability for any event occurring with-in their own not-One corpo-reality and accounts for the difference of such response-ability from the phallic order. The matrix intends the cultural Symbolic, Imaginary, and Real spheres no less then the phallus, which even though indexing the male penis in the Real and imaginary "castration" anxiety is mainly acknowledged as a concept loaded with broad cultural implications.
11. Sigmund Freud, "Three Essays on the Theory of Sexuality" (1905), *Standard Edition,* 7:219.
12. Ibid., note 1915.
13. Sigmund Freud, "The Infantile Genital Organization" (1923), *Standard Edition,* 19:145.
14. Freud, "Three Essays," note 1924, and "The Infantile Genital Organization," 142. Freud states this even though "unfortunately we can describe this state of things only as it affects the male child; the corresponding processes in the little girt are not known to us" (ibid.).
15. Jacques Lacan, "The Meaning of the Phallus," in *Feminine Sexuality: Jacques Lacan and the Ecole Freudienne,* ed. Juliette Mitchell and Jacqueline Rose, trans. Jacqueline Rose (New York: Norton, 1985), 84.
16. Joan Rivière, "Womanliness as Masquerade," in *Formations of Fantasy,* ed. Victor Burgin, James Donald, and Cora Kaplan (London: Routledge, 1989), 39.
17. The scope of this article does not allow me a detailed presentation of the *objet a.* For further explanation see my essay "Woman as *objet a* between Phantasy and Art," *Complexity—Journal of Philosophy and the Visual Arts,* no. 6 (London: Academy Editions, 1995).
18. Jacques Lacan, "D'un autre à l'Autre," unpublished seminar, March 12, 1969. *Jouissance* is a term that designates archaic events of pleasure and/or pain on the level of the Real that are neither symbolized by words nor articulated in speech.
19. Desire in Lacanian theory is a concept that treats the Freudian libido as a metonymy subjected to the signifying network; that is, the desire is predetermined by means of the symbolic Other that is in charge of meaning attribution.

20. Since Merleau-Ponty emphasizes reciprocity, while for Lacan the universe of the Other is prior to the subject who is born into it.

21. Lacan, *Four Fundamental Concepts,* 77.

22. Ibid., 73.

23. Freud's late self-criticism deserves attention: "The discoveries touching the infantile sexuality were done on men, *and the theory which emerges from them* was elaborated *for the male infant.*" Sigmund Freud, *Sigmund Freud présenté par lui-même* (Paris: Gallimard, 1991), note from 1935, 61 (my italics).

24. Lacan, *Four Fundamental Concepts,* 77.

25. Ibid., 96–97.

26. Ibid., 83. The partition between the gaze and seeing, in Lacan's view, makes it possible to count the scopic drive among the drives (as suggested by Freud) and the gaze among the *objets a* of the drive, which leans upon an organ possessing orifices (such as the mouth, the ear, or the anus).

27. Jacques-Alain Miller, "Du symptôme au fonction et retour," unpublished seminar, May 4, 1983.

28. Lacan, *Four Fundamental Concepts,* 193.

29. Ibid., 88.

30. Lacan, *Le séminaire: Encore,* 58.

31. Lacan, "D'un autre à l'Autre," May 14, 1969. At the same time, in the later stages of his theory, the concept of the phallus retains its status more weakly. With great difficulty, and with very many constraints, the concept somehow—in all kinds of "negative" variations (such as minus phallus)—still maintains a correlation with the "feminine" reality that Lacan seeks to designate.

32. In Lacan, *Le séminaire: Encore.* I have discussed this in *The Matrixial Gaze* (Leeds: FAHN, Dept. of Fine Arts, Leeds University, 1995).

33. Miller, "Du symptôme," March 2, 1983 (my italics).

34. Playing on "symptom" and "saint-homme" (holy man).

35. Jacques Lacan, "Le sinthôme," unpublished seminar, September 9, 1975.

36. Lacan, "D'un autre à l'Autre," March 12, 1969.

37. Gilles Deleuze, *Proust et les signes* (Paris: Presses Universitaires de France, 1964), 186, 192.

38. Jacques Lacan, "Les non-dupes errent," unpublished seminar, 1973–74; "Le sinthôme," 1975–76.

39. Lacan, "Les non-dupes errent," May 21, 1974.

40. Miller, "Du symptôme," March 16, 1983.

41. Lacan, "Les non-dupes errent," May 21, 1974.

42. Jacques-Alain Miller, "Silet," unpublished seminar, 1995.

43. It is important to note that the concept of the unconscious does not cover the whole field of what is not conscious in the individual. I write *non-conscious* wherever I refer to zones that are not conscious yet are not included within the realm of (or covered by the definition of) the Lacanian unconscious that is "structured like a language" and includes repressions. The *sub-unconscious* is a term I suggest for the connectionist sphere of severality and encounter, which treasures traces of borderlinks (metramorphosis) and subsymbolic elements. The sub-unconscious is a non-unconscious sphere that is not included within the definition of the Unconscious.

44. Lacan, "Les non-dupes errent," January 15, 1974.

45. Thus Lacan sums up his teaching in 1973–74.

46. Jacques Lacan, "Subversion of the Subject," *Ecrits, a Selection,* trans. Alan Sheridan (London: Tavistock, 1977), 321. French version in *Ecrits* (Paris: Seuil, 1966), 825.

47. That is how it is usually considered. See, for example, C. Soler, "Hysteria and Obsession," presented at "A Seminar of the Freudian Field," Tel Aviv, December 3–4, 1989, 43. Soler continues accordingly: "Lacan says: Desire is the desire of the Other. And now I say: If desire is the desire of the other, phantasy is not the phantasy of the Other," etc.

48. Lacan, "L'identification," May 1962 (my italics).

49. Miller, "Du symptôme," June 8, 1983.

50. Lacan, "D'un autre à l'Autre," May 14, 1969.

51. Jacques Lacan, "Le malentendu," *Ornicar?,* no. 22 (1980). In French, *parl'être* evokes "a being by the speak," "speak/through-being," "by-being," "speakbeing," as well as "by the letter" and "speak by letter."

52. See, for example, Sigmund Freud, "On Sexual Theories of Children" (1908), *Standard Edition,* 9:205–26. The conceptualization of a "universal and neutral" narcissism, supposed to serve both sexes, is constructed by Freud upon the male organ of the subject, even when the subject (i.e., she) doesn't have it. The sexual difference represented by the womb and the male's envy of it are presented then negated by the Freudian theory *while the issue of its meaning for sexual difference from the female's side is rejected in advance.* I treat this matter in "The Feminine/Prenatal Weaving in the Matrixial Subjectivity-as-Encounter," *Psychoanalytic Dialogues* (New York: Analytic Press, issue forthcoming).

53. I disagree with Julia Kristeva, who believes that giving birth must emerge as psychosis in culture (Julia Kristeva, *Desire in Language: A Semiotic Approach to Literature and Art,* ed. Leon S. Roudiez, trans. T. Gorz, A. Jardine, and L. S. Roudiez [New York: Columbia University Press, 1980]). I suggest that this is so only in a Symbolic articulated

within the phallic pardigm. Evocations of the prebirth are not psychotic either, provided a wider-Symbolic in-formed by the matrix. For an extensive criticism of Kristeva's position on this matter, see Judith Butler, *Gender Trouble* (New York: Routledge, 1990), 79–93.

54. Lacan, "Le sinthôme," December 9, 1975.

55. Jacques-Alain Miller, "Extimité," unpublished seminar, November 20, 1985.

56. Jacques-Alain Miller, "Matrice," *Ornicar?*, no. 4 (1974). The "too early and too late" is an expression used by the poet Paul Celan to describe poetry.

57. Jean-François Lyotard, *Discours, Figure* (Paris: Klincksieck, 1985).

58. Janine Chasseguet-Smirgel, *Creativity and Perversion* (London: Free Association Books, 1985).

59. In agreement with Lacan's account of perversion in the 1960s. It is interesting to note that psychoanalytic experience in general shows perversion to be a male "speciality."

60. The first quote is from Mary Douglas's *Purity and Danger* (London: Routledge, 1969) as quoted in Butler, *Gender Trouble*, 132; further quotes in *Gender Trouble*, 132, 133, 134, 139. For Butler, parody is the way to achieve these aims.

61. Francisco Varela, *Autonomie et conaissance* (Paris: Seuil, 1989).

62. Jacques Lacan, "Le moment de conclure," unedited seminar, April 11, 1978.

63. Lichtenberg Ettinger, *The Matrixial Gaze*.

64. Freud, *The Uncanny*, 244, 248–49.

65. Lacan, "Le sinthôme," 1975–76.

66. A "becoming-woman" is an expression of Gilles Deleuze and Félix Guattari in *Capitalisme et schizophrenie: Mille plateaux* (Paris: Minuit, 1980). The matrixial "becoming" relates to but deviates from Deleuze and Guattari, whose "becoming-woman" is mounted on a sphere of infinity (while, in the matrix, *the several orients* the *becoming*).

67. An expression of the poet Henri Michaux.

68. Jacques Lacan, "Ou pire," unpublished seminar, March 8, 1972.

69. Lacan, "Les non-dupes errent," February 19, 1974.

70. Georges Perec, *Je suis né* (Paris: Seuil, 1990), 86.

71. An expression of the poet Paul Celan.

72. Maurice Merleau-Ponty, *Le visible et l'invisible* (Paris: Gallimard, 1964), 181–82.

73. Maurice Merleau-Ponty, *Résumés de cours*, Collège de France, 1952–60 (Paris: Gallimard, 1968), 179.

74. Maurice Merleau-Ponty, *L'oeil et l'esprit* (Paris: Gallimard, 1964), 21, 23.

75. Lacan, *Four Fundamental Concepts*, 65.

76. Merleau-Ponty, *L'oeil et l'esprit,* 37.

77. Merleau-Ponty objects to the touch as an aesthetic field for painting while Didier Anzieu suggests it. Didier Anzieu, *Le corps de l'oeuvre* (Paris: Gallimard, 1981), 71–72. Unlike Anzieu, I propose to examine the touch first of all as prenatal and in the framework of intrauterine relations of coemergence with minimal differentiation, not as postnatal and in the framework of symbiotic relations with the mother.

78. Merleau-Ponty, *Le visible et l'invisible*, 188.

79. Lacan, *Four Fundamental Concepts*, 84.

80. Merleau-Ponty, *Le visible et l'invisible*, 113–14 (my italics).

81. Bracha Lichtenberg Ettinger, "The Red Cow Effect," in Act 2 (London: Pluto Press, issue forthcoming).

82. To borrow a term from Winnicott.

83. Merleau-Ponty, *Le visible et l'invisible*, 113–14 (my italics).

84. An expression of Dori Lawb, in Shoshana Felman and Dori Lawb, T*estimony: Crises of Witnessing in Literature, Psychoanalysis and History* (London: Routledge, 1992).

85. See Lichtenberg Ettinger, *The Matrixial Gaze*.

86. Miller, "Extimité," June 18, 1986.

87. Griselda Pollock speaks of *écriture matrixiale* in "After the Reapers," *Generations and Geographies: Critical Practices and Critical Theories in Feminism and the Visual Arts*, ed. Griselda Pollock (London: Routledge, forthcoming), and in the exhibition catalogue *Bracha Lichtenberg Ettinger: Halala—Autistwork* (Jerusalem: The Israel Museum; Aix-en-Provence: Arfiac, 1995).

PARTS OF/FOR

Denkmal II: Eitelkeit (Monument
II: Vanity), from the series
Aus einem ethnographischen
Museum (From an Ethnographic
Museum), 1926.
Photomontage. 25.8 x 16.7 cm.
Collection of Rössner-Höch,
Backnang, Germany.
© 1996 Artists Rights Society
(ARS), New York/VG Bild-Kunst,
Bonn.

Denkmal I: Aus einem ethno-
graphischen Museum (Monument I:
From an Ethnographic Museum),
1924.
Photomontage. 19.6 x 15.5 cm.
Berlinische Galerie, Berlin.
Photo: Herrmann Kiessling.
© 1996 Artists Rights Society
(ARS), New York/VG Bild-Kunst,
Bonn.

The Mess of History or the Unclean Hannah Höch

Maud Lavin

> The abject shatters the wall of repression and its judgments. It takes the ego back to its source on the abominable limits from which, in order to be, the ego has broken away. . . . Refuse and corpses *show* me what I permanently thrust aside in order to live. These body fluids, this defilement, this shit are what life withstands, hardly and with difficulty, on the part of death. There, I am at the border of my condition as a living being. My body extricates itself, as being alive from that border.
> —Julia Kristeva, *Powers of Horror: An Essay on Abjection*

Cleaning Up History

Just four days after the Wall came down in 1989, the Hannah Höch symposium commemorating the hundredth anniversary of the artist's birth convened at Berlin's Akademie der Künste. What could have been a quaint, well-mannered delivering of papers was instead a massive, joyous, cantankerous women's event. The auditorium was filled with (mainly) women from East and West Berlin. Most of the papers were boring. The audience wasn't. The audience was vociferous and well-miked. West Berlin art historian Ines Lindner stood up after one particularly repressed paper and said, and I'm paraphrasing here, "You know, what is interesting here is the psychology of the speakers. You have these fragmented, complex photomontages, and most of you are spending all your time trying to nail each fragment to one meaning. This tells us nothing about the photomontages and everything about the need of the speakers for order." I felt relieved that she wasn't criticizing me—exonerated since I'd been talking about ambiguity in montage and the flowering of allegory. Beyond escaping my own fear of criticism, though, I was also buoyed by Linder's comment because I thought it explained part of the pleasure I'd gotten from the montages—a pleasure in their messiness.

Now, by the mid-nineties, Hannah Höch, whose status in Germany for some time has been roughly akin to Georgia O'Keeffe's here—historical, modern, admired—finally has been discovered in the U.S. My book *Cut with the Kitchen Knife: The Weimar Photomontages of Hannah Höch* has had something to do with that and simultaneously has ridden on a wave of interest stirred by Höch as a hip, whimsical, bisexual, bobbed-hair, dadaist icon. The book, first published in 1993, made it out of the academic ghetto, was reviewed in mainstream publications—*The New York Times Book Review, Newsweek, Harper's Bazaar, Ms, The Guardian,* etc.—and has come out in paperback. I've given many, many lectures in the U.S. and some in Europe in conjunction with the book and benefited from discussion with audiences. Now the Walker Art Center and the Museum of Modern Art are preparing a show, and smaller exhibitions of Höch's work have been traveling around.

I'm enjoying all of this but I also get angry from time to time because I see that as the U.S. marketing of Höch continues, slowly something messy is being made clean. It's not only the pieces of the montages that are being identified and labeled—and why not? It's interesting to know which images from which newspapers and magazines were the raw material. But Höch's art and Höch herself are being forced into what I'll call a *straitjacket of dichotomy*, with Höch being constructed as the savior/artist and the mass media of her time as the duper of women. The female viewer, of course, is cast as the hapless dupe. It's all too familiar. It's a familiar simplification of art history. It's the reductive good vs. evil to which women's history is too often reduced, as if a specific cohort of women either moves forward toward progress or back toward oppression, as if women's (and men's) lives aren't usually an asynchronous mix of the two experiences. It's an ignorance about how aesthetic and emotional responses work.

In contrast, to research my book I spent a lot of time playing in the mud, making Höch's messy Weimar photomontages even messier in interpretation. The photomontages almost all include images of women, so I learned about what was happening in women's lives in twenties Germany and complicated that with questions about how women were depicted in the Weimar mass media. I researched institutional structures of mass media at the time and questioned my contemporary, personal motivations for my writing. I like Höch's work and the book reflects that bias, but I refrained from making her a heroine. I saw her as a very intelligent and talented woman swimming in the soup of what it meant to be feminine in Weimar culture. Implicated and self-implicating. In the thick of it.

Because the montages are so ambiguous, a lot of the scholars (almost all women) working on Höch in Germany had different interpretations. I exchanged work with many of them when I lived there and after. We often disagreed. I didn't mind. I even thought that together our interpretations made another kind of montage. But this new sanitized view of Höch floating in the U.S. makes me angry. It goes something like this: despite media claims to the contrary, as seen in glorified photographs of the New Woman, women's lives in Weimar Germany were terrible, and Höch as artist/seer/hero recognized this. Her montages (good) are a condemnation of these dishonest, slaphappy media images of the New Woman (evil). The fact that Höch fragmented women's bodies, goes the simplistic aesthetic argument, means that she wanted to show that women were unhappy. One example of such reasoning is Maria Makela's essay on Höch in a 1994 Des Moines Art Center catalogue *Three Berlin Artists*. In it, Makela declaims (pp. 16–17),

> The "new woman" of the Weimar Republic was really not all that different from her counterpart in the Empire, and if the mainstream press did not acknowledge this in their upbeat photographs of modern women, many liberal women's journals did. . . . Hannah Höch did, too, in an *Untitled* photocollage from 1921 that has as its central image the photograph of Claudia Pawlowa. . . .
> Apparently saddened by but nevertheless resigned to her lot in life, she passively endures the condescending gesture of the man to her right. . . . Severed from the original photograph, Pawlowa's body no longer seems energetic, lively, and in control. Rather, it appears inert, and frozen into a mannequin-like pose. In fact, Höch's Weimar photocollages depict "new women" again and again as immobilized mannequins, dolls, or puppets, in stark contrast to the mass media image of the dynamic modern woman. . . . *Zerbrochen (Broken)* of 1930 . . . consists of overlapped fragments of a doll's chubby yet curiously adult face. . . . The title refers not only to the formal fragmentation of the image, but also, no doubt, to the destruction of female subjectivity.

This argument makes me want to throw up.

History is not that simple, and visual fantasies do not always come with clean, unbroken outlines. Well documented by German women's historians like Claudia Koonz, Renate Bridenthal, and Atina Grossmann, women's lives in Weimar were a contradictory mix of emancipation and deprivation. Sure, it's hard to say how the liberated New Woman images of women with short hair and smoking jackets or Isadora Duncan–like dance costumes played into all this. But fantasy and excitement are an important part of life, especially at times of transition. Höch's montages, conveying a compelling mix of anger and pleasure, are full of this excitement. To me, it's the mix and the confusion of representations and emotions that are interesting, that determine the move from one complex, transitional state of experience to another. Höch didn't have all the answers, but she had some great, wide-open questions and in her photomontages gave viewers room for complex, ambiguous emotional responses. Strongly opinionated and wonderfully complex, Höch's montages both celebrate and critique (to different degrees in different works) myths of the New Woman.

In discussions after lectures (in Los Angeles, Detroit, New York, Nashville, etc.) I found that audiences enjoyed the ambiguities. There was always some anxiety too about contradictions and unresolved questions. This surfaced not in opposition to the idea that it was possible for Höch to both celebrate and critique images of the New Woman but in relation to biographical facts. There were inevitably questions about Höch's relationship to the Nazis (she fled to the exurbs of Berlin and stayed), her bisexuality (she never proselytized for bisexuality or lesbianism), her irony (why couldn't she be more like John Heartfield with his bold, propagandistic slogans?). In fact, Höch is no hero, or maybe more of an everyday one, piecing together (literally) comments on her femininity and her culture.

Keeping Höch Messy: Looking Again at the Ethnographic Museum Series

I'm glad Höch's work is being shown in *Inside the Visible,* which does not present a dichotomized view of the history of women artists, instead looking at recurrent issues like fragmentation of the body and psychoanalytic motivations. And it's fortunate that the exhibition includes Höch's Ethnographic Museum series, one of her messiest.[1] Here she juxtaposes parts of modern European women's bodies with ethnographic objects, often presenting the conglomerate figures for display on bases. This series deals in a sophisticated way with feminist issues like presenting the self as abject other and in an introductory, groping way with issues of race like the simultaneous elevating and demoting of primitive cultures in German museums, zoos, and art studios. Höch implicates herself in these montages: There's something deeply personal—although no one but her will ever know exactly what was personal about it—in the way she blurs boundaries between the self and the other, between proud display and shame, and between a sense of self and selflessness. In this spirit, Höch wrote, in a statement published in conjunction with a 1929 one-woman exhibition in The Hague: "I want to blur the firm boundaries that we as people tend self-assuredly to draw around all that we can achieve." The Ethnographic Museum series, which Höch also called *der Sammlung* or "the collection," consists of eighteen to twenty works made over a period of more than five years. These include *Masken* (c. 1924), *Entführung* (1925), *Trauer* (1925), *Denkmal I* (Nr. VIII) (c. 1925), *Mit Mütze* (c. 1925), *Die Süße* (before 1926), *Nummer IX (Zwei)* (c. 1926), *Hörner (Nr. X)* (c. 1926), *Denkmal II: Eitelkeit* (1926), *Der heilige Berg* (1927), *Negerplastik* (1929), *Fremde Schönheit* (c. 1929), *Untitled* (Museum für Kunst und Gewerbe, Hamburg, 1929), *Untitled* (Museum für Kunst und Gewerbe, Hamburg, 1930), *Mutter* (1930), *Indische Tänzerin* (1930), *Buddha* (c. 1930), and *Untitled* (Kunst-Sammlung der Bundesrepublik Deutschland, c. 1930), and possibly other related works. It is doubtful that all of the montages of the Ethnographic

Museum series were ever exhibited together, though Höch included twelve of them in her one-person photomontage exhibition in Brno, Czechoslovakia, in 1934.

In the series Höch was not particularly critical of contemporary ethnographic attitudes; instead she used images of tribal objects and the exhibition format in ethnographic museums almost exclusively to comment on contemporary European gender definitions. Höch never substantively or explicitly challenged contemporary racist or colonialist ideas, although her irony often functions as implicit criticism. Her montages too are an important early exploration of representing tribal cultures in a way that did not completely subsume their artifacts in Western identity: difference as well as sameness is represented. Höch's intentions are distinguishable from those of the German expressionists, who borrowed images from tribal cultures with the conceit that an analogy operated between primitive power and the primordial creativity embedded in the spirit of the artist. Höch ironically focused on Western representation of racial difference and its application to gender politics. She created allegories of modern femininity, montages that question the status and representation of Weimar women. Boundaries between self and other and between private identity and public display are established and blurred in a way that in places elicits irony and distance and elsewhere a more frightening closeness.

For example, the viewer senses an oscillation between distance and closeness in *Fremde Schönheit (Strange Beauty)*. Höch used this photomontage to question contemporary norms of feminine beauty. A photograph of a young, naked white woman in a traditional alluring pose—lying on her side with one elbow angled behind her head—is dramatically surmounted by a dark, grotesquely wrinkled, possibly shrunken head. To exaggerate this shocking juxtaposition, Höch added to the face a pair of skewed eyes, magnified by eyeglasses that distort the figure's gaze and in turn emphasize the viewer's own act of looking at the figure's eyes, face, and body. Through the alienation effect of montage, both the European body and the tribal shrunken head (or grotesque mask) appear strange. In many of Höch's Ethnographic Museum montages, the New Woman as an icon is fractured, brought into question, and made to appear as a construction. But the New Woman is not parodied; rather, contemporary femininity is aligned disturbingly with ugliness in such a way that differences and similarities are confused. If one interprets *Fremde Schönheit* as a statement about the contradictions and arbitrariness of canons of feminine beauty, one is reading the montage as an allegory; many montages in the Ethnographic Museum series lend themselves to such readings.

The use of tribal objects and references immediately invokes the embattled tradition of Western ethnographic interpretation. Poised between scientific "objectivity" and a sort of moralistic storytelling, ethnographic representations are, according to anthropologist James Clifford, often thinly masked allegories. "Allegory prompts us to say of any cultural description," Clifford writes, "not 'this represents or symbolizes that' but rather, 'this is a (morally charged) story about that.'" This comparative mode, Clifford points out, is fundamentally humanist, producing "controlled fictions of difference and similitude" in which the standard for locating either the self or the other is a universalizing humanism. Clifford also describes how many ethnographic writings establish distance through the use of irony: "We note . . . the ironic structure (which need not imply an ironic tone) of such allegories," he writes. "For they are presented through the detour of an ethnographic subjectivity whose attitude toward the other is one of participant-observer, or better perhaps, belief-skepticism."[2]

If white Europeans looked at this image as a representation of the self, this blurring, this self-identification with the dark, grotesque face could have brought them to the brink of the abject, the terror at the edges of the ego, the dark side of self. In this montage, the grotesque is defined on the most basic level with racist overtones since the dark part of the body is classified as ugly. Yet in other ways Höch was ahead of her times in the respectful analysis of the commodified display of tribal objects in museums. Summarizing Höch's racial attitudes as evident in her work, it seems that while critiquing some of the racist assimilation of tribal culture in Weimar Germany, she also at times practiced a subtle degree of racist caricature (see her *Bauerliches Brautpaar [Peasant Wedding Couple* of 1931], for example). She was both of her times and ahead of them. A purified view of Höch, in contrast, would try to deny that the artist in any way participated in the hierarchical racial views of her time. The potential differences between the twenties and the nineties would be erased.

In *Denkmal I (Monument I),* perhaps the most abject work in the entire series, the figure's sculptural trunk (with flattened, stylized breasts) has an amphibious quality. The "monument" has three montage legs. One is identifiable as human, but its "foot" looks like an animal hoof; another is attached from behind and appears to be a trousered leg, perhaps amputated at the knee (extra trouser material is folded upward at the end); the third is a woman's leg wearing a dancing shoe. The "woman" appears to shrug one shoulder, lurch forward, and look askance. Both tense and flaccid, she digs her chin into her chest and clenches her fist. The face is an abstract sculptural mask, with long, slit eyelids through which the eyes are just barely visible, giving the face a mysterious expression. The figure stands on a base or platform. The body's slinking, ungainly quality appears to be a bitter comment on the heroic pose of the (usually male) figure commemorated in the conventional monument. The standard heroic pose is supplanted here by a self-denigrating one with the head buried in the chest, a shoulder uncomfortably raised, the body misshapen. The effect is of turmoil, black humor, and an inwardly inflected anger. If it were not for the barely visible eyes and the tangled posture, this would be merely a repellent figure without identification for the viewer. But these attributes, together with the New Woman's leg, argue for a reading of this image that could involve a threatening degree of closeness for the female viewer.

"The Medicine Man,"
from *Uhu* 56 (June 1930).
Kunstbibliothek, Staatliche Museen Preußischer
Kulturbesitz, Berlin.
Photo: Knud Petersen.

In *Denkmal II: Eitelkeit (Monument II: Vanity),* a figure poses on a tall base in a classical posture of self-display, turned three-quarters in contrapposto, against a background of pink and blue colored papers. From the waist down, the figure is a seminude female, but its chest and dwarfed arms are male. This combination is typical of a large body of Höch's works that deal with androgyny. In these montages, the central figure cannot be identified as either male or female; it is always two genders. In preserving ambiguity, Höch encourages oscillation and suggests fluctuating gender roles. In *Denkmal II,* the head, an African mask, bears a wide, fanned headdress. This dominant photographic image appeared in the June 1930 issue of

Uhu, where its caption read: "The medicine man: Masked dancer and sorcerer of the African Masai tribe." The magazine text draws a parallel between the Western magician and the African medicine man. The photograph is a particularly apt illustration: instead of making the African medicine man exotic, it shows him sitting in an everyday pose of rest and contemplation, dressed to practice his trade, with villagers and huts in the distance. Höch made the image exotic by appropriating the medicine man's symbolic headgear and recontextualizing it within the frame of the sculptural monument or museum display. She has also given the figure human legs, which make it appear to display him/herself. Hence the title *Vanity.* If Höch retained any sense of the magical and religious from the original *Uhu* photograph, it is here mixed with parodic commentary on the vanity of monuments and self-display.

In this montage Höch used the base on which the figure stands as a frame within a frame. This important device, deployed often throughout the Ethnographic Museum series, comments ironically on the categorization and display of people as objects. The base, which traditionally presents the wholeness and perfection of an object on display, is used here as a pedestal for Höch's fragmentary, grotesque, and sometimes humorous montages of multicultural fragments. Mocking the ideal of plenitude, with its illusion of homogenization (difference subsumed by wholeness), the discordance of Höch's montages raises fundamentally political issues regarding the representation of race and gender.

The tension that Höch established between self-display (one that follows the cultural dictate that women redefine their bodies as commodities and men embody power) and selflessness (according to European myths about African religion as represented in their art objects) was discussed at the time in terms of non-Western ideas of transcendence and anonymity. In particular, these ideas were identified with the work of cultural critic Carl Einstein, author of the first German book devoted to African sculpture, *Negerplastik* (1915), and a member of the same dada and protodada circles as Höch and Raoul Hausmann. Einstein coedited the dada journals *Der blutige Ernst* (*Bloody Seriousness*) and *Der Pleite* (*Bankruptcy*) with George Grosz and John Heartfield in 1919. Both Hausmann and Höch probably knew Einstein personally. Given Höch's interest in ethnography, she probably read *Negerplastik* and Einstein's later *Afrikanische Plastik* (1921).

One idea in Einstein's work that may have engaged Höch was the tension established between individualism and anti-individualism. In *Negerplastik,* Einstein wrote of African masks:

> With this transformation [the mask-wearer] becomes a balance to negating adoration. He prays to the god, performs an ecstatic tribal dance, and the mask transforms him into both the god and the tribe. This transformation gives him the most powerful idea of the objective; he incarnates the objective itself and becomes that in which all particularities are destroyed. Therefore the mask only makes sense when it is inhuman and impersonal; that is, constructive and free from the experience of the individual. It is possible that he reveres the mask as a deity when he is not wearing it.[3]

Once again, we return to a slippage between self and other, here self and object. In bringing this confusion home to displays and identities of European women, Höch's representation of fluidity between a focus on self and an identification with the abject other has the potential to map deeply personal relationships to the self and its boundaries as manifested within culture. The messiness and fluctuations possible within that map are significant for the viewer.

To conclude, I want to return to Höch's *Fremde Schönheit.* In this montage, the figure's eyes, which would usually be the site of identification for the female viewer, are located in the face of an abject other. They are also magnified, suggesting identification with the disfigured face

Fremde Schönheit
(Strange Beauty),
1929.
Photomontage.
32 x 23 cm.
Private collec-
tion, Paris.
Courtesy Timothy
Baum.

as well as the conventionally beautiful body. The self is re-presented as the other—revisited and rendered abject. Thus, as in other Ethnographic Museum montages, there is a shifting between identification and differentiation with tribal peoples (and the myths attached to their objects on display). By emphasizing this fluctuation, Höch deviated from the unambiguous, folkloric representation of African and other tribal peoples in the illustrated weeklies and laid the foundation for a critique of racism, even if she did not pursue it further. The series's primary referent is not race, however, but how race is socially coded in ethnographic museums. What concerned Höch in these works is the display of culture marked as different—for the other as well as the self in Höch's photomontages is the modern European woman.

There is no clean-cut between the experience of women's lives in Weimar and the fantasies and images depicting women's lives in Weimar, no well-marked boundary to represent the divide. The status of women in Weimar culture was undergoing rapid change in terms of social mores yet paralyzed in terms of money and power. The challenge was to expand the areas where changes were occurring. Höch's montages then are all the more important in that they open interpretative avenues suggesting deep, protean transitions rather than offer themselves to a coagulated reading of dichotomized meanings. For Höch, montage led away from the orderly and toward an exploration of the confusions between self and other, self and selflessness, ego and the abject, Western legs and African headdresses, lived femininity and images of the New Woman. She leaves us today, as we undergo yet another contradictory period of transition in women's lives, blurred boundaries to enjoy and further to confuse if we want. Anything but wipe clean. Or perhaps for me, that image of the montages wiped clean is the abject underside of interpretation—the end of discourse.

NOTES:
1. For a lengthier and different discussion of the Ethnographic Museum series, see chapter 5 of my *Cut with the Kitchen Knife* (New Haven: Yale University Press, 1993); for a full analysis of androgyny in Höch's montages, see chapter 6.
2. James Clifford, "On Ethnographic Writing," in *Writing Culture*, ed. James Clifford and George E. Marcus (Berkeley: University of California Press, 1986), 100–1, 111.
3. Carl Einstein, *Gesammelte Werke* (Wiesbaden: Limes Verlag, 1962), 102.

Self-Portrait, c. 1928.
Gelatin silver print. 10 x 7.5 cm.
Courtesy Galerie Berggruen & Cie, Paris.

Radical Transformations: Claude Cahun and the Masquerade of Womanliness

Laurie J. Monahan

"Miroir," "fixer," voilà des mots qui n'ont rien à faire ici.
—Claude Cahun, *Aveux non avenus*

In *Gender Trouble*, Judith Butler asks,

> To what extent do *regulatory practices* of gender formation and division constitute identity,
> the internal coherence of the subject, indeed, the self-identical status of the person? To
> what extent is "identity" a normative ideal rather than a descriptive feature of experience?
> And how do the regulatory practices that govern gender also govern culturally intelligible
> notions of identity? In other words, the "coherence" and "continuity" of "the person" are
> not logical or analytic features of personhood, but, rather, socially instituted and main-
> tained norms of intelligibility by which persons are defined.[1]

Such questions and problems frame the work of writer/artist/photographer Claude Cahun
(1893–1954), an important participant in the Parisian cultural scene between the two world
wars. Active in prominent literary and artistic circles, Cahun produced a wide range of surre-
alist-inspired objects, collages, photographs, and writings that explore identity and gender
through her own image and autobiography. Ironically, Cahun's success in engaging the cultural
contingencies that Butler describes can be measured by the fact that Cahun fell into complete obscurity at the onset of World War II—indeed, her identity became so uncertain that
for a time it was unclear whether she was male or female. Her works were ascribed to an
anonymous artist, and the circumstances of her life were essentially unknown.[2] A further irony
is that the first extensive scholarly work on Cahun is a biography, *Claude Cahun: L'écart et la
métamorphose,* by François Leperlier:[3] for if Cahun's entire oeuvre was devoted to investigating
the very notion of a stable subject position through her own autobiographical inquiry,
Leperlier—drawing on an interesting array of unpublished letters, manuscripts, and documents—seeks to *fix* Cahun's identity by explaining her through the very ambiguities that she
seized as her own critical project. While Leperlier produced a very useful book that provides
the opportunity to reassess and reexamine Cahun's work and affords some interesting reflections on Cahun herself, a psychoanalytic biography seems antithetical to Cahun's problemati-
zation of her own identity.[4]

Born Lucy Schwob, daughter of the publisher Maurice Schwob and niece of the prominent writer Marcel Schwob, Cahun eliminated any affiliation with her famous family by

changing her name to the sexually ambiguous "Claude Cahun" in 1918. Under this name she first published in the prestigious *Mercure de France,* reporting on the trial of Oscar Wilde. Moving from Nantes to Paris with her stepsister and lifelong lover, Suzanne Malherbe, Cahun befriended writer-publishers Adrienne Monnier and Sylvia Beach. She wrote for a variety of journals, including Henri Lefebvre and Pierre Morhange's *Philosophies,* Henri Michaux and Franz Hellens's *Disque vert,* and the avant-garde homosexual review *L'Amitié.* In 1930 her book *Aveux non avenus* was published, featuring poems, prose, and photomontages (the latter being collaborative efforts with Malherbe, publishing under the pseudonym "Moore"). Alarmed by the burgeoning fascist movements throughout Europe, Cahun joined the Association des Ecrivains et Artistes Révolutionnaires (AEAR) at the end of 1932 but within a year became disenchanted with its close affiliation with the Communist Party and attendant hostility to anything but a socialist-realist aesthetic. Her critique of AEAR's politics and, more pointedly, of those of Louis Aragon was published as *Les paris sont ouverts,* a brochure that André Breton later described as providing "une image vraiment évocatrice de cette époque."[5] In 1934 Cahun joined Contre-attaque, the short-lived antifascist political coalition formed by Georges Bataille and André Breton. Concurrently, she produced photographs and objects to illustrate Lise Deharme's *Coeur de Pic* and participated in the surrealist "object" exhibitions in Paris and London. By 1938—probably because of the threat of war—Cahun had left Paris permanently, moving to her family's summer retreat on the Isle of Jersey, where she was active in the Resistance during the Nazi occupation and was finally arrested and condemned to death (a sentence from which she was spared with the liberation of the island in 1945). In failing health exacerbated by her time in prison, she remained on the island until her death in 1954.

Humanité Figure (Poupée),
1936.
Silver print.
18.5 x 15.3 cm.
The Sackner Archive of
Concrete and Visual
Poetry, Miami Beach,
Florida.
Courtesy Zabriskie
Gallery, New York.

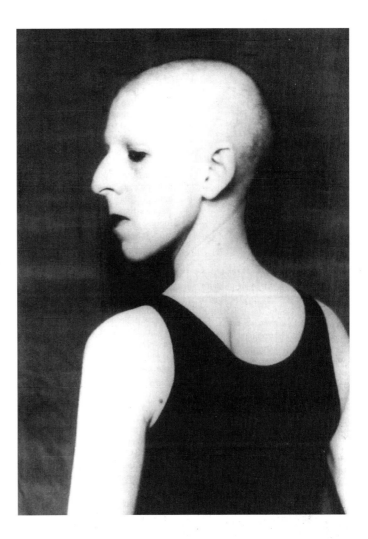

Self-Portrait,
from *Bifur*, no. 5
(April 1930).
Editions du
Carrefour, Paris.

These details fill in the necessary "facts" lacking in previous accounts of Cahun's life but tell us precious little of the enigmatic personae that appear in her self-portraits and writings, or of her personal notoriety. As early as 1919 she consciously spurned conventional femininity by shaving her head, then took to dyeing pink or green the crew cut that she sometimes allowed to sprout. She stained her skin and wore outlandish batiked, vaguely orientalized clothing. Surrealist Marcel Jean noted in his memoirs that Cahun's appearance—"her face like that of a little bird of prey"—at the Café Cyrano with her companion Malherbe by her side was enough to drive Breton into temporary exile, giving up his favorite café and regular meeting place: "Ce n'est pas contre vous, cher ami, me dirent-ils [Breton and Eluard], que nous avons changé d'adresse, provisoirement. Cahun-Malherbe n'insistèrent pas, on ne les revit plus place Blanche [where the Cyrano was located]."[6]

Breton's homophobia would probably sufficiently account for his discomfort in Cahun's presence,[7] but I suggest that the uneasy tension that Cahun inspired was as much cultural as personal and was linked to a more general anxiety about identity itself. In this respect, her work engages current feminist concerns, as well as providing the opportunity to examine the ways in which her own avant-garde aspirations converged and intersected with contemporary debates about sexuality and identity.

The strength and difficulty of Cahun's work can still be sensed in her self-portraits from this period: take, for example, a photograph that appeared in a 1930 issue of Ribemont-Dessaigne's *Bifur*. Cahun depicts herself in stark profile, her expression cold, almost menacing; harsh lighting underscores her severe, unadorned appearance, stripped of any mediating "props"—including hair—that might soften her image. This portrait aggressively militates against the normative ideals of femininity and, more broadly, exposes the viewer's expectations of intelligible identity as grounded, specifically, in gender. "So who *is* this, anyway?" we ask; Cahun made it her business to keep the question in play by constantly exposing her "self" as nothing but a series of constructions. In perhaps her most ambitious undertaking, *Aveux non avenus*—a book of prose, poems, dreams, and autobiography, accompanied by several photomontages that invariably include self-portraits—she undercut the seemingly revelatory nature of its self-descriptive material (its title translates variously as *Disavowed Confessions* or *"Voided" Confessions*).[8] What begins as an autobiographical "diary" soon departs from traditional autobiographical form, losing its coherence as a narrative of specific events and feelings and becoming a complex weave of aphorisms, dream sequences, and imaginary dialogues and encounters. Cahun takes her own subjectivity as the means of revealing the impossibility of fixing the self; her text and images speak of its dissolution, fragmentation, and transformations, as biography itself becomes suspect, another mask among many. Cahun recounts a dream:

> Il m'en souvient, c'était le Carnaval. J'avais passé mes heures solitaires à déguiser mon âme. Les masques en étaient si parfaits que lorsqu'il leur arrivait de se croiser sur la grand'place de ma conscience ils ne se reconnaissaient pas. Tenté par leur laideur comique, j'essayais les plus mauvais instincts; j'adoptais, j'élevais en moi de jeunes monstres. Mais les fards que j'avais employés semblaient indélébiles. Je frottai tant pour nettoyer que j'enlevai la peau. Et mon âme comme un visage écorché, à vif, n'avait plus forme humaine.[9]

Without a mask, without identity—not even human form. Or, alternatively, the self as nothing but masks, a point reiterated in a photomontage from *Aveux non avenus*, where a series of faces—all Cahun's, in various guises—spring from a single neck, framed by the lines "Sous ce masque un autre masque. Je n'en finirai pas de soulever tous ces visages." The succession of painted eyes and lips underscores the artifice and versatility of a single face, becoming a series of masks that in and of themselves obscure their own "identities": male here, female there, and elsewhere impossible to tell. In any case, revealing is never to be confused with knowing: Cahun writes in the section entitled "Psychological Portraits," "Non. Je ne tracerai que des ébauches. Quand on a fini de démonter la mècanique, le mystère reste entier."[10]

Cahun's constantly shifting and transforming self sought to make gender itself ambiguous, although this ability to mask and masquerade was something that Joan Rivière, an analyst writing in 1929, attributed specifically to the character of woman. Rivière argued that "womanliness could be assumed and worn as a mask, both to hide the possession of masculinity and to avert the reprisals expected if she was found to possess it—much as a thief will turn out his pockets and ask to be searched to prove that he has not stolen the goods. The reader may now ask how I define womanliness or where I draw the line between genuine womanliness and the 'masquerade.' My suggestion is not, however, that there is any such difference; whether radical or superficial, they are the same thing."[11] Rivière was specifically addressing the case of an "intellectual woman" who, to assuage the anxieties of being highly

Self-Portrait,
c. 1929.
Gelatin silver print.
13.7 x 6.5 cm.
Private collection,
New York. Courtesy
Zabriskie Gallery,
New York.

successful in a masculine world, engaged in "compulsive ogling and coquetting" to assure that she would not be punished for her intellectual proficiency. Of interest for our purposes is Rivière's denial that any "essential" identity exists for woman: the masquerade, the construction "woman," could not be distinguished from the woman herself. The increasing difficulty in sorting out gender and behavior was symptomatic of the problem, as Rivière noted: "Not long ago intellectual pursuits for women were associated almost exclusively with an overtly masculine type of woman, who in pronounced cases made no secret of her wish or claim to be a man. This has now changed. Of all the women engaged in professional work today, it would be hard to say whether the greater number are more feminine than masculine in their mode of life and character. . . . It is really a puzzle to know how to classify this type psychologically."[12] Rivière was relatively sympathetic to this type—indeed, the piece perhaps unwittingly describes her own situation in the male-dominated psychoanalytic community—but critics roundly decried such ambiguities in the "natural" order of things. If there was no stable ground on which to secure the essence of woman, the mask itself became a serious threat, making the "deviant" woman a category hardly separable from women in general. Recent and important work by Carolyn Dean[13] has brought this historical debate to light; she quotes Léon Bizard writing on prostitutes' lives in 1934:

It has become very difficult to differentiate at first sight an honest woman or a pure young girl from a whore. . . . All women, from the adolescent to the grandmother are molded according to the same model: they wear lipstick and powder their faces, have pearly eyelids, long black lashes, painted nails, platinum or red hair . . . they all smoke, drink cocktails, loiter at dancing halls, drive cars. . . . Given the promiscuity of these bodies that are not always comparable to Venus, how can we place them? Which is the marquise, the wife of the wealthy industrialist? or simply the woman of easy virtue? What an embarrassing question and what a difficult problem to solve![14]

A difficult problem, indeed: such developments, fretted Bizard and other guardians of the moral order, not only jeopardized social morals but threatened class order. Masked with lipstick and rouge, all women were equally suspect and—even more alarmingly—were suspiciously equal: smoking and loitering, drinking and driving, traditionally masculine prerogatives, were fast becoming a part of woman's masquerade. This posed problems extending beyond prostitution, as Dean notes:

After the [first world] war prostitution became a metaphor for the uncertain status of female gender identity, for the *dissolution* of distinctive female nature. The deviant woman no longer affirmed sexual difference, she metaphorized sexual *sameness*. . . . When she acted as an autonomous individual, she usurped male prerogatives and, in so doing, acted out the insatiable longing and lack of self-control which purportedly characterized female nature. When she acted as a man she did not transgress or invert her so-called nature but expressed it. In other words, the deviant or criminal woman no longer transgressed or inverted gender roles but marked their fluidity, marked the reification of gender itself.[15]

Gender slipped precisely where it was supposed to be distinguished, fixed: woman as Other, but by her very nature impossible to identify. When she appeared as a man, she was more than ever a woman, but this in itself signified nothing but appearances, a series of representations. Even when the masquerade was exposed, the mystery remained intact.

Cahun's work revels in the ambiguities afforded by the fluidity of "womanliness"; it was precisely through this indistinct subject position that the coherence of the self was most vulnerable, and therein lay the revolutionary potential of subjectivity itself. Cahun's constructed, shifting identities were but a prelude to the radical dissolution of individual subjectivity itself:

Je ferme les yeux pour délimiter l'orgie. Il y a trop de tout. Je me tais. Je retiens mon haleine. Je me couche en rond, j'abandonne mes bords, je me replie vers un centre imaginaire. . . . Ce n'est pas sans arrière pensée. . . . Je me fais raser les cheveux, arracher les dents, les seins—tout ce qui gêne ou impatiente mon regard—l'estomac, les ovaires, le cerveau conscient et enkysté. Quand je n'aurai plus qu'une carte en main, qu'un battement de coeur à noter, mais à la perfection, bien sûr je gagnerai la partie.[16]

A desire to dissolve the body itself, to become nothing but a heartbeat: to reach Cahun's imaginary center, recognizable features are transformed, effaced, producing a subjectivity that turns on its own ambiguities and through these attempts to transcend its own limits. In this respect, the photomontage from *Aveux non avenus* presents a series in the evolution of the individual's identity, her own critical transformation through the "stages of life": fetal

Self-Portrait,
c. 1925.
Vintage gelatin
silver print.
11.2 x 8.2 cm.
Leslie Tonkonow,
New York.

development (in which the self develops a "double" in the final stage, shown on the left) gives way to a childhood in which mother, father, and infant are inseparable, torsos linked by bands of flesh. This sequence is framed by a chevron that points to the succession of Cahun's "adult" faces emerging from a single body, a relation reversed by the prone statue that abuts them: its genitalia broken, head obscured, this body produces sensory fragments derived from Cahun's self-portraits rather than a "complete" face. A triangle below this figure echoes the chevron at the top, this time depicting Cahun—first with eyes masked, then wearing false eyes—looking "in" then "out." Finally, in an overlapping of heads the lines designating each become hopelessly blurred, impossible to discern. Cahun's subjective inquiry hopes to do away with its *self:* "C'est assez dire que j'écris, que je souhaite écrire avant tout *contre moi.*"[17]

In what might seem paradoxical, the individual became the site on which a kind of "collectivity" was founded—but only through a radical reconceptualization, a being deconstructed through self-scrutiny. Cahun was not alone in this desire to "dematerialize" the limits of the self: Michel Leiris, who also took autobiography as the primary material for his writings, noted in his journal:

Le chemin de la découverte[:] s'habituer à une certaine multiplication de la conscience, et s'opposer son coeur comme d'ordinaire on s'oppose un arbre ou un maison. J'ai l'impression . . . d'une espèce de révolution qui se produit en moi,—de mouvement tournant dans lequel ma pensée semble décrire un demi-cercle et ainsi se tenir face à face avec elle-même. . . . Un tel état correspond moins à la dispersion du moi dans le monde extérieur qu'à la concentration du monde extérieur dans le moi. Toutefois, plus que retour de la périphérie au centre, il y a identité—sans mouvement dans aucun sens—entre la périphérie et le centre.[18]

Through a detached, methodical investigation of himself, Leiris conceptualized a complex geometry between individual and external world, in which identity emerges from the exchange between these poles. For Cahun and other contemporary leftist intellectuals who sought alternatives to the straightforward political agitation advocated by the Communist Party, a potential space of disruption was the subjective transcending its own bounds. In a society where the coherent subject was central to social stability—its structure, moral codes, rules—a radical reconceptualization of the self promised fundamental change.

The ways in which the contemporary "external" world impinged upon Cahun's personal experience were no doubt considerable: as a woman, a lesbian, a Jew, her own identity was particularly circumscribed by existing social labels and stereotypes. Yet while these categories imposed constraints, the fact that they were themselves somewhat unstable and ambiguous provided the possibility of imagining an identity radically reconfigured. This was grounded in her experience as a woman and a lesbian: if the "experts" were baffled by their attempts to define "woman," the homosexual woman posed an even more vexing problem. Havelock Ellis—whose work Cahun translated into French in 1929[19]—theorized that the lesbian was actually a "third sex," uniting masculine and feminine traits but existing as neither one nor the other.[20] While Ellis and others treated this as a pathology, it offered Cahun a way to imagine, through her own experience, the self outside the conventional constraints of gender. Being a lesbian—separate from the "norms" of heterosexuality—enabled her to produce work that so insistently turns on ambiguities of gender. In this sense, although she never directly addresses her own sexuality, her own experience was very much an impetus for her production. That lesbians were a prominent presence in Paris—some of the most fashionable literary circles of the interwar period were constituted by "notorious" lesbians[21]—provided both a community and an avenue for public expression; yet this heightened visibility also invited what Michel Foucault has called "the policing of sex."[22] If lesbians were able to come out of the closet at last, this offered an opportunity further to categorize, study, and control them. The seemingly permissive culture was quick to reassert control with employment rising, the birthrate dropping, and war on the horizon; by the early 1930s, the period of cultural flexibility seemed to be coming to a close, and Cahun herself produced far fewer of her enigmatic self-portraits, turning to the production of objects instead.

To move from the confines of the individual to a space that can be described only through negation—a world without barriers, where identity itself becomes impossible to distinguish—could this exist in any space other than the imaginary? For Cahun, the point was not to imagine what this might "look like" as a reality but simply to indicate its possibilities, as she would make clear in her discussion of writing as a revolutionary practice: "Il s'agit de mettre en marche et de laisser en panne. Ça oblige le lecteur à faire tout seul un pas de plus qu'il ne voudrait. On a soigneusement bloqué toutes les sorties, mais la porte d'entrée, on lui laisse le soin de l'ouvrir."[23] She could access this space through the instabilities embodied in her own identity, particularly as configured around the problematic categories of gender and sexuality. In our age, in which identification with a particular group or cause often replaces revolutionary politics and radical thinking, Cahun's example is still instructive. She encourages us to imagine a different world where identity does not fix the individual but radically transforms the culture that would define her: "Car devant son miroir Aurige est touchée de la grâce. Elle consent à se reconnaître. Et l'illusion qu'elle crée pour elle-même s'étend à quelques autres."[24]

NOTES:

This essay was originally published in German in *Texte zur Kunst,* vol. 3, no. 11 (September 1994): 101-108, under the title "Claude Cahuns Radikale Transformationen."

1. Judith Butler, *Gender Trouble: Feminism and the Subversion of Identity* (London: Routledge, 1990), 17.
2. For example, the catalogues to two relatively recent exhibitions that "rediscovered" Cahun's work speculate that she died in a concentration camp during the war and note that relatively little is known about her life: see Rosalind Krauss, Jane Livingston, and Dawn Ades, *L'Amour Fou: Photography and Surrealism* (New York: Abbeville Press, 1985), 205 (from an exhibition at the Corcoran Gallery of Art, Washington, D.C.), and Sidra Stich, *Anxious Visions: Surrealist Art* (Berkeley: University Art Museum, University of California at Berkeley, 1990), 237. Significantly, Cahun was not featured in the relatively comprehensive exhibition "La femme et le surréalisme" (Musée des Beaux-Arts, Lausanne, 1987–88) nor in Whitney Chadwick's *Women Artists and the Surrealist Movement* (Boston: Little, Brown, 1985). An object that Cahun showed in the 1936 surrealist exhibition of objects (Gallerie Charles Ratton) was listed as "Anonymous" in the 1978 exhibition "Dada and Surrealism Reviewed" (Tate Gallery, London).
3. François Leperlier, *Claude Cahun: L'écart et la métamorphose* (Paris: Jean-Michel Place, 1992).
4. Although Leperlier's book is the most exhaustive study on Cahun to date, two important articles examine her work from a feminist perspective: see Honor Lasalle and Abigail Solomon-Godeau, "Surrealist Confession: Claude Cahun's Photomontages," *Afterimage* 19 (March 1992): 10–13; and Therese Lichtenstein, "A Mutable Mirror: Claude Cahun," *Artforum*, no. 8 (April 1992): 64–67.
5. André Breton with André Parinaud, *Entretiens* (Paris: Gallimard, 1969), 171. Originally published in *Le Point du Jour*, 1952.
6. Marcel Jean, *Au galop dans le vent* (Paris: Jean-Pierre de Monza, 1991), 27.
7. For his vehement refusal to allow the discussion of homosexuality among the surrealists, see Breton's comments in "Recherches sur la sexualité," January 1928–August 1932; reprinted in *Archives du surréalisme*, vol. 4, ed. and annotated by José Pierre (Paris: NRF/Gallimard, 1990), 67–68.
8. Lasalle and Solomon-Godeau, "Surrealist Confession," 10; Lichtenstein, "A Mutable Mirror," 6.
9. Claude Cahun, *Aveux non avenus* (Paris: Editions du Carrefour, 1930), 15–16.
10. Cahun, "Portraits psychologiques," in *Aveux non avenus*, 59.
11. Joan Rivière, "Womanliness as Masquerade," *The International Journal of Psychoanalysis* 10 (1929); reprinted in *Formations of Fantasy*, ed. Victor Burgin, James Donald, and Cora Kaplan (London: Routledge, 1989), 38.
12. Ibid., 35–36.
13. Carolyn Dean, *The Self and Its Pleasures: Bataille, Lacan, and the History of the Decentered Subject* (Ithaca: Cornell University Press, 1992); see especially chapter 2, "Gender Complexes." Although this is only one aspect of a larger argument and analysis of the "self" during the interwar period, Dean's is by far the most thorough and well-documented work to date on the phenomenon and impact of the "new woman" of the 1920s and 1930s.
14. Léon Bizard, *La vie des filles* (Paris: Grasset, 1934), 45, as quoted (in translation) in Dean, *The Self and Its Pleasures*, 70.
15. Dean, *The Self and Its Pleasures*, 71.
16. Cahun, *Aveux non avenus*, 35.
17. Cahun, as quoted in Leperlier, *Claude Cahun*, 154.
18. Michel Leiris, entry from May 1929, *Journal 1922–1989* (Paris: Gallimard/NRF, 1992), 137.
19. Havelock Ellis, *La femme dans la société, I. L'hygiène sociale*, Etudes de psychologie sociale, trans. Lucie [sic] Schwob (Paris: Mercure de France, 1929).
20. For a brief overview of the debate around lesbian sexuality see Esther Newton, "The Mythic Mannish Lesbian: Radclyffe Hall and the New Woman," *Signs: Journal of Women in Culture and Society* 9, no. 4 (Summer 1984): 565–68. See also Lilian Faderman, *Surpassing the Love of Men* (New York: William Morrow & Co., 1981).
21. Natalie Barney was perhaps the most prominent of these; her weekly salons, frequented by the Parisian (and expatriate) literati, were the subject of much attention; Djuna Barnes, writing under the ironic pen name "Lady of Fashion," produced a satire of this circle, *The Ladies Almanack*, in 1928. For accounts of the lives of lesbian women in Paris in this period, see Shari Benstock, *Women of the Left Bank* (Austin: University of Texas Press, 1986), passim.
22. Foucault writes that this policing is "not the rigor of a taboo, but the necessity of regulating sex through useful and public discourses. Michel Foucault, *The History of Sexuality*, vol. 1 (New York: Random House/Vintage Books, 1980), 25. For a historical account of how this affected lesbians specifically in the late 1920s and early 1930s, see Lillian Faderman, "Love between Women in 1928: Why Progressivism Is Not Always Progress," *Journal of Homosexuality* 12, nos. 3–4 (May 1986): 23–42.
23. Claude Cahun, *Les paris sont ouverts* (Paris: José Corti, 1934), 14.
24. Cahun, *Aveux non avenus*, 58.

Totems outside of country house, Easton, Connecticut, c. 1947–49.
Courtesy Robert Miller Gallery, New York. Photo: Allan Finkelman.

Louise Bourgeois: Deconstructing the Phallus within the Exile of the Self

Rosi Huhn

> I have no ego. I am my work. I am not looking for an identity. I have too much identity.
> —Louise Bourgeois[1]

In 1947 Louise Bourgeois produced a series of nine prints, consisting of engravings and texts, entitled *He Disappeared into Complete Silence*.[2] Through nine abstract and enigmatic episodes she created scenarios and actors of a theater of the absurd lacking continuous action and coherent narrative. The engravings do not illustrate the texts, nor do the texts provide commentaries on the images. Rather, narrative devices are thwarted. To provoke a game of multiple interpretations, the conventional meanings of the motifs employed (towers, houses, easels, lighthouses, ladders) and their symbolic values are thrown into question. As if in a reality made of dreams and paradoxes, everything is subsumed in a process of destabilization and disintegration. Nevertheless, these texts and images reveal a series of missed encounters and situations that are tragicomic, if not futile: stood up by the man she loves, a girl copes with emptiness while waiting next to the "eighth street station of the sixth avenue subway" (text of plate 1). In the absence of the gaze of the other, "her good clothes and a new hat" worn for the occasion will go unnoticed. In offering us an image, the artist proposes to fill this gap. But what she shows—an abstract, anonymous sketch of a towering house—merely bolsters the notion of vacuousness and oddity.

Houses and imaginary anthropomorphic towers, inspired for the most part by New York's skyscrapers, are the main players of this actorless theater, whose sets and characters are identical. The different episodes, which do not lend themselves to easy reading, focus on solitude and emptiness, exclusion and confinement. They also evoke fragility and alienation, rage and destruction, mourning and mockery.

In the early plates, the house figures, which the artist identifies as *moi* and *toi*,[3] appear proud, closed, and impenetrable. Bourgeois characterizes them as "creatures of dignity."[4] Then there appears what lies behind the facades: a skeleton, an interior, virtual void and transparency. The successive exploitation of these structures stripped bare brings out feelings of solitariness and claustrophobia, violence and distress: in a word, a whole gamut of emotions, moods, and states of mind, confined in the enigma of their representation.

Bourgeois uses the basic elements of geometry as figures in a game of construction. She superimposes the different elements and subordinates them to an overall verticality. In the first prints of the series, the figures refer to the elementary canon of drawing. They refuse both the richness of graphic art and the perfection of classical art, which the artist endeavors to deconstruct. In subsequent plates, the geometric components lose rigidity, are rendered more and more fragile, and are dislodged by nonrational elements that signify chaos and disorder or refer to fiction and dreams. The engravings appear frail and meager; the motifs are made up of only the simplest forms. Reduced to a minimum of lines, the prints do not go beyond the state of sketches and at times even resemble children's drawings.

Through texts and images, Bourgeois's artistic enterprise corresponds to a journey that starts out with what she characterizes as an "architectural idealism,"[5] for which the skyscraper is the metaphor. But she parodies the buildings' sheer size, beauty, and monumentality, as well as their modernity, not only in the minimalist and childlike appearance of the engravings but in the texts, which, through their absurd, futile, and disconnected constructions, lead to nonsense. As the series continues, the representations veer increasingly toward what the artist calls "more realism,"[6] for the later plates include what is hidden behind appearances.

The body of prints comprises an artistic program that abandons both the heroic subject and heroic representation. Bourgeois strives to deconstruct grandeur and power, the monolithic and the megalomaniacal, emphasizing instead fragility and temperaments not revealed or dissembled, in most instances, behind an outward facade.

This attitude also dominates the sculpture that she produced at this time (the postwar years), in which she rejects monumentality and any totalizing concept of art. By staying close to the sculptural vocabulary of the so-called "primitives" (African art in particular), the abstract figures that she constructs vertically are made up of simple forms. Just as in the prints, they are anthropomorphic. The material is predominantly wood, sometimes combined with industrial elements (nails, paint), in most cases salvaged, ranging from simple (plaster) to noble (bronze), sometimes painted and often hybrid. Depending on their respective compositions and constitutions, the sculptures convey characters and moods mapped and deployed as in a *carte du tendre*. These forms and materials, as much as their arrangement, evoke psychological states in which meaning is neither fixed nor static but shifting, changing, ambiguous. Horizontality, for example, conforms to "a desire for abandonment, slumber, passivity and withdrawal. Ascending verticality is an affirmation or even an onslaught. Descending verticality, and wavering, is a sketch of compromise, a desire for acceptance."[7] The content of the antagonistic forms lies in between, or in the space between several meanings, where the apparatus that we use for symbolic interpretation, our capacity for multiple and infinite associations, is suspended. The suspension Bourgeois investigates aspires to "a state of ambivalence and doubt."[8]

The sculptures may be solitary or linked, fragile or potent. They often stand in groups of two or more. Each is defined by the others or remains isolated, even while comprising part of the "crowd." They often complement one another. When one is fragile, the other can lend support by virtue of its own strength and stability. The figures may sustain each other, share a secret, display either consensus or discord. They can be proud and confident, or weak and vulnerable. Through various constellations and innumerable possibilities of encounter, their different and changing natures are revealed. "Now even though the shapes are abstract, they represent people. They are delicate as relationships are delicate. And they look at each other and they lean on each other."[9] Through these sculptures, Bourgeois reconstructs, interprets, and recomposes the characters she knew in France before she left for the United States in 1938. Lent a new physical and psychological presence, these characters transposed into sculptures attest to absence and presence alike, to intimacy as well as to strangeness.

In the postwar years, Bourgeois's commitment to unmasking the facades of monumentality and grandeur in order to reveal their underlying fragility amounted to a stand against everything that dominated art during the 1930s and 1940s—the *retour à l'ordre,* neoclassicism, fascist

Louise Bourgeois and her son Alain. Courtesy of the artist and Robert Miller Gallery.

art, and socialist realism. However, the great surrealist exhibition of 1939, held in New York under the banner of antifascism and in keen opposition to everything rational and operative, must have had a considerable impact on the artist, who had just arrived in the city. Bourgeois shared the surrealists' fascination with the unconscious and "primitive art" (African art), incidentally the focus of her husband Robert Goldwater's research. While Goldwater was publishing his major work on the influence of primitivism on modern art (he was then director of New York's Museum of Primitive Art),[10] Bourgeois was orienting her work toward a contemporary and personal context. She found archaism not only in the art of the so-called primitives but also in childhood, in the unconscious and in the actual forms and structures of human communication. She held a solitary position among modernists and surrealists and defended it against the major postwar tendencies in the U.S.: abstract expressionism and minimalism. Many styles and movements, including those of the past and those that would follow, played a part and coexist in her work. She seeks to violate artistic trends and aesthetic doctrines in the pursuit of her own personal research.

In the series *He Disappeared into Complete Silence,* Bourgeois deconstructs the ideal image of the Self in order to unveil what, for her, is the "drama of the self."[11] Assembled like a riddle, the nine plates show the sides of the Self that are narcissistic and secret, aggressive and destructive, grim and paradoxal. She describes the evolution of the series as a journey into depression: "The mood starts out very fine; but it declines . . . it goes down and down."[12] The pivotal point of her artistic practice is indeed depression and "low self-esteem." "What helps me is understanding my foibles and blunders, and displaying them."[13] The representation of skyscraper facades, proud and impenetrable, with which she identifies at the start of the series (*moi* and *toi* in her later commentary), stands for her introspection, where fragility and vulnerability predominate. She exhumes and exorcises the uncontrolled and unconventional instincts of the unconscious. She borrows this approach from psychoanalytic practice. While her images and texts remain extremely controlled, they strive to attain what lies beyond control and reason, precisely in order to make it visible and apparent to consciousness.

From one plate to the next, she carries out a self-analysis in order to discover the multiple and matrixial nature of the Self.[14] "His" disappearance (He Disappeared into Complete Silence) would seem to be the sine qua non condition for the Self (as feminine subject) to appear. With "(His) disappearance into Complete Silence," Louise Bourgeois suspends the symbolic father figure and, with it, the phallic order, which in so many ways has turned silence into its terrain of exclusion. Through silence, absence, and negation woman has been excluded from the symbolic.[15]

Through her absurd and nonsensical little texts and strange engravings, Bourgeois orchestrates a world that is self-absorbed and autistic, in which she herself adopts an autistic attitude. Silence, which, according to the artist, is nonviolence, forms part of it. The set of prints and texts is presented as a sequence of hampered situations and dialogues of the deaf. The man fails to show up for the meeting. The girl who loves him and is waiting for him is left alone, her beauty unseen (I). A "very good story" is told so fast that nobody understands: it makes only the narrator happy (III). A man in an elevator hails his friend: laughing too hard, he sticks his head out and is decapitated (V). An American who served three years in the army hears his friend's voice twice through his ailing ear, then never hears anything again, which cuts him off from a part of the world (VIII). A mother's love for her son, and her need to protect him, go unrequited because the son has other things on his mind. She dies but he does not even know it (IX).

Set in the past, the texts take a form akin to that of "once-upon-a-time" fairy tales. They are constructed bit by bit, with things left unsaid and abrupt and unexpected linkages.

Text pages:
He Disappeared into Complete Silence, 1949. Text and engraving. Double page spread: 10 x 14 in. Courtesy of the artist and Robert Miller Gallery, New York.

Plate 4

In the mountains of Central France forty years ago, sugar was a rare product.

Children got one piece of it at Christmas time.

A little girl that I knew when she was my mother used to be very fond and very jealous of it.

She made a hole in the ground and hid her sugar in, and she always forgot that the earth is damp.

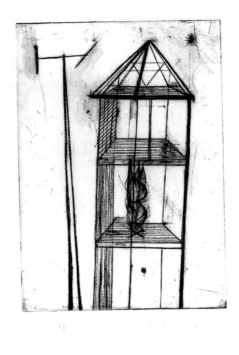

Plate 5

Once a man was waving to his friend from the elevator.

He was laughing so much that he stuck his head out and the ceiling cut it off.

Plate 8

Once an American man who had been in the army for three years became sick in one ear.

His middle ear became almost hard.

Through the bone of the skull back of the said ear a passage was bored.

From then on he heard the voice of his friend twice, first in a high pitch and then in a low pitch.

Later on the middle ear grew completely hard and he became cut off from part of the world.

Plate 9

Once there was the mother of a son. She loved him with a complete devotion.

And she protected him because she knew how sad and wicked this world is.

He was of a quiet nature and rather intelligent but he was not interested in being loved or protected because he was interested in something else.

Consequently at an early age he slammed the door and never came back.

Later on she died but he did not know it.

Communication, exchange, and the give-and-take of human relationships are constantly upset, cut off, violated, and even fail to exist. Images and texts attest to a reality that is partial and fractured, disconnected and empty. Through different characters, the body appears more and more fragmented: a head decapitated (V), a woman cut into pieces and turned into a stew (VII). The various senses also atrophy. Visual and aural perception jam, the eye seems to be screened or blinded, the ear troubled, even deaf, taste is warped as it becomes associated with a cannibalistic meal. In the sequence of images, objects and space are increasingly shattered. The laws of gravity are put on hold, and stability is suspended. The moods of the nine episodes, which start off in a state of motionlessness, proceed by way of outburst and eventually reach the ultimate depression, recall a cycle of hysteria.

Seeking to represent the unbridled as much as an unbridled representation, Bourgeois borrows her artistic language from hysteria. She refers to it explicitly in her recent work, *Cells* (1989–93). By staging an atmosphere that confines the sensory body, displaying its fragments (eyes, ears, hands), and by reinstating the "arch of hysteria" in one *Cell* (1992–93), she pays homage to the suffering and sickening bodies that featured so prominently in Jean-Martin Charcot's late nineteenth-century experiments.[16] They had served then as models not only for studying the symptoms of an ailment (whose problematic definitions remain controversial and contested today) but also for formulating a typology of expressions that was taken up in artistic practice, particularly in photography and sculpture.[17] The famous public sessions at La Salpêtrière, where the sick were brought out like actors on a stage, became something of a spectacle.[18] Bourgeois's arch, in its mutinous setting and headless state, becomes the sign of a corporal language disconnected from cerebral control: like all of the other physical organs and reminiscences, it repudiates the body. Its fragmentation and the dissociation of the sense organs refuse synesthesia.

Bourgeois's artistic commitment is founded, in part, on the attempt to identify with a perception close to that of schizophrenia,[19] a perception that, originating from a *regard aveugle* and from beyond the rational and structured, has neither perspective nor vanishing point. This field *outside* focus, traditionally associated with woman, madness, and hysteria, allows the artist to find a place opposed to the phallic, where the representation of the feminine subject is possible.[20] The body that features in the hysterical arch of the cell is, however, male. Bourgeois thus challenges the traditional paradigm, in which the model (of the hysteric) is associated with the female, but the subject with the male. She explores a field somewhere between the loss of the Self and its formation. Her Trojan horse is made up of autism, hysteria, and madness, all traditionally associated with woman. Bourgeois detects unconscious conversions between psychic suffering and physical release and uses these in her sculptures.

The experience of hysteria and madness combines with the experience of the *unconscious image of the body*,[21] fundamental to the formation of the subject, where the female factor is not repressed. This "image" is not really an image. Defined by Françoise Dolto as an elementary organizer of narcissism, it belongs to a complex prelinguistic reality established in a relationship between the child and the mother's speech and bears the memory of the body's satisfaction with itself. The unconscious image of the body conveys physical sensations. It is re-formed on the basis of an uncoordinated perception and appears in a fragmented, incoherent form unraveled from the center and from all recognizable order. It operates partially, by way of multiple liaisons and divisions, the result of exchanges with the Other, whose mother, instead of being supplanted by the phallus, is at the origin.[22]

The girl all alone at her meeting (I), the woman cut into pieces and turned into a stew by her husband (VII), the mother dying far from her son—are not all of these self-portraits in which the artist summons up different aspects of her self-analysis? Is not the missed meeting a chance to discover the Other of oneself? Is not the woman cut into pieces a metaphor for the sacrifice and loss of identity? Is not the separation between mother and son, and the nonreciprocity of feelings, a metaphorical narrative in which mourning is revealed—the mourning for the substitution of the "maternal function" by the "artistic function"? Is not the son's indifference the indifference of the works themselves? While traditional theories of artistic creation are based on the theory of sublimation, or even the elimination of the maternal function, Bourgeois continues to maintain this function through melancholy. She represents this separation from the standpoint of the woman and mother in mourning. As an allegorical figure, melancholy infuses the present with the past, instead of doing away with and repressing the past.[23]

Bourgeois operates in a matrixial field, where the feminine subject is asserted instead of fading away in front of the Other.[24] In denying the principle of Oneness, the matrixial subject forms by means of divisions and multiplications, fragmentations and montages, in borderline areas and transit zones, between two spaces and among several. Meanings waver, in fact, between poles. Bourgeois's works represent a figure with two (or more) faces, which recalls the mythological theme of Janus. Her *Janus fleuri* (1968), for example, proposes an infinite field of meanings between the phallus and the vulva. I quote just a few descriptions, summarized by Alain Cueff: "a sort of fetus," "a double mammary phallus," "a double introverted vulva," "the enshrinement of a vulva between two phalluses," "transition from vulva to phallus."[25]

The partial links and intersections between sexual and sense organs give rise to a process of *metramorphosis*. In metramorphosis—*metra*, like matrix, etymologically refers to the uterus—as the subject encounters the Other, it changes its nature as much as it changes the nature of the Other. Without either elimination or domination, each one adopts aspects alien

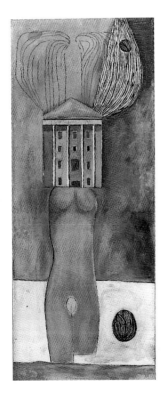

Femme-Maison, 1946–47. Oil and ink on linen. 91.3 x 35.6 cm. Private collection. Courtesy Robert Miller Gallery, New York. Photo: Allan Finkelman.

Femme-Maison, 1947. Ink and gouache on paper. 12 1/4 x 9 1/4 in. Private collection. Courtesy Robert Miller Gallery, New York. Photo: Allan Finkelman.

Les voleuses de gratte ciel
(Women Stealing a Skyscraper), 1949.
Pencil on paper. 20.3 x 12.7 cm.
Courtesy Robert Miller Gallery, New York.

to it. This *metramorphic* energy between phallus and matrix crosses the boundaries and limits of oppressive phallic symbolism, which Bourgeois strives to demystify and deconstruct. Rather, she underscores the vulnerability of the phallus that she tries to protect: "The phallus is the subject of my tenderness. It has to do with vulnerability and protection. . . . Although I feel protective about the phallus, that doesn't mean I'm not afraid of it."[26]

In the processes of metramorphosis, Bourgeois's motifs and symbols are forever being exposed to doubt. The artist justifies her line of reasoning by turning Descartes upside down from the point of view of a feminine subject: "I try to be Descartes. I am Descartes' daughter: I think therefore I am, I doubt therefore I am, I am disappointed therefore I am."[27] All iconography is subverted and converted into ambiguous imagery. In the *He Disappeared into Complete Silence* series, the lighthouse (III) has lost its power as a (phallic) symbol of knowledge and truth. Set somewhere between *moi* and *toi,* it attests to impotence rather than superiority. As a figure *inter alios,* no more nor less powerful, it no longer acts as a guide in an overtly difficult world: "The lighthouse is there to throw light . . . to give guidance. But it is a difficult world."[28] The motif of an easel (V) becomes muddled with that of a guillotine. Like an ambiguous, creaking plaything, the easel-guillotine parodies the act of painting and (artistic) execution in general. Not relying exclusively on violence, Bourgeois deploys game, parody, and irony as counterparts.

Bourgeois achieves her work in a terrain of mental exile: not only her real and deliberate exile in the United States, but also her position of exteriority within the domain of art and language. Outside systems and established ideas, she reveals her Self, as a woman, as an artist, and as a subject. Her personal and artistic revolt takes place in the space between the phallic and the transphallic (silence, blindness, deafness). Her work is the outcome of the coexistence of vital forces, destructive and creative alike. She seeks out aesthetic and psychological terrains where the real, the imaginary, and the fictional, the conscious and the unconscious, the outside and the inside intermingle and where the intimate and the anonymous merge into something strange. Anonymity and strangeness heighten her otherness and her disintegration as an artist and as a subject.

A woman walks on tiptoe so as not to draw attention to herself: she carries a skyscraper on her back. *Women Stealing a Skyscraper* (1949) is undoubtedly Bourgeois herself. She furtively removes the object of her desire, the phallic symbol of modernity, in order to appropriate for herself and dismantle it.

Translated from the French by Simon Pleasance and Fronza Woods

NOTES:

I wish to thank Catherine de Zegher and Bracha Lichtenberg Ettinger for their encouragement and support throughout this project, and Alain Morel and Michael Orwicz for their critical reading, valuable comments, and help in
refining the French and English versions of this text.

1. As quoted in *Louise Bourgeois. Sculptures, environments, dessins 1938–1995* (Paris: Editions de la Tempête, 1995), 220.
2. *He Disappeared into Complete Silence*, 1947, nine engravings. Background and references in Deborah Wye and
Carol Smith, *The Prints of Louise Bourgeois*, exhib. cat. (New York: Museum of Modern Art, 1994), 72.
3. With regard to plate 2, Louise Bourgeois annotates the scene by identifying the two houses: "The right is moi, the
left is you." Wye and Smith, *The Prints of Louise Bourgeois*, 78.
4. Ibid., 80.
5. "The early plates 1, 2 and 3 have something of an 'architectural idealism,' while the later plates have more 'realism.'" Wye and Smith, *The Prints of Louise Bourgeois*, 76.
6. Ibid.
7. As quoted in *Louise Bourgeois. Sculptures, environments, dessins 1938–1995*, 81.
8. Ibid.
9. As quoted in *Louise Bourgeois* (New York: Museum of Modern Art, 1988).
10. Robert Goldwater, *Primitivism in Modern Art* (New York: Alfred A. Knopf, 1938).
11. "This is a drama of the self. . . . It is about the fear of going overboard and hurting others." Wye and Smith, *The
Prints of Louise Bourgeois*, 72.
12. Ibid., 76.
13. As quoted in *Louise Bourgeois. Sculptures, environments, dessins 1938–1995*, 133.
14. The matrix is proposed as a model of a feminine symbolism by Bracha Lichtenberg Ettinger; see her "Matrix and
Metramorphosis," *Differences* 4, no. 3 (1992).
15. Bracha Lichtenberg Ettinger, "La femme n'existe pas et ne signifie rien," in *Feminin presence*, exhib. cat. (Tel
Aviv: Tel-Aviv Museum of Art, 1990). Also see Rosi Huhn, "Moving Omissions and Hollow Spots into the Field of
Vision," in *Bracha Lichtenberg Ettinger: Matrix Borderlines* (Oxford: Museum of Modern Art, 1993), 5–10.
16. Charcot (1825–1893), French physician, founded the school of neurology at La Salpêtrière. Using La
Salpêtrière's patients, he studied the development of *l'hystéro-épilepsie* in the last three decades of the nineteenth century. In the famous "Tuesday evenings at La Salpêtrière," he provoked fits in the patients so as to
show them to the Parisian public. The arch featured as well as a "typical position and as a variant" of the hysterical fit in Charles-Robert Richet's *Tableau synoptique de la grande attaque hystérique complète et regulière*. Also
see Georges Didi-Huberman, *Invention de l'hystérie, Charcot et l'iconographie photographique de la Salpêtrière*
(Paris: Macula, 1982).
17. In fact, Charcot's public experiments lured the literary and artistic circles of Paris, which derived inspiration
from them for spectacular representations of hysteria in art and literature. Together Charcot and Richet published
Les difformes et les malades dans l'art; Charcot founded the body of work for *La nouvelle iconographie de la
Salpêtrière*, claiming that "les images parlent plus vivement à l'esprit que les paroles." Didi-Huberman, *Invention de
l'hystérie*, 36.
18. Sigrid Schade, "Charcot und das Schauspiel des hysterischen Körpers. Die Pathosformel als ästhetische
Inszenierung des psychiatrischen Diskurses: Ein blinder Fleck in der Warburg-rezeption," in *Denkräume zwischen
Kunst und Wissenschaft* (Berlin: Dietrich Reimler Verlag, 1993).
19. Rosalind Krauss refers to the impact of schizophrenia on the conception of partial objects in Louise
Bourgeois's work with reference to Gilles Deleuze and Félix Guattari's *Anti-Oedipus*. Rosalind Krauss, "Porträt
der Künstlerin als Fillette," in *Louise Bourgeois*, ed. Peter Weiermair (Schaffhausen: Edition Stemmle, 1989),
23. For a recent Kleinian reading of Bourgeois's partial objects see Mignon Nixon, "Bad Enough Mother,"
October 71 (Winter 1995): 71–92.
20. Rosi Huhn, *Bracha Lichtenberg Ettinger et la folie de la raison* (Paris: Goethe Institut Paris, Ocre d'Art, 1990).
See also Rosi Huhn, "Le problème du traitement des résidus dans l'art et dans la culture, en tant que passage vers
une barbarie positive," in *Passages (d')après Walter Benjamin* (Mainz: Hermann Schmidt, 1992), 92–109.
21. Françoise Dolto, *L'image inconsciente du corps* (Paris: Edition du Seuil, 1984).
22. Rosi Huhn, "L'image des cas-limites—autoportraits," in *Borderline Conditions and Pathological Narcissism:
Bracha Lichtenberg Ettinger* (Villeurbanne: Le Nouveau Musée, 1992).
23. Ibid., chapter 3, "Entre allégorie et image du corps: Mélancholie et mamalanguc."
24. The phallic determination of the Other in Jacques Lacan's "Schéma L." See Bracha Lichtenberg Ettinger,
"Matrix and Metramorphosis."
25. Alain Cueff, "Une et autres. L'oeuvre impaire de Louise Bourgeois," in *Louise Bourgeois. Sculptures, environments, dessins 1938–1995*, 45–49.
26. In *Louise Bourgeois. Sculptures, environments, dessins 1938–1995*, 117.
27. Ibid., 122.
28. In *The Prints of Louise Bourgeois*, 80.

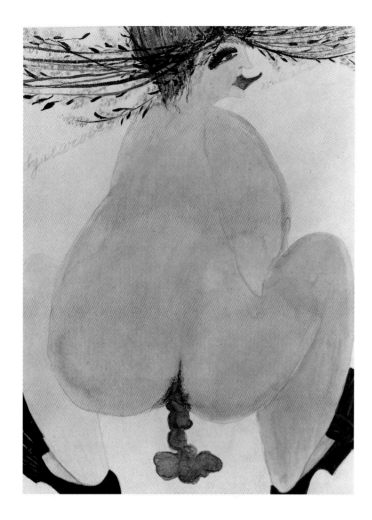

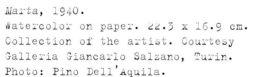

Marta, 1940.
Watercolor on paper. 22.3 x 16.9 cm.
Collection of the artist. Courtesy
Galleria Giancarlo Salzano, Turin.
Photo: Pino Dell'Aquila.

Opera no. 34, 1940.
Watercolor on paper.
92 x 71 cm. Collection of
Andrea and Paolo
Accornero, Turin. Photo:
Pino Dell'Aquila.

Carol Rama: Heroic, Exotic, Heretic

C arol Rama is a vast and unexplored site.

When, in the summer of 1979, I browsed through the catalogue of her exhibition in the Galleria Martano, Turin, depicting her scarcely known watercolors from the years 1936–41 —superbly unseemly works—I realized that Rama's stature as an artist reached beyond Europe.

The following year, at the international exhibition "L'altra metà dell'avanguardia 1910–40" (The Other Side of the Avant-Garde 1910–40) at the Palazzo Reale, Milan, Rama's works were among the most astonishing; her images elicited terrifying and ambivalent echoes from the audience. Where did that unruly witchcraft, apart from the Italian mannerisms of the 1940s, come from? Shoes, stoles, dentures, brooms, horses' limbs, shaving brushes, tongues: intimate and infamous clues of imaginary and hyperreal, shining and crumbling universes, shown with a tauntingly shameless style. Rama showed drawings marked by a sophisticated and seductive fierceness; hallucinated, violent and bloody fluctuations, celebrating luxurious joys but always ruled by the idea of decomposition. These works were an apotheosis of puritan pornography, a crucible where suffering and abjection became ornate with gay colors, pink and purple pastel transparencies. Despite Rama's elegant style, the painful and dissolute meaning of her pictures, metaphors, and distressing exorcisms never weakened. Every object had a hidden meaning—the heels, the razors, the teeth, the empty shoes—each item recalled something, each was both tender and cruel. Explosive madeleines!

The dreadful display of sweetness became more visible at the Swedish version of "L'altra metà dell'avanguardia," where more works from that period were exhibited. Titled *Appassionata*, the pieces were a shockingly intense series of horrors and wonders. The tragic quality of the images, the innocent familiarity with pain, and the rigorous management of nightmares became more explicit, unrestrained, and astonishing. Rama displayed belts, beds with restraints, wheelchairs, severed nudes, busts, and ambiguous garlands: the black abyss of the unconscious, the eye-opening exploration of the abject, the obscene, the forbidden. Sex is always humiliation, mystery, wonderful tearing, morbid harshness, and hints of tenderness. These were surprisingly prescient psychological insights for Italian culture.

Rama's talent is extraordinary; not only was she a painter but also an artist who—even before the 1940s—touched on loss, failure, and loneliness, the most intense and dramatic conflicts. For her, reality is either tragedy or guilt; the truth is unknown. Grotesque ghosts, obscene puppets, mournful screams, painful silences, and indecent slivers of her puberty will probably never be fully realized. From those early stages, neither Cartesian *passion de l'âme* nor *intermittenze del cuore nor cognizioni del dolore* were unknown to her.

However, Carol Rama surrounded her vivid imagination with a disturbing aura of fairy tales: why separate memories from hallucinations? We don't know and cannot know whether we are facing a picture, entering a dream, reading a diary page, or browsing through a list of the unavowable. . . .

What happened afterward?

Rama is one of few artists who—despite many hysterical weaknesses and unruly rebellions—does not fear anything. Therefore, in the 1950s, with her own radical determination, she worked through abstraction. She painted a series of esoteric and archaic geometric canvases. In these pictures squares, lozenges, and diamonds (kites, flags, musical notes perhaps) float against lunar backgrounds. These elusive marks preserve the fascination of a coded microcosm, parts of mobile and varied threads, agents of mysterious relations within a simulation of vital and organic rhythms.

Her rough purity and her ability to juxtapose rage with detachment, refined formalism with passion, made Carol Rama part of the Informal movement of the 1960s. She played her role with magnificence and fatality. A wonderful example is the black surface of her *Riso nero* of 1961, an image of both destruction and mundane attachment. The *Bricolages* of the following years seem to come out of the underworld, encompassing its magical darkness and its glow, its nectar and its cyanide. The brutal and corrosive beauty of these works springs from Rama's own tears, prayers, and roars. The *Bricolages* are dark cosmogonies thirsting for all kinds of wounds. All the sorrows and pity of life are present. Carol Rama knows what life and death are made of.

Clots of matter, streams of lava, debris of colors and marks, along with the ultimate creation of combined canvases. Claws, needles, syringes, twined wires, bundles of thread, and glass eyes juxtaposed with words by the poet Edoardo Sanguineti become original paint, sculpture, words. Through symbolism and allegory Rama continues her anguished and intrepid search within herself, outside and backward. Memory is always archetypal, obsessive, amorous, caricaturing, even in the clefts between pieces of cloth, waste, scratches, and patches.

Around 1970 Rama became interested in materials such as convertible car roofs, car and bicycle tires, and plastic sheets. She modified these materials: tires become smooth. Pirelli and similar brands imitate painting. Rama created the balanced compositions of the *Arsenali*. She is capable of everything, she can even be a physiologist of perception.

In the midst of diptychs and polyptychs, in 1977, the dismal magnificence of *Movimento ed immobilità di Birnam* burst out. A bundle of plastic pipes, flickering bladders, and industrial bowels hangs from a hitch against a black leather background. Birnam is not a forest but the group of camouflaged soldiers that advances to beat Macbeth. Again, here are those damned passions, Rama's pious and obscene attitudes, the pink and dirty bowels, her tropism for decadence and expiation. The spices that Rama adds to the ostensible triviality of everyday things are plastic tubes, hitches, and leather pieces.

Demiurge of her own specters, prophet and follower of her own rituals, repressed werewolf, deserter of rules and social impostures, intemperate like a heretic, unbounded in her passions like a mystic, Rama keeps on plunging us and herself into the less explored swamps of the unconscious. At the same time, she narrates through "fragments of a lovers' discourse."

It is not fair to consider her role in the history of the visual arts of the last forty years as purely confined to painting; her contribution is more diverse. While we usually go into other people's experiences, and more rarely use our own, Rama is totally possessed by her own memories. Her sole source of inspiration is her own "insanity." As the absolute eccentric, she carefully avoided getting professional help for her "troubles." Fearing "healing" and afraid of being stripped of her fears, Rama has pruned, manured, sharpened, and rashly fondled her troubles. Since she uses "illness," difference, and remedy as her endless sources, Rama hides her good health and her strength as if they were vices, shames, and disgraces. Few "lunacies" are left hanging in her closet.

*Gli Scopini
(Opera no. 7),
1937.
Watercolor on
paper.
17.5 x 25 cm.
Private collec-
tion, Turin.
Courtesy Galleria
Giancarlo
Salzano, Turin.
Photo: Pino
Dell'Aquila.*

The tragic verve of many of her reveries came back in the drawings of the last five years: *La macelleria, Ritratto di Huguette, I miei tristi capitani, Soffitte e pittura, Trofei,* and *Amoroso.* Allusions flow on surveyor's maps, marked with land and private estates, and on maps of Turin. A small seed makes the paper expand in innumerable branches and makes nonsense bloom.

Animals stand for either virtues or occult powers, as in medieval literature. The spell consists of what is hidden. Rama continues to show all of her paraphernalia, her flora, and her fauna in disguise. She uses ordinary objects such as maps, which look normal and discreet. On one of her bewitched maps three winged or plumed creatures—angels, perhaps—thrive with folded and unfolded wings, placing garlands on each other. Again worms, snakes, serpents, insects, frogs, green lizards, even a bull with wicked wit emerge from blooming branches and vegetable shoots, bringing back scents and odors of decaying rubbish, freshness and stench, and all of those exquisite contradictions that make Rama's work a continuous odyssey. Again we are overwhelmed by something beyond what is inscribed in these "little pictures," as formal pleasures are shattered by the spleen's evils. We are unable to maintain composure while we feel secret emotions erupt, melt, and scuffle, echoing within us.

No doubt many personal tragedies must have occurred to produce such an artist.

So, who is Carol Rama, really?

She is a devilish angel, kind and wild; she is a supreme amateur; a survivor hunting for originality; she is a Manganelli's fool and a blazing kobold; she is an artifice, a perfect mise-en-scène; a mosaic of ruins, of rotten leftovers of the past; she is a character of literature, she is a poem by Sanguineti and a passage from Baudelaire; she is exotic, erotic, and heroic.

Besides, she is "damned and beautiful," primitive and blasé, beaten and impermeable, strong and asthenic, sparkling and rascally, aristocratic and plebeian, pervert and naive, humorous and sorrowful, educated, shy and diligent, a wandering minstrel and a hermit. Is she Molly Bloom or Alice, Lady Ramsay or Pandora, Sisyphus or Icarus, Gorgon or Cagliostro, the Medusa or Eurydice without Orpheus?

Nobody, absolutely nobody, can answer these questions. The artist gives and denies herself, cloaked in permanent mystery.

Translated from the Italian by Marcella Beccaria.
First published in *Carol Rama* (Milan: Mazzotta, 1985).

Poster for "Driving Image Show" at the Castellane Gallery, New York, Spring 1964.
Courtesy Richard Castellane, New York.

Yayoi Kusama: · surface · stitch · skin

J. F. Rodenbeck

P riestess of Nudity, Psychotic Artist, the Polka-Dot Girl, Obsessional Artist, publicity hound: in the 1960s Yayoi Kusama was the target of a number of epithets, some of them self-inflicted, all of them part of an exhibitionist's notoriety. A self-professed visionary mad-woman, fantastically dressed, distinctly eccentric and unconventional, Kusama was also a realist and, as one longtime supporter put it, "firmly devoted to the promotional necessities of artistic success."[1] Within a decade of her arrival in New York in 1957 Kusama was a fixture on the "scene"—that social configuration whose uncertain borders overlap the art world, fashion, the underground, and the unsavory. By the end of the 1960s, through an unfortunate combination of her aggressive pursuit of publicity and her erratic behavior, Kusama had worn out her apparent success. In 1972 she returned to Japan and soon thereafter voluntarily entered a mental hospital, where she continues to produce work, including paintings, fabric sculptures, ceramics, and novels.

Born in 1929 in Nagano prefecture, Japan, into a traditional and rather conservative bourgeois family (which owned a successful nursery business), Kusama claims to have had her first hallucinatory experiences in the early 1940s, hearing voices and seeing the world covered in patterns. Drawings dated from around 1939 of quite ordinary subjects are covered with a hail of graphite spots said to represent the consuming patterns in her visions.[2] By the early 1950s, after an uneven education interrupted by World War II, Kusama was committed to being an artist and had begun experimenting with Western-style painting techniques. These early works—painted fields of repeated marks or strokes, some with biomorphic foci embedded in the dots or mesh, others unhinged grids that seem to expand beyond the canvas—were well received in Japan. But Kusama found the postwar Japanese art world restrictive, cliquish, and sexist. Like a number of her compatriots, she carefully set her sights on New York City, using the opportunity of her first U.S. one-person show (in Seattle) to apply for a visa.

Kusama's first solo show in New York, at the Brata Gallery on East 10th Street in October 1959, featured five expansive, noncompositional canvases covered with pale, irregular lattice fields in light impasto, part of a series continuing the earlier work done in Japan called *Infinity Nets*. Reviewed very favorably in the press, pieces from this series were included the next year as the only Japanese contribution to the important exhibition "Monochrome Malerei" held in Leverkusen, Germany, alongside work by Yves Klein, Piero Manzoni, Lucio Fontana, Günter Uecker, and Otto Piene, among others. It was a promising beginning for the ambitious painter, and the resulting linkage with European artists from Group Zero and Nul proved fortuitous throughout the 1960s.

In the fall of 1961, possibly prompted by a show of assemblages held at the Museum of Modern Art, Kusama began to expand her repertoire by experimenting with various material "accumulations." In hanging works, for example, large fields of repetitive elements were fixed to wall supports, as with the *Airmail Stickers* (1962)—hundreds of nearly identical postal stickers mechanistically glued to a roughly 6-by-5.5-foot surface—or the *Egg Carton* series, in which Kusama modified these familiar prestamped forms by sewing them convex-side-out onto canvas and adding mattress stuffing to the depressions (photographs of her studio at the time show entire walls covered with these). A related group of works, the *Accumulations*, are domestic objects—furniture, clothes, toiletries, often salvaged from the New York streets—covered with small fabric sacks roughly the size and shape of cucumbers and stuffed with cotton batting (also from local refuse) and then painted white. The first of these, *Accumulation #1,* is an ambiguously droll, oversized armchair completely infested with phallic protrusions except for the slightly menacing and curiously sexual fringe along its bottom edge—"hardly the answer to Eliza Doolittle's yearnings, aggressively octopus-like and not in the least metaphoric."[3] It was included in the "NO Show," a sampling of aggressive neodada art self-consciously posed in critical relation to the perceived commercial banalities of pop, at the Gertrude Stein Gallery in 1963.[4]

During 1964 and early 1965, in a transition from sculpture to environments, the *Accumulations* became part of larger arrangements. In a long (but mixed) review of Kusama's retrospective "Driving Image Show" (Castellane Gallery, Spring 1964), Donald Judd observed, "The . . . masses of white protuberances are more alike than their underlying forms are unlike.

Kusama varies the protuberances, but they are seen collectively, as she intends, before they are seen individually. The collective impression is the more important anyway; the point is obsessive repetition."[5] Claes Oldenburg, who began producing his soft sculptures the same year as Kusama, put it slightly differently: "The topic was not the object, [but] the thing that was on the object. Her sculpture is a small thing that covers."[6] Taking into account this textural, skinlike quality and using work generated by the various "obsessional" series on which she was concentrating her productive energies (*Sex-Obsession, Food-Obsession, Compulsion Furniture, Repetitive Vision, and Macaroni Room*), Kusama began to constellate the objects into room-sized environments.

Aggregation: One Thousand Boats Show, Kusama's first complete environment, was installed at the Gertrude Stein Gallery in December 1964. At the end of a sequence of narrow halls one came upon a small room: in the center was a rowboat with readied oars, both covered with the stuffed fabric phalli; hundreds of poster-sized black-and-white photo-reproductions of the same boat composed the wallpaper. Jill Johnston, reviewing the show, noted that "the photographs do not simply play tricks with the spectator by way of startling him when he sees the real thing; they are actually a reiterated extension of the boat, suggesting an infinite expansion of the image."[7] Kusama had herself photographed nude in this environment, standing coyly sandwiched between the wall and the boat; in this publicity shot the wallpaper's repeated pattern abstracts the snubbed-bullet shape of the boat—which juts in a low, menacing diagonal from right to left—into the cinematic yet static form of a penis, or

Traveling Life (Ladder), 1964. Mixed media. The National Museum of Modern Art, Kyoto, Japan. Courtesy Richard Castellane, New York.

multiple penises, with a suggested anatomic detail oddly in tension with the stark lip of the boat's edge and more childish, yamlike fabric blobs that crowd across its planar surfaces. (Thus when Johnston, echoing Oldenburg and Judd, adds that "Any object will do, and if it were practical, the walls might have been covered with the [fabric] projections instead of the photographs" she is only partially correct, for it is the flattened restatement, the inverted textural *mise-en-abîme* that gives the piece its particular synecdochic qualities; similarly, the particularity of the signifier "boat" is spatially dislocated on wall and floor differently than, say "armchair" or "shoes"—though all, it must be added, are objects to be filled.)

By 1965 Kusama had also settled on the motif of the polka dot as surface ornament. Present in her work in various forms since childhood, the polka dot now became ubiquitous, covering virtually every available surface, from fabric elements to living skin. In a typically viscous statement she proclaimed: "The polka dot has the form of the sun, signifying masculine energy, the source of life. The polka dot has the form of the moon, symbolizing the feminine principle of reproduction and growth. Polka dots suggest multiplication to infinity. Our earth is only one polka dot among millions of others. . . . We must forget ourselves with polka dots! We must lose ourselves in the ever-advancing stream of eternity."[8] The first of her mirrored environments, *Infinity Mirror Room—Phalli's Field* (Castellane Gallery, 1965), incorporated the polka dot by covering the floor of the enclosure with red-dotted stuffed forms. Photographs of this environment show, variously, a Dalmatian puppy crawling through the spotted agglomeration and Kusama herself, in a red leotard, lying or standing in the sporogenic field, arms outstretched cruciform. The choice of color here again suggests the synecdochic linkage of surface to surface, the extension this time of Kusama's surface as a spot in the infinitely reflected image—in a sense, the dematerialization of the tactile, of skin itself, through the very mechanism of its visual extension.

Continuing her work with mirrors, Kusama temporarily abandoned both the polka dot and the phallic pillow in the spring of 1966 in one of her most ambitious environmental pieces, *Kusama's Peep Show—Endless Love Show* (Castellane Gallery). The viewer approached the outside of an empty hexagonal room roughly nine feet in diameter lined with mirrors and illuminated by a concentric arrangement of sequenced red, blue, green, and white light bulbs on the ceiling. A tape loop of Beatles music accompanied the clacking of the lights overhead, which flashed in increasingly vertiginous cycles. Two head-sized openings in the walls allowed viewers to look into the chamber, catching themselves and, perhaps, someone else—"ideally someone you're in love with, judging from the title," wrote the *ArtNews* reviewer[9]—infinitely reflected. Viewers were also invited to walk on the mirrored floor. Like Andy Warhol's *Exploding Plastic Inevitable,* the psychedelic proto-disco that opened on St. Mark's Place in April of the same year, *Endless Love* was greeted as a sensory pleasure chest.

But was the person in the other window really the viewer's interlocutor, the "someone you're in love with"? If so, the sense is hardly benevolent, given the extreme disorientation produced by the infinite and decentered mirroring of one or the other peeper and the void at the center of the room, the pulsating colored lights, the aural overload. The decentering is remarked again in the double register of the title: if "endless love" is a romantic banality, the "peep show" is unquestionably a voyeuristic display. Originally Kusama had wanted the lights to flash "Love" and "Sex" alternately (this proved technically too difficult), and in this context the display is unmistakably Times Square, as Kusama literally cites the hardware of the sex industry—from cheap commercial lighting to mirrored peep booths to pop music to the size of the viewing windows—and marks the phantasmatic conditions of romance itself. Missing from the center of *Peep Show* is the performer who usually occupies such a mirrored chamber doing an erotic dance for the usually invisible viewer. The reflective skin, endlessly interpolating the viewer, is an infinite barrier. Indeed commercial erotic exchange relies precisely on this inaccessibility, the impenetrability of the surface, the tactile impossibility of vision. Unlike, say, Warhol's *Silver Clouds,* shown the same season at Leo Castelli and composing a playful, if melancholy, mass, *Endless Love* is a loud and terrible vacuum.

The Venice Biennale of 1966, for which Kusama was given the lawn in front of the Italian pavilion, was the scene of what she calls her first happening.[10] Making use once again of the mirror theme and combining it with her polka dots, Kusama installed fifteen hundred pumpkin-sized plastic mirrored balls (ordered from a local manufacturer) on the grass in a piece she

called *Narcissus Garden.* In a Biennale described as "conservative," "less exciting than the last one," "no impact," "weak and insipid," a large asterisk—both isolating and indicating—interrupts the litany: "Except for Kusama['s] . . . way-out exhibition of mirror-balls."[11] Kusama had herself photographed lying among the spheres in her red leotard and juggling them dressed in a gold kimono. Scandalously, she occupied her "garden" in kimono and handed out promotional flyers; when she began to sell the balls for two dollars each, the Italian authorities protested that to "sell art like hot dogs or ice cream cones at the Venice Biennale" was not appropriate.[12]

Happenings continued throughout the late 1960s, including events designed for the theater as well as street performance and demonstrations against the Vietnam War, notoriously using nude performers. These events—usually highly publicized, with well orchestrated press campaigns—often had the morphology of guerrilla nudist actions (one did result in Kusama's arrest), targeting such high-profile locations as the sculpture garden at the Museum of Modern Art and the New York Stock Exchange. During this period Kusama also established a number of marginal businesses connected to psychedelic culture—among them Kusama Polka Dot Church, Kusama Fashion Co., Ltd., Body Paint Studio Co., Ltd., and the Homo Social Club "KOK"—and even contracted her name out to a start-up pornographic magazine, *Kusama's Orgy,* for which she served as "House Geisha." In April of 1969 she opened a Nudist Design Clothes Workshop for Department Stores and a Fashion Boutique, which produced fantastic clothing cut with holes designed to reveal the (naked) body underneath. In November, Kusama provided the wedding gown for a gay wedding, which she conducted; in an inversion of the (visual) propositions of *Endless Love,* both partners wore the "orgy gown" together: "Clothes ought to bring people together, not separate them," she said.[13]

But as Kusama's notoriety increased in the mid and late 1960s, she moved increasingly into activities rather than objects, and the reviews grew hostile; "the basic flaw in her *oeuvre,*" Johnston wrote in 1966, "is that it has no autonomous life, but depends for its effects, such

Anatomic Explosion at the Statue of Alice in Wonderland in New York's Central Park, 1968.

as they are, on its references to Miss Kusama herself and her very, very personal problems."[14] The work, in other words, was too obviously narcissistic, too close to its maker. By 1969 the *Village Voice* published this scathing comment: "Kusama, whose gross lust for publicity never leaves room for taste, managed to put on the year's most boring freak show for members of the press this week. . . . Kusama is definitely suffering from over-exposure of over-exposure."[15] In the early 1970s Kusama moved back to Japan, to enter the mental hospital.

Like Andy Warhol and Joseph Beuys, to whom Johnston's words might just as easily have applied, Kusama in New York was a mythic being; but her process embraced neither mechanical reproduction nor the kinds of auratic evocations for which Beuys is known, falling somewhere in between. Otto Piene remarked, "There is a phobia in her painting, like a compulsive stitching. It is more psychological, more specifically women's painting."[16] If one can set aside the sexism of such a remark and read it, instead, as a certain postwar realism, if one can talk about the work as labor, it is a kind of driven sweatshop labor, the artisanal reduced to repetition, to a production timetable or quota. (Indeed Kusama kept an extremely demanding schedule, often working in her studio, forgetting to eat or sleep, until she was exhausted.) Painting polka dots on everything reduces surface to the status of surface, as does attaching pods to every available expanse: the skin of labor, representing labor, enacting labor for the photograph: labor leaks out, staining the diaphanous inscription of the artist in the artwork, failing to be swallowed by the repetitious void.

The apparent lack of distinction between Kusama's psychic state, her body, and her art, the unstable surface of her production, from canvas to "Co., Ltd.," draws troubling links between art, sexuality, and commodities in which Kusama embeds her accumulations. Though this subtext has correlates in pop art (one thinks in particular of Warhol, but also of Oldenburg), in Kusama's work and pronouncements it is rendered so literal, so legible that it seems unreadable. An apocryphal tale tells how as a child Kusama was given a work assignment in a factory making parachutes during the Second World War; allegedly it is there— assembling lengths of fine stuff in such a way as to render the porous material impermeable for the few minutes it would take to catch and cradle the air, dampen the fall from damaged aircraft to earth below—that she learned how to sew. Sewing is, in this myth, an apotropaic measure. The silk in its taut state is a kind of skin, then, a barrier against sheer drop, but only when its harness is occupied.

NOTES:

1. Udo Kulturmann, "Yayoi Kusama and the Concept of Obsession in Contemporary Art," *Obsession: Yayoi Kusama* (Tokyo: Fuji Television Gallery, 1982), unpaginated.

2. See Yayoi Kusama, Bhupendra Karia, and Alexandra Munroe, *Yayoi Kusama: A Retrospective* (New York: Center for International Contemporary Arts, 1989), fig. 1, p. 13, and p. 69 for examples.

3. Edward T. Kelly, "Neo-Dada: A Critique of Pop Art," *Art Journal* 23, no. 3 (1964): 200.

4. "Although in some ways similar, the imagery of NO often goes quite beyond that of Pop Art," wrote Edward Kelly. "With a far more violently satiric iconography, NO renders the social message of Pop Art tame and harmless by comparison. In fact, it has been suggested that the Pop Art movement itself was inspired by an attempt to make NO Art a more palatable commodity for a public willing to invest in satiric games, but no more." Kelly, "Neo-Dada," 194.

5. Donald Judd, *Arts* 38 (September 1964): 69.

6. As quoted in Alexandra Munroe, "Obsession, Fantasy and Outrage: The Art of Yayoi Kusama," in *Yayoi Kusama*, 24.

7. Jill Johnston, "Reviews and Previews," *ArtNews* 62 (Fall 1964): 12.

8. As quoted in Kulturmann, "Yayoi Kusama."

9. Peter Schjeldahl, "Reviews and Previews," *ArtNews* 65 (May 1966): 18.

10. Although, as Alexandra Munroe notes in her indispensable essay, Kusama had been posing for photographs in the streets of New York with various costumes and props since the early 1960s. See Munroe, "Obsession, Fantasy and Outrage," 28.

11. Norman Narotzky, "The Venice Biennale: Pease Porridge in the Pot Nine Days Old," *Arts* 40 (Summer 1966): 42.

12. As quoted in Bhupendra Karia, "Biographical Notes," in *Yayoi Kusama*, 87.

13. Kultermann, "Yayoi Kusama."

14. *Arts* 40: 61.

15. As quoted in Karia, "Biographical Notes," 92. This is in fact a vicious review of the gay wedding mentioned above.

16. As quoted in Munroe, "Obsession, Fantasy and Outrage," 20.

Yayoi Kusama with "Love Forever" buttons, 1966.
Photo: Hall Reiff. Courtesy of the artist.

Tron (Amputee), from the series *Bringing the War Home*, 1969–72.
Photomontage printed as color photograph. 24 x 20 in.
Courtesy of the artist and Jay Gorney Modern Art, New York.

The Inadequacy of Seeing and Believing:
The Art of Martha Rosler

Laura Cottingham

Since the late sixties, Martha Rosler has been making art, very political art, that refuses to rest neatly within any one medium, ideology, or aesthetic but rather seeks to explain the world by revealing the fallacies inherent in most explanations. Her work, in video, photography, and text, persistently evokes a dialectic of meaning wherein meaning is constructed, broken, and, by virtue of its very dismantling, reconstructed again. Although it has been called so, hers is no "postmodern" art in the sense that challenging the verity of our signifying practices is only the beginning, not the end, of Rosler's aim. Her work problematizes the taxonomies of thought that regulate both theoretical and quotidian thinking while refusing to abandon—as have so many postmodernist thinkers—the reality of the observable, the experiential, and the real. She is less a Baudrillard than a Habermas and more a Kafka than either—a historical materialist with a subjectively metaphysical bent.

Her interrogation of categories, both social and philosophical, and the disturbance she brings to bear on the organizing principles of everyday life as well as those of art production, includes her own refusal to participate in a dominant convention of contemporary art production: the gallery system. For more than twenty-five years, until 1993, she was without commercial gallery representation. Despite her rare status as a twentieth-century artist who has been recognized but commercially excluded, she is one of the most influential American artists of her generation.[1]

Among Rosler's earliest works is a series of photographs critical of the Vietnam War that were published in the California-based alternative press in the early seventies but, until 1991, were never exhibited in an art context.[2] Made during the peak of U.S. military involvement in Vietnam, *Bringing the War Home* (1967–72) grew out of Rosler's involvement in antiwar activities, reflecting the artist's "frustration with images we saw in television and print media, even with antiwar flyers and posters. The images we saw were always very far away, in a place we couldn't imagine."[3] In this remarkable series, images taken from *Life* and other mainstream American magazines are reassembled, then rephotographed, thus reconnecting two sites of human experience—the war in Vietnam and the American home—which the media, and the American popular consciousness, insist(ed) on falsely separating. Rosler's rephotographs don't reflect the unconscious or irrational inspiration central to the collage experimentation of surrealism or dadaism, nor do they evidence the randomness or ironic play typical of sixties British and American pop assemblages. Rather, like the consciously political photo works of the Berlin-based dadaists, especially John Heartfield, and the self-reflective cinematic technique with which Jean-Luc Godard began experimenting in the late sixties, Rosler utilizes found images not to produce "another" reality but to expose a material connection buried, denied, and mystified in dominant signifying practices, i.e., in popular magazines. Like all of the politically conscious members of her generation of American thinkers, artists, and activists, Rosler was influenced by her involvement with civil rights organizing against racism, the critique of imperialism and violence central to anti-Vietnam organizing, and the new demands for female autonomy that coalesced in the women's liberation movement. The collage technique employed in *Bringing the War Home* is politically axiomatic and executed with deliberate precision: the war images literally "fit" into the space of American domesticity. In a white, high-tech kitchen equipped with the most stylish contemporary consumer conveniences, two men in combat gear bend to the ground as if setting up another mortar round—but they do so as casually as if they were searching for a lost button. In another, set in a boy's bedroom, a young white boy is asleep while another is preoccupied at his desk; outside the room's window protesters are being brutally attacked by police, yet both boys are as oblivious to the struggle outside their own window as they might be to a Beatles poster hanging on the wall. In another, Pat Nixon smiles into the camera, surrounded by the elegant, French-inspired luxury of the White House, seemingly unaware of the bloodied woman pictured in a heavy gilt frame that hangs securely above the mantlepiece.[4]

Like Jean-Luc Godard's *Ici et ailleurs* (1974), which connects French consumerism ("here") with the Palestinian struggle ("elsewhere"), Rosler's *Bringing the War Home* asks us to consider the real social and economic connections between our comfortable sofas and some else's dead body. Rosler forefronts the false separation between "us" and "them," between "here" and "there," and suggests that this separation is an illusion that we, as a war-profit society and as immediately war-free individuals, are economically and emotionally invested in maintaining. While politically specific to the military aggression of the United States against the people of South Vietnam and visually coded via images produced and circulated within dominant popular media, Rosler's *Bringing the War Home* series asks viewers to confront the most basic philosophical question: Are you aware of who you are and what you are doing? This question rests at the basis of Rosler's aesthetics; all of her work urges an epistemology of the self that situates the "self" within an awareness of how individual identities and actions are bounded by political parameters.

During the eighties, many so-called postmodernist theoreticians denounced the proposition that any "self" is possible (or responsible) or that any representation can claim a hegemony of truth. Rosler's work is ambitious in its refusal to accept easy solutions to the theoretical problems that attend representation and in its concomitant insistence that real communication must be attempted. While theoretically motivated (Rosler's theoretical writings and lectures have been as influential as her visual works), she remains committed, to paraphrase Marx, to the idea that the purpose of theory is not to change theory but to change the inequity of social and political relationships. Or, as she informed one interviewer a few year ago: "You're not going to catch me saying there's such a thing as direct, unmediated truth, but there is more truth and less truth, better explanation and poorer explanation, better social practice and worse social practice."[5]

In one of her earliest videos, *Semiotics of the Kitchen* (1975), Rosler stands in a kitchen before a table piled with ordinary culinary utensils. As she recites the alphabet, she lifts an item to illustrate each letter ("A, apron, B, bowl, C, chopper . . ."); but the last six letters are represented only by sound and the image of a woman (Rosler), slicing the air with a knife. This glib performance suggests that any "semiotics of the kitchen" is only a fetish unless it is useful in liberating women from the tyranny of domestic servitude; with uncanny prescience,

Rosler's 1975 tape anticipated the depoliticization of Roland Barthes's potentially useful method. Like her contemporary Adrian Piper, Rosler adheres to an aesthetics of engagement that requires viewers to bring their lives with them to the art experience.

One of a first generation of video artists, Rosler began working with the then-new technology because "it could be used in some way to reverberate against television."[6] Like other first-generation feminist artists, Rosler includes her own body, and often her own experience, in much of her work. But the most distinctive personal attribute in her video works is usually her voice. As Amy Taubin has written, "Rosler's voice is one the strongest elements in her work. . . . Rosler's voice is tough, intelligent and unmistakably of Brooklyn origin." Writing of Rosler's *Vital Statistics of a Citizen Simply Obtained* (1977), Taubin heralds the "specificity" of Rosler's voice: "The voice of a specific person who grew up in a specific time, place and social class . . . her voice is her best argument against the social standardization that is the target of her tape."[7]

*Vital Statistics
of a Citizen
Simply Obtained*,
1977.
Color video,
39:20 minutes.
Electronic Arts
Intermix, New
York.

While attention to the specificity of lived experience is a guiding principle in Rosler's work (gender, class, race, and international concerns are always multivalenced in Rosler's representations, even in her projects from the early seventies, when such considerations were less in the forefront of most art practices), she also uses her voice as a problematizing mechanism. In *Martha Rosler Reads Vogue* (with Paper Tiger Television) (1982), her voice is the central carrier of meaning in a tape that literally enacts the title: the artist is visually and aurally presented, in real time and space, reading *Vogue* magazine. Her voice in this and other tapes is a curiously controlled instrument that speaks neither with heartfelt conviction nor with its opposite, adamant derision. An opening created from the tenor of her delivery excuses neither the narrator nor the viewer from the information; nor does it overly implicate her/us. Rather, the voice functions as a sign of distance and consideration, a Brechtian device that coaxes us to reflect on information with critical intelligence rather than easy emotion. In her first video, *A Budding Gourmet* (1974), a middle-class white American woman (Rosler) narrates her desire to learn to cook gourmet food (for her husband), as the camera shifts around from images of the woman to images of fancy food to images of starving people. The flat, monotonal

Laura Cottingham

the worse for liquor

top heavy   moon-eyed   owl-eyed

pie-eyed   shit-faced

snockered

shicker

The Bowery in Two Inadequate Descriptive Systems, 1974. Black and white print. 8 x 10 in. Courtesy Jay Gorney Modern Art, New York.

plastered   stuccoed

rosined   shellacked

vulcanized

inebriated

polluted

comatose   unconscious

passed out   knocked out

laid out

out of the picture

out like a light

T H E   B O W E R Y

in
two
inadequate
descriptive
systems

enunciation of this semiconfessional narrative helps reveal the multiple contradictions brought forth by the text, including national identity and imperialism ("I'm thankful we can give them [our children] the advantages of living in America. We can take the best of all times and places and make them our own"); classism ("Some people have money but no old-fashioned breeding"); blindness to the starvation of others (we, the viewers, see the starving, but she only talks of recipes); and, finally, ignorance of one's own subordination (it is for her husband and children that the woman must learn "to cook gourmet"). Rosler always keeps her voice at a mild variance with the words it is communicating, producing constant uncertainty about what is being said, why, and for whom: her voice is one of the most effective critical devices that any artist has yet used in video or film.

In one of her most influential projects, *The Bowery in Two Inadequate Descriptive Systems* (1974–75), black and white photographs of Bowery storefronts hang adjacent to clusters of typewritten words that mean "drunk." This piece challenges the inadequacy of pictures and words, simply stated, to reveal social reality, especially the reality of the "other," specifically the reality of "Bowery bums." As Craig Owens observed: "Most importantly, Rosler has refused to photograph the inhabitants of Skid row, to speak on their behalf, to illuminate them from a safe distance (photography as social work in the tradition of Jacob Riis). For 'concerned' or what Rosler calls 'victim' photography overlooks the constitutive role of its own activity to be merely representative (the 'myth' of photographic transparency and objectivity)."[8] Rosler insists that her critique "Doesn't mean that photography and, in particular, documentary, can't work in a project of social change, only that photography's role has to be re-thought."[9]

A piece produced for the traveling exhibition "Unknown Secrets: Art and the Rosenberg Era" synthesizes many of Rosler's concerns with the ideological (mis)recognitions activated by the categorical imperatives of gender, ethnicity, and nationalism. *The Secret of the Rosenbergs* (1988) is composed of three parts: a large framed canvas covered with silkscreened images taken from various printed sources, a simple wooden pedestal that holds a fourteen-page essay written by Rosler, and a wooden rack holding a printed dish towel and a box of Jello. The dominant image on the canvas is Ethel Rosenberg standing before a kitchen sink, wearing an apron, drying a dinner plate. Ethel Rosenberg is surrounded by various fifties icons: of motherhood, the arms race, and media photos of both Rosenbergs—including a display of their open coffins, which ran in Time magazine.

Rosler's text analyzes the 1951 trial and subsequent death sentence of Julius and Ethel Rosenberg for conspiracy to commit espionage. Her essay includes excerpts from the judge's hyperbolic sentencing speech, the rhetoric of which was reproduced, and amplified upon, by every major American news agency. It accuses the Rosenbergs of a "crime worse than murder," of altering "the course of history to the disadvantage of our country," and of "sacrificing their own children." Of course, as many thought then, the Rosenbergs could never have been important Soviet spies.

Rosler's piece re-presents Ethel Rosenberg as a psychic instance from the popular consciousness—a charged symbol that Rosler knows America would prefer to keep hidden. Given that the anticommunist hysteria of the fifties was an irrational national pathology, what were that actual fears that the Red scare sought to veil? According to President Eisenhower, whose words are printed on the dishtowel in *The Secret of the Rosenbergs,* Ethel Rosenberg "is the strong and recalcitrant character," and unless she receives the death sentence, "from here on in the Soviets would simply recruit their spies from among women." Rosler's text recounts the same exaggerated fear of women communists from a more recent *New York Times* editorial by

Richard Nixon. Commenting on the Alger Hiss case in 1986, Nixon cautioned that: "In the case of Communist couples . . . the wife is often more extremist than the husband." While suggesting that men's need to control women helped marshal the murderous scapegoating of the Rosenbergs, the Jello box included in the piece also forefronts the complete absurdity of the whole situation. Although Rosler could have presented the Jello box as a blind signifier of the empty artificiality of fifties America in general and the kitchen-wife imprisonment of women in particular, it actually refers specifically to the Rosenberg trial. The primary witness against the couple, David Greenglass, claimed that Julius Rosenberg used half of a Jello box as a (Communist spy) recognition device. In Rosler's tableaux, the box that rests atop a towel rack is whole; and, like the severed one offered as evidence during the trial (in replica, as Rosler notes), it is imitation raspberry flavor.[10]

Rosler's latest project, *In the Place of the Public* (1980-93), is an installation of color photographs taken in airports and circumscribed by wall texts. These images—advertisements, motorized walkways, baggage carts, rolls of empty chairs, and other standard airport props—obliquely question the relation between public and private space. One photograph of empty, worn upholstered seats evokes the weary loneliness of air travel and the impersonality of communal space in most industrialized societies while recalling a living room couch that isn't really as inviting or comfortable as we'd like to think it could or should be. Other images of stewards and stewardesses between flight shifts or passengers navigating the walking patterns proscribed by airline terminals reveal the subtle play of human action within institutional situations. In another photo, taken in Chicago's O'Hare Airport, a reflection of moving passengers is captured on an advertisement for channel 7, where a glare blankets the eyes of featured newscaster Peter Jennings, blinding him. This image of his lost vision renders ironic the ad copy printed beneath Jennings's head—although, as a literal statement, it aptly summarizes Rosler's twenty-five-year practice: "Look at the news with more intelligence."

In the Place of the Public, 1980-93. C-prints. 26.6 x 40 in. each. Vinyl wall lettering. Courtesy Jay Gorney Modern Art, New York.

Notes:

This essay was originally published in a slightly different form in *Frieze* (November-December 1993): 52-55, under the title "Crossing Borders: Laura Cottingham on Martha Rosler."

1. In 1993, Rosler joined a commercial gallery, Jay Gorney Modern Art, New York. Before that, her influence resulted from various independent and group exhibitions and the art education system. Since the mid-seventies, she has been a visiting lecturer at nearly every art school in America; she is currently professor of visual art at Rutgers University.
2. For instance, one of Rosler's antiwar montages appeared in the October 13, 1970, issue of *Goodbye to All That*, a feminist newspaper in San Diego. Ten of the images from this series were exhibited, for the first time in a fine art context, at the Simon Watson Gallery, October 1991. Some of my comments here originally appeared in my "The War Is Always Home: Martha Rosler," which accompanied that exhibition. Rosler's art was first shown publicly in 1973, when *Monumental Garage Sale* was installed/performed at the University of California, San Diego, where Rosler was a graduate student in fine arts. The piece included tables piled with used clothes, personal letters, records, magazines, and other discarded items assembled from the artist's possessions and those of her friends. It also included a show of personal slides that Rosler had purchased from a dead man's garage sale and an audiotape that accompanied the projected images. It was, as Rosler remembers, her "attempt to produce a portrait of a person through things" and a reflection on America's, especially southern California's, "reliance on commodity culture as a substitute for human relations."
3. Rosler, telephone interview, New York, September 23, 1991.
4. In the Pat Nixon piece, the bloodied woman is not taken from documentary photos of the war, like most of the violence represented in this series, but is the police-bulleted Bonnie (Faye Dunaway) from Arthur Penn's 1967 film *Bonnie and Clyde*.
5. Steven Edwards, "Secrets from the Street and Other Stories," *TEN 8 Magazine*, no. 35 (Winter 1989–90).
6. From an interview with Martha Rosler included on program 2, tape 1, of "The First Generation: Woman and Video, 1970–75," curated by Jo Ann Hanley for Independent Curators Incorporated, New York, 1993.
7. Amy Taubin, "'And what is a fact anyway?' (On a Tape by Martha Rosler)," *Millennium Film Journal*, no. 4/5 (Summer/Fall 1979).
8. Craig Owens, "The Discourse of Others: Feminists and Postmodernism," in *The Anti-Aesthetic*, ed. Hal Foster (Port Townsend, Wash.: Bay Press, 1983), 57–77.
9. Edwards, "Secrets from the Streets."
10. The absurdity of the Jello Box evidence reverberates against an equally bizarre and fantastic item of "evidence" produced in the McCarthy-led hysteria during the testimony of Whitaker Chambers against J. Alger Hiss, who, like the Rosenbergs, was convicted on fabricated charges of Communist espionage (but, unlike the Rosenbergs, not executed). Chambers claimed that Hiss kept rolls of conspiratorial film inside a pumpkin in a pumpkin patch! That a Jello box and a pumpkin emerged as two of the dominant iconic containers of nationalist betrayal perhaps indicates just how far-flung was the displaced anxiety that motivated the Red Scare. While the dominant rhetoric claimed Communism as the threat, the coextensive targets—and perhaps the real social and emotional threat to American popular identity—were Jews, homosexuals, and, as Eisenhower's and Nixon's words make clear, women.

Silueta Works in Mexico, 1973-77.
Color photograph documenting earth/body work. 20 x 16 in.
Courtesy The Estate of Ana Mendieta and Galerie Lelong, New York.

Bloody Valentines: Afterimages by Ana Mendieta

There is no original past to redeem: there is the void, the orphanhood, the unbaptized earth of the beginning, the time that from within the earth looks upon us. There is above all the search for origin.
—Ana Mendieta[1]

The souvenir speaks to a context of origin through a language of longing, for it is not an object arising out of need or use value; it is an object arising out of the necessarily insatiable demands of nostalgia.
—Susan Stewart[2]

Ana Mendieta's body disappeared long ago. A sudden passage that lasted about four seconds . . . a lifetime.

September 8, 1995, marked the tenth anniversary of her dramatic death from a fall through an apartment window in Greenwich Village in New York City. But the lack of clarity concerning her final moments and the subsequent irresolution of the exact cause of her death still loom large as the fact of the event continues to cast its dark shadow over her art works, infecting all possible readings and interpretations of them. Like many others now, I come to Mendieta's work as a stranger, infected to be sure by the partial and fragmentary knowledge of her nomadic life as an exile from Cuba at age thirteen, the painful years of isolation and alienation growing up as an "orphan" in Iowa, and her early death under dubious circumstances at age thirty-six, when she was just beginning to receive serious critical attention for her work from the New York and international art communities.[3] The looping temporality of retrospection seems inescapable, and the desire to narrate a direct, meaningful connection between her art and her life/death is overwhelming—setting up one as the manifestation and explanation for the other and vice versa. But such an interpretation would do a disservice to both as it would not only decontextualize her body of work and her body as source of her work from their historical and cultural specificities, but also suspend a recognition of my own writing as undeniably located. Mid-1990s, New York City. Mine is the moment of so-called postfeminisms.

Recent exhibitions and critical debates focusing on feminism (most often as subject matter and not so much as a structural problematic) reveal a common, albeit complicated, double imperative. On the one hand, there seems to be a need at this particular moment to consider the legacies of the feminist art movement primarily from a historical perspective, an attempt to clarify the various political, artistic, and intellectual shifts of the past thirty years or so via periodization. On the other hand is a related need to grapple with this legacy in order to redefine or reformulate what (post)feminist art and cultural practices might/should look like for the present and future.[4] This project of writing the history of feminist practices (always with a secret desire to be prescriptive in some way) is a highly contested and controversial enterprise with as many positions of allegiance as there are individual feminists. But within this multifaceted, complex, and emotional struggle, a vague and uncomfortable, embarrassingly simplistic but undeniable distinction of at least two seemingly irreconcilable "camps" emerges. At the crux of this distinction is the status of the body *in* representation and *as* representation. That is, the body as a transparent signifier of identity and self versus the body as a nexus of arbitrary conventions of meaning, the body as signature or sign.

Feminist artworks that foreground(ed) the physicality of the female body, sometimes celebrating its biological functions (menstruation and childbearing) as well as valorizing socially ordained "women's work" (the domestic labor of cooking, cleaning, and sewing), and artworks that treat(ed) the female body as a direct source of meaning and imagery have been cast as belonging to (or directly aligned with) an earlier moment in the feminist movement. Problematically, the diverse practices from the late 1960s through the 1970s of artists including Judy Chicago, Miriam Shapiro, Carolee Schneemann, Audrey Flack, Hannah Wilke, and others are loosely grouped and associated with "a belief in female sexuality as an innate quality . . . produced [at a time] when women's demands for an autonomous and self-defined sexuality became a metaphor for the struggle for personal liberation."[5] Fairly or not, many contemporary feminist critics berate this strategy as essentialist because the "feminine" and "woman" are presented as ahistorical categories with characteristics belonging naturally and universally to one gender. This strategy thus upholds rather than challenges the patriarchal hierarchies of sexual difference, which is in fact engendered by specific sociocultural conventions and ideologies.

Silueta Works in Mexico,
1976-78.
From portfolio of twelve
color photographs.
20 x 13 1/4 in.
Courtesy The Estate of Ana
Mendieta and Galerie
Lelong, New York.

In turn, this antiessentialist or constructivist position, generally associated with the feminist practices of the 1980s that engage(d) psychoanalysis, poststructuralism, and Marxist-influenced social critiques, in directing its attention to a critical analysis of the body (and identity) as a fluctuating, coded *effect* of social and cultural contingencies, has been attacked for its perceived inability to deal with the primacy of the "real" physical body. Theoretically driven postmodern feminist works that attempt(ed) to understand the categories of "feminine" and "woman" as functions of language and systems of representation rather than as a given biological distinction (I'm thinking of works by Mary Kelly, Silvia Kolbowski, Cindy Sherman, Barbara Kruger, Sherrie Levine, and others) have been accused of intellectual elitism.

While most feminist practitioners would agree on the need to do away with this kind of binary opposition, some going so far as to embrace all forms of women's art as manifestations of a healthy pluralistic diversity *within* a very broadly conceived feminist art practice and history, the poles of this opposition nevertheless remain a framework for current debates concerning feminism(s). Within this context, how might one reconsider Ana Mendieta's work? Or, more productively, might a reconsideration of Mendieta's work complicate the terms of the current feminist debate?

In the conceptual framework outlined above, Mendieta's work, especially the well-known projects from the 1970s, such as the *Silueta*, *Fetish*, and *Rupestrian Sculptures* series, veer strongly toward the essentialist pole in both intention and reception. The *Silueta* series, for example, was executed originally as outdoor performances in various locations in Iowa and Mexico throughout a seven-year period, from 1973 to 1980. In the series, which now exists primarily in the form of documentary photographs, the artist marked various natural landscapes with traces of her own body. Sometimes she molded mud, sand, and stones alongside a creek bed to register a thick and wet outline of her five-foot figure. Sometimes she gathered flowers to decorate her body or to follow its contours. Sometimes she imprinted barely visible silhouettes of herself onto grassy meadows. Sometimes she "drew" the perimeter of her body with an arrangement of burning candles. Sometimes, in a more explosive gesture, she burned gunpowder to create ash pits the size and shape of a human being or ignited fireworks whose blazing form in the night sky echoed the artist's upright, open-arm stance.

Untitled, 1983. Photo of carved clay bed, Iowa. Courtesy The Estate of Ana Mendieta and Galerie Lelong, New York.

Of the *Silueta* series, perhaps the most reproduced if not the most powerful set of Mendieta's works, the artist wrote in 1981, "My art . . . is a return to the maternal source. Through my earth/body sculptures I become one with the earth . . . I become an extension of nature and nature becomes and extension of my body. This obsessive act of reasserting my ties with the earth is really the reactivation of primeval beliefs . . . [in] an omnipresent female force, the after-image of being encompassed within the womb, in a manifestation of my thirst for being."[6] Both male and female critics, perhaps taking their cues from the artist, continue to view the strength of Mendieta's work as essentially female—as artistic imagery and power exclusive to women. William Zimmer commented rather crudely in 1979, "Mendieta offers photographs of alterations she has made on landscape sites. These marks are dubbed 'silhou-ettes' but are really vaginas on the hillside or on the grass. The Abstract Expressionists wished to identify their bodies with the earth, but as men couldn't come this close."[7] A more recent reviewer stridently asserted: "Mendieta hails women as omnipotent creators, not slavish bio-logical reproducers. . . . Female body one with the earthen core, the feminine creative spirit reasserts her fertile sovereignty. The female force becomes primary mover."[8] Fellow artist Nancy Spero in a tribute to Ana Mendieta noted the timeless quality of this feminine creative force: "If one of her sculptures were sent to a distant planet, or were kept sealed for thou-sands of years on earth, it would still convey the imagery, strength, mystery, and sexuality of the female human form—woman's body and spirit inscribed."[9]

Countless others have interpreted Mendieta's schematic and iconographic use of the female body in her earth/body works of the 1970s as an "affirmation of female power, the female body, the female will, and women's bonds and heritage."[10] But often projected as a kind of (feminist) primitivist fantasy, this female power has been configured as a primordial natural force, exceeding historical and cultural specificities. In characterizations like "Ana Mendieta's Primal Scream: With Fire, Water, Blood, and Earth as Her Medium, This Cuban-Born Artist was the High Priestess of Performance Work,"[11] and "Ana *became* the earth and the earth goddess became Ana. By 1980, when the [*Silueta*] series ended, Ana and the god-dess were one,"[12] the willful identification of the artist with some elemental, (super)natural feminine power was emphatic. Recruiting the imagery, ritual, and symbolism of various god-dess-worshipping religions and traditions, Mendieta, like many other women artists of the period, claimed power through a process of self-othering—a self-primitivizing that located the "feminine" and "woman" anterior to historical time (moving to *pre*history) and outside "civi-lized" cultural spaces (siting the work in the "other" space of nature or treating the body as a natural site).[13] Mendieta, of course, did both. And the allure of her identity as a Third World woman artist surely added to the exoticism of her works in light of the entrenched primitivist tendencies of 1970s feminist discourse and in the general discourse on Western modernism.

Yet something enigmatic remains, especially concerning the configuration of the *Silueta* series, a peculiarity that spills over and exceeds this feminist framing. Mendieta's use of her/the body almost always approached erasure or negation: her "body" consistently disap-peared. This is striking given that most feminist artists during the 1970s vied for visibility and self-affirming expression through figurative, literal, sometimes "in-your-face" presence. It is curious that Mendieta traced her absence instead. Even when considered within a broader context of other contemporary experiments in earth/body works, such as Dennis Oppenheim's *Rocked Hand* (1970) or Charles Simonds's *Landscape—Body—Dwelling* (1970), Mendieta's substitution of negative imprints for positive figures seems anomalous. Her sensi-bility as expressed in exemplary works like the *Silueta* series, in other words, cannot be attributed simply to her sex.

Some critics have sought to explain the dominant presence of absence (as well as other macabre themes) in Mendieta's work as indicative of an "aesthetic lust for death" provoked by her traumatic separation from her family and homeland during childhood and further intensi-fied by her obsessive longing throughout her adult life for a reunion with them.[14] This desire for reunification, having accumulated a familiar romantic sheen, is described in Mendieta's case as a spiritual wandering of an exile's quest for her origins—a quest in which the "origi-nal" site prior to civilization (nature) is conflated or confused with a personal origin. The artist herself claimed that the overwhelming feeling "of having been cast from the womb (nature)" was a motivating force in her work. "My art is the way I reestablish the bonds that unite me with the universe."[15]

Silueta Works in Mexico,
1976-78.
Color photograph docu-
menting earth/body work.
20 x 16 in.
Courtesy The Estate of
Ana Mendieta and Galerie
Lelong, New York.

Silueta Series, 1979.
Color photograph of gun-
powder. 8 x 10 in.
Courtesy The Estate of
Ana Mendieta and Galerie
Lelong, New York.

The perception of mythic power associated with the various images of negative empty bodies in Mendieta's tracings is reinforced by the ways in which documentary images of these performances have come to stand in for the production of them as events—indeed as surrogates for the artist's experience of "making" them. The importance of understanding the role of Mendieta's images in relation to her actions in the landscape, however, does not rest solely on the fact that photography can no longer sustain its position as innocent documentation. Rather, even as we acknowledge photographic documentation as integral to the construction of meaning around performance and earth art, we must give special attention in the case of Mendieta's work because photography here serves a specific function. As delayed relays, photographs of Mendieta's work register at another level an absence already contained *within* her work. If the performative aspect of her work represented an unrelenting desire to reach an origin forever irretrievable, the photographic mediation that records this effort structurally echoes and mimics the impossible longing. Always pointing to a singular moment unavailable to the viewers of her images, the original act of creation is distanced by the photographs as an irretrievable origin. The possibility of repetitive reproduction afforded by photography determines the unrepeatability of experiential events: the appropriation of distance in time and space engendered by photographs never delivers on its promise of contact.

Silueta Works in
Iowa, 1976-78.
Color photograph.
16 x 20 in.
Courtesy The
Estate of Ana
Mendieta and
Galerie Lelong,
New York.

The double void—the missing body *in* the image and the missing event *of* the image—articulated in Mendieta's body tracings and translated through photography, then, highlights a distinction between the photograph as documentation and the photograph as souvenir. While a document is predicated on the belief of an authentic moment of origin, the souvenir is based on a recognition of its loss. If for no other reason, Mendieta's photographs function like souvenirs. As Susan Stewart has remarked,

> We might say that this capacity of objects to serve as traces of authentic experience is, in fact, exemplified by the souvenir. The souvenir distinguishes experiences. We do not need or desire souvenirs of events that are repeatable. Rather we need and desire souvenirs of events that are reportable, events whose materiality has escaped us, events that thereby exist only through the invention of narrative. Through narrative the souvenir substitutes a context of perpetual consumption for its context of origin.[16]

In other words, unlike documents, which maintain a connection to the moment of creation, souvenirs are material markers of events recognized, perhaps unconsciously, as too distant or already lost, and they provoke the production of narratives as compensation for this loss.

The narrative that has come to "substitute . . . for [the] context of origin" in relation to Mendieta's artistic production, as with all souvenirs, is intimate and biographical. Indeed, references to aspects of her personal life, full of emotionally traumatic losses, displacements, and separations, are offered frequently to explain the sense of loss and absence that strongly resonates in her work; her work is almost always seen to be material expressions of her subjectivity and identity. The common attribution of the violence implicit in so much of Mendieta's work to her "fiery" Latin nature is one caricaturish example of this tendency. But the gap or void that is "embodied" in her work is inherent in all longing for an original (re)union. And the biography to which many critics and viewers turn to understand this gap is not so much the source of the work as a product of it. Negative residues of actions, the essence of Mendieta's work through the 1970s, provoke mythification through biographical storytelling, filling precisely the space of absence that is so impossible to narrate. The biographical turn, indeed, is the narrative invention that continuously misrecognizes its "context of perpetual consumption" for the "context of origin."

One might say that Ana Mendieta was a rather selfish artist, not only because she sought remote and secluded areas to execute her work, often in solitude, but because she seems to have consciously "hidden" her work as a secret origin. In order to make her work (in)visible, she recruited the camera to (re)discover for her audience the traces of her actions after the fact, seeking to authenticate the experience for herself and others, but ultimately authenticating it for no one. As viewers, we always arrive too late on the scene. The immediacy of her experience of marking the landscape, guaranteed by the image that registers its distance in space and time, has already been transferred from origin to trace, transformed from event to memory to desire.[17]

NOTES:

1. Undated note by Ana Mendieta, as cited by Robert Katz in *Naked by the Window: The Fatal Marriage of Carl Andre and Ana Mendieta* (New York: The Atlantic Monthly Press, 1990), 123.
2. Susan Stewart, *On Longing: Narratives of the Miniature, the Gigantic, the Souvenir, the Collection* (Baltimore: Johns Hopkins University Press, 1984), 135.
3. As is well known, Ana Mendieta's husband, the famous minimalist sculptor Carl Andre, was charged with murder in the second degree for her death. He was acquitted of the crime in a juryless trial in 1988.
4. Exhibitions "Bad Girls," organized by the New Museum of Contemporary Art (1994), "Sense and Sensibility," organized by the Museum of Modern Art (1994), and "Division of Labor," organized by the Bronx Museum (1995), are recent curatorial endeavors exemplary of this phenomenon. See also the special issue on "Feminist Issue(s)" edited by Silvia Kolbowski, *October* 71 (Winter 1995); Norma Broude and Mary Garrard, eds., *The Power of Feminist Art: The American Movement of the 1970's, History and Impact* (New York: Abrams, 1994); and Judith Butler and Joan W. Scott, eds., *Feminists Theorize the Political* (New York: Routledge, 1992), as examples of the historical and critical counterpart to this examination.
5. Whitney Chadwick, *Women, Art, and Society* (London: Thames and Hudson, 1990), 355.
6. Ana Mendieta, as quoted by John Perreault in "Earth and Fire, Mendieta's Body of Work," *Ana Mendieta: A Retrospective*, exhib. cat. (New York: New Museum of Contemporary Art, 1987), 10.
7. William Zimmer, "Artists Only," *Soho Weekly News*, 1979, as quoted by Petra Barreras del Rio in "Ana Mendieta: A Historical Overview," *Ana Mendieta: A Retrospective*, 33.
8. Nancy Shalala, "Artist Gets Physical for Feminism," *Japan Times*, September 27, 1992, 11.
9. Nancy Spero, "Tracing Ana Mendieta," *Artforum* (April 1992): 77.
10. Chadwick, *Women, Art, and Society*, 324. See also Lucy Lippard, *Overlay: Contemporary Art and the Art of Prehistory* (New York: Pantheon, 1983), for a similar characterization.
11. Title of an article by Heidi Rauch and Federico Suro in *Américas* 44, no. 5 (1992): 45–48.
12. Rachel Mendieta, "Ana Mendieta: Self-Portrait of a Goddess," *Review: Latin American Literature and Arts* (January–June 1988): 39.
13. Of course, many male artists of the period invoked and searched for "other" sites, too, often in nature—Charles Simonds, Dennis Oppenheim, Robert Morris, Robert Smithson, Richard Long, and Michael Heizer, among others. But as many feminist art historians have noted, their works tended to be gestures of control and domination of nature rather than respectful homages to it. Such a critique, however, is based on a problematic identification of the female body with the earth, which puts into equivalence women's itinerant vulnerability, in sociopolitical terms, with the earth's physical vulnerability. In contradistinction to the male artists' ventures into nature, Nancy Spero wrote of Mendieta's work: "Ana did not rampage the earth to control or dominate or create grandiose monuments of power and authority. She sought intimate, recessed spaces, protective habitats signaling a temporary respite of comfort and meditation."
14. Gregory Galligan, "Ana Mendieta: A Retrospective," *Arts Magazine* (April 1988): 49. See also Donald Kuspit's review of the exhibition "Ana Mendieta: A Retrospective" in *Artforum* (February 1988): 144. Kuspit notes, "Mendieta's art often takes the form of a peculiar violation of Mother Earth, who has abandoned her, and with whom she is perpetually trying to remerge. . . . The ultimate, literal reunion with Mother Earth is of course death."
15. Ana Mendieta, as quoted by Galligan, "Ana Mendieta: A Retrospective."
16. Stewart, *On Longing*, 135.
17. Ibid., 134.

BURNT ORANGE GIRL

Burnt Orange Girl (Colored People), 1989-90.
Monochrome color print, 30 x 30 in. matted.
Courtesy of the artist and P.P.O.W. Gallery, New York.

Carrie Mae Weems:
Diasporic Landscapes of Longing

bell hooks

> We take home and language for granted; they become nature and
> their underlying assumptions recede into dogma and orthodoxy.
> The exile knows that in a secular and contingent world, homes are always provisional. Borders and
> barriers, which enclose us within the safety of familiar territory, can also become prisons, and are often
> defended beyond reason or necessity. Exiles cross borders, break barriers of thought and experience.
> —Edward Said, *Reflections on Exile*

When I was a little girl in the rural South, we would sometimes go to country churches. Traveling down narrow, dusty, unpaved roads, past fields and fields of crops and chewing tobacco, we would ride into a wilderness of nature, arrive late, and yet be welcomed into a hot, crowded sanctuary full of holiness and grace. To awaken a spirit of ecstatic reverie, the choir would sing this song with a line that just made folks shout and cry out with joy, "I wouldn't take nothing for my journey now." This line affirmed a vision of life in which all experience, good and bad, everything that happened, could retrospectively be seen as a manifestation of divine destiny. It called on believers to lay claim to an inclusive spirit of unconditional acceptance that would enable all of us to see every path we had taken in life, whether chosen or not, as a necessary one—preparing us for that return to a home we could only dream about. The multilayered vision of life's journey celebrated in this old-time black church song, where every bit of history and experience is seen as essential to the unfolding of one's destiny, is rearticulated in the artistic practices of Carrie Mae Weems.

Traditionally trained in mainstream art schools where there was little or no awareness of the way in which the politics of white supremacy shaped and informed academic pedagogies of photographic practice, Weems made a conscious decision to work with black subjects. This choice preceded contemporary academic focus on decentering Western civilization, which necessarily requires that attention shift from a central concern with white subjects. Ironically, for the most part, cultural criticism that calls for acts of intervention that would decenter the West tends to reprivilege whiteness by investing in a politics of representation that merely substitutes the central image of colonizing oppressive whiteness with that of a *newly* reclaimed radical whiteness portrayed as liberatory. Whiteness then remains the starting point for all progressive cultural journeying—that movement across borders which invites the world to take note, to pay attention, to give critical affirmation. The much talked-about discourse of postcoloniality is a critical location that, ironically, often maintains white cultural hegemony. The less well-recognized discursive practices of anticolonialism, on the other hand, decenter, interrogate, and displace whiteness. This discourse disrupts accepted epistemologies to make room for an inclusive understanding of radical subjectivity that allows recognition and appreciation of the myriad ways individuals from oppressed or marginalized groups create oppositional cultural strategies that can be meaningfully deployed by everyone. This constructive cultural appropriation happens only as shifts in standpoint take place, when there is ongoing transformation of ways of seeing that sustain oppositional spheres of representation.

The work of Carrie Mae Weems visually engages a politics of anticolonialism. Concretely decentering the white subject, she challenges viewers to shift their paradigms. Although her work encourages us not to see the black subject through the totalizing lens of race, it is often discussed as though the sign of racial difference is the only relevant visual experience her images evoke. This way of seeing actively reappropriates the work and reinscribes it within the dominant cultural hegemony of Western imperialism and colonialism. By choosing to concentrate attention on black subjects, Weems risks this oversimplification of her artistic practice. In her work, however, she consistently invites us to engage the black subject in ways that call attention to the specificity of race even as we engage an emotional landscape that challenges us to look beyond race and recognize the multiple concerns represented. Unfortunately, the failure to move beyond a conventional practice of art criticism that consistently confines black artists within a discourse that is always and only about racial otherness characterizes much critical writing about Weems's work. Transforming ways of seeing means that we learn to see race—thereby no longer acting in complicity with a white-supremacist aesthetic that would have us believe issues of color and race have no place in artistic practices—without privileging it as the only relevant category of analysis. Carrie Mae Weems's photoworks create a cartography of experience wherein race, gender, and class identity converge, fuse, and mix so as to disrupt and deconstruct simple notions of subjectivity.

While Weems's decision to concentrate on black subjects was a challenge to white cultural hegemony, it signaled, more importantly, the emergence of a lifelong commitment to recover and bring to the foreground subjugated knowledge relating to African-American experience. Although Weems was initially captivated by mainstream documentary photography, learning from the work of photographers from Henri Cartier-Bresson to Roy DeCarava, she critically engages a process of image making that fuses diverse traditions and engages mixed media. Early in her artistic development, she was particularly inspired by DeCarava's visual representations of black subjects that invert the dominant culture's aesthetics, in which, informed by racist thinking, blackness was iconographically seen as a marker of ugliness. DeCarava endeavored to reframe the black image within a subversive politics of representation that challenged the logic of racist colonization and dehumanization. Moving among and within the public and private worlds of poor and working-class black experience, which mainstream white culture perceived only as a location of deprivation and spiritual and emotional "ugliness," DeCarava created images of black folks embodying a spirit of abundance and plenty; he claimed blackness as the aesthetic space of ethereal beauty, of persistent, unsuppressed elegance and grace.

Such work fits most neatly into the category that the critic Saidiya Hartman identified as artistic practice aimed at "rescuing and recovering the black subject" via a "critical labor of the positive. It is a resolutely counterhegemonic labor that has as its aim the establishment of other standards of aesthetic value and visual possibility. The intention of the work is corrective representation." Weems extended DeCarava's legacy beyond the investment in creating positive images. Her images problematizing black subjectivity expand the visual discursive field. Weems's journey, beginning with this "critical labor of the positive," is fundamentally altered and refigured as her relation to the black image is transformed by a politics of dislocation. In her early work, Weems's perception of black subjectivity departed from a concern with the positive and refigured itself within a field of contestation, wherein identity is always fluid, always changing.

Weems is engaged in a process of border crossing, of living within a social context of cultural hybridity. Her understanding of black subjectivity is informed by what Paul Gilroy identified as "the powerful effects of even temporary experiences of exile, relocation, and displacement." Indeed, it is the effort to recover subjugated knowledge within the realm of visual representation that brings Weems face to face with the limitations of essentialist constructions of black identity.

Contrary to critical discussion that sees Weems as laying claim to an "authentic" black experience, her explorative journeys of recovery and return merely expose how reality is distorted when a unitary representation of black subjectivity is reinscribed rather than consistently challenged. When Weems made the decision to focus on black subjects—as she put it, to "dig in my own backyard"—she was motivated by a longing to restore knowledge, not by a desire to uphold an essentialist politics of representation. (A distinction must be made here between the critical project that seeks to promote a notion of authentic blackness and efforts to reclaim the past that are a gesture of critical resistance and remembrance.) While Weems drew on her family history in the series *Family Pictures and Stories,* her narrative deflects any one-dimensional construction of these works as "positive" images deployed to challenge racist stereotypes. She not only named her location as that of the outsider who has journeyed away from family and community of origin to return with new perspectives, she juxtaposed and contrasted her memories of people with the present reality. Balancing image making that commemorates the past with the act of highlighting the ways in which the meaning of this past is changed by interrogations in the present, Weems celebrated what Roger Simon called "processes of collective remembrance." He explained: "Central to these processes is a procedure within which images and stories of a shared past are woven together with a person (or group's) feelings and comprehension of their embodied presence in time and space. These processes of remembrance are organized and produced within practices of commemoration which initiate and structure the relation between a representation of past events and that constellation of affect and information which defines a standpoint from which various people engage such representations."

Commemoration is central to Weems's artistic practice. From early work that focused on constructing images and narratives of families, she moved into an exploration of the journey from Africa to the so-called New World. There she looked at African-American ideas of home, community, and nation, particularly as expressed in vernacular, working-class culture. Visually revisiting slavery, the Middle Passage, Reconstruction, the civil rights era, and on to militant black power activism, Weems has created images that chart the passion of rebellion and resistance. Commemorative plates remind us of the nature of that journey. Simon called this process "insurgent commemoration" that "attempts to construct and engage representations that rub taken-for-granted history against the grain so as to revitalize and rearticulate what one sees as desirable and necessary for an open, just and life-sustaining future." In the series *Ain't Jokin,* Weems used wit and satire to exorcise the power of racist representation. Referencing racist iconography, as well as highlighting folklore used to perpetuate white supremacy in everyday life, that makes this iconography appear matter of fact, while contrasting these images with narrative statements that problematize, Weems deconstructed these ways of knowing. Throughout her work, she has relied on strategies of deconstruction to challenge conventional perceptions created by our attachment to fixed ways of looking that lead to blind spots.

EBO LANDING

One midnight at high tide a
ship bringing in a cargo of Ebo (Ibo)
men landed at Dunbar Creek on the
Island of St. Simons. But the men refused to be sold into slavery; joining hands
together they turned back toward the
water, chanting, "the water brought us,
the water will take us away." They all
drowned, but to this day when the
breeze sighs over the marshes and
through the trees, you can hear the
clank of chains and echo of
their chant at Ebo Landing.

Sea Islands Series, 1992
Two gelatin silver prints, one
text panel.
20 x 20 in. each panel,
edition of 10.
Courtesy of the artist and
P.P.O.W. Gallery,
New York.

Installation View of
Sea Islands, 1992.
Courtesy of the artist and
P.P.O.W. Gallery,
New York.

In the installation *and 22 Million Very Tired and Very Angry People,* Weems created an assemblage of carefully chosen political narratives—the declarative confessions of working-class activists, the lyrical prose of the novelist—and placed them with specific images. No fixed, authentic black subject is represented in this piece. The common bond is not race or shared history but, rather, an emotional universe inhabited by individuals committed to ending domination, oppression, and injustice around the world; who are linked together across the boundaries of space, time, race, culture, nationality, and even life and death, by a shared commitment to struggle. As this installation makes clear, rage against injustice, as well as the weariness that comes with protracted struggle, is not the exclusive property of black people. As the image of the globe suggests, it is present wherever oppression and exploitation prevail in daily life.

In this installation, Weems laid claim to a diasporic vision of journeying in search of freedom and strategies of resistance and fulfillment. She has staked her claim by inhabiting the space of blackness in the United States, but also by refusing to stay in her place and rejecting a narrow identity politics imposed by systems of domination. The radical black subjectivity mirrored in this installation audaciously unites that particularity with a universal transcendent emotional landscape wherein the desire to be free is the tie that binds and creates continuity in the midst of discontinuity. Within the emotional landscape of this work, the *Sea Islands* series, and the images of *Gorée Island,* Weems established a commonality of longing, of yearning for connection, for home. Here home is not a place but a condition—felt only when there is freedom of movement and expression. It is the seeking that is shared, not what is found.

The will to search out spaces of recovery and renewal led Carrie Mae Weems to Africa. Articulating with satiric wit the contemplative significance of that search in *Went Looking for Africa,* she problematized this dream of exile and return, of homecoming. She found in the Sea Islands African cultural retentions that link blackness in the diaspora, that create an imaginative world wherein Africa can be represented as present yet far away, as both real and mythic. To distinguish this search for subjugated knowledge from nostalgic longing for the mythical, paradisiacal homeland that is so often the imperialist vision imposed by contemporary Afrocentric black neonationalism, Weems presented images of specific locations. She arranged these sites to compose a ritual of seduction that evokes an emotional connection between Africans and African-Americans, even if that common bond cannot always be documented with visual proof of African cultural retentions in the United States. Her work offers documentary "proof' even as it tells us that this is ultimately not as important as the abiding sense of emotional and spiritual connection that imperialism and colonialism have not been able to suppress.

Within a political context of anticolonialism, Weems positions her work on Africa as a counterhegemonic response to the Western cultural imperialism that systematically erases that connection—that diasporic bond—which links all black people. To do this she decenters the West by abandoning notions that reason is the only way to apprehend the universe. This serves to promote alternative means by which we can know what connects us to distant places, to folks we have never seen but somehow recognize in our hearts as kin. Jane Flax challenged progressive thinkers to resist investing "in the primacy of reason," to prevent it from occupying "a privileged place within our subjectivity or political hopes." With her images of African sites, Weems has insisted on rituals of commemoration that can be understood only within the context of an oppositional world view, wherein intuition, magic, dream lore are all acknowledged to be ways of knowing that enhance our experience of life, that sweeten the journey. When Weems looks to Africa, it is to rediscover and remember an undocumented past even as she simultaneously creates a relationship forced in the concrete dailiness of the present. For example, in the *Gorée Island* series, captivity is evoked by the depiction of spaces that convey a spirit of containment. A cultural genealogy of loss and abandonment is recorded in the words Weems stacked on top of one another: "Congo, Ibo, Mandingo, Togo." These markers of heritage, legacy, and location in history stand in direct contrast to those words that evoke dislocation, displacement, dismemberment: "Grabbing, Snatching, Blink, And You Be Gone." Whereas the *Sea Islands* series marks the meeting ground between Africa and America, the *Gorée Island* images articulate a decolonized politics of resistance. They represent a return that counters the loss of the Middle Passage, the recovery that is made possible because of revolution and resistance, through ongoing anticolonial struggle. Weems is not attempting to create an ethnographic cartography to document diasporic black connections. Her work does not record a journey to unearth essential, authentic black roots, even though it will likely be critically discussed and arranged by curators in a manner that makes this appropriative reinscription possible. Weems is most concerned with ways such knowledge remakes and transforms contemporary radical black subjectivity. A spirit of contestation that emerges with the *Went Looking for Africa* series exposes the way Western imperialism informs the relationship of African-Americans to Africa. Yet the failure to embrace a progressive, anticolonial standpoint as the perspective that might enable everyone in the West, including black folks, to see Africa differently in no way delegitimizes the longing to return to Africa as origin site, as location of possible spiritual renewal. The Africa Weems visually represented in the *Gorée Island* series is both a site for insurgent commemorative remembrance and a contemporary location that must be engaged on its own terms, in the present.

Weems has centralized architectural images, linking traditional dwellings with modern space. In these images, Africa is both familiar homeland and location of Otherness. Fundamentally, it is a place that awakens the senses, enabling us to move into a future empowered by the previously subjugated knowledge that we cannot allow reason to overdetermine constructions of identity and community. As Bernard Tschumi declared, we have an experience of space that is registered in the senses, in a world beyond words: "Space is real for it seems to affect my senses long before my reason. The materiality of my body both coincides with and struggles with the materiality of space. My body carries in itself spatial properties, and spatial determinations. . . . Unfolding against the projections of reason, against the Absolute Truth, against the Pyramid, here is the Sensory Space, the Labyrinth, the Hole . . . here is where my body tries to rediscover its lost unity, its energies and impulses, its rhythms and its flux." Weems seeks such reunion in her imaginative engagement and remembrance of Africa—past and present. Her visual quest to recover subjugated knowledge is fulfilled in a process of journeying that, as Mary Catherine Bateson proclaimed, makes learning a process by which we come home: "The process of learning turns a strange context into a familiar one, and finally into a habitation of mind and heart. . . . Learning to know a community or a landscape is a homecoming. Creating a vision of that community or landscape is homemaking." In her art practice, Weems imagines a diasporic landscape of longing, a cartography of desire wherein boundaries are marked only to be transgressed, where the exile returns home only to leave again.

Previously published in bell hooks, *Art on My Mind: Visual Politics* (New York: The New Press, 1995)

The Shape of Things, from the Africa Series, 1993.
Three Silver Prints. Overall dimensions 25 x 60 in.
Edition of 10. Courtesy of the artist and P.P.O.W. Gallery, New York.

Untitled, 1992. Diptych. Black and white photographs. Courtesy of the artist.

The Mannerism of Nadine Tasseel

Leen De Backer and Lieven De Cauter

Nadine Tasseel adopts a seemingly archaic stance toward the time-honored duel between photography and painting. She opts for pictorial photography. She inverts photography's realism. Her photographs are not in accordance with truth; she doesn't catch reality in snapshots. Rather, she makes use of this medium to construct another, artificial visual world. In her studio, Tasseel selectively combines objects and textures to stage them as *tableaux vivants* or frames a human body as a still life, *nature morte*. This process generates many-layered images. Once photographed, these shots are further elaborated in the darkroom. Framing and toning enhance the artificial character of the reproduction, shrouding the texture of the reproduced materials with a veil of alienation, creating the aura of old photographs.

Tasseel relates her photographs to mannerism. They are emphatically constructed, rely on artificiality, on hypersophistication, on stylization. The image is replete with tensions and inversions: the flesh becomes defunct, cardboard masks are alive. Heads in profile become plaster busts. Children's legs petrify and suggest a putto stumbled from its pedestal. The tension in each photograph is enhanced by the serial character of the work. The images become variations on a type of reproduction. The photographs are stereotypes in the most literal sense of the word: each work is counterbalanced by a pendant that acts as its counterpart or its completion. In the diptychs of female nudes with masks from famous paintings, for instance, she refers to typologies of the female figure throughout the history of art.

Mannerist works refer to other works of art. They refer to a *maniera,* a style, a manner of painting or rendering, painting "in the manner of." Mannerism is not so much about specific quotations as about the "model" of art: not "nature" but aesthetic language is imitated. This tradition only exists in ruins, fragments that are both meaningless—because cut off from their original contexts—and mysterious—because they suggest a plethora of meanings. We find only remnants of these meanings, traces; the key to their interpretation is lost to us.

Mannerism is time and again considered the expression of a certain *decadence*—whence its negative connotation. It surfaces in epochs marked by uncertainty, by a feeling of transition, as in sixteenth-century Italy and at the turn of the past century. It is a style of decay as much as an approach fascinated by decay. Mannerism (and this also goes for Tasseel's mannerism) wallows in the sensuality of materials; hence it is all the more acutely conscious of appearances, of the irretrievable vanity and transitoriness of all matter. Attitudes become poses, portraits turn into personifications in Tasseel's photographs. Gestures appear to be symbolically coded; objects become attributes. Each object, each figure is part of a configuration that renders the whole enigmatic. Everything may have a hidden meaning. In her most recent series, the image has become an image puzzle, a rebus. Precisely because objects are attributes and characters are personifications instead of persons, her photographs are heavily allegorical. They address the transitory (vanity)—the very theme of allegory—on different levels: the transitoriness of matter, the vanity of all flesh, but equally the transitoriness of meaning. However, Tasseel's photographs signal neither regression nor nostalgia, no fashionable pastiche of bygone styles, no quest for a neo- or pseudo-historical style. They reflect on the allegorical self. The fish in her still-life photographs not only show the "beauty" of dead staring eyes, a memento mori, but index the absence of (symbolic or allegorical) meanings.

Allegories supersede the first meaning of an image in favor of a second, arbitrary meaning (e.g., the dog in Dürer's famous print *Melancholia I* is not so much a real dog as a symbol of melancholy, but it could have symbolized fidelity or idleness as well). The horns are objects with a specific shape and beauty as well as the remaining repository of all meanings they may ever have had in the blurred, lost tradition of allegorical representation (in which they refer to satyrs, devils, adultery, rutting, perversion, and the like). A third semantic level reflects on the decay of allegory; in other words, it is an allegory of the decay of meanings.

Not only the use value, the authenticity of objects dwindles, but equally the ability of representations to transmit meanings expires as a result of the lack of codified symbols and icons. The photographs express a fascination with this silencing of meaning. This fascination constitutes what the artist calls "the silence" in her work.

But silence does not have the final word. Matter acquires a new power because her works express a longing for lost artificiality and sophistication and meditate on the decay of the allegorical tradition, beneath the haze that shrouds her photographs and meaning, whence it is sublime, unrestrained, and surpassing all comprehension. This paradox underpins Tasseel's works: things have lost their meaning, but loss produces their ultimate meaning: their intrinsic materiality, their worldliness, their weight. The restraints imposed upon them by time (the decomposition of fruits, scars on bodies, wrinkles) express their transitory, ephemeral, and consequently "futile" nature. But this very futility is the final confirmation of the lust for life, of an almost ecstatic sensuality. Often the images contain emblems of lust and pain. In some instances, the demonic and obsession are near. As a result of this and despite the stylized rigor, Tasseel's photographs are dominated by the paradoxical atmosphere of eros and violence.

Translated from the Flemish by Jan Foncé

Untitled, 1993. Black and white photographs. Courtesy of the artist.

Condition, 1995. Performance object (and video made with Ana Torfs), at the Béguinage of Kortrijk (Belgium).
Metal wire, casters, leather straps.
146 x 230 x 50 cm. Collection of the artist.
Courtesy of the artist.

Scenes of Seduction: Reflections on the Work of Jana Sterbak

Desa Philippi

Anachronisms

> What are those lascivious apes doing, those fierce lions, monstrous centaurs, half-men and spotted
> pards, what is the meaning of fighting soldiers and horn-blowing hunters? You can see several
> bodies attached to one head, or, the other way round, many heads joined to one body.
> Here a serpent's tail is to be seen on a four-footed beast, there a fish with an animal's head. There is a
> creature starting out as a horse, whilst the rear half of a goat brings up the rear; here a horned beast
> generates the rear of a horse. Indeed there are so many things, and everywhere such an extraordinary
> variety of hybrid forms, that it is more diverting to read in the marble than in the texts before you,
> *'ut magis legere libeat in marmoribus quam in codibus,'* and to spend the whole day gazing at such
> singularities in preference to meditating on God's laws.
> —St. Bernard in a letter to Abbot William of St. Thierry (1135)

There is nothing medieval about the work of Jana Sterbak except perhaps the pleasure it exhibits in a certain unruliness; her art suggests a becoming, a taking form and transforming which, if not timelessly of the world is not self-consciously modern either. The body turned memento mori and inside out in the flesh dress, myth materialized into objects, and bodies attached to machines, internal organs formed from metals chosen not just for their appearance but for the metaphorical potential of their reactive, chemical qualities. . . .

An ancient flux is within and part of the contemporary surfaces of these works. We become aware of its presence as soon as we arrive at the point where "gazing at singularities" intrudes on the contemplation and analysis of what exactly this art presents. The installations, objects, and performances belong to the tradition of conceptual or idea art insofar as they do not automatically privilege the visual as autonomous and disembodied perception. Unfailingly, we are given an inseparable entanglement of often complex ideas with the most stubborn physicality: food for thought. The refusal to separate mind and body, spirit and matter, forms an underlying condition that connects otherwise diverse works.

Particular works allude to myths (Sisyphus, the Golem) and to tragedy (Medea). These narratives are less interpreted than provided as references of who we are as existential rather than historical subjects. Destructive passion, search for origin, punishment, and meaningless labor may take different forms historically but are never entirely absent from human activity. From this point of view, mobility (and actual movement in many of the works) is itself immobile, a movement that goes round in circles and folds back on itself. Conceptually, Jana Sterbak's work

185

occupies the same ground in shifting constellations. Each piece is ambivalent; in its composite nature it always belongs to more than one category at a time: object/image, object/performance, body/machine. The absence of formal continuity from one piece to the next underlines the belief that representation is irrevocably split and the recognition that this gap can no longer be bridged by the imagination. Sterbak's work, conscious of its romantic legacy in its play with irony, paradox, and ambiguity, always stops short of unequivocal statements. A possible synthesis of the disparate elements is out of the question. It is worth remembering at this point that the lack of clear distinctions in art—of recognizable materials and forms or what we have become accustomed to calling style or signature—has always introduced a measure of anxiety. Already the early medieval author of the *Libri Carolini* was worried by this: "How was one to distinguish between the Virgin and the ass in representations of the Flight into Egypt, since both were painted in the same color?"[1]

Sterbak's work refuses to "sweep us toward the object which it designates," to use Maurice Merleau-Ponty's phrase.[2] Yet if instead of forming judgments about form and content, truth and falsehood, we confront the question of what exactly we want from this work, we are up against our own demand for reason, identity, and meaning in the face of seduction. We long for the protected territory of the disembodied mind to safeguard against paradoxical bodies that mock and question, "What about this?" "And this?"—displacing "What does it mean?" with "How do you respond to what has become your own fascination?" Sterbak's art stages the kind of amorous encounter where seduction and denial become pivotal points around which our perception is structured. At this point the question of gender and the feminine arises, not in relation to some perceived object or content but in the affective and amorous lining of our powers of cognition and analysis.

Sisyphus II, 1991 Chrome, aluminum, and projection. 127 x 152 cm. Courtesy Galerie René Blouin, Montreal. Photo: Louis Lussier.

Eros/Woman

Enters Diotima.

The ancients knew that love is a matter of indirect speech, of relays, detours, and the feminine. Diotima, the woman of Mantinea who instructs the great Socrates in the art of love, who had taught him many years ago even then, or so Apollodorus tells a friend. Apollodorus tells what he in turn only knows secondhand from Aristodemus, who was present when Socrates held forth on love. Diotima is absent from the company of men who sing the praises of Eros, of beauty, and of young boys—all of those reputable men of Athens giving speeches in praise of love. They also postpone and set the scene for Socrates, the self-proclaimed expert on the subject—thanks to the woman who, as commentaries on the *Symposium* are quick to point out, is entirely fictional. However that may be, and it doesn't really matter, Diotima's voice is needed to delineate truth and distinguish it from the eulogies of the men. She had to be invented, conjured, for Socrates to expound the truth of love in her name. But what did Diotima have to teach him? What did the woman know so well that the philosopher couldn't pronounce in his own name?

Love, we are told, is a halfway state between wisdom and ignorance, between mortality and the immortal. "Having true convictions without being able to give reasons for them," Diotima replies to Socrates' questioning.[3] Eros cannot be a god, she explains, because the gods are beautiful, good, and without lack, whereas Love is in a state of desire and need for beauty and the good. Halfway between god and mortal, the role of Eros is "to interpret and convey messages to the gods from men and to men from the gods." This position is extremely precarious. Guided by desire, Love is a spirit rather than a god, and a supplement which

Sisyphus II, 1991. Still image from Sisyphus (16 mm. film). Courtesy Galerie René Blouin, Montreal.

"bridges the gap" between men and gods insofar as "through this class of being come all divination and the supernatural skill of priests in sacrifices and rites and spells and every kind of magic and wizardry." Propelled by longing and need, Eros is at the same time "weather-beaten" and "homeless." As mediator he is torn and driven. Untouched by the sovereignty of the gods, Eros, according to Diotima, means proximity to desire's disorganizing powers. Needy and longing, we are far from rule of the logos; instead we find ourselves exposed to signs that we interpret in the absence of a clear distinction between desire and its object: "On one and the same day he will love and flourish . . . and also meet his death. . . . What he wins he always loses, and is neither rich nor poor, neither wise nor ignorant."

But could Diotima, could Plato, have left Socrates there at the dinner party, halfway between wisdom and ignorance and vulnerable to the ridicule of his friends? And how better to forestall accusations of frivolousness and lack of intellectual rigor than by introducing the notion of work, of production? Eros as desire and neediness is thus swiftly transformed into love as a striving toward immortality. Love then becomes "desire for the perpetual possession of the good," achievable through procreation as "the nearest thing to perpetuity and immortality that a mortal can attain," or through creative and intellectual begetting—"poets and . . . craftsmen as have found out some new thing may be said to be begetters." Not only do we witness the formulation of production as reproduction and guarantee of the continuation of life beyond death, but also and congruently it becomes clear that, in order to function is this way, love must be understood as active exertion toward a telos: the continuation of the species and the creation of great works of art.

Henceforth labors of love thus transformed into work will be haunted by denial. At the same time, denial becomes a productive force allowing us to produce and to reproduce our own and other bodies as work, as artifice, as art. Except that these bodies are beset by needs and desires. They always turn out to be feminine, a succession of masks, jokes, and paradoxical performances that are in turn excessive, hilarious, and deprived in their ambivalence. Their very artifice—in Sterbak's work the extreme dresses, crinolines on wheels, the uniforms and jackets rendered useless with arms sewn together, the metal organs and imaginary prostheses, the tattoos and shaven heads—simultaneously renounces and enacts this denial.

Machine Love

> Look, there's something peculiar going on here, very peculiar—
> Maybe if you could send somebody over here or, better yet, come yourself—
> All right then, I'll be waiting for you at the corner—I don't *know* what's going on.
> —Karel Capek, *Tales from Two Pockets*

In the recent piece *Condition,* a bizarre contraption of aluminum wire on wheels that looks like a giant stylized snail or caterpillar is strapped to a man's back; the man moves around in circles executing incomprehensible maneuvers. This action, apparently necessary, seems like an act of pure will. Whether we are dealing with an external command or an internalized rule is impossible to determine; in either case the rationale for the performance remains entirely outside of the performance itself.

Modernist literature teems with descriptions of absurd and paradoxical events prompted by the unpredictable and irrational workings of social institutions, usually but not always the army or the police. Yet what makes these works so fascinating is the way in which they refuse to reduce these events to the sociopolitical arena. It is never simply a question of the struggle between individual and society, or of opposing political forces. Thematized in endless variations in Jaroslav Hasek's novel *The Good Soldier Svejk,* and again differently in Karel Capek, Franz Kafka, and Milan Kundera, to stay with some of Sterbak's early literary influences, is a certain fundamental obscurity or disproportion in the relation between cause and effect. These and other works intimate a particular form of power both modern, in that it is technological and bureaucratic, and timeless in its arbitrariness and despotism.

Art and literature at their best express how this power is not restricted to political totalitarianism or even to what is still and often misleadingly called the public sphere but can inhabit our most intimate thoughts and actions. Thus, the protagonist of Kundera's first novel, *The Joke*, is not simply the victim of political repression. His disaster, triggered by desire and jealousy, can never be explained purely in terms of external events. Instead, the novel moves through a specter of emotional twists and turns that often follow their own "authoritarian" agenda. The narrative examines the desire for verbal artifice—the joke—as directly linked to sexual desire by placing it on the political construction site, here the "building of socialism," which allows for the joke to be made while guaranteeing its failure to be funny. Once the bureaucratic machine gets going, events unfold automatically, just as the joke itself was an automatic response, prompted by jealousy and without consideration of its possible consequences. Of course, the novel's interest lies not in an analogy between two separate technologies (one psychic, one social) but in the automatism that displaces the transparency and intentionality in both.

Absorption, 1995.
Performance.
Courtesy of the
artist and
Galerie René
Blouin, Montreal.

Sterbak's work is pitched at precisely this level. In her installations and performances, machines and bodies are inextricably linked in mutual mimesis, modification, and construction. Is it to this "condition" that the title of the latest piece refers? In this collaboration with the filmmaker Ana Torfs, the mechanical extension somehow prompts the performer to walk very quickly, on the verge of running, around a small airfield. In the background are round hangars, closer up a runway cast in large squares of concrete. The camera mimes the man's circling: sweeping 360-degree shots reveal in black and white the strange sight of an airport without planes, with plains instead of water, concrete, and distant fields. The video is accompanied by a sound track of the performer's breathing and sniffling and the occasional whistle of wind. In mingling visual and audible rhythms, machine and body become dreamlike extensions of each other, a record and simultaneous canceling of a fixed, recordable reality. The wire construction, this curious prosthesis of an imaginary phantom limb, exists doubly as machine and driving force and as object "parked" just outside the exhibition space.

As machines give concrete forms to the laws of nature, they also provide a mirage of human will and understanding in projecting the functions of bodies and organs, both physical and social. To the extent that technology can isolate particular functions—point of view (camera), flying (planes), rolling (wheels), etc.—it also produces these functions as autonomous objects that can then be recognized in and as part of the natural world. Technology thus projects back onto human subjects who, among other things, begin to act automatically and dream in slow motion or fast-forward. The double, one of romanticism's favorite themes, is thereby rendered dialectical: the universal robot is increasingly hard to distinguish from the human and vice versa.[4]

189

Desa Philippi

Not Knowing

Another thing we are not supposed to do is to explain the inexplicable. Men have learned to live with a
black burden, a huge aching hump: the supposition that "reality" may only be a "dream." How much
more dreadful it would be if the very awareness of your being aware of reality's dreamlike nature were
also a dream, a built-in hallucination! One should bear in mind, however, that there is no mirage without a vanishing point, just as there is no lake without a closed circle of reliable land.
—Vladimir Nabokov, *Transparent Things*

In *Prometheus,* Kafka tells us that the inexplicable is not the dream or fantasy but the "reliable land" itself from which our dreams and myths arise. He presents four versions of the myth of Prometheus and observes that in each case "there remained the inexplicable mass of rock," the foundation from which the myth and also the story arise. Trying to explain the inexplicable constitutes the truth of the story insofar as "it had in turn to end in the inexplicable."[5]

In this way, art is shackled to the rock of not knowing, and its irreducibility or truthful-ness resides in giving shape to that space of not knowing. We can look at and recognize the mirage but we cannot recognize its vanishing point, and only because we cannot determine the latter do we acknowledge the authenticity of the former.

According to this romantic/modernist legacy, understanding the work of art in all of its determinations would mean to reduce it to a historical, social, or psychological document. Recognizing the work of art as art, on the other hand, involves the recognition of its limit as work, an unworking whereby art's very materiality is understood to interfere with any defini-tive meaning or destination that we may wish to attribute to it. This argument is well rehearsed and perhaps most subtly elaborated in the collection of essays *L'espace littéraire* by Maurice Blanchot. What interests me in Sterbak's work is the way in which not knowing can be construed as a machine, an automatism.

Right at the beginning of *Transparent Things,* Nabokov suggests a relationship between the attention that we pay to material objects in artistic representation and time. "Perhaps if the future existed, concretely and individually . . . the past would not be so seductive," he writes, "but the future has no such reality (as the pictured past and the perceived present possess); the future is but a figure of speech, a specter of thought." To do justice to the inde-terminacy of the future, to keep it that way, we must avoid "sinking into the history" of the object. Only attention to the surface will keep us in the present and prevent us from reducing "man-made objects, or natural ones" to their history, thereby simplifying the story of those objects. Attention to material, to surface, keeps the future open by rendering things transpar-ent, "transparent things through which the past shines."

Not knowing, then, rallies to the future, which we cannot know concretely, which is also the future of writing and of art. For art to be made, the future must become the future of art—a figure of speech, specter of thought—and must remain unpredictable. In the natural sciences, too, every new hypothesis shifts and thereby reproduces a space of not (yet) know-ing. It is difficult not to regard this perpetual production of not knowing, of openness toward the future as a *conditio sine qua non.* In Sterbak's *Remote Control,* the performer is suspended in a motorized crinoline on wheels, mobile yet entirely subjected to a machine that she can-not leave or enter without assistance. Even when the remote control remains in the her own hands, the performer's movements are more or less reduced to those of the machine. The machine turns out to be a mobile prison. In *Condition,* however, the performer hastens around in circles until suddenly and for no apparent reason, he abandons the wire contrap-tion in the middle of the airfield and leaves the scene.

190

Sometimes machines can be stopped, that's part of their beauty. If they can't be stopped altogether, at least we can begin to think about their automatism. One such moment occurs in the writings of Walter Benjamin, who, before Nabokov, wanted to see the past light up outside the "once upon a time" of historical continuity. For Benjamin, "the past can be seized only as an image which flashes up at the instant when it can be recognized and is never seen again," in what is at once a foreboding and a possible means of liberation.[6]

In 1986 Sterbak did a performance entitled *Artist as Combustible*. The room was completely dark until gunpowder was ignited in a small dish that the artist balanced on her head. For a few seconds the room was illuminated, showing her standing naked and motionless. This humorous enactment of the stroke of genius revealed that the artist doubles seductively as model and muse, but before we could comfortably settle into the place of voyeur, the performance was over. Again, we didn't quite get what we saw.

Condition, 1995.
Performance
object and video
made with Ana
Torfs.
Courtesy Kanaal
Art Foundation,
Kortrijk
(Belgium).

NOTES:
1. Michael Camille, *Image on the Edge: The Margins of Medieval Art* (Cambridge, Mass.: Harvard University Press, 1992), 55.
2. Maurice Merleau-Ponty, *The Prose of the World,* trans. John O'Neill (Evanston, Ill.: Northwestern University Press, 1973), 3.
3. Quotations are taken from Plato, *The Symposium,* trans. Walter Hamilton (Harmondsworth: Penguin Classics, 1951).
4. Karel Capek's famous play *R.U.R.: Rossum's Universal Robot* (1921) traces and elaborates the thin line between human and robot. (The word *robot* is derived from the Czech *robota*—work, labor.)
5. Franz Kafka, *The Complete Short Stories* (London: Minerva, 1992), 432.
6 .Walter Benjamin, "Theses on the Philosophy of History," in *Illuminations,* trans. Harry Zohn (New York: Harcourt, Brace and World, 1968), 257.

Cultivated Want: Ana Torfs's Video Vocabulary

Edwin Carels

Anamnesis: "To become a kaleidoscope gifted with consciousness was the goal of the lover of universal life." Nearly one and a half centuries after Baudelaire formulated this motto for modern man, the Belgian video director Ana Torfs conforms to his words in a particularly intuitive manner. From the start, her work has been varied and systematically fragmented, playfully naive yet precisely measured. She works stringently and harmoniously yet always remains fragile and elusive. Torfs gives us generous amounts of small, precise data about each of her subjects rather than providing a general overview. She asks her spectator to be just like a child with its kaleidoscope, to close one eye against the bright light of the present so as to enjoy a few sparkling pearls from the past, seen through her construction of mirrors. Her striking, selective interest in cultural names and past periods is as surprising as it is uncommon, especially given the framework of the nineties and the norms of postmodernism. It is as if she wanted, in her videos, to sketch the prehistory of a disease (her own context or postmodernism?) by bringing suppressed or lost ideas back to life.

Jeanne la Pucelle (1988): a contemporary version of the life of Joan of Arc based on testimonies by her friends and enemies, as transmitted in the translation of the trial documents by historian Régine Pernoud (U-matic, color, 25 minutes).

Anabiosis: Torfs has the medieval texts recited in their proper bourgeois environment by a multitude of simple characters in old-fashioned costumes. Set in static frames and bare lighting, the anonymous models address their statements to the camera in a totally unemotional, almost indifferent manner. A comparison to Robert Bresson's equally dry-as-dust *Procès de Jeanne d'Arc* (1962) is apt. More than any other video artist, Torfs shows in her rigidly stylized tapes a relationship with the clear-cut image and text constructions of modernist filmmakers such as Bresson, De Oliveira, and Straub. Sober, rigid, and serene, sound and image appear separately and without a calculated hope of response. Torfs also uses her medium primordially as a means of preserving latent (spiritual) life, of registering texts and faces in a state of apparent death.

Marco Polo, une histoire de brodeurs (1990): a contemporary and very fragmented version of Marco Polo's travelogue as dictated to Rustichello of Pisa, a writer of chivalric romances who shared Polo's prison cell in Genoa (Betacam, color, 35 minutes).

Condition, 1995. Video stills. Video made with Jana Sterbak. Courtesy Kanaal Art Foundation, Kortrijk Belgium).

193

Anachronism: The episodic life story of this Renaissance traveler is even less fashionable than the spiritual testament of a medieval saint, at least in the manner in which Torfs evokes it. Just as the possibility of a proto-feminist interpretation is nowhere explicitly suggested in *Jeanne la Pucelle,* Torfs does not seize the opportunity to present us here with a topical discourse on migration, Moslem tradition, economic expansion, or denigrating exoticism. Despite the emphatic play with props, her *tableaux vivants* remain deliberately sparse in meaningful references. Of prime importance here, as in the works that follow, is the physical representation of oral tradition: the extremely literal, clear-cut, and sometimes even neutral reading of a text. Nevertheless, this solemn minimalism endows the unintentional expression of the models, the materiality of their faces, and the timbre of their voices with an important gravity. Everything should speak for itself; the camera only registers each slightest intonation, accent, or spontaneous gesture. Ancient words pass through strange mouthpieces, resound in contemporary spaces, and thus reach a new era in the form of vague echoes. This simple alienation technique betrays Torfs's crucial obsession, in which she exceeds her concrete themes: the simple sensual experience of a cultural time warp.

Jeanne la Pucelle
1988.
Video stills.
Courtesy of the
artist.

Akarova, M. L. Baugniet: L'entre-deux-guerres (1991, in cooperation with Jürgen Persijn): a portrait of two surviving protagonists of the 1920s Belgian avant-garde, she a dancer, he a painter and furniture designer. A fragmentary story develops, based on the testimonies of contemporaries and on archival footage (Betacam, color and black and white, 53 minutes).

Analecta: Again a time warp; Torfs reminds us of the forgotten glory days of Belgian (Brussels) modernism, between the two world wars, now that it is on the verge of disappearing forever. The last representatives of this movement are still alive and their memories are just sufficient to recall this limited (and internationally almost unnoticed) movement. Their verbal reconstruction of Belgian modernism is in unusually strong contrast with the physical decay seen on their faces. Even though these forgotten, aged pioneers try as they can to maintain self-respect, each wrinkle and each trace of transience stands out in pitiless sharpness via Torfs's choice of a black background and frontal lighting. As Henri Bergson used to say: "At the intersection of mind and matter lies memory." Once again, tracing the course of time is the most important theme underlying this tape. Instead of working toward a conclusion, Torfs, as always, confines herself to the experience of evasive duration. Instead of drawing a double portrait, she confronts us with a gallery full of anonymous and yet authentic faces. Contemporaries, friends, and colleagues are interviewed at random and without names. Their hesitations are as revealing as their words. At each occasion, the associative, kaleidoscopic function of memory is an important structural principle. The fragmentary character of the reminiscences is simultaneously remedied and emphasized by her selection of illustrations: an anthology of climaxes taken from interwar dance, film, architecture, and the arts.

Mozart Material (1993, in cooperation with Jürgen Persijn): a playful survey of the conception and execution of Rosas's choreography *Mozart/Concertarias: Un moto di gioia*. An insider's view on the working process and aesthetic vocabulary of a contemporary dance company (Betacam, color and black and white, 52 minutes).

Anaglyph: Following questions on this documentary (a commissioned work), Torfs described her eclectic, consciously incoherent approach as "an evidently incomplete cookery book or an encyclopedia of movement." Even more striking than the way in which the famous Akarova and Baugniet are reduced to the level of their peers is how choreographer Anne Teresa De Keersmaeker is ignored, in order to show the collective, multivoiced creative process of dancers of equal merit. Of all Belgian dance videos (a genre that has kept pace with the new developments in contemporary dance and gained an international reputation thanks to Walter Verdin, Eric Pauwels, and Wolfgang Kolb), Torfs and Persijn's dance study is the most humble, yet probably also the most clarifying and enriching to date. In fact, Torfs also applies the principle of scaling down an individual's ego to herself. Each tendency toward autobiography or individual affirmation is suppressed by continually presenting subjects from an archaeologically distant past or from a contemporary yet clearly defined context. Only the spontaneous affinity, the simple ease with which Torfs approaches these subjects, may suggest something about her own character. This must be seen in the perspective of her close cooperation with film/video director Jürgen Persijn. The alternate presentation of two views—black and white and color, panoramic movements and close-ups, real time and slow motion—creates a constant ambiguity further stressed by the discrepancy between sound and image. This endows the most simple, face-on documentary shots with an extra dimension and a broader, stereoscopic nature.

Mozart Material,
1993.
Video stills.
Courtesy of the
artist and Jürgen
Persijn.

Background (Endless) (1993, in cooperation with Jürgen Persijn): a film essay on "the city."
Looking for the unnoticed in diary entries, cultural-philosophical quotations, panoramic
views, survey centers, networks, shop windows, buildings, and interiors in order to discover
the essence of the city (Betacam, color and black and white, 28 minutes).

Anamorphosis:

> So no special significance should be given to the name of the city. Like all big cities, it consisted of
> irregularity, change, of going with the flow, of not keeping in step, of collisions between things and
> objects and of fathomless points of silence in between paved and dirt roads, of one great rhythmic throb
> and the perpetual discord and contrary movements of opposing rhythms; and, as a whole, it looked like
> a seething, bubbling fluid in a vessel formed by the solid material of buildings,
> laws, regulations and historical traditions.
> —Robert Musil, *The Man without Qualities*

Besides this typical Musil quotation, Torfs and Persijn also quote Paul Auster, Walter
Benjamin, and Henry David Thoreau to evoke a city (here Antwerp, but it could just as well
have been Brussels) outside time, without inhabitants, without beginning or end. The ambitious combination of visual essay and lyrical documentary is also expressed in the sound
track: behind the feeble voice of an aged guide, bookbinder Petrus Pluym, we hear a young
woman trying to refresh Pluym's literary memory. The many contrasting image clusters suggest a universe in suspension between past and present, between modernism and postmodernism, between utopia and dystopia, between dream and reality. The double point of view of
the voices further extends through identification with a falcon's eye, a surveillance camera, a
television personality, a peep show customer, etc.: the city as a deformed and marked character, an intangible construction only seen correctly through a warped mirror.

Il combattimento (1994): the video adaptation of a video installation of the same name. Opera
reduced to its essence: three faces, shown face-on and in profile, singing Monteverdi's scenic
cantata based on the twelfth canto of Tasso's *Gerusalemme Liberata*. (Betacam, color and
black and white, 21 minutes).

Anaphase: This most radical of Torfs's works, this most naked, self-contained representation
of the human face and its voice consists of a harmonious triptych. Three static, vertical
tableaux vivants of neutral faces in close-up, as measured and sharp as the famous portraits in
profile by Piero della Francesca or the dramatis personae from a Straub film. Torfs reduces
opera to pure breathing, swallowing, vibrating, and the location of a voice in a body, to
mouths that open and close. The body's gestures are reduced to the gestures of the face and
the physical act of singing. The only visual counterpart of the verbal information from the
libretto (about war, anger, belief, and agony) is the effort of the singers' facial muscles.
Through the complete absence of historical setting and period costumes the text regains its
explosive directness. Here Torfs's fascination with music and architectural composition
results in particularly tense video images, the condensed beauty of which may at each
moment turn into uncontrollable aggression, as if in the penultimate phase of nuclear fission.

Condition (1995): on a deserted airfield, a neat, anonymous young man angrily marches in circles.
This physical effort is hampered by the metal frame of what looks like an enormous larva, which
the hurried man drags along on wheels behind him (Betacam, black and white, 7 minutes).

Analemma: This installation tape combined with a sculpture by Jana Sterbak is Torfs's most recent commissioned work and seems to be her least personal, least typical work to date. Nevertheless, it contains familiar components such as the contribution by Jürgen Persijn (here as a model) and the discrete emphasis on architectural structure shown in the patterns of the road surface and in the symmetrical warehouses in the background. Again, we are confronted with the radical simplicity of the planned sequence, although in this case the panoramic camera movements convey exceptional dynamism. Even more important here is the play with the indirect experience of time. Instead of using the abstract effect of classic, elliptic editing, Torfs gives her images a shaky, implicitly fragmentary character through simple handling of the video, without influencing the real duration of the film. This she combines with the shadow play resulting from the camera's circular movements to create the effect of a very unusual time scale. According to Torfs's astrolabe, each tape represents a step (backward) toward authenticity. Within the context of postmodernism she undertakes a continued search for authentic time experience, without getting lost in nostalgia, and adopts Rimbaud's simple radicalism: "Avant tout, il faut être absolument moderne."

Translated from the Flemish by Catherine Thys

Plates

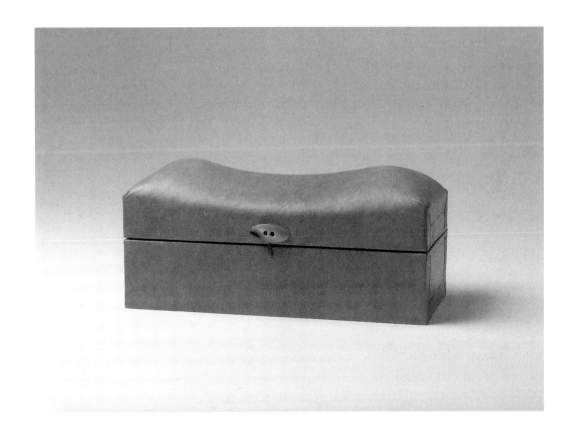

CARRIE MAE WEEMS, *From the Very Beginning*, 1995.
Leather, wood, and audio component. 3-5 narrative/music boxes.
13 3/4 x 5 3/4 x 5 3/4 in. each.
Courtesy of the artist and P.P.O.W., New York.

NADINE TASSEEL, *Untitled*, 1992.
Black and white photograph. 30 x 40 cm.
Courtesy of the artist.

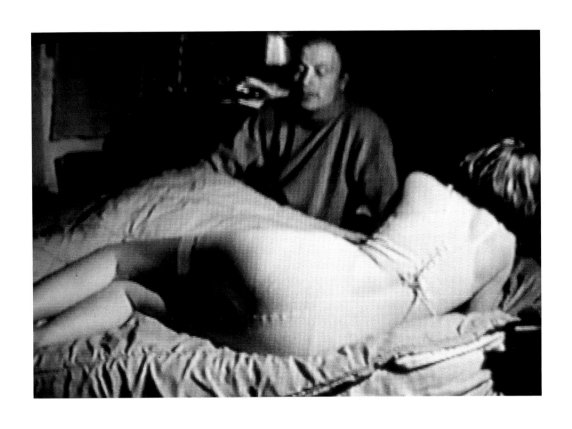

ANA TORFS, *Jeanne La Pucelle*, 1988.
Video still. Courtesy of the artist.

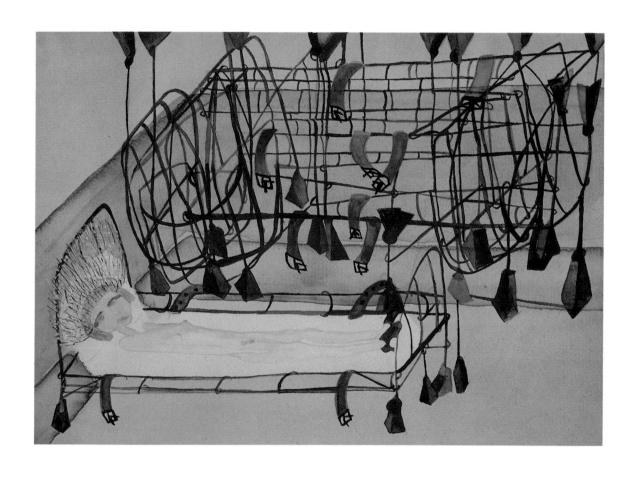

CAROL RAMA, *Appassionata*, 1940.
Watercolor on paper. 33 x 23 cm.
Museo Civico di Torino, Italy.

CAROL RAMA, *Nonna Carolina*, 1936.
Watercolor on paper. 24 x 35 cm.
Collection of the artist. Courtesy Galleria Giancarlo Salzano, Turin.

CLAUDE CAHUN AND MOORE, *Untitled*, from *Aveux non avenus*, plate VI, 1929–30.
Gelatin silver print. 6 x 4 in. Collection of Helen Kornblum,
St. Louis, Missouri. Courtesy Zabriskie Gallery, New York.

Absorption. Work in progress.

In 1970, nine years before my first wearable pieces, Joseph Beuys created the first of his felt suits.

I became aware of it in 1986 and its existence has bothered me ever since...
At the beginning of the nineties I conceived of a solution: the absorption of the suit. To this end I have metamorphosed myself into a moth (see photo), have proceeded systematically to eat one after another of the 100 suits Beuys sold to private and public collections around the world.

In some cases, my activity was temporarily disrupted by misguided conservation efforts... Nevertheless, it would not be immodest or inaccurate to state that I have already put more than one suit out of its exhibition condition.

My work is not easy, but it's not without reward, and, most important, it continues.

JANA STERBAK, *Absorption*, 1995.
Text, photograph, and Joseph
Beuys's *Felt Suit* (1970).
30 x 41 cm.
Collection of the artist.

HANNAH HÖCH, *Untitled*, from the series *Aus einem ethnographischen Museum*
(From an Ethnographic Museum), 1930.
Museum für Kunst und Gewerbe, Photographische Sammlung, Hamburg.
©1995 Artists Rights Society (ARS), New York/VG Bild-Kunst, Bonn.

HANNAH HÖCH, *Mutter: Aus einem ethnographischen Museum* (*Mother: From an Ethnographic Museum*), 1930. Photomontage. 18 x 24 cm.
Musée National d'Art Moderne, Centre Georges Pompidou, Paris.

MARTHA ROSLER, *Balloons*,
from the series *Bringing the War Home*, 1967-72.
Photomontage printed as color photograph. 24 x 20 in.
Courtesy of the artist and Jay Gorney Modern Art, New York.

MARTHA ROSLER, *House Beautiful: Giacometti*,
from the series *Bringing the War Home*, 1967–72.
Photomontage printed as color photograph. 24 x 20 in.
Courtesy of the artist and Jay Gorney Modern Art, New York.

ANA MENDIETA, *Untitled (Silueta Series)*, 1977.
Earth/body work with snow in Iowa. Courtesy The Estate of Ana Mendieta
and Galerie Lelong, New York.

ANA MENDIETA, *Silueta Works in Mexico*, 1973-77.
Color photograph documenting earth/body work. 16 x 20 in.
Courtesy The Estate of Ana Mendieta and Galerie Lelong, New York.

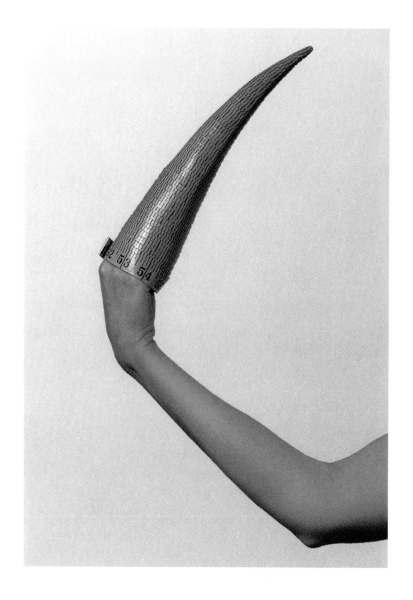

JANA STERBAK, *Cone on Hand*, 1979.
Dressmaker's cone.
Courtesy Galerie René Blouin, Montreal.
Photo: Louis Lussier.

CAROL RAMA, *Opera no. 9*, 1938. Watercolor on paper. 50 x 38 cm.
Private collection, Milan. Photo: Pino Dell'Aquila.

LOUISE BOURGEOIS, *Untitled*, 1950.
Painted wood. Height c. 180 cm.
Courtesy Robert Miller Gallery, New York.

Yayoi Kusama, *Baby Carriage*, 1965.
Mixed media.
Courtesy Richard Castellane. Photo: J. Wollach.

THE BLANK IN THE PAGE

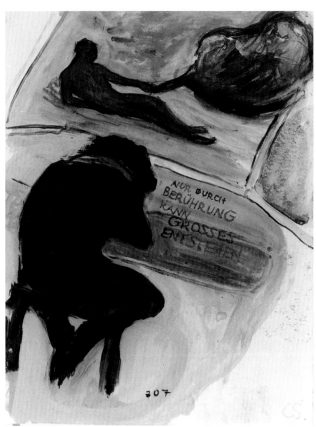

Leben? Oder Theater? (Life? or Theater?) series
(nos. 4698, 4685), 1940-42.
Gouache. Each approx. 32.5 x 25 cm. ©Stichting Charlotte Salomon.
Collection Jewish Historical Museum, Amsterdam.

Charlotte Salomon:
Autobiography as a Resistance to History

Ernst van Alphen

I

Charlotte Salomon's[1] painted life history differs from most examples of its own genre. Life histories tend to take the form of written autobiographies or diaries, sometimes illustrated with drawings illuminating specific passages, themes, or events. Salomon's life history consists of a complex whole of narrative images, text fragments, and musical citations. The work took shape during the Second World War, when many German artists had to flee the country because they were Jewish, Communist, or homosexual. Not only was the political situation in which Salomon lived gruesome; her family history was also terrible. Her mother, grandmother, aunt, great-uncle, great-aunt, and cousin committed suicide. At the time that she made *Leben? oder Theatre? (Life? or Theater?)* she was the only surviving member of her mother's side of the family.[2] Except for her grandfather, they all had killed themselves.

Life? or Theater? is a musical-theatrical piece, with Salomon herself as narrator. It consists of 769 compositions and thirteen painted text pages. According to the subtitle, it is a "songplay." In the history of theatrical music, this genre is a predecessor of opera. It makes use of existing melodies, mostly provided with new texts. Salomon's songplay, however, is not destined to be played and sung but to be looked at. The work is tightly structured. It consists of a prelude subdivided into two acts, which are in turn subdivided into scenes. Next comes the body, composed of sections, the first of which has eleven scenes and the second five. An afterword closes the work. Salomon numbered the total work as serial pages.

The event stages within this classical three-tiered structure are commented on and questioned in the accompanying texts, which contain statements by the characters as well as the narrator's commentary. They also contain quotations from literature, opera, and songs. Thus a layered text takes shape within which voices speak and comment on different levels. There are also loose sheets, preliminary studies and variants, which Salomon did not include in the finished *Life? or Theater?*

This complex work, its historical moment, and the cultural place that the work has occupied after the fact—the work as afterimage—make a particularly good case for inquiring into the relationships among history, biography, and art, or public history, personal expression, and the ways in which the history of art mediates between them. Salomon's *Life? or Theater?* has so far attracted partial responses addressing any one of these aspects. Historians place the work in its personal and/or sociopolitical context. For them, it is an important document illustrating one of the most dramatic moments of Jewish history. That it documents a personal, private history makes identification easy for postwar readers/lookers. In this respect *Life? or Theater?* is equivalent to Anne Frank's *Diary*. Although Salomon's life history is not as well known as Frank's, both have become cultural icons in the commemoration of Jewish history and the Holocaust.

Although Jewish history is obviously relevant to Salomon's work, its very obviousness has resulted in a neglect of the art historical significance of *Life? or Theater?* The historical value seems to preclude realization, even visibility of its significance as a work of art: its autonomy is under pressure. Art historians tend to analyze art in relation to other art—to place it within an autonomous stream of artistic tradition. Confronted with a work so blatantly addressing history while equally blatantly transgressing the artistic genres, historians treat it *either* as history *or* as art history.

For art historians, the problem is the work's undefinable genre. Visually, it is often characterized as expressionist because of its drawing style. This label seems justified by the fact that Salomon's artistic context was Germany of the twenties and thirties: the period of German expressionism. But this label makes it difficult to take into account other aspects of *Life? or Theater?* What to do with the texts, with their content as well as their visual qualities? One is also puzzled by the ironic relations between text and image and between the music quotations and the represented events. Nor do the intertextual references to other works of art, especially Michelangelo's frescoes, and to Western mythologies come into play in this reading.

The situation becomes yet more complicated when we consider gender, a third framework within which to place this art. Salomon narrates a life history in which female family members are central by their absence: they all commit suicide. Her role model, however, is a man, who initiates her into conceptions of art in which creativity is an exclusively male asset. Hence, male creativity and female suicide are the two central motifs in *Life? or Theater?* This leads to a paradox for Salomon herself. Her life history in art seems to tell the story of the impossibility of the female artist. We readers must consider questions such as how her work of art relates to the (male) conceptions of art that she describes *in* her work of art. This raises the question of the difference between *Life? or Theater?* as autobiography and the conventional autobiography generated by her gender, on the one hand, and between this work and the gendered histories of which she partook: the history of European Jews, her family history, and the history of art.

Shoshana Felman has addressed the question of women's autobiography with acuity in "What Does a Woman Want? The Question of Autobiography and the Bond of Reading."[3] Felman demonstrates the specific complications present when women attempt to inscribe their gendered becoming. She argues that under the current symbolic regime, women can only tell their stories through the stories of others. Woman's autobiographical voice has to be traced within each text as "its own specific, literary, inadvertent textual transgression of its male assumptions and prescriptions"(6). She continues:

> None of us, as women, has as yet, precisely, an autobiography. Trained to see ourselves as objects and to be positioned as the Other, estranged to ourselves, we have a story that by definition cannot be self-present to us, a story that, in other words, is not a story, but *must become* a story. And it cannot *become* a story except through the *bond of reading*, that is, through the *story of the Other* (the story read by other women, the story of other women, the story of women told by others), in so far as this story of the Other, as *our own* autobiography, *has as yet precisely to be owned.* (14)

The narrative frameworks that women have at their disposal to write their autobiographies are the products of a culture dominated by men. It is impossible for women to "confess" their stories because those stories are not self-present to them. Women's lives can only *become* stories in the act of representation or narration, that is, in the resistance to and transgression of the unavoidable male frameworks with their male assumptions and prescriptions. Only in this negative performance, in this act of resistance and transgression, according to Felman, can women tell their life histories.

I will argue that Salomon, indeed, tells her story "between the lines." She can only represent herself in the ironic distance toward the story of others that she is telling, in the resistance of and toward the stories of women told by others. But if gender becomes a primary guideline in my reading of this work, this is also because gender enables me to overcome the binary opposition between history and art history that has so far dominated readings of Salomon's work, an opposition that makes either one of these two frameworks invisible. Reading through gender, in contrast, will turn out to be an integrative mode of reading that not only accommodates but even foregrounds both history and art history and how they function in Salomon's work.

I will focus my reading on two mythic motifs of creativity by means of which Salomon structures *Life? or Theater?*: the story of God's creation of Adam and the story of Orpheus and Eurydice. Both stories thematize creativity, and in both it is male creativity that is at stake. Salomon has not rendered these myths with the attitude of a serious believer. She uses them ironically, and it is exactly there, in the distance created by her irony, that she is able to tell her story.

First, she elaborates the very act of narrating her life history as an act of creativity through an implicit "discussion" or working through of the intimate relationship between art and death. Death, and the relationship between death and life, is a recurrent motif in *Life? or Theater?* The first images of the first act represent a moment of Charlotte's prehistory, introducing a tight relationship between life and death, a mutual dependency. In 1913 a family member leaves the house and goes to Lake Schlachten outside Berlin to drown herself. This is Charlotte's Aunt Charlotte, her namesake and her mother's sister. In the following images, her mother, Franziska, announces that she wants to become a nurse in order to save the lives of soldiers fighting the First World War. Just as Charlotte decided, at the end of the work, to do something wildly eccentric after her grandmother's suicide, so did her mother. After her sister's suicide, Franziska starts saving lives instead of joining her sister in death. Although this causal relation remains implicit, it is clearly suggested by the similitudes structuring the narrative against the grain. Thus, the opening scenes introduce the leitmotiv that structures Charlotte's life and life work: situations in which life slips into death and death motivates life, moments of transition where the passage between life and death and between death and life is almost indiscernible.

The tie between life and death is not experienced as tragic or dramatic. On the contrary, it becomes the site of Charlotte's access to art, and this access is strongly gendered. She achieves it through the teachings of a young man called Daberlohn, her stepmother Paulinka's teacher and Charlotte's guru, with whom she falls in love. He occupies an important place in Charlotte's life history as well as in her personal artistic development, her private art history.

Salomon has Daberlohn declare that the frontier between death and life is indispensable for the emergence of art. That frontier is an ideal nourishment for art. This rather conceited young man, entirely inspired by romantic views of art, searches for moments of transition between life and death because they are the moments of creation. "Between life and death there must be a stage of high concentration that can be filled by singing" (435), he affirms.[4]

His teaching is based on his theory of the soul and the voice. To arrive at the transition between death and life he does not sing but instead has a death mask of himself made while still alive. While the wax is pressed against his face, a sensation is triggered in his mind. Salomon's images show that the impression dominating his senses mixes color with music,

and that mixture produces a theatrical mask of Paulinka, the woman with whom he is in love and whom he wants to use as nourishment for his theory of music and the soul. The commentary on his vision by the voice-over (Salomon) is ironic: "He is pervaded by a deep sense of satisfaction from his exhausting labors and he feels that he has penetrated far into the mysterious depths of human existence" (435). The mysterious depth of human existence consists, however, of the image of his utterly personal obsession of the moment: Paulinka. Salomon creates ironic distance between what she shows us (Daberlohn's vision) and the range of the thoughts that she has Daberlohn think.

The link, ironic as it is, between this personal obsession and the universalist view of art is represented by a visual reference to myth. When the mask is taken off, Daberlohn thinks of the story of Orpheus going into the underworld to awaken Eurydice back to life. Helped by Amor, he has the strength to appease the god of the underworld with his song. In the frontier situation between death and life, supported by love, it is possible to soften a god or to create art.

The Orpheus myth is central to *Life? or Theater?*, but in Daberlohn's imagination it transforms into a gendered conception of creativity. This is the version of the myth, the theory of creation, against which Charlotte must tell her story, and which she will resist and transgress. For Daberlohn, Eurydice is no longer the ultimate goal of his descent; she is merely its precondition. Orpheus descends into the underworld not in order to awaken Eurydice but to seduce the god of the underworld by means of the art of music. He must excel in his art to impress the god. His ambition to create such an art overrules his love for Eurydice. His love for her *supports* and *sustains* his creative pursuit.

In the text of one unnumbered page Salomon makes Daberlohn quite explicit about the serving role of women in the project of redemption through art. Daberlohn says to himself: "Yet for me also I believe in the redemption by means of woman."[5] In the story of *Life or*

Theater? Charlotte's stepmother Paulinka Bimbam first serves this eroticized creative project. That Daberlohn is in love with her does not mean that she is his love object, however; she serves rather as a narcissistic mirror for Daberlohn. He wants her to reflect his own value back to him. Felman describes men's use of women as narcissistic mirrors in analyzing Balzac's short story "Adieu." She characterizes the meaning of Stéphanie for Philippe: "In Philippe's eyes, Stéphanie is viewed above all as an object whose role is to ensure, by an inter-play of reflections, his own self-sufficiency as a 'subject,' to serve as a mediator in his own specular relationship with himself. What Philippe pursues in the woman is not a face but a mirror, which, reflecting his image, will thereby acknowledge his narcissistic self-image" (36). Salomon gives Daberlohn exactly these words when he reflects on his love for Paulinka: "And when I look deep into her eyes I see only my own face + that mirroring of yourself is for me nothing more than a symbol for that when you believe to love somebody else, just you your-self are object and subject."[6]

But the situation in *Life? or Theater?* is even more complex and already transgressive in itself, because Paulinka and Charlotte not only serve as narcissistic mirrors or nourishing mediators in Daberlohn's creative pursuit; they have creative ambitions themselves. Paulinka is a famous singer, and Charlotte is a student at art school. They are both influenced by Daberlohn's aesthetic conception and his role model Orpheus, but gender is a sticky problem here. In the story that Salomon's narrator tells, Daberlohn is not an artist himself but a music teacher. How does he then equal his own role model Orpheus? And how does Salomon have him deal with the fact that Paulinka and Charlotte as artists have more in common with Orpheus than he does himself?

The text of another unnumbered sheet is again revealing:

> It is an easy job to prepare Mrs. B. for the fact that the Orpheus which she has to per-form is nobody else than herself who has suffered this loss of soul and who only has to descend in her own inner world in order to refind herself. Probably you have noticed, how much big talk goes into her affectation with which for years she had seduced many people. And the interesting thing is that behind her pose there is a real fantastic woman to whom men can look up . . . and won't I pull the unique figure into life with languorous violence? A Maria, a Helena, a Mona Lisa, My God stop this. . . . Your philosophical bab-ble means nothing more than that you are head over ears in love with here.[7]

As Paulinka's teacher, it is Daberlohn's task to impel her to identify with Orpheus, for Orpheus is the symbol of, and hence role model for, the artist. However, Daberlohn presents Orpheus's descent in search of a lost soul (Eurydice) as an inner quest for her true essence. He knows or sees already that she is, in essence, "a fantastic woman to whom men can look up." He wonders if he should pull "with languorous violence" this unique inner woman out of her into life. When he starts to compare Paulinka's true womanhood with Maria, Helena, and Mona Lisa, his own fantasy begins to seem absurd to him, and he suddenly diminishes every-thing by claiming that his idealization of Paulinka only means that he is in love with her. Here we can hear the narrator's voice both resist the discourse of the character she represents and transgress the gendered system of thought he embodies and utters. She renders his thoughts at the moment that he himself becomes aware of how pathetic they are. This scene needs no ironic comment of the external narrator Salomon.

Although Daberlohn suddenly distances himself from his aesthetic and ecstatic outcry, he takes over Orpheus's pursuit when he wants to pull Paulinka's unique essence into life. He as the teacher becomes Orpheus—making Paulinka—instead of wakening the Orpheus quest in Paulinka. Hence there is no room left for Paulinka as creator of art. Felman's conception of the conditions under which women have access to their own life stories plays out with precision in Salomon's overworking of Daberlohn's gendered vision. Salomon cannot tell her life story without framing it within the ideology within which Daberlohn speaks, judges, and loves. But while endorsing that framework as the only one available to her, she also resists it by means of irony and transgresses it by displaying its inner contradictions. This is for her the only way, the way of indirection, through which she can achieve this autobiographical representation—through which, in other words, she can gain access to her own history *and* her own project.

Something of the same order happens in Salomon the narrator's relationship to the history of art. Daberlohn's ideas about film also influenced Charlotte's work. Salomon represents them in a scene in which Daberlohn sits at a small table in his room, waiting for inspiration for a book that he wants to write (525–37). Michelangelo's Sistine Chapel fresco of the creation of Adam appears in the image, suggesting that Daberlohn is thinking of it. That fresco appeared earlier, when Charlotte traveled through Italy with her grandparents. Charlotte was then deeply impressed by Michelangelo.

Later, Daberlohn imagines these frescoes. Salomon's narrative voice-over does not comment on Daberlohn's thoughts as much as on her own view: "The following images are those which to the author seem the strangest. Without doubt they have their origin in the Michelangelo Rome series of the main section that was sung with the loudest and most penetrating voice of this entire work" (527). The commentary indicates that the following images are, in a sense, the work's core. This arouses a keen interest in the story that they show and tell. Daberlohn begins to write his book. He writes about Michelangelo as the greatest genius of all times. God's creation of Adam marks the end of God's total domination over mankind. It is no longer the same God who creates Eve. "This is the tragedy of the king who must hand over his dominion to his son" (529). Daberlohn uses this homosocial competition to justify that women have no role in this story of creation. On the next sheet Salomon has him say: "That is why the path led from Adam to Christ, so that the words might be spoken: 'Woman, what have I to do with thee?'" (530). According to Daberlohn, Adam is reincarnated in Christ, and Daberlohn in turn resembles Christ. In the second instance, however, Salomon lets him take a more modest position: he is a conqueror and a redeemer, but only of his own underworld. Yet he hopes that many will follow his example. Of what does that example consist?

According to Daberlohn, man must learn to know himself, to descend within himself first, before he can transcend himself and reach beyond. One means of getting outside himself, Daberlohn thinks, would be through film, because it is a machine through which we can produce ourselves. This holds for the hero of the film as well as for the spectator who identifies with the hero: "At the movie, on an equal level with the hero passing before his eyes, he feels the equal of his ideal. At the movie he follows his path to the heights, to his refuge, the dream world that is to help him ignore the dingy harshness of daily life" (536). In keeping with the experience of the height of the Sistine Chapel, Daberlohn presents Adam– Christ– Daberlohn himself–the film hero–the film spectator all as God's rivals. Because they all, each in his own way, create a world—a new, alternative world—they are able to deny or forget the God-created world.

This view is the framework in which Charlotte will intervene with resistance and transgression. Riddled with rivalry and ambition, the process is emphatically represented as Daberlohn's vision: it is he who sits at the table and thinks it up. Charlotte must now find a way to relate to this series of God's rivals. Eve, the only woman mentioned in Daberlohn's fantasy, is assigned the function of nurturing Adam's creative power or is a sign that Adam can reproduce himself. God's creative power has thereby lost its exclusivity; Adam can do it, too. Salomon's commentary on this familiar sexist presentation is quite subtle. It provides a wonderful example of resistance and transgression through visual means and of Salomon's revision of art history. On sheet 321 (p. 539) we see her and Daberlohn sitting in a canoe, Charlotte adopting the position and pose of Adam in Michelangelo's fresco. Hence, the creative power is here attributed to Charlotte herself while Daberlohn is used to paddle for her. She draws explicit albeit convoluted attention to the reversal of Daberlohn's fantasy in the accompanying text:[8] "Please compare this pose 1) with no. 22 of the prelude (p. 30) 2) with Michelangelo's 'Night,' no. 308 (p. 528), also no. 325 (p. 545)" (541). Before tracing these comparisons, I want to note that Salomon painted several sheets with the same scene where, even more remarkably, she reversed the positions.[9] We see Daberlohn at the left occupying Adam's position while Charlotte sits in the middle. Salomon, however, did not select these images for *Life? or Theater?* One can only guess her reason, but the *gesture* of excluding them must be taken seriously and interpreted as part of the work itself. It seems plausible that her conscious or unconscious motivation was tied to her resistance to Daberlohn's gendered conception of creativity. Her resistance is not explicitly stated but shaped in the form of a complex intertextual reference to Michelangelo that acts out the transgression of the limits even of her own work. Her subtle comment on Daberlohn's view is, however, lost in the images with Daberlohn at the left in Adam's position; hence, I speculate, these had to be discarded in the finished composition.

Leben? Oder Theater?
(Life? or Theater?)
series (no. 5025),
1940–42.
Gouache.
Approx. 32.5 x 25 cm.
© Stichting Charlotte
Salomon.
Collection Jewish
Historical Museum,
Amsterdam.

It seems worthwhile, therefore, to trace the gesture in some more detail. On the first page to which she refers in this convoluted commentary (p. 30 in the prelude), we see Charlotte's mother also in the pose of Michelangelo's Adam. However, far from taking this as a pose of empowerment, at the moment she adopts the pose she decides to kill herself. The second sheet to which the narrator refers (p. 528) contains the Adam of the fresco by Michelangelo. The text that goes with this sheet refers, however, to another work of Michelangelo: the figure Night on the tomb of Lorenzo de' Medici in Florence. There is indeed a remarkable similarity in pose between Michelangelo's Adam and his personification of Night. This similarity results also in a contamination of what these two figures stand for. While Adam is the main, victorious character in a story of creation, Night signifies, together with the figures Day, Morning, and Evening, the fluctuation of time; hence, it signifies life and death, or the transition of life into death. This meaning is intensified by the fact that the sculptures are part of a tomb.

The reference to Michelangelo's works contaminates the idea of creation by death—or the other way around. Again, Salomon suggests a narrow link between creativity (art) and death, which explains the passivity of Charlotte's Adam. This pose, signifying creativity, is not associated with activity or productivity but with the transgression of death.

On the third sheet to which she refers (p. 545) we see Charlotte again in the position and pose of Adam and, we can now add, in the pose of Night. Daberlohn lies on top of her and kisses her. The accompanying text states: "but suddenly his hypersensitive nerves are touched by a firelike current—which is only natural considering that this picture was created to the tune of: I love you as no one has ever, ever, loved before!"

The text suggests that Daberlohn sends out this firelike current of love/creativity. The next page reveals, however, that Charlotte is responsible for this God-inspired moment: "It was only a second. Charlotte is lying there as if it were not she who had brought about this fiery stream. If Daberlohn had known old Mrs. Knarre, he would once again have noted a family resemblance—just as you can after reading the epilogue" (546). We see Charlotte lying down, totally passive, Daberlohn next to her. In the epilogue Mrs. Knarre, Charlotte's grandmother, commits suicide. Daberlohn fails to understand the full implications of Michelangelo's view of creativity because he failed to understand that the relationship between art, love, and death is reversible. Daberlohn assumes that contact with death is a precondition for creativity, while Salomon is frightened by the reverse relation: for her, creativity is equally strongly an enticement to the desire for death. Her grandmother's (and her mother's) suicide is an example of failed creativity, but of creativity nevertheless.

Salomon's resistance to the tradition of megalomaniac creators in which Daberlohn places himself is not, however, focused on the reversal of gendered positions as such. Daberlohn in fact notices the reversal within the story. In chapter 11, titled "Interesting discoveries, For us too," the external narrator[10] again gives the reader access to Daberlohn's thoughts. *He* makes the following discovery: "He is struck by a remarkable resemblance between Charlotte's pose and that of Michelangelo's 'Night'" (p. 539). Daberlohn then takes this decision: "That is my new religion." Daberlohn's new religion seems to be his task to bring creativity to life in fantastic women like Paulinka and Charlotte. While in the earlier scene he projected Orpheus onto Paulinka, now he projects Night/Adam onto Charlotte at the moment he notices their similar poses. In both cases this implies that he thinks that he possesses the power to bestow creativity on them. But as in the Paulinka-Orpheus scene, after his act of bestowal he is not so much *facing* a creative woman as looking into a mirror of his own creative act.

This becomes clear in the next scene, where the couple has left the canoe. We see Charlotte and Daberlohn lying next to each other and Daberlohn start to make love to Charlotte. So far, this is a conventional scene, framed within conventional representations of relations between men and women. One of the sheets on which this scene is represented is the one to which Salomon the narrator impelled us to compare sheet 321. There Salomon has Daberlohn assume unjustly that he produced the firelike current. A text of one of the unnumbered sheets that, one assumes, goes before the latter text, addresses Daberlohn's failing creativity more explicitly. The following from this unnumbered sheet comments on the amorous scenes of sheets 323 and 324: "Charlotte remains unyielding. That has never happened to him in his long-standing practice. He feels something cold which borders upon death—he is amazed, interested. He continues 'his experiment' which interests him as always a lot."[11] These commentaries complicate the seemingly traditional scene—woman lies still, man makes love to her—considerably. Now, read in light of this text, it is as if Daberlohn, even in lovemaking, is the entire product of Charlotte's creative power. From guide, teacher, and guru, he becomes her puppet.

Salomon resists Daberlohn's conceptions of creativity in two crucial ways, integrating history and art history as well as personal history and artistic subjectivity and is so effective in this because these pairs are strongly bound to the gendered problems of women's autobiography that Felman pointed out. First of all, Salomon has Daberlohn fail in his Orphic project of awakening creativity/love in the women he admires. His "experiment" in creativity by means of lovemaking fails while Charlotte succeeds in emitting a firelike stream. Second, she uses this creative energy to create an alternative tradition for her female family members who committed suicide. The external narrator Salomon relates Charlotte's Orphic-Adamic moment of creativity to the suicides of her mother and grandmother. They form a contiguous line.

II

So far, I have read words and images in *Life? or Theater?* as if they formed complementary elements: they illustrate, represent, the narrated events, or they give form to, present, Salomon's narrative comment on those events. This implies that we experience both the series of texts and the series of images in their continuity and that the two support each other as mutual illustrations. But this handling of words and images ignores the visual and material features of the texts. At most one might remark that the texts are visually expressive: this intensifies the content of the narrated story, which is, however, mediated by coded language and illustrative, realistic images. In this view, the materiality of the texts does not "tell" itself, it only "adds" emphasis and intensity.

It is hard to sustain this reading when we consider the form of Salomon's work. The first 210 sheets (the prelude and the first few sheets of the main section) have accompanying texts written on sheets of tracing paper, which were pasted over the gouaches. The sheets that follow have the texts written on the gouaches themselves. One assumes that Salomon ran out of tracing paper, forcing her to write the texts on the images.

The book edition reproduces all of the gouaches but without the semitransparent sheets of tracing paper that belong on top of them. The texts written on the tracing paper sheets have been transcribed as captions to the images. This is legitimized as follows: "It was decided that we could not do justice to the complete allusive complexity of *Life? or Theater?* in the 'reading edition' we had in mind. The decision was made to limit ourselves to the gouaches and to a typographically neutral rendition of the text" (xiv). This tacitly acknowledges only the expressive features of Salomon's handwriting, ignoring the semitransparent sheets. When we read the work in the form it was made, the texts on transparent sheets partly hide or distort the visual images underneath. The first thing we see is the written text; only at second sight do we see the images. In some cases the lines of the tracing paper texts correspond with the underlying image.

In the second part Salomon wrote her texts directly on the images. There is never a distinct part, isolated from the image, reserved for the text as in comic books. The texts appear in the representational space of the narrated story; the words fill the represented space together with the characters. In the epilogue, which tells of the grandmother's suicide and Charlotte's decision to make her life work, the words begin to overrule the other elements. More and more they look like graffiti aggressively inscribed onto the surface.

One could argue that the epilogue is the most dramatic part of the whole work. Here Charlotte must choose between committing suicide or starting her life work. That the words come more to the fore in this section expresses this dramatic situation. But such an interpretation fails to account for the fact that the overruling of images by words is already the case in the sheets covered with tracing paper; there it happens in an even more literally material way.

The epilogue delivers another possible reading of the increasing *inscription* of words onto images. One sheet shows Charlotte's grandfather in bed, after his wife has committed suicide (753). The text covers almost the whole surface; only the grandfather's head is free of text. This sheet forces us to choose between the ambiguous meanings of *to cover*. The words here no longer *match* the grandfather, whom we see in the image, although in content they do: they render his words. The words literally cover him up, *hide* him, as the blanket covers him within the representational space. Salomon has covered her grandfather with words because that is her artistic way of resisting, covering up, this male family member. She cannot avoid or silence him as a character in her life history, but in the act of telling *his* story, she resists him by covering him with words.

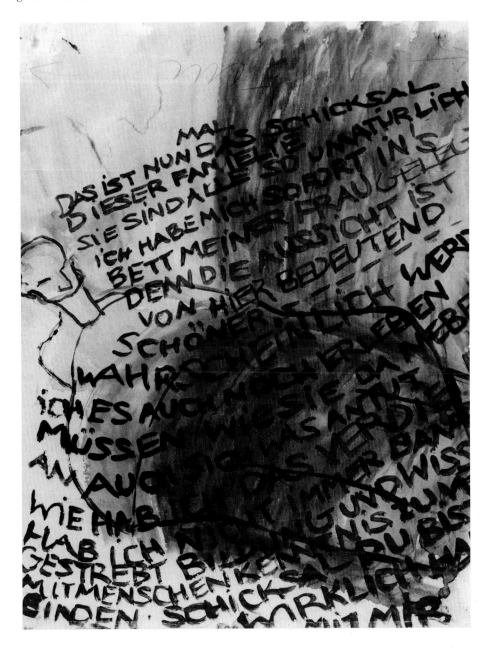

Leben? Oder Theater? (Life? or Theater?) series (no. 4905), 1940–42. Gouache. Approx. 32.5 x 25 cm. © Stichting Charlotte Salomon. Collection Jewish Historical Museum, Amsterdam.

The act of resisting her grandfather has several meanings, all equally dramatic for Salomon. In the sheets that follow shortly after this crucial image, Charlotte refuses her grandfather sexually. After his wife has killed herself, he presses himself upon Charlotte. Salomon decides to have her grandfather say the following words: "I don't understand you. What's wrong with sharing a bed with me—when there's nothing else available. I'm in favor of what's natural" (764). Charlotte answers: "Don't torment me. You know that I know exactly what I have to do." This reply effectuates the integration of Charlotte's gender-specific life history as a young woman—she is all but overwhelmed by a powerful man—and her artistic vocation. The grandfather thus stands for the tradition in family life that subjects female children to the power of the father and for the tradition that excludes women from artistic subjecthood.

She resists her grandfather artistically in yet another way. When she tells him that the whole world has to be put together again, his response is cynical: "Oh, go ahead and kill yourself and put an end to all this babble" (774). She resists his advice and instead begins making her life work. Her life work thus not only tells her life history but it does so as an act of creation that remakes the world. The sheets that follow contain only text. Only the very last sheet contains another visual image. We see Charlotte at the beach working. She draws or writes on a transparent sheet that is still empty. Like Proust, who ends his autobiographical masterpiece by the scene of writing, beginning the creation of the work we have just finished reading, Charlotte's work ends with the start of that very work her grandfather told her *not* to bother to make.

But there is a third way in which she resists her grandfather. This character not only plays a negative role for Charlotte in the history of her family; he is the symbol of all of the people against whom she fought in making her work. The narrator makes this claim on one of the unnumbered sheets. "My grandfather was for me the symbol of all the people I had to fight against."[12] This statement is remarkable in several aspects. First it suggests that her grandfather also symbolizes the people of Nazi Germany. She did not made her life work only to repudiate the family fate to commit suicide but also to put the world, which was being destroyed by the Nazis, together again. Making her work, she tried not only to turn around the fate of her family but that of the European Jews.

This symbolic condensation of functions projected onto the character of the grandfather explains the astonishing absence of any explicit resistance against the Nazis within Charlotte's project. The history of Nazi oppression that affects Charlotte's life quite dramatically is not represented up-front; it is the context in which her narrative is set, a backdrop that invades her life only tangentially. By stating her ambition to remake the world, however, she includes that history within her personal struggle. The grandfather thus embodies evil and destructiveness on all levels of her life.

Yet her remark "My grandfather was for me the symbol of all the people I had to fight against" also makes explicit that her work is a way of *fighting history*, her family history and political history. This fight takes place between the words and images comprising her work. Visually, she writes history, she renders the story of her family, and by doing so she exemplifies the history of the European Jews, now known as the Holocaust. But she also writes the history of her gendered becoming and of her artistic becoming. The two latter histories could only be written as inscriptions of the other histories. In her texts Salomon comments on the stories she tells; in her intertextual references she appropriates the artistic conceptions of others; in her ironic composition of words, images, and music citations,[13] she opens up gaps in which she is able to tell her story and to work through the histories in which she partook.

The triple resistance against the grandfather demonstrates that (and also why) interpretations of Salomon's work in the exclusive terms of either Jewish history and the Holocaust or a phase in the history of art profoundly misread this work. She produced the fictional representation of her alter ego's struggle against this man who threatened her private life, her art, and, by extension and symbolically, even the collective history in which she lived. Salomon thus transgresses the boundaries between the categories that confine our readings, and she resists the traditions—of art, of history, of autobiography—that preclude her access to creation. Or would have, if it weren't for her resistance.

NOTES:

I am very grateful to Carol Zemel for her critical suggestions and generous comments on my essay.

1. In this paper I will use the last name Salomon to refer to the artist, the first name Charlotte to the character in the autobiographical work *Life? or Theater?* In a third role the persona appears as a narrator within the work. I will indicate those cases by using the term *narrator*.
2. Mary Lowenthal Felstiner, in her important study on Salomon, *To Paint Her Life: Charlotte Salomon in the Nazi Era* (New York: Harper Collins, 1994), has convincingly shown that the suicides in Salomon's family are not anomalous but exemplary of German Jews in the Nazi era. The suicide rates of Prussian inhabitants between 1923 and 1927 legitimize Salomon's statement: "So Fränze Salomon's suicide took place in a nation with one of the highest rates in the world, in a province and capital with the highest rate in the nation, in a city with the highest ration of female suicides, in a class with the highest rate among classes, in a faith with the highest proportion among faiths" (14).
3. Shoshana Felman, "What Does a Woman Want?" in *What Does a Woman Want? Reading and Sexual Difference* (Baltimore: Johns Hopkins University Press, 1993).
4. These peculiar conceptions of Daberlohn become slightly more understandable against the background of the experiences of the real person represented: Alfred Wolfsohn. During World War I, he was eighteen years of age and served as a stretcher bearer in the army. He incurred a serious shock when he remained buried for several days under dead and dying soldiers. After the war, while attempting to restore his psychic balance, he developed a theory of the human voice. The sounds that he had heard from the dying soldiers had been far from normal in range and volume. Afterward he experimented with his own voice and took singing lessons but failed to find vocal heights and depths to equal the extreme emotions he had experienced and perceived in the dying soldiers. He concluded that the voice and the soul are inseparably bound and that the limitations of the voice reflect those of the soul. He believed, however, that development of the voice can help to cure the soul.
5. "Doch glaub ich auch für mich an die Erlösung durch die Frau" (unnumbered sheet, C 34876, JHM 4948). All the sheets of *Life? or Theater?*, as well as the unnumbered sheets not inserted in the final selection that forms *Life or Theater?*, are in the collection of the Jewish Historical Museum in Amsterdam. The unnumbered sheets have been not reproduced in the book edition of *Life? or Theater?*, but the Jewish Historical Museum will show them on request. I refer to the codes of the unnumbered sheets as they are used in this museum.
6. "Und wenn ich ihr ganz tief in ihre Augen schau dann seh ich nur mein eigenes Gesicht + sich spiegeln ist mir + dies nicht ein Symbol dafür dass wir wenn den anderen zu lieben glauben nur immer selbst Objekt und Subjekt sind" (unnumbered sheet, C 34872, JHM 4963).
7. "Künste Frau B klar zu machen, dass dieser Orpheus, den sie darstellen soll, nichts anderes ist als sie selber, die diesen Seelenverlust erlitten hat und nun in ihr eigenes Inneres herabsteigen muss, um sich selbst wieder zu finden. Du wirst vielleicht gemerkt haben, wieviel Bluff hinter ihrem ganzen Getue ist, mit dem sie schon eine Reihe von Jahren sehr viele Menschen betört. Und das Interessante ist nämlich, dass darunter eine ganz phantastische Frau steckt, eine Frau zu der man aussehen konnte . . . und sollt ich nicht mit sehnsüchtiger Gewalt in's Leben ziehn, die einzigste Gestalt. Eine Maria, eine Helena, eine Mona Lisa. Mein Gott hör auf. . . . Hinter deinem ganzen philosofischen Getue steckt nichts weiter, als dass du bis über beide Ohren in sie verliebt bist" (unnumbered sheet, verso C34406, JHM 5045).
8. As I will argue shortly, this text is not simply an accompaniment but more precisely a literal overwriting of the traditional image—as well as of its reveal.
9. See the unnumbered sheets C34870, JHM 5000–5003.
10. The term *external narrator* refers to the narratological notion of a narrator who is not at the same time a character within the fictional universe. Here the narrator marks her exteriority by speaking of Charlotte in the third person and by demonstrating access to Daberlohn's thought. These two signs mark the text generically as a fiction, a genre in tension with both history writing and autobiography.
11. "Charlotte bleibt unbeweglich. Das ist ihm in seiner langjährigen Praxis noch nicht vorgekommen. Er hat das Gefühl von etwas kaltem Totenähnlichem und ist erstaunt interessiert. Er setzt 'seine Experimente' die ihn wie immer sehr interessieren fort" (unnumbered sheet [transparent], C 34381, JHM 4998).
12. "Mein Grossvater war für mich das Symbol für die Menschen gegen die ich kämpfen sollte" (unnumbered sheet, JHM 4928, N4).
13. For an analysis of how Salomon uses music citations to create an ironic distance toward the events and experiences of her characters, see Ernst van Alphen, "Salomon's Work," *Journal of Narrative and Life History* 3, nos. 2 and 3 (1993): 239–54.

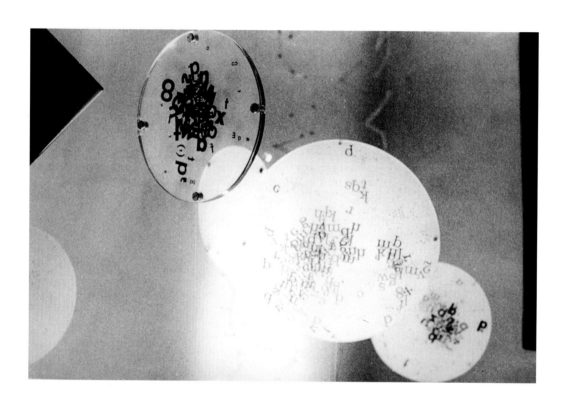

Discos, 1972.
Paper between Plexiglas. Diameter 25 cm.
Courtesy Gallery Ralph Camargo.

Mira Schendel: Resisting the Present

Sônia Salzstein

I t seems significant that Mira Schendel's career, begun in the mid-fifties, attained public visibility only in the early eighties, just a few years before her death in 1988. In some measure, the reasons can be found in the work itself. From the start it demonstrated a need to develop at a slow pace, concentrated on a restricted number of basic issues; above all, it remained relatively isolated from the noisy upheavals of the cultural agenda of the time. Considering Schendel's decisive disposition for obliqueness, it is hardly surprising that the Brazilian artistic milieu, still at odds with the incipience of Brazilian art history, has only superficially absorbed her contribution.

By the time it gained visibility, Schendel had developed a highly original body of work. From the beginning she combined the demand for distilled conceptual maneuvers and a disconcerting adherence to things from daily life—to what daily life could provide of the entropic, arbitrary, and brutal. Perhaps the work depended on this obliqueness, since its main interrogation originates in a necessarily solipsistic subject, incessantly calling into question the ideological nature of all incitement to communication. Such a methodical reticence toward language, or better, toward what the work would perceive as permissive in language, in its incessant attrition in practical life, is one of its essential characteristics.

The *Droguinhas,*[1] objects produced around 1966, based on the alternation between the random and methodical braiding of strips of rice paper, resulting in an indefinite and informal progression of knots, exemplify the cohabitation of opposites that marks all of Schendel's work. They are objects whose very existence speaks of an ethical humility of action (at just the moment at which the solipsistic subject is captured into practical life) because the obstinate attempt at formalization, enmeshed in a complex topological and vertiginous reasoning, reacts at the same time to the mundane need to supplant the abstruseness of the material.

The combination of these opposing principles appears in her paintings and drawings in the form of an extremely reduced repertoire of signs—a minimal expressive coefficient that accounts step by step for the socialization and generalization of a purely personal and self-reflective instance. But what distinguishes Schendel's confrontation of this patiently extracted personal sphere is that she relates to things on an intimate scale and in a colloquial way. She reveals profound indifference toward all that evokes the idiosyncrasies of petty personal dramas, in favor of the depersonalized and anonymous (and consequently to the reality testing of the self-reflective nature of the work). Schendel's work addresses the movement toward interiorization without falling into psychologizing.

Mira Schendel with
Droguinhas, 1966.
Courtesy Ada Schendel
Bento, São Paulo.

Here we must recapitulate the most significant passages of the artist's trajectory. Born in 1919 in Zurich, Schendel emigrated to Brazil in 1949, after a long period of living in Milan. Some of her first paintings, done during the second half of the fifties, prepare for the genesis of an elementary vocabulary of forms: weights, pliers, scissors, bottles, and containers, condensed little by little, over the course of her career, into a nearly empty white spatiality, punctuated by a few interventions.

The works from that period are still lifes elaborated more or less conventionally in the manner of a Morandi and perfectly integrated into a certain tendency of the time (found in the work of her Brazilian contemporaries Milton da Costa and Maria Leontina). They point to the interest in welcoming objects in their literalness, thus establishing a tense relationship between an affective and complacent perception of things and the resistance of the medium—a heterogeneous surface forced to maintain its unity and not to unfold its objects to view. It is well to remember, nevertheless, that what is in question here is beyond the modernist dialectic between a system of representation and the unavoidable evidence of the medium. Differently, and by a very particular route, Schendel called into doubt the notion of naturalization, the process by which things become familiar to our eyes.

After this first moment, in which the work was developing its fundamental features, there were no abrupt ruptures or great contrasts, nor can one trace a chronologically cumulative stylistic development in the artist's career. Perhaps the best image is that of a whirlwind, where the changes actually emerge from an ever renewed perplexity; a few germinal questions are indefinitely revisited in a circular motion and an incessant expansion. Within this movement, one notices growing simplicity of medium—the language becomes more economical and enigmatic; the material thin, casual, and oblivious to any drama of excess or extravagance.

In the sixties, Schendel produced a vast body of monotypes, the above-mentioned *Droguinhas* and the *Objetos Gráficos (Graphic Objects)* as well as the surprising work presented at the last São Paulo International Biennial (*Ondas Paradas de Probabilidade [Standing Waves of Probability]*), consisting of an "ambience," a diffuse impenetrable landscape of bundles of white strings hanging from the ceiling. The artist also continued to paint, concentrating on a figuration that pushed the limits between abstract perception of virtual space and the physical qualities of the medium. Predominant in all of these works is a tense alternation between transparency and opacity, between what permits and what impedes reflection.

To understand better this play of oppositions (without possible resolution), one needs to examine specific works. The monotypes, on superfine rice paper, show simple linear forms, segments of writing, hints of landscapes, or just ambiguous spatial landmarks. The virtual space is frequently denied by the literal space of the written inserts, but at times these are incorporated in the landscapes, completing lines or featuring small anthropomorphic characters who get lost on the lines of the horizon. Through this procedure, the artist succeeds in restoring the homogeneity of the plane, even while combining various orders of representation. Thanks to the transparency, the monotypes invite an exchange of points of view between the front and back sides of the paper. The fusion between the writing and the topographical images equally suggests a transitivity between diverse orders of representation—between a "natural" and an "intellectual" perception.

The same lack of differentiation between the material and the virtual, the natural and the intellectual, appears in the *Objetos Gráficos*, a series of drawings produced from the late sixties to the early seventies, most featuring a tangle of letters, lines, and graphic signs repeated insistently. The *Objetos Gráficos* were produced on translucent paper, mounted between transparent acrylic plates intended to be viewed suspended in space to allow a simultaneous vision of the anterior and posterior faces of the drawings.

In this way these drawings are presented as circular writing, transformed into a magma of all representations, requiring an integral apprehension, as in sculpture, and suggesting indecision between purely sensible and conceptual perception. In others, the ambiguity of the expressive tenor with which the industrial and handwritten letters emerge and the lines repeat more or less automatically—sometimes casual, sometimes schematic—again reveals an inquiry into what is natural.

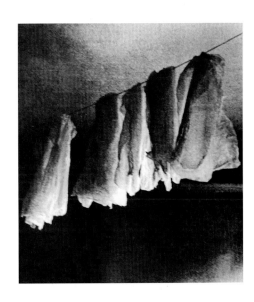

Trenzinho (Little Train), 1964. Paper with rope. 23 x 47 x 5 cm. Courtesy Ada Schendel Bento, São Paulo.

Among the works relevant to the personal sphere, understood in this case as an endless, patient apprenticeship of its limits, are the *Sarrafos (Beams)* of 1987, the last series produced by the artist, a year before her death. The *Sarrafos* are the most violent and emphatic expression of all prior formulations. They give to the virtual recess constituted by the crossing of two lines—the preeminent stronghold of the subject's idealizations and projections—a literal materiality. The most important aspect of this series of white temperas with black wooden *sarrafos* (recalling a modernist assemblage, adapted to the circumspection of recent times, arid and laconic) is the exasperating obviousness with which the same constructive operation is always performed—a line erupting from a plane.

But what catches one's attention in the *Sarrafos* is that the visual thinking that they insistently affirm, as if it were the stages of some analytic reasoning of form, brings to light nothing interior. Further, they resist any identification; they do nothing more than arbitrate a public and social inter-face, affirming the possibility of ideological freedom and responding only to their productive élan.

Objetos graficos, 1968. Installation at the XXXIV Venice Biennale.

Schendel's work is thus based on the effort continually to present the personal sphere in the context that serves it as a background, where this materializes historically and socially. What does this mean other than that such work is there to confront us with the ambiguous forms that notions of public and private life have taken on in contemporary life? Does it not finally embody for us the ever more labile limits of contemporary privacy? If it is true that this work locates a fundamental issue in inquiring into such limits, the experience of privacy here has nothing of the intense confessional compulsion to which contemporary subjectivity is frequently reduced, in its eminently behavioral forms of appearance. On the other hand, the experience of the public dimension contrasts absolutely with the merchandising impulse that we frequently detect in private demands that vie for public attention.

Before touching on these questions, it is well to remember that the presence of something necessarily contemplative and intimate in Schendel's work does not even remotely evoke an idealistic nostalgia (a kind of modernist classicism, outside time and space, for example). The availability for contemplation comes from the genetic interest in things that these works reveal, from the inextricable materiality with which such things impose themselves to compose the forms of our daily experience of reality. Recurrent procedures in the drawings of the sixties, such as the repeated enumeration of groupings of fruit above or below the horizon line, the dehierarchization of things to the point of alphabets and handwritten segments walking unhindered on the landscape—in sum, a figuration based on the random, on repetition—supply evidence that there the subject retreats from the center of the scene to inaugurate a nonanalytical and nonexplicative relationship with language.

Beyond this, the drawings simply affirm their elemental and colloquial mode of seeing, as if they had suspended all analytical thinking toward the hermetic and intransitive in language. These observations seem important to me, to dismiss from Schendel's work any pretense of conceptualism or even the epithet "intellectual" that frequently accompanies it. Her work would be then, from the start, profoundly anchored in the real, even when it could be said that introduced there, like a species of extra productivity, is a time dedicated to contemplation and to the slow ripening of vision.

Returning now to the constitution of the work as the topos of the reciprocal movement between the personal sphere and its public and anonymous dimension, it seems important to restate how Schendel could indifferently cast aside the scenographic dimension and the declaratory compulsion of the "I" in the familiar forms of contemporary privacy. This in no way means that she would value a position safely distanced from present-day cultural dilemmas. In the end, the obliqueness of the work, its suspiciousness of skin-deep expressiveness, its valuing of a subject that exposes itself (that's what the work is about) but knows how to retreat from the center—all of this suggests that her work recognizes the world around it as an instance little receptive to the subtleties of subjectivity. For this reason, the works always respond with unavoidable objectivity to a pedagogy of the artistic clichés of a psychological tonality and with skepticism to the extroversions of a world psychologized to the extreme but paradoxically hostile to any operation of inscribing subjectivity in the public dimension.

Considering the work's affinity for the little, at root it contains an idea of productivity methodically disinterested in the product as a result, as something that could be detached from an existential totality. Everything in this work evokes a slower tempo, slowly unraveling itself, indifferent to the innumerable or the quantifiable—art not as a specialty, as a linguistic repertoire that can antedate and serve as a receptacle for things, but as the gathering place of discipline and of personal maturation.

Translated from the Portuguese by Ann Puntch

NOTE:

My thanks to the philosophers Bento Prado, Jr., and Eric Alliez, whose article "Words at Market Value" inspired my title. I want to thank Ada Schendel for having put her collection of Mira Schendel's work at my disposal, and also Paulo Malta Campos, whose research on the artist's life and work was useful in developing this text.

1. Literally "little drugs"; in the colloquial sense the term designates something unimportant—"whatever"—an artifact drawn at random from the universe of common objects.

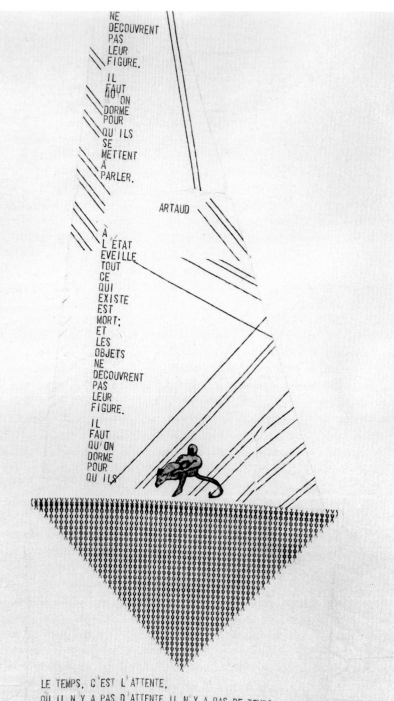

NE
DECOUVRENT
PAS
LEUR
FIGURE.

IL
FAUT
QU'ON
DORME
POUR
QU'ILS
SE
METTENT
A
PARLER.

ARTAUD

A
L'ETAT
EVEILLE
TOUT
CE
QUI
EXISTE
EST
MORT;
ET
LES
OBJETS
NE
DECOUVRENT
PAS
LEUR
FIGURE.

IL
FAUT
QU'ON
DORME
POUR
QU'ILS

LE TEMPS, C'EST L'ATTENTE,
OU IL N'Y A PAS D'ATTENTE IL N'Y A PAS DE TEMPS,
ATTENTE ___ ESPOIR,
ATTENTE ___ DESESPOIR
L'UNE TOURNEE EN AVANT,
L'AUTRE EN ARRIERE,
L'UNE VOYANT VENIR,
L'AUTRE VOYANT FUIR,

Codex Artaud XXI,
1972. Detail.
Painting and type-
writer collage on
paper.
68 1/2 x 20 1/2 in.
Courtesy of the
artist.
Photo: David
Reynolds.

Spero's Other Traditions

Benjamin H. D. Buchloh

In choosing Artaud, I chose a pariah, a madman. He was the Other, a brilliant artist,
but a victim running in circles.
—Nancy Spero[1]

The (failed) reception of Nancy Spero's work within the context of mainstream critical debates and institutional evaluations of artistic production of the sixties and seventies, in both Europe and the United States, points to a larger complex of social, psychological, and aesthetic investments that have remained powerfully latent and have thereby governed aesthetic judgment all the more. Obviously the first obstacle one would have to mention is the fact that Spero is a woman artist and has been a practicing and often radically outspoken feminist for the past thirty years. Any attempt to understand the conditions of discrimination that have excluded her work consistently from critical evaluation, from public and private collections during the past three decades would have to start from this inevitable perspective. But what exactly determined the patriarchal criteria of choice and exclusion seems insufficiently explored in the feminist accounts of Spero's works. In fact, they have even obscured some of the persistent obstacles to reading Spero's "other traditions."

In what follows I will, therefore, suggest a different and complementary perspective: instead of positioning Spero once again outside of the established practices of the sixties and seventies and thereby perpetuating her marginality, I will attempt to compare certain aspects of her artistic production with so-called canonical works of the period. This comparison could first of all clarify some aspects of Spero's work that have made its acceptance difficult if not impossible. Furthermore the comparison could illuminate the specific investments of modernist canonical criticism and why it had either to ignore or to marginalize Spero's attempts to establish "other" traditions within the territory of modernism. I will sketch such a project of historical contextualization by affiliating Spero (born in 1927) with artists that were her generational and historical "peers," as for example Cy Twombly (born in 1928).

Spero's early work originated—like Twombly's—in the continuing dialogue with abstract expressionism, but both artists had voluntarily taken on positions as aesthetic and geographic outsiders facing the impact of the New York School. Spero resisted that impact stylistically by continuing to paint in a mode of figurative representation and considering Dubuffet's alternate model of *art brut* as one of her foundations. Furthermore she deliberately placed herself outside of the New York School orbit by moving from Chicago to Paris in 1959 and remaining there until 1964. In a similar manner Twombly adopted pictorial devices manifestly derived from European artists such as Fautrier and Dubuffet, and he settled in Italy in 1957. By focusing on Spero's *Artaud Paintings* from the late 1960s and more specifically on the *Codex Artaud* (1971), I hope to demonstrate that Spero articulated specific critiques of New York School–derived concepts of painting still prevailing at that time, articulating an alternate model of visuality and definitions of avant-garde practice; but I also want to illuminate the differences in her deployment of language and the displacement of the pictorial in the *Codex Artaud* by comparing her work with other, contemporary practices of inserting fragments or textual quotations within the field of painting. This trajectory, emerging in the American context at first within the work of Jasper Johns in the early 1950s, would lead eventually to the emergence of a rigorously textual and linguistic definition of artistic production in the moment of conceptual art in 1968, thus encompassing the exact period of the development of Spero's own oeuvre up to the *Artaud Paintings* and the *Codex*.

At first glance, the painterly projects of Spero's peers seem to have been altogether different from her own, inasmuch as Jackson Pollock remained the central figure for the male artists of that generation (both of venerating reference and of patricidal articulation). For Spero, by contrast, it was precisely the initial—and continuing— *doubt* about Pollock's status as the most important (American) artist of the postwar period that set her radically apart. Yet in the development of a critical opposition to the figure "Pollock," she would inevitably develop similar strategies, directed not necessarily or solely at Pollock's painting but rather at the terminology developed in the work's critical reception. One such strategy would be Spero's insistence on the continuing possibilities and functions of figurative representation, a strategy she clearly shared with most of the artists emerging in the late fifties and early sixties later identified as the "pop artists." The other strategy—and possibly the more consequential one—would be Spero's programmatic departure from traditional painting altogether in 1966 and her work's increasing retrieval of collage techniques, the insertion of mechanically produced imagery and the extensive quotation and graphic articulation of language elements within the visual construct, leading up to primarily textual and graphic constructions on paper such as the *Codex Artaud*.

Pollock, not unlike Picasso, represented for Spero first of all the culturally hegemonic definition of painting as an exclusively male-gendered practice, and Pollock's hagiographers until this day leave little doubt that they perceive his greatness as a painter as having been intricately intertwined with the performance of his virility. But in the beginning of the sixties, at the time of Spero's own initial articulation as an artist, Pollock had also come to represent modernist visuality, or rather *opticality*, the core concept of American modernism as it had been formulated by Clement Greenberg and Michael Fried.

The construction of this concept as a central term of critical evaluation had depended upon a series of maneuvers that would henceforth determine the course of the most visible and official American art throughout the 1970s. The first maneuver was to eliminate the avant-garde's inextricable involvement with literary practices, since literature had proven to be incompatible with medium-specific modernist art and the increasingly specialized eyes of its viewers. This specialization of perception, *de facto* amounting to an accelerated division of the labor of the senses, was accomplished furthermore not just by banning all forms of figurative representation from the field of painting but also by barring all traces of cultural and historical memory from the pictorial pursuit. Lastly and perhaps most importantly, as the recent critical revisions of the Pollock literature have convincingly clarified,[2] the modernist account of his work had not only eliminated an understanding of the base, physiological underpinnings of his production procedures but it had also banned the sexual and the somatic dimensions from perception and artistic production altogether.

JE
CONSERVE
DANS
LE
COIN
LE
PLUS
PRÉCIEUX
DE /
MA
TETE
CETTE
PRÉOCCUPATION
DU
SEXE
QUI
ME
PÉTRIFIE
ET
M ' ARRACHE
LE
SANG.
ARTAUD

odex Artaud XIA,
971. Detail.
ypewriter and
ainted collage
n paper.
1 x 84 in.
ourtesy of the
rtist.
hoto: David
eynolds.

Yet even in the immediate aftermath of abstract expressionism's critical triumph—if not already at its apogee—the first voices emerged, even if tentatively, to oppose the one-dimensional restructuring of modernism developed by Greenberg. One such instance would be a paradoxical editorial venture undertaken by one of the abstract expressionists' slightly younger and slightly less authentic and respected members. Robert Motherwell's collection *The Dada Painters and Poets,* published by George Wittenborn in 1951, not only attempted to open up the horizon of New York School artists to a radically different moment of textuality in recent avant-garde history, but it already opposed explicitly the seemingly ineluctable teleology of modernist visuality from cubism to surrealism to abstract expressionism that had been prominently established by Greenberg and Alfred Barr by that time. Motherwell's anthology attempted to reestablish a correlation between the poetical language of the avant-garde and the visual production of its artists, a correlation that had been constitutive of modernism since its origins in the nineteenth century, as exemplified in the affiliations between Courbet and Champfleury, between Baudelaire and Manet, between Mallarmé and Degas, between Apollinaire and the cubists. But Motherwell's editorial emphasis on the poetical and literary complements of avant-garde painting seems to have been presented not just as a form of countermemory but also with an underlying critical agenda: namely to destabilize, within the very moment of its formation and at the site of its increasingly chauvinist convictions, the supposed genealogy of abstract expressionism, and to oppose the instrumental specialization of Greenberg's modernism and its hegemonic concepts of medium specificity and opticality on their proper territory.

It is of course not accidental that the impact of Motherwell's collection would only become evident in the next generation of artists (rather than in his own work, let alone that of his peers). Thus—for the first time in the New York School context—the function of poetical and philosophical texts, or more specifically the status of linguistic signifiers within painterly representation, or, ultimately and most importantly, the status of painterly representation *as a linguistic signifier,* would be systematically explored in the work of Cy Twombly (who had met Motherwell at Black Mountain College) and of Jasper Johns from the early to mid-1950s onward.

It is now evident that the rigorous autoreflexive logic of modernist painting, in its persistent paring down to its constitutive features, would make it inevitably approach the condition of a "language," inasmuch as it would function like a regularized structure and system following its own laws. Thus painting—presumed to be essentially incommensurable with language—fulfilled its inherent subjection to the forces of enlightenment and technology, with which it had been involuntarily or intentionally allied ever since the avant-garde made the cause of the collectively dominating, social conditions of perception its own. And in doing so, painting programmatically eliminated the last traces of its traditional affinity with myth and its "natural" association with the forces of the unconscious.

One would have to take into account that it was at that very moment that the Freudian theorization of the unconscious and conceptions of sexuality as the last domain of the natural, the irrational, and the profoundly prelinguistic were giving way to theorizations such as Jacques Lacan's, where the unconscious was conceived for the first time in analogy to the structuring principles of language. In the context of painting, more precisely surrealist automatism and its aftermath, the traditional Freudian models of the libidinal seemed to have found their most compelling evidence in the specifically male-encoded procedures of abstract expressionism. Inasmuch as the myth of the pictorial gesture as the self-evident correlative of the "natural" and of the "unconscious," as a prelinguistic "presence," was embodied in gestural performance, it was primarily on the level of pictorial execution that—at the beginning of

Benjamin H. D. Buchloh

the 1950s—this new process of an increasing secularization and demythification of painting
would occur. Inevitably, this "denaturalizing" critique of the painterly gesture would entail
also the critique of the latent and profoundly gendered assumptions about painting's intricate
association with virility. The transition from Jasper Johns's mid-1950s work to the late 1950s
and early 1960s work of Robert Ryman and Frank Stella illustrates the rapid and consequential demythification of the gestural mark-making process and the critical deconstruction of
this last mythical site of painting. Yet this traditional account of a seemingly ineluctable
development from Johns to Ryman and Stella necessarily had to omit figures like Twombly
and Spero from its narrative, since they represented positions that were quite evidently more
complicated and contradicted the evolution of the logic of modernist painting in its final
stages. What demarcates the differences in Spero's and Twombly's response to the dialectic of
enlightenment produced within the reflection on the discursive traditions of painting is the
fact that they both reinvest painting with a reconsideration of history's (and painting's) profound entanglement with myth. These contradictions were articulated both in their particular
way of incorporating language within the pictorial construct as well as in the manner of reinvesting the painterly mark-making process with a profoundly different type of corporeality.

It seems to have been left precisely to the generation of Spero as a woman/feminist artist
and to Twombly as a gay artist to develop a countercritique for the first time from the perspectives of radically different models of sexual identity. Spero's work would be based on an
altogether different model of the relationship between painting and sublimation and would
set out from a radically different conception of painting as the site of the articulation and
inscription of the unconscious. It is certainly not accidental that Spero and Twombly shared a
deep involvement with the structure and morphology of the *graffito* as much as with its poeti-
cal/textual equivalent of written *profanity*. Pictorially speaking the *graffito* is a type of random
and anonymous mark-making process; in its conscious artistic deployment, however, it rein-
vested the emptied and routine gesture of modernist painting and its deconstruction with a
rather different type of spontaneity and immediacy altogether. The *graffito* inscription was no
longer imbued with a celebration of (male) mastery and the sublime achievement of competence and skill, but rather emphasized the libidinal ineluctability of the pictorial mark-making
process that is as intensely compulsive as it is confined and incompetent.

The dialectical nature of all artistic practice as sublimation is instantly evident in this
emphasis on the contorted conditions of articulation. It is apparent in the continuous oscillation between retentive disgust and elated discharge between which all graffiti gestures—
authentic or consciously adopted—hover: *disgusted* with the conditions of confinement and
the evident absence of the linguistic competence to articulate oneself publicly, a condition
that condemns the speaker precisely to the clandestine forms of speech, and *elated* at finding
any means and sites of articulation at all in an overall regime of interdiction.

Artaud's famous title "All Writing Is Pigshit"—a text especially important to Spero's reading of Artaud[3]—announces precisely this dialectic, and it formulates the countersublimatory
impulse at work in certain artistic oppositions that refuse the compensatory functions of artistic production. One could argue that Spero's *Codex Artaud* functions as a manifesto of coun-
tersublimation and counterenlightenment at the moment of modernism's climactic completion of the project of demythifying painting in the formation of conceptual art. It is here that
we find the continuous invocation of a radically different model of culture: as literature it is
different from modernist visuality, and as historical referent it points toward a different set of
cultural topoi and tropes. In Spero's *Codex* this appeal points not only to the fate of the out-
cast writer Artaud but to literary culture at large, to the continuation of writing in painting
and to the somatic dimension of writing. But Spero's consistent references to medieval

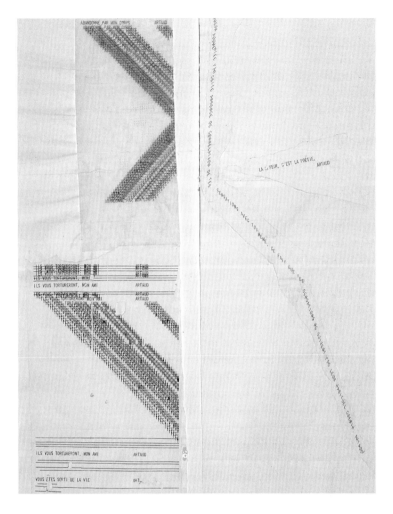

Codex Artaud XVIII
& XIX, 1972.
Detail.
Typewriter and
painted collage on
paper.
140 x 16 in.
Courtesy of the
artist.
Photo: David
Reynolds.

imagery and Egyptian mythology point equally to painting's lost resources in myth. Image types taken from Egyptian scrolls and the *Book of the Dead*, a text that had been of considerable importance to both Artaud and later to Spero herself correspond to Other elegies on lost cultures: Twombly's consistent appeal to the memories of classical antiquity or Marcel Broodthaers's continuous evocation of the central poets of modernity, Baudelaire and Mallarmé, and the loss of *their* literary legacies in the present instrumentalization of language.

The duality of painting as writing and of writing as painting is central to the inversion of a modernist trajectory at that moment. Not only are the literary dimensions of culture invoked in a gesture that mourns the hermetic inaccessibility of those cultural legacies, but the literary dimension is also reinscribed as an aggressive challenge to the myopic definitions of the *pictorial* in the modernist framework and of the *linguistic* in conceptual art. "Writing" and the invocation of Artaud as Spero's "male muse" therefore also assumes a double function in its emergence in Spero's work in the late 1960s: first of all, as argued above, it resituates "painting" within the larger context of speech, language, and poetical representation, and it frees painting from the exclusively perceptual forms of experience to which it had been restricted by modernism. Yet paradoxically, "writing" in Spero's work now also assumes a function of opposing precisely the patent congruence of the "writing" of conceptual art. The underlying model of conceptual art, the analytic proposition, claimed to have sublated the dialectic of painting between pure physicality and spiritual transcendentality, between the pre- and the paralinguistic, and it had pronounced the final reduction of the painterly to the textual. Spero positions the *Codex Artaud* explicitly in the crucial discussion of the early seventies by donning the appearance of a related enterprise and by adopting the conceptualists' most cherished design device, the "radical" reduction of all painting to the typewriter text. In the late sixties and early seventies this ready-made typography was evidently perceived as a quintessential anti-design feature signaling a new "objectivity." By now it appears to have been merely the aesthetic of the tautological and of the totality of administrative order.

Thus for Spero in the *Codex Artaud* the "scene of writing" is a dialectical project of both defacing painting in the name of literature and poetry as well as challenging if not erasing the "writings" of conceptual artists in the name of painting. It is crucial to see, for example, how reductivist painterly concepts such as monochromy and textuality are radically transfigured in their deployment in Spero's *Codex*. The paradigm of monochrome painting had been registered throughout its modernist history as a strategy of reductivist logic, as a consequential paring down of the chromatic and textural elements of painterly representation. Monochromy appears now in Spero's large-scale scrolls as an aggressive assault on that very reductivist logic and pictorial visuality altogether in favor of the definition of the painting as a "page," as a receptacle of writing.[4] The countersublimatory impulse operates thus throughout Spero's work, consistently negating the privilege of the pictorial over the literary just as much as it defaces the triumphant claims of the "language" of conceptual art to have done away with pictorial representation and painterly practice altogether. Thus Spero's dialogue with conceptual art inverts practically every single claim of that movement's primary figures.

The oversize typeface of Spero's (deliberately chosen) *Bulletin*-typewriter mocks the "avantgarde" claims of the conceptualists, their commitment to the purity of language functions and analytical thought. Again, Spero's counterenlightenment impulse reveals suddenly the hidden folly and violence of the rationalist project of conceptualism, its mere affirmation of a rigorous and all encompassing control of instrumentalizing rationality even within the sphere of artistic production. It is against this totalizing claim that Spero mobilizes her dialectic project of painting and writing, and it is against this order that she implores Artaud's testimony. The fragments of pictorial representation, disseminated like shards throughout the scrolls of the *Codex* allegorize the teleology of progressivist pictorial modernism as a failed and insufficient project just as much as the continuous attempts to organize the fields of language fragments in purely graphic, not to say, pictorial terms, denounce the premature sublation of the pictorial within the linguistic as fraud.

NOTES:
1. Interview with Barbara Flynn, in *Nancy Spero: 43 Works on Paper. Excerpts from the Writings of Antonin Artaud* (Cologne: Galerie Rudolf Zwirner, 1987), 1.
2. The revision of the modernist account of Pollock has been accomplished most notably in Rosalind Krauss's study *The Optical Unconscious* (Cambridge: MIT Press, 1992).
3. Amy Schlegel, currently at work on a doctoral dissertation on Nancy Spero, was kind enough to provide me with the information that this particular text is marked by Spero in her copy of Jack Hirschman's *Artaud Anthology*, published by City Lights Books in San Francisco in 1965 and the major—if not the first—source of Spero's encounter with the writings of Artaud.
4. One could of course make an argument that this process had been prefigured in Twombly's paintings of the mid- to late 1950s, where the baring of the canvas as a white ground resulted from both the reductivist logic of pictorial self-reflexivity and the desecratory impulse as it transformed the canvas as a site of privileged pictorial visuality into a "mere" white page of writing.

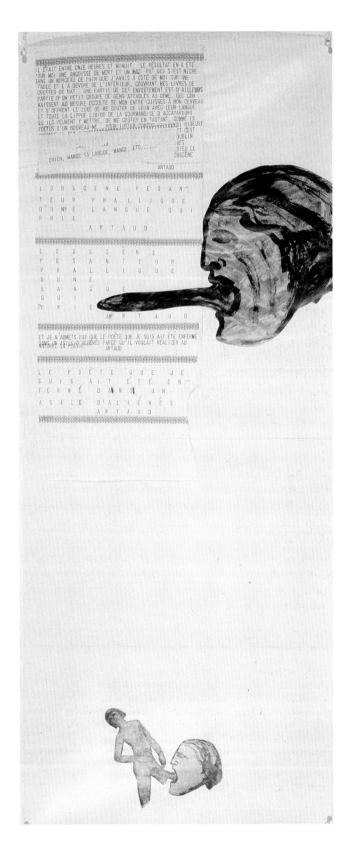

Codex Artaud XIII, 1972.
Handpainted and type-
writer collage on paper.
51 1/4 x 24 1/2 in.
Courtesy of the artist.
Photo: David Reynolds.

Oct, 6, 1973, aubburgberg
dear mmm dear sol
and what an irony —
i choose liberal writing —
i choose number- "date"-numbers — liberal writing —
not to be used
and vice versa it developed
and even i have to use dates
now by using them —
ironical —
but as i wrote to you, SOL:
reason follows reason/creates "iA"
Call "iA" "iA"
and i do hope/will, return
to "iA" dash i will dash
writing liberal writing —
writing as quiet as pencil and
paper as writing is writing —
this is my belief→ "iA"
this is my limit →"iA"
this is my desire→"iA"
and i will work for this→"iA"
and i will work, this for→"iA"
for writing-writing —
"iA" "iA" / dear SOL
call "iA" "iA" / dear SOL
page ④

Untitled (letter
with statements),
1976.
Ink on paper.
Courtesy The
LeWitt
Collection.
Wadsworth
Atheneum,
Hartford,
Connecticut.

Work ennobles—I'm staying bourgeois (Hanne Darboven)[1]

Isabelle Graw

> It is harder to commemorate the nameless than the famous.
> —Walter Benjamin

Hanne Darboven's status seems to be self-evident: notable German artist with international reputation. But how is this seemingly unassailable position to be explained? How do the following elements influence the acquisition and consolidation of a reputation: cultivated middle-class background, German culture, period in New York, family, educational system?

These themes have never actually been discussed in relation to Darboven's work. Yet the titles of her pieces themselves—such as *Evolution 86* and *Ein Jahrhundert (One Century)*—make it fairly obvious that Darboven is committed to a specific notion of culture, history, and education. Most commentators nevertheless pass this by and launch straight into a discussion of the dimension of time in Darboven, conducted in the language of metaphysics.[2]

I will confine myself to the books that Darboven has published, either as catalogues to accompany exhibitions or as "artist's books" in their own right. In books, as distinct from exhibitions, it is possible to read—to take literally—the texts handwritten or typed by Darboven. Her books transmit signs that stand for German culture, for the cultivated bourgeoisie, for a work ethic, and for family relationships.

German Lesson

Darboven has fostered the impression that her work is bound up with an idea of German culture. The work confirms the cliché of a German identity. By giving one book the title *Bismarckszeit (Bismarck's Time,* 1979), she involves herself with a name that epitomizes what is understood by "German history." The texts copied or retranscribed are mostly by the country's great "poets and thinkers": Goethe, Rilke, and Heine.[3] Typically German themes are just what one would expect from a German artist. Unobtrusively, the idea takes root that the artist's nationality gives legitimacy to what she does.

The idea of a specifically German culture is closely tied to the positivist desire for knowledge that regards that culture as a manageable concept (because tied to a single nation). The concept of specific, national knowledge may bring in its train the desire to bring that knowledge under control. Encyclopedias are the correlative to that desire. Darboven frequently consults reference books, copies definitions out of Brockhaus, or compiles indexes.[4] The photographic section at the back of *Bismarckszeit* presents objects "from my collection" that symbolize the bourgeois urge to accumulate culture: a type case (microcosm of the world) or a set of library steps.

A person who has a library in his or her house, complete with library steps, usually lives in style: a member of the upper middle classes or the nobility, with an assured grasp of culture. How are these relics of a high-minded lifestyle to be united with the industriousness of the cultivated bourgeois? To be susceptible to the promptings of the cultivated bourgeois mind, one need not belong to any particular class. Sociologists have in any case abandoned the distinction between upper and lower middle classes. In the presence of manifold identities and allegiances, it seems reductivist to think in terms of class antagonisms. Yet in most countries class thinking is once more increasingly coming to correspond to social reality. In Pierre Bourdieu's behavioral classification, Darboven would qualify as a member of the lower middle class. Many characteristics of her work (asceticism, rigor, strict discipline, predilection for the classics, sense of duty) are defined by Bourdieu as typically *petit bourgeois*.[5]

In fact, however, Darboven grew up in an upper-middle-class—or *grand bourgeois*—environment.[6] Unlike the *petit bourgeois*, she was able to choose her lower-middle-class behavior patterns of her own free will. Not that there is any such thing as unrestricted freedom, even for artists.

Revolt Versus Payoff

Darboven's works often yield two mutually contradictory interpretations. Her thick books connote education and cultivation—which they simultaneously negate. Their bulk bears no relation to their content: indeed, it seems to reduce that content *ad absurdum*. Some of the books are filled with nothing but lines and loops.

Darboven produces books that are more likely to be owned than read. Even so, it has been said of Bismarckszeit that the photographs of her bric-a-brac collection at the end of the book "show the whole of human evolution as manifested in the history of culture and technology."[7] Indeed, she aims to capture and engage vast tracts of time, whole centuries, and the entire history of civilization.[8] Can so comprehensive, so encyclopedic an undertaking ever simultaneously criticize the impulse that drives it?

Art critics who employ the method known as deconstruction[9] might object at this point that even the act of copying out or retranscribing is tantamount to a critique. In the 1980s, many theorists argued that repetitive appropriation displaces or dislocates the original content. I am skeptical about this, if only because I can reread Darboven's texts—or at least those that remain intact and are not broken down into numbers—without ever finding that the copying provokes a different and more critical reading. Far from it: the selection and the types of text used (autobiographical, in the case of Jean-Paul Sartre's *Words* or Charles Baudelaire's *My Heart Laid Bare*) rather suggest that Darboven identifies with the words she copies.[10]

Official Confirmation

Does the accumulation of great names (Bismarck, Goethe, Rilke, Heine, Rainer Werner Fassbinder) express a desire to be part and parcel of this official culture?

That is one possible explanation. The many chronological tables incorporated in the work further indicate that the official canon is never repudiated and that a consensus view of history, culture, and historical personalities is adopted. Ultimately, chronologies are the instruments of the official, linear interpretation of history.

Darboven has also produced books that express her own predilections. Yet they never stray outside the limits of official culture. In *Quartett '88*, she offers an appreciation of four women, none of whom is an unknown. These women are the classic exceptions to the rule; they are official female personalities, individual destinies that testify to a history of female achievement: Marie Curie, Rosa Luxemburg, Gertrude Stein, and Virginia Woolf.

For political events, too, the source is an official one: the German news magazine *Der Spiegel*. Darboven's book *Wende 80 (Turn of the '80s)* contains a reprint of a *Spiegel* interview between Franz Josef Strauss and Helmut Schmidt,[11] in which Strauss's answers have been blacked out. I regard this tendentious intervention on Darboven's part as less significant than the fact that she gives preference to Schmidt. This is foreshadowed in the Fassbinder book, in which the following sentence forms a leitmotiv: "My goat didn't eat Schmidt but she does eat Kohl,"[12] from which we may draw the conclusion that Schmidt and the Social Democrats are preferred as the lesser of two evils.

Among the political figures who find their way into Darboven's books there are no "extremists" or radicals.

Formalities

On the formal level, Darboven's work lays claim to an official function analogous to that of *Der Spiegel*: the red border that runs round many of Darboven's pages is *Der Spiegel*'s graphic trademark.[13]

Does Darboven cater to the needs of an enlightened and critical art public, just as *Der Spiegel* supplies information to its antiestablishment readership? The red border on *Der Spiegel* suggests urgency. Darboven lays claim to a contemporary relevance comparable to *Der Spiegel*'s; or is the red border around the page intended to indicate that the signal it conveys is false?

So we might well suppose, given that Darboven's work confronts us not with important tidings but with historical material either retold or numerically dissected and therefore of little or no news value. Much the same goes for *Der Spiegel*: with regular reading it starts to become predictable. So there are two alternative readings of the red border around Darboven's pages: as with *Der Spiegel*, there is a claim to purvey important information; but that claim is undermined by the fact that the contents are negligible.[14] This dialectic is typical of Darboven's work: it cannot be reduced to either an affirmative or a critical statement. The outcome is not an impasse but a set of productive contradictions.

School Days

The act of copying a text, which dominates Darboven's work, is among the techniques of subjectivization that take shape in institutions. The process of appropriation and internalization that begins in school continues in Darboven's work.

Her handwritten books, and especially those consisting entirely of loops, recall the ritual exercises performed by schoolchildren. Such exercises also regiment the child's thinking: a regular hand brings measured thoughts. Good handwriting implies the avoidance of extremes: unconventional thinking is channeled and disciplined. Social pressures can be internalized through writing.

The sheer bulk of Darboven's books is also a sign of discipline. She has a tightly organized daily routine[15] and once told Sol LeWitt that she always finishes a piece once started.[16] This indicates a sense of duty and suggests that in her eyes all distraction is bad. There are countless other intimations of scholastic rigor. Darboven is pointing to the scholastic mentality that pervades her work. The many timetables that she includes have the same effect.[17] Timetables make the day predictable: they give one a hold on it, by visibly imposing order on the inconsequential. Darboven's work, with its handwriting exercises and checklists, carries us back to our own school days. As Lucy Lippard observes: "It recalls the pleasure of counting rhythmically out loud."[18]

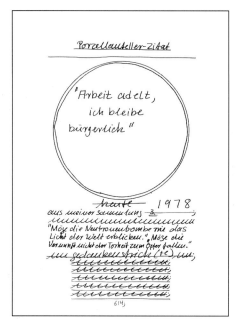

Others approach Darboven's work as they would a math problem, for which there has to be a solution somewhere. The process of cultural reenactment and appropriation that Darboven herself undertakes in her acts of "copying and repeated writing" conveys itself as an obligation to her viewers. Jean-Claude Ammann stresses that Darboven's system is fully worked out;[19] Klaus Honnef pursues total comprehension. Darboven's time system is based, he tells us, on adding together the digits of those numbers that denote years and decades, while keeping those of days and months as double-digit integers.[20]

No attempt is made to carry the interpretation farther. Why is reenactment considered enough? Because Darboven's pages are intended for a viewer who reenacts. Lippard is the one critic, to my knowledge, who has *not* immediately gone along with Darboven's number system. Instead of giving an account of its logic, she sets out to reflect the impulse itself: as she says, she could not imagine anyone encountering Darboven's work without being absorbed into the activity that underlies it.

I have felt this powerful force myself. While working through Darboven's books, I found myself lapsing into a mode of action that anthropologist René Girard describes as "mimetic rivalry." I appropriated Darboven's gesture of writing, as if to compete with her, and myself wrote out by hand those of her retranscribed sentences that seemed important to me. My writing increasingly came to resemble hers.

Conflict at Work

If it is true—as Michel Foucault and Judith Butler assert in relation to psychoanalysis—that all subjectivization is inseparable from submission and creates constraints, then Darboven has produced a visual equivalent for these processes. She cultivates those practices that shape the subjective self (such as a regular work schedule or reading assignments) and produces something of her own that consists of matter not her own: quotations from writers and politicians.

Darboven herself does not think of her work as an identity-creating process but accepts it as work that is there to be done.[21] She transfers the meaning of the work into the work itself,

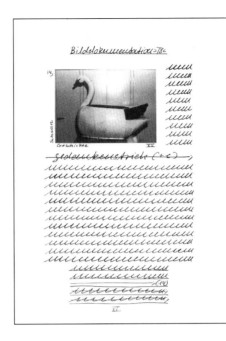
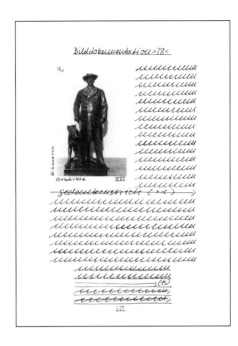

Drawings from
Bismarckszeit
(Bismarck's
Time), 1979.

as if the work were her employer. Anyone who sees work as its own ultimate rationale is accepting the present-day status of work, the universality of the work fixation, and the general acceptance of work as an ironclad duty. Work is regarded as intrinsic to human nature—as the anthropological constant of present-day social life. This primacy of work partly springs from the fear of its contrary: unemployment. To have no work is to be catapulted into a zone right outside this society; and so work becomes an absolute necessity. Hardly anyone (in the Western world) is free from the belief that one has to work, or from the feeling of guilt about not doing enough work.

Darboven commits herself to piecework and remains subject to the time-and-motion production methods of the manual worker in industrial society; equally, however, her work bears witness to a work ethic closely related to the bourgeois sense of duty. Here two class-specific modes of work coexist: Darboven's concept of work cannot be confined to one class alone.

Even superficially, a piece by Darboven points to the countless hours of work that have gone into it; often her books include a note to the effect that the work is "done." The Fassbinder book closes with a list of tasks accomplished. And in the printed items that Darboven sends to friends and acquaintances she alludes to work done.[22] She explicitly draws attention to the fact that individual work sheets and books contain time; the artist's lifetime. Their eventual owners can regard themselves as the possessors of a segment of her life.

Whereas conceptual artists commonly attach value to the Idea,[23] for Darboven "time spent actually working" forms part of the content of her works. She also introduces her subjective self by reporting on how much she has done. Her work is incompatible with the depersonalizing strategies generally associated with conceptual art.

Experience Abroad

Looking through the chronological outlines of Darboven's career, I have noticed that great importance is still attached to her stay in New York and her encounters with conceptual artists. Ever since the catalogue *Ansichten* (*Views*, 1985), her New York period has been mentioned in many publications roughly as follows: "1966–68: living in New York. Contacts with Sol LeWitt, Carl Andre and others."[24] Her two years in New York attract a great deal of attention in relation to their relatively short time span.

There is more to this than the general propensity of First World dwellers for writing CVs in which all foreign travel is totted up in detail as an investment in experience. Darboven did more than spend time in New York: she made contacts that are still worth discussing. In *Evolution 86*, Ulrich Bischoff (who extended Darboven's New York period from two to three years) writes that she came into close contact with the leading exponents of minimal and conceptual art: Sol LeWitt, Carl Andre, Lawrence Weiner, and Hilla and Bernd Becher. The message goes beyond the mere record of those contacts. If a contact is to go down in art history, the parties must have made statements indicative of mutual respect. Without official declarations of affinity by LeWitt for Darboven and vice versa, it would not have been possible to write today (or rather in 1991) that an "intensive dialogue" existed between the two: "LeWitt clearly introduced her to a number of influential people and was seen as her adviser."[25] The figure of LeWitt is significant, in that in the 1960s he not only supported Darboven but also championed Eva Hesse. His role as a forceful advocate of women artists calls for closer study on some other occasion.

Concepts

LeWitt's description of the serial artist (1967) certainly owes something to his knowledge of Darboven's work: he says that the serial artist works like a clerk, cataloguing the outcome of his assignment. Benjamin Buchloh seizes on this statement to criticize conceptual art for mimicking the logic of capitalism and for being the artistic equivalent of a world under total administrative control. It was, writes Buchloh, entirely suited to a technocratic society by virtue of its renunciation of individuality and manual skill.[26] Buchloh reduces conceptual art to the lowest common denominator of an "aesthetic of administration." Aside from the problems raised by any such sweeping generalization, it is worth asking what such an aesthetic would actually look like—an aesthetic composed of bureaucratic principles? The coupling of artistic with social tendencies is a classic device used by art historians to lend relevance to the work under consideration and authority to their own opinions.

In Darboven, however, there are elements that subvert or complicate Buchloh's thesis. The "aesthetic of administration" that he detects in conceptual art is not there in her work— unless, that is, an aesthetic of administration can incorporate and systematize the irrational and the personal. Darboven has never (in the sense argued by Buchloh) called individuality into question. True, her subjective presence emerges through a set of dependent relationships (dependency on authors, on books, on structures, and on systems); but it has always retained an identity of its own, or at least a sign for that identity: an individual handwriting. She has never delegated the "creative process," as LeWitt or Weiner habitually did. This is true even of those of her books that contain type, produced in a manner that entails a division of labor. We are told that a secretary typed up the pages "according to precise instructions."[27] The original formulation remains Darboven's alone. Division of labor does nothing to weaken the status of the inventor—quite the contrary.

Recognition Processes

How did Darboven manage to secure recognition among the artists of the American avant-garde, with their predilection for structures and systems? In 1967 Darboven was invited to participate in "Normal Art" (Lanis Museum of Normal Art), and in the same year her work was in the "Art in Series" show at Finch College: two legendary sites of early conceptual art activity.[28]

Did the other artists not feel her use of handwriting to be a subjective, retrograde element? Lippard cites a letter from Darboven to LeWitt in which the artist herself adopted the language of systems and declared her own to be a vital necessity: "A system became necessary, how else could I see more concentratedly, find some interest, continue, go on at all?"[29] In the first of LeWitt's "Sentences on Conceptual Art," he had written that conceptual artists were mystics rather than rationalists.[30] In light of this publicly proclaimed irrationalism, it must surely have been possible to accept the signs of personality and individuality in Darboven's work.

Family as Powerhouse

Hanne Darboven was born in 1941 to a Hamburg merchant family.[31] She alludes to this context in her work. *Schreibzeit (Writing Time,* 1982) incorporates advertising postcards used by the Darboven firm, to which the artist has "family ties,"[32] and in *Evolution* 86 the photographs at the bottom are of a family party.[33]

Though the work itself ascribes significance to the family, I do not believe that the family explains everything or that it totally determines any of the steps that the artist has taken. Modes of working and personal ambitions can often be traced back to parental standards and expectations, but parental hopes alone do not supply sufficient motivation. According to Bourdieu, one's inclination to acquire professional skills increases in line with the growth of one's social skills and of the social image of oneself as a person who is both worthy and obligated to acquire those skills.[34] The awareness of social status causes the individual to think that a specific achievement is incumbent on her or him.

Darboven was always concerned to prove to her parents that her work was orderly and meaningful. Her letters from New York are revealing in this connection. We learn from Eva Keller that expressions of gratitude to her parents run like a scarlet thread through those letters.[35] In surprisingly dutiful and formal terms, Darboven wrote: "I look up to you, thank you, and hope that my 'work' leads to something, and that I as your daughter can thereby give you pleasure."

Sigmund Freud regards detachment from parental authority as a necessary achievement of individual development.[36] With Darboven, detachment from parents went along with orientation toward them. This may have been a function of distance. Relationships often gain in intensity when people are far apart. Additionally, in New York Darboven depended on her parents for financial support. In the letters it all started with Darboven minutely describing the events of her day. So was her eventual choice of artistic technique initially prompted by family constraints?

Darboven's obsessive and systematic mode of working may well have played a part in proving her determination to her parents: she must, after all, have had a hard time convincing them that her work was art. What kind of work would hold up in her parents' eyes? One that made a "worthy" contribution to the history of art. So was the incorporation of official history, culture, and great names a way of impressing her parents? Darboven's predilection for German history and for "official" knowledge points to the influence of her family's cultural tastes. The work ethic that emanates from the work and its reproduction of cultural input reveal a familiarity with the convictions typical of the higher bourgeoisie.

Darboven's work, with its thick books and pointless activities, presents the hunger for

253

culture and the thirst for knowledge as absurd; yet it appeals to the consciousness of an art public principally composed—now as always—of members of the ruling classes: an encounter actually out of keeping with the implied purpose of the artist's actions. Most often, the distinguishing strategies of the producers and those of receptive consumers coincide without having to look for each other.

Translated from the German by David Britt

NOTES:

1. "Arbeit adelt, ich bleibe bürgerlich." Inscription on a china plate illustrated in Darboven's book *Bismarckszeit* and recorded as being in her own collection.
2. For example, Jean-Christophe Ammann in the Darboven publication *Atta Troll* (Luzern: Kunstmuseum, 1975); Klaus Honnef in the exhibition catalogue of the Westfälischer Kunstverein (1971); and Margarethe Jochimsen in *Wende 80* (1982) (the latter writes "on the principle of temporality").
3. See the book *Johann Wolfgang von Goethe* (1988) or Darboven's work based on extracts from *Atta Troll* by Heinrich Heine (1975). *R. M. Rilke—das Stundenbuch* (New York: Leo Castelli, 1987) contains photographed pages from Rilke's *Stundenbuch*.
4. See the index at the end of *Histoire de la culture* (Paris: Musée National d'Art Moderne, 1980–83).
5. See Pierre Bourdieu, *Le distinction* (Paris: Minuit, 1979).
6. See Eva Keller, "Konstruktionen 1966/67," in *Hanne Darboven,* exhib. cat. (Basel, 1991).
7. Quoted from Klaus Honnef, *Bismarckszeit* (Bonn: Rheinisches Landesmuseum, 1979).
8. As her projects *Histoire de la culture* (History of Culture) and *Ein Jahrhundert* (One Century) demonstrate.
9. According to Jacques Derrida, there can be no such thing as a method of deconstruction. I refer to a ensemble of currents of thought that found their way into art criticism in the mid-1980s through poststructuralism and deconstruction.
10. See the Darboven publication of 1975 in which Baudelaire's *Mon coeur mis à nu* and parts of Sartre's *Les mots* are copied out.
11. Rival German politicians: Strauss of the right-wing Christian Social Union (CSU), Schmidt of the left-of-center Social Democratic Party of Germany (SPD). Hanne Darboven, *Wende 80* (Bonn: Bonner Kunstverein, 1982).
12. "Schmidt hat meine Ziege nicht gefressen, aber Kohl frißt sie." The conservative Christian Democratic Union (CDU) politician Helmut Kohl has been chancellor since 1982. (The word *Kohl* means "cabbage.") His predecessor as chancellor (1974–82), Helmut Schmidt, led the SPD in the general election of 1980.
13. This red border is present, for example, in the book *Quartett 88* and in the Fassbinder book.
14. Which suggests the converse: that much the same can be said of the news in *Der Spiegel*.
15. In the catalogue *Schreibzeit, Biennale Venedig* (1982), Johannes Cladders speaks of her "inexorable rhythmic discipline."
16. See Lucy R. Lippard, "Deep in Numbers," *Artforum* no. 2 (1972).
17. See Darboven's book *Ansichten* (1985).
18. As cited by Lippard, "Deep in Numbers."
19. See Ammann, *Atta Troll*.
20. See Honnef, *Bismarckszeit*.
21. See Lippard, "Deep in Numbers."
22. See the information given by Ammann, *Bismarckszeit*.
23. In "Sentences on Conceptual Art" (1969), LeWitt writes that only ideas can be works of art.
24. The wording of the biographical note on Darboven in the Kunsthalle Basel catalogue (1991).
25. Keller, "Konstruktionen 1966/67."
26. Benjamin H. D. Buchloh, "From the Aesthetic of Administration to Institutional Critique," in *L'Art conceptuel, une perspective* (Paris: Musée d'Art Moderne de la Ville de Paris, 1989).
27. In *Bismarckszeit,* Honnef quotes Evelyn Weiss: "Among other things, Darboven writes her tabulation of one century in a series of more than 100 books. They are all typed by a secretary according to precise instructions, just as is done in producing the manuscript for a book."
28. She was involved in "Information" at The Museum of Modern Art in 1970, and in 1971 she took part in the "Guggenheim International." She was also included in the touring survey exhibition "Europe in the Seventies: Aspects of Recent Art" (1977–79), organized by the Art Institute of Chicago.
29. As quoted by Lippard, "Deep in Numbers."
30. The third "Sentence" contains the statement that irrational judgments lead to new experience.
31. See Keller. "Konstruktionen 1966/67."
32. See Cladders, *Schreibzeit, Biennale Venedig.*
33. See Ulrich Bischoff, *Evolution 86* (Munich: Staatsgalerie Moderner Kunst, 1991).
34. See Pierre Bourdieu, *Questions de sociologie* (Paris: Minuit, 1980).
35. See Keller, "Konstruktionen 1966/67."
36. See Sigmund Freud, *Der Familienroman der Neurotiker.*

October, 19, 1973, allburgberg
dear sol at hesterstreet ——
i do like to write
i don't like to read
this world is real
this word is frightening
this word is real
i don't like to read
i do like to write
all what is written i read
all what i write is written
i write
i d'out describe
writingwriting
there is nothing to describe
writing writing
i d'out describe
i write
all what i write is written
all what is written i read
i do like to write
i d'out like to read
this world is real
this world is frightening
this world is real
i d'out like to read
i do like to write
—————   all —————— /

Untitled, 1976. Ink, paper, envelope. Courtesy The LeWitt Collection.
Wadsworth Atheneum, Hartford, Connecticut.

Élan, 1982. Detail.
Thirteen c-type photographs with colored ink,
each 30 x 20 in., block-mounted, and stereo soundtrack,
11 minutes duration. Overall installed dimensions
12 ft. 10 in. x 8 ft. 4 in. Courtesy of the artist and
Pat Hearn Gallery, New York. Photo: Zindman/Fremont.

Susan Hiller: *Élan* and Other Evocations

Jean Fisher

The aim of this essay is to trace one strand of Susan Hiller's work that makes specific use of "automatic writing" or its auditory equivalent, nonverbal vocalization. This choice is both arbitrary and paradigmatic, as all of Hiller's work concerns unraveling the knots of everyday language, freeing a space for a more productive play of the imagination. *Midnight Tottenham Court Road* (1982) recalls early Renaissance predella panels. Four rephotographed and enlarged Photomat self-portraits, slightly less than life-size, are arranged side by side. Each head has been cut and displaced from its background while an erratic script, partly obscured by a wash of color, faintly Islamic but in any case not alphabetic, lingers like a semi-transparent screen over both. The facial features, stained with colored markers, possess the androgyny of painted angels, the eyes closed in an ambiguous gesture: sleep, death, trance, or ecstasy? The sitter therefore seems withdrawn into herself, strangely uninterested in the presence of the mirror/camera and resistant to the desire for reciprocal self-affirmation through an exchange of gazes. The projection of a public identity through the seeming transparency of the exterior—the assumption that the outer aspect reveals the nature of the inner being, which is our expectation of the portrait—is refused. The face is veiled, reinscribed, and rendered partially opaque, the gaze turned inward to a private, interior space of reflection.

Hiller's self-portraits nevertheless make no claim to a privileged or transcendent subjectivity. Her source material (the set of Photomat miniatures) undergoes several transformations: decoupage, montage, inscription. Always more or less, or variable within the same work, as in *Midnight Liverpool Street* (1984), the vacillation of scale means that the viewer can never stabilize. Others, like *Midnight Kings Cross* (1984) and *Midnight Oxford Circus* (1987), do not center their objects as do professional portraits; rather, as in amateur snapshots or mannerist paintings, the object is cropped or faintly distorted, so that the frame draws attention to the eye, mouth, or ear: the organs of perception and communication, complementing earlier works that focused on the back, shoulders, and particularly the hands. We are given not representation's mirrored body but an allusion to those *acts*—seeing, hearing, speaking, making—by which the self constantly reinterprets and reinvents itself in its relations with the world.

The suggestion of a performative or narrative space in excess of the given view is also implied by Hiller's manipulations and the serial format of the Photomat. If the mechanism promises to fulfill the realist (and bureaucratic) demand that the photographic portrait provide "evidence" of an "authentic" and stable identity, in Hiller's hands it produces multiple, shifting identities whose expressions are controlled by the subject herself, not legislated by the mediating authority of the photographer. Moreover, while referring to minimalism's seriality and its reification of the frame, the order of Hiller's "grids" is transgressed by overlaps, slippages, and variable contents such that the frame never restrains its object.

Hence, although at first glance these works apparently subscribe to familiar aesthetic genres and modernist codes of representation—photographic reproduction, montage, and projection, combined with the color and gesture traditional to painting—it quickly becomes clear that these codes subtly contaminate one another. A continuous dialogue occurs between the "authenticity" or "originality" assumed for the handmade mark and its mechanical reproduction, between the demands of the photograph as mirror or analogue of nature and its status as no more than surface illusion. Consequently we move beyond any secure notion of pure categories or determinable identities: rather, we are drawn into a imaginative field of permeable or shifting boundaries, where vision is no longer the guarantor of "truth" and in which we are invited to reflect upon the duplicity of representation and the uncertain nature of seeing.

The artist's work plays between the dual meaning of vision: in the post-Enlightenment rationalist sense of the mechanics or physiology of sight, and in the nonrational sense of what is *beyond* the purely retinal, in the domains of psychic processes and the supernatural. Western thought has given priority to vision as the guarantor of the truth of the world, until recently developing a succession of technologies of vision—the camera obscura, photography, the magic lantern and slide projection, film and video, to which the artist has made constant reference—designed to "improve" the veracity of visual representation. This view of the world relies on the existence of stable or essentially unchanging entities; indeed the identity and status of its privileged subject is guaranteed by identification with fixed positions that objectify the world and deny other subjectivities, a system idealized in Western perspective.

Technologies are, however, far from ideologically neutral. Rather, they are inextricably bound to the thought processes, fears, and desires of the culture that invents them. Hiller's work makes manifest this tension between the drive to stabilize identity and an inherent but disavowed instability. Despite the apparent self-assurance of the Western representational system, it is possessed by an underlying anxiety. Its traditional, centered point of view is symmetrical with and dependent on its other—the vanishing point; where "I" am summoned as a subject is also the place where "I" cannot be and where "I" become the object of another's gaze. What prevents me falling into this hole is the framing apparatus as it positions and anchors me in relation to the imago/object isolated in the visual field.

The mechanism of photography is thoroughly implicated in this capture of the object, as Hiller's Midnight series shows. While *Midnight Tottenham Court Road* produces such an object, its various veilings and displacements deflect our narcissistic desire that it function as an affirming mirror of the self. Nor do the veilings promise some hidden meaning ready to be revealed by the author; on the contrary, they suggest that representation is itself the veil behind which there is "nothing" but what we don't know we know—the "blind spot" that sits like an invisible stain in the retinal field. What it reveals is, in the end, nothing but our desire to know.

Here, too, framing offers no security. Insofar as the retinal takes up only a narrow angle of the total spatial field occupied by the viewer, there is always a "behind-sight"—a tenebrous terrain beyond the edge of the frame, outside the periphery of vision. The frame, then, occupies an ambivalent and precarious zone between the "there" and the "elsewhere," order and chaos, the known and the not-known. It is to this that the titles of this series of works refer: the train station as a no-place between being here and being there; "midnight" as the space between "before" and "after," past and future. In effect, midnight is an interval of suspended time, when the mind's censors relax their vigilance and surrender the body to its erotic and morbid imaginings: to an intimation of death.

The instability to which Hiller's work ultimately refers is produced by the lack of coincidence between the image of the self as understood through its own psychosocial history and its image as the image of the other that calls the subject into being, that inscribes its place within the imaginary symbolic order. The order is that of inherited language, the "voice of the dead" that precedes us and that, in naming us, displaces us from the body where we feel ourselves to be, henceforth condemning us to a desire that perpetually pursues a lost unity. Yet the very lack of coincidence points to the indeterminacy of language, the fictional edifice upon which cultural identity is founded, and its inability to give an account of the complexity of existence. There, in the minute fractures in the apparent seamlessness of language, in disturbances in the coherence of the visual field, the subject can play with its own reinscription. Hiller's work stirs up these disturbances, articulated around the question of inscription itself.

The artist's "automatic writing" is central to this inquiry. It appeared, unsolicited, so to speak, from the artist's hand while on a trip to France—a semi-alphabet scrawl covering several pages that announced itself as the voice of the "Sisters of Menon." First exhibited in 1974 and then mislaid for several years, the pages reappeared in 1979, and from them the artist made *Sisters of Menon,* first as a set of annotated panels arranged in a cruciform (1979) and later as a book (1983).[1] Hence, the ecstatic moment that brought forth the writing underwent a further transcription into a symbolic order that, on one level, might seem to be an attempt to give a "reasoned" account of its appearance yet, on another, enacts the language of desire's characteristic deferral as it seeks but never finds its impossible object—a perpetual writing performed throughout Hiller's successive works.

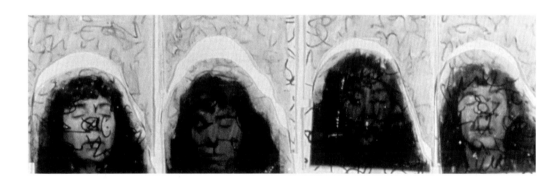

idnight
ottenham Court
oad, 1982.
-type photograph
nlarged from
andworked photo-
ooth images.
ourtesy of the
rtist and Gimpel
ils Gallery,
ondon.

Automatic writing is not amenable to rationalist interpretations, which is not to say, however, that it does not possess its own order or sense; we may simply not know what this is. It has long been practiced by psychic mediums to "get in touch" with the dead and was keenly practiced by the surrealists as a means of getting in touch with psychic processes, following their interest in Freud's analysis of dreams and the workings of the unconscious. Hiller's involvement in this practice has nonetheless little to do with "conjuring" or with revelations of modernism's unique, autonomous self; it does however reclaim the spirit of this earlier writing, whose significance was lost in its aesthetic mutation into the reified gestural mark of late modernism.[2] If this came to signify an authentic, creative self, by contrast, Hiller's performative gesture speaks of the *creative process*.

The inscriptions of *Sisters of Menon* are handwork comparable to the wordless vocalizations of works using time-based media, such as *Élan* (1982) and *Belshazzar's Feast/The Writing on Your Wall* (1983–84), both of which express the yet-to-be-deciphered movement of desire as it inscribes the body prior to or in excess of any sublimation to determinable referents. In relation to these vocalizations, the artist refers to the liberating experience of hearing a recording of Kurt Schwitters's *Merz* poem *Sonata for Primeval Sound,* in which the uncoupling of signifiers from any determinable signifieds releases laughter, the free play of association, and the possibility of unexpected meanings and of the uses of language in non-Western cultures such as the Native American, whose songs condense ideas, often incorporating the language of animate and inanimate spirits—a lightness of language that counterpoints the weight of its rhythm. In any case, these codes lie beyond the scope of Western thought.

Vocalization has, then, a special role in the artist's work: a materiality of sound that vibrates with the body and its reminiscences in nonvisual and nonverbal ways—rhythm and spatiality, touch and volume, movement and stillness, lightness and weight, sound and silence. In *Élan* both the soundtrack and the scale of the photographic construction appeal directly to these bodily sensations.[3] "Élan," the only decipherable word to appear in the calligraphic dance of this particular body of scripts, may be loosely translated as an "ardor of the spirit," evoking the sense of weightlessness that is part of the ecstatic moment. The color photographs, derived from negative projections of the scripts (a negativity that perhaps alludes to the *absence* of the self in language), are installed floor to ceiling and grouped in four sets of three panels to form a cross, with an "empty" space at the center. This open "figure"—it is more than a ground—is of such a scale that one might imagine oneself bodily within it. The approximate size and position of a mirror, it nevertheless reflects nothing. It functions rather like the blank page before the initiation of the *Sisters* script, the fire in *Belshazzar's Feast,* or, as the artist has pointed out, the Tibetan Tantric meditation image called *me-lon* (mirror)—a screen for meandering reverie and the projection of fantasies. One photographic panel—less a writing than a joyful arabesque—sits alone beside the larger configuration as a strange supplement or a part displaced.

The notion of decipherability is traced throughout the soundtrack, in which the artist's improvised wordless singing (whose vocables are not all common to Western speech patterns) alternates with fragments of the Raudive recordings.[4] Prefacing these (literal) "voices of the dead," with their cryptic "messages" struggling to emerge through the crackling of tape noise, are two other voices, male and female, which, in the authoritative tones of the anthropologist or scientific researcher, instruct the listener on how to interpret what they are about to hear. Yet these commentaries make no more sense than the utterances themselves. The artist's voice closes the soundtrack on a quasi-pedagogical note:

> Language as system, language as symptom, language as shock. The fragmented body. They build walls out of fragments. She builds a wall against silence. Five seconds of silence for the dead, starting—now. Their silent memorial. The enigma of divided origins, tradition and inspiration. Fruitful incoherence, formless production, aimless production as expression. Here, language breaks free. Outside of its own quotation the voice is a relic.

Élan moves as a continuous involution of inner and outer space. It presents us with a heterogeneity of textual allusions in which "meaning" is continuously displaced: the scientific text in which the machine—as above for the photograph—produces "objective evidence" of a truth to which we are urged to bear witness; the social text in which "hearing voices" is construed skeptically as a sign of psychosis; and the psychic text in which our minds and bodies are captive to the work's pulsations through our desire to believe the improbable.

The artist, however, makes clear that the significance of ecstatic writing lies not as content but as utterance, an act of saying.[5] The "I" who is an other in *Sisters* figures a leap into a weightless gravity where the "becoming-absent and becoming-unconscious of the subject"[6] finds regeneration. Hiller's insistence on the need to retranscribe "other" possible subjectivities, not only against the grain of dominant discourses but against those who make a virtue of the marginal, gains support from cultural inquiries outside the field of art. Her rhythms and cadences, her evocations of the terror and ecstasy that accompany the pleasure of art, find echoes in Julia Kristeva's notion of the "pre-Oedipal *chora*,"[7] an ungendered, rhythmic pulsion or pressure on symbolic language. Although the *chora* cannot displace this language, it produces interferences in the form of nonsense, silences, and absences, opening a space for a transformation and resymbolization of the self.

The body that speaks in hieroglyphs is that which finds no representation in the economy of dominant discourse. This ecstatic utterance is commonly associated with the mystic or visionary or with the sense of the sublime in art. But it is clear from Hiller's work that to a greater or lesser extent it is integral to human experience: what emerges as visual or verbal hallucination is fundamentally an effect of language to which we are all subject. Nevertheless, the rapturous moment of writing has been negatively gendered: when uttered by a male, it is valorized as poetic; when uttered by those outside this privileged position, it is marginalized as mad, nonsensical, exotic.

For the most part Hiller explores collective utterances and vernacular images deriving from experiences within the everyday that defy rational explanation and that therefore are typically marginalized and dismissed as folk/popular superstitions, hallucinations, mis-sightings, pathological aberrations or, in earlier times, the ecstatic visions of saints. Far from marginal, however, they are central to culture insofar as they speak from the place where society's unacknowledged fears and desires sediment. Like Freud's return of the repressed, these fears and desires cannot be wholly contained by society's mechanisms of censorship and tend to seep to the surface, often projected in strangely allegorized forms.

Such is the theme of the artist's video installation *Belshazzar's Feast/The Writing on Your Wall,* which draws on reverie (a state of near-trance in which the mind wanders down unpremeditated pathways) and hallucination (a phenomenon that corresponds to no determinable recollection and whose source—like the "Sisters of Menon"—is invariably located *outside* by the subject who experiences it; in this respect, there is a correlation with the mystic narrative).

One version of *Belshazzar's Feast* presents a cluster of video monitors arranged to suggest a campfire around which one might gather at night to tell and listen to stories. Somewhat abstracted and constantly metamorphosing images of tongues of fire emerge with the persistent cracking of fire, a reference to the role that the hearth once played as a site of reverie and imagination—a role since usurped by television. A somewhat authoritarian voice ("What the fire says, Take One . . .") periodically introduces a faintly exotic improvised vocalization, alternating with the voice of a child. Midway through the video, a secretive whispering recounts published newspaper reports of people who claimed to have received transmissions from "aliens" through the television screen *after* broadcast hours. These messages were often apocalyptic.

The artist draws parallels between these mysterious communications and the phantasms of fire gazing, which were also interpreted as premonitions of disaster. The artist links these to the biblical story of Belshazzar's feast (connecting also with art, since this is the subject of a painting by Rembrandt), which tells how a society's punishment for transgressing divine law was forewarned in cryptic writing traced on a wall by a disembodied hand—signs that could only be deciphered by the mystic Daniel. Fragments of this story reappear throughout the video, spoken in the often faltering voice of a young boy as if repeating a lesson.

Memento M, 1987.
Ripolin, gesso, and Conte
crayon on wallpaper, mounted
on canvas.
85 x 54 in.
Courtesy of the artist.

How should we interpret such apparitions except as projections of an inner conflict—the ejected voice of the inside that, like a thief in the night, makes a guilty return from the outside? Hiller's juxtaposition of three modes of saying—nonverbal singing, the adult voice of interpretation, and the child's efforts to re-collect the fragments of a story into a meaningful whole (in effect, to narrate himself into the social)—realizes the tension between the experience of the body and the constraints of language: between the pulsions of desire and the demands of the Law that it conform to its own narrations, a struggle played out across competing forms of authorized and unauthorized representation.

If language nominates a subject in distinction to others, Hiller's nonverbal scripts and vocalizations dissolve such categories. They are not identifiable in any strict linguistic sense; rather they suspend language, feign writing, nevertheless expressing a rhythmic scriptovisual space. In the Photomat portraits, the script disfigures not the face but its representation. Like a tattoo, it "stains" the exterior of the body while mapping its extension beyond the limits of perception or speech.

In the artist's collaged paintings, this calligraphy emanates from an existing cultural ground—mass-produced domestic wallpapers—to suggest the tension between an unrepresentable field of existence and society's institutionalized interpretations of reality. Thus, the wallpaper both frames and is partly obliterated by layers of semiopaque scriptural veils: a double inscription of erasure and disclosure. Although the wallpaper deliberately evokes pop art's engagement with mass media or kitsch, Hiller does not celebrate this but reflects on certain slippages in signification, reinvesting familiar cultural artifacts with those social and historical narratives that pop art relegated to the aesthetic realm. Thus, the still-life motif of the kitchen wallpaper in *Memento M . . .* (1987) has its roots in the *vanitas*, a death-and-mortality theme hardly appropriate to accompany the preparation of food and that consequently suffers a burial or inversion of meaning. More sinister, perhaps, are the designs selected for children's rooms, which are gendered according to crude stereotypes of what should concern girls and boys. Wallpaper is conventionally regarded as an invisible backdrop to aesthetic pleasure. But Hiller's paintings unfold its latent meanings, bringing into focus what is visible but unseen or what is invisible but potentially seeable, otherwise obscured by encrusted cultural baggage or blind habit. These paintings render visible how the home and the child's unconscious become colonized and manipulated by dominant ideologies and how perception is directed toward mediated conventions of seeing and identity. Yet we should not mire this work in a ponderous seriousness; as Italo Calvino said of an ancient writer, in poetry "knowledge of the world tends to dissolve the solidity of the world, leading to a perception of all that is infinitely minute, light, and mobile."[8]

The work seeks to lighten the apparent seamless unity of this ideological vision, to disclose other, heterogeneous meanings through which the self might reinscribe its own narrative. Hiller's transcriptions—the handmade marks, enlarged, projected through light, and painted onto the wallpaper ground—mime and undermine photography's documentary truth. And as this truth reveals itself as a fiction, it summons more intimate projections: memories of childhood's twilight reveries when the mundane familiarity of the wallpaper pattern dissolved into strange, often animated configurations. This imaginative space, glimpsed only briefly in the everyday, is also the productive space of art.

This "other" spatiality, where desire ceaselessly transcribes itself, announces the dissolution of the boundaries that define the subject. We might speak of an unsignifiable space of nonentities, of pure relation, of the dance of dust particles in the sunlight of which Calvino is so enamored. At this limit of the representable is the lightness of thought before it knows itself as thought, a joyous liberation of desire into a space of pure production—the tracings and retracings, resonant with the carnivalesque humor, passion, horror, and ecstasy of an itinerant and heterogeneous self in the process of continuously making and remaking itself.

NOTES:

An early version of this essay appeared in *Lifelines/Lebenslinien: Four Artists in Great Britain/Vier Künstler aus Großbritannien* (Liverpool: Tate Gallery Liverpool; Ludwigshafen: Ausstellung im BASF-Feierabendhaus, 1989).

1. For a more extended discussion of *Sisters of Menon* see my essay "The Echoes of Enchantment," in this volume.
2. See the interview with Catherine Lacey in *Susan Hiller: Belshazzar's Feast* (Tate New Art/The Artist's View Series, 1984), reprinted in *Thinking about Art: Conversations with Susan Hiller*, ed. Barbara Einzig (Manchester: Manchester University Press, 1996).
3. The description of *Élan* is developed from my book *Susan Hiller: The Revenants of Time* (London: Matt's Gallery; Sheffield: Mappin Art Gallery; Glasgow: Third Eye Centre, 1990).
4. During the late 1960s the Latvian psychologist Konstantin Raudive conducted a series of experiments in which he left a tape recorder running in an empty, soundproofed room. He claimed that the resultant amplified sound recordings were the voices of historical figures (mostly famous modernist men like Mayakovsky, James Joyce, Winston Churchill) who had their own transmission station.
5. See also "Beyond Control: Susan Hiller Interviewed by Stuart Morgan," *Frieze*, no. 23 (Summer 1995), 52–57 and cover.
6. The phrase is borrowed from Jacques Derrida, *Of Grammatology*, trans. Gayatri Chakravorty Spivak (Baltimore: Johns Hopkins University Press, 1974), 69.
7. Julia Kristeva, "Revolution in Poetic Language," in *The Kristeva Reader*, ed. Toril Moi (Oxford: Basil Blackwell, 1986), 93.
8. Italo Calvino, *Six Memos for the Next Millennium*, trans. Patrick Creagh (London: Jonathan Cape, 1992), 6.

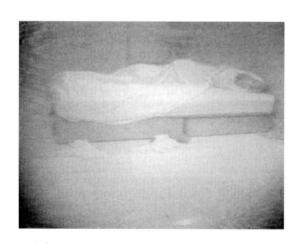 

Hommage à (Homage to) (I, II), 1972.
Video still.
Video, originally 16 mm. film, 30 minutes.
Courtesy of the artist.
Photo: Hans Sonneveld.

Homage to . . .:
The Pensive Images of Lili Dujourie

Marianne Brouwer

More than twenty years ago, Lili Dujourie made a small series of video works. They stand distinct at the beginning of her oeuvre, as well as at the beginning of the seventies, when video art was new. Because video—unlike film—couldn't be edited or otherwise manipulated, the notion of "real time" became important in the battle against the "idealized time" of the art object. Video was therefore intimately linked to the real time of performance art, which it often recorded. Dujourie's videos—made around 1972—make expert use of the tension of performance in real time, yet they are unique for those days in that they are first and foremost artworks in their own right. Undemonstrative and quiet, they are recordings of waiting, of the imperceptible passing of time, of a Proustian sense of ennui, agonizingly beautiful and—whether because of or in spite of their beauty—sometimes almost unbearable to watch. The first of them, *Hommage à . . . (Homage to . . .),* is also the most monumental, anticipating what was to become her main sculptural work in the eighties, in both form and content.

The video shows a naked woman on a large bed that stands in what seems to be a corner of a light and spacious room. The camera is directed at her slightly from above in such a way that the space frames her like a painting. The woman seems to be asleep at first. She is young and very beautiful. Perhaps she is taking a siesta. Perhaps she is also dreaming—for we see her restlessly tossing and turning, rolling over and over on the bed. Clutching at the sheets, she throws her limbs about, furls up like a fetus or stretches like a cat. Sometimes she slowly rolls off the bed, then searches for the edge of the bed, hoists herself up and starts tossing and turning again. Gradually we may begin to recognize something familiar about her, resembling a déjà-vu. It is there in the very poses of the woman, as though her attitudes were part of a repertory. It is there in the axis around which her movements rotate, at the center of the painterly perspective. The sheets through her gestures seem to undergo a metamorphosis and become the rich drapery we associate with Titian's Venus or Manet's *Olympia.* There is the arm, flung aside or bent under the neck like the one of Goya's *Maya.* The long, curved back that we know from Ingres. The legs, opening up or dangling from the bed, give us Courbet. Each posture recalls yet another famous painting, as though in a *tableau vivant.* She lies there like a painter's dream, presenting herself, opening herself up to the gaze: the perfect painter's model.

Time gradually changes us into the uneasy voyeurs of this naked woman's body, by the very ambiguity of its intimacy and the attitudes she seems to offer up for choice. What are we to make of her—naked woman or Female Nude? In the former case she might be judged provocative or shamelessly seductive. In the latter she belongs to the wholly different category

265

Marianne Brouwer

of sculpture and painting, of the woman's body as sublime. But sleep renders her innocent and totally self-contained, unaware of whoever looks at her. Her passiveness is total, maddeningly so perhaps. Maybe we, the public, cannot look at her without wishing her to wake up, maybe worse.

A woman's body, fast asleep. The closed eyes do not look at the painter, at the public. She seems unaware of herself, of us. Yet she poses in the nude. But how do we know for sure that she poses? Whose model is she? What kind of awakening will it take for her to become courtesan, full-length portrait, nymph, madonna? For wake up she must, rise and freeze into one of the attitudes she seems to offer up for choice; if ever she is to acquire meaning, she must undergo the transformation into whatever we, the public or the painter, want her to be. As yet, we don't know what to make of her. As yet, her body is nothing but place, *lieu, Ort.*

She is nothing but our gaze.

Hommage à . . . contains many layers of meaning. For Dujourie is both the artist and the model. The woman on the bed and the woman directing our gaze through the camera are the same person. We watch her through the eye of the camera exactly as she wants us to see her; exposed to the public for an eternity of real time. Hers is not a "pure" body, because meaning is already inscribed within it; the implicit meaning culture attributes to woman as an object. In fact it is the artist who offers us this object—herself—as her own subject. She does not

Hommage à (Homage to) (III, IV), 1972. Video still. Video, originally 16 mm. film, 30 minutes. Courtesy of the artist. Photo: Hans Sonneveld.

say "I," or "me"; her body exists at the frontier of subject and object, of word and flesh. There is nothing natural in her seemingly languid poses. So difficult, so unnatural are they that it is agony to adopt them and to hold still for any longer period of time. What seems to be sleepy abandon is in fact total concentration on movement, on the rhythm of transposition between one pose and the next, on the duration of each pose. Although the video shows us the artist, it certainly doesn't show us a self-portrait in any usual sense. It denies the self-consciousness of the inquisitive gaze, the scrutiny by measured distance. The soul bared through the eyes, the implicit judgment the painter asks his public to wage while he looks at himself in the mirror—all of that is absent; instead there is just the pose, the framing. Yet she wants us to look at her. Is that the same as being seen? And whom or what does she want us to see? Does it make a difference who is looking at her—man or woman?

To pause and look more closely than is required, to look at what one is not supposed to look at in the context of cinema action, cinema affection, cinema superproduction, upsets

266

the established order in all its forms, to the degree that the very duration or intensity of the gaze is controlled by society. Hence, the outrageous nature of certain films when they escape this control, not because they are indecent or aggressive but simply because they foreground the "pose." Because what one can call the movement-image, which characterizes the concept of filmmaking in mainstream cinema and equates action to movement, is being challenged here by the time-image in which time is no longer made the measure of movement, but rather, through movement, a perspective of time is made visible. The image is subversive, not through violence and aggression, but through duration and intensity. . . . It unsettles the male apparatus of the gaze, in which men own, articulate, and create the look, while woman is either being looked at (displayed for the gaze of male protagonists as well as of male spectators), or she only holds the look to signify the master's desire.[1]

The painter decides what his model is to represent. Whatever she is in the real world, whether she is called Marie or Jeanne, she is shortly to become Diana, Mary, Eve, or the Republic of France. The artist has cast his look at her and decided that she is the chosen one; he will tattoo his meaning on her, from a nobody she will become Pygmalion's woman, the one to whom *he* gives life—for she does not live by herself; he made her, he discovered her, he breathes life and meaning into her. The model needs to be transformed by the artist, in order to *be*, to exist at all. As to the real Jeanne or Marie, she is just the raw material, which has no place in history. Her own life is of no account; she only lives within the sublime transfiguration of art.

Framed by painterly space, woman's body for centuries has been the product of our gaze. Dujourie offers us woman as a live, mute body, invested with whatever meaning we may attribute to it, and yet independent of it, because she will not allow us to share her own space. Reversing roles, she becomes the lake into which Narcissus gazes—Narcissus being anyone, man or woman. Her body gazed at since time immemorial and absorbing all the gazes. Invested with meaning and reflecting all. Not offering realism, nor stereotype, nor opinion, but suspended time. She is whatever we make of her, the projected image of desire, of art, of beauty, of memory. She herself is *no place*. If a mirror existed that could absorb our every gaze, she would be that mirror. We would not know it was there. There would be the drapery, the empty place, just abandoned, the imprint of her foot, but not herself.

The waiting. The interval. The consciousness, the intended pose, the transition between poses, the endlessly repeated.

In this way *Hommage à* . . . evokes Dujourie's later sculptures, done in the eighties; the draperies, the velvet curves and bows, all around bodies that are no longer there. Ornaments, frames, indicating the figure, all signifying, never the signified. How does one describe an empty frame, an abandoned pedestal? How to describe something that is not there? Not there any more, except for the tension that concentrates within these marks of absence. The tension of the interval.

She knows art, knows it with no place for self-hatred or self-depreciation. Knows the backgrounds and velvet draperies against which, for centuries, she has stood or lain, which for centuries have celebrated her. A celebration that as an artist she is about to repeat and intends to continue, because this is what painting, what art is about, and especially the art that is hers by history: Flemish painting.

But now she has become a painter herself and, while from knowing painting she knows everything about herself as the painter's model, she knows nothing about herself as the author as yet, about her place in history, her image of it. Another video shows an adolescent boy

267

whom she directs into the same classical painterly attitudes of Adonis, Mars, Christ asleep. But clothed, this time, not in the nude.

Most important; her videos do not comment on sexual politics. They are first and foremost a testimony about art, about her relationship to the making of art, about the kind of artist she will be. But by this very commitment, she has to challenge the way we look at art. This challenge alters the very text by which we have to describe her work, a text that starts from within dislocation and can only be written from within the silence of the interval, through the enduring of that time.

The waiting, the surrender to ennui, the muteness and sometimes failures or impatience shown in her videos are all related to the process of the making of art. Rather than the artist being victorious over the subject, they show the artist's surrender to it. The artist does not discover her subject; instead it finds her. Sometimes it takes a long time passed in waiting before it reveals itself. All of her works show a quest for the sublime, which cannot be named nor designated beforehand. From this conviction springs her intensely ethical inquiry, starting with her very first works, into the nature of her own relationship as an artist to the subject, which now has become hers to subjugate in turn, if she chooses to do so. *American Imperialism* (1972) repeats the forms of minimal art while provoking the issue of what those forms, in spite of all theory, dominate and deny: the hidden, the unseen, the

Hommage à (Homage to) (V), 1972. Video still. Video, originally 16 mm. film, 30 minutes. Courtesy of the artist. Photo: Hans Sonneveld.

overlooked. She is no longer, perhaps, a victim, but she will not become a victor. For the victor's world is one-dimensional.

What crystallizes is "a space offered, but never occupied."[2] Like the woman's body in *Hommage à . . .*, art is itself the interval, the duration, dislocation, is *no place*.

Dujourie's video's have been described as "boring"; her consequent works were never allowed fully to enter the mainstream of the art world. Hers is what the writer and filmmaker Trinh Minh-ha has called "the pensive image": "the image that speaks—and speaks volumes for what it is not supposed to say."[3]

NOTES:
1. Trinh T. Minh-ha, *When the Moon Waxes Red* (London: Routledge, 1991), 114–15.
2. Marguerite Duras, *Duras by Duras* (San Francisco: City Lights, 1987), 71.
3. Trinh Minh-ha, *When the Moon Waxes Red*, 115.

American Imperialism, 1972.
Monochromatically painted wall and steel sheet.
Collection Christian Mys, Oudenaarde (Belgium)
Courtesy Paul Robbrecht.

Marking Time: Memory and Matter in the Work of Avis Newman

Michael Newman

After the invention of the monochrome there can be no tabula rasa. There is no pure beginning to a painting. The raw, untreated, unstretched canvas is already a work. The artist must therefore take responsibility even for laying a ground or the first brush marks, which alter something already there, covering and concealing as much as offering something to be seen.

The canvases of Avis Newman's *Webs (Backlight)* series (1993–) involve either dark marks on a light ground or light marks on a dark ground. No colors other than white and black are used. The artist makes a set of marks on a canvas covered with a wash, then covers these with a further wash of paint, whereby the marks may be lost to the eye, to be retrieved by a further mark on top of the obscured one. The superimposed mark indicates, without occluding, the mark beneath, which shows around the edges of the new mark.

The restriction to black and white has at least two effects: first, it implies a relation to the "absolute" monochrome that begins with Malevich's *Black Square*—although not an identity, since Newman introduces difference and repetition; second, the palette alludes to writing, the black and white of the page, which comes to the fore in the spacing of Stéphane Mallarmé's poem "Un coup de dés." Both effects feature in works of the early 1990s, which reached the "zero degree" from which the *Webs* series departs in a group of works exhibited in 1993 under the collective title *Vicious Circle*. In *A Book of Numbers,* before a dark gray graphite-covered monochrome canvas, stands a closed white-linen-bound book inaccessible in a perspex box on a graphite-covered base. Seen from the front, the book appears like a white image in the dark field. The box contains ten sets of ten lithographs printed with the numbers 0 to 9 in Wolpe's sloping Albertus typeface: in the book a rational numerical system from which the viewer is excluded, on the canvas a somber, brooding dark field.[1] Both this work and the *Webs* convey the sense of a radical outside. On the one hand the marks in the *Webs* series could be disseminations from the book; and on the other, the closed book in its container alludes to Newman's *Boxes* series, which parallels the canvases. If the canvases concern memory in relation to loss and retrieval, a number of the *Boxes* concern the sheer obduracy of matter. Both—in somewhat different ways—address the question of alterity.

Marks Lost and Refound

The configuration of marks in the *Webs (Backlight)* series suggests a web, an image with no volume. Newman layers the marks that make the "webs": for the drawings, on sheets of tracing paper, sometimes alternating with gauze; for the canvases, alternating with layers of

*Untitled,
Webs series,
1995.
Drawing, ink on
tracing paper.
24 x 18 cm.
Courtesy of the
artist.*

wash. Yet these procedures create no spatial depth. Nonetheless, when one mark on the painting is superimposed on another, the two do not fuse, nor does one "imitate" the other. One mark, in effect, recalls the other without denying difference. The situation is not quite the same with the marks aligned beside each other so that they appear to repeat. There a tension is set up between the singularity of the mark and the rule generated retroactively by the relation of similarity and difference of the marks to each other, which depends upon repetition. In general, by breaking up the web while still evoking it, Newman shifts the emphasis from the whole to the parts, mediated by the forces of attraction and repulsion to suggest movement around a central void.

Nor do the marks cross. Marks that cross imply volume, as in Piet Mondrian's painting *Pier and Ocean* (1915) and related drawings (1914–15), the austerity of which is comparable to that of Newman's *Webs*. But where the marks of the *Pier and Ocean* works center on the cross, which cannot actually crystallize since that would stop their oscillation, the dynamism involved in their stability, the center of Newman's *Webs* and related drawings is empty, or at least gives the impression of emptiness. The web is fragmented and reconfigured, turned upside down, inside out, rotated into a vortex. Mondrian multiplies the horizon and the projection centered in the pier; Newman, by rotating the image, abolishes any horizon and empties the center. The implied temporality also differs: Mondrian suggests a utopian movement toward the future, Newman's work is governed by a rhythm of retrieval and loss.

The layering of marks and the repetition whereby contiguous marks on the point of disappearance may be recalled, literally re-membered, invoke the experience of time. The marks, having been "repeated" over successive layers of wash, assert identity through the very difference interposed by time. Difference here is apprehended as the temporalization involved in the "fading" of the earlier marks. The time of making is in a certain sense reversed by the viewer: the artist layered marks one above the other; the viewer is drawn from the uppermost layer back into the past. Since this layering and repetition do not produce volume, there is no reduction of time to space, of duration to instantaneity; rather, repetition and layering, spacing and temporalization are inextricability intertwined. Duration is interrupted, broken open by the possibility, never far from the surface, of an irrecoverable loss. We thereby undergo the double work of time: the trauma of loss and a recovery, but without returning that which is lost as it was. If there is a movement back into the past of the making of the work, it is without origin, and if there is a movement of anticipation, it is without a predetermined goal or final consummation. The temporality of the canvases is thus an attentiveness, an awaiting, that inheres between these two movements. Even having reached their final form, the Webs are, through the experience of the viewer, spun and unraveled, worked and unworked, endlessly. This may be likened to the thread of Penelope, wife of Odysseus, woven into her father-in-law's shroud during the day to be undone at night; yet there is, in Newman's canvases, complete and "right" as they are as works of art, no final closure, no sense of a return home. They are as dry as the desert.

The canvases hold not so much webs themselves or representations of webs as the *shadows* of webs, indications of something absent or at least not present. Yet paradoxically, for all the works' reticence and austerity, they are intensely *there,* almost blindingly so. Something has been made, been given—a work—to circumscribe a void. The marks give the impression of having been spun off from, or striving toward, an emptiness, which governs their repetition and their search—as if only that which is repeatable and thereby identifiable can figure. Yet this very repetition defigures, empties out the mark insofar as its being now refers to the other marks. On the one hand, only that which is repeatable is memorable; the repetition draws back into the visual field those marks about to disappear beneath the layers of wash.

On the other hand, if memory depends on repeatability, it also involves the loss of singularity: in the very recovery of the mark something falls away. Hence the tension between singularity and the remarking of that singularity upon which memory depends and in which singularity is lost. But how, then, may the singular be remembered?

The Gift of Memory and the Origin of Drawing

To think of memory in terms of representation is to think of it from the perceiver's point of view. From the maker's point of view, it is not the case that something is retrieved in order to be represented; rather something is *given* to be remembered. This does not preclude that such a gift is always already a response. Memory as representation occludes memory as gift. We find this movement of gift and occlusion in Pliny, in the account of what has come to be known as the story of the origin of drawing, where the daughter of the potter Butades, who lived in Corinth, "was in love with a young man, and when he was going abroad she drew a silhouette on the wall round the shadow of his face cast by the lamp."[2]

By making marks around a shadow and thus forming a line ("umbram ex facie eius ad lucernam in pariete lineis circumscripsit," literally "she circumscribed with a line the shadow of his face projected on the wall by the light of a lamp"), the potter's daughter created a silhouette of her lover, a gift of memory, to herself and to the other. In the grief of departure, her anticipation of the absence of her lover and her substitution of an image recall another story, that of the child in Freud's *Beyond the Pleasure Principle* who throws and retrieves a bobbin, accompanied by sounds that Freud interprets as meaning *fort* (gone) and *da* (there).[3] Why does the child repeat the unpleasurable experience of the mother's absence? Because the excitations that arise from this loss and cause the trauma must *first* be bound before they can be subject to the pleasure principle, that is to say, discharged. To bind the excitations means to associate them with signifiers or representations—as here the binary *fort-da* occupies the very space of the inaugural loss—whereby their traumatic effect is lessened. This is what it means to transform repetition into memory. The trauma is to be "worked through" in order that it may be left behind.[4]

Rather than simply transforming repetition into memory, Newman's *Webs* canvases reenact loss and retrieval through remarking the mark that has all but disappeared under the wash. The second, "retrieving" mark responds to the near loss of the first, in an act of "saving." Yet the "first" mark made in the field can be read as a violent act of separation. One reason that repetition cannot in this case be converted into representational memory is that this would involve forgetting the original violence of separation reenacted through the process of marking.

It is not a matter in the canvases of the "mastery" of the traumatic but rather of its acknowledgment or avowal. At stake here is *singularity*: to bind the singular to signifiers already possessed of meaning, or to representations, is to occlude it. In the canvases of the *Webs (Backlight)* series Newman holds the marks to the moment of repetition and difference before meaning, a state in between the singular, or traumatic, and the aftereffect of having-been-bound to meaning whereby the singular and the traumatic are at once concealed and made possible, represented and left behind. We are confronted, then, with a double trauma: of singularity and of loss. The mitigation of the loss will occlude the singularity of the other, not least by binding it to the general through representation. This process is precisely what is articulated through the relation of shadow, mark-making, and resemblance in Pliny's story of the origin of drawing.

Thinking of Joseph-Benoît Suvée's painting *The Invention of the Art of Drawing,* Jacques Derrida writes:

> [Butades's daughter] does not see her lover, either because she turns her back to him—more abiding than Orpheus—or because he turns his back to her, or again, because their gazes simply cannot meet . . . it is as if seeing were forbidden in order to draw, as if one drew only on the condition of not seeing, as if the drawing were a declaration of love destined for or suited to the invisibility of the other—unless it were in fact born from seeing the other withdrawn from sight. . . . From the outset, perception belongs to recollection.[5]

Derrida moves from discussing the myth of the origin of drawing to a general claim concerning the inseparability of present perception from the recollection that enters into its constitution but cannot be appropriated and represented in terms of present experience. Butades's daughter, in order to draw her beloved, in a declaration of love that is also an anticipation of his absence, must look away, no longer seeing him in the present; present perception depends on the trace of the past, which cannot itself be made present. This trace may also be understood as the trace of the other in its irreducible singularity.[6] How, then, may the trace of singularity, as that which does *not* appear in the mark, be remembered?

Pliny's account is not, in fact, of the origin of drawing but rather of the origin of the modeling of portraits. The woman whose name we do not know, who is defined by her relationships with men (who, nonetheless, in turn ultimately depend upon her), is "framed" by her father the potter thus: "It is now time to say something about modeling. By taking advantage of the earth itself,[7] Butades, a potter from Sicyon, was the first to introduce the modeling of portraits [*similitudines*, likenesses] in clay at Corinth. . . . Her father pressed clay on this to make a relief [*typum fecit,* to make a figure, image, form, or type] and fired it with the rest of his pottery." Butades displaces his daughter's indexical inscription of a loss, the memorial of a shadow, with a work that transforms sheer matter, "earth," into a form or imitation. This imitation, the relief image of the face, hides the absence in the shadow. It is possible to see the father's act also as one of love: he wishes, perhaps, to make a gift to his daughter of the effigy of the face of her lover, and in that way gently to reconcile her to an unavoidable separation, to teach the necessity of accepting lack and metaphoric substitution, to free the memory of her lover from being fetishized by a place, a patch of wall, and to prevent her from sinking into melancholy. Nonetheless, in seeking to detach her from a possibly too immediate attachment to her object, he replaces a tracing of absence, the memento of a shadow recalling in advance the death of the other (in Suvée's painting, the shadows of the couple merge as if anticipating a union of shades), with a substitute presence. The clay formed into a resemblance will cover the marks around what will have been the index of the absent lover.

What is involved in Pliny's story of origin is not, first of all, a mirroring of reality but rather a series of responses—of the daughter to the anticipated absence of her lover, of her father to his daughter's tracing—the latter a relation of response, involving absence and desire forgotten when displaced by the mimetic model installed *within* this very series of responses. The difference is that the daughter's tracing does not involve an act of substituting an object, in the literal sense, for that which is about to become absent, whereas the father substitutes an object, a relief sculpture, which displaces that which is to be lost, and conceals this very act of displacement through the substitution. Thus to resist the idealizing sublimation is also to open the space of a certain unforgetting (*aletheia*) in which there is acknowledgment of concealment and withdrawal.

As the "backlight" in the title of Newman's canvases suggests, there is "something"—an origin or an Other—that may be "seen" or remarked only by being covered, as in an eclipse of the sun. One may think also of the candle flickering behind the skull in Georges de la Tour's painting *The Repentant Magdalen,* the candle illuminating the side of the Magdalen's face as she gently touches the dark side of the skull with the fingers of her left hand, "endeavouring to grope their way toward a recognition of the contours of death,"[8] contemplating the reflection in a mirror of the illuminated side of the skull. Death cannot be seen face on but perhaps it may be touched or appear indirectly, backlit, as that which is concealed, even as the very place where concealment itself, the origin of things, is hidden. While the painter creates appearances through the touch of the brush, the touch of the hand in de la Tour's painting signals the undoing of appearances. As in Pliny's story and Suvée's representation of it, where the lover grasps the potter's daughter who reaches for his shadow, neither looking at the other directly but rather anticipating the absence of the other just as the painting hints at their shadowy reunion, if the scopic regime serves to conceal loss, the hand, perhaps through the reversibility of touching and being touched, activity and passivity, feels for it.

Butades's daughter does not make an imitation of the loved one's face but rather, looking away, forms the image by tracing the shadow. To take a *shadow* as an origin is to suggest that drawing begins not in the imitation of something present but rather in a withdrawal.[9] The drawing is given-to-remember. The mark remains as close to touch as it is given to be seen: the gift is of the hand. Turning away, Butades's daughter seeks the other not through vision but through touch, and with her hand she gives something to be remembered. On this side of the scopic regime, she invents an art of the memory of the touch, and she does so by turning away from, by not looking at, the one she desires. In Suvée's painting the lover grasps the "present" woman, who in turn reaches out to his shadow, his absence. Vision itself contains the memory of what comes before it. Her gesture, stroking the shadowed surface with a medium, perhaps a stick of charcoal, evokes the difference between a grasp and a caress, which seeks not so much the presence of the other as that which withdraws from it.

The muteness of touch is not simply the deprivation of speech. If vision is tied to naming, there is no "innocent eye." To see the things as the things that they are is to see them as named, as disclosed through speech. However, one task of modern painting, together with Newman's earlier canvases, has been to seek a visuality before names, to reach back to the origin of the world, which is also the origin of language. The caress, perhaps, extends even further, to seek that which withdraws from, or approaches from elsewhere than the horizon of the world, and from which one does not have time to establish a distance, the earliest touch. If a work were to be made of this, it would be one in which the artist had to create a paradoxical object without closure, or a work the formal closure of which was in the process of being shattered, or one in which form became sheer repetition. Impossible, perhaps, yet an attempt to turn the activity of the maker toward a primordial passivity, the capability of being touched by the outside, by a shadow, a withdrawal.

How, then, may the touch of the caress be remembered without being reified? What if the touch of the caress, of the mark, were already to give something to be remembered, not by representing itself but by leaving and recalling marks and by conveying not some*thing* marked but the very movement of marking, losing, and remarking? That which is marked—on the rock, the wall, the paper, the canvas—is given to the visual through touch. But the trace of the other always exceeds the mark, even the most indexical; the other's alterity, which is absolute, can never be present as such in their marks. So this visual art is not an art of the visual but rather of what exceeds vision, an exteriority at its heart.

Butades's daughter's gesture, in which there is no mastery however well it is done, is quite different from that of her father. The outline that she has traced is treated by the potter as a plan or blueprint, an *eidos* or form, an end in view of which he makes an object. Thus his act declares her outline a finished thing and transforms it into the basis for a detachable object. But his daughter's activity has been a touching without seeing, without *eidos*, an opening of herself to nonknowledge, to not knowing the end. She seeks to touch, to respond to, an absence rather than to project an object. There is thus an excess in what she does over any work directed toward an end, and if she moves toward the other, it is through the gift in response to a withdrawal and not because she wants to possess him forever in a memorial or monument.

Butades uses his daughter's shadow drawing to make an imitation of the head of her lover while making the marks traced by his daughter function as the contour or outer limit of a figure. Becoming thus contour through the mediation of the line, the ambiguity of the trace— that it at once unites and separates, that relates to both the physical mark and to that which is not visible, that it makes possible presentation while withdrawing from it—is foreclosed. This occlusion involves a series of substitutions: marks for shadow, line for marks, contour for line. The character of the substitution fundamentally changes between the first and the second moment, in a move from negativity and absence to positivity and presence, and from plurality to unity, while the "first" substitution makes the subsequent ones possible. Hubert Damisch, in his treatise on the mark, writes: "According to Pliny, the first step forward, the really decisive progress, which opens the field of history properly speaking, being that of painting, would have consisted, once the possibility of encompassing the contour of the shadow with a plurality of marks [*traits*] had been discovered (*repertam*), in the invention of line (*inventam liniarem*) which substitutes for them."[10] The contour made from the line is both the sublimation and the idealization of the mark, opening "the field of imitation." The mark is ambiguous insofar as it both touches the shadow or stain and anticipates its sublimation into the continuous line as contour. On the one hand, the origin of drawing, and thereby modeling and sculpture, indeed art as such, lies in the experience of absence, loss, and lack: "Art, in the very moment of what is presented as its 'origin,' is linked to absence, to loss, to lack. As is, without having need of the myth to pronounce it, the mark which distributes [*fait le partage entre*] figure and ground. The mark grasped, outside all consideration of the figure, in its difference, its departure from the surface. But it is the mark that equally abolishes itself in the line, which arises from it as the sublimated aspect [*l'espèce sublimée*]."[11] The contour, the line taken as describing the edge or limit of a body, will define a presence supposedly permanent and independent—the relief will develop into the freestanding statue—rather than indicating absence and separation. In the father's gesture, absence, separation, and loss are, indeed, physically obscured, supposed to be recuperated in the transubstantiation of matter, earth or clay, into art that will be taken as a mimicry of divine creation. But, as the story also shows, contrary to any simple opposition, imitation depends on what it occludes.

Newman's practice in her canvases, closer to drawing than to painting, works precisely *against* (insofar as this is possible since the relation is not one of simple opposition) the "idealizing" sublimation of mark into line and line into contour. The marks in her earlier canvases, up to those in the *Earth of Paradise* installation (1990), tended to emphasize contour with a reference to the body (and by implication the origin of the whole tradition of the representation of the figure) and to the imagined object, the object of fantasy and fixation, the Image worshiped and attacked, torn apart and repaired. By contrast, in the *Webs* the marks do not denote a boundary and therefore are not sublimated into contours, perhaps not even into lines: the web as an image without volume emphasizes the mark as such. By using the web, rather than a body or solid object, as the organizing principle of her canvases, Newman struggles to hold the mark at the moment *before* it becomes line: instead of the mark "elevating" itself into line, and into the beautiful contour, there is a working back, a movement not of obliteration of the mark in the line but of repeated loss and retrieval. The application of a new ground over the marks prevents them crystallizing into a figure and mitigates the separation that gives even the gentlest touch of the brush its violence. Yet this overlay also obscures,

.. a day without
 day, 1991.
ilver gilded box
ith glass.
1.7 x 36 x 7.2 cm.
nstallation at
he Béguinage of
ortrijk
Belgium).
ourtesy Kanaal
rt Foundation,
ortrijk.
hoto: Rien van
en Eshof.

and, lest it become like potter's clay, the marks it covers—or at least some of them—must be retrieved without themselves being covered. These marks have become invisible to the eye yet continue to exist, calling, in their relief, rather to the touch. The question to which these various approaches respond: How can one make a thing that is outside the self yet does not fetishistically forget its status as substitution, as dependent on absence and loss?

The marks inscribed and remembered in the *Webs (Backlight)* canvases do not result in a monument, upright and centered. Rather, the center of the web is empty. Here we find another sense of sublimation, this time no longer as an elevating distillation that suppresses difference but rather, as Jacques Lacan would have it, as signifiers encircling a void: "In every form of sublimation, emptiness is determinative."[12]

The Outside on the Inside

Almost all of Newman's *Boxes* give the impression of being sealed off from the viewer, condensed and hermetic. Often the frame is strongly emphasized, or the edge is sharply defined. This is quite the opposite of the canvases, where the curved edges deemphasize the limit, suggesting an unlimited space that envelops the viewer in proximity with the work. In a sense the web is a frame *within* the painting, leaving the canvases themselves unframed. The web marks the limit of the human and the nonhuman, the spider's web and the artist's marks. However, while as fields the canvases envelop the viewer, at their heart is a movement toward an another kind of alterity. The *Boxes* convey the impression that something is being withheld from the viewer; the canvases concern a fundamental withdrawal—the difference between a secret and a mystery. The *Boxes* filled with untransformed "stuff" convey the static sense that something is sealed off rather than involving, as the canvases do, a movement of withdrawal. The withholding of the *Boxes* is the obverse of the gesture of the hand in the gift. Taken together, these two modes of work reveal an ambivalence in love and in the caress of Eros.

Both *Boxes* and *Webs* concern separation: the loss and recovery of the other in the case of the canvases, the separation of contents from viewer in the case of the *Boxes*. In neither case does the work return the gaze of the viewer, which, for Walter Benjamin, was a condition for the aura of the work of art,[13] in the canvases because of their fragmentation and the void at the center and in the *Boxes* because of the opacity of their contents. However, whereas the canvases, insofar as they involve marks and, through the reference to the origin of drawing, evoke the human other, the *Boxes* provoke an experience of the inhumanity of matter, the

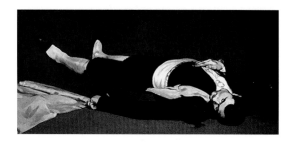

sheer indifference of the universe to human feelings and purposes. They are melancholic works of art in the strict sense, objects emptied of significance, removed from the circuits of meaning, knowledge, and gratification.

Simply to present matter as if it were unmediated would provide only an imaginary solution, implying a metaphysical realism, that the Real predates symbolic mediation rather than being its remainder or fallout. Hence Newman's recourse to exaggerated framing—silvered in *The Salt Box* (1989), graphite-covered in *Wax, to Feel the Unwritten* (1989–90), copper-gessoed in *Dazzling Emptiness, Supreme Burn* (1991), which is filled with copper dust—drawing attention to Symbolic mediation only to frustrate it through closure, in terms of both physical separation and visual tautology. The salt and the copper dust provide an almost undifferentiated surface. While their subliminal metallic and crystalline shimmer attracts the gaze, their flat, uninflected smoothness repels the eye. While the salt and copper are flat against the glass that encloses them, the wax is concave, as if softened, warmed by the eye that desires a place—yet finally this too is an impress without meaning in impersonal matter.

These *Boxes* invert the normal way in which the frame mediates the relation between inside and outside: instead of the transformation being worked on the interior, framed by a frame whose function is largely to be forgotten, the frame itself is worked; the framed material is untransformed by the artist or, if changed, is unexpressive. Objects without mercy, which care nothing for us. If in a traditional painting the interior is the subject and returns the gaze, here—as in certain works of the rococo—the frame is subject. But whereas in the rococo the effect is of an inside on the outside, in Newman's *Boxes* it is of an outside on the inside, incorporated as a "crypt" without being introjected as an image or object of identification and means of self-transformation for the subject.[14] As in the canvases, which remain at the level of the mark that does not become line or contour, so in certain *Boxes* sublimation, as an idealizing work, is also blocked. And this is so without hypostatizing transgression, which would reinforce the law of the limit.

At the Limit

Remaining this side of representation in Newman's *Webs (Backlight)* canvases involves insisting on the singularity of the mark, even if the latter is inseparable from repetition. Turning to her *Boxes,* we find the attempt—perhaps in the end impossible—to make works of art that do not auratically return the gaze, where matter is not "spiritualized." If this can be achieved, an art will be possible that is not a cipher for resurrection, for the overcoming of death and the unifying synthesis with the other, for the resuscitation of the corpse.[15]

Manet, remarkably, achieved this opacity within the figurative tradition in a painting that is one of Newman's favorites, *The Dead Toreador* (1864). The painting was cut by Manet from a larger canvas, eliminating all narrative to focus attention on the stillness of the cadaver, its left hand holding the edge of the flesh-pink cape beneath the lumped folds of which something—we will never know what—seems to be concealed.[16] How to paint a death without transcendence? Considering Manet's canvases of dead bodies, Georges Bataille remarks: "Modern painting attains through absence what Goya, in a world freighted with solemnity and grave respect, attained through *excess*."[17] If the corpse in this painting barely casts a shadow, it is because it has itself become shadow, an image in the trace of its own absence. The object, removed from the circuit of signifiers, becomes opaque, a placeholder for the unpresentable.

NOTES:

This essay was jointly commissioned by Camden Arts Centre, London, the Ikon Gallery, Birmingham, the Kanaal Art Foundation, Kortrijk, and The Institute of Contemporary Art, Boston. A shorter version is published in the catalogue *Avis Newman* (London: Camden Arts Centre; Birmingham: Ikon Gallery, 1995).

1. Avis Newman's installation *Earth of Paradise* (1990) included three boxes, *The Salt Box, The Soot Box,* and *The Graphite Box,* and four canvases shown together in another room together with an additional box, *Wood in Wood.* An excellent discussion of this work and of *A Book of Numbers* appears in Patricia Bickers's "Vicious Circle," in *Avis Newman, Vicious Circle,* exhib. cat. (Dublin: Douglas Hyde Gallery; Amsterdam: De Appel Foundation, 1993). On Newman's earlier work, see Jean Fisher, "On the Margins of Forgetfulness," in *Avis Newman,* exhib. cat. (London: Lisson Gallery; Chicago: Renaissance Society of the University of Chicago, 1987).
2. Pliny the Elder, *Natural History: A Selection* (London: Penguin Books, 1991), book 35, §151, p. 336. For an account of the many works of art from the seventeenth to the nineteenth centuries based on this legend, see Robert Rosenblum, "The Origin of Painting: A Problem in the Iconography of Romantic Classicism," *Art Bulletin* 39 (1957): 279–90.
3. Sigmund Freud, *The Standard Edition of the Complete Psychological Works,* 24 vols. (London: Hogarth Press, 1953–74), 18:14–15.
4. Cf. Sigmund Freud, "Remembering, Repeating and Working-Through," *Standard Edition,* 12:147–56.
5. Jacques Derrida, *Memoirs of the Blind: The Self-Portrait and Other Ruins,* trans. Pascale-Anne Brault and Michael Naas (Chicago: University of Chicago Press, 1993), 49–51.
6. For a more detailed discussion of these topics, see Michael Newman, "Derrida and the Scene of Drawing," *Research in Phenomenology* 24 (Fall 1994): 218–34, and "The Trace of Trauma: Blindness, Testimony and the Gaze in Blanchot and Derrida," in *Maurice Blanchot: The Demand of Writing,* ed. Carolyn Bailey Gill (London: Routledge, 1996).
7. Jean-Michel Croisille translates "eiusdem opere terrae" as "en utilisant lui aussi la terre" ("he too by using earth") in his translation of Pliny, *Histoire naturelle* (Paris: Belles Lettres, 1985), p. 101, which also contains a useful appendix on *skiagraphia,* shadow drawing or painting (297–300), for which see also Plato, *Theatetus* 208e, *Parmenides* 165c, and *Sophist* 266b–c; and Aristotle, *Rhetoric* 3, no. 12:1414a. These passages refer to scene painting in which an image resolved at a distance falls apart or becomes something else close up, revealing itself as illusion, which implies that what is true is seen as the same from all perspectives and to all perceivers. Pliny's story perhaps evokes another possibility, which becomes dangerous for philosophy if not limited to art, where truth is based on loss and desire rather than on the constancy of the *eidos* and is closer to the touch—and hence to the movement of response and gift of the artist—than to the contemplative gaze, *theoria,* of the onlooker.
8. Pascal Quignard, *Georges de la Tour,* trans. Barbara Wright (Paris: Flohic, 1991), 12.
9. This is of course to change the order of priority given to the source of light, ultimately the sun, over shadow in Plato's allegory of the cave: see *Republic* 7:514ff.
10. Hubert Damisch, *Traité du trait* (Paris: Louvre/Réunion des Musées Nationaux, 1995), 67 (my translation).
11. Ibid., 76. Damisch is playing on the senses of espèce, including sensible appearance, coinage or cash, species or kind, and, in the plural, the body and blood of Christ under the appearance of bread and wine, after the transubstantiation.
12. Jacques Lacan, *The Seminar of Jacques Lacan: Book VII, The Ethics of Psychoanalysis 1959–1960,* trans. Dennis Porter (New York: Norton, 1992), 130; also 112 ("The object is elevated to the dignity of the Thing"), 120–21, 140.
13. Cf. Walter Benjamin, "The Work of Art in the Age of Mechanical Reproduction," in *Illuminations,* ed. Hannah Arendt (New York: Schocken Books, 1969), 222–23; and "A Small History of Photography," in *One Way Street and Other Writings* (London: Verso, 1979), 247, 250.
14. For discussions of the distinction between introjection and incorporation and the incorporated "crypt," see Nicolas Abraham and Maria Torok, *The Wolf Man's Magic Word: A Cryptonymy,* trans. Nicholas Rand (Minneapolis: University of Minnesota Press, 1986), including a foreword, "Fors," by Jacques Derrida; and Nicolas Abraham and Maria Torok, *The Shell and the Kernel,* trans. Nicholas Rand (Chicago: University of Chicago Press, 1994).
15. Cf. Rebecca Comay, "Facing History/Memories of Resistance: Boltanski, Benjamin and the Aura of Fascist Architecture," *Alphabet City* (Toronto), nos. 4–5 (1995).
16. Manet submitted the larger canvas to the Salon of 1864, under the title *Épisode d'une course de taureaux.* His other submission, *Christ with Angels,* stresses the inertia of the dead, seminaked body, the corpse that is flesh turning into image.
17. Georges Bataille, *Manet* (Geneva: Skira; New York: Rizzoli, 1983), 50.

Matrixial Borderline, 1990-91.
India ink, pencil, pastel, and photocopy on paper, Plexiglas.
Four panels with twenty-five elements, 160 x 35 cm.
Courtesy of the artist.
Photo: Yoram Lehmann.

Bracha Lichtenberg Ettinger: Images of Absence in the Inner Space of Painting

Christine Buci-Glucksmann

> Although the signs have a fixed form and place on paper the multitude of "resemblances" they contain sets them in motion. Virtual resemblances that are expressed with each brush stroke form a mirror which reflects the thought of this resembling, resonating atmosphere. Consequently, the resemblances do not exclude one another; they overlap, constituting an ensemble that sways thought as a breeze sways a gauze veil.
> —Walter Benjamin[1]

I. That Which Cannot Be Looked At: An Art of Palimpsest

Suppose, at the outset, a game of languages, playing on that Hebrew letter in Latin script whose repeated mark punctuates Bracha Lichtenberg Ettinger's borders work. Suppose, then, this *a*, this *aïn*, irreducibly ambiguous since it signifies at once "eye" and "nothingness, naught, void" when kept in a Latin script. As though it were necessary to gaze into the void in order to see again, as though the nothingness and the quiver of these extenuated materials, cut up and reassembled, stood here for a failing memory, faded and threatened by what it can see. In the likeness of these anonymous—even if family—photographs, which emerge here, continually reproduced and effaced, ruined and reframed by the compulsive work of that false memory machine, the photocopier. People seen from behind, faceless, a Jewish couple strolling in the streets of Warsaw, if not Lodz, with their insistent gaze of absence, of testimony, their eyes emptied on timelessness, between expression and being deprived of expression.

For here, effacing is not forgetting but remembering, in a case history of absence, of the far off and encrypted, which organizes all of these heterogeneous materials—images and signs, outlines and pictorial materials diluted in India ink—like traces subjected to the tight-knit play of repetition-variation. We might think of those sixteenth-century theaters of the memory with their images and their places, their symbolism and their secrets (by Giulio Camillo, for instance, that Venetian friend of Erasmus who warped the perspectivist theater founded by Vitruvius to create a theater without spectators, where imaginary doors opened onto the "nothing" of recollection). Supported by the Seven Pillars of Wisdom, the theater interweaves a multiplicity of cultural references. Seven Pillars, seven planets, seven Sephirot—those emanations from God described in the Kabbala; seven is the symbolic numeral of a magic, cultural, and mystical memory that crypts the languages descended for the Tower of Babel.

Traces, then, a theater of memory, where images of words and images of things intersect in the pure disappearance of the visual, to the point where nonplaces and borderline situations replace the classical "places" of remembrance. Copying, effacing, veiling, covering by layers and superimposing, emptying or suspending—this whole art of quivering that inhabits Lichtenberg Ettinger's work ends up creating what I would call *images of absence,* distributed by the intentional haphazardness of signs. Dictionary pages, title pages of works of clinical psychiatry, Latin and Hebrew letters: writing functions here like a linguistic combination that spells out the world in a giant palimpsest. A world of beyond-the-visual, subjected to the constant double violence of the sexual and of history, in a single attempt to destroy bodies reduced to pieces, partial objects or the infinite metaphor of what has been or what could have been. Further ambiguity: that other Hebrew word, *p'nim,* which echoes the *aïn* and means "face," "there once was," "before," and "that which moves toward the inside."

Mamalangue–*Borderline Conditions and Pathological Narcissism, n. 5,* 1989–90.
India ink, pencil, charcoal, and photocopy on paper, Plexiglas.
Composed of three elements, 122 x 40 cm.
Nouveau Musée, Villeurbanne (France).

But if the face is no longer an appeal and if ethics are no longer an optic—to borrow
Emmanuel Levinas's expression—is it not because the conversion of the event of the face, its
"there once was," is no more than the pure interiority of memory? A nothing, a void, something of the universe before birth or after destruction. Accordingly, this triple composition of
the face-event-interiority could serve as a model for all of the micro-forms and micro-stagings,
where the minutiae of the details are a prelude to the musical variation of the whole. For the
original stage of this theater is, of course, the image. But it is there only as an image abstract,
an image affect, which emerges and disappears, in these reprocessed papers of memory, more
apt to suggest haziness and obliteration than outlines and sharpness. Purified, stripped, these
"images" evoke wanderers, "fleeting travelers" ripped away from the immemorial. It is thus not
enough to present that from which the images originated, loss, anonymity, fleetingness. They
must also be submitted to the violence of cutting, which makes them into strips, fragments,

Installation at le
Nouveau Musée,
Villeurbanne (France),
1992.
Courtesy of the
artist.

in order to serialize them better, to distance them, in a composition under glass, in a diptych
or triptych. In the gaps between fragments we see the fractured real but also the real brought
to the surface, in the tradition of the "thin" of surface effect, specific to contemporary art. It
is a fundamentally cruel space where, as in Kafka, violence links the letter to the body. The
image is what remains when it is all over, like the "mama tongue" of a written will. For if the
bodies here are only partial pieces, floating white shapes, like the projection of a psychotic
universe, it is precisely because nothing can be articulated about them. A red leg here, drawn
over with Indian ink, the ubiquitous faces of this doll substitute, little Hans's graph accentuated with the same phantasm red ("He began by draw[ing]"), a madwoman borrowed from the
cover of a book on *The Lunatic Ward in France* and encircled with pain and indifference;
everywhere bodies are merely bodily states and ultimately pure graphs, places of a hesitant
and faded memory. Between table and *tableau* we have here an entire geography, a cartography of "borderline cases" of our history and our society.

The fragile materiality of these photocopier-assisted images and texts, their ghostly, readable surfaces, recall Foucault's *The Birth of the Clinic* with its classificatory medicine and the relations between what is visible and what is stated. "The form in which truth appears at the origin is the surface, where the relief simultaneously manifests and abolishes itself—the portrait."[2] Surface of symptoms, as in *Borderline Conditions and Pathological Narcissism, Infantile Autism,* or *Symptoms under the Control of the Will,* to cite three painting titles. This glass truth, with its entire cold surface, pins the illness—hysteria or autism—and its written form onto reproduced plates. It is a flat classificatory space that meets the nongaze of the couple or the doll. For between these empty seeings, of Nothingness and nothings, and the gaze of Bracha Lichtenberg Ettinger, there is more than a simple structural homology. There is that which founds her work, this *aïn* dispersed like a peripheral gaze onto the world. We need only consider the "plate" in *Pathological Narcissism* where the shadowy spaces of language-languor and of the mama tongue above alternate with the effaced photographs below of carriages in the country or the return of the haunting couple. Yet between the pre-Oedipal narcissism of a psychotic world and the historical pathology of effacement appears the play of this psychiatric plate, clarifying the illnesses, where all is visible-readable, without secrets.

Confronted with the dumb, aimless, expressionless gaze, the letter scans a truth that indicates itself. Everything is a *tableau,* in the sense of clinical analysis, in the connection between seeing and visualized knowledge. Yet the elements introduce variations and permutations, a rhythm like an infinitely reexposed musical motif. All of these graphs of bodies seek only to efface the effacement, to rid themselves of any immediate reference, to stage an inner gaze, a phantasm script that would derhetoricize the strengths of the image and nevertheless exploit their metonymic powers. For between a "there has been"—but what?—and a "there no longer is"—but why?—the image explores the possibilities of what the Hebrew word in *Case History and Analysis, s(a)f,* designates as the threshold: *s(a)f* and the end: *s(o)f.*

That the art of the threshold, which from Walter Benjamin to Peter Handke has relentlessly "fractalized" the beautiful, could be the art of the end accounts for this paradox of the photocopier-assisted work. Pages from dictionaries, Latin languages, Hebrew, the plate of the word *language* are a matter neither of a simple realism of the letter nor of a simple play on language. In Lichtenberg Ettinger's work, the letter is dismembered, in what Edmond Jabès called the *manque à la lettre.*[3] Not the real letter but the letter reinscribed as that o which introduces the series: obscurum, obscure, objective . . . A colossal slip of the tongue by a machine that is all the more efficient for its objectification of anonymity; the letter recurs like the *P'h* in Hebrew, a what is "here" and what has been expelled from the "mouth," that primary cavity of emptiness and of *jouissance.* As in the art of Raymond Lulle, the notation of the letters is displaced onto the figures, sketching a composite and strict space from the pure letter to the diagram and to the breath of the image.

The fact that the here of presence is foreclosed, expelled by this first void that is the cavity of the mouth, delivers letters and images for the construction of "existential deterritorialized territories," those "ritornellos of bygone time" to quote Félix Guattari. These territories fastidiously constructed in infinite detail, these bodies permanently isolated from the image, do not translate a simple act of historical or castrating violence, as a first approach might suggest. For the arrangements always explore threshold-borders of a meeting of worlds, where the pre-Oedipal space of psychosis intrudes upon that of a scattered "banality of evil" that obliterates faces, bodies, and letters, and that obliterated even the name of death, reducing corpses to mere *Figuren.* Might these reddened lines and suddenly vivid purples testify, through their effect of discontinuity, against effacement within the effaced? For it is very much a matter, here, of fighting against a forgetting of oblivion, of introducing into the diptychs and triptychs this memory of strata and cutouts, this interior space of the event, through its disconnectedness and its being out of grasp. Between the abstract and the concrete, between the inscription and the support, between appearance and disappearance, Lichtenberg Ettinger turns the gaze to that which cannot be looked at, in an art of the palimpsest, as in the work of Christian Boltanski and Anselm Kiefer.

II. The Annulled Gaze: An Art of Memory

Thus we have to return to that astonishing memory machine, both abstract and concrete, capable of reproducing whole series but also effacing as it preserves, capable of maintaining the ephemeral of the visual while transforming it: the photocopier. For working with a photocopier means working at a first remove that determines "the object" by distancing materiality from the material.

The photocopy, in its very reproducibility, actualizes the Benjaminian loss of the aura, of the singularity of the far off, of the event. It flattens, impoverishes, and in doing so serves as an accountant for acts of memory, just as the magic pad, the *Wunderblok,* served Freud as a metaphor for the inscription of the unconscious, with its tracks, its traces, its appearances and disappearances. One might even say that the photocopier functions as a magic pad on which past and present, actual and virtual intersect.

The same image-photo, the same plate-text, can pass again and again by different circuits of inscription and effacement, so that there are always only traces and even "archtraces." The real is obliquely deferred, in a glimpse of what survives. Consequently, the game (in a sense of a game of draughts or of chess) oscillates between rendering the material uniform and altering the ever-different traces. On the one hand is an elementary, minimalist grammar of poverty, composed of photocopies, reprocessed papers, more or less diluted Indian inks, transparent or opaque, in the double range of the black/white, purple/red. And on the other hand, depending on your starting point (what I would call the "kernel" of the image), is tremendous heterogeneity. Thus, everything is uniform, like anonymity, and unique, like a memory. One might think of what Hindu philosophy calls the *nama-rupa* (name-and-shape), which aims to classify the ungraspable of the world, the fluidity of shapes. The name-and-shape is the mental-physical of all these flashing yet always tremulous and effaced memories. Everything is grayed, neutralized, quivered, and then a certain name-and-shape will break off, depending on the point of view, within the mental combinatory of these table-*tableau.*

The machine in itself materializes the *aïn* in the sense that the contemporary technological eye sees everything and nothing: empty, in the ghostly fragility of a "shadowy space." The very choice of drawing with diluted Indian ink authorizes these states of haziness between being and nonbeing, from the most transparent to the most opaque. To remember, as in a fog, is always to replay the tension between the line and the vacuity, the inhuman space of suspense, of drifting, of the veil.

From Veronica's veil to the veil of modesty, from Eros's veils to those of the shrouds of death, the technique of the veil has never been absent from the scene of Western painting.[4] With veils, you are able to show by hiding, to uncover by covering over, to reach the space of shadows and ghosts by choosing surfaces as a space for truth. As Benjamin wrote with great foresight: "In the spectral, all the forms of reproduction (scission, co-presence) are represented as forms of existence." Neither the pure reproducibility, nor the pure aura, neither the impossible mimesis of an art of the true, nor the generalized simulacrum of an art of the false, but the image specter, trapped by the lure of itself.

Must we then take literally, on the surface level, that which announces itself in the intentional, framed, purely Lacanian scansion of those sequences that distributes the principal knots of the topology of the unconscious: the Woman, the Other, and the Thing? Too abrupt a reading of the photocopied texts might lead us to look for some kind of metaphor or metonymy of the whole. The question, in fact, is whether they should be read or seen. Or even seen-read? Or are they only there for some wholly "other-thing"? *Das Ding,* the Thing, this first that cannot be beheld, that stands outside the signified, is foreign, like the pure power of absence, like the absolute Other. The relentless question from within these frames: What do we love, what can we love?

To frame in this way that which slips away, in the most Lacanian of motifs of the wholly "feminine" *jouissance* of the other, of the other Whole, is surely not to answer with a decision that which is undecidable in memory. It is much more an attempt to offer to see-read the metaphor of the artistic act when it tackles "the thing," the unnamable. It is to represent what Shoshana Felman calls the "events without witness."[5] Yet when we inscribe psychic or historical events without witness, we find ourselves with an *annulled gaze.* This gaze is not nothing, even if it shatters our amnesia into images of absence. Could this annulled, unfinished, or prehuman gaze be the gaze of the projection-disjunctions of image-making from a lost, forgotten, and almost unattainable world?

This place, this loss, this destitution of a Being-in-distress, *infans* or lost, leads us back to the "I/non-I" that Lichtenberg Ettinger discusses in her writings: constitutive heteronymy of the intimate-anonymous, heteronymy of memory itself, where the memory is mourning for the thing.

We need only look at the large series of languishing—she is languishing, she says—with its graduated purples, its whitened grays suddenly underlined, like double-exposed images in the cinema. We know that these superimposed faces create a composite image, where one image is diffused into another, onto another, in a diaphanous in-between, to the point where the overabundance of images inverts itself. Everything is drowned, and we all end up "visualizing thought"[6] and absence. Such, then, is the annulled gaze of events without witness. It visualizes thought, beyond names-and-shapes. It is located in that in-between of the letter, between the *aïn*—"eye" and "void"—and the *eïn*—"of the eye" and "there is not." For the event is indeed this meeting of the eye and of the "there has been": an uncertain and ever-threatened meeting.

A nonevent, faded but present, which alone sets the stage of the painting. Taken up again, between destitution and motifs, between letter and image, it draws the strata of a cartography of "border situations." For these effaced, cut-up, and reassembled papers are never more than the forms of a theater of a memory set free, where outside and inside exchange parts. The superimposed layers reveal to our gaze the novelty of these images of absence, the light and almost impalpable substances of a blank memory. Our own.

III. *Halala*—Autistworks in the Between-Space of Image-Thought

According to Benjamin, the great lesson in Chinese aesthetics is that a surface or plane can—through virtual signs—create nonsensitive resemblances that sway thought much like a mirror or a veil. In the between-two of the sign and the figure, an uncertain space solicits the slippage from the visible to the readable, from the painted to the thought. The image beyond reference and context becomes an image-thought in which a multitude of signs and planes melt into a kind of suspense—a gauze veil—or into a reflexive, musical mirror and its resonances.

Lichtenberg Ettinger has for a long time positioned her work in this site. From photos reworked on photocopy machines—effaced textures, blurred acuities, reframed effects—she creates what I have called images of absence, images without witness, carriers of an annulled gaze on the history of a historical and individual violence. There are also images of memory, in the between-two of a word that becomes polysemic and evocative when written in Latin script: *aïn*— "eye" and "empty"; and *eîn*—"eye of" and "there is not." As if seeing were conjugated with nonseeing, seeing through, in the virtual unfixableness of these composite, superimposed images, these image-thoughts. Painting was then nothing but trace (*trait*). The intimate or anonymous memory still demanded the blur of black and white, with gray tones difficult to pin down.

And what if this painting were to embody the gauze veil, the mirror, and reflect little by little the blur of just-sketched, phantomlike images? In this respect the series *Autistwork* marks a decisive change in the image-thought: the entrance *of and into* painting. And even in its play of particularly ambivalent pictorial color schemes—violet and its components blue and red, its lilac gradations. Violet is the very color of trouble, a kind of "elective nothingness"

 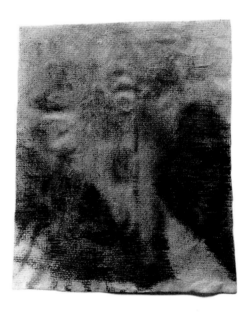

...tistworks,
...93–94.
...l and photocopy
...n paper mounted
...n canvas.
...5 x 26.7 cm.
...he Israel
...useum,
...erusalem.

in the words of Goethe. Both hot and cold it attracts and repulses at the same time, giving rise to a pensive space. A double symbolic then, sign of detachment and even mourning, while in Egypt it is also a remedy for pain. This screen and veil violet invades everything to such an extent that the series reveals its own laws of composition. While in the first painting the photograph can still be seen in the double frontality of a face and two naked backs, the last canvas is covered with oil paint—like skin. Better yet, gray is superimposed within violet. What has happened here?

Entering painting today cannot be (and never has been) an innocent act. The crisis of pictorial modernism—planeity, abstraction, purity of the medium, and self-definition of each art—has shattered the very notion of plane. As Leo Steinberg analyzed as early as 1968 in *Other Criteria,* his critique of Clement Greenberg, the "flatbed" plane could become composite, invaded by the world, and affected by deteriorated images or incorporated objects. Images of images, the plane-*tableau* is a plane of impure inscription and impression, a billboard or control panel, a projection screen open to all the readymades of the world, as in the work of Robert Rauschenberg or Jasper Johns. "A painting of ideas," as Duchamp would put it. In any event, "painting after painting."

Yet the question remains open, and the pictorial plane, while maintained, is necessarily rethought in keeping with effects produced by other mediums, including photography (cf. Gerhard Richter, Arnulf Rainer, Sigmar Polke). To such an extent that it has undergone "heterogenesis": a "deterritorialization-reterritorialization," to use Guattari's terms. Painting is an art of constant remapping, an art of passages, a crossing of real or virtual surfaces and screens where the pictorial and nonpictorial battle it out, as do the image and the thought, the abstract and the figural, the singular and the reproducible, the word and the thing. Entering into painting recalls the Freudian magic pad, the Wunderblok, that machinery of the unconscious whereupon inscription is an impression made by the contact of two distinct surfaces, the piece of resin and the sheet of paper, a veritable membrane sheet.

In this play of contact between presence and absence, reproduced photo and painting, image and abstract, Lichtenberg Ettinger's series of eight *tableaux* go exploring. In addition the series is constitutive of that *between-space in image-thought*. While one can say that the series has imposed itself in art as a play on singularity, placement, and repetition, it can also be said that all series are not identical. From the series of elective signifiers of Raymond Roussel to Andy Warhol's series by multiplication of a single image; from Joseph Beuys's, Christian Boltanski's, and Arman's series collections to Wim Wenders's series of "the state of things"—the series creates a gap between the signifier and the signified, disconnects the image, and most often gives rise to an effect of surface without depth. If there is a serial "eroticism," it oscillates between the anonymity of the disaffected and the exploration of "the surface's erogenous zone."[7] Lichtenberg Ettinger has made a series of "states of painting" always screened on the surface, in the "infra-thin." She has treated the initial image as a pure fantasy in which the too-full of photographic reality is progressively emptied of all visibility. Painting that discovers and recovers (covers over) the image functions as a matrix of separation-contact, analogous to the prelanguage ego-skin of which Didier Anzieu speaks. As surface of reception and protection, as interface of interior and exterior, as a kind of "interior mother," the ego-skin is "an experience of the frontier between two bodies in symbiosis as surface of inscription."[8] This symbiosis through contact and separation is accomplished by the play between the photocopied photographic image on recycled paper and the entrance into painting.

At the start, the photo from the 1940s—the bodies from behind and the quasi-Klimtian shadowed face looking at you—remains visible but difficult to position. The "veil" of the violet oil paint, screen veil and veil overprint, is there as if in shadow. It gives way to the memory-image. But this same image becomes enlarged fragment-image. In the second painting only the empty space between the two heads is apparent. Erasure is again pronounced in the third painting: the photo no more than a ghost image that suggests skin seen from behind but that is in fact an abstracted image. The painting through repetitive strokes is the quasi-screen of the initial image, which is little by little invaded by a purplish blue, and the degradation of the violet-blues and reds, in which what remains of the image is overprinted in the color. To such an extent that the slippage from the seventh to the eighth painting marks this progressive erasure of the image with a lilac painting that creates strange floating beings, Klee-like figures arising from an unknown "between world." At the end of the series the whole is finally covered and the image is no more than virtual trace, energy of dissipation, flux that opens onto the necessity of painting. The series is ripe with displacement rather than variation. It sets up an obscure circulation between the quasi-invisible of photocopied photography—in which presence undoes form and results in an image of the dreamed—and the transparent opacity of a painting restoring its uncertain being by covering it up so as to better annul it. Throughout these displacements, the contact between the two surfaces results in an inversion of the point of departure: *the painting is but the screen, the vibration, the modulation of the photographic image.* Contrary to Veronica's veil, which makes the "true" image of Christ appear, here the pictorial veil erases all image while nevertheless conserving its constituents: its fragility, its screen, its blur, its abstract character, its "shadow space" (Henri Michaux).

Lichtenberg Ettinger's magic pad is rather more photo-fantasy than memory; it is veil painting and violet skin. One goes from varnished black and white in the beginning to all shadowed violet at the end. As if, in the same movement, the image disappeared to leave room for the *inner space of painting,* which would be the equivalent of autistic, indeed schizophrenic, space. For while the painting obstinately hangs onto its regular-irregular strokes and striations—superimposed and discontinuous—the effect is rather one of global indetermination. Neither the painting nor the blurred photo can be fixed, positioned: it deterritorializes the gaze to such an extent that the image is but a *displaying of affects.* At best it is an index, as in Duchamp's *Tu m',* where projected shadows are brought to the painted surface. It designates a before, a visual prehistory, an emptied and dematerialized sensibility. This nevertheless remains *necessary* in order for the painting to reach the event that little by little covers up the initial matrix—of memory, no doubt. The bursts of blood—matter of the intolerable—finally give way to violet redemption treated with very light pigments. In killing the photographic aura of an invasive memory-screen, it saves the unconscious truth, image-thought. The veil-mirror of signs proper to painting would be nothing more than the anamnesis of photography, the passage from a visible image to an invisible image made of virtualities.

Perhaps this strange violet is but the trace and transposition of an invisible signifier that recurs in Lichtenberg Ettinger's writings: "halala."[9] While as a masculine substantive *halal* is common and used to signify both "dead" and "space" (one could say, the space of the dead), the feminine *halala,* absent in modern Hebrew, on the other hand, is gifted with a particularly strong significance: it points back to the acts of desacralization and profanation in ancient Hebrew. The painting in its violet, in its *halala,* would be this act of profaning (*hiloul*) a space of the dead (*halal*), indeed it would be the conquest of an impurity as ambiguous as the color violet. The magic pad of *Autistwork* could then be interpreted in the following manner: it brings into contact a *photo-halal*—shadow space, death space—and a *painting-halala,* a power of life as troubling as the aggressive, metaphysical violet it makes from a kind of transparent lighting, the inner space of painting with its modulations and its resonances.

Translated from the French by Annemarie Hamad, Scott Lerner, and Joseph Simas

NOTES:

The first two sections of this essay are reprints of my essay "Images d'absence" in the exhibition catalogue *Matrixial Borderline* (Cahiers des Regards, 1993), translated by Annemarie Hamad and Scott Lerner as "Images of Absence" in *Complexity—Journal of Philosophy and the Visual Arts,* no. 6 (London: Academy Editions, 1995). The third section is a reprint of my essay "Inner Space of Painting," translated by Joseph Simas, in the exhibition catalogue *Halala—Autistwork* (The Israel Museum and Arfiac, 1995).

1. Walter Benjamin, *Ecrits français* (Paris: Gallimard, 1991), 261.
2. Michel Foucault, *La Naissance de la Clinique* (Paris: Presses Universitaires de France, 1963).
3. Translator's note: "literal lack; missing for the letter; missed by the letter; lack of the letter."
4. See Christine Buci-Glucksmann, *L'Enjeu de beau. Musique et passion* (Paris: Galilée, 1992).
5. See Shoshana Felman and Dori Lawb, *Testimony: Crises of Witnessing in Literature, Psychoanalysis and History* (London: Routledge, 1992).
6. See Marc Vernet, *Figures de l'absence* (Paris: Editions de l'Etoile, 1988), 64ff.
7. Gilles Deleuze, *La logique du sens* (Paris: Minuit, 1970), 50ff.
8. Didier Anzieu, *Le corps de l'oeuvre* (Paris: Gallimard, 1981), 72.
9. Bracha Lichtenberg Ettinger, *Matrix. Halal(a)—Lapsus: Notes on Painting 1985–1992* (Oxford: Museum of Modern Art, 1993).

Plates

NANCY SPERO, *Stalks I*, 1974.
Handprinting and
painted collage.
94.5 x 21 in.
Photo: David Reynolds.

MIRA SCHENDEL, *Droguinhas*, 1966.
Knotted rice-paper.
Various sizes, approx. 50 x 50 x 30 cm.
Ada Schendel Bento, São Paulo.

MIRA SCHENDEL, *Untitled*, 1968.
Paper between Plexiglas. 1 x 1 m.
Collection of Konrad Gromholt, Hovikodden (Norway).

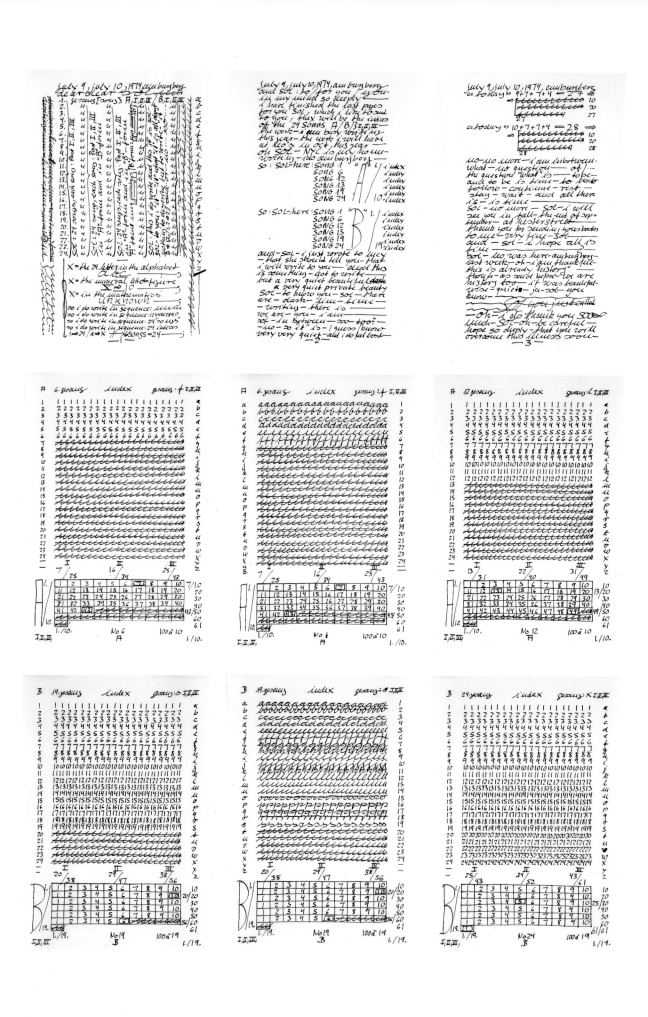

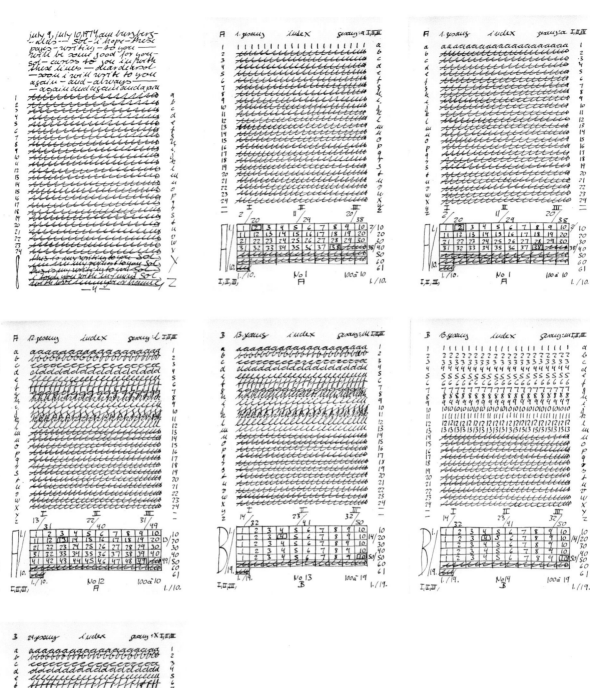
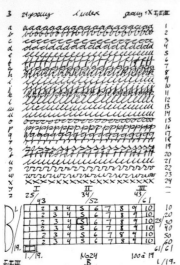

HANNE DARBOVEN,
Letter and Indices to 24 songs A/B I, II, III; 1976.
Ink on vellum.
Courtesy The LeWitt Collection.
Wadsworth Atheneum, Hartford, Connecticut.

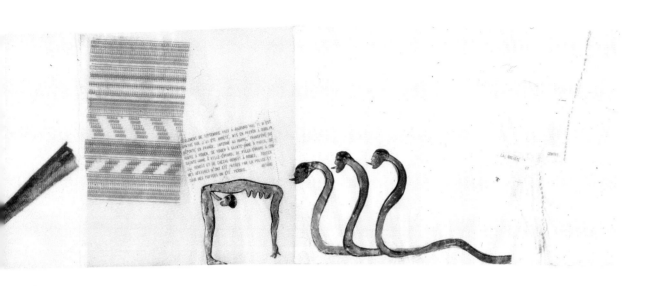

NANCY SPERO, *Codex Artaud VI and VII*, 1971.
Typewriter, painted collage on paper.
20.5 x 124.5 in. and 20.5 x 150 in.
Photo: David Reynolds.

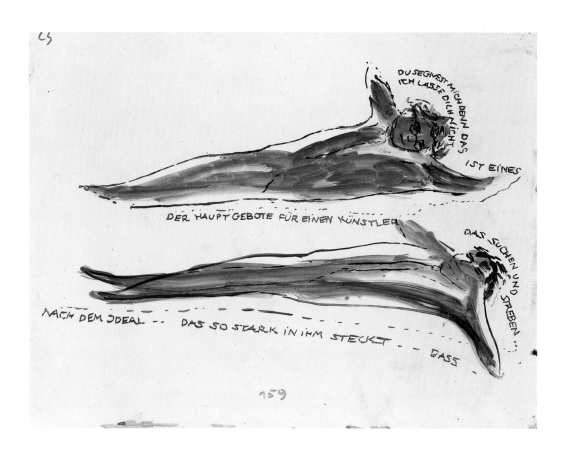

CHARLOTTE SALOMON,
*Leben? Oder
Theater?* (Life?
or Theater?)
series (nos. 45–
2159, 2160, 2171
2172), 1940–42.
Gouache. Approx.
32.5 x 25 cm.
Stichtung
Charlotte
Salomon. Jewish
Historical
Museum,
Amsterdam.

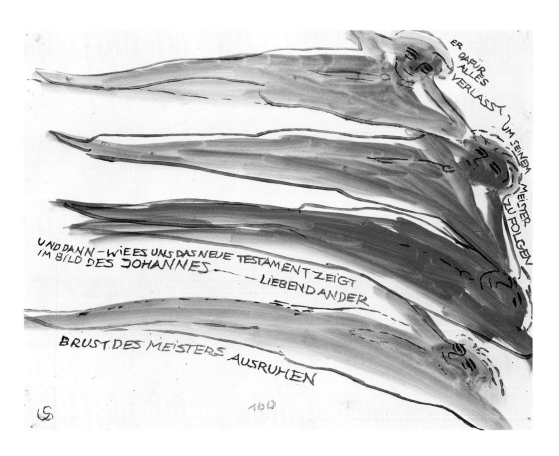

ER DAFÜR
ALLES
VERLASST
UM SEINEM
MEISTER
ZU FOLGEN

UND DANN — WIE ES UNS DAS NEUE TESTAMENT ZEIGT
IM BILD DES JOHANNES — LIEBEND AN DER

BRUST DES MEISTERS AUSRUHEN

160

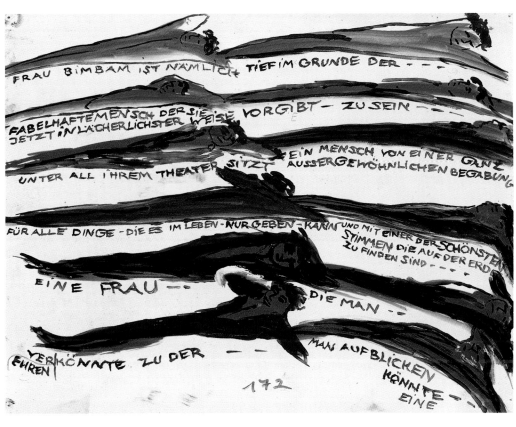

FRAU BIMBAM IST NÄMLICH TIEF IM GRUNDE DER — — —

FABELHAFTE MENSCH DER SIE VORGIBT — ZU SEIN — — —
JETZT IN LÄCHERLICHSTER WEISE

UNTER ALL IHREM THEATER SITZT EIN MENSCH VON EINER GANZ
AUSSERGEWÖHNLICHEN BEGABUNG

FÜR ALLE DINGE — DIE ES IM LEBEN — NUR GEBEN — KANN UND MIT EINER DER SCHÖNSTEN
STIMMEN DIE AUF DER ERDE
ZU FINDEN SIND — — —

EINE FRAU — — DIE MAN — —

VER KÖNNTE ZU DER — — — MAN AUFBLICKEN
EHREN KÖNNTE — — —
EINE

172

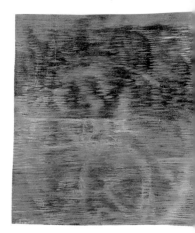

BRACHA LICHTENBERG ETTINGER,
*Autistworks, n. 1, 4, 3,
5, 9, 1993-94.*
Oil and photocopy on
paper mounted on canvas.
Approx. 35 x 27 cm.
Courtesy of the artist.

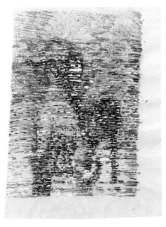

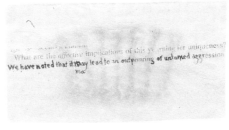

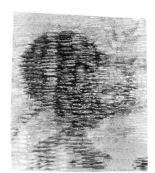

Bracha Lichtenberg Ettinger,
*After/Behind the
Reapers, n. 3 (2nd
series)*, 1990-92.
India ink, pencil, and
photocopy on paper,
Plexiglas. Composed of
two elements,
41 x 84 cm.

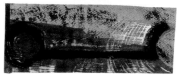

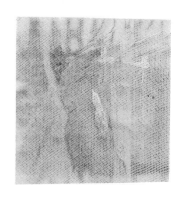

Bracha Lichtenberg Ettinger,
*Halal(a)-Lapsus, n. 2,
Halal(a)-Lapsus, n. 3*,
1985-93.
India ink, pencil, char-
coal, acrylic, pastel,
and photocopy on paper,
Plexiglas. Composed of
three elements,
80 x 40 cm.
Courtesy of the artist.

AVIS NEWMAN, *Webs (Backlight) III*, 1994.
Acrylic, graphite and pigment on linen. 254 x 254 cm.
Courtesy Kanaal Art Foundation, Kortrijk (Belgium).
Photo: Rien van den Eshof.

AVIS NEWMAN, *Webs (Backlight) IV*, 1994.
Acrylic, graphite and pigment on linen. 254 x 254 cm.
Courtesy Kanaal Art Foundation, Kortrijk (Belgium).
Photo: Rien van den Eshof.

SUSAN HILLER, *Midnight, Charing Cross* (Photomat Self Portrait), 1982.
C-type photograph. 20 x 36 in.
Courtesy of the artist and Gimpel Fils Gallery, London.

LILI DUJOURIE, *Enjambement* (Enjambment), 1976.
Video, originally 18 mm. film.
Still: Hans Sonneveld.

LILI DUJOURIE, *Contrapunt* (Counterpoint), 1981.
Video, originally 18 mm. film.
Still: Hans Sonneveld.

AVIS NEWMAN, *Webs (Backlight) IV*, 1994.
Detail.
Acrylic, graphite and pigment on linen. 254 x 254 cm.
Courtesy Kanaal Art Foundation, Kortrijk (Belgium).
Photo: Rien van den Eshof.

THE WEAVING OF WATER AND WORDS

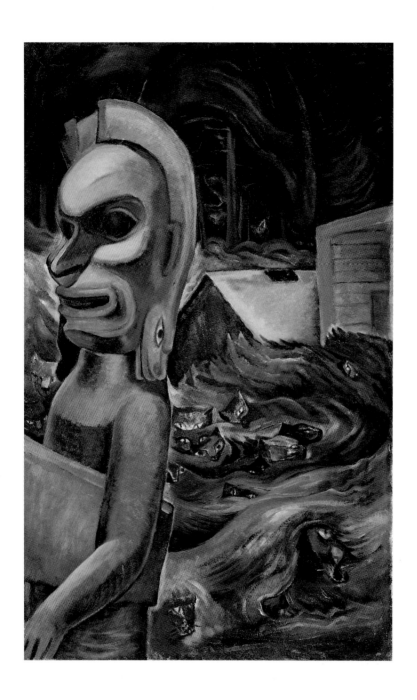

Zunoqua of the Cat Village, 1931.
Oil on canvas. 112.5 x 70.5 cm.
Courtesy Vancouver Art Gallery, Emily Carr Trust.
Photo: Trevor Mills.

Hysterical Histories:
Emily Carr and the Canadian West

Judith Mastai

E mily Carr has become an iconic artist of the Canadian West and the North American Pacific Northwest. A modernist painter, trained in the United States, England, and France at the turn of the century, Carr was a prolific and recognized female artist whose landscapes were to influence succeeding generations. Her paintings of First Nations' villages, particularly totem poles, distinguished her as an advocate for the First Nations' people at a time when racism toward them prevailed. In recent years, half a century after her death, her work has been accorded additional significance as a symbol in a national agenda that attempted to deprive the First Nations of their legitimate claims to the land. During the 1970s, she was embraced as a feminist, whose style established an essentialist signature for women's art.[1] More recently her veiled sexuality has provoked much innuendo. Hysteria seems to have marked both factual and theoretical constructions of Carr's histories. I will suggest that in Carr's case there has been a clouding of the critical distinction between historical narratives, which reconstruct the artist's life and intentions, and contemporary theoretical readings of her work. I will compile these complexities rather than offer yet another "definitive" reading. The occasion of *Inside the Visible* provides an excellent opportunity to map these various positions on Carr's work, because the curator's stated intention is to generate a "space of amazement shared by the artwork, the maker, and the beholder, which could be called 'participatory relation.'" My remarks are framed in this spirit.

I

Born in Victoria, British Columbia, in 1871, the year of the Paris Commune as well as of British Columbia's entry into the Canadian confederation, Carr grew up in a frontier society amid a family of British expatriates. Fort Victoria, situated on Vancouver Island, was a Hudson's Bay outpost primarily serving the interests of the fur trade until gold was discovered on the mainland in 1858. The presence of a British stronghold was also important in the struggle to establish the Canada/U.S. border at the 49th parallel. At the time of Carr's birth, First Nations' peoples were a strong presence on Vancouver Island, and from the turn of the century Carr traveled the West Coast, "documenting" native culture, particularly totem poles.

In 1890, at the age of eighteen, Carr embarked on the first of many travels to study art. At the California School of Design in San Francisco she apparently came under the influence of "the French professor," Amédée Joullin,[2] and decided to dedicate her life to recording the indigenous peoples of the Pacific Northwest in Canada. This anthropologically oriented project was fashionable at the time as researchers like Franz Boas, Edward Curtis, and Marius Barbeau pursued what they imagined heroically as the project of documenting these "noble" peoples before they "disappeared" in the face of western expansion. Carr had grown up adjacent to these Native communities, but ironically her European art education led her to represent them through the stylistic conventions of British watercolors and impressionist and postimpressionist landscapes.

In 1899 Carr enrolled at the Westminster School of Art in London, later moving to St. Ives where she studied under Julius Olsson and the Canadian Algernon Talmage, then director of the Cornish school. Soon after, she entered an English sanitorium, where she was treated for hysteria. After returning to Canada for a brief period, during which she continued to paint, Carr set out again, in 1910, to continue her European studies. This time, on the advice of Victoria painter Sophie Pemberton, she traveled to France and enrolled in the Academi Collarossi. However, the majority of her time in France was spent in Brittany, under the tutelage of William Phelan Gibb, who appears to have been at the center of the prewar Parisian art community. In 1911, two of Carr's works appeared in the Salon d'Automne in Paris.

Emily Carr in her caravan at Metchosin (British Columbia), 1936. Photo: Edythe Hembroff-Schleicher. Courtesy Victoria City Archives and British Columbia Archives.

Carr remained single all her life, painting, teaching art, and, when she failed to earn a living with these pursuits, running a boarding house, breeding sheepdogs, and crafting pottery and hooked rugs for the tourist trade. In 1929, after many years of discouragement, Carr received recognition on the national scene through an invitation to participate in the exhibition "Canadian West Coast Art: Native and Modern" at the National Gallery of Canada in Ottawa. Here for the first time she met members of Ontario's Group of Seven, particularly Lawren Harris, who became a mentor and lifelong friend. Through Harris, Carr was attracted to theosophy for a number of years, finally abandoning it as too cold and intellectual a form of spirituality[3] and returning to Christianity, with liberal sprinklings of transcendentalism. Her sojourn with theosophy also brought her into contact with the American artist Mark Tobey, who was living in Seattle and visited Carr in Victoria.[4]

Carr's art career came to an end in 1945 as a result of angina and a number of heart attacks. As her ability to paint weakened during the last eight years of her life, she took up writing, producing seven autobiographical volumes that won her a Governor General's Award for Literature, the highest form of recognition offered in Canada at that time.

II

In recent years Carr's work has enjoyed renewed notoriety because of her representation of Native culture. While still a student at the University of British Columbia and in response to a survey course on Canadian art, Native art historian Marcia Crosby stated:

Carr not only painted what she called Indian pictures; she gave public lectures about the "Indians." She stated in the Supplement to the *McGill News,* June 1929, "I used to wish I had been born an Indian;" in 1941 she wrote in a letter to Nan Cheney that she was "homesick for Indian"—I don't know if she meant, homesick for the Indians, or an Indian, or being Indian, or things considered to be Indian. It seems to me that since she uses the word "Indian" as a state of being, or as an adjective or an adverb to modify something else, it would be logical to conclude that it acts as a symbol or signifier for something that had personal meaning for Emily Carr. When she was writing her short stories around 1937, she states that she tried to be "plain, straight, simple, and Indian."[5] Yet, how could she be someone or something she was not—much less, be something that did not really exist, except as a construct.[6]

For Crosby, Carr was only one of a growing number of artists, historical and contemporary, who had prospered from representing Native culture and traditions. Like others of her day, Carr had "gone native."[7]

At the time of Carr's birth, there was still ample evidence of the presence of the First Nations peoples on Vancouver Island (among them, the Nuu-Chah-Nulth, the Kwagiut'l, and the Cowichan), and Carr traveled to the sites of other Native nations—the Haida, Gitksan, Wet'suwet'en, Bella Coola, and others—sojourning with Christian missionaries and hosted by the villagers as she carried out her program of documenting their cultures. One of the First Nations gave her the name "Klee Wyck" ("the laughing one"), seemingly in recognition of her friendship. However, Crosby's critique is well founded in light of the fact that Carr, like many of her contemporaries, believed that she and her colleagues were the last witnesses of a "dying" culture.[8] Even as her documentary efforts advocated on behalf of Native culture, Carr's project emanated, as James Clifford has pointed out, from a "salvage paradigm."[9] Crosby states, "We did not all die. We are still here—altered forever, and without the 'authenticity' that some, nostalgically, would like to impose."[10] Along with this positioning of Carr as a representative of the paternalistic, white, colonizing culture of Canada, the people of many of the First Nations are now engaged in a series of celebrated struggles with the governments of Canada and the provinces over land claims. In these struggles, culture in general, and specifically the appropriation of images from their cultures, has been a central issue.

Tom Berger, former justice of the Supreme Court of British Columbia and a longtime advocate for Native rights, wrote:

> The defence of Native land rights is the issue upon which Native peoples base claims to their identity, culture and political autonomy, and ultimately to their survival. Throughout the New World, Native people understand that without a secure land base they will cease to exist as distinct peoples; their fate will be assimilation.
> These claims can only be achieved, however, where Native collective identity is acknowledged and their claim to land itself entrenched in the law.[11]

Regarding the land claims of the Gitksan and Wet'suwet'en peoples, Chief Justice Allan McEachern of the Supreme Court of the Province of British Columbia concluded that "the plaintiffs' aboriginal interests in the territory were lawfully extinguished by the Crown during the colonial period."[12] Berger, however, notes that "these issues are increasingly being determined by the Supreme Court of Canada in favour of the Indians."[13] These different judgments indicate the need of the provinces, such as British Columbia, firmly to establish jurisdiction with the federal (not the provincial) government so that the fiduciary and financial responsibilities for settling the claims also rest with the federal government. While the Native people of Vancouver Island entered into treaties with the colonial government of James Douglas, those on the mainland did not. Therefore, many Native nations of the Pacific Northwest have never acquiesced to the authority of the Crown. There is a well-documented history of their resistance to the claims of the Crown over their lands. In 1982 Canada's new constitution guaranteed Native rights, and in 1991 the Province of British Columbia agreed to become a party to land claims negotiations. The issue of appropriation, then, is not academic. Works like those of Emily Carr have been used by Canadian society to point out the diffusion of Native culture into Canadian culture in order to deny Native peoples' claims for aboriginal title.

III

In addition to the increased attention that Carr's work has enjoyed in recent years as a result of these changing political conditions, many art theoreticians have found her work a convenient example for their musings. Carr has become an irresistible subject for postmodern inquiry. At a 1991 seminar convened by the Vancouver Art Gallery on the occasion of the exhibition "Emily Carr in France," a group of Canadian artists, historians, critics, and theorists exchanged views and investigated the application of contemporary theoretical approaches to Carr's life and work. During two days of engaged discussions, these fifteen people speculated beyond the limits of the presumed objectivity of an empirical paradigm. While gently insisting on "the facts," each spoke from his or her individual subjectivity, sharing ideas and information, niggling about details, agreeing and disagreeing about things that can never be ascertained regarding Carr's motivations, drives, and desires. The spirit of the gathering was not avant-gardist—to claim new ground—but rather involved risking and rehearsing possibilities.

Artist Sara Diamond was interested "in the ways that Carr entered a 'symbolic' that hinged a great deal on her femininity but also operated to erase difference, to erase her femininity," as well as how the presence of Carr's Trust Collection at the Vancouver Art Gallery might have reduced the gallery's interest in acquiring work by contemporary women artists.[14] Diamond also drew attention to claims that have been made for Carr's imagery as Freudian and phallic,[15] suggesting that Carr may have exhibited a masculinity complex manifested in self-sufficiency and autonomy. Art historian Carol Williams pointed out that institutional narratives have sought to authenticate Carr's work as ethnographic, even though in her own day it was rejected by the museum community as not being accurate enough to serve as a document of Native life. Charles Hill, a curator at the National Gallery of Canada, who introduced a series of extracts from a variety of sources on didactic labels accompanying an anniversary exhibition of Carr's work, argued that this device did not validate but rather pointed out the contrast between Carr's own narratives and those of anthropologists dealing with the same subject matter. Hill argued that Carr's work expressed her spiritual search, her attempt to achieve ecstasy in landscape painting, but also her desire to interpret landscape as a national symbol—to find a distinctly Canadian form of representation.

Scott Wilson, director of the Morris and Helen Belkin Gallery at the University of British Columbia, pointed out that our versions of Carr have also been constructed by her friends and biographers, such as Lawren Harris, who helped Carr select which works to donate to the Emily Carr Trust Collection; Ira Dilworth, who edited her writings and wrote about her; artist Jack Shadbolt and curator Doris Shadbolt, who have lectured and written extensively about Carr's life, work, and influence; historians Maria Tippett and Paula Blanshard, who have been her biographers. Quebecois art historian Johanne Lamoureux, who teaches at the University of Montreal, was interested in "the geographical factor" as a motive for Canadian

art history. Her historiographical analysis suggested a gendering of geography, outlining how "Carr became the cultural representative of the West Coast," which was being colonized under the Canadian banner, just as contemporary women artists in Quebec have been colonized as representatives of Canada at international events such as the Venice Biennale, at a time when Canadian unity was threatened by separatism in Quebec. "Through Carr's identification with Native cultures," wrote Lamoureux, "Carr helped Canada to assert its own identity and to found the legitimacy of its existence as one modern country."[16] Critic Joanne Sloane was interested in representations of the landscape. Contrasting Carr's images to the "unhappy wilderness" imagined by the Group of Seven in Ontario, Sloane argued that Carr imagined "a geography with a history"; however, her pictorial language was "a centuries-old European tradition of painting ruins," and this was the major influence on her representation of Native artifacts and culture as those of a "dying" people.

Quebec artist Nicole Jolicoeur introduced the idea that Carr's form of hysteria, unlike Charcot's theatrical hysteria or Freud's Viennese talking cure, was a Victorian hysteria—mute and ironic. Carr's Christianity was discussed, as were other subjects as diverse as her spirituality, her sexuality, her abjection, her desire to be the surrogate mother of a young Victoria girl, Carol Pearson, her relationships with the Native woman Sophie and the Chinese painter Li Man, as well as fauvist influences on her painting as a result of her sojourn in France. Artist Landon Mackenzie discussed the discomfort and physical hardship that Carr endured in the forests and on the waters of British Columbia in order to paint her subject matter. Others investigated the content of her imagery, suggesting metaphorical readings of Carr's work as a picturesque garden, of the image of the path as a symbol for a search leading from darkness to light, of the vertical orientation of her compositions as suggesting figuration, personifying totem poles and trees. Heather Dawkins, an art historian from Simon Fraser University, cautioned participants not to separate Carr's visual texts from her written texts, suggesting that they be "read" together. Such are the complexities of our relationships with Emily Carr, whose life and work have come to represent many obsessions and contradictions in the narratives of the Canadian West.

IV

In a lecture on the work of Vancouver artist Ken Lum at the Witte de With Centre for Contemporary Art in Rotterdam in 1990, Jeff Wall introduced his subject by stating: "I want to draw out some ideas about cultural traditions which have formed artistic attitudes in Western Canada, and particularly, Vancouver. To do so, it is necessary to begin with the work of Emily Carr. She is known as the originary figure in modern art in the area, and is thereby a kind of emblematic representative of traditions in which all of us who work there are in some way or other involved."[17] Wall ties his positioning of Carr, as the founding mother of the traditions of art in western Canada, to pantheistic romanticism and to "the great Western adventure of British colonialism . . . an intensely modernistic thing which projected itself all over the globe, moving from frontier to frontier."[18] He sees Vancouver as the final Western frontier and proposes that Carr's work, seen in the greater context of British imperialism, participated in a "Commonwealth romanticism" that embraced Victorian values, imbuing them with the new national aspirations of former colonies. Wall particularly used the phrase "Victorian values" to connote the culture of the home that would domesticate the wilderness. Carr both participated in this program and transgressed it. Wall states:

> [Carr's] subjectivism destabilized British Romantic ideas, even though it grew out of them. It did so, maybe, because her impulses were constantly linked with a protest against the vanishing of the Native cultures and against the abuse of the forest environment by logging. Certainly by 1912, the economy of the region was firmly set in the direction of maximum extraction of lumber for the export market, a direction which continues up to today, when we can see the exhaustion of the forests and are alarmed and ashamed by it. At the same time, her work can be seen as an ideological reconciliation with the destruction of the forest; that is, reconciliation with nature as it is experienced in Carr's painting can be seen as the mark of a fantasized reconciliation with the economy, a means by which an acceptance of the actuality of forest-destruction is lived through and acquiesced to.

Wall's concise descriptions of the complexities of Carr's historical situation and their importance as a founding logic for the practices of West Coast artists beg interpretation as simply another modernist practice. Many artists, historians, and theorists focus not on the obvious parallels of Carr's practice with that of other modernist artists but on the discrepancies and lack of fit. The simultaneous presence of many contradictory impulses remains with us to this day, and thus Carr's work still holds meaning for us, here on the West Coast and beyond.

In outlining the purpose of *Inside the Visible,* curator Catherine de Zegher asked if it is possible to consider "sameness" and "difference" in a perpetual state of mutual negotiation, after the ideas of artist and theorist Bracha Lichtenberg Ettinger. A central feature of Lichtenberg Ettinger's psychoanalytically based writing is the concept of *metramorphosis,* which she defines as a creative principle, inducing instances of coemergence of meaning, such as those that I propose are being suggested by Wall. Metramorphosis relates to *matrixial* rather than phallic relations. Lichtenberg Ettinger cautions that while "matrix" means womb, she does not mean to imply that the body has a hold on the mind in an essentialist sense; nor does she mean to suggest that knowledge of it is solely the privilege of women. "The *matrix* is at the service of both sexes. It should not be reduced to the womb, just as the *phallus* should not be reduced to the penis even though it is linked to the male in the Real and to the masculine in the Imaginary. The Matrix is oriented toward the feminine in men and women, toward Woman *not as Other* but as *a different kind of relations between* the I and the *non-I.*"[19] She suggests that matrixial "making sense" does

316

not involve opposition of the subject and the object, as in the phallic paradigm, but recognition of the borderlines and borderlinks between *I* and *non-I*. In her view, transgression is not represented by alternations between presence and absence, but by the shareability of factors that constitute the shifting and changing borderlinks. Here "woman" is preserved as both subject and object, not only as object; and borderlines between subjects and objects become thresholds for creation.

Such a psychoanalytic model well suits the "hysterical" histories and theoretical narratives that have come to be associated with Emily Carr as an iconic figure. The contradictions and occurrences of Carr's life and the work that she produced as a result have appealed to modernists and postmodernists alike, as well as to formalists, postcolonial theorists, nationalists, and regionalists. Certainly these debates and attributions have contributed to her popularity and increasing recognition as an artist.

NOTES:
1. Lucy Lippard, "Quite Contrary: Body, Nature, and Ritual in Women's Art," *Chrysalis* 2 (1977): 31–47. Carr's influence is compared to that of Georgia O'Keeffe.
2. Ruth Ann Appelhof, "Emily Carr: Canadian Modernist," *The Expressionist Landscape*, exhib. cat. (Birmingham, Ala.: Birmingham Museum of Art, 1988), 33.
3. Emily Carr, *Hundreds and Thousands: The Journals of Emily Carr* (Toronto and Vancouver: Clarke, Irwin & Co., 1966), 112. Carr wrote: "Having Christ in one's life should waken one to a far bigger sense of life, far bigger than the sense of life that comes through theosophy, that static, frozen awfulness, sort of a cold storage for beautiful thoughts, no connect-up with God by Christ. At one time I was very keenly interested, thought perhaps it was the way. Now it numbs and chills me. It's so bloodless, so tied up with 'states' and laws and dogma and by what authority?"
4. Mark Tobey painted *Emily Carr's Studio* in 1928 (oil on canvas, 75.6 by 62.9 centimeters).
5. Carr, *Hundreds and Thousands: The Journals of Emily Carr,* 291.
6. Marcia Crosby, *Emily Carr,* ed. Judith Mastai (Vancouver: Vancouver Art Gallery, 1992), 38.
7. Among those who capitalized on a Native persona were the Canadian poet Pauline Johnson (Tekahionwake) and the Englishman George Stansfeld Belaney, who adopted the name Grey Owl and became a renowned wildlife advocate.
8. Gerta Moray has pointed out that Carr's paintings of Northwest Coast Native people and their culture were produced within a context of colonization, at a time when racism was an instrument for the acquisition of their resource-rich lands by the Canadian government. Moray goes to great lengths to point out that Carr attempted to contest prevailing views about Native people; however her work did indeed depict an "other" race and construct an "imaginary" Indian. Moray's defense of Carr is not intended to exonerate the artist of complicity with these national agendas but rather to understand better how she was also a product of the social, political, and economic conditions of her day. The so-called "primitivist" works of French artists were known to Carr, but Moray also takes pains to propose that Carr's work attempted to counteract prevailing negative views, challenging social attitudes and public policy by creating a body of work in homage to these cultures and their traditions. Gerta Moray, "Northwest Coast Native Culture and the Early Indian Paintings of Emily Carr, 1899–1913," Ph.D. diss., Department of Art History, University of Toronto, 1993.
9. James Clifford, *The Predicament of Culture: Twentieth Century Ethnography, Literature and Art* (Cambridge, Mass.: Harvard University Press, 1988).
10. Marcia Crosby, "Construction of the Imaginary Indian," *Vancouver Anthology: The Institutional Politics of Art,* ed. Stan Douglas (Vancouver: Talonbooks/Or Gallery, 1991), 270.
11. Ibid., 140–41.
12. Chief Justice Allan McEachern, Reasons for Judgment, No. 0843 Smithers Registry, In the Supreme Court of British Columbia, Between DELGAMUUKW, also known as KEN MULDOE, suing on his own behalf and on behalf of all the members of the HOUSE OF DELGAMUUKW, and others (Plaintiffs) and HER MAJESTY THE QUEEN IN RIGHT OF THE PROVINCE OF BRITISH COLUMBIA and THE ATTORNEY GENERAL OF CANADA (Defendants), March 8, 1991, p. 254.
13. Ibid., 142.
14. Diamond's point is that the large number of Carr's works in the gallery's holdings greatly increases the gallery's percentage of work by women artists in the collection in general. This fact has been used to argue against the gallery's acquiring more work by women artists, particularly contemporary Canadian women artists.
15. Robert Linsley, "Painting and the Social History of British Columbia," *Vancouver Anthology,* 225–45.
16. Lamoureux was quoting from her paper "Emily Carr's Territory," presented at the colloquium "Defining Canada" April 20, 1991, at the Barbican Centre, London, on the occasion of the exhibitions "The True North" and "Unnatural Traces."
17. Jeff Wall, "Traditions and Counter-traditions in Vancouver Art: A Deeper Background for Ken Lum's Work," *The Lectures 1990* (Rotterdam and Ghent: Witte de With Centre for Contemporary Art and Imschoot, Uitgevers, 1991), 67.
18. Ibid., 67–68.
19. Bracha Lichtenberg Ettinger, *The Matrixial Gaze* (Leeds: University of Leeds, Feminist Arts and Histories Network, 1995), 25.

Les drapeaux rouges, 1939.
Oil on canvas. 80 x 140 cm.
Kunstsammlung Nordrhein-Westfalen, Düsseldorf.
Photo: Walter Klein.

The Taming of the Saccadic Eye:
The Work of Vieira da Silva in Paris

Serge Guilbaut

I t might sound strange to a North American public reading about the Portuguese painter Maria Helena Vieira da Silva that in international circles she is one of the most well-known, respected, and beloved painters. As is often the case in modern art history, Vieira da Silva had a very different reception on either side of the Atlantic Ocean. In Europe she is considered one of the most important figures in modern art history and even recognized as a master of postwar French abstraction. Although the artist had worked in Paris since the 1930s, only upon returning to Paris in 1947 after a stay in Brazil during the war did her work become recognized as one of the finest expressions of contemporary Parisian production. She was recognized by the Museum of Modern Art in Paris, where her work was acquired as early as 1948 (*La partie d'échec*, 1943). She soon had exhibits all over Europe (Paris, Stockholm, London, Basel, etc.) and also in the Americas, where she won a series of prestigious prizes: São Paulo Biennale in 1953, Caracas Biennale in 1955, Carnegie Institute, Pittsburgh, in 1958, etc. Although many other female artists in Paris in those days were taken seriously,[1] Vieira da Silva was exceptional in being able to keep her place in the European art world while others were fading away with the arrival of new stylistic fads.

What makes her even more interesting these days is that her career has taken the opposite trajectory of painters such as Lee Krasner and Elaine De Kooning, wives of famous American artists whose work was long eclipsed by their husbands and only lately are being fully recognized. The reverse is true in Vieira da Silva's case. Her Hungarian husband, Arpad Szenes, whom she married in Paris in 1930, was himself a sensitive and sophisticated abstract painter who was never able to attain the level of recognition that his wife achieved. Her recognition occurred while the Parisian art scene was being reorganized after the war, amongst the clamor of critical disputes centering around the validity of abstraction confronted with a still aggressive realist tradition. I contend that Vieira da Silva's work was luckily caught in the struggle to establish a reformulated School of Paris and that she provided crucial elements for this reconstruction. To perform this role, her work had to be seen through a classical Parisian grid, leaving aside what was, interestingly, a somewhat destabilizing and vacillating artistic proposition.

For many American painters, musicians, and writers for a while—let's say between 1946 and 1953, before lyrical abstraction became hegemonic—Paris was a sort of heaven for intellectuals. One could live cheaply, possibilities were numerous, and the liberal atmosphere was tremendously productive for many artists who would have had a hard time expressing their unconventional views at home during reactionary political moments. Gay artists, for example, flocked to Paris to find breathing space, understanding, and productive support. African-American writers, painters, and musicians also discovered a city open to difference, often to the point of *indifference,* as James Baldwin put it. Paris still, for a few years, carried the bohemian myth of the 1920s and 1930s. These were times of high hopes for the French, in general, and for intellectuals, in particular, because possibilities for radical changes were envisaged with a certain sense of realism. It seemed unthinkable that France would ever go back to a social and political system as corrupt and cynical as the last, which could not even prevent the ascension of Fascism and war. The enthusiasm for change after such a horrendous past was such that André Breton, still in North America, published in a new liberal newspaper ironically called *Terres des Hommes* a powerful piece calling for a dramatic transformation of world values. If dominant male behavior was responsible for the war and its massacres, Breton wrote, then it was high time to look for other alternatives: women's values.

Maria Helena Vieira da Silva painting *Les drapeaux rouges,* 1939.

His attempt, if not universally accepted, was characteristic of other postwar/revolution moral crises: "Artists should definitely be suspicious of destructive male culture and replace it as soon as possible by female culture in order to avoid a global disaster. Time has come to promote women's ideas rather than the totally bankrupt ones of men. It is the artist who should, in particular, only if in protest, promote female systems of ideas." These words, written while he was in exile in North America as part of his book *Arcane 17,* resonated when published in February 1946, and in particular because they came just after women were finally allowed to vote in France (October 5, 1944). A new era seemed, indeed, to flourish. This, supplemented by a euphoric feeling that French culture was being rebuilt on respected grounds—Matisse, Bonnard, Villon, Braque, and Picasso were still active and visible—produced a short but intense elation during which everybody seemed to have a chance to participate in the reassertion of a very specific French Renaissance.

The year 1947, nevertheless, when Vieira da Silva went back to Paris, saw this nationalistic euphoria ebb somewhat, due to the progressive realization that the postwar world was going to be a world in which France would have only a small part to play. During the cold war, Paris became the site, the playground, for a raucous debate about contemporary culture in which artistic styles became the nodal point for political positions. Vieira da Silva's paintings were caught in the maelstrom, as they seemed to express several key elements that critics thought to be emblematic of what the new Parisian culture was or ought to be in its search for universal values.

Her work was clearly related to a modern, even cubist vocabulary. While analytic cubism was often seen by French critics as too intellectual, Vieira da Silva's idiosyncratic formations brought together two elements that revitalized Parisian tradition. Her study with Hayter, Torres García, and Bissière gave her work a soft constructivist vocabulary, addressing some of the post-Mondrian questions posed by artists at the end of the war: How could one produce meaningful but emotional abstract statements about everyday experiences without falling into the hated decorative? Also beneficial was her decision not to censor her non-French identity. On the contrary, she played with it, without fear of offering a modern exoticism to wary and hungry Parisian eyes. She introduced famous Portuguese blue tiles in her paintings that cleverly phagocytized Cézanne's blue constructivist brush strokes. Square tiles overwhelmed the faceted cubist surface, giving coherence to an otherwise traditional cubist space.[2] These complex tiled spaces provided a tumultuous depth, a maelstrom of accelerating and decelerating curves and broken perspectives. By the same token, Vieira da Silva was also recalling the beautiful, intimate red squares inhabiting the work of another giant of French art, the luscious Bonnard (she remembered vividly Bonnard's show of checkered tablecloths at the

Galerie Georges Petit in 1928). This, allied with what she learned of spirituality in Bissière's studio, was literally too much to bypass for certain Parisian critics in search of a renewed expression of Parisian qualities.

Vieira da Silva was prolific within a reduced, well-defined corpus of topics referring to privacy, in particular when representing modern cityscapes. In constructing this new modern space, she pulled many traditional modern strings. She recalled Cézanne (*La forêt des erreurs,* 1941), reworked through Marcel Duchamp (*La partie d'échec,* 1943), Robert Delaunay (*Les portes,* 1947), or Bonnard and Villon. What was new was the seemingly realist urban landscape couched in abstract terms. Her abstraction carried in its folds enough realistic figuration to lead the viewer into a monstrous faceted labyrinth, which nevertheless offered enough clues that one could follow a trail designed and lined as if by some wicked Ariadne.

Like other painters of her generation (Franz Kline or Pierre Soulages), Vieira da Silva attempted to express the spiritual and structural qualities of cities but with more attachment to the recognizable. Hers are also lyrical expressions of the city. If Soulages and Kline articulated their virility through speed (Kline) or through quiet, monumental, and archaic force (Soulages)—the confident and optimistic relation with representation of the sites of everyday living—Vieira da Silva displaced unmediated experiences into maps, into dreamed and distanced metaphorical cityscapes difficult to grasp but as a consequence visually exciting. These cityscapes are places where thinking and dreaming intertwine, where action is minimal, where physical display is restrained, where representation is more intellectual than physical. She was quick to explain: "Painting is very consoling. One can paint with a tremor, or almost blind. One's physical condition does not matter, almost."[3] If Soulages in his constructions has the seriousness of a monk, Vieira da Silva in hers is like a magician. Under a gracile surface, she represents, nevertheless, a disconnected world, always in turmoil, fast moving, strident, and cutting, charged with cool phantasmagoria.

The picture of contemporary life in her work is as disconcerting as the drawings of cities by Wols. It is as if she was scrutinizing the world from the wrong end of a telescope or, more accurately, binoculars. Wols drew *The City* (1951) after a close-up glance at his environment, which becomes threatening by the sheer claustrophobic jumble of unengaging things and people that he represented, clustered together like a colony of suffocating mussels. Wols investigated the dirty water stagnating between the cobblestones of the winding, archaic streets, looking for his reflection in the sullied water of the gutter. More detached, Vieira da Silva saw herself in the constellation of the map. She turned the binoculars around and gazed from the other end, overlooking the scene from afar, protected from the crushing forms that she knew are so destructive, a gaze that rapidly produced a kind of out-of-body experience. To protect herself from the crushing hustle of the modern city, she constructed an apparently modern point of view: from the top of a skyscraper or from an airplane. It is a place to enjoy the view without wanting to know too much about it, or at least to be able to manage a heterogeneity there for the taking but too close for comfort: the ethereal conflicts with the libidinal.

Michel de Certeau well describes this phenomenon. Looking down from the new World Trade Center in New York, he mused:

> To be lifted up to the summit of the World Trade Center is to be lifted out of the city's grasp. . . . An Icarus flying above these waters, he can ignore the devices of Daedalus in mobile and endless labyrinths far below. His elevation transfigures him into a voyeur. It puts him at a distance. It transforms the bewitching world by which one was possessed into a text that lies before one's eye. It allows one to read it, to be a solar Eye, looking down like a god.[4]

This is what Parisian critics read in Vieira da Silva's pictures and evaluated positively, without seeing that her vision from above was a bit trickier, mediated by the construction of a labyrinthine grid that renders the reading, the grasp of the city elusive and the transparent fiction of display opaque. This distorted grid, in fact, produces a complex, baroque space, a multitude of fragmentary glimpses. As the geographer Derek Gregory writes of city spaces, Vieira da Silva's cultural production seems to be one of "consolation" rather than one of "resistance,"[5] a place to dream rather than to act. Those public spaces, through distantiation, are transformed into private areas. She often superimposes architecture and plans of cities onto the labyrinthine rows of libraries, as if, structurally speaking, they were similarly baffling. Indeed, her two major themes are city plans and labyrinthine libraries, where the sweetness of reading and learning is as terrifying as the Tower of Babel. As any book lover knows, and as Walter Benjamin has explained, a library simultaneously shows the pleasure of private delightful reading and knowledge and the anxiety resulting from the sheer number of books collected but not read, of unprocessed knowledge. One has the illusion of owning the totality of knowledge while simultaneously knowing the impossibility and arrogance of the project. In fact, the library in its structural diversity can be said to be the empire of non-sense. This was a space used in the nineteenth century by modernist writers, paradoxically, to express a wild imagination. Michel Foucault discusses Gustave Flaubert's use of the "library" of the book in order to carve out a space where "the visionary experience arises from the black and white surface of printed signs, from the closed words; fantasies are carefully deployed in the hushed library. . . . The fantastic is no longer a property of the heart, nor is it found among the incongruities of nature; it evolves from the accuracy of knowledge, and its treasures lie dormant in documents."[6] The city and the library became sites of tourism, waves of distorted perspectives on which one could surf without too much danger but with much exhilarating delight, slaloming around the everyday.

Bibliothèque en feu, 1974. Oil on canvas. 158.6 x 178.5 cm. Fundação Calouste Gulbenkian, Centro de Arte Moderna José de Azredo Perdigão, Lisbon (Portugal).

Several times Vieira da Silva commented on her interest in private isolation, an isolation that she rapidly realized was peopled with dreams and fantasies. She mentioned that, being the daughter of the owner of a large Lisbon newspaper, in her youth she could hear the noise of history crashing at her doorstep, a hum produced by an ungraspable history. She was a witness without engagement—an attitude no doubt extremely interesting to French intellectuals distressed by so much intellectual engagement in the late 1940s. Her art was miles away from political social realism or the depressing existential realism of Bernard Buffet. Her studio was another world, a place of morality, an abstract space similar to that occupied by Lewis Carroll, a funny philosophizing space. Commenting on Zurbarán, for example, she said: "Those people in monasteries, who led such austere lives. I am not a believer, but for me that would have been paradise, that cloistered, concentrated life."[7] That is precisely why in 1954, when her career was developing rapidly, she hired Guy Weelen to be her business partner, a go-between with the world.

Vieira da Silva understood her position as a modern painter confronted with an accelerating modernity with all the implied anxieties and decided to represent it from her specific vantage point. By the same token her complex vision allowed a French critical establishment in search of a renewed Parisian school to extract and use part of her discourse for its own interests.

The modern city does become an excuse for the production of a powerful modernist grid but serves also as an excuse to project the viewer out of a traditional way of looking. Once caught by the net of flickering lines, the viewer becomes suddenly the floating psychoanalytical Redon eye over the land of our miseries, a kind of a crazy Nadar looking down from his balloon at a strange world that seems, nevertheless, to make sense when seen from so high.

In picture after picture her work addressed the new city spaces developed during the postwar reconstruction of France: representations always on the verge of collapsing due to the thinness, the arachnid quality of lines that convey an airiness more appropriate to the representation of impressionist landscape than to modern architecture but that suggest impending doom or a palpable fragility inherent in those new utopian cities (*villes nouvelles,* as the French called them). In the late 1950s, her paintings are full of new glass buildings, transparent, translucent, intimidating in their openness, their fake communicative appeal replacing private thinking and isolation with spectacularization and decodification of urban activities comparable to what Jacques Tati was presenting in his films during those same years (*Mon oncle, Playtime*). Vieira da Silva offered not so much a radical critique of Mondrian's utopian grid as an enrichment of it, more tactile, less visual. Her sophisticated and elegant grid corresponded to desires of part of the Parisian intelligentsia, always uneasy about Mondrian's dryness, to find a representation of contemporaneity between rigid realism and wild, unchecked and unformed abstraction. Part of Vieira da Silva's work responded to this, but, I would argue, Parisian critics' cursory glance at the work, necessitated by the urgency of their task, left many facets in shadow, in particular those that contradicted their theoretical constructions.

Vieira da Silva's paintings, then, must be seen in connection with the electric debate unfolding in Paris in the middle 1950s around the issue of abstraction versus figuration and, inside this debate, about what type of abstraction (geometrical or lyrical, "hot" or "cold," as they were called then) should represent Parisian talent and civilization. Her private world intersected so deeply with a form of public critical discourse in the early 1950s that it was never really dislodged from the reconstruction of a phantasmic "School of Paris."

Certain characteristics of her work described above explain why recognition came so early and so strongly. At the end of the war, the Parisian establishment wanted to restore their city's cultural hegemony to counteract its loss of political, military, and colonial power. Several attempts were made to recover this blessed time, without much success because of internal schisms, on the one hand, and the American challenge on the other. The arguments promoted in books by Bernard Dorival (*Les étapes de la peinture contemporaine, 1911–1944*), *Les peintres du XXe siècle*), and even by Pierre Francastel in his *Nouveau dessin, nouvelle peinture: L'école de Paris* (1946), defined the specific qualities of Parisian painting. They were the opposite of what German art was supposed to be: expressionist. French art was somewhat Cartesian, with flair, delicacy, and reasonable beauty. These reconstructions were rooted in deep nationalistic convictions. A large part of the French elite that came out of the war unscathed by collaboration was still clinging to a world rapidly passing them by; they were still articulating a cultural position that had been powerful and progressive under the Third Republic. Writers like Diehl, Dorival, and Francastel, to name only a few, were reestablishing old ideas of French culture in new garb. This ideology saw man as part of nature but without the destabilizing effect of instincts: in man, nature is confused with reason because the nature of man is nothing else than instinct controlled by reason. Thus Dorival dismissed Mondrian and Kandinsky, preferring Léger's and Modigliani's elegant reserve. French genius is exactly this Dionysus tamed by Apollo, but a Dionysus still present and visible, in order to show the force and the passion being controlled. The struggle has to be visible, but the victory of taste over instincts must also be displayed on the canvas for everyone to see. Dorival writes in *La peinture française* (1946): "French painting is foremost about discretion. It is weary of color and thickness. . . . A particular characteristic of French tradition is poetical realism." For Dorival, humanist measure is so important and so ingrained in Parisian soil that it touches and transforms every form that comes in contact with it. Even the air of Paris pacifies, one would even say colonizes, the rough foreigner's habits. "The climate of our country has imposed itself onto painters, who were profoundly different from our genius—oriental Jews in particular—with such a soft convincing strength (force) that it modified their spirit and their forms, and made their art a kind of province or protectorate of real French art."[8] This identification became standard in the aesthetic and political discourses of people who could not understand abstraction or social or bourgeois realism. This question of identity was hotly debated until 1956.[9]

The important role played by Vieira da Silva's work in this construction is shown in the first text written about her in 1949 by Michel Seuphor, the famous expert on abstract art, early defender of Mondrian, and friend and collaborator of Torres García. He saw in her work everything for which "real" progressive Parisians were looking:

> The beauty of this work is this canalized power, this explosion seen in slow motion, so to speak. A severe discipline, hidden by a certain elegant playfulness, the apparent improvisation of lines and colors produces every brush stroke but is never overwhelmed by personality [temperament]. Or rather, this personality in Vieira da Silva is tempered, is order, orchestration. . . . Rigor and freedom here produce an exalting marriage. The art of Mondrian was pure style, that of van Gogh pure scream. With Vieira da Silva, Style and Shout are simultaneously produced in each painting, closely intertwined in each moment of the painting.[10]

Once more Paris was coopting, refining, pacifying the exaltations of the world, forcing vehemence through the sifter of coherence in order to shape a civilized product. Noise became harmony, scream was transformed into song. Seuphor's superimposition of a woman's work on top of Mondrian's strict harmony would, recalling Mondrian's coolness about the feminine, have made the Dutch artist turn in his grave. But the moment was such that the defense of "cool," curvilinear abstraction was more important than theoretical purity. Important in this reading, which was later endlessly repeated and on which Vieira da Silva's reputation and success were based, was this balancing act, this mixture of emotion and coolness, this taming of the apocalyptic, swirling landscapes in which instability was seen as being checked by the often-quoted, happy Bonnard checkered tablecloth. A nightmarish series of spaces pacified by a protected net knitted by an elegant and cultured woman able to fuse eighteenth-century Portuguese Azulejos (blue) with the red Bonnard tablecloth.

No wonder that when, in 1952, Charles Estienne tired of the reckless international avant-garde pronouncements made by his rival Michel Tapié, he enrolled Vieira da Silva and Marie Raymond, among others, in his new French counterattack. In a bold move, while America was involved in an all-out cultural propaganda blitz in Paris and while Tapié, showing Jackson Pollock, pleaded for Pollock to help French abstraction win the cultural civil war ("Pollock with Us" as the title of his catalogue put it), Estienne in a surge of national pride proposed a show at the Galerie de Babylone called "Peintres de la Nouvelle Ecole de Paris." Estienne planned to reorganize the school along new, more modern lines, an up-to-date version of the old one in order to disassociate himself from Tapié's all-encompassing and amorphous grouping. Estienne's art, was not going to be an "art autre," but a Parisian one produced by an international community of artists learning a few tricks from the Parisian history, atmosphere, and environment. "What is the school of Paris?" Estienne asked in his catalogue.

> It is, first of all and simply, a name and a fact, which means that maybe the time of national schools is over but that Paris is the privileged site, where the best painting in the world—from the four corners of the world—gives the best of itself without losing its deep indigenous savor. Maybe there is no longer a French school in the strict sense of the term, but the glory of Paris is that Paris is still located in France. It is then in Paris that twentieth-century painting becomes self-conscious. . . . And so what is the new School of Paris? From the specificity of the plastic fact—I mean abstraction—from this fact then . . . it is the discovery of reality behind it that is important, the marvel of this reality. Two antagonistic brothers connecting the most profound surrealism and the extreme freedom of abstraction. Art does not imitate nature, it is its signification.[11]

For Estienne, this particular mixture defined the new art, not formalist abstraction transformed into academic exercises or extreme expressionist experiments but a poetic, controlled, and meaningful trade with reality. Vieira da Silva here fits with Pignon, Estève, Hartung, de Staël, and Poliakoff in an international, if eclectic, school. The French saw her work as sophisticated and reasonable; she knew classical music, opera, painting, literature; in a word, she was cultured. Abstraction could then continue the elevated task of traditional painting.

The French found what they were looking for, but her work is actually situated in a cultural sphere that lovers of the School of Paris could not possibly appreciate. Vieira da Silva articulated a complex image of modernity parallel to that proposed by Walter Benjamin just before the war: pessimistic and baroque. Like Benjamin, she was fascinated with Marseilles's new transporter bridge arching over the harbor, a huge, moving structure, symbol for many of the most advanced technology. As she drew, this modern structure became the point of departure for her career as a painter: "Nobody told me that a moving bridge could be beautiful; a strong structure with a multitude of wiry parts able to connect distant parts was fascinating."[12] This, as Benjamin saw it, was the epitome of modernity, the opposite of architecture, which was too close to historical traditions. The engineer, as the Marseilles bridge proved, was inventing a new equilibrium, a new organization of form in order to produce a beautiful new aesthetic rooted in efficiency. This fairy-tale quality of modern life was imprinted in her work.

"When I arrived in Paris, I was enchanted by the metro, by the organization of the metro. It is like a fairy tale. The doors that open and close when and how they should, and the way you infallibly find the right route."[13] Vieira da Silva was perhaps the last modern artist to try to continue the modernist tradition in attempting to represent the new city. But she avoided the overpowering male gaze, a gaze that she understood but placed in an antagonistic relation to modernist tradition. Eager to emulate Cézanne's space, she was also serious about putting it in jeopardy, shredding it through a maelstrom of distorted tiled environment. This was a last attempt to represent the essence of modernity formulated only through phantasmagoria, activated by a surrealist notion of the marvelous. Everybody noticed this last component but took it as influence, when in fact it was a tool to connect with the grand old project of description important to early modernism. It is no accident that she and Benjamin were interested in similar topics and had similar reactions to modernity. Her paintings of city plans seen from above are a kind of futuristic vision that, paradoxically, relate to past representations. In fact, these images are syncopated, breathless in their shift of perspective and sinuous lines, returning to a medieval, premodern city. The roller-coaster perspective of ancient streets evokes medieval Lisbon rather than Haussmann's boulevards, remnants of the past city also present in Eugène Atget's early photographs: small, old, stubborn, primitive empty spaces lodged, forgotten, between the newer boulevards. Vieira da Silva's images represent cities emptied of humans, as if people had been systematically stamped out, annihilated, sucked out by the speed with which the painter propels us across the canvas, just as early cameras depicted empty streets because they could not register human activity due to the low sensitivity of the film.[14] These are monuments to failed, aborted progress, reflecting a strange, speechless fascination with modernity, its precious fairy-tale quality, the world transformed into empty Parisian "passages." These views are located between Wols's pessimistic views and Mondrian's optimistic and utopian ones. Hers are nostalgic, protected views of a city that cannot be known or processed but can be enjoyed from afar as a fascinating touristic uprooting (if not alienation), a personal resistance through nostalgia.

Although agoraphobic, Vieira da Silva seemed to be sucked into heights, to be interested in the towering point of view. Her constructions offer a high-speed push-and-pull travel through space, a Donna Haraway "integrated circuit" that aspires to a global polymorphous network; the female, high-bourgeois Portuguese view of the world can finally have a place, can describe the heterogeneous world without fear. Vieira da Silva's grid is all about the unwillingness to give (or the impossibility of giving) the eye a specific place from which to read the world. As Martin Jay writes:

> Baroque vision is deeply antiplatonic, hostile to the ordered regularities of geometric optics. As such, it opposes both Cartesian philosophy and perspective in painting. The space it inhabits is more haptic or tactile than purely visual, more plural than unified. It presents a bewildering surplus of images, an overloading of the visual apparatus. Resistant to any panoptic God's eye view, any *survol global*. . . . It strives for the representation of the unrepresentable and, necessarily failing to achieve it, resonates a deep melancholy.[15]

I do not want to transform Vieira da Silva's work into a postmodern guerrilla tactic because she was obviously not into this mode, but her work proposes a structure in which the well-understood modernist formal lessons and teaching mix with her own experience, which too often clashed with what she knew. This destabilization of tradition nevertheless kept enough in its folds to make her work appealing to a critical establishment that wanted to revive a middle-of-the-road-production, far from the shapeless extremes of the *informel* painters. Vieira da Silva's subject matter (libraries, city plans, erased by flooded railway stations) and her way of representing her detached self produced a fantasy of limitless multiple embodiments, whose openness made it possible to kidnap parts of her project without fear: a Portuguese woman's decentered eye became again, thanks to her untheorized position, a Parisian modern art through misreading and appropriation.

Consider a discussion that she reported with the German abstract *informel* and *maudit* painter Wols: "One day, right after the war, Wols asked me: 'Tell me, I like what you're doing a lot, but why are you doing perspective?' I answered that I knew it wasn't done in modern art, but that I had to do it anyway."[16] It was as if the modernist project in its tango with tradition was unavoidable for her. "Cartesian perspectivalism," as Jay calls it, was identified with the modern scopic regime *tout court* without allowing other ways of seeing. Vieira da Silva's cultural and gender experience of modern life proposed a different point of view. What was missing in the unique eye of Cartesian perspective was a certain emotional component unable to surface under the technology of the grid. The bodies of the painter and viewer were forgotten in the name of an allegedly disincarnated, absolute eye. In her modern baroque, despite her traditional commanding gaze, Vieira da Silva restored the repressed blinking eye. It becomes dynamic again, moving with saccadic jumps from one focal point to another, opening up a different pleasure of seeing, procuring simultaneously an individual, protected space, undisciplined description bringing emotional elation. Neutrality is shattered by the active, emotional involvement of a canvassing eye.[17] Too bad that the Parisian critique was relentlessly taming precisely this liberating saccadic quality of the eye in order to recast it into a well-worn Cartesian point of view.

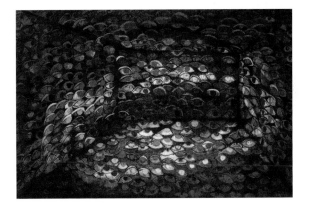

La scala or Les yeux, 1937. Oil on canvas. 60 x 92 cm. Courtesy Galerie Jeanne Bucher, Paris. Photo: Jacques Faujour.

What was confusing was that Vieira da Silva used a modernist grid, managing to push it a notch over the formal, materialist project toward the construction of a staircase to the universal. Her work is located between the grid, which, according to Rosalind Krauss, declares its own surface, and Renaissance perspective. It is as if the modern grid was inflated with a dose of a perspective so unsure of itself that it loops in and out, allowing, insisting on, multiple points of view: a cubist space rendered hallucinatory by the rapidity, the acceleration of the reading provided by the collision of multiple sets of squared networks. It is a grid put into perspective with all the visual havoc it creates, permitting a dose of mysticism usually repressed by the grid to appear here as heterogeneity, as spirituality. Krauss has mentioned that if "perspective was the science of the real, the grid is 'a mode of withdrawal from it.'"[18] Vieira da Silva is close to Mondrian in this case, but in the way two positive magnets reject each other when forced to face their similar poles. *Paris la nuit* of 1948 stands at the opposite end from Mondrian's *Victory Boogie Woogie,* but also from Dubuffet's representation of the city with walls, graffiti, and dirt. Grid and perspective, usually historically separated, here fuse in a breathless ascent recalling baroque painting, a rush toward the heavens, forcing the viewer to "desire the impossible spiral of ascending desire foredoomed to the earthly representation of appearances."[19] But here the spiral, accentuated by the tile squares, produces a roller-coaster ride in and out of a shallow space giving us tremendous pleasure of speed and vision before slamming our gaze against the surface again: a world without center, without fixed point of reference, a puzzle written by each viewer. If not spirituality (she did not like the word), then it was the unexpected meandering of the baroque that Vieira da Silva appreciated, the surprising vistas that baroque constructions give the eye, the illusion of independence and individual discovery. "I adored Bernini's colonnade. I could have gone forever walking between the columns," she said to Schneider. It is this decentered vision, this multiplicity of appreciation, this pleasure of play that she integrated into her modernism. When one reads French criticism of her work, one is always directed by the word toward a form of classicism, of modern classicism, closer to Braque than to Wols. But her work pulls us literally out of classicism. She is a *femme de la ville* all right, as she herself said, but the space that she inhabits and displays is baroque. Libraries, like cities, are symbols of baroque culture. Libraries are collecting discourses in the world, but also dissonances, contradictory voices; they are Towers of Babel representing the impossibility of universality, as Roger Chartier explains.[20]

Vieira da Silva's importance in the postwar French landscape is that she proposed a comprehensible representation of the modern city, allowing recognition of complexities and shifting meaning but producing a vocabulary more compelling in its baroque glitz than pessimistic

Composition le rêve, 1949–50. Oil on canvas. 130 x 180 cm.

and incoherent. She was simultaneously being destabilized by the drastic transformation of her own identity through the new consumerist culture and the realization that her power to universalize culture was fading as fast as her power to colonize the world. Her active engagement in the art scene (not her academic recognition) faded away in the late 1950s when consumerism pushed women back into their new, clean, and modern kitchens. Vieira da Silva's reputation continued but rapidly became an archaeological artifact of modernity, an example of a historical style that lost out against *art informel*. Moreover, women artists' visibility in Paris faded proportionally to the success of *nouveau réaliste* art and to Yves Klein's ascension to the new bourgeois pantheon. Women lost the rank of recognized creators and moved to the role of object, not only of painting but literally of tools, as Klein loved to use them as brushes. That one of the most gifted painters of the period, Marie Raymond, was symbolically obliterated by Klein's female brushes should give psychoanalytic art historians pause, given that Raymond was in fact Klein's mother.

NOTES:
1. While many other women artists were working and visible in the late 1940s in Paris, including 1949 Kandinsky prize winner Marie Raymond, American artist Claire Falkenstein, Iranian painter Fahr-el-Nissa Zeid (defended with force by the art critic Charles Estienne), the other visible American Shirley Jaffe, Day Schnabel, the gestural painter Marcelle Loubschansky, and Christine Boumeister, none sustained visibility as did Vieira da Silva through her career.
2. This system was so important for her that she is almost always represented in photographs of the time wearing blouses or skirts with the squares motif: a total identification with her logo.
3. Cited in Pierre Schneider, *Louvre Dialogues* (New York: Atheneum, 1971), 169. She also identified with some of the characteristics of Mantegna's *San Sebastian* at the Louvre: "This [is] my painting. . . . Those gradations of gray in the volume of the bodies. . . . That very sharp drawing. The tense, sustained, sharp drawing. Look at the arrows, how they are made. A great strength that conceals itself. One cannot be harder and quieter than an arrow. A pianist needs great strength to play without making noise. Bach's suites for violin and violoncello seem to me to be the loudest possible sound—louder than a large orchestra" (ibid., 165).
4. Michel de Certeau, *The Practice of Everyday Life* (Berkeley: University of California Press, 1984), 92.
5. Derek Gregory, *Geographical Imaginations* (Cambridge, Mass.: Blackwell, 1994), 303.
6. See Michel Foucault, "Fantasia of the Library," in Donald F. Bouchard, ed., *Language, Counter-Memory, Practice* (Ithaca: Cornell University Press, 1977), 90–91.
7. Schneider, *Louvre Dialogues*, 168. One should also note that, according to de Certeau, Erasmus said that "the city is a huge monastery" when it comes to managing growth of human agglomeration and accumulation (de Certeau, *The Practice of Everyday Life,* 93).
8. Bernard Dorival, *Les étapes de la peinture française contemporaine* (Paris: Gallimard, 1944), 320–24.
9. See Laure de Buzon-Vallet, "L'école de Paris: Eléments d'une enquête," in *Paris 1937–Paris 1957* (Paris: Centre Pompidou, 1981), 252–55.
10. Michel Seuphor, "Le style et le cri," preface to Vieira da Silva's show, Galerie Pierre (Paris, 1949), cited in *Vieira da Silva* (Paris: Cercle d'art, 1987), 184–85.
11. *Peintres de la nouvelle école de Paris,* exhib. cat. (Paris: Galerie Babylone, 1952).
12. Cited in Yvon Taillandier, "Parmi les peintres dont on parle le plus, une femme: Vieira da Silva," *Connaissance des Arts* (December 1957).
13. Schneider, *Louvre Dialogues,* 171.
14. Her pictures are only crowded when she tries to portray the horror of war. It's like a hymn to death in the tradition of Brueghel (*Le désastre,* 1942). But this experiment is unique, as she prefers soft music to declarative, bombastic expression.
15. Martin Jay, *Force Fields* (London: Routledge, 1993), 108. She often mentioned that she "wants to paint what is not there."
16. Schneider, *Louvre Dialogues,* 170. This difference is understandable when one knows the enormous gap between their two lives. Wols was stateless and proud of it, a male not sure of his maleness (see a portrait of himself that he overdrew with lines showing that he did not know who he was—a question mark on his forehead and lines on his crotch transforming himself into a woman), compared with Vieira da Silva, a Portuguese woman keeping her identity in Paris with a certain amount of success.
17. See Jay, *Force Fields,* 116–17.
18. See Rosalind Krauss, "Grids," in *The Originality of the Avant-Garde and Other Modernist Myths* (Cambridge, Mass.: MIT Press, 1985), 8–22.
19. See Christine Buci-Glucksmann, *Baroque Reason: The Aesthetics of Modernity* (London: Sage, 1994), 130.
20. See Roger Chartier, *L'ordre des livres* (Aix-en-Provence: Alinea, 1992), 71–75

Flower in the Wind, 1963.
Oil on canvas. 190.5 x 190.5 cm.
Courtesy Thomas Amman Fine Arts, Zurich.

Agnes Martin: The /Cloud/

Rosalind E. Krauss

Do you remember the hilarity, as a child, of playing the game that takes the form: if you were a vegetable (or a color, an animal, etc.), what vegetable (color, animal) would you be? The surrealists were fond of rewriting children's games in the register of adult desire. I remembered that when I stumbled on the information that Agnes Martin had made a film. Agnes Martin? A film? If you were Agnes Martin, I thought, and you made a film, what film would it be?

Zorns Lemma, I thought.

In order to achieve its peculiar transubstantiation of matter, Hollis Frampton's great film reorganizes both the real world of cinema's photographic support and the temporal dimension of its continuous unreeling into the atemporal, nonspatial order of the grid. *Zorns Lemma* (1970) is, for that reason, profoundly abstract. As its one-second shots present us with the regular beat of disjunctive bits of reality, each one bearing a word discovered in the urban landscape beginning with the letter appropriate to its place in the alphabetic organization of the work, a linguistic matrix seems to settle over the visual field. Cycling again and again over the alphabetic ground—*eagle . . . hair . . . wagon . . . yacht*—the film gradually replaces each "letter" with a fragment of landscape that, in this arbitrary play of substitutions, takes on the character of a pure emblem, the insubstantiality of an idea. Indeed the first four substitute images—reeds, smoke, flames, waves—capture a thought of the real as primordial separation: earth, air, fire, water. And behind that separation, as its very condition of being, is light.

Zorns Lemma ends with a long stationary shot of two people with their dog in a snowy field, walking away from the camera and toward a stand of trees in the distance. As the image is increasingly absorbed by the continuous whiteness of the snow-struck frame, the sound track completes the reading of a text by the thirteenth-century theologian Robert Grosseteste, called *On Light, or the Ingression of Forms.* "In the beginning of time," it says, "light drew out matter along with itself into a mass as great as the fabric of the world." And at another point it says, "Matter cannot be emptied of form; form is light itself, and the bringer of dimensions into matter."

Gabriel, for this is the name of Martin's film, also watches the movement of a subject through nature, in this case silently tracking a young boy walking through a mountain landscape in the American West. Martin made this film in 1976, two years into her renewed involvement with painting, having left New York and art behind her in 1967 only to begin again in 1974 in New Mexico. An hour and twenty minutes long, *Gabriel* was screened at the Institute of Contemporary Art in Philadelphia with a certain amount of fanfare in April 1977

Rosalind E. Krauss

and subsequently shown at White Columns, New York (1982). Martin herself gives no indication of wanting to bracket the work away from the rest of her art.

Yet it should be. For *Gabriel* constructs a reading of Martin's own work as crypto-landscape, a reading that, produced by the artist herself, tends to carry the weight of interpretive proof. The terrain of the work, in both film and painting, it seems to say, is that of the abstract sublime, behind which, underwriting it as its field of relevance, is the immensity, the endlessness, the ecstasy, the *terribilità* of nature.

Gabriel begins with a shot of the boy seen from behind. He is staring at a vastness of sky, water, and beach, which fills the frame with six luminous horizontal bands of color. He does this, motionless, for a very long time: Caspar David Friedrich's *Monk by the Sea*. He then begins to walk, with the camera following close behind, moving steadily upward along a mountain stream. At a certain point in this ascent the camera passes beyond him to capture the target of his gaze—revealing in shot after shot, each held for a very long time, one after another "Agnes Martin" painting: a turquoise river filling the frame with a rushing, transparent luminosity vertically laced by the burnished whiteness of stalks of sage; the all-over pattern of aquamarine shallows washing over the nearly uniform indistinctness of a ground of pebbles; the horizontal bands of a falls dividing into green, white, brown, white, green, white.

There is aid and assistance in all of this for the kind of reading of Martin's painting that was initiated early on by Lawrence Alloway, in the catalogue of Martin's 1973 retrospective, and has continued ever since. This reading comprehends the canvases as analogues of nature, "both," as Alloway wrote, "by inference from her imagery and from judging her titles."[1] And indeed, like the film *Gabriel*, Martin's titles have always held out an invitation to experience the work as an allusion to nature: *The Beach, Desert, Drops, Earth, Field, Garden, Happy Valley, Islands, Leaf in the Wind, Milk River, Night Sea, Orange Grove, Wheat, White Stone, Falling Blue.*

Nonetheless Alloway is careful, in his text, to acknowledge the admonitions Martin herself has always pronounced against understanding her work as an abstracted nature: "My paintings have neither objects, nor space, nor time, not anything—no forms," he quotes her saying. Or again, he cautions, "Referring to one of her poems she notes: 'This poem, like the paintings, is not really about nature. It is not what is seen. It is what is known forever in the mind.'"[2]

It is one thing, however, to listen to Martin insisting, "My work is anti-nature," and it is another to hold this claim steady as one approaches her paintings. Alloway's reading became the standard for interpreting Martin, as the rubric "abstract sublime" slid into the space between her work and its succession of interpreter/viewers. Characteristically, Carter Ratcliff referred Martin's work to Edmund Burke's *Philosophical Enquiry into the Sublime and the Beautiful,* which, in the mid-eighteenth century, laid down a recipe for satisfying the growing taste for "sublime effects," turning on ways the artist could produce a sense of limitlessness by abandoning the measure parceled out by traditional modes of composition and working instead with forms "melted as it were into each other." Burke's description of "a perfect simplicity, an absolute uniformity in disposition, shape and coloring," his call for a succession "of uniform parts" that can permit "a comparatively small quantity of matter to produce a grander effect than a much larger quantity disposed in another manner" seemed made for Martin's work, just as that work—as paired down and simplified as it might appear—could be thought nonetheless to smuggle within it diffused references to the repertory of natural "subjects" that followed from Burke's analysis: "the sea (Turner), the sky (Constable), foliage (Church) and, simply, light."[3]

The category *abstract sublime* has come to imply this covert allusion to nature, with the abstract work always able to be decoded by its romantic double: Rothko read out through Friedrich; Pollock through Turner's storms; Martin through Turner's skies.[4]

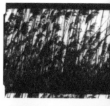
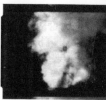
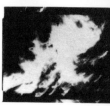

Four frames from Hollis Frampton, *Zorns Lemma*, 1970.

332

Second frame from
Agnes Martin,
Gabriel, 1976.

But again Martin herself has consistently cautioned against a romantic context for her work. Repeating that she sees herself joined to an ancient tradition of classicists—"Coptic, Egyptian, Greek, Chinese"—she defines this tradition as something that turns its back on nature. "Classicism forsakes the nature pattern," she writes.[5] "Classicists are people that look out with their back to the world/It represents something that isn't possible in the world/More perfection than is possible in the world/It's as unsubjective as possible. . . . The point—it doesn't exist in the world."[6]

And this same text, written three years before Martin made *Gabriel,* contains an extraordinary condemnation of the trope at work in her own film: "The classic is cool/a classical period/it is cool because it is impersonal/the detached and impersonal/If a person goes walking in the mountains that is not detached/and impersonal, he's just looking back."[7]

In the exceedingly superficial and repetitive literature on Agnes Martin, there is one arresting exception: Kasha Linville's careful phenomenological reading, which for the first and only time includes a description of what it is actually like to see the paintings, which, she explains, "are sequences of illusions of textures that change as viewing distance changes."[7]

First there is the close-to reading, in which one is engaged in the work's facture and drawing, in the details of its materiality in all their sparse precision: the irregular weave of the linen, the thickness and uniformity of the gesso, the touch in the application of the penciled lines. "Sometimes," Linville explains,

> her line is sharp, as in an early painting, *Flowers in the Wind,* 1963. Sometimes its own shadow softens it—that is, it is drawn once beneath the pigment or gesso and then redrawn on top, as in *The Beach.* Most often, her line respects the canvas grain, skimming its surface without filling the low places in the fabric so it becomes almost a dotted or broken line at close range. Sometimes she uses pairs of lines that dematerialize as rapidly as the lighter-drawn single ones. As you move back from a canvas like *Mountain II,* 1966, the pairs become single, gray horizontals and then begin to disappear.[8]

But this "moving back" from the matrix of the fine grids of Martin's 1960–67 work, as well as from the more grossly calibrated bands of her post-1974 painting, is a crucial second "moment" in the viewing of the work. For here the ambiguities of illusion take over from the earlier materiality of a surface redoubled by the weave of Martin's grids or bands; and at this place the paintings go atmospheric. Again, Linville's description of this effect is elegant and precise. "I don't mean 'atmosphere' in the spatially illusionistic sense I associate with color field painting," she writes. "Rather it is a non-radiating, impermeable . . . mist. It feels like, rather than looks like atmosphere. Somehow, the red lines [she is speaking here of *Red Bird*] dematerialize the canvas, making it hazy, velvety. Then, as you step back even further, the painting closes down entirely, becoming completely opaque."

That opaqueness of the third "moment," produced by a fully distant, more objective vantage on the work, brackets the atmospheric interval of the middle-distance view, closing it from behind, so to speak. Wall-like and impenetrable, this view now disperses the earlier "atmosphere." And this final result, as Linville again writes of Martin, is "to make her paintings impermeable, immovable as stone."

The "abstract sublime" consideration of Martin's art, never so careful or accurate as this one, implies that *atmosphere* or *light* is a given of the paintings, which, like a certain kind of landscape subject—clouds, sea, fields—can simply be observed from any vantage one might take on them. The landscape subject, no matter how reduced or abstracted, simply defines the work, is an objective attribute of it, like the color blue or red. But Linville's three distances make it clear that /atmosphere/ is an effect set within a system in which an opposite effect is also at work, and that it both defines and is defined by that opposite.[9] Linville's three distances, that is, transform the experience from an intuition into a system and convert *atmosphere* from a signified (the content of an image) into a signifier—/atmosphere/—the open member of a differential series: wall/mist; weave/cloud; closed/open; form/formless.

By a curious coincidence, just as Linville was noticing Martin's production of the three distances, Hubert Damisch was completing his study *Théorie du /nuage/*, a book that rewrites the history of Renaissance and baroque painting according to a system in which the signifier /cloud/ plays a major, foundational role.[10] This role, which is that of a "remainder"—the thing that cannot be fitted into a system but that the system nevertheless needs in order to constitute itself *as* a system—finds its most perfect illustration in the famous demonstration performed by Brunelleschi at the opening of the fifteenth century, which both invented and supplied the complete theory of perspective.

Having painted the image of the baptistery in Florence on a wooden panel into which a tiny peephole had been drilled at the exact vanishing point of the perspective construction, Brunelleschi devised an apparatus for viewing this image. Its reverse side would be placed up against the brow of the observer, whose eye, right at the peephole, would gaze through the panel, while in front of the panel, at arm's length, the observer would hold up a mirror. The depicted baptistery, reflected in this mirror, would thus be guaranteed a "correct" viewing according to the theory of perspective's *legitimate construction,* in which the vanishing point and viewing point must be geometrically synonymous. In this sense the representation is the function not of one but of two constructed planes: that of the "viewer" (stationary, mono-ocular) and that of the display (constructed in terms of measurable bodies deployed in space, thus capable of being submitted to the determinations of geometry).

But between those two planes of the perspective apparatus something was necessarily added, slipped into the construction as though it were a measurable, definable body but giving the lie nonetheless to this very possibility of definition. This something was the /cloud/. For the sky above the baptistery on Brunelleschi's panel was not depicted in paint; rather the area given over to it was executed in silver leaf so that, acting as a mirror, it would capture onto its surface the reflections of the real sky passing over the head of the viewer staring into the optical box of the perspective construction.

Perspective was thus understood from the first to be a matter of architectonics, of a structure built from delimited bodies standing in a specific space and possessing a contour defined by lines. The immeasurability and ubiquity of the sky, however, and the unanalyzable surfacelessness of the clouds render these things fundamentally unknowable by the perspective order. "The process to which Brunelleschi had recourse for 'showing' the sky," Damisch writes,

> this way of mirroring that he inserted into the pictorial field like a piece of marquetry and onto which the sky and its clouds were captured, this mirror is thus much more than a subterfuge. It has the value of an epistemological emblem . . . to the extent that it reveals the limitations of the perspective code, for which the demonstration furnishes the complete theory. It makes perspective appear as a structure of exclusions, whose coherence is founded on a series of refusals that nonetheless must make a place, as the background onto which it is printed, for the very thing it excludes from its order.[11]

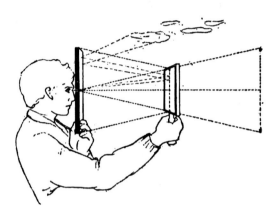

Reconstruction of Brunelleschi's first perspective experiment, as reproduced in Damisch, *Théorie du/nuage/*.

It is in this sense that painting understands its scientific aspirations—toward measurement, toward the probing of bodies, toward exact knowledge—as always limited or conditioned by the unformed, which is unknowable and unrepresentable. And if the /architectural/ came to symbolize the reach of the artist's "knowledge," the /cloud/ operated as the lack in the center of that knowledge, the outside that joins the inside in order to constitute it as an inside.

Thus, before being a thematic element—functioning in the moral and allegorical sphere as a registration of miraculous vision, or of ascension, or as the opening onto divine space; or in the psychological sphere as an index of desire, fantasy, hallucination; or, for that matter, before being a visual integer, the image of vaporousness, instability, movement—the /cloud/ is a differential marker in a semiological system. This can be seen for example in the extent to which cloud elements are interchangeable within the repertory of religious imagery. "The fact that an object can thus be substituted for another in the economy of the sacred visual text," Damisch writes, "this fact is instructive: the /cloud/ has no meaning that can be properly assigned to it; it has no other value than that which comes to it from those serial relations of opposition and substitution that it entertains with the other elements of the system."[12]

Meaning, according to this argument, is then a function of a system that underpins and produces it, a system—/cloud/ vs. /built, definable space/—with its own autonomy, that of painting, which precedes the specifics of either theme or image.

Autonomy, of course, has come by now to have indescribably bad associations; like formalism, it is thought to be the blinkered product of ideological construction. Yet much art has been produced within this ideology and in relation to a conception of autonomy, and the rush to move beyond the circumscribed aesthetic sphere to the *hors texte,* the context, the legitimating "real" text, often produces superficial readings, as in the case of leaching out Agnes Martin's painting into the concealed landscapes of the "abstract sublime."

But if we allow ourselves for a moment to entertain this transgressive thought of autonomy, we come upon a position, itself the founding moment of art history as a discipline, that sets up a model, along with Damisch's, for Martin's three distances. This is the work that Alois Riegl developed over the course of his *Stilfragen* (1893) and *Spätrömische Kunstindustrie* (1901), studies that fend off all hypotheses about the putative effect of external factors on art's development—whether in the material field, as in Semper's theories of art's genesis out of building practices; in the field of the "real," as theories of mimesis would have it; or due to the contingencies of history, as the "barbaric invasions" explanation of the supposed decline in late Roman art would imply. Instead, Riegl posits an entirely internal or autonomous evolution that continues without gap or deflection from the most ancient civilizations of the Near East up through Byzantium.

This evolution, "dialectic" in nature, arises from the desire, externalized via art, to grasp things in the most objective way possible, untainted, that is, by the merely happenstance and contingent vantage point of the viewing subject. But in acknowledging the object in terms of almost any level of sculptural relief (that is, in promoting an experience of its tactility), shadow is necessarily admitted into the confines of the object—shadow that, marking the position of the spectator relative to the object, is the very index of subjectivity. "The art of antiquity," Riegl wrote, "which sought as much as possible to enclose the figures in objective, tactile borders, accordingly was bound from the very beginning to include a subjective, optical element; this, however, gave rise to a contradiction, the resolution of which was to pose a problem. Every attempt to solve this problem led in turn to a new problem, which was handed down to the next period, and one might well say that the entire art history of the ancient world consists of a developmental chain made up of such problems and their solutions."[13]

The development that Riegl charts goes from what he calls the haptic objectivism of the Greeks—the delineation of the clarity of the object through an appeal to and a stimulation of tactile associations—to the optical objectivism of Roman art, in which the need to set the figure up in space as radically freestanding led to the projection of the rear side of the body and hence to the use of the drill to excavate the relief plane. This course arrives finally at the most extreme moment of this opticalism carried out in the service of the object. When the relief plane itself becomes the "object" whose unity must be preserved, this leads, in examples that Riegl drew from late Roman decorative arts, to the construction of the object itself in terms of a kind of moiré effect, with a constant oscillation between figure and ground depending—and here this begins to get interesting for Martin—on where the viewer happens to be standing. Writing that now "the ground is the interface," Riegl describes the fully optical play of this phenomenon once what had formerly been background emerges as *object:* "The relationship of the bronze buckle alters with each movement of its wearer; what was just now the light-side can become at the next moment shadow-side."[14]

Since this figure/ground fluctuation varies with the stance of the viewer, one might argue that the object, now fully dependent upon its perceiver, has become entirely subjectivized. And indeed, although Riegl argues that this development ultimately gave rise to the subjective as a newly autonomous problem for the history of art, one that would fulfill itself in the efforts, for example, of seventeenth-century Dutch portraitists to portray something as nonobjective as states of attention, he does not read this late Roman moment as itself subjective. Rather, he wants to argue, with this optical glitter organized into the very weft of the object, it is the subject-viewer who has been fractured, having now been deprived of the security of a unitary vantage. This is still the *Kunstwollen* of objectivism at work, but in the highest throes of its dialectical development. The filigrees of late Roman relief, far from being a regression to a more ancient or barbaric linearism, are the sublation of this aesthetic problem. "The screw of time has seemingly turned all the way back to its old position," Riegl writes, "yet in reality it has ended up one full turn higher."[15]

Martin's claim to be a classical artist—along with the full complement of Egyptians, Greeks, and Copts who make up Riegl's objectivist *Kunstwollen*—has been in the main disbelieved by her interpreters. How can her interest in formlessness, it is argued, be reconciled with such a claim, given classicism's complete commitment to form? When Martin observes, approvingly, "You wouldn't think of form by the ocean," or when she says that her work is about "merging, about formlessness, breaking down form," this is thought to underwrite the idea that she has transcended classicism for a newly ardent and romantic attitude toward the sublime.

Yet let us take Martin at her word and allow her her affiliations to a classicism that, in Riegl's terms, would commit her to an objectivist vision, no matter how optically fractured, and to a place within a development internal to the system of art, a system within which the marker /cloud/ has a foundational role to play.

This objectivism, unfolding within the twentieth century, would itself have to be seamed into the fully subjectivist project that was put in place following the Renaissance, a Cartesian project that has only intensified steadily into the present. Except that at the beginning of the century, modernist painting opened up, within an ever growing dependence of the work on the phenomenology of seeing (and thus on the subject), what we could call an "objectivist opticality," namely, an attempt to discover—at the level of pure abstraction—the objective conditions, or the logical grounds of possibility, for the purely subjective phenomenon of vision itself.

In this context the grid achieves its historical importance: as the transformer that moved painting from the subjective experience of the empirical field to the internal grounds of what could be called subjectivity as such, subjectivity now construed as a logic. Because the grid not only displays perfectly the conditions of what could be called the visual—the simultaneity of vision's grasp of its field dissolving the spatial (tactile) separation of figure against ground into the continuous immediacy of a purely optical spread—but also repeats the original, antique terms of a desire for objectivity and extreme clarity. Like the Egyptian relief, the grid both enforces a shadowless linearity and is projected as though seen from no vantage at all. At least this is so in what could be called the classical period of the modernist grid, for which Mondrian would stand as the prime figure.

Let us say further that this attempt to grasp the logical conditions of vision was, like the dialectic of the ancient drive toward the utterly independent object, continually forced to include its opposite. For as the grid came to coincide more and more closely with its material support and to begin actually to depict the warp and weft of textiles (not only in Annie Albers's work but in that of a host of followers such as Al Jensen), this supposed "logic of vision" became infected by the tactile. Two possible outcomes of this tactilization of what I've been calling an "objectivist opticality" are: (1) to materialize the grid itself, as when Ellsworth Kelly constructs the network of *Colors for a Large Wall* out of sixty-four separate canvases (nonetheless retaining the optical or the indefinite in the form of chance);[16] and (2) to make the optical a function of the tactile (kinesthetic) field of its viewer, that is to say, the succession of those viewing distances that the observer might assume. This latter is the case with Agnes Martin, and in her work it also remains clear that the optical, here marked as /cloud/, emerges within a system defined by being bracketed by its two materialist and tactile counterterms: the fabric of the grid in the near position and the wall-like stele of the impassive, perfectly square panel in the distant view. This closed system, taken as a whole, preserves—like the moiré belt buckle—the drive toward the "objective," which is to say the fundamental classicism of its *Kunstwollen*.

To say all of this is, of course, impossibly outmoded, formalist, determinist, empty. But the /cloud/ remains bracketed within its peculiar system; and it is what Agnes Martin painted for these last thirty years. She destroyed all the rest.

NOTES:

This essay was originally published in *Agnes Martin*, ed. Barbara Haskell, exhib. cat. (New York: Whitney Museum of American Art, 1992).

1. Lawrence Alloway, in *Agnes Martin,* exhib. cat. (Philadelphia: Institute of Contemporary Art, University of Pennsylvania, 1973), reprinted as "'Formlessness Breaking Down Form': The Paintings of Agnes Martin," *Studio International* 85 (February 1973): 62.
2. Ibid. Martin's text is published in Dieter Schwarz, ed., *Agnes Martin: Writings/Schriften* (Winterthur: Kunstmuseum Winterthur, 1992), 15.
3. Carter Ratcliff, "Agnes Martin and the 'Artificial Infinite,'" *Art News* 72 (May 1973): 26–27. For other discussions of Martin's work in relation to the abstract sublime, see Thomas McEvilley, "Grey Geese Descending: The Art of Agnes Martin," *Artforum* 25 (Summer 1987): 94–99; and for her general placement within the category, Jean-François Lyotard, "Presenting the Unpresentable: The Sublime," *Artforum* 20 (April 1982), and "The Sublime and the Avant-Garde," *Artforum* 22 (April 1984).
4. Robert Rosenblum's "The Abstract Sublime" (*Art News* 59 [February 1961]), in which such comparisons are made for Pollock and Rothko, laid the foundation for later discussions in this vein.
5. In Schwarz, *Agnes Martin,* 15.
6. Ibid., 37.
7. Kasha Linville, "Agnes Martin: An Appreciation," *Artforum* 9 (June 1971): 72.
8. Ibid., 73.
9. In the formal notation of semiological analysis, the placement of a word between slashes indicates that it is being considered in its function as signifier—in terms, that is, of its condition within a differential, oppositional system—and thus bracketed off from its "content" or signified.
10. Hubert Damisch, *Théorie du /nuage/* (Paris: Editions du Seuil, 1972).
11. Ibid., 170–71.
12. Ibid., 69.
13. Alois Riegl, "Late Roman or Oriental?" in Gert Schiff, ed., *Readings in German Art History* (New York: Continuum, l988), 181–82.
14. Quoted in Barbara Harlow, "Riegl's Image of Late Roman Art Industry," *Glyph,* no. 3 (1978), 127.
15. Riegl, "Late Roman or Oriental?" 187.
16. For an important analysis of Kelly's recourse to chance, see Yve-Alain Bois, "Kelly in France: Anti-Composition in Its Many Guises," in *Ellsworth Kelly: The Years in France: 1948–1954,* exhib. cat. (Washington, D.C.: The National Gallery of Art, l992), 24–27.

Untitled/Grey Bird, 1964.
Ink on paper.
22.9 x 22.9 cm.
Private collection.

Untitled, 1963.
Watercolor on paper.
22.9 x 22.9 cm.
Private Collection.

Reticulárea (Ambientación), 1969.
Steel and iron wires. Variable dimensions.
Installation at the Museo de Bellas Artes, Caracas (Venezuela).
Collection Galeria de Arte Nacional, Caracas.
Courtesy Americas Society, New York.
Photo: Paolo Gasparini.

Gego: Weaving the Margins

Rina Carvajal

We can think the invisible only as invisibility, but we can grasp it in its complex relation to the visible.

—Edmond Jabès

T oward the end of the 1960s, Gego created her first series of *reticuláreas*.[1] Among them was an environmental sculpture, an immense, weblike structure made up of fine steel wires of varying thicknesses forming discrete geometric modules that came to occupy—without visible weight or means of support—an entire room. These wire lines drew space, intertwining planes and grids in a dynamic rhythm of tensions, forces, and layers. As if it were a live, growing body, the *reticulárea* projected an architectonic energy into space. Open, inconclusive, on the edge of dematerialization, the sculpture seemed to expand infinitely while maintaining a delicate and subtle equilibrium.

The enigmatic vitality of this reticulárea—its weave of grids and spaces—conveys something of the singularity of Gego's work, an art that moves freely between the logic and rigor of geometries and an unlimited subjective field. The reticuláreas marked the beginning of Gego's mature career, summarizing her lucid and passionate exploration of structural language and opening up a new sphere of possibilities in which she could rethink form and the role of expressiveness and subjectivity in her work. With these sculptures, Gego began to experiment with the grid and repetitive modules, gradually destabilizing the objectivity of these forms to arrive at an organic space that would restore both self and nature to her work.

Throughout her career, rational structure was the path to Gego's most intuitive and subjective sources. All of her work derived from experimentation with different structural systems, whether of lines or simple figures, combined and transformed with various linkages.[2] She began as a sculptor, engraver, and draftsperson in the mid-1950s, deploying parallel lines to produce planes and virtual volumes. By the end of the 1960s, she devised monumental structures to be integrated into architecture as well as environmental and individual sculptures of great complexity that progressively heightened the importance of expressiveness. From the mid-1970s until a few years before her death in 1994, Gego simplified her techniques and formats, recycling discarded and ephemeral materials with a subtle, playful irony, emphasizing the intimate, ambiguous, and impermanent character of her work.

From her early training as an architect and engineer, Gego acquired a rigorous scientific precision and over many years of work became a skilled craftsperson.[3] Thus, she gradually learned how to combine the processes of manual labor and the possibilities of structural systems, materials, and spatial and modular organization. Innovative in her manipulation of aluminum, iron, and stainless steel, Gego devised systems of connections that permitted her to work independently of welders. Such technical skills allowed her to construct enormous sculptures that defied gravity and combined great delicacy with structural power. In her later years, Gego softened the technical element in her work and subtly connected gesture with geometry, arriving gradually at a model closer to weaving than to engineering.

A reexamination of the complex influences and relationships between Latin America and Europe lies at the root of Gego's sculptures. Like many European artists of her generation, she lived through the experience of war, exile, and adaptation to a new land. She was born Gertrude Goldschmidt in 1912 to an intellectual and liberal Jewish family in Hamburg and completed studies in architecture and engineering at the Technical University of Stuttgart, which carried on a constructivist and interdisciplinary tradition close to that of the Bauhaus. Forced to leave Germany at the outset of World War II, Gego emigrated to Venezuela in 1939. These experiences, although hidden in her work behind a formalist veil, generated an intricate and enigmatic body of relationships and tensions that profoundly shaped her work. Gego never completely abandoned the constructivist bases of her European training, but her work—informed by the experience of displacement and the contradictions and vitality of Venezuela—led her to see the "concrete" in all its transitoriness and constant destabilization. Thus her forms fluctuate ceaselessly between two distinct notions of order—one fixed and rational, the other vulnerable, dynamic, and indeterminate.

Gego rarely spoke about her personal life. Nevertheless, she inscribed a dimension of her self in her art through the rituals of her working methods—the rhythms and repetitions in the shaping of her grids and modules, the constant linking of lines and forms, the folding and unfolding of the work beneath its constant superposition of layers and planes—and through the flexible materiality with which her structures relate to space. Through intense repetition and multiplication, her forms resist closure, rather expressing an infinite expansion of space. While always maintaining a structural form, the sculptures evolved toward an ever more open relationship with space. Resistant and malleable, strong and delicate, logical and irrational, inclusive and intact, they seem to participate in a process of healing and renewal, to both apprehend and integrate with their surroundings.

Gego began her artistic activity in the 1950s, a time of great artistic fervor and radical transformation in Venezuela. A flourishing oil-based economy stimulated the country's rapid urbanization, accelerating the process of modernization. The Venezuelan abstract geometric movement arose in the first years of the decade, resuming a debate begun in the 1940s—and contested in Paris and Caracas—between a nationalist, realist tradition and the striving for an international modernity. Optimistic and combative, the young artists who returned from Europe after having absorbed its constructivist legacy constituted the vanguard of the movement. They found in the rational language of science and geometry the possibility of a new order in which to explore form and a way to establish a dialogue with the international artistic currents of the time.

Gego participated in her own way in the artistic establishment of her period, relying on the support of public and private commissions to carry out her work, but she deliberately remained on the margins of the abstract geometric movement. Highly independent and introspective, she always resisted categorization and followed a personal style very different from that of the geometric artists, who were more concerned with assimilating the scientific and technological aspects of European modernism into their work than with the contradictions and realities present in Venezuela. Gego, on the other hand, found both her own dialogue with the environment and a way to combine the European and the Venezuelan in her work. For her, science and technology became a means to reconstitute life, to configure an expressive space that would assimilate and transform her relationship with reality and with nature.

In its response to nature, Gego's work establishes subtle links with nature's structural principles of growth.[4] The work does not imitate, but rather recognizes and reflects upon the rhythms, patterns, and tensions that arise from the vital order of forms. Gego analyzed and reworked such perceptions, never forgetting to include the random, the irregular, and the poetic within her logic. The *Chorros* (*Folds*), a series begun in 1970 and often installed in outdoor spaces among the exuberance of tropical vegetation, at times erase their boundaries with the natural world. Composed of irregular groups of lines of aluminum rods of varying thicknesses whose delicately interwoven mesh is often interrupted by curves and unexpected doublings, they seem to be falling weightlessly, impregnated with the organic, mutable energy of nature, dwelling equally in impermanence and continuity.

Even in the epic, monumental sculptures integrated into architecture, in which she resolves intricate spatial problems by connecting and assembling forms with mathematical precision, Gego favors an organic sense of form and a dialogic treatment of space. These structures seem to hold the secret of lightness: they gradually free themselves from the ground, rising as fluidly as a weave in a rhythm of flexible adaptation, of serene dialogue with space. In *Nubes* (*Clouds*; Pasaje la Concordia, Caracas, 1974), Gego builds an environmental sculpture composed of two immense webs of aluminum tubes joined together by specially designed cast copper links. The larger web measures 4.3 by 4.3 meters, the smaller 3 by 3 meters. Suspended on light, almost invisible tensors attached to the walls of an open court, the individual structures are formed by a multiplication of irregular grids made up of intersecting triangles and squares that fold, twist, and break continuously. These structures expand and contract dynamically in a flux of lines, tensions, and spatial paradoxes.

 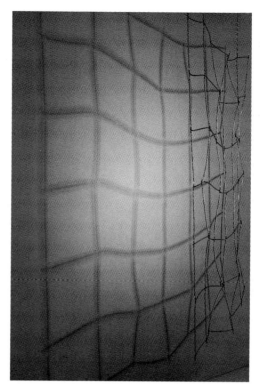

Left:
Chorros (Ambientación), 1971.
Rods of various metals. Variable dimensions. Installation at the Galería Conkright, Caracas.
Photo: Paolo Gasparini.

Right:
Malla cuadrada, 1971.
Plastic and steel wire. 143 x 143 cm. Collection Frank Porter, Cleveland, Ohio.
Photo: Paolo Gasparini.

Gego's use of line became the unifying element in all of her attempts to solve spatial problems, whether in her graphic or sculptural work, two genres that the artist continually transgressed.[5] In every stage of her career, she produced prints and drawings along with her sculptures; only at the beginning of the 1970s, however, did she create a series of "sculptural drawings." In these, the *mallas* (meshes) and the *dibujos sin papel* (drawings without paper), Gego continued to subvert the traditional order of rational structure and the grid. The first work in the series, *Malla cuadrada* (Square Mesh, 1971), is an outgrowth of the *reticuláreas* and is organized around a grid-shaped net carefully made by hand. Overcoming the resistance of her materials—steel, iron, and copper wires—and continuing to break with the idea of a fixed genre and space, Gego created a drawing with wires as lines and floated it suspended in front of a wall. Through this superimposition, the interplay of light in the work produces constant, shifting tensions between volumes and planes. The *mallas,* in turn, led in 1976 to the *dibujos sin papel.* Freer and more irreverent than the earlier series, these pieces expressed a new playfulness and subtle irony in Gego's work. Rather than resolving complex structural problems, these "drawings without paper" appear to spring from chance and random gesture, and they manage to incorporate, with great economy of means, discarded materials and remnants from her larger sculptures.

In the last stages of her work, during the 1980s and early 1990s, Gego introduced ever more subjective references into her art. The *bichos* (animals), the *cuadrículas dislocadas* (dislocated grids), and the *tejeduras* (weavings), among other works from this period, form a multifaceted, intimately scaled set of postulates that combine various materials and processes in the manner of a collage or "assemblage." These subtle exercises, in which Gego humorously embraces the precarious and the intimate, evoke the essentially elusive and transitory nature of the object and of life itself.

By the time of her death, Gego had reconciled extremely diverse realities in her work, affirming through her methods the value she held most dear—the self-renewing continuity of life. The work, without conscious premeditation and under its own formal terms, acknowledged an autobiographical content. It allowed her to create an inclusive, flexible identity that continuously erased and reconstructed its own boundaries. Through her transgression of the grid, her paradoxical construction of space, and her perpetual mediation between the mathematical and the organic, Gego wove and unwove, carefully, constantly, a history and a meaningful relationship with the world.

NOTES:
1. *Reticula* means "web design"; the *reticulárea* is an environment made from these webs.
2. These structural systems, as well as Gego's methods of construction and assemblage, are discussed by Hanni Ossott, in collaboration with Gego and Alvaro Sotillo, in Ossott's *Gego* (Caracas: Ediciones Museo de Arte Contemporáneo, 1977).
3. Gego's art making was the result of a patient, fruitful process of experimentation that interwove diverse disciplines and media. During her first years in Venezuela, before she turned to art, she worked in the design and production of furniture and objects while setting up an architectural practice. From the 1950s through the end of the 1970s, she taught extensively in schools of art, architecture, and design in Caracas, an experience that allowed her to work systematically in the development of her ideas.
4. Marta Traba analyzes at length the relationship of Gego's work to nature in *Gego,* exhib. cat. (Caracas: Ediciones Museo de Arte Contemporáneo, 1977).
5. The role of line and drawing in Gego's work is discussed by Lourdes Blanco in Gego: Reticulárea (Caracas: Ediciones de la Galería Conkright, 1969); and in "Gego libre y abstracta," *El Diario de Caracas,* September 24, 1994.

I set a loom in the street
looming above
a puddle of rain.

"We are the thread,"
                    says she
"To weave is to speak."

A thread in the air
a cloud in the mud.

Cecilia Vicuña, 1995

The Shadow of a Loom, 1993.
Courtesy of the artist.
Photo: César Paternosto.

Cecilia Vicuña's *Ouvrage*:
Knot a Not, Notes as Knots

M. Catherine de Zegher

Crisscrossing the Antivero River, a single white thread joins rocks and stones under and over the clear water. In this remote place, high up in the Chilean Andes, Cecilia Vicuña—an artist and a poet—is tracing the fragrance of the *ñipa* leaves and tying one verdant side of the river to the other with cord. Flexible, straight, and light, the line that she draws is a visible act. When suddenly two boys come up the river, jumping from stone to stone, they watch her carefully dropping lines inside the water. Without saying a word they slowly approach closer and closer in the prints of her hands. While Vicuña is securing the yarn as into a warp—the loom of the Antivero: the river is the warp, the crossing threads are the weft—their curiosity turns into interest. Sitting on a rock they observe her gestures/signs and finally ask her what it is. When she returns them the question, the boys reply that they do not know, but that they would like very much to get the string. With a laugh Vicuña grants their request and immediately they start to untie all of the rocks and plants, gradually dissolving the spatialized drawing or geometric pattern of woven lines into the current.

A drawn game. To the boys the line is a valuable length of cord used with or without a rod for catching fish. To Vicuña the line—as a single row of words in a poem—is a trail of communication, and the gift is the completion of the circle, where the process of forming in the present by disappearance is taken up again in the flow of events. Perhaps to some the line is a contour of an overtly romantic and idealistic story about "nomad space," because it blurs the border between the "real" and the "imaginary," between art and life—the object consumed in the act; because it circumscribes and "protects" the mountain water as a source of life before contamination; because it alludes to joy, play, and ramble; because it refers to the whole meaning in the action—even more, to the perpetual motion of "doing" and "undoing" in weaving as in language; and because it recovers in a distant past our sensory memory of a children's game at school: "cat's cradle."

In the widespread game of cat's cradle one makes geometric string figures, looped over fingers and stretched between two hands, as the string is passed from one person to another. As if speaking and listening to each other with the fingers alternately restricted and free, the players seek not only to take over the string but to recast the pattern without losing it. Hundreds of individual patterns can be generated from the same loop of string. Drawing patterns of construction/dissolution, cat's cradle is a play of "beginnings," an interplay between the new and the customary without which a beginning cannot take place. Similarly, in Vicuña's work *Antivero* (1981), the rocky banks of the river can be considered two hands; the intertwined

Antivero, 1981.
Courtesy of the
artist.
Photo: César
Paternosto.

thread functions as the cradle and the communication, as the "nest" and the "text." Etymologically "nest" derives from "net,"[1] an open-meshed fabric of cord, hair, or twine used for protecting, confining, or carrying. This meshwork relates to the framework of interwoven flexible sticks and twigs used to make walls, fences, and roofs in which to rear the young. To give birth and to protect the lineage, women needed to weave nests into wattle-and-daub shelters.

Word-spinning. Although we cannot recapture details of prehistoric women's lives, weaving has always been associated with caring: child care and food preparation. In *Note on the Division of Labor by Sex* Judith Brown states that whether or not the community relies upon women as the chief providers of a given type of labor depends upon "the compatibility of this pursuit with the demands of child care."[2] This is particularly the case for the crafts of spinning, weaving, and sewing, which are "repetitive, easy to pick up at any point, reasonably child-safe, and easily done at home."[3] Being perishable, the textiles themselves at best only provide fragmentary evidence about women's lives, but materials and metaphors of weaving do inform, since they permeate both childbearing and food. "Weaving (resulting in cloth) and parturition[4] (resulting in babies) both display women's generative capability. Tzutujil Maya use anatomical terms for loom parts (i.e. head, bottom, ribs, heart, umbilical cord), indicating that weaving is equivalent to giving birth. . . . In Chenalho, fine *huipiles*[5] are thrown into the nearby lake when women dream that the Virgin Mary needs this nourishment."[6] According to Vicuña, caring and weaving fuse in naming: to care and carry, to bear children, to bear a name.[7]

Odds and ends. Considering the linguistic relation of text, textile, and architecture, it seems appropriate to introduce the French word *ouvrage* to describe Vicuña's art practice as an open-ended work, an ongoing practice with links to writing, weaving, constructing. Since January 1966, when Vicuña made her first outdoor piece, *Con-con,* on the beach at the junction of the

348

Aconcagua River and the Pacific Ocean in Chile, she has examined transience and named her work *precario*. "Precarious is what is obtained by prayer. Uncertain, exposed to hazards, insecure. From the Latin *precarius*, from *precis*, 'prayer.'"[8] Prayer understood not as a request but as a response is a dialogue or a speech that addresses what is (physically) "there" as well as what is "not there," the place as well as the "no-place." Prayer is dialogue as a transition from what is to what could be. "Sacrifice" is an act made sacred and transcendent by the awareness that it is not only physical but retains another dimension and thus has a double meaning, is ambiguous. Vicuña quotes a Vedic text: "The first sacrifice is 'seeing,' because the act of seeing is a response." The root of the word *respond* is "to dedicate again," to receive something and to donate it back. Born of contemplation and made of refuse, Vicuña's *precarios* since the mid-1960s consist of small, multicolored assemblages of found materials such as fragments of driftwood, feathers, stones, lumps of shredded plastic, herbs, thin sticks, electric wire, shells, bones, and thread (e.g., *Balancin*, 1981; *Velo y Verde*, 1994; *Poncho Brillante*, 1992). Recognizing the inherent value of disregarded materials, her desire to order things is a response to their language: garbage/language, in the sense that garbage has a signifying potential and impulse that gives new tension to the signifier. Furthermore, about her *basuritas* ("little nothings") she relates: "'We are made of throwaways, and we will be thrown away,' say the objects. Twice precarious, they come from prayer and predict their own destruction. Precarious in history, they will leave no trace. The history of art written in the North includes nothing of the South. Thus they speak in prayer, precariously."

By name. From 1966 to 1972 Vicuña often practiced her work in the streets of Santiago de Chile, where she created various unannounced performances and events. In 1971 she had her first solo exhibition at the National Museum of Fine Arts in Santiago with the work *Otoño (Autumn)*, for which she filled the main room with autumn leaves three feet deep. In 1972 she traveled to London with a fellowship for postgraduate study at the Slade School of Fine Arts; in 1973 she had an exhibition at the Institute of Contemporary Art. When the military coup occurred in 1973 and President Allende died, Vicuña decided not to return to her country and remained in exile in Great Britain. She became a political activist and founded, together with Guy Brett, David Medalla, and John Dugger, the organization Artists for Democracy to oppose the military dictatorship in Chile. Their ideas were linked to her first revolutionary group action in 1967: the formation of Tribu No (the No Tribe), which issued

Con-con, 1967. Courtesy of the artist.

manifestos and staged public interventions. However, confronted with a sense of loss and isolation, Vicuña left London in 1975 to return to South America, where she stayed in Bogota. Since 1980 she has lived between New York and Santiago de Chile.

In Vicuña's artistic practice and particularly in its relationship to political protest, the investigation of language and the politics of definition are always at stake, because for her "naming" is the most political act of all. *Arte precario* is the name she gives to her independent artistic voice within the Southern Hemisphere, challenging her colonized position. Her art belongs to the urban Andean mestizo culture and not to the Western purist version of it. Her work concerns *la batalla de los significados* (the battle of the signifieds). Vicuña explores the symbolic function of weaving and language, stressing the fundamental place of textiles in the Andean system of knowledge.[9] Technically, a woven fabric consists of two elements with different functions: the fixed vertical threads (warp) and the mobile horizontal threads (weft or woof), which pass above and beneath the fixed threads. Stake and thread, warp and woof have been analyzed in basketry and weaving as figures of "supple solids."[10] Determined by the loom (the frame of the warp), the textile can be infinite in length but not in width, where it is closed by a back and forth motion. Warp-patterned weaving, characteristic of all remaining Andean weaving today, was slow to be recognized as valuable to studies of gender, social identity, economic

networks, and modernization. As a strong indicator of cultural patterns—what the Maya of Mexico and Guatemala call *costumbre*—textile has communicative but also poetic, economic, ritual, and political power. Weaving is meaning in multiple ways.

Mistresses of the needle. Vicuña, using thread and cloth as her main medium, proposes weaving as a form of participation issuing from popular culture, but has always perceived and understood it as an alternative discourse and a dynamic model of resistance (as do most indigenous Latin American women). Janet Catherine Berlo points out that "all of the cultural cross-currents and overlaps in textile art of Latin America are not, however, simply a 'making do.' They are not merely a passive, defensive response to five centuries of colonialism." In "Beyond Bricolage" she argues that "the improvisations and appropriations in women's textiles are deliberate and sometimes culturally subversive." Although world-famous as tourist items, the fabrics are signs of renewal, of new forms and topical themes coming directly from the people. Women in Latin America transform alien objects, influences, materials, and ideas in purposeful collages, as they adopt multivocal aesthetics to indigenous culture. The textiles are thus active texts that play out the ongoing intercultural dialogue of self-determination and

Left:
El guante, 1968
(1994).
Bus performance.

Right:
Hilo en el cerro
1994.

Courtesy Kanaal
Art Foundation,
Kortrijk
(Belgium).
Photo: Catherine
de Zegher.

cultural hegemony, as well as the dialogue of exchange between conservatism and innovation, continuity and transmutation.[11] Although both women and textiles are crucial to the study of postcolonial representation, Western biases have until recently viewed women's textiles as subprimitive art.

Word and thread. Vicuña actively participates in defining culture and the social fabric of language by disrupting the grammar imposed by figures of authority and by recovering the texture of communication. During the sixties, when she daily rode buses in Santiago, she decided to wear a different woven invention as a multicolored glove over her hand every day. For weeks she manufactured many types of sometimes funny gloves in all colors and forms. As an operator of signs, she wanted these handfuls of threads to function as a surprise—"as art"—each time she raised her hand to reach for a hand grip. Her use of the body as a material for performance art inscribed itself in the city and its human movements. Both the artist and the "person in society" were liberated by awakening to each gesture. Questioning a familiar material and gesture, she shattered the passengers' quiescent habits and intensified the desire and capacity to reformulate modes of signification.

Vicuña's glove performance was prompted by the necessity to restructure the language of creativity, so that the artwork could remain a force for opposing authority (be it military or multinational) and its concepts of meaning. Art here was a tool to retain independence and to nourish resistance. On the one hand, her action seems to relate to the earlier dissatisfaction of rebellious young poets, writers, and painters in South America—such as Violeta Parra,[12] José Luis Borges, Xul Solar, and the manifesto-issuing *vanguardistas*—with the prevailing norm of Spanish literary language as a system of repressive and deadening constraints. For them, "a model of a perpetually reinvented language, constantly shifting to accommodate new concepts and information, was close at hand—again, in the streets of Buenos Aires, where Argentines daily enriched the staid speech of Castille with Italianisms, fragments of German and English, and their own surprising coinages."[13] On the other hand, Vicuña's glove performance seems to retrace an ancient Mapuche practice in Chile, where an old myth tells that the Mapuche women learned how to weave from observing spiders at work and from contemplating their cobwebs (both nests and traps). When a baby girl is born, mothers walk out to catch a spider and let it walk on the baby's hand: the movements of the spider will stick to her hands, and the spider will teach her.

El mirar cruzado.[14] More recently, in 1994, two outdoor works in Chile reframe Vicuña's concern with transgressing the individual and the collective, the private and the public, the local and the global, the "smooth" and the "striated," the "nomad space" and the "sedentary space."[15] For *Hilo en el cerro (Thread in the Mountain)* at Cerro Santa Lucia in the public park, the trysting place of lovers and others in the center of Santiago, she wove with a bowl of red yarn spun in the house of a Mapuche woman. Was she using the thread in order to find her way out of the labyrinthine garden or to enweb the little mountain? Does the string indicate the solution of a problem, or does it entail a question? *12 Hilos en un corral (12 Threads in a Corral)* was made in the corral of a farm in the mountains near San Fernando. The corral is a trapezoidal space created by stone walls for the mestizo purpose of domesticating horses. Inside the irregular corral Vicuña's woven striation is suspended in midair at wall height. Emphasizing the spatial "imperfection" of the corral, it is an open weaving, an open work for the viewer to enter, to slide one's head in and to look upon. Essential in both weavings is the crossing of threads, the crossing of straightened lines at right angles, the intercrossing of opposed forces, the intertexture. Vicuña's art exists at the crux, where fertility sprouts and change or transformation happens through the encounter. However, if the former weaving consists of her usual unrolled woolen lines revealing an optional trajectory around trees and flowers, local linkages between parts, and multiple orientation or constant change in direction, the latter weaving represents a most regular grid structure.

In principle a fabric has a certain number of characteristics that define it as a striated space. However, this conventional view of weaving should be suspended and observed within some specific processes. For example, felt is a supple solid product that proceeds altogether differently, as "an antifabric." Since it implies no separation of threads, no intertwining, only an entanglement of fibers obtained by fulling, it constitutes a smooth space.[16] Like paper, felt uses a matrix without entering it. But, according to Gilles Deleuze and Félix Guattari, striated space is not simply opposed to smooth space. Although there is a distinction between the two, in fact they only exist in mixture and in passages from one to another. In this sense, and conversely to one's expectation about the striated in a fabric, most of Vicuña's weavings seem to belong to smooth space, where variation and development of form are continuous and unlimited, where the lines go all directions, where "the stop follows from the trajectory." To quote Deleuze and Guattari: "Smooth space is directional rather than dimensional or metric. Smooth space is filled by events or singularities/haecceities, far more than by formed and perceived things. It is a space of affects, more than one of properties. It is *haptic*[17] rather than optical perception. Whereas in the striated, forms organize matter, in the smooth, materials signal forces and serve as symptoms for them. It is an intensive rather than extensive space, one of distances, not of measures and properties."[18] Vicuña's sites (beaches, sea and river, streets) and works—in Chile, Bogota, or New York—are "local spaces of pure connection." Her linkages, signals, and orientations change according to temporary vegetation, occupation, and precipitation. The abstract line that she draws is "a line of flight without beginning or end, a line of variable direction that describes no contour and delimits no form."[19]

Yet Vicuña's two recent outdoor weavings, *Hilo en el cerro* and *12 Hilos en un corral,* seem to enact respectively smooth space and striated space and almost literally the crossings, passages between both spaces, as though one emanated from the other, "but not without a correlation between the two, a recapitulation of one in the other, a furtherance of one through the other."[20] Her unexpected use of the woven grid in the corral piece visualizes the striation of space as a way to subordinate and measure it within anxiety in the face of all that passes, flows, or varies. As the grid since the Renaissance has been applied on a vertical plane to master the three-dimensional space in painting, so the grid applied on a horizontal plane in Vicuña's open weaving brings to mind an archaeological method for mapping ancient sites. Additionally, it is important to mention that there are among the Quechua of Chinchero (Peru) profound conceptual and linguistic links between the processes of working the loom and working the earth, both providing life's fundamentals—clothing and food. Here the word pampa refers both to the agricultural plain and to the large, single-color sections of handwoven textiles. *Khata* is a furrowed field ready for planting as well as the textile warp configuration ready for pattern formation.[21] Since Vicuña's materialization of the grid in this work seems to be projected without vantage point, it perhaps, more importantly, figures and embalms the connection in weaving that protects. In this sense we can recall two examples of protective clothing: the plain weaving of Penelope's fabric that—because of its possibilities of doing and undoing—kept not only Penelope but also Odysseus alive; and the plain weaving of the poncho, which is made like a blanket with a central slit for the head. Since its structure is part of "an eternal order," as Anni Albers tells us, the open (corral) weaving "protects" the entering viewer/reader and the land against the multinational grip of North American corporate agro-industry—which eliminates the "inferior" native corn to replace it with its own "rich" corn treated so as not to run to seed. The Chilean farmers thus become completely dependent on the corporations.[22]

Knots in wool as notes. Moreover, taking up the grid's geometrized flatness, its ambivalent relation to matter and to spirit, and its "capacity to serve as a paradigm or model for the antidevelopment, the antinarrative, the antihistorical"—as described by Rosalind Krauss[23]—Vicuña extends the grid to transfer modernity onto Andean culture, and vice versa. Apparently, her spatial weaving considers both the plain surface of the grid and the subversion of the line. With enormous perspicacity she disorganizes and redefines the forms of meaning transmitted to her from her Andean culture and from dominant Western cultures, in order to overturn distinctions between the vernacular and the modern and to shift the international models of language. Her use of multiple fluctuating referents and of ambiguity applies to her visual art as well as her poetry. Simultaneously approaching and distancing herself from so-called international movements or institutions, such as body art, land art, and arte povera, she chose a flexible though firm position unassimilable to different cultural programs. Her first spatial work, *El Khipu que no recuerda nada* (*The Khipu That Remembers Nothing,* 1965), was a line carrying these convergences, where the aesthetic of silence was embraced to initiate a critique of the self-reflexive model and its enforced hermeticism; here she challenged and refused the quietism of modernism from within.[24] During the 1960s, in one of the anthologies about twentieth-century European modernist thought and art[25] that were translated and published in Buenos Aires and found their way to Chile, Vicuña noticed a photograph of Kurt Schwitters's *Merzbau* (1923–36) in Hannover. Very soon thereafter she outlined a bare thread in her own bedroom and titled the work significantly: *El Khipu que no recuerda nada.* Consisting of woolen cords with knots, the *khipu* is an Inca instrument that registers events, circumstances, and numerals. Ancient documents tell us that these registering artifacts continued to be used during the first period of the *conquista,* to be replaced later by written systems. The largest and most complex *khipu* found within the extensive region of Tawantinsuyu is on display in the Museo Chileno de Arte Precolombino in Santiago.[26]

The entire *khipu* carries meaning: the length, the form, the color, the number of knots. The endless tying and retying of knots allow continuous marking and modification. In contradistinction to other writing systems, the substance of the *khipu* provides the opportunity of infinite inscription since the "inscribed" is never fixed. The act of doing and undoing, ins and outs, as in weaving, offers multitudinous possibilities or beginnings, flexibility and mobility. In this sense Vicuña's *Khipu que no recuerda nada* synthesizes an attitude toward life, language, memory, and history in a postcolonial country where transformation generated the foundation for a new socialist collective culture. Almost willing to lose any trace of representation, Vicuña oscillates between the constructivist strategies of transparency of procedure, self-referentiality of signifying devices, and reflexive spatial organization, on the one hand, and on the other hand the strategies of differentiation of subjective experience and historical reflection. Taking into account the experience of colonialism (and even more of neocolonial dependence) with its legacies of oppression and destruction, from which her identity emerged, she holds on to the name: *khipu.* Taking account of the desire of a new generation to be "absolutely modern," Vicuña wanted to articulate a beginning and to position herself at this beginning, but within pre-Columbian and colonial history.

Knot in a handkerchief. Perhaps, at first, the connection seems incongruous. However, I wish to analyze and emphasize the relationship between the work of Vicuña and of Schwitters in the context of Chilean colonial history. There is an affinity worth exploring, since both artists' oeuvres agree on several issues: nonrepresentational multimedia constructions, a "nonobjective" art, emphasis on connection and interaction—the "directional" rather than the "dimensional"; the use of refuse, the strategies of naming (Merz and precario), and experimentation with other art forms, for example poetry. However, besides aesthetic considerations and formal analogies, both focus on naming and the use of waste materials in specific socioeconomic environments. The oppression during Schwitters's time in Germany before World War II parallels that of Vicuña's in Chile before the dictatorship. The German connection[27] has also played an increasingly important role both progressively (e.g., at the universities) and repressively (on a military and political level) in Chile's colonial and postcolonial history.[28] These historical facts remind us of the context in which Vicuña acted while elucidating her attention to dadaism, particularly to Schwitters, in her visual art and her interest in the German romantic poets, such as Novalis, in relation to her poetry.[29] The German avant-garde art of the late nineteenth and early twentieth centuries dissolved identities and shattered the communicative, representative aspect of language in favor of a dynamic conception of art. These artists created a theory of the subject in process, a subject equally constituted by symbolic and semiotic elements. Considering them rebels in a restraining German society, Vicuña embraced their modernist vanguard aesthetic and poetry as a liberating force useful to both: the newly defined social production of culture propagated by the Unidad Popular of the Marxist President Salvador Allende and to the resistance against German colonization and its ramifications in an emerging totalitarian regime.

Desire of the hand. If this presumed equation were based not on aesthetic and sociopolitical recurrences and convergences in time but on the linear notion of filiation and

Hilumbres/allqa, 1995. Installation at the Béguinage in Kortrijk (Belgium). Courtesy Kanaal Art Foundation, Kortrijk. Photo: Rien van den Eshof.

belatedness, it would constitute yet another neocolonial attempt to create predecessors of South American art in Europe. Still, at the same time it is imperative to read Vicuña's work, which fuses the knowledge of a colonial Chilean and local Andean culture with the quest for a global avant-garde, in reference to the work of her contemporaries in South America. Her determination to break away from the universalist claims of geometric abstraction, without abandoning a nonfigurative, geometric vocabulary and the general social concerns of constructivism, and her desire to take on complex human reality and to remain receptive to her immediate environment parallel the earlier attitude of the neoconcrete group in Brazil.[30] This group affirmed the values of modernity and eschewed "regionalist realism," but in the *Manifesto neo-concreto*[31] (1959) it attacked the positivism and mechanistic reductionism of the philosophy of Max Bill and the Hochschule für Gestaltung Ulm, designed for an advanced capitalist/industrial society, and restated the problem of subjectivity in a specific Brazilian context.

Significantly, the neoconcrete work of Lygia Clark and Hélio Oiticica "gradually lost the technological sheen associated with constructivism and moved (in very different ways) towards the use of common and relatively valueless materials that were 'at hand' in the everyday environment of Rio."[32] Notwithstanding the isolation of these artists and the lack of communication at that time among most countries in South America, it appears that, in 1966, at the moment when Vicuña in Chile was naming her works *arte precario*, Clark in Brazil was proposing "*precariousness* as a new idea of existence against all static crystallization within duration; and the very time of the act as a field of experience."[33] At the same time, in the 1960s and 1970s, these South American artists positioned themselves in relation to the international claims of *arte povera,* resolutely stressing their own terminology and its intrinsic differences. In a 1968 letter to Clark, Oiticica states:

> For European and North American expression, this is the great difference: the so-called Italian *arte povera* is done with the most advanced means: it is the sublimation of poverty, but in an anecdotal, visual way, deliberately poor but actually quite rich: it is the assimilation of the remains of an oppressive civilization and their transformation into consumption, the capitalization of the idea of poverty. To us, it does not seem that the economy of elements is directly connected with the idea of structure, with the nontechnique as discipline, with the freedom of creation as the super-economy, in which the rudimentary element in itself liberates open structures.[34]

Basting the space with large loose stitches, Vicuña recently constructed *Hilumbres/allqa* (1995) at the Béguinage of Saint Elizabeth in Kortrijk.[35] To realize a double "weaving in space" she used industrial black and white cotton spun in Flemish factories out of raw materials mainly imported from the so-called Third World (Turkey, Egypt, Peru, etc.). "I speak to the moment in which the visible becomes invisible and vice versa," said Vicuña, "to the moment when the cognition, the definition, has not yet been formed. Moving through the room people should discover the limits and traps of their own perception, the wandering attention." *Hilumbres,* a word invented by Vicuña, is composed of two words, *hilo/lumbre* (thread/light), meaning "the thread catching light" or "the thread of light"; *allqa* is an Aymara word and a textile term that refers to a sharp contrast in the play of light and shadow. In weaving, it applies to the connection or encounter of things that can never be together: black and white. In Andean weaving this union of oppositions generates a degradation—or, as Vicuña formulates it, "a soft stairway" (or as Bracha Lichtenberg Ettinger theorizes it, "a matrixial borderspace"—and "metramorphosis"), which argues for a model of subjectivity not rooted in binary thought: self/other, love/hate, aggression/identification, rejection/ incorporation.

Similarly, in Andean and Mayan textiles the joins between two woven panels are often the focus of articulation and elaboration. "The seam itself is not rendered unobtrusive as it is in our apparel. Instead it is emphasized by silk or rayon stitching of bold color and emphatic form. This is called the *randa*."[36] Dealing with the past and the Other, the crossing of border-lines and seams of cultural articulation are often highlighted in this work.

Poetry in space. If Vicuña's *ouvrage* challenges questions of recent art such as the status of the object, the relation of the artist and the viewer/reader, bodily action, the space-time relation, the environment, inner and outer, the connection of the visual to the other senses—at once moving viewers away from their habit of compartmentalizing artistic production into separate media—it also evokes a polemical attitude toward modernity, investigating a universal artistic development without negating local forms of expression. In the knowledge that the elaboration of popular elements shows links with bricolage and that bricolage involves continual reconstruction from the same materials (earlier ends are called upon to play the part of means),[37] Vicuña reconsiders the changes of the signified into the signifying and vice versa. Vicuña dwells in im/possibility, as do Violeta Parra and Xul Solar. She demands a laying open of the mechanism that produces meaning: the formation of a language. Her ideal is a discourse characterized by plurality, the open interplay of elements, and the possibility of infinite recombination.[38] However, Vicuña concludes that "(visual) language speaks of its own process: to name something which can not be named."

NOTES:

1. Cecilia Vicuña, "Metafisica del textil," in *Revista Tramemos II* (Buenos Aires, 1989).
2. Elizabeth Wayland Barber, *Women's Work: The First 20,000 Years: Women, Cloth, and Society in Early* Times (New York: W. W. Norton, 1994), 29–33.
3. Ibid.
4. Cecilia Vicuña creates the new verb *palabrir,* which means "to open words," noting that *abrir* (to open) originally meant *parir:* to give birth.
5. *Huipil* is a rectangular or square shirt, sewn on the sides, with a circular opening for the head, made of cotton or wool, and usually embroidered. Worn in Mesoamerica since pre-Columbian times, it is still used in southern Mexico and Guatemala, where indigenous women continue to weave huipiles both for their own use and for trade.
6. Janet Catherine Berlo, "Beyond Bricolage: Women and Aesthetic Strategies in Latin American Textiles," in *Textile Traditions of Mesoamerica and the Andes: An Anthology,* ed. Margot Blum Schevill (New York: Garland, 1991), 437–67.
7. Cecilia Vicuña, *Unravelling Words and the Weaving of Water* (Minneapolis: Graywolf Press, 1992).
8. Cecilia Vicuña, *Precario/Precarious* (New York: Tanam Press, 1983).
9. Barbara and Dennis Tedlock, "Text and Textile: Language and Technology in the Arts of the Quiché Maya," *Journal of Anthropological Research* 2, no. 41 (1985): 121–46: "Affirming a basic congruence among the realms of writing, agriculture and weaving, the opening lines of the Popol Vuh (the Quiché Maya's ancient sacred text) have two possible translations: 'This is the beginning of the Ancient Word, here in this place called Quiché. Here we shall inscribe, we shall implant the Ancient Word'; or 'Here we shall design, we shall brocade the Ancient Word.' This multivocal translation suggests that the Maya recognize these three realms as diverse yet congruent paths of knowledge."
10. André Leroi-Gourhan, *L'homme et la matière* (Paris: Albin Michel, 1943), 244.
11. Berlo, "Beyond Bricolage."
12. The art, poetry, and music of Violeta Parra (1917–67) have been of great influence on Vicuña's propositions. Parra was a Chilean peasant woman whose research on Chilean weaving, oral poetry, and music, as well as her own work, were the foundations of the movement La Nueva Cancion Chilena. Her music, political and contemporary yet retaining the ancient mestizo rhythms of traditional music, influenced all of South America.
13. Naomi Lindstrom, "Live Language against Dead: Literary Rebels of Buenos Aires," *Review: Latin American Literature and Arts,* no. 31 (New York) (January–April 1982).
14. *El mirar cruzado* is an expression for looking at something from (two) different points of view, mixing the sources. See Cecilia Vicuña "Fragmentos de Poeticas," unpublished manuscript.
15. Gilles Deleuze and Félix Guattari, *A Thousand Plateaus: Capitalism and Schizophrenia,* trans. Brian Massumi (Minneapolis: University of Minnesota Press, 1987), 474–500.

16. Ibid., 475.

17. Ibid., 429: "'Haptic' is a better word than 'tactile' since it does not establish an opposition between two sense organs but rather invites the assumption that the eye itself may fulfill this nonoptical function."

18. Ibid., 493.

19. Ibid., 499.

20. Ibid.

21. Berlo, "Beyond Bricolage," 446–47.

22. In fact this situation is part of an ongoing destruction of native agriculture since colonial times. First most of the wild wheat was devastated by the *conquistadores,* to be replaced by imported Western wheat, which the Indian population had to buy. A great number of alpacas and llamas were killed; these herds had to be replaced by sheep and cows sold at very high prices. See also Cecilia Vicuña, "The Invention of Poverty," in *America: Bride of the Sun,* exhib. cat. (Antwerp: Royal Museum of Fine Arts, 1992), 514–15.

23. Rosalind E. Krauss, *The Originality of the Avant-Garde and Other Modernist Myths* (Cambridge: MIT Press, 1986), 8–22.

24. Benjamin H. D. Buchloh, "Refuse and Refuge," in *Gabriel Orozco,* exhib. cat. (Kortrijk: Kanaal Art Foundation, 1993).

25. Examples are Jean Cassou's *Panorama de las artes contemporáneas* and J. E. Cirlot's *El arte otro; also Antología de la poesía surrealista de lengua francesa,* trans. Aldo Pellegrini (Buenos Aires: Fabril Editora, 1961).

26. *A Noble Andean Art,* exhib. cat. (Santiago: Museo Chileno de Arte Precolombino), 72–73, no. 0780: *Khipu,* Camelid fibers, Inca, 1470–1532 A.D.; main cord length 168 cm. According to the catalogue this *khipu* was excavated from an Inca cemetery in Mollepampa, in the valley of the Lluta River, near what is now the city of Arica. Seven white cords without knots, joined to a main cord by a red bow, divide six sets of ten groups of cords each. Near the end of the instrument are nine white, knotless cords and one with only one knot. The *khipu* ends in eleven sets of cords. These sets of cords, each one with their knots, are formed by a main cord from which secondary ones derive, some of which produce more cords. The location of these sets and that of the cords and knots within, the way of twisting each cord, and the colors used are part of a symbolism still not completely deciphered. We know only that the pattern of knots used the decimal system according to position on the cord. It seems that the colors encoded nonnumerological information.

27. Some remains of the German language still pop up daily in Chilean Spanish. The most remarkable example is the word *ya,* which means "already" in Spanish, "yes" in German, and "yes, already" or "yes, instantly" as a contraction of both meanings in Chilean Spanish.

28. During the nineteenth and twentieth centuries several presidents eventually established a concrete policy of "Germanization" and facilitated the German immigration to southern Chile "in order to bring prosperity to a forsaken land and to improve the Indian race." Thus they encouraged "populating" the southern provinces of Valdivia, Osorno, and Llanquihue by taking the land from the Mapuche. During World War II a German fascist presence in southern Chile appeared through groups supporting the Nazis (two National Socialist parties). After the war this presence was enforced by the arrival of exiled and former Nazis, who later participated in the dictatorship of General Pinochet.

29. Vicuña's grandfather, the writer, civil rights activist, and lawyer Carlos Vicuña Fuentes (dean of the University of Chile and a deputy in the Chilean Parliament), had received a group of refugees from the Spanish Civil War in his home. Among them were the playwright José Ricardo Morales and editors Arturo Soria and Carmelo Soria (the latter was later murdered by Pinochet's secret police). These men and their families became part of Cecilia Vicuña's family and education. The Nazis were also instrumental in Franco's rise and the defeat of the Spanish Republic. Carlos Vicuña Fuentes was made an "honorary Jew" by the Jewish community in Santiago as a result of his antifascist activities.

30. Members of the neoconcrete group were Lygia Clark, Hélio Oiticica, Lygia Pape, Amilcar de Castro, Franz Weissmann, Reynaldo Jardim, Theon Spanudis, the poet Ferreira Gullar, and the art critic Mario Pedrosa.

31. Reproduced in Ronaldo Brito, *Neoconcretismo: Vertice e ruptura* (Rio de Janeiro: Funarte, 1985), 12–13; reprinted in French in *Robho,* no. 4, and in English in *October* 69 (Summer 1994): 91–95.

32. Guy Brett, "Lygia Clark: The Borderline between Art and Life," *Third Text* 1 (Autumn 1987): 65–94.

33. Lygia Clark, "Nostalgia of the Body," *October* 69 (Summer 1994): 106.

34. "Isso é a grande diferença para a expressão européia e americana do norte: a tal *povera arte* italiana é feita com os meios mais avançados: é a sublimaçao da pobreza, mas de modo anedótico, visual, propositalmente pobre mas na verdade bem rica: é a assimilação dos restos de uma civilização opressiva e sua transformação em consumo, a capitalização da idéia de pobreza. Para ns, não parece que a economia de elementos está diretamente ligada à idéia de estrutura, à não-técnica como disciplina, à liberdade de criação como a supra-economia, onde o elemento rudimentar já libera estruturas abertas." From *Lygia Clark e Hélio Oiticica,* exhib. cat. (Rio de Janeiro: Funarte, 1986–87).

35. Vicuña exhibition in the series *Inside the Visible: Begin the Béguine in Flanders,* organized by the Kanaal Art Foundation as Cultural Ambassador of Flanders (1994).

36. Berlo, "Beyond Bricolage," 453.

37. Claude Lévi-Strauss, *The Savage Mind* (Chicago: University of Chicago Press, 1966), 21.

38. Naomi Lindstrom, "Xul Solar: Star-Spangler of Languages," *Review: Latin American Literature and Arts,* no. 25/26: 121.

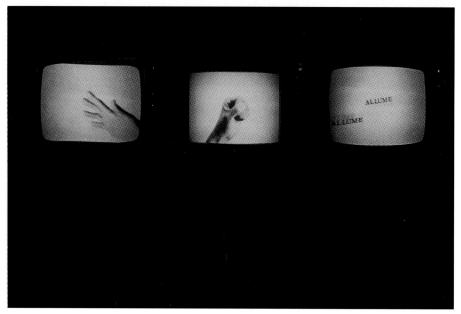

Passages Paysages, 1978.
Three-channel video.
University Art Museum, University of California, Berkeley.
Gift of the Theresa Hak Kyung Memorial Foundation.

Theresa Hak Kyung Cha: *Passages Paysages*

Lawrence Rinder

I have seen Theresa Hak Kyung Cha's *Passages Paysages* many times, yet it has left no coherent impression. It is what Roland Barthes called a "free text": "free of all subjects, of all objects, of all symbols, written in the space (the abyss or blind spot) where the traditional constituents of discourse (the one who speaks, the events recounted, the way they are expressed) would be superfluous."[1] It is tightly wound, measured to the second, three channels of video in perfect counterpoint. Image, text, sound, blank screen, silence. Concrete elements stripped bare: impoverishment, poetry.

In an earlier work, Cha expressed succinctly her understanding of the medium:

Vide
Video
Vide o eme[2]

There are words, in English, French, Korean. Some are known to me, others simply register as inflection, emphasis, articulation. The words I know lead me on to . . . what?

not gone
not yet
not gone not yet
a few remaining
a few
a few remaining moments moments
it should be as
it should be as good as
gone
it should be as good as gone
good as gone . . . gone.
but still—but still remaining moments yet
still remaining moments yet
remaining moments
wait.[3]

It is almost over before it has almost begun. "Wait," she says. Impossible.

I cannot describe the whole because to do so means describing the parts and even that cannot be done. Isolate one channel, and you will hear and see things imperceptible in the whole. Take in the whole and you will hear and see things imperceptible in each part.

Her voice is haunting, like the ringing of a glass.

A word appears again and again, but I cannot find it in a dictionary: *etteindre. Eteindre,* to extinguish, misspelled? Or a conscious archaism? The word as seen centuries ago, before the addition of the accent aigu made the second t obsolete . . . extinguished. The *t* in *lointain* comes unmoored and drifts between two distant halves of the word: "loin T ain." *T* for Theresa. Elsewhere, "see" is so faint it's almost invisible. I struggle to hear words, led to the threshold of perception. On the second channel, each letter of the title appears in quick succession, a chain of small, typewritten black marks flashing one after the other. Meaning is the retrieval of the past.

So much of this has to do with letters: letters flashing, letters obscured, letters in different typefaces, letters displaced, letters disappeared. Then, toward the end, as correspondence, a tied bundle of them. A male voice reading a letter to Cha. Then her voice overlying his, reading another, this time in French. Last, a letter read in Korean. The dates of each one receding further into the past than the one before: 1975, 1974, 1973. Meaning is the retrieval of the past.

Passages Paysages, 1978. Three-channel video. University Art Museum, University of California, Berkeley. Gift of the Theresa Hak Kyun Memorial Foundation.

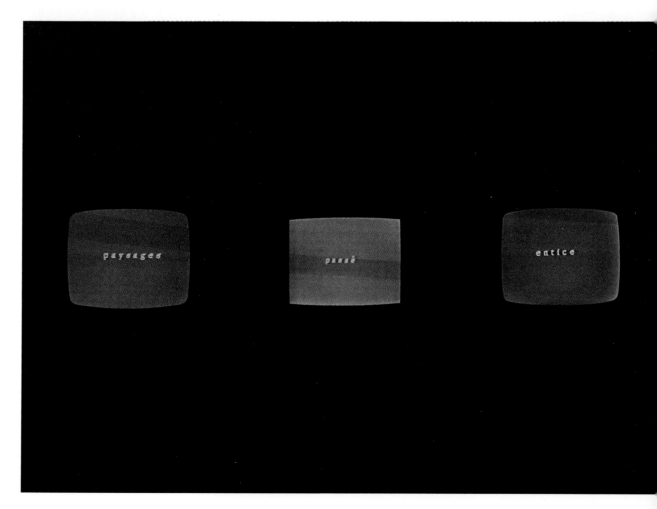

Her notes tell me that the empty room is her lover's room; the empty bed his too. The opening and closing hand is meant to signify the clarity of that which is known but cannot be seen. In Carl Dreyer's film *Vampyr*, a skeletal hand reaches out with a vial of poison. Another Dreyer echo: David Gray watches from inside his own coffin as the vampire lowers a candle onto the small window cut out above his face. But in *Passages Paysages* even the candle is extinguished.

Traditional Korean music, an ink brush landscape, an old family photo. Cha was born into exile in 1951, her parents fleeing the advancing Chinese army that was pushing south toward Pusan. Exiled from a land that was itself nearly extinguished: its language forbidden, its population scattered or enslaved, its culture obliterated by the Japanese during forty years of occupation. She writes, "My work, until now, in one sense has been a series of metaphors for the return, going back to a lost time and space, always in the imaginary. The content of my work has been the realization of the imprint, the inscription etched from the experience of leaving."[4]

passage: thoroughfare/literary extract/transition
paysage: scenery
passé: past
mot de passe: password
pays: country/land/home
sage: wise/virtuous/quiet

From adolescence on, Cha deeply identified with St. Thérèse of Lisieux: ascetic, passionate, and self-effacing. Yet Confucianism, deeply ingrained in Korean culture, teaches that spiritual healing is to be found in the extended family. Thus, in another work, Cha writes:

You are the audience
You are my distant relative
i address you
as i would a distant relative
as if a distant relative
seen only heard only through someone else's description.[5]

Cha's suffering dissipates as it is absorbed into the collective consciousness. Although it is intensely personal, *Passages Paysages* does not address us personally. . . . It is incomprehensible as such. Rather, it scatters its meanings and effects among us, Cha's innumerable relatives.

NOTES:
1. Roland Barthes, "Preface," in Pierre Guyotat, *Eden, Eden, Eden* (London: Creation Books, 1995).
2. Theresa Hak Kyung Cha, *Videoeme*, 1976, black and white video, 4 minutes, Collection University Art Museum and Pacific Film Archive, University of California at Berkeley.
3. Theresa Hak Kyung Cha, *Passages Paysages*, 1978, three-channel black and white video, 10 minutes, Collection University Art Museum and Pacific Film Archive of the University of California at Berkeley.
4. Theresa Hak Kyung Cha, "Personal Statement and Outline of Postdoctoral Project," ca. 1978, typed manuscript, p. 2, Theresa Hak Kyung Cha Archive, University Art Museum and Pacific Film Archive, University of California at Berkeley.
5. Theresa Hak Kyung Cha, *Audience—Distant Relative*, 1977, artist's book, Collection University Art Museum and Pacific Film Archive, University of California at Berkeley.

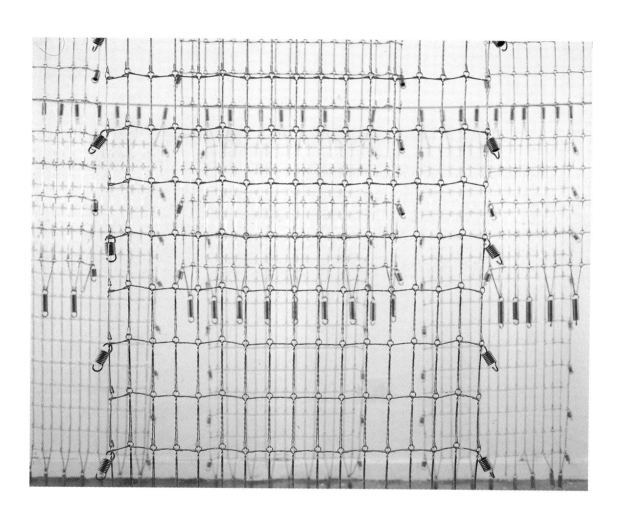

Short Space (In Progress), 1992.
Artist's studio. Courtesy of the artist.
Photo: Paul Bevan.

Mona Hatoum: Some Any No Every Body

Desa Philippi

Mona Hatoum's recent work consists primarily of installations. In a gradual move during the 1980s from time-based work (performance and video) to installations produced for specific spaces, the work has become less narrative and more associative and open-ended.

The installation + *or* −, made for an exhibition at the Arnolfini Gallery, Bristol, in 1993, clearly evidences a particular way of thinking about materials and space that underlies Hatoum's work. A wall forty feet long and twelve feet wide is clad in sheets of metal. At a right angle to the wall, between two existing pillars, panes of glass run from floor to ceiling. Small magnets are positioned in a regular grid on both metal and glass. On closer inspection these magnets reveal a strange, fuzzy surface. Clusters of fine iron filings on the magnetic cubes produce chaotic and organic-looking microcosms that, in turn, make up the regular and structured macrocosm of the larger surfaces.

The large smooth surfaces, similarly defined and punctuated by the magnets with their organic, furry texture, establish an economy of oppositions only to render it inoperable. The two large elements appear to mirror each other but in fact establish a connection that cannot be reduced to repetition and inversion. In the most ordered and rational of arrangements, habitual ways of categorizing and rationalizing become problematic. The accustomed alternative, the relief of a "new way of looking at things," is not forthcoming. Instead we are left with the trappings of structure and symmetry. Aesthetically referring to minimalism, in everyday language to "things falling into place," these identifications are immediately rendered superficial and unsustainable. On closer examination the connection to minimalism is minimal, and whatever falls into place is also out of place. Careful spacing and installing turn continually into measures of displacement that form a threa/d/t through all of Hatoum's work. To my mind, a primary concern in these pieces is the process of negotiating proximity and distance.

In *Short Space*, bedsprings hang from the ceiling in three rows that slowly move up and down at regular intervals. Only the soft humming of the motors can be heard; the neon lighting is weak but cold. The bedsprings hanging in midair look perversely like meat or flayed skin. Yet such a connection seems far-fetched. In Jannis Kounellis's *Untitled* beds of 1969, the bed remained bed and because of that could be fully transformed into the place of dreams, birth, sex, torture, and death. Where Kounellis elaborates a poetics of the symbol and of identity, Hatoum's work both suggests and withholds metaphors. Using many of the materials and formal devices of the *arte povera* artists and Kounellis in particular, her installations include something that militates against the inevitable transposition of form into aesthetic form and work into artwork.

Short Space is also a machine and shares with other symbolic machines, such as those of Rebecca Horn, for instance, an uncanny quality. While in the work of Horn or Tinguély the strange and threatening connotations are mediated through and often canceled by humor and absurdity, Hatoum's installations are uncanny in the classic sense of estrangement; things that were familiar and commonplace—beds, chairs, lockers, heating elements—metamorphose into something remote and somehow threatening.

The uncanny of machines resides less in what is hidden (the mechanism) than in the transparency of the machine. In mechanics and electronics, where the machine extends and ultimately replaces the human body as tool, rationality is functional and predicated on the exact predictability of movements. Only when the machine is transported into a symbolic context does its automatism begin to reveal its proximity to the uncanny and to death. While in the discourses of technology and physics repetition indicates the functioning of the system— the engine runs, an experiment produces the same results each time it is repeated—in psychoanalytic theory repetition signals lack of control and self-determination. Instead of ensuring the smooth working of the psyche, it is regarded as symptomatic and indicative of breakdown.

Measures of
Distance,
1988.
Video still.
Color video,
15.26 minutes.
Courtesy of
the artist.

Inscribed in the scenarios of repetition and machine, utility and symbol is a notion of the body as a mechanical apparatus in contrast to mind, spirit, or psyche. In Hatoum's recent work this body rarely appears as an image; instead it supplies proportions and measurements. The standardized body of average size is used as a measure of spacing. According to Foucault, this standard body is the product of modern social technologies and institutions. It is also linked to the panopticon as a building type that institutes a particular regime of vision. Hatoum's work too proposes a relationship between architectural spacing, the body, and vision. However, where Foucault's theory of the panopticon stresses internalization—the subject acts as if continually under a regulating and punishing gaze—these installations emphasize the external and tactile. Nothing is hidden from the spectator. The eerie feeling that I have when entering one of these spaces has to do precisely with the fact that while I can see the entire scene, predict the movements of the kinetic elements, and orient myself in the space, I am nonetheless caught in it. My movements are restricted and authoritatively directed when, for instance, I make my way into *Untitled* (1992), which consists of thin wires stretched across the room in such a way as to leave only a narrow corridor. The visual delicacy of the work—parallel wires in an entirely white space on two levels resemble a giant stringed instrument—exposes its cutting edge perfectly measured at ankle and throat height. One wrong step . . . This physical danger is matched by the symbolic threat of a visible yet transparent "trap." Hatoum's work suggests that often we find ourselves in a situation where danger and error are not related to lack of knowledge or (in)sight. There is nothing mysterious or obscure in her installations, which, on the contrary, are uncluttered and direct.

Take *Light Sentence*. In a windowless room with a single lightbulb at the center, two rows of lockers are stacked too high to see over. As you walk around and into this cage structure, you are also surrounded by the shadows of the wire grids on the walls including your own shadow. Slowly, the lightbulb moves up and down. This movement is amplified in the shadows: a contemporary version of Plato's cave but with no outside. In this space the spectator becomes both subject and object, experiential body and its shadow, object and representation, all set in place by a central light. Suddenly you are no longer sure whether the shadows, the metal lockers, or the floor is moving, a disorientation like that felt when sitting in a train and waiting for it to pull out of the station. In *Light Sentence*, the movement of the light makes the shadows of the empty metal lockers creep up and down the walls and across the floor. The geometric wire grids, orderly, transparent, rational, and symmetrical, slowly spread out and expand into imaginary architectural configurations on the surrounding surfaces.

Abandoning yourself to the play of light and projection, you become part of the scene observed. Your body multiplies into a body of sense perception and a body of multiple surfaces, a seeing body and a body seen, caught in the play of light and shadow. These shifting sites and moments of physicality and their refusal to coincide in a self-identical, bounded unity pervade much of Hatoum's recent work. This is perhaps most apparent in an installation of 1989 titled *The Light at the End*. In this piece six glowing heating elements are held vertically in a solid steel frame. This structure is placed at the apex of a triangular room and dimly lit from above by a single light. On entering the practically dark space only the red lines are visible. As you draw nearer, sight is supplanted by the sensation of heat. The structure's proximity is acutely felt, and a small niche behind it becomes visible. At this point at the very latest, imaginary scenarios begin to enfold. You picture somebody behind the metal structure; associations of electric fences, prison cells, torture instruments, more generally confinement, and perhaps possible routes of escape, or simply a vague but paralyzing feeling of menace, emanate from the piece. Knowing that the spaces between the glowing metal rods measure the average width of a human head and that the space between the steel frame and the floor is calculated so that an adult could, hypothetically, crawl through the gap, does not really explain this phenomenon. It seems, rather, that the structure literally constitutes a barrier that partitions off a space (if not a person) on one side from the spectator on the other. This effect is heightened by the possibility of getting too close, of becoming the imagined victim oneself, of getting hurt. Hatoum hints at the subtle irony of this freedom of the imagination in the title. *The Light at the End* turns out to be literal and descriptive rather than metaphorical, and the power of the imagination in this piece evolves around the power to imagine all the ramifications of imprisonment.

In many of Hatoum's installations there is a strong sense of being submitted to a particular order. The distance between spectator and work is minimized and the physical proximity to the materials creates a claustrophobic closeness rather than a distanced and disinterested overview. The feeling of being subjected to a situation is particularly acute in those works that constrain movement while offering an unrestricted view of the space. The use of furniture that directly relates to the placement and positioning of bodies—chairs, bedsprings, a cot in recent work—further accentuates the prospect of physical manipulation and suggests the possibility of harm to the body in an installation with the ironic title *Alive and Well*.

Several artists, Bruce Nauman and Kounellis among them, have worked with the symbolic ambivalence of furniture to orchestrate the doubling of comfort with danger, safety with vulnerability, and protection with violence. In Nauman's work, furniture is often identified in the title, with what is already a string of complex metaphors, combinations of synecdoches and personifications in works such as *White Anger, Red Danger, Yellow Peril, Black Death* (1984). In Hatoum's work, metaphor often operates through inversion and through idiomatic registers. The combined effect results in an intensely mobile relation between word and image. This mobility is directly exploited in the pieces that use what in linguistics are called shifters, words that are "empty" in the sense that their referent keeps changing, for instance personal pronouns. Thus, whoever looks in the engraved mirror of the multiple *You Are Still Here* will at that moment be the "you" addressed in the work. The way in which idioms and metaphors shape bodies is intimated in Hatoum's *Over My Dead Body*, a billboard project of 1988, which juxtaposes image and text and playfully inverts, in terms of scale, the power relationship between aggressor and victim. The large black and white image shows the artist balancing a toy soldier on her nose with the caption "over my dead body."

Where Nauman proposes the translation of a verbal expression into a visual work in *From Hand to Mouth*, in Hatoum's work language often figures as ready-made material that presents a particular aspect and only ever offers a partial translation of the visual and vice versa. This helps to foreground the performative aspect of much of her work, which allows us to treat her installations as spaces of fantasy where we occupy different imaginary positions all at once. In many ways, the video installation *Corps étranger* (1994), one of Hatoum's most complex works to date, develops and focuses her persistent preoccupation with the metaphorical power of the body.

Corps étranger consists of a round enclosure, 240 centimeters in diameter, that can be entered via two opposite narrow openings. The center of the floor is occupied by a circular video projection, a close-up scanning of the artist's body inside and out. In the gallery but still outside the cylinder, the sound tape is already audible, and once you have entered the enclosure you are engulfed by the rhythm of heartbeat. Here the machine-produced sound of the heartbeat is overlaid with the sound of breathing, but the two rhythms remain distinct. When, with the camera, our gaze enters the body through one of its orifices, the breathing stops and all we hear is a whistling sound, at moments ephemeral and "windy," at other moments heavier—depending, I was told, on where on the body the pulse was recorded. So there are different locations on the sound tape too, but we cannot relate them to the image. We cannot match. There is no equivalence. Unlike the format of the tondo, these images do not have a "right way up." The circle within a circle and our circulation around the circular projection seem at odds with the determined directionality of the camera until we realize that the video is on a loop without recognizable beginning or end. The close scanning of the body's surfaces creates a topography only loosely connected to the familiar figure that we think of as "the body." In the erasure of difference that would allow us to identify this body as belonging to a particular individual, only sexual difference remains. We recognize the body as female. But what does this mean here? We momentarily glimpse a vagina and a nipple in what has become a bodyscape of skin, hair, and flesh.

The camera has abolished the body as the physical thing with a visible outside and an impenetrable and opaque interior. Entirely visual, this body can no longer harbor a soul or keep a secret. What at first appears to be a directed and determined search does not in fact

Jardin Public,
1993.
Wrought iron
chair and pubic
hair.
H. 89 cm. ⌀ 38 cm
Collection of
Yannick Thiroux
and the artist.
Photo: Edward
Woodman.

arrive anywhere or at anything. The camera goes over the same ground again and again without stopping. But this is not simply the scenario of the fetishist's disavowal of a perceived lack. There is also a strange orality to this vision that cannot leave out anything and systematically and inclusively traces the surfaces of the body in an endless circularity. Alongside the mastery and objectification suggested by the technology of the medical gaze, there is another relation in which the boundaries between object and subject are less marked and projection is also a form of introjection. In order to see anything at all, we must first enter into a sound-box that, womblike, both shelters and exposes. We incorporate as we are incorporated, and while visually penetrating the inside of the body we are also swallowed up by that body.

The viewer, then, is placed in an ambiguous relation to this body that he or she surveys and masters and that at the same time engulfs and swallows the controlling gaze. It is surely no coincidence that this ambiguity presents the two sides of the coin that constitute the stereotype of femininity: on the one hand the passive and (natural) body submitted to the operations of science (culture), on the other hand the Sphinx, preying mantis, vagina dentata, and other such phantasmagorias of the female body that recall the violence toward and the fear of women that accompany and often characterize the processes of signification and culture.

In much of her work in performance and video, Hatoum uses images of her own body. Both subject and object, "the body" can suggest victimization on the one hand and empowerment on the other, often within the same piece. In this way the body is elaborated as a site of momentary and often contradictory identifications. Unlike the conventional self-portrait, which suggests a level of imaginary coherence of the subject as object, in Hatoum's work the body is staged as the very stuff of symbolic substitution. In *Corps étranger* the body as figure is no longer contained or containable.

"Failure is given at the outset," Jean-Luc Nancy observes in a paper entitled *Corpus*. He continues: "a double failure . . . to produce a discourse on the body, also the failure not to produce a discourse on it. I have finished talking about the body and I have not yet begun. I will never stop talking about it, and this body from which I speak will never be able to speak,

Light Sentence,
1992.
Installation at
Chapter Cardiff.
Wire mesh lockers
and a single
slow-moving
motorized light
bulb.
198 x 185 x 490 cm.
Photo: Edward
Woodman.

Corps Étranger
1994.
Video installa-
tion.
Edition of 2.
3.50 x ⌀ 3.05 m
Courtesy Centre
Pompidou, Paris
and White Cube,
London.

neither about itself nor about me."[1] This, at least, is how the "question of the body" is often presented in continental philosophy; in theoretical discourse it becomes a question and at the same time a "double bind" and a "psychosis."[2]

In art the body and especially the female body, signifying anything from liberty to truth and from evil to redemption, has become synonymous with allegory. By the same token it has been voided of anything intrinsically belonging to it, and in this move from property to propriety, the question of property and the proper has turned into the question of representation and its rules.

Corps étranger relates two attitudes toward the human body that have dominated the history of Western art since antiquity: on the one hand the idealized body as the sign of culture per se. This body is suggested by the perfect symmetry and "classical" geometry of the space in which the image is projected. The doubling of the body as architectural space gestures toward the long history of architecture modeled on the measurements, proportions, and structure of the human body. It also recalls the ancient and still current understanding of the body as a container inhabited by feelings, intelligence, and consciousness in general. At the same time another attitude is suggested by the video, where the gaze of the camera fragments and fractures. Precariously balanced in such a way that the images still read as close-ups of a female body, we are constantly aware of how easily identification slips into a terrain of associations that quickly turn the body into other figures such as tunnels, landscapes, and labyrinths.

An installation made for the Béguinage of Saint Elizabeth in Kortrijk (Belgium) in 1995 and entitled *Recollection* again uses the artist's body in a play of presence and absence. Here the body supplies the raw material for the piece—hair—and in that very gesture disperses the body and makes it collectable and recollected. At first the large room appears practically empty except for a small wooden table in the far corner. A roughly made miniature loom is attached to the tabletop with metal brackets. Hundreds of small hair balls sit on floor and window sills. As you walk into the room, something keeps brushing against your face: hanging from the wooden ceiling beams are rows of individual hairs six inches apart. The weaving on the loom is also made from hair, and looking around the space I noticed a piece of used soap with a row of pubic hairs "growing" out of it on one of the window sills.

For years, Hatoum has collected her own hair from combs and brushes; what is usually discarded as debris is instead collected and installed to juxtapose pattern with unordered matter, emphasizing the narrow line between the two. Hair stuck onto a piece of soap rather than a piece of soap with hair left sticking to it, woven fabric surrounded by balls of hair drifting across the floor like dust . . .

Much can be said about the symbolic power of hair as that part of the human body considered least human, as fetish, and as elaborately staged delineation of nature and culture. In the context of Hatoum's work, it seems to me that what is at issue in *Recollection,* as in previous installations, are the ways in which structures, proportions, and materials derived from the human body function instrumentally and cognitively, on the one hand, and expressively on the other. Hatoum's work unsettles distinctions between order and chaos by presenting material continuity between these states. Chaos, debris, or dirt as transgression, in Mary Douglas's words as "matter out of place," simultaneously refer to the social and cultural processes through which objects and materials are invested with symbolic significance.[3] Hatoum's work, then, involves both the recognition and creative modification of knowledge and experience as it is collected and figured, refigured and recollected through the body.

NOTES:
1. Jean-Luc Nancy, *The Birth to Presence* (Stanford, Calif.: Stanford University Press, 1993), 190.
2. Ibid.
3. Mary Douglas, *Purity and Danger: An Analysis of the Concepts of Pollution and Taboo* (London: Routledge, 1966), 40.

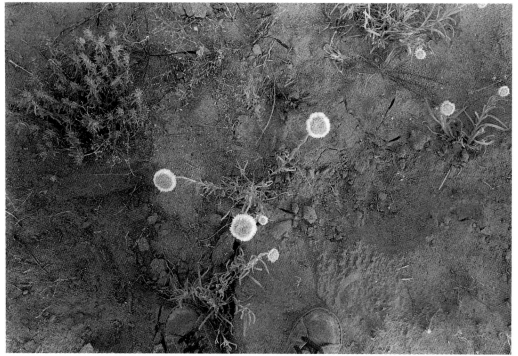

Horizons
(Southern End,
Birdsville Track
South Australia)
1979.
Black and white
print.
Courtesy of the
artist.

Reveries on Lynn Silverman's *1:1*

Jean Fisher

When we first spoke, Lynn Silverman and I, it was to discover a shared love of the desert. To those who do not know it, experience of the desert is traumatic; or, perhaps, the desert figures a trauma that cannot otherwise be spoken. Perceived by the European as menacing and life-threatening, for him or her it is a place of frightening homogeneity, of emptiness. For those who cannot see its life, it is the absolute Other of nature as a source of plenitude. It is treacherous; it leads one astray with its seductions and mirages. In Australia, where Silverman encountered the desert, it is the center, which is also the *horror vacui* of the (aboriginal) Other. The European cannot dwell in the desert; he can only cross it, or map it, in his attempt to master it. But the desert cannot be colonized by the imperial gaze. One can see how the desert has come to be designated as a space of the feminine . . .

Space in the desert (or in other flatlands like the plains of the American Midwest) is experienced strangely—in the absence of perspective provided by vertical territorial markers one cannot find its measure, and, as a consequence, one's own orientation. We seem unable to focus the intermediate distance, and, as Silverman says, it seems to "drop out." To arrest this vertigo of dislocation, we try to orient ourselves to the horizon, but its expansiveness only reinforces the sense of "no-where." Alternatively, our attention is drawn to the ground beneath our feet; this has a material reality, it is tangible, it is the "now-here." Why is precisely the middle distance, the continuity between the now-here and no-where, absent in Silverman's photographs of the Australian desert? The desert defies the totalizing demand of the gaze; rather, it is a tactile space, characterized by the "event": the movement of clouds, the sudden and unexpected scurrying of a small creature, the flurry of an impromptu wind. My desire, I must admit, is to lie down; not to submit, but to empower a different nature: to feel its texture, to embrace its expansiveness, to find its energizing pulse or matrix. And, looking up, there is the sky . . .

There is a comfort, at first, standing in front of Lynn's photographs of sky and clouds. They seem to mime the position and scale of my body, like portraits. They do not overwhelm or threaten. Indeed, the first image instills a sense of airiness and lightness of being—like a summer sky. Yet in my passage through the images I begin to feel their differences, and an unease—or uncertainty—gradually enfolds me. Here, the black field has an alluring density; it would absorb me were it not for a certain resistance of the surface and the band of cloud at the foot of the image, which anchors me this side of the picture plane. There a reversal takes place; the blackness that elsewhere seems to be sky becomes a brooding pall of cloud trailing an ominous scud. Time and speed are imagined variably: in places the wisps of cloud drift and dissolve leisurely into nothing; elsewhere they boil and foment at the edges, like time-lapse photographs of sunspots. The sky, too, is a space of the event: winds, rain, changing luminosities, shooting stars, and orbiting satellites.

These are images of light, formed through light, yet the source, as in a Rembrandt interior, lies mysteriously beyond the edge of the image or is only partly glimpsed behind the darkness, seemingly emanating from a different set of coordinates than the one that I occupy. The scene is not called forth by the radiating gaze of a romantic visionary: I am not positioned as the author of the event. In any case, this light obscures as it illuminates, which is indeed the very nature of the photographic apparatus. The artist calls the dense black of the photographs "maximum black"—a technical term suggesting an absolute, but one that I visualize as an infinite number of holes puncturing the surface, so infinite that the surface itself becomes a hole where the cloud or whiteness is not . . . a punctured veil, alluding to the veil of Western pictorialism that shows by concealing.

Zones of gray break into the black and white to either side: the edges of things lack precise focus; boundaries waver, but the image is neither fragmentary nor boundless in the manner evoked by the romantic sublime. The "event" in the image—a hovering cloud, for instance—produces a symmetry that centers me, but only *provisionally*: the space invoked is unstable. What figures as a horizon lacks substance, floats, glimmers faintly as a pale light. Above all, the angle of the shot belies the verticality of the photographic format; the viewer is positioned *as if* seeing from the place of, say, Caspar David Friedrich's mountaintop *Wanderer above the Mists* (c. 1818), but this is clearly impossible. As in the desert, there is a disorientation, not because there is no intermediate distance but because neither foreground nor background is determinable. In contradistinction to the romantic tradition, these photographs offer no "scene" as such for the viewer to command and by which he or she might be aggrandized. Silverman's work thus calls attention to the masculinist and narcissistic romantic convention that summoned the terror or "awesomeness" of the sublime Other only to colonize and thence to internalize and obliterate it.

It may seem paradoxical at first that Silverman's photographic images of cloud and sky emerged from a reverie on her experience of the Australian desert. Yet on further reflection it becomes clear that what is at issue is the image of the cloud not as an index of some tangible referent "out there" in the "real" world but as a signifier of other layers of experience deeply embedded in imaginative and cultural life, whose investment in representation is itself problematized. From the point of view of culture's symbolic structures, the link between cloud/sky and desert is found in the romantic imagination and its discourse of the sublime as the paradoxical desire to transcend the human and the search for a redemptive narrative in the wake of the "death of God."

But if the cloud/sky purports at first to mark an elevation of spirit, like the desert, in an inversion of meanings in the romantic narrative, it comes to figure the abject or nothing at the origin. At the most pragmatic level, the cloud is no more than a mass of water droplets and particulate matter—an insubstantial and unstable no-thing, an opaque "atmosphere" that catches and reflects sunlight. In this sense it reminds me of the material properties of photographic paper: little more than a thin veneer of particles whose density, from "maximum" black through tonal variations to "maximum" whiteness, depends on the level of projected light. This particulate surface, which has no meaning in itself, also becomes the image of a seemingly amorphous "atmosphere" when the negative is blown up past the level of object definition.

In these photographs, however, not only the black but the white is the site of obscurity, the place where nothing has (yet) appeared, a lack of light (of "reason" or "knowledge" in the

European philosophical schema). In this the cloud sometimes seems to function as a veil. However, the blackness that whiteness obscures here is also a nonappearance, the effect of a relative excess of light. Yet it is not so much to photography as to the history of painting that we might look to understand the cloud's performance.

Brunelleschi, in his graphic demonstrations of geometric perspective, introduced, somewhat curiously, a mirrored metal plate to reflect the image of "real" clouds passing. Hubert Damisch has pointed out this need to introduce an unmeasurable element as the very condition of creating a pictorial system that could structure the orientation of the body in space. Thus, as Rosalind Krauss suggests, the cloud, "before being a thematic element—functioning in the moral and allegorical sphere as a registration of miraculous vision, or of ascension, or as divine space; or in the psychological sphere as an index of desire, fantasy, hallucination . . . is a differential marker in a semiological system."[1] We are therefore given in this pictorial tradition a binary relation of the grounded and the ungrounded; which is to say, an ordering of the world through language and a sign of what has no order or representation.

But is not this binary system precisely what is undermined in these photographs—a refusal of a determinable order, a refusal of the relations of power inherent in the romantic visionary's pacification of his sublime, or traumatic, Other? Figured in the photographs are only the traditional markers of the unordered and the unrepresentable; hence, the absence of any geometric space into which we can comfortably inscribe ourselves. Unable to project ourselves, we are thrown back constantly onto the material presence of our own bodies—the sentient body that, in being made over into a picture in the European pictorial tradition, was progressively eliminated.

We may more properly say that Silverman's photographs of a deferred evanescence offer something like a *scriptural* event; for what the images most closely resemble in terms of aesthetic practice is drawing or writing—the marking of the open white sheet that is the beginning of symbolizing the self and its reality. Here, however, in the instability of the relation between cloud and sky, light and dark, presence and absence, the image and myself, remains the suggestion of a constant rhythm of emerging and dematerializing of the body image: a positive lack of fixity. Thus, if the cloud tracings sometimes have the character of a hallucination, it is not that of the narcissistic mirror (Silverman takes pains to minimize the reflective tendencies of photographic process and presentation) or the paranoid mask, both of which turn away from a traumatic reality, but of a confrontation with the strangeness or otherness of myself. This strangeness also draws me into a relation with another and is, like Silverman's images, both intimate and infinitely unapproachable; a relation of "one-to-one" in which sameness and difference are in perpetual negotiation, with neither absorbing nor ejecting the other.

Finally, these images suggest a presymbolic (or pre-Oedipal) space of the "feminine": the traumatic Other, which the romantic sublime sought to suppress and master as the nothing at the origin. In these photographs, this space is also unknown, but it is refigured positively as a space of potential, of an ongoing emergence and transformation. A different sense of human subjectivity emerges, no longer trapped in rigid oppositions with its others but mutable and negotiable, more capable of being the agent of its own realities.

NOTES:

This essay was originally published as *1:1*, photographs by Lynn Silverman, text by Jean Fisher (Nottingham: Angel Row Gallery, in collaboration with Camerawork, London, and the University of Derby, 1993).

1. Rosalind Krauss, "The /Cloud/," in *Agnes Martin*, ed. Barbara Haskell, exhib. cat. (New York: Whitney Museum of American Art and Harry Abrams, 1992), 155–65; reprinted in this volume.

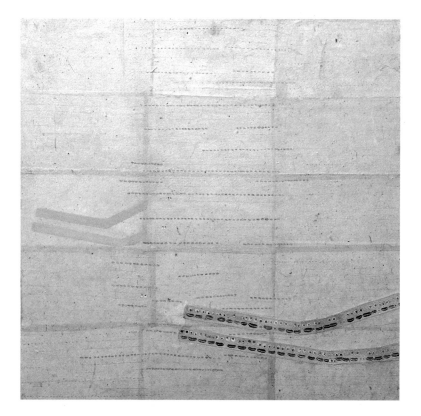

Untitled, 1995.
Oil, pencil, and
paper on canvas.
24 x 24 in.
Collection
Marjory Jacobson
and Marshall
Smith.
Courtesy Mario
Diacono Gallery,
Boston.

Untitled, 1995.
Oil, pencil, and
paper on canvas.
24 x 24 in.
Mario Diacono
Gallery, Boston.

Sniffing Elephant Bones: The Poetics of Race in the Art of Ellen Gallagher

Judith Wilson

What she said once, unforgettable, was that
the stereotype is the distance between
ourselves—our real, our black bodies—& the image[1]

The greatest thing by far is to be a master of metaphor;
for to use metaphors well is to see the similarity in dissimilars.
—Aristotle, *The Poetics*

Image, body, text: these three sites have been crucially linked in recent cultural theory and practice. Thirty years old and a native of New England, painter Ellen Gallagher has been described as working "in the gap between image and body (the gap that is language)."[2] That understanding of her project, of course, simultaneously echoes and significantly revises a late modernist agenda epitomized by Robert Rauschenberg: "Painting relates to both art and life. Neither can be made. (I try to act in that gap between the two.)"[3] Postpop, postpainterly, and postminimal, Gallagher operates in a space cleared by contemporary feminist, semiotic, black, and cultural studies discourses. Yet her art negotiates these busy intersections in a starkly independent fashion.

In conversation, she readily shifts from charting the ancestry of Walt Disney's Mickey Mouse (whose origins, she informs me, include both the legendary black "river rat" Steamboat Willie and the once-despised Irish "Mick") to quoting nineteenth-century New England's quintessential poet, Emily Dickinson. Indeed, poetry and pop culture are key sources of Gallagher's art—a conjunction that aligns the painter with the Dark Room Collective, a Cambridge-based group of African-American writers. Authors of poetry and fiction, their diverse literary manners and modes cohere around a shared ability to "code-switch with the same fast dazzle" and a common pool of black pop cultural knowledge.[4] Given her fascination with troublesome bits of Americana like minstrelsy, in which she sees a theatrical "embodying of language," as well as her preoccupation with "culturally-embedded imagery," it makes sense that one of Gallagher's first exhibitions took place at The Dark Room in 1989.

Despite these literary ties, Gallagher insists on mining imagery from the process of painting. In each canvas, she explains, "the narrative comes from the legacy of the marks." While she favors simple forms, they often have complex genealogies. In many of her paintings of the past two years, for example, tiny, coffee-bean-shaped lozenges mass in various formations. They stem from a cloud of red pigment that appears in a 1992–93 canvas, *Untitled (Doll's Eyes)*. Reading the red smudge as a lipstick stain eventually led the artist to draw small, disembodied pairs of stylized black lips: the sort of rubbery, banana-shaped lips that were standard elements of the grotesque rendition of African features in nineteenth- and twentieth-century U.S. mass media, advertising, and entertainment, as well as in objects ranging from tea cozies to children's toys.

In an untitled painting (1995), large blocks of paper are collaged onto canvas, and smaller, stacked rows of lips are painted over them. Both types of semirectangular forms have concave or convex edges, instead of Gallagher's usual straight sides. These flexed contours come from the round opening of the hoop skirt worn by a minstrel puppet or doll in a pencil drawing called *Delirious Hem* (1993). The title, in turn, comes from an Emily Dickinson poem in which a suicidal urge is evoked by the image of a woman being tugged into a well by her skirt's "delirious hem."

Such practices of generating imagery or formal elements via synecdochic allusion give Gallagher's work the rich multireferentiality and semantic compression of the best poetry. But the resultant textuality is profoundly visual, producing a lexicon of forms based on fragments of other forms and/or images. A pair of small (twenty-four-inch-square) paintings in oil and pencil on canvas make clear the artist's will to merge socioculturally "thick" references with imagery arising solely from a confrontation with her materials. The blond canvas features large, rectangular patches of blue-lined penmanship paper. In all but one case, these patches are covered with rows of tiny eyes. A single patch, positioned somewhat lower than and left of center, is filled with faintly penciled "lips." Slight differences of scale in the various panels' eyes create tonal shifts and produce visual rhythms that seem to emanate from the one block of lips.

The second painting consists of the same materials—paper, paint, pencil—applied in reverse. Color relations have been inverted, too. Now, instead of being covered with pale beige, mottled fields of eyeballs and a single patch of fugitive graphite lips that are partly blurred by a veil of paint, the papered ground is blackened with inky paint and a spiraling cluster of silvery graphite heads has been superimposed over a central block of the canvas. In these light/dark contrasts, reversed application of materials, opposing configurations of circles and rectangles, and the metonymic relationship between the isolated eyes and lips of one canvas and spooky faces—in which Munch or Ensor's wraiths seem to have been morphed into the "Have a Nice Day" smile—of the other, Gallagher practices intertextual play as a kind of visual call-and-response.

One recent painting is entitled *Elephant Bones*. Here the printed lines of penmanship paper have been carefully superimposed with hand-drawn lines and, in a further elaboration of process, cerulean blue ink has been forced through a hole poked in each coffee-bean pair of lips, then scraped out to reveal the burr of the paper. Recent scientific investigations indicate that elephants may recognize the bones of their kin by scent. Thus, at one place in her canvas, Gallagher shows the trunk of a suspicious pachyderm sniffing a white minstrel. This small area serves as a "microcosm of the rest" of the composition, a device she employs in all of her canvases.

Another recurrent trope is color. The golden tones of many of Gallagher's canvases are meant to evoke skin—i.e., the various skin colors associated with racial hybridity as a mode of transgression and as a source of ambivalence and/or alienation in a strictly color-coded society. As always, though, symbols function on more than one plane for this artist. Thus, the sociohistorically fraught questions of color and race subsumed under the artist's palette are balanced by aesthetic references—on one hand, to the materiality of paint, which forms a type of skin on the canvas; on the other to Byzantine icons with their enormous, all-seeing eyes.

The double-voiced character of Gallagher's imagery is conscious and strategic. It reflects her awareness of the profound presentness of both verbal and visual images, their power to endure well beyond the limits of their historical rationales. At the same time, it coincides with the artist's interest in making "history paintings" that "want to be present—to say 'Remember.'"

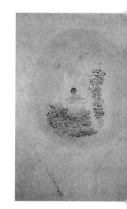

Delirious Hem, 1993. Pencil on paper. 32 x 15 in. Courtesy of the artist.

titled, 1995.
tail.
l, pencil, and
per on canvas.
x 24 in.
ivate collec-
on.
urtesy Mario
acono Gallery,
ston.

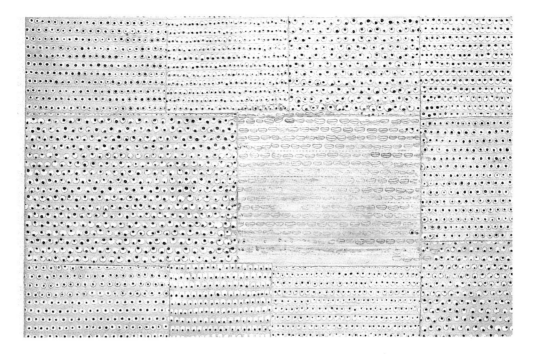

To fulfill this mandate, she deftly deploys visual conventions that act as narrative cues—making the act of viewing an "unfolding of time" in the process of "putting the story together"—while maintaining a degree of visual reticence that seduces the viewer into visceral engagement with images about which we have learned to feel numb. This is risky art, venturing to wed supposedly irreconcilable artistic missions: probing the formal nature of painting and pushing the politics of representation past existing thresholds. Risky, too, in what it asks of viewers, daring us to see intimately and make connections collectively forgotten.

NOTES:
1. Kevin Young and Ellen Gallagher, "Paraphrases," in *Altered States: American Art in the 90s*, exhib. cat. (St. Louis: Forum for Contemporary Art, 1995), n.p.
2. Ibid.
3. Robert Rauschenberg, "Statement," in Dorothy C. Miller, *Sixteen Americans* (New York: Museum of Modern Art, 1959), 58.
4. In a tribute to the collective, nonmember poet Elizabeth Alexander writes:

> …I
> drove my car to
> Cambridge in nineteen-
> eighty-nine and read
> …
> and The Dark Room
> listened, the house
> came down because
> we knew how to read
> each other, could code-switch
> with the same fast dazzle,
> knew Gladys from Patti
> from all the other divas,
> knew which commercials
> had black people in them
> from 1965 forward…

Elizabeth Alexander, "The Dark Room: An Invocation," *Callaloo 16*, no. 3 (1993): 554–55.

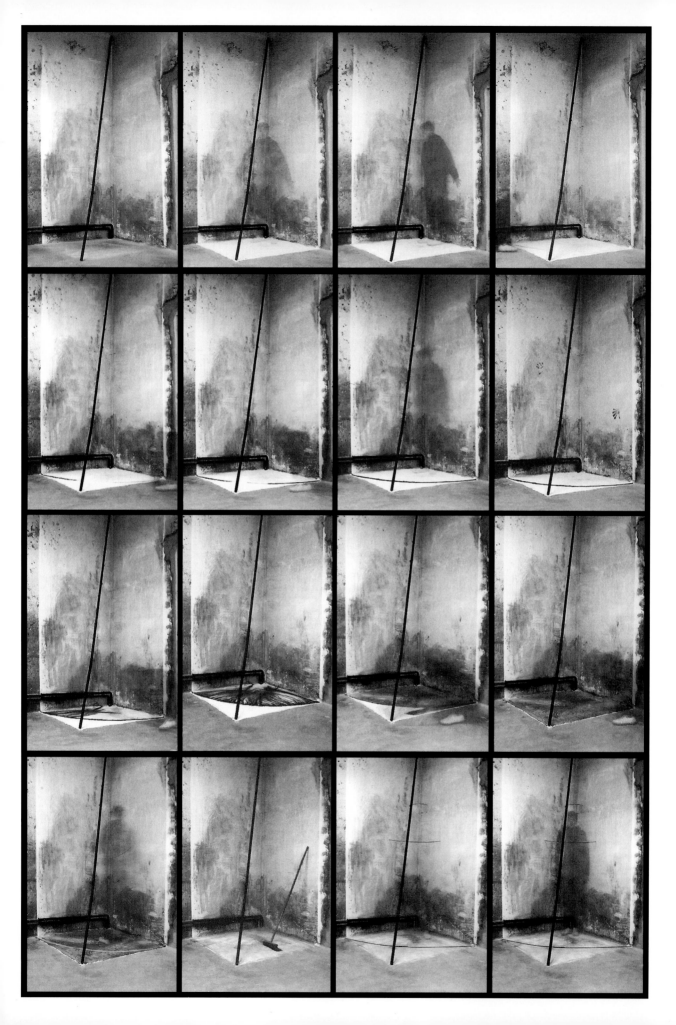

Inter-Image: Preliminary Observations on the Work of Nathalie Hervieux

Christophe Domino

> Everything happens as if
> within the group of images I call the universe
> nothing really new can take place
> except through the intermediary of certain personal images
> whose model is provided to me
> by my body.
> —Henri Bergson[1]

I n less than ten years, Nathalie Hervieux has built a solid corpus of work out of a sustained preoccupation with the body and, principally, its existence as image. Her work is by no means in the vein of postexpressionist corporeality common to much recent artistic production and often too easily satisfied by a corporeal presence guaranteed in terms of ontological drama, including gestural violence, mutilation, and a variety of wounds. At a distance from such matters, with neither naive dream of presence nor simplistic visual passion nor the fetishism of dyed-in-the-wool iconicity, Hervieux grounds her undertaking in an awareness that the body is only subject to apprehension and conception to the extent that it offers itself as a visible object. The body in focus here is not of a preexisting order; the aim is to manifest its existence only by means of its spatial and temporal inscription. The body invents itself through the image, in the image.

The recourse to photography is both central and nonexclusive, making no presumptions about the forms that the work may adopt or masking those from which it already borrows, such as painting. Yet photography as a technique, a mechanism, allows representational invention to play a special role within the folds, so to speak, of the image. The successive stages of the image's elaboration—from the shot to the print and from the placing of the subject to its being placed on exhibit—constitute as many moments of decision and possible manipulation for the artist. In the discrete evidence of the photographic rendering Hervieux constructs a contemporary subjectivity, in accordance with a mode of self-invention that, beyond the self-contemplation of Narcissus, builds an experiential space at once intersubjective and personal. It is personal because—repetition allowing the spectator to subsume it— the photograph always depicts the same model, perhaps recognizable from print to print and soon identifiable, due to coherence more than resemblance, as the photographer herself. Through this portraitless self-portraiture, Hervieux situates an individual subject who, without abandoning herself to the first effusion on psychic drama, is situated at the center of an exis-

ans titre, 1988.
lack and white
hotograph.
0 x 60 cm. each.
ourtesy of the
rtist.

379

tential questioning. She is not afraid to discover and confront mortifying vision and theatrical masquerade, something between an angelic apparition with ironic reference to religious iconography and a news-story figure turned mythical, such as the image of the *Inconnue de la Seine* (*Unknown Woman of the Seine*), that anonymous drowned beauty, a sort of modern Ophelia who reinvents, most likely involuntarily, a sequence of images like *Bain no. 1* (1990). Outside reference, outside citation, Hervieux inscribes the body between present and represented, through the logic of an image that invents for itself an extension at once spatial and temporal, halfway between technique and action.

Since 1990, Hervieux has shown photographic prints (or, less often, projections) presented in series and in series of series. Here appears a face (in *Lits* [*Beds*], a series begun in 1990), there a body (series entitled *La première chambre de Babel* [*The First Room of Babel*], 1990–93): figures manifesting themselves in collapsed space, deliberately lacking depth of field, without points of reference or spatial order analogous to that of lived experience. The photographic frame may be a colored zone, densely crowded with banal decorative motifs (flowers, stripes) borrowed from ordinary wallpaper or upholstery fabric, to the point of saturation (*Lits*), or full of overlapping colored pictorial and gestural traces, freely inscribed (*Babel*). Often at the center of this dense space, ghostly and sometimes divided with an ubiquitousness confined by strangeness,[2] the figure reveals itself as a discrete utterance,[3] a fragile apparition: the gaze encourages interrogation of the nature of the image, beyond any referential echo, between evidence and ambiguity.

Communicating with these images presumes a reentry into the photographic structure, within its *arché*.[4] Suggesting a significant displacement of the examination of the photographic fact, to paraphrase Nelson Goodman's pertinent formula[5] substituting traditional aesthetic essentialism's *what is art* with *when is art?*, Hervieux, by articulating the photograph in terms of duration, questions the *when* of photography over its *what*. A major feature of her work entails constituting not only the image (in the case of even the simplest photograph) but also the figure itself within the *durée* of sensory perception, in the absolute singularity of the present tense of each shot, within a drawing out that fosters the Barthesian *punctum*.

The image may be considered either as the manifestation of an entity or as factual documentation, as proof of the existence of a repeatable state or as proof of an event's occurrence.[6] Each of Hervieux's prints treats an entity (the body's presence) as document, as a performance,[7] thus inscribed in duration, as a specifically photographic piece of evidence defined by a certain mode of construction within the "memory" of photonic flux—in other words, the refractive capacity of luminous flux directed toward the sensitive surface. The photographic image is made from the temporal prolongation of the shot that allows the registration of a photonically unstable refraction. This controlled distortion defines the nature of the object that it reveals. Taken in time, apprehended as performance before becoming thing, the body finally constitutes itself as an entity in adding to its state of factuality the photograph's capacity of presentness.[8] The photographic structure conceived of in this way manifests a present beyond the actual moment, a Bergsonian present, site of reductions and foldings of temporal extension.

Without deliberately refusing or denying technique, Hervieux's work nevertheless involves operational as well as material archaism. The tools are simple: camera obscura, simple pinhole cameras, casings rudimentary to the exclusion of any complex operation. Her experimental mastery of process has more to do with (ritualistic) action than with work. Only essential principles are brought to bear, with neither gimmickry nor fixed methodology. The image displays no other manipulation than that which it reveals: nothing to hide. In this way, *techné* is foiled in favor of *arché*, taking the photograph as a pure field receptive to action.[9] Against the grain of technological one-upmanship, Hervieux locates the shortest path in the world to the image, taking as a model the image of the looking glass that owes much to Alice, a model that allows a glimpse at the thick complexity within the apparent filminess of reflection.

"To place duration in space is, by true contradiction, to locate successiveness in the very heart of simultaneity,"[10] as Bergson points out. The transfer of space into time gives rise to a unique space, complex yet directly accessible, like that of a mirrored reflection. It is after all the vocation of photography and artistic work to make visible, i.e., evident, a space whose many dimensions overlay to the point of seeming to form a spatial covering, dense but without depth. In Hervieux's works, conversion respects unity to scale, a 1:1 ratio between object,

hambres obscures LITXXIX nos. 1 nd 2), 1994. olor print. ourtesy of the rtist.

place, and representational material. Such a requirement may originate in the painter's rather than the photographer's practice. For the photographer, the image becomes autonomous, constituting its world in its own independent dimension, a rightfully imaginary space. Such a division retraces the classical separation between the *imago* (the image) and the *vestigium* (the footstep, its trace, its print), a distinction "brilliantly used in classical Scholasticism to problematize, through reasoning still instructive in our time, man's relation to the *Imago Dei*, in other words, the image's bases."[11] Strangely, the works in the *La première chambre de Babel* series grant the foot, the image of the foot, a role as spatial marker and a function as *vestigium*, between painting and photography, serving as a pedestal for both.

The persistence of the 1:1 ratio is often dissimulated. It is a question of a tendency rather than an algebraic norm, a symptom rather than a quotient. There is a 1:1 ratio when the photograph displays an actual-size panel painted on corporeal scale;[12] there is a 1:1 ratio between negative and image through contact printing;[13] there is, above all, a 1:1 ratio, of which the print is the result even more than the witness, between the studio space and the photographic apparatus, between the place of the artist's action and the method of exposure.

Thus, studio and photographic apparatus are one and the same: the studio becomes the encasing; the chambers, one in the sense of camera obscura and the other constituting an existential and banal frame, overlap. The lived-in and representational spaces are thus superimposed. The persistence of the square frame, already seen in works from 1987 in the form of a cubic volume, contributes to this unity, as do the various boxes (for example in the 1992 projects such as *La petite chambre noire à l'échelle humaine [The little room at human size])* The square format predominates in the negatives (2 1/4 by 2 1/4) as well as in the exhibition prints, a fullness that the artist registers in qualifying the work's space as "a cube traversed by the body and subject to impression on one of its sides." Bergson, once again, seems to provide a precise program for the artist's work when he notes that the conversion into representation of a thing of the world entails not "shedding light on the object, but on the contrary, obscuring some of its parts, in diminishing the largest portion so that the residuum, instead of remaining encased in its surroundings as a thing, detaches itself from them as a *picture.*"[14]

The figure's manifestation in the image carries a charge independent of the specificity of the medium and its effects, a charge that suspends the main question of identity. As space of representation and represented space change course without coming to terms, two figures of the artist are superimposed: subject and object of the photograph; *manipulans and manipulandum* of the work of art. In Hervieux, blindness, isolation, and solitude are the image constitution's central conditions: again, a 1:1 ratio in which the unity of reference is the body as image, much more than an intangible truth of being. If the question of identity lies herein, it does not choose the naive path of reducing the image to the saving scale of its referent, of its model, in an overlapping that reabsorbs alterity. If there is death here, it is, as Legendre—and Narcissus—says, because the question of the image is always that of the "representation of absence" and the "representability of absence," in other words of "the relation (of the subject) to disappearance, to the very plausibility of loss, and, beyond that, of death as a condition of life."[15] Hervieux's image seeks more to learn separation than to forge reunion, to "conceive of the necessity of a subjective void—called distance, digression, or separation—thanks to which identity constitutes itself as a relation to identity."[16] In *La chambre de Babel*, in *Lits*, it is a matter of retracing the paths of Narcissus and of the enormous effort of self-separation. The goal is never to get there nor to indulge in the old passions of the icon, nor to give credit to the fact of the image without questioning its nebulous cultural and anthropological bases.[17] The issue is rather to give oneself all of the means of producing an image, without constraints other than that of engaging the subject that accepts itself as present, that accepts itself as a duration that illustrates photographic latency, as a "constituting principle of the Third";[18] a subject that also realizes the risks involved in seeing itself as temporal.

Translated from the French by Stacy Doris

NOTES:

1. Henri Bergson, *Matière et mémoire* (Paris: Presses Universitaires de France, 1959), 170.
2. A disquieting strangeness (a sort of *unheimlich*) whose visual consistency, by indirect analogy, evokes mental images of dreams, memories, or hallucinations.
3. In the mathematical or linguistic sense, where each element, number, or utterance in a finite group is at once separate, distinct, and indissociable from the whole of which it forms a part.
4. That is, the photonic status of the photographic signal, a semiotic condition of the photographic structure and the implicit knowledge of the recipient, according to the description by Jean-Marie Schaeffer in *L'image précaire* (Paris: Le Seuil, 1987).
5. Made known in France only in the past five or six years.
6. As discussed by Schaeffer, *L'image précaire*, 69, who points out that it is not a question of the image's different semiotic nature but of the functioning of the relation of the *analogon*, to use his term, of the form of reinsertion in the world of which each photograph posits an interpretation.

 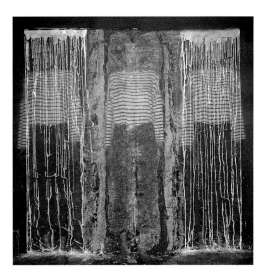

 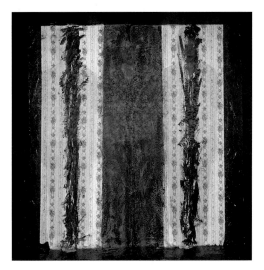

7. Not in the artistic sense but rather to the extent that it can be said of any work in terms of its execution (cf. Gérard Genette, *L'oeuvre de l'art* (Paris: Le Seuil, 1994), 66ff.

8. This often-remarked capacity entails the photograph's transformation of temporality into an indexical notation, since in involving the print in immediate identification it is able to allow the apprehension of the *durée* outside the real duration of perceptual flux.

9. If this is the case for the central photographic event, the artist remains not entirely protected from technicality, even if delegated, for example in printing, where, on the contrary, it demonstrates demands of mastery and delivery necessary for the proper access to its protocol.

10. Henri Bergson, *Les données de la conscience* (Paris: Presses Universitaires de France, 1959), 148–71.

11. Pierre Legendre, *Dieu au miroir* (Paris: Fayard, 1994), 45.

12. At the presentation at the Ecole des Beaux-Arts de Paris in 1993, where the panels started at floor level, like doors through which one couldn't pass.

13. In hanging the *La première chambre de Babel* series at Issy-les-Moulineaux and at Kortrijk in 1994.

14. Bergson, *Matière et mémoire*, 186.

15. Legendre, *Dieu au miroir*, 44–45.

16. Ibid., 69.

17. Very much in fashion, as evidenced by the undertaking of Jean Clair in the 1995 Venice Biennale.

18. In Legendre's vocabulary, this Third is the operator of all reflexivity.

Plates

EMILY CARR, *Forest, British Columbia*, 1932.
Oil on canvas. 130 x 86.6 cm. Courtesy Vancouver Art Gallery,
Emily Carr Trust. Photo: Trevor Mills.

LYNN SILVERMAN, *Untitled (94.47.12)*, 1994.
Black and white print.
36 x 47 3/4 in.
Courtesy of the artist.

LYNN SILVERMAN, *Untitled (95.4.12)*, 1995.
Black and white print.
36 x 47 3/4 in.
Courtesy of the artist.

CECILIA VICUÑA, *Con-con*, 1967 (1987).
Mixed media. Courtesy of the artist.

CECILIA VICUÑA, *Spiral Weaving*, 1992.
Mixed media. University Art Museum,
University of California, Berkeley.

MARIA HELENA VIEIRA DA SILVA, *Composition*, 1936.
Oil on canvas. 84 x 103.5 cm.
Fundação Calouste Gulbenkian,
Centro de Arte Moderna Jose de Azredo Perdigão, Lisbon, Portugal.

MARIA HELENA VIEIRA DA SILVA, *Normandie*, 1949.
Gouache on canvas. 40 x 47 cm.
Courtesy Galerie Jeanne Bucher, Paris.
Photo: J. Hyde

AGNES MARTIN, *The Rose*, 1964.
Oil, red and black pencil, and sizing on canvas.
182.6 x 182.7 cm. Art Gallery of Ontario, Toronto.
Purchased with Assistance from Wintario, 1979.

Mona Hatoum, *Recollection*, 1995.
Installation at Béguinage,
Kortrijk (Belgium).
Courtesy Kanaal Art Foundation,
Kortrijk.
Photo: M. Catherine de Zegher
and Rien van den Eshof.

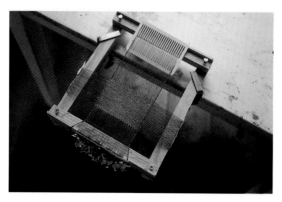

Previous pages:
Gego, *Reticulárea* (installation
view), 1969.
Environmental wire sculpture,
size of room 20.5 x 21.5 x 11.5 ft.
Installation at the Americas
Society, New York.
Photo: Charles Uht.

ELLEN GALLAGHER, *Untitled*, 1995.
Oil, pencil, and paper on canvas. 84 x 71 3/4.
Collection of Charlene Engelhard.

ELLEN GALLAGHER, *Untitled*, 1995.
Oil, pencil, and paper on canvas. 84 x 71 3/4.
Whitney Museum of American Art, New York, gift of Charlene Engelhard.

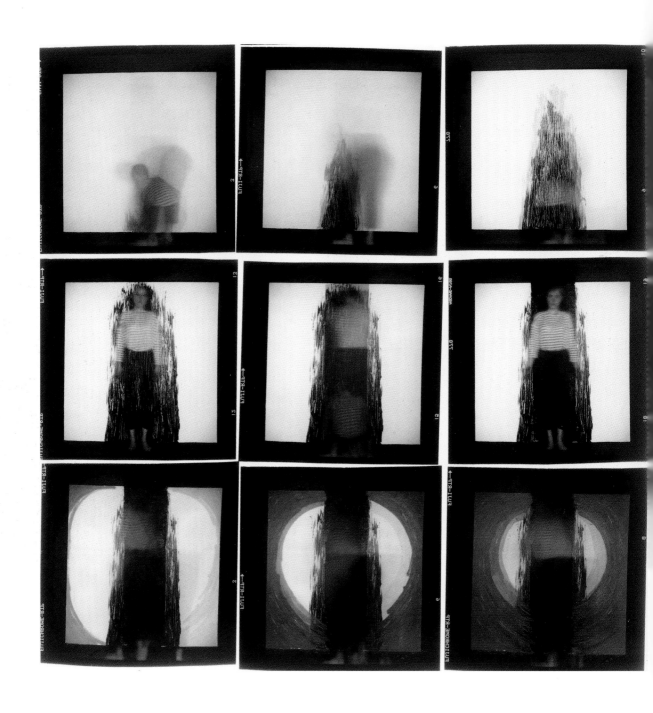

NATHALIE HERVIEUX, *La première chambre de Babel*
(The First Room of Babel), 1990-93.
Color photographs.
Courtesy of the artist.

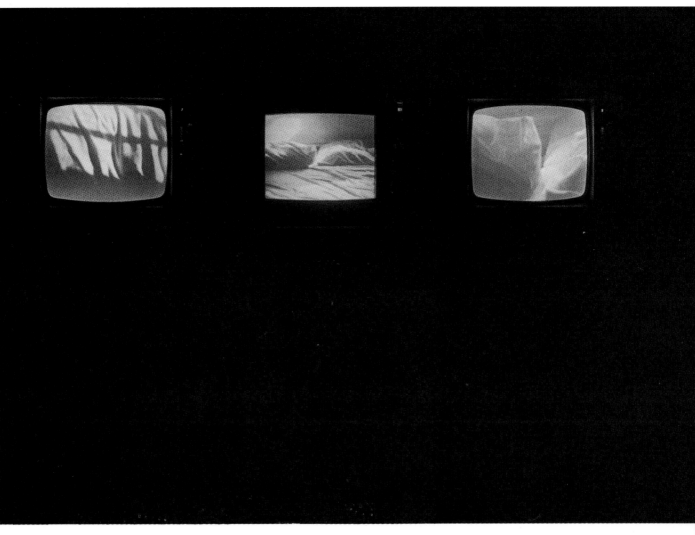

THERESA HAK KYUNG CHA, *Passages Paysages*, 1978.
Three-channel video. University Art Museum,
University of California, Berkeley.
Gift of the Theresa Hak Kyung Cha Memorial
Foundation.

ENJAMBMENT: "LA DONNA È MOBILE"

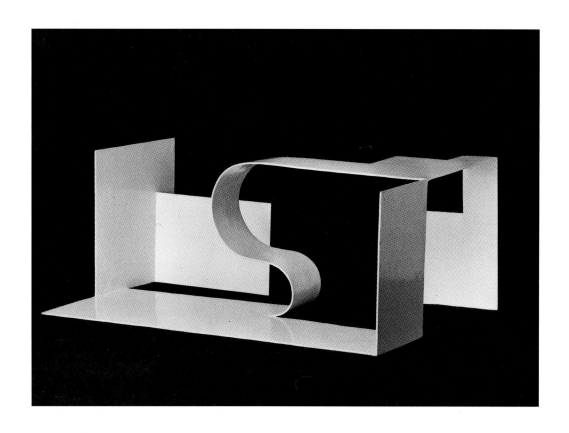

Space Composition 5, 1929-30.
Welded steel, monochrome white. 25 x 64 x 40 cm.
Muzeum Sztuki, Lodz (Poland).

Kobro's Disjunctive Syntax

Yve-Alain Bois

S ome works appear too early and make a comeback too late, their very precocity interfering—and continuing to interfere—with their reception. The belated discovery of such works plunges us into confusion: we confront them in the same way as we would confront an improbable species that does not fit comfortably into the categories of our evolutionist reading of natural history. Wladyslaw Strzeminski's and Katarzyna Kobro's texts and works from the 1920s and 1930s belong to this category. We would wish to call them "seminal," so much do they seem to have influenced the art and aesthetics of the 1960s. But this is impossible, since they have been condemned to a double oblivion. First, as part of the Eastern European avant-garde, they were tightly covered up by the lugubrious lid of Stalinization (this is common enough, but in their case this oblivion was abetted by the Nazi destruction—only about fifteen of Kobro's sculptures have survived, six of which are reconstructions). Second, their work was ignored by artists and critics in the West, who would later ask the same questions and often adopt the same solutions, despite the fact that, with Gomulka's return to power in 1956, nothing prevented the rediscovery of this work. ("*Re*discovery" is slightly inaccurate, in fact, for in comparison to those of the Russian avant-garde of the 1920s the ideas and works of the Polish avant-garde had not circulated very widely in Europe prior to World War II.)

Given the historicist bias of our aesthetic judgment, our first impulse is to "rehabilitate" Strzeminski's and Kobro's work and to contest the novelty of what was produced later—to argue, for example, that Yves Klein invented nothing with his monochromes, or that Frank Stella was truly presumptuous in claiming that European art had never been anything more than a balancing act ("You do something in one corner and balance it with something in the other corner").[1] However well intended such rehabilitation may be, it has the perfect uselessness of an academic debate. For we "discover" Strzeminski and Kobro at a time when the system of values we call modernist has floundered—a system that they themselves formulated very precisely, some thirty years before the theories that are more familiar to us. So that rehabilitation is no longer the order of the day; what is in order is an attempt to understand the causes, mechanisms, and effects of the mortal crisis, or declared death, of modernism (which means, by the same token, the necessity to reexamine its history).

It is precisely this task that a close reading of Strzeminski and Kobro's work and theory, which they baptized unism, can help us to achieve. Why? Because the historicism that makes us evaluate a work of art as a function of its date, that is, of its position within an unbroken chain of events, this very historicism was an essential condition of modernism. Because our disarray before their works and their texts, itself the product of a theory of history they had

405

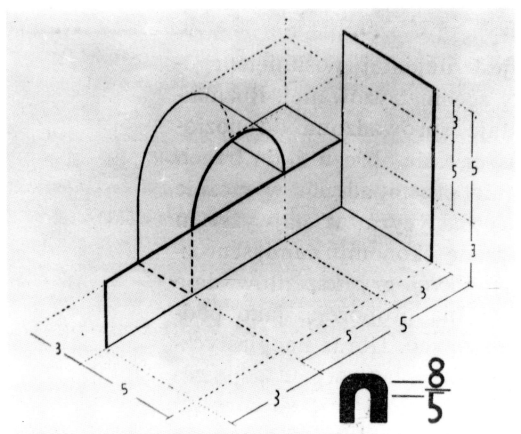

Calculation of numeral relatio: (Golden Section especially for *Spatial Compostion 3*, 1928. Courtesy Muzeum Sztuki, Lodz (Poland).

coined better than others, should help us understand that this theory is wrong (that history is not linear and that temporalities are not synchronous), and that it is partly because modernism was explicitly grounded on such a theory that it is nowadays in crisis and might have reached the end of its course.

The fact that the oblivion to which they have been consigned continues is itself instructive and can no longer be explained by circumstances alone, since their works have been exhibited widely during the past twenty years in the major museums of modern art in the West, several studies have been published in English, German, and French, and many of their texts are available in languages other than Polish (not to speak, of course, of the remarkable work accomplished by Polish scholars over the years, and most recently by Jaromir Jedlinski, to publicize their extraordinary achievement). This lasting oblivion, it seems to me, stems from the specific historical situation of these texts and works, a situation of "in-between" that obliges us to periodize history differently and to rid ourselves of such traditional conceptual tools as genealogy, influence, and style.

Strzeminski and Kobro's theory of sculpture is one of the most elaborate of our century, and the fifteen or so sculptures that illustrate it—all by Kobro—are among the most astonishing. Following what they call the "law of organicity" (the modernist dictum according to which each medium is governed by specific rules), the theory begins with the difference between painting and sculpture:

The painting has natural limits which are determined by the dimensions of the canvas. It cannot go beyond its natural limits. This is why the construction of the painting takes its limits as a point of departure. . . . A sculpture, on the other hand, does not have such natural limits, defined a priori. Hence the natural law must be for a sculpture not to enclose itself within a volume, but to unite with the totality of space, with the infinite space. The union of the sculpture with space, the saturation of space by the sculpture, the fusion of the sculpture in space and its link with it constitute the organic law of sculpture.[2]

Since it does not have "limits which would exist prior to its conception,"[3] a sculpture must be considered as a part of space, must exhibit the same characteristics as space. In exactly the same way that a figure, in one of Strzeminski's "architectonic" paintings, must be in an "unde-cidable" relationship with the ground of the painting (a positive/negative relationship) and consists only in the "motivated" division of the surface of the painting (since this division, in a typical reductionist manner, is based on various reduplications of the proportional relation-ship between the height and the width of the canvas), a unist sculpture must divide and shape interior as well as exterior space. For Kobro, "the most important problem" in the entire history of sculpture is

the relationship between the space contained within the sculpture and the space situated outside the sculpture. Aside of this fundamental problem, the following issues are rela-tively secondary: the static or dynamic character of the sculpture, the predominance of line or of volume, the use or non use of color, the handling in lights and shadows or in masses. From the solution given to this principal problem will stem both the type of sculpture and the solutions found for the secondary questions.[4]

I shall not try here to retrace the extremely complex typology of sculpture from antiquity onward proposed by the theoreticians of unism (Egyptian sculpture: a volume sculpture, which does not raise the issue of exterior space; Gothic sculpture, which reaches a union

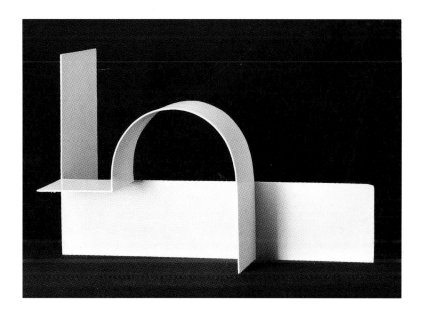

Space Composition 3,
1928.
Painted steel.
40 x 64 x 40 cm.
Muzeum Sztuki, Łódz
(Poland).

with that portion of exterior space contained within the limits of architecture; baroque sculpture, where "the limit of form is the limit of the zone of influence of its dynamic forms" and which reaches a union with that portion of exterior space contained within this "limiting limit").[5] Despite the odd terminology, art historians could learn a lot from these analyses; but more important here is Strzeminski and Kobro's insistence on "union with space." The issue is to avoid what Rosalind Krauss has called "the logic of the monument"—a commemorative logic that "distinguishes sculpture from the ongoing phenomena of daily life" and plunges the viewer "into a state of passive contemplation which cuts him off from the concerns of everyday life."[6] Why would anyone want to avoid this logic, when it has already demonstrated its effectiveness? Because it denies that sculpture inhabits the same space as the viewer, that is, the space of our experience in the world. Thus: "unist sculpture does not produce sculptures. Unist sculpture sculpts space, condensing it within the limits of its sculptural zone. The unist sculpture, based upon the organic unity of sculpture and space, does not want the form to be a goal in itself, but only the expression of spatial relationships."[7]

Even if Kobro subscribed to the ideology of transparency that defines, as Krauss demonstrated, a good portion of the constructivist production,[8] she did not employ the axes of spatial coordinates as a grid conceived as the sign of a universal language. If unism conceived space as an a priori category of our sensibility, it was always concerned with the space of our experience: "The union of man and space is the action of man in that space. We come to know space through our actions. The vectors traced by the actions of man in space are: the vertical station of man and every object, the horizontal of the environment which he encounters on both sides, and the depth, before him, of forward movement."[9] Space, according to Kobro and Strzeminski, is homogeneous and infinite, in a state of constant equilibrium (an equilibrium that is neither dynamic, based on movement, nor static, based on weight—that is, on a type of movement).[10] As a result, every dynamic form will subtract itself from space and reintroduce the logic of the monument. Moreover, every figure is necessarily dynamic because it is opposed, as center and foreign body, to the homogeneity of surrounding space: "The sculpture must not be a foreign body in space, nor the center which dominates illicitly the rest of space. It must create the prolongation of space. If sculpture is to be united with space, the fundamental laws of space must govern its construction."[11]

With the exception of her six earliest sculptures, which were influenced by suprematism and Russian constructivism,[12] all of Kobro's work from 1925 on is composed of open planes, orthogonal or curved. The intersection of these planes, according to the theory, renders space visible ("the division of space, the interruption of its continuity, the partial closing of one of its parts, all that renders it visible, plastic, for us, for space is by itself ungraspable and almost imperceptible").[13] These planes, whose division and articulation were determined according to a constant proportional system (the same one used by Strzeminski in his "architectonic" paintings), were conceived as materializations of the axes of the space of our experience: "The lines of space are continued in those of the sculpture";[14] or, "Each part of space which is not filled can be transformed into a sculptural shape."[15] But if Kobro had stopped here, nothing would have distinguished her work from constructivism in general, except for a rigor of mathematical specification (which has allowed the reconstruction of several lost works). The real inventiveness of her work lies in the two methods that she employed to prevent her sculptures from being perceived as figures in space, both based on an extreme syntactic disjunction.

The first is the use of polychromy to destroy the "optical unity" that would separate the sculpture from space; contrary to unist painting, unist sculpture must include the harshest contrasts possible (hence the use of primary colors—the only way to avoid chromatic harmonies, which would read as separate unities).[16] Contrasting the formal arrangement of the sculpture, the disposition of colors causes it to explode in three dimensions: not only are two sides of a single plane painted different colors, but each color is also distributed noncontiguously in the three dimensions of depth, width, and height. Strzeminski and Kobro's text precisely describes the works themselves:

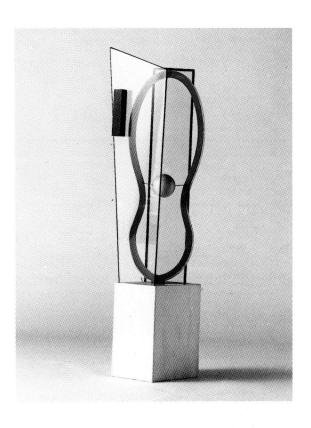

Abstract Sculpture 1, 1924.
Glass, metal, wood, colored.
72 x 17.5 x 15.5 cm.
Muzeum Sztuki, Lodz (Poland).

Because of their different color intensity, we cannot see all the various planes at once. . . . We do not unite adjacent colors but those who bear the same amount of energy. Thus we do not attempt to diversify the various forms by color but to lay a given color on various planes of the sculpture, perpendicular to one another and separated from the other color planes. . . . Each color creates within the sculpture new spatial forms, more and more numerous, which fit into each other. The spatial forms, related by the given common color, hinge and create many "corridors" which link them together and with the exterior space. . . . We have thus a system of spatial forms created by color. This system is analogous to the system of forms of the sculpture itself [prior to the application of color], with one important fact however: both systems do not overlap. . . . In this manner the extreme diversity of spatial partitions is emphasized in unist sculpture: they are independent from one and other and yet create through their connections an incalculable diversity of links between the sculpture and space. The arrangement of the sculpture's forms determines intersections which make space concrete and "corridors" which give to the sculpture the internal unity of the spatial phenomenon, linking it to space. The same happens for each color used.[17]

Yve-Alain Bois

True, Kobro made few polychrome sculptures (if the number of surviving works are any indication). But this system of optical disjunction is so effective in her work—in, for example, *Space Composition 4* (1929), one of her masterpieces and in my opinion one of the most extraordinary works of twentieth-century sculpture—because she grafted it onto another disjunctive principle used to greatest advantage in her white sculptures such as *Space Composition 5* (1929–30), another highly successful work. This second method (to which the color syntax is analogous) takes into account explicitly, perhaps for the first time in the history of sculpture, the duration of aesthetic experience. In unist theory, sculpture, unlike painting, mobilizes time:

> The spatio-temporality of the work of art is related to its variability. We call spatio-temporal the spatial changes produced in time. Those variations are functions of the third dimension, of depth which, although momentarily hidden, nevertheless reveals its existence while transforming the appearance of the work of art, the appearance of each form, in creating variability; when the spectator moves certain forms present themselves, other hide: the perception of these forms changes constantly.[18]

Wanting to stage the "transformation of depth into breadth," to render visible that invisible object which is depth ("wherever we stand to observe the work of art, depth is always hidden from us"), to solicit the spectator's movement, Kobro made sculptures in which no elevation can be inferred from any other. As we circulate around her best sculptures, what was negative (empty) becomes positive (full), what was line becomes plane or point, what was straight becomes curved, what was wide becomes narrow. An entire stream-of-consciousness novel would be necessary to describe the transformations that occur as we circulate around the two works mentioned above. While her theory participates in the constructivist ideology of transparency, Kobro's sculptural practice undermines that ideology, as David Smith would later in using the same disjunctive language.[19] Rather than presupposing the existence of a generative core or spine, the rationality of which would be immediately intelligible (an image of our clear consciousness, to refer again to Rosalind Krauss's analysis of constructivism), these sculptures have the opacity of material objects, whose space they cohabit (the base has been eliminated). But unlike objects whose meanings are discovered through use, Kobro's sculptures treat our experience in the world abstractly—without finality. Although we can apprehend them physically (measuring their variability as we move around them), neither the naked eye nor the intellect is sufficient to comprehend them. The philosophical foundation of unism, albeit implicit, was phenomenology, as it would later be for minimalism, this time explicitly: "The form of existence produces the form of consciousness."[20]

Notes:

This text is excerpted from "Strzeminski and Kobro: In Search of Motivation" (1984), reprinted in *Painting as Model* (Cambridge: MIT Press, 1990).

1. Frank Stella, in Bruce Glaser, "Questions to Stella and Judd," 1966, reprinted in Gregory Battcock, *Minimal Art* (New York: Dutton, 1968), 149.
2. Strzeminski and Kobro, "La composition de l'espace. Les calculs du rythme spatio-temporel" ("Composition of Space. Calculations of Spatiotemporal Rhythm"), in Wladyslaw Strzeminski and Katarzyna Kobro, *L'espace uniste*, ed. and trans. Antoine Baudin and Pierre-Maxime Jedryka (Lausanne: L'Age d'Homme, 1977), 86.
3. Ibid., 87.
4. Ibid., 85.

5. Ibid., 97.

6. Strzeminski, "Modern Art in Poland," in *L'espace uniste,* 149. For Rosalind Krauss's analysis of the "logic of the monument," see "Sculpture in the Expanded Field" (1978), in *The Originality of the Avant-Garde and Other Modernist Myths* (Cambridge: MIT Press, 1985), 279–80.

7. Strzeminski and Kobro, "Composition of Space," 106.

8. Rosalind Krauss, *Passages in Modern Sculpture* (New York: Viking, 1977), 56–67. Krauss's vision of constructivism is somewhat partial, for she takes the work of Naum Gabo as the essential model (Rodchenko's wood sculptures of 1921, whose additive structure is very close to that of Carl Andre's minimalist works of the late 1950s, could in no way be reduced to Gabo's "transparent" diagram).

9. Strzeminski and Kobro, "Composition of Space," 104.

10. "A summary analysis of the notion of weight is enough to reveal all the dynamism it contains." Ibid., 103.

11. Ibid., 102.

12. To my knowledge, only one of these early sculptures survives, but the team of Polish scholars working on unism at the Muzeum Sztuki in Lodz have been able to reconstruct another four from photographs, largely thanks to Kobro's rigorous system of proportions. The first, not reconstructed, is a dense, quasi-cubist conglomerate of heteroclite objects and materials made in 1920, when Kobro and Strzeminski were living in Russia. The second, *Suspended Sculpture 1* (1921, reconstructed in 1972), looks likes the translation into space of a painting by Malevich; the third, *Suspended Sculpture 2* (1921–22, reconstructed in 1971), reflects the aesthetics of the Obmokhu group and resembles both a work by Medunetsky in the collection of the Yale University Art Gallery and Rodchenko's hanging sculptures (all works exhibited at the third Obmokhu exhibition in Moscow in May 1921). *Abstract Sculptures 1, 2, and 3* (all from 1924, the first one preserved, the last two reconstructed in 1972) are related to Naum Gabo's "transparent" constructivism, which has been analyzed by Rosalind Krauss (see note 8). Kobro's real genius did not appear until 1925, with *Space Sculpture.*

Three things are worth noting here, concerning the relationship of Kobro's art to the production of the Obmokhu group:

1. In his "Notes on Russian Art" (1922), Strzeminski describes this relationship as that of a fellow-wanderer: "Close to them we find the most talented of these young artists, Kobro, whose suprematist sculptures are a phenomenon of European importance. Her works represent a true breakthrough, the conquest of still virginal values; they do not imitate Malevich's work but are parallel to it." *L'espace uniste,* 50.

2. In their "Composition of Space," Strzeminski and Kobro reproduce a work by Medunetsky. The work, now lost, is visible in one of the two photographs of the Obmokhu show mentioned above; see Christina Lodder, *Russian Constructivism* (New Haven: Yale University Press, 1983), 66. (Lodder labels this work *a* on the photograph.)

3. The elements combined in *Suspended Sculpture 2* are in fact tools, as if Kobro's only answer to the productivist position advocated at the time (but not yet put into practice) by some members of the Obmokhu group was an aestheticization of labor.

Despite Kobro's obvious ties with this group, one should not overestimate its impact on her work and imagine her a follower: she seems rather to have been open to the various trends of the Russian avant-garde, without any dogmatism. This explains, for example, why Strzeminski calls her work suprematist (before Kobro left Russia with Strzeminski, in 1922, she had been a member of the Smolensk branch of Unovis, the organization founded by Malevich), while according to Janusz Zagrodzki she might also have studied with Tatlin at the Moscow Free State Artistic Studio in 1919 (*Katarzyna Kobro—i kompozycja przestrzeni* [Warsaw: Panstwowe Wydawnitcwo Naukowe, 1984], 31).

13. Strzeminski and Kobro, "Composition in Space," 105.

14. Ibid., 104.

15. Ibid., 87.

16. Ibid., 109.

17. Ibid., 107–8.

18. Ibid., 115.

19. Krauss, *Passages in Modern Sculpture,* 147–73.

20. Strzeminski, "B=2; to read," 1924, translated in *Constructivism in Poland 1923–1936* (Essen: Museum Folwang, and Otterloo: Rijksmuseum Kröller-Müller, 1973), 81. Of course, Strzeminski could not have read Husserl; I am just underlining a striking similarity.

Temporary studio for the project of "Café Aubette" (1926-27),
placed at the disposal of Sophie Taeuber-Arp by the Horn, 9 Place Kléber,
Strasbourg.

Sophie Taeuber-Arp against Greatness

Yve-Alain Bois

Why is so little tribute paid, in standard accounts of twentieth-century art, to the maker of works as beautiful and intelligent as *Relief rectangulaire, Cercles découpés, Cônes surgissants*, with its cut-out background and menacingly protruding elements, or the painting entitled *Cercles mouvementés*, whose play on regularity and irregularity was so brilliantly analyzed long ago (in 1943) by Max Bill?

The ready-made answer—that Sophie Taeuber-Arp had to live her too-short life in the shadow of a much more famous husband, the sculptor Jean (or Hans) Arp, and was thus a typical victim of patriarchy—does not satisfy me. By all accounts Taeuber-Arp was "modest" in character, but she is also known to have been quite forthcoming: she was an excellent dancer, for example (to the point that she considered a professional career), and she played a stellar role in numerous dada performances. She conducted her career quite independently from Arp, was active in areas far removed from his concerns (puppet theater, textile and furniture design, architecture, pedagogy, editing), and it is obvious that in their collaborative work (from the duo-collages of 1918 to the duo-drawings of 1939) she never felt herself—nor, for that matter, was she ever felt—to be a lesser half of the pair. Furthermore, Arp was never tired of promoting her work, especially after her death, nor of underlining what he owed to it, not only in his writings but also in life: attentive visitors to Arp's studio in Meudon were invariably shown, almost as a reward, a good number of Taeuber-Arp's paintings and reliefs.[1] In short, it would be wrong, but for the tragic and absurd accident of her death by asphyxia at fifty-four, to posit her as a victim.

I would suggest instead that, if anything, her reputation has suffered from too much piety, in part enhanced by the tragic death. Leaving aside Bill's essay, the Taeuber-Arp literature divides for the most part into two categories: on the one hand, poignant memoirs by her friends (Georg Schmidt, Gabrielle Buffet-Picabia, Wassily Kandinsky, Emmy Ball-Hennings, Camille Bryen, among others), often written shortly after her death, and on the other hand, art historical studies at pains to reconcile the various threads of her extremely diverse production.[2] No value judgment seems ever to have been allowed: first mourning forbade it, then the sheer necessity to document her work transmuted into a general desire to present it as that of a "universal" artist, similarly able in any field and successful in all her endeavors.

This was the wrong tactic: appraising all things identically is not much better in the end than ignoring them altogether; the lack of differentiation that results from unreserved applause, no matter how well intentioned, is not far from mere indifference. Arp sensed as much when he urged Hugo Weber, compiler of the succinct (and so far, only) catalogue of

413

Taeuber-Arp's oeuvre, to leave aside her forays into "applied arts." He felt that, given the formal similarity between her textiles and some of her paintings and reliefs, her art would be read as a simple extension of principles of design into the realm of "fine" art.[3] To be sure, one cannot but notice the emancipatory role that the textiles played in Taeuber-Arp's discovery of abstraction (enhanced, from 1916 on, by her teaching of this craft at the Kunstgewerbeschule in Zurich). She liked to challenge the hierarchy between "applied" and "fine" art: not only did she devote equal attention to both, seemingly as engaged in embroidering a pillowcase or a purse as in making a painting, but she also deliberately confused the issue (for example, in using almost identical compositions for her decorative frescoes in the Café Aubette in Strasbourg—her most ambitious collaborative enterprise, with Arp and Theo van Doesburg— and for a series of highly colored reliefs, realized at the same time, which she invariably called *Composition Aubette*). She was evidently an extremely talented craftsperson; yet, though she might have approved of it, there is a double danger in measuring all her activities with the same yardstick. A notion such as "decoration," imported into the domain of her independent work, becomes the great leveler, exonerating her mediocre paintings (there are quite a few) while diminishing the scope of her real inventions. There is little glory in designing an all-over motif for a tapestry, for example, but the same gesture is of major historical significance if it concerns a picture.

But "glory" and "major" are words that do not quite fit when dealing with Sophie Taeuber-Arp's achievement, and this may be what is lying at the core of most writers' embarrassment about it. What if she had found glory and "majorness" repulsive? What if she had seen heroism, in its phallocratic bravado, as that which her art should try to undercut? (After all, it was under the antimilitarist spell of dada that she emerged as an artist during World War I.) Kandinsky, though himself more prone to unleash vociferous canvases, gently compared the general tone of Taeuber-Arp's work to a whisper, adding (perhaps thinking of his own production) that a murmuring voice is often more persuasive than a loud one.[4] What if she had tried to make effectively "minor" art?

I used a similar phrase in a discussion of Ad Reinhardt's painting, both to underline what distinguishes his aesthetic from that of the abstract expressionist artists with whom he is usually associated and to account for the lack of interest of a critic like Clement Greenberg in his work. I added that the term "minor" was inappropriate, but that the impossibility of finding an antonym for "major" devoid of deprecating connotations demonstrates the hold that the aesthetic of heroism has on our culture. This is as valid with regard to Taeuber-Arp's work as it was with Reinhardt's. If I am drawn to such a comparison, however, it is because in discussing Reinhardt's work I offered this quote from Greenberg's archrival G. L. K. Morris: "It was interesting to hear Arp mention this a few months ago: 'I don't want to be great—there are too many forces throughout the world today that are *great*.' This was not spoken in modesty; it merely represents a new relation between the artist and his work." Although Arp's statement was directed at his own endeavor, I think it is not unlikely that he had his recently deceased wife in mind. (Morris's article dates from June 1948; Taeuber-Arp died in January 1943.)[5]

Morris's "this was not spoken in modesty" is important here, for the acknowledged "modesty" of Sophie Taeuber-Arp blinded her friends and admirers to the originality of her best work (just as it provided them with an explanation of what they saw as her lack of desire to differentiate her art from her craft activities). In certain ways, nothing is more difficult than attempting to be "minor," nothing more ambitious, for nothing involves a greater risk of being misunderstood. Reinhardt certainly knew this, and it is not by chance that he shared with her an interest in what I would call the noncompositional (which is different in tone from the anticompositional: it is quieter).[6]

Left: Ascona, ca. 1925.

Right: Sophie Taeuber-Arp
dancing in a costume
designed by Hans Arp at
the opening party of
"Galerie Dada" in Zürich
(March 23, 1916).

One has to distinguish, of course, between two modes of being minor: the involuntary (Gleizes and Metzinger were minor cubists in this sense) and what I would label, for want of a better word, the programmatic. The first is common (often simply a failed attempt at greatness): not everyone can be Picasso. The second is much rarer (and particularly difficult to realize for the simple reason that, if the affirmation of the "program" itself becomes too forceful, it tips into "majorness"). It is to such a programmatic "minorness" that I attach Taeuber-Arp's best inventions. Her lesser works often fall into the involuntary minor category: it is impossible for me to see what Hugo Weber called her "Pompeii" series (1926) or her "constructive abstractions" (1927–28), for example, as anything but unsuccessful efforts to tame down abstraction with a dash of art deco figurative stylization; and many of her abstract paintings, particularly in the early thirties, perfectly illustrate the type of academic European postcubism that Frank Stella later attacked under the label of "relational art."[7]

Although I am far from pretending that the following choice is enough to summarize Taeuber-Arp's artistic accomplishment, I would like to concentrate on several key moments of her production that epitomize for me her unique position in the development of twentieth-century art.

1. The duo-collages of 1918. Realized in collaboration with Arp, these regular grids are to be counted among the earliest noncompositional works ever, preceding by several months Mondrian's series of modular paintings dating from 1918–19 and going further than the Dutch artist in the search for impersonality that was prevalent at the time: commenting later on these collages, Arp pointed to their introduction of a certain degree of chance in the color distribution, and the mechanical (nonautographic) procedure of cutting colored paper with scissors. Yet a certain lack of purposefulness in this demotion of authorial choice, noticeable in the arbitrary subdivision of certain modular units or the sudden use of a differently textured paper for others, prevents the duo-collages from being on a par with other works such as Delaunay's famous *Disk* of 1913–14, Malevich's *Black Square* of 1915, Duchamp's "unassisted" readymades (the 1914 *Bottlerack,* for example), or Rodchenko's *Monochrome Triptych* and modular sculptures of 1921. One could say that these last works were deliberately anticompositional: the duo-collages did not carry such a high-voltage message.[8] They resemble the first noncompositional works ever, Balla's various *compenetrazioni iridescenti* of 1912, in that they were conceived as private experiments. (According to Arp, Taeuber-Arp at first did not wish to exhibit them.)

415

 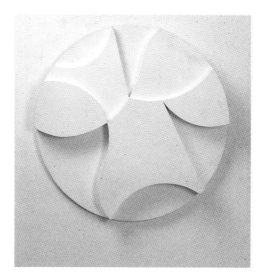

Left: Composit:
dans un cercle
blanc (Composi:
in a White
Circle), 1936.
Relief, painted
wood.
49 cm. diameter
x 4 cm.

Right: Relief
circulaire en
trois coupes
(Circular Relie
in Three Layers
1936.
Painted wood.
60 cm. diameter
x 6 cm.

Courtesy Stiftu
Hans Arp und
Sophie Taeuber-
e.V., Rolandsec
Germany.
Photo: Fotostud
Wolfgang Morell

2. The Aubette low reliefs of 1927–28. Although their motif is similar to that of the Aubette frescoes, its stark modularity is far more conspicuous once transposed into the independent realm of easel painting (relief). However, it takes some effort to perceive them as modular. They consist of brightly painted rectangles of thin cardboard glued on a white support. Except for a white margin surrounding the overall pattern, the "ground" itself is entirely regulated by the module and thus loses its character as ground. But it only loses this character here and there, inconsistently: a white unit interrupting a field of colored ones is not perceived as ground, nor is a similar hole made by two contiguous white units, but what about a continuous white field consisting of nine such units, or thirty-six? Its effect depends entirely on the distribution of the neighboring areas. Some areas display a strictly binary opposition of "negative" and "positive" units (as in a chessboard), but in general conglomerates are markedly unequal so as to destroy any perceptive certainty. One of Taeuber-Arp's most cherished strategies is obviously that of the greatest diversity within utter regularity.

3. The "multispace" paintings of 1932–39. These are among Taeuber-Arp's most intriguing works: they use the syntax of the "relational works" of the same period while undermining it. The canvas is divided into four, six, or twelve equal areas, usually square, each being treated as a potentially independent composition. The ground of each zone is of a different color, but its composition acknowledges that of its contiguous zones—something like an abstract *cadavre exquis*.

4. The semi-irregular compositions with circles, or dots, of 1934 (the most celebrated, and rightly so, being *Cercles mouvementés*, mentioned above), followed by the more systematic high reliefs of 1936. Strict modularity is abolished, but it is always looming at the horizon. Or rather, one could say that regularity is affectionately teased but playfully frustrated. Various possible groupings constantly cancel one another: these works must be a nightmare for Gestalt psychologists. The best reliefs are those in which half circles are cut out from the periphery of the wooden ground, allowing the wall behind to enter the space of the work.

5. The tondo reliefs of 1937–38, sometimes polychrome (like *Envol*) but far more engaging when they are white on white (like *Relief circulaire en trois coupes*). As in the multispace canvases, the issue is once again that of contiguity and continuity: the two notions are antithetical, but Taeuber-Arp plays at undoing the opposition. The reliefs comprise several layers (often four), each the irregular cut-out portion of a disk. Their superimposition locks into

an elegant puzzle of illusionistic transparency, yet the possibility of an independent rotation of each layer is always implied. These works are highly compositional, but composition itself is given as transient.

6. The colored pencil drawings of curved lines dating from 1939–42.[9] The lines are agitated yet deprived of any sign of autographic expression: mechanical, textureless, evenly traced, each of a different color. Wormlike when seen individually (but that is almost impossible to achieve), these lines form spaghetti meshes so intricate that one quickly renounces the effort to entangle them. They can often be found in two different thicknesses in a single drawing, the thinner lines inducing an illusion of depth that gets undone when one begins to group the curves by color. Superimposition is the rule, and also near-parallel doubling. Almost never fulfilling a function of contour, close to being doodles yet carefully penciled in, Taeuber-Arp's lines harbor a sense of purposelessness while remaining sheer trajectories. Despite the industrial draftsmanship, these drawings are perhaps the first truly automatic ones in our century: unlike their surrealist antecedents, they never appeal to an unconscious reservoir of images in order to signify. Pure transit and pure transitivity.

Many other things could be singled out in Taeuber-Arp's voluminous oeuvre: I have no doubt that my selection will seem arbitrary to some, especially since, partly for reasons of space, it brackets out her work in fields other than painting and relief. I do not wish to dismiss the rest of her activity, though I admit to finding it less innovative. As a matter of principle, it seems to me that the major works of an artist have to be understood first, especially if they invent a way of forcefully being "minor."

NOTES:
1. Ellsworth Kelly told me how relieved he was that Arp was touched by his enthusiasm upon discovering of Taeuber-Arp's work at Meudon around 1950. Embarrassed by his own preference yet finding it difficult to hide, he was encouraged by Arp to express his admiration freely.
2. The first (and still most complete) monograph, beautifully designed by Max Bill, was edited by Georg Schmidt (*Sophie Taeuber-Arp* [Basel: Holbein Verlag, 1948]). It contains numerous memoirs by Taeuber-Arp's friends and the catalogue of her work by Hugo Weber. The only full-length study, as far as I know, is Margit Staber's *Taeuber-Arp* (Lausanne: Editions Rencontre, 1970). The most complete exhibition catalogue was jointly published by the Musée d'Art Moderne de la Ville de Paris and the Musée Cantonal des Beaux-Arts, Lausanne, in 1990. Rather than providing a general overview, the texts included in this catalogue consist of monographic studies of specific areas of Taeuber-Arp's production and activities (her "vertical-horizontal compositions," dance, puppet theater, the Aubette and her other interior "designs," pedagogy, textiles, the publication of the journal *Plastique*, and line drawings). Rather than synthetic, the approach is kaleidoscopic, but the effect is similar: the importance of her reliefs, for example, is utterly obliterated.
3. Information provided by Staber, *Taeuber-Arp*, 81.
4. Kandinsky, as quoted in Schmidt, *Sophie Taeuber-Arp*, 88.
5. On this episode and on the issue raised here, see Yve-Alain Bois, "The Limit of Almost," in *Ad Reinhardt* (New York: The Museum of Modern Art, 1991), 25.
6. Frank Stella's 1959 black paintings represent a case of anticomposition (rather than of noncomposition): the program was so assertive that the "minor" mode was transmuted into a "major" one. This might explain why this artist returned to a highly compositional manner shortly thereafter.
7. See Frank Stella as quoted in Bruce Glaser, "Questions to Stella and Judd" (1966), reprinted in Gregory Battcock, *Minimal Art* (New York: Dutton, 1968), 149.
8. Delaunay's case is enigmatic, to say the least: although he was aware of the radicalism of his *Disk* (calling it his *coup de poing*), it represents a unicum in his oeuvre and can possibly be regarded as a fluke. As for the duo-collages, see Christian Besson, "Les *Compositions verticales-horizontales* de Sophie Taeuber," in Schmidt, *Sophie Taeuber-Arp*, 35–41.
9. On the line drawings, see Agnieszka Lulinska, "Sous le signe de la ligne," in Schmidt, *Sophie Taeuber-Arp*, 113–19.

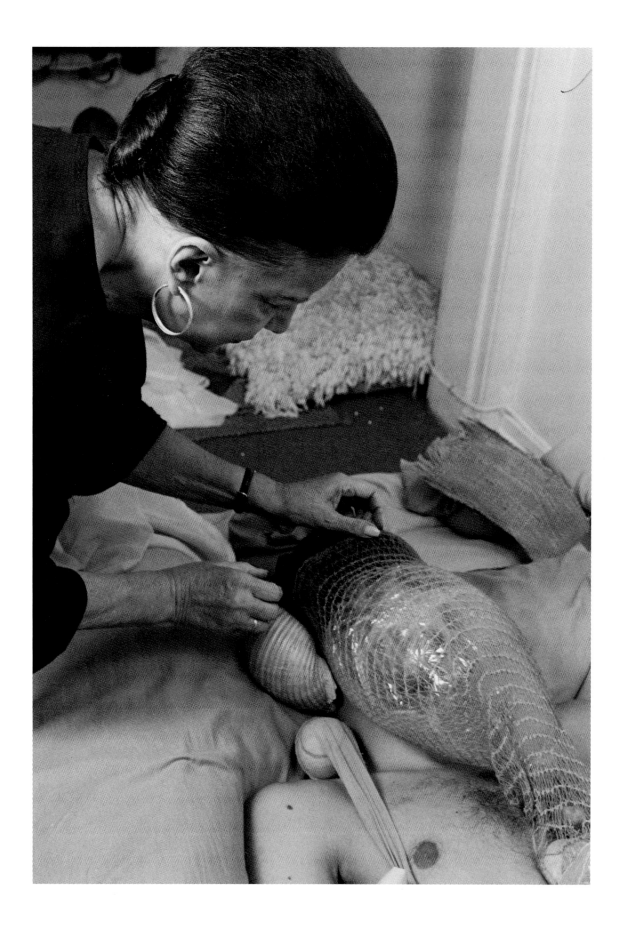

The Proposal of Lygia Clark

Guy Brett

The evolution of Lygia Clark's work is one of the most fascinating in recent cultural life. I think it is correct to speak broadly in terms of culture because the implications of Clark's research reach far beyond the limits of the art world. In chronological terms her work began in the sphere of art and ended in a practice that she termed "therapeutic": a form of experimental freedom, reparation, or "healing." This came about through a temporal evolution of compelling audacity and logic, but in another sense it was not a move from one sphere into another. Both remain simultaneously present, and both are changed. Just as it is valid to trace the evolution of Clark's work forward from her early geometric-concrete abstract art to her eventual therapeutic practice, it is equally valid to trace her work backward from the eventual therapy to a beginning in the aesthetic consideration of space and time.

Looking back from the position of the therapy, her use of relational objects working one-on-one with "patients" to help them through psychological crises, one can see that Clark arrived there by questioning the traditional subject/object, artistic/spectator relationships that constitute the world of "art" and all of its institutions in the West in the mid-twentieth century. Instead of an object in which her own expressivity was encoded, she proposed one that had no identity of its own. This object only took on meaning in relation to the participant's fantasy, and "only in the act of a relation established with the body" (Wanderley).

Clark believed that her work anticipated or accompanied a change in consciousness: that the whole cultural tradition in which we have projected our poetics outward onto a god figure or an artist figure was coming to an end, and that we would "rediscover our own poetics in ourselves." It is in this light that we must approach what is offered here: photographs of Clark's work and a selection of words written or spoken about it.

I believe the beginnings and ends of Lygia's evolution were in the relationship she made between the subjective, visceral flux, and the objective sense of order and clarity. Today it is easier to speak of subjectivity than of objectivity; indeed the very notion of objectivity is under suspicion. But a powerful element of the objective, from the firmly construed structure of her early *Bichos* onwards, persists through all Lygia's experiments and is important to her aesthetic (the way in which she remained an artist). This lies in the simplicity and brevity, I would say the wit, of her propositions. *Baba Antropofágica*, for instance, for all its intense immersion in subjectivity and "lived experience," its disturbing and destabilizing aspects, does not become something lugubrious or literal. It remains in the delicacy, the levity, of the metaphor of the cotton reel, a poetic structure, reminiscent of the magic of the conjurer's legerdemain.

—Guy Brett

But he who could
observe the beast within,
see his paradise of veins,
his dark humours

he who could
turn around the beast like
turning around a centripedal force,
he who could place his hand on the cold
cell which the beast delivers to torture.

He who could construct an amorous insomnia
in the belly of the beast,
he who could
awaken the beast
amid marks of horror, and awake with it
vigorously holy.

He who could unveil the beast in silence, and study with love
the innocence of the beast!

He who could
above all
lose himself
any moment in the power of the beast. . . .
He would have seen the first order of memory
which the beast inhabits.

—Walmir Ayala[1]

*Linear Egg
(Unidade series
1958.
Nitro-cellulose
paint on wood.
13 in. diameter
Collection of
David Medalla.*

Lygia Clark, the most universal we have produced in the field of the visual arts. . . .
Reviewing her development, the coherence and the intuition of her ideas immediately stand
out, a general intrinsic greatness which comes from inside: optimistic. Above all, the affirmative courage of her line of development impresses me. Therein lies, in my opinion, the link
with post-Mondrian development, the initiating link which, among us, initiated everything
new and universal to be done in this line of development. Lygia Clark did not limit herself to
understanding superficially the "geometrism" of Mondrian, but went back to the root of
Mondrian's thought, generating insight into his most important lines of action, and opening a
new way for art. Her primary comprehension is related to "space," as the fundamental element tackled by Mondrian, to which she gave a new meaning; this was the real matter of her
relationship with Mondrian—not "geometric form," as in the case of so many others. She
understood the meaning of Mondrian's great intuitions, not from outside but from inside, as a
living thing. Her need to "verticalize" space, to "break the frame," for example, are not
thought-out needs, or "interesting" as an experiment, but highly aesthetic and ethical needs,
surprisingly noble, placing her in relation to Mondrian like Cubism in relation to Cézanne.

I could even say that not since Mondrian has the "picture plane" been so "lived" as [in
Lygia Clark's *Unities* series of paintings]. . . . What matters here is not "geometry" or "form,"
or even viewpoints (as still happens in Albers), but spaces in counterpoint creating their own
time. This experience will remain valid as one of the most surprising in the creation of the

spatio-temporal sense in painting, with black not functioning as a "graphic colour" next to white, but an elemental colour/non-colour, the limit where light (white) and dark (black) meet and vitalise each other through space-time counterposition.

—Hélio Oiticica[2]

Out of these impressions and analogies there was born, one does not know how, probably, the name *Bicho* (beast). In many of them, because of their complexity and because of the super-posed structural parts, a kind of internal gear causes the generation of a plane in space, or a simple displacement of this, to have an immediate repercussion on the group, and all parts commence to move, as if of their own accord, in search of a new position. Sometimes the work moves about like an insect, or else the idea of a strange machine for constructing space is suggested. They are fabulous architectonic units which are designed in the air. The spatial articulation, which is extremely rich, shows us, from this or that angle of vision, from the other side of the polyhedric planes, spatial projections which cannot be transposed by unob-structed vision. . . .

The new art of Lygia Clark invites the subject-spectator to enter into a new relationship with the work, that is to say, with the object, so that the subject may share in the creation of the object, and this, transcending itself, may make him reach the fullness of his being.

—Mário Pedrosa[3]

Tout l'effort de Lygia Clark est, à l'inverse, de plonger dans le contradictoire, de l'absorber, de coller passionnément à ce qui l'exclut, de se maintenir à toute l'entropie cosmique, comme si elle jouait là, à travers son oeuvre, l'impossible fusion avec le monde dont elle sait bien, d'autre part, que tout homme est à la fin séparé par sa mort.

La complexité de cette oeuvre vient de ce que la dynamique en est double. La logique de la démarche, nourrie au départ de Mondrian, Malevich, Albers, est constamment élargie, perturbée par les coups de sang d'une impérieuse intuition organique. Lygia Clark vit son oeuvre comme une épreuve, un psychodrame où elle est tout entière engagée—sans que cette oeuvre perde pour autant les caractères rationnels d'une progression intellectuelle très logique.

—Jean Clay[4]

Lygia Clark arrives at sensuality in her work, not by the old-fashioned means of illustration but by the modern means of relations. She does not *recreate* more or less exact images of the visible world; she *creates* forms whose textures and metamorphoses generate continuous rhythms which are analogous to the sensuous rhythms we experience in life.

—David Medalla[5]

Several tables were covered with pebbles connected by small rubber bands tied together, one or two pebbles at each end. Lygia showed me what interested her in these precarious assem-blies, and how to "use" them. You draw a pebble or a group of pebbles toward you, and, at a given always unforeseeable moment, the mass at the other end of the elastic will follow, and will jump suddenly toward you as if moved by a spring, or will drag feebly like a slug. It was the interaction between different forces that moved Lygia (your own pulling, the extensibility of the elastic, and the weight of the pebbles), and the fact that the incommensurable action that results cannot fail to be perceived as a phenomenological metaphor for the relationship of your body with others in the world.

—Yve-Alain Bois[6]

Lygia Clark in her studio with *Tensions* in the foreground, Paris, 1966. Photo: Michael Desjardins.

We would wait for mother to go out and open the wardrobe door, worried about the noise the movement made, a loud creaking like the whining of a mare. Lygia would pull out the glove drawer and blow soul into them, concentrating on the forms they took. Her eyes, more open still, Clarked this experience into a work which consisted of wearing gloves made of different materials, sizes and types and trying to catch balls of different sizes and textures. After combining all the different variations, using large gloves to grasp little balls, Lygia would take off the glove and hold the ball normally and point out: "This rebirth of the tactile is experienced as joy, as if the person were reliving the discovery of his own touch."

—Sonia Lins[7]

Arriving home after midnight, uncles already home from their evening fun, we stood next to grandma whose insomnia kept her awake waiting for explanations. We were put under observation by older uncles who would glare when they saw us learning tango steps with the younger ones.

One sunless and beachless morning, taking advantage of the fact that Carlos was naked from the waist up, Lygia decided to transform him into a woman and was caught by the thick brows of older uncles who had stopped playing backgammon, as she tried to give his breasts volume by tying them with a string.

—Sonia Lins[8]

I remember that when Lygia arrived back in Brazil from Paris in the mid-1970s she said to me literally: "One of my greatest happinesses in being back in Brazil is to be able to walk in the streets of Copacabana and feel my body brushing other people's bodies." Because I live here (the USA) I understand why she said that. Here if by any chance you touch, without intention even, someone else's body in the streets, in a store, or even in your own house, it's more than likely you'll hear a strange "Excuse me," said in a sort of angry or bothered way. Every Brazilian I know complains about that. Another thing I remember Lygia said: "Paris was my concentration camp in terms of the body." She told me that the vision we have in Brazil that the French are very sensual is completely wrong. . . . I wonder if in some way Paris was not good for Lygia in helping her to confirm and highlight the intuitions she put into *Nostalgia do corpo*.

—Regina Vater[9]

Nostalgia do corpo. I think it is important not to transliterate this title. Nostalgia is so often in English considered to be a sort of fake memory, a description almost of the commodity fetishism of memory. In Latin languages, there is not so hierarchical a split between memory and nostalgia, and nostalgia has much to do with longing, with homesickness, with a displacement or absence which is centrifugally related to visceral and sensorial aspects of identity.

—Martha Fleming[10]

[Lygia Clark and Hélio Oiticica] produced their works, they asked their questions, outside the frame of the provincial v. international, archaic v. modern dilemmas, those polarities which have dominated Brazilian cultural processes up to today. What is most striking is the way in which the popular SUBSTRATUM in Brazilian society appears in their work, not as a theme—that's clear—but as a kind of strategy for being placed immediately, completely, in life, as a process, assigning to art the power to constitute social life which is, in my opinion, a very Brazilian cultural demand.

—Sônia Salzstein[11]

São Paulo, Sunday May 5, 1994. Lying on the floor with my eyes blindfolded, aware of a stirring of anonymous bodies around me, I don't know what is likely to happen. A complete loss of references, disquiet, apprehension. I give myself up to it. Parts of bodies, detached and without visible form, take on an autonomy and begin to act upon me: anonymous mouths are holding cotton-reels inside them, from which the thread, coated with saliva, is being noisily pulled by equally anonymous hands and allowed to drop upon my body. Covered little by little from head to foot with a mass of entangled threads, falling in an improvised pattern from the hands and mouths surrounding me, I gradually lose my fear of seeing my body-image, myself, dissolve: I begin to be that slobber-tangle. The sound of the reels unwinding in the mouths ceases. Then the hands delve into that sort of moist and warm mass which envelopes me, in order to remove it: some nervously pull it away in fistfuls, others delicately lift the threads with their fingertips as if they feared to see them unravel. And so it goes on until there is nothing left. My blindfold is removed. I return to the visible world. In the flux of the slobber-tangle a new body is molded, a new face, a new me.

I am dizzy. What happened to me? I feel compelled to confront the enigma. . . .

I think of the "body without organs," which Antonin Artaud referred to, and which was taken up again and developed by Gilles Deleuze and Félix Guattari at the same period when Lygia Clark was making her *Baba Antropofágica*. The body without organs is that nonformal matter of the flux-dribble, which I had experience of on a totally different plane to that on which my form is usually figured, whether subjectively or objectively. . . . I begin to see that the body without organs of the flux-dribble is a sort of reservoir of worlds—of modes of existence, bodies, me's. . . . It is an "outside of me" which, strangely, inhabits me and at the same time distinguishes me from myself—as Lygia says, "the inside is the outside. . . ." To come back to *Baba Antropofágica*: from this "outside" is produced a new "inside" me.

—Suely Rolnik[12]

[The Relational Object] may be described as small bags filled with earth, small grains, small styrofoam balls, water, air; small rounded pebbles enclosed in woven shopping bags; a net enclosing a stone at one end and a bag of air at the other end, etc.

The R.O.s proposed by Lygia Clark for use in setting up the relationship with a participant—unlike those seen today in contemporary art—are doubtless of a surprisingly formal simplicity. As one looks at them they are seen as a pellicle with which some elemental material flows. Their sensuousness as to texture, weight and temperature, the way the elements move inside, as well as the specificity of each one, makes them differ from one another. Simultaneously experienced they remind one of or retain a certain analogy to the body's primary surroundings. Primary because this analogy does not refer to the formal aspects of surroundings but to the pluri-sensorial qualities registered by the body. It is in the flow—between full and empty, the interchange of absence and presence, of inside and outside, of lightness and heaviness, of hot and cold—that objects acquire unity in this relationship of body/space/object/surroundings.

The relationship established between objects and body is not attained through the meaning of shape (visual image of the object) but through its sensorial image: something vague "lived" by the body. Not a sensorial outlining of shape nor some quality of the surface, but something that dilutes the notion of surface and makes the objects to be lived in an "imaginary inwardness of the body" where it finds signification. This is where the frontier is broken between body and object.

—Lula Wanderley[13]

Clothing-Body-Clothing: "the and the You," Rio de Janeiro, 1967. Touch dialogue between a man a: a woman, linked with a rubber umbilical cord, who each discov in the pockets the other's sui metaphorical suggestions of their own gende:

  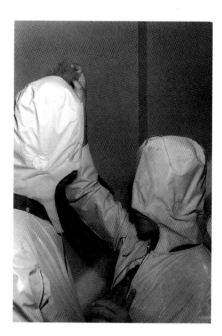

[Clark said] her work had nothing to do with any performance whatsoever nor with the offering on a platter, for the secondary benefit of a voyeur, of her fantasies and her impulses. It was impossible to "attend" one of these "courses," to retreat from it as a spectator. Anyone not wishing to take part in the great collective body fabricated there, each time according to a different rite, was sent packing. She saw her practice as a type of social electric shock, at the limits of psychodrama: it had no relation to the padded space of the museum or the gallery (no object), or with the exhibitionism of the avant-garde (she saw no interest in shocking the bourgeois).

—Yve-Alain Bois[14]

PRODUCING TRANSFORMATIONS: this formula permeated the work of the Brazilian artists Hélio Oiticica and Lygia Clark. It meant, in one aspect, that they engaged themselves radically in their own lives, living a process of permanent actualisation, through self-construction, deconstruction, and experimentation. Unlike body-artists, however, their main support was not their own bodies, but those of others. The pattern:

> YOU the spectator
> ME the artist

was sensorially reversed by them into the conceptual flux:

> YOUwillbecoME

not through a simple mirror-like inversion, but in the sense of moving "YOU" from the spectator's passive position to the active and singular role of being the subject of your own experience.

—Ricardo Basbaum[15]

NOTES:

1. Walmir Ayala, "'The Beasts': pour Lygia Clark, à propos de ses bêtes" (1961), trans. Sebastian Brett. Reprinted in *Signals* (London) 1, no. 7 (special issue on Lygia Clark) (May–July 1965): 5. *Signals,* edited by David Medalla, 1964–66, has been republished in facsimile (London: Institute of International Visual Art, 1995).
2. Hélio Oiticica, diary entry 31/8/65, in *Hélio Oiticica* (Rotterdam: Witte de With, 1992), 56.
3. Mário Pedrosa, "The Significance of Lygia Clark" (1960). Reprinted in *Signals* (London), 1, no. 7 (special issue on Lygia Clark) (May–July 1965): 5.
4. Jean Clay, "Lygia Clark: Fusion généralisée," *Rhobo* (Paris), no. 4 (c. 1966): 4.
5. David Medalla, "Participe présent: L'art de Lygia Clark," *Rhobo* (Paris), no. 4 (c. 1966): 16.
6. Yve-Alain Bois, "Lygia Clark: Introduction," *October* 69 (Summer 1994): 85.
7. Sonia Lins, Lygia Clark's sister, in *Artes,* her memoirs of their childhood, privately published (Rio de Janeiro, 1994).
8. Ibid.
9. Regina Vater, letter to Guy Brett, 8 September 1994.
10. Martha Fleming, letter to Guy Brett, 7 July 1994.
11. Sônia Salzstein, letter to Guy Brett, 16 November 1993.
12. Suely Rolnick, "Um singular estado de arte" ("Lygia Clark and the Singular State of Art without Art"), *Folha de São Paulo,* 4 December 1994, 6 (16).
13. Lula Wanderley, "Nostalgia do corpo," unpublished lecture, 1993.
14. Bois, "Lygia Clark: Introduction."
15. Ricardo Basbaum, "Clark & Oiticica," *Blast 4: Bioinformatica* (New York) (December 1994).

Eva Hesse's studio, 1966. Courtesy Robert Miller Gallery, New York.

Eva Hesse: On the Threshold of Illusions

William S. Wilson

Eva Hesse wrote in her notebook, October 28, 1960: "I will paint *against* every rule I or others have invisibly placed. Oh, how they penetrate throughout and all over." Violating rules gives one a good look at the edges—where rules can be broken down, where they might break down or just stop. At the edge of a system of rules one may be on one's own, but needing to do perhaps what one needs to do—to invent one's own rules, or to decide which rules to preserve and to extend those into the future.

For some artists, a world of objective external facts precedes investigation of the facts, and such facts can be imitated or represented, with verisimilitude or expressionist interpretation, in realistic pictures. But construction, or constructivism, pertains to objects constructed by the methods that investigate those objects. In this sense, as Michael Dummett writes, *constructs* or *constructivist objects* "did not exist for our statements to be true or false of before we carried out the investigations which brought them into being."[1] Etymologically, the *struct* of *construct* concretely suggests *to pile up*, and *con* suggests *with* or *together: to pile up with.*

The vocabulary of construction and investigation was familiar to Hesse. She wrote in her notebook, "The less pressures and strains that personally effect me the more relaxed and thoughtful can my powers be directed to constructive meaningful work" (September 9, 1958). "I have become a painter, working in isolation, constructively" (August 8, 1960). And even earlier, the eighteen-year-old Hesse was quoted in *Seventeen* magazine (September 1954): "For me being an artist means to see, to observe, to investigate." Her verb *to investigate* suggests that she is questioning conventional "facts," and that she might already think that some entities would not exist apart from the investigations that bring them into existence on a visual plane among other observables.

Hesse had studied art in one way or another at the High School of Industrial Arts, Pratt Institute of Design, Art Students' League, The Cooper Union, and the Yale School of Art and Architecture. At Yale her teacher, Josef Albers, had worked out a theoretical system of interactions of color, and since he taught about how to think with and about color, he taught how to think. He would argue in lectures, or prove in his paintings, that no one ideal "red" could exist and that conventional or verbal ideas of red can cause imprecisions in seeing. He would show that red *is* as red *does* in a context of interrelations of color where an apparently self-identical patch of red *becomes* lighter or darker and even something other than what one would call red. For Hesse, Albers's teaching had two aspects: (1) the interactions of colors for their own sake—which could not be the system for her, if only because it was someone else's system; and (2) the ability of the artist to construct colors that might not have been seen as individual colors before. The lesson she taught herself, inspired by Albers's teaching, was that to become able to construct a color, or an experience of color, is to become one who is able to construct. Hesse, who was trying to answer her questions of who she was and who she wanted to become, slowly brought some answers into focus through her work: she was becoming one who wanted to construct.

The most abstract lesson that one could learn from Albers was that if one could construct a color, then one *could construct,* and Hesse knew that she had already been doing that, which was why she had trouble with other people's rules and systems for construction. At Pratt Institute: "I waited until I was getting A's instead of C's and declared I was quitting." Hesse, after showing that she could succeed within a system by following its rules, would then position herself outside the system so that she could see its limits and edges, because at the edges and limits of rules was the place where she could begin. Because no rules exist outside a system of rules, or between two systems of rules, such ruleless anarchy is an anguish, yet she would preserve her position both *within* a set of rules and *without* a set of rules. Her further task, as she eluded anyone else's rules, would be to work without building a closed and seamless system of her own—to leave loose ends and rough edges—and so to work without developing her own set of rules or conventions or systems that might close over her in a totality.

Positioned at the edge of a system—wherever rules come to an end—Hesse would feel anxious and unhappy, sometimes declaring that she experienced only extremes and had never been happy. These are not statements that picture actual facts—they are statements that construct the position she needed to occupy in order to be able to think through her work. When she thought in extremes, the effect was to break up orderly transitions or continuities into oppositions and discontinuities. Then when she attached parts or left them unattached or combined parts in a match and/or mismatch that joined pieces in absurd juxtapositions, her motive was to call attention to edges and to how, when, and where edges fit together. If two pieces match and are joined seamlessly, they become one piece. But if nineteen pieces—seamless objects—are grouped, then what holds them together as a group? Are they with each other, or *almost with* each other?

The meaning of a work of art is a function of how parts are combined. If two pieces mismatch and the seams are visible, then the construction of the pieces into a whole has attention called to it, and that becomes thematic. Hesse's complaints in notebooks require interpretation because she lamented some of the very positions she had worked ingeniously to get herself into—where she could see the boundaries of the systems that threatened to govern her. Because she needed to be able to see that the systems *had* boundaries, she would move from the middle of any system to its edges, even if she sometimes had to make the edges herself by

Eva Hesse in group's photo by Peter Hujar, 196

breaking up or violating a system. Then she would become anxious because she would not be within a system that could govern her, or she would become anxious because a system *was* governing her. But Hesse became an artist because she had the courage of the anguish in her favored position—almost outside a worthy system that would have included her if she had agreed to its rules. She worked both *within* and *without*, straddling an edge, at an extreme where edges don't meet and merge. Extremes are what she needed to begin to become one who felt constructive.

A photograph of Hesse in a corner was made by Peter Hujar, who wanted to include the "young geniuses" in a historic documentation. Hesse, wary of being included in someone else's order yet miserable if she were excluded from the groups she thought she wanted to be included in, posed at the bottom on the left of the rectangle, clearly *with* Mike Todd. She is not at the governing center of the rectangle but, and characteristically, at the *edge* of the rectangle as well as at the edge of a group. She leans against Todd, who holds her in his arms without binding her; she is *with* him, but she isn't adhering to him.

In a letter to Sol LeWitt, Hesse wrote: "I am constantly at ends with the idea, myself and or what I am about" (March 18, 1965). The conventional expression is "at *odds* with the idea," but the truth is that she was constantly at *ends*, because "at ends" was where she could begin again to see thoughtfully how the ends of two things, or how two ends of one thing, were to be joined. At ends, she began again to begin to be able to see what happens to an object, or

Washer Table, 1967.
Rubber, wood, and metal.
Courtesy The LeWitt Collection.
Wadsworth Atheneum, Hartford,
Connecticut.

to a system, where it begins and ends, as when an edge is reached and so might be left as a raw edge, or joined to another edge, or two edges of something are wrapped around and adhered to each other. When she was "at ends with the idea," she became a woman who saw how to construct without setting herself up for disappointments or disillusionments.

Hesse decided to become an artist in junior high school but attended a high school of "industrial arts," not fine arts. Learning how to make window displays, she learned the differences between actual materials and salesmanly display of evanescent illusions. I think, given the disillusionments in her childhood, that even in high school, where she received her lowest grades in art, she was giving herself industrial-strength lessons in the connoisseurship of illusions. She learned, as one learns by doing, distinctions between any ordinary unfounded illusions and aesthetic illusions. Within the aesthetic, she taught herself to trust the sturdy aesthetic illusions that are so objective that one can return to them later, for something more that seems to have been there the whole time. Such an illusion is not mere subjective imagining projected like a movie upon a blank screen.

While Hesse was married to the sculptor Tom Doyle and was trying to paint in a disused factory in Germany, he suggested that she use some of the materials lying around rather than painting illusionistic pictures. She took a heavy metal screen that workers use to sift or sort materials and pushed lead wire, then rags soaked in plaster, through the holes. This metal screen displaced anything like a projection screen on which images are focused. With projected images, the spectator focuses not on the screen but within it or beyond its surface into an illusory or virtual space. A metal screen, which has no rules for its use in the visual arts, can scarcely evoke ethereal or idealist experiences or have imaginings projected onto it. Few disillusionments could await the spectator of such a found object reconstructed into art.

Hesse experimented with seriality and with systems, processes, procedures, and even mathematical operations, but she was not committed to any such systems except as places where she could work herself toward an edge. At those edges she could contemplate the transitions from separate parts to any wholeness. She could see how separate pieces could become parts of a system, as in the interdependencies of parts in an organic wholeness, and she could see that the pieces lost their separateness when they functioned within such a system. *Organic wholeness* would not do for her because she wanted to preserve in visibility the threshold where the parts begin to enter a system but have not done so completely.

Art is necessarily illusory, existing in consciousness, not in materials. Hesse wanted to evoke self-consciousness about the question whether something was or was not art. Because she was constructing aesthetic illusions but did not want to provide an opening through which disappointment or disillusionment might enter aesthetic experiences, she worked toward an art of nondeceptive illusions. The illusions in her art could not be further reduced without the materials becoming the mere undesignated materiality of unconstruction. So she constructed works of art at the thresholds of aesthetic illusions, where she would catch the poignancy and pathos of the very moment of transition into and out of illusion as illusion. Her late works are poised on the verge of an illusion of wholeness, or internally necessary form, or permanence, and never misrepresent the fact that even illusions worth preserving will perish.

By 1966, back in New York, she could see that the way that illusions exist in relation to materials is an expressive resource, and that what can be expressed is the relation of meanings and values to physical events. Which values exist? How do they exist? What are their relations to materials? Many of her artist friends were working against perceptual illusions, against literary meanings, against symbol and myth and allegory and metaphor (as they understood and/or misconstrued them), against idealisms, and against any power of language to describe, account for, or interpret mute visual experiences. Friends may have taught her much and helped to build her works, but no one had anything to teach her about how a visual construct might outwit both the verbal and the nonvisual, yet not evoke misleading or consoling visual illusions. She had worked herself toward the final edges or limits of the systems of art, and so brought herself to the questions of what a work of art is and of how she could construct a system that would work for her, but without extrapolating to a totality that would enclose and smother her. What possible system could this woman, who had excluded herself from so many systems that would have included her, propose as the way to go on with life?

The word *system*—which in its Greek origins meant "a composite whole"—is most concretely visualized as "to cause to stand together." Precisely. In her late work, she caused parts to stand together, but not to do much more than stand together. Her point of view on systems was her perspective on how parts are to be *with* each other. The task was to create a complete whole that was not a false image or example of completeness or of wholeness. Some parts lean against a wall, some lie on the floor or slump across each other, while others are tied together and suspended from exposed wires in the ceiling or secured to hooks on the wall. Because weight is a function of position in a gravitational field, weight is not concealed but used to hold parts together in a sketch for a system never to be completed. So Hesse worked to bring her own truth into an art without false magic or consoling enchantments or seductive bewitchments—an art that would not support false optimism or wishful thinking. She learned from her experiences to let materials hang, droop, or sag or to sit on the floor where they can sink no further. Thus she solved the problem of works of art and disappointment by building disappointments right into the art.

What then are the fewest relations among parts that show how they stand together—with each other—as the transition into or out of a composite visual system or visual wholeness? What is the least relation among parts that is a relation of a part being *with* other parts? It is the relation of *with*. Hesse wrote in her journal (March 30, 1961): "Want to be alone and/or only with one person I can love." Two weeks later she wrote—emphasis mine—"I have been *with* Tom Doyle the last 3 days." For Hesse, gradually, to exist was to *stand out and/or with*

Repetition Nineteen I, 1967. Aluminum screening, papier-maché, Elmer's glue, polyester resin, and Dutch Boy Diamond Gloss paint. Each of nineteen units: 23.2–26.7 x 16.5–23.2 cm. Collection Museum of Modern Art, New York. Gift of Mr. and Mrs. Murray Charash.

upon thresholds of the undecidable, uncertain, and uncompletable, with the courage to construct inconclusive experiences of visual moments in transition from meaningless materiality to—almost—*being together with in a whole.*

Hesse—sometimes with the help of the people who worked with her—took two ends of a piece of material and joined end with end, but not with invisible seams. If the ends were joined any less, they would not be with each other. If the ends were joined seamlessly, so that the seams would not show, then an end would not be seen as *with* another end—one would see a falsifying seamlessness. When a unit is seamless, like a bucket shape in *Repetition Nineteen,* then the units are placed apart from each other, just enough *with* each other to evoke the transition to a whole without completing the transition. Hesse avoided a seamless whole because it falsified relations of being *with*. Any whole, for her, is a rough construction that is stitched or glued, with parts placed near enough to each other to be with each other but not lost in each other. The construction then shows, for the sake of truth, how obviously or tentatively or awkwardly parts are joined *with* each other, however impermanently. Any smoother wholeness would mislead the spectator as to the means of producing wholeness and would falsify how wholeness and unity could be believable ideals in the Manhattan of 1968, 1969, and 1970.

So Hesse eventually defined wholeness in visual works in which if the parts were any less with each other, they would be too separate to be parts of a whole, and if the parts were any more with each other, they would render invisible or transparent the material means and physical methods of production. The spectator is not invited to wander into pictorial illusions or to calculate serial ideas, but confronts responsible participation in the visual construction of the physical event in the radical present—Now!—*here*, and *now*—where systems and rules don't seem to be in force yet. The experience is to be out of the reach of any rules and conventions and ideas that would come between the spectator-participant and an experience of being in direct visual touch with the parts that are held in antic arrangements *with* other parts.

Hesse's friendly acquaintance *with* Josef Albers as a teacher would provide an example of how to respond to loss and impermanence. Albers would describe constructions in glass he had made at the Bauhaus—sometimes using broken wine bottles to make stained-glass "paintings"—and tell how most of them had been destroyed. Yet he would shrug and smile, as though something about what had been destroyed was indestructible. The indestructible part is in construction itself, because construction necessarily affirms the materials, methods, and objects of construction. Those positive affirmations—which don't destroy anything that should have been preserved—are not themselves so easily destroyed.

Hesse's late sculptures are masterpieces. If they entail negations, the negations are in behalf of affirmations, as she continued to affirm even as she lay in a hospital bed. She wrote, within a few months of dying, "The lack of energy I have is contrasted by a psychic energy of rebirth. A will to start to live again, work again, be seen, love."

Hesse's choice to construct was her choice to invent opportunities for herself to affirm that which she could affirm without illusions from which one could be disillusioned. She found too much *with* difficult, and too much *without* difficult. She wrote to herself in 1964: "I survived, not happily but with determination, goals, and an idea of a better way. Now cope with it, no longer hide from the consequences but face them." As I have suggested, she was able to use some of the suffering in her life as part of her working method, and even when not suffering she moved herself to extremes where she could go against the edges of the rules, just so that she saw herself in the act of *coping with*. "Now cope with it" includes the *with* that she was working to define. Successfully *coping with* was a conduit for joy.

Being with this art now is not like being with Eva Hesse, but it is an experience of the moral values and truth that her sculptures make visually available. The most constructive affirmation I can make is to suggest that everything that happens between a spectator and her art continues the story of her life. That story begins: "Eva Hesse was born a Jew in Germany, January 11, 1936."

NOTES:
1. Michael Dummett,"Wittgenstein's Philosophy of Mathematics," in *Wittgenstein, The Philosophical Investigations: A Collection of Critical Essays*, ed. George Pitcher (Garden City, N.Y.: Anchor Books, 1966), 447.

Eva Hesse, c. 1968.
From Bill Barrette, *Eva Hesse: Sculpture*,
Timken Publishers, New York, 1989. Courtesy The Estate of Eva Hesse.

Untitled, from *Space Squared*, Providence 1975-76.
Black and white photograph. 5 7/8 x 5 3/4 in.
Courtesy Betty and George Woodman.

Vanishing Points:
The Photography of Francesca Woodman

Margaret Sundell

> I was shown a small book with pictures. Francesca Woodman: Born 1958. First photograph 1970. Suicide 1981. The points of a life like a chart, graphed on a line from A to B to C. But the pictures inscribed a geometry that was far more complex. Like tangents, they shot off, sometimes dipping back to meet the line but, in the end, always slipping beyond its strictures.

Helen Wilson, a painter and close friend of Francesca Woodman, calls her photographs "diary pictures." The term refers to their intimate scale (with the exception of a series of monumental blueprints, none exceed eight by ten inches and many are smaller still), but even more to their exceedingly personal sensibility. There are few close-ups; views of Woodman's face are rare, and she often used friends as models. Yet it is hard not to read these works, produced during Woodman's late teens and early twenties, as an ongoing series of self-portraits, a map of the artist's own evolution—both as a potential object of others' desire and as a creator of images.

Behind the search for self in Woodman's photographs, however, lies the insistent cultivation of a liminal space. Woodman's frequent use of serial images pushes the limits of the photographic frame, as does the voyeuristic complicity that many of her works establish with the viewer. In content, Woodman's photographs seek out and surpass the borders between subject and object, self and environment, and in sensibility they reveal a moment hovering precariously between adolescence and adulthood. The *House* series (1975–76) exemplifies this play of physical and psychic limits. Crouching beneath a fireplace, or blurring her body into a ghostly specter through overly long exposures, Woodman stages an elaborate game of hide-and-seek with the peeling walls and chipped floors of an abandoned dwelling. Like Charlotte Perkins's *The Yellow Wallpaper,* this series can be seen as a nightmare of femininity, the literal engulfing of a woman by her domestic role. But Woodman's childish attire—her flowered dress, white stockings, and black Mary Janes—recall a second work of fiction, *Alice in Wonderland.* In addition to the potentially feminist message, the series conveys a sense of "playing house," of the way a child feels at once overwhelmed and omnipotently invisible when infiltrating a place that adults once owned.

If Woodman's preoccupation is limits, the examination of them is consistently grounded in the body or, more precisely, in the act of bringing the body into relation with an outside element that destabilizes it and renders it liminal. Rosalind Krauss has defined Woodman's aesthetic strategy as "the subjectification of the objective language, the immediate instinct to register the formal within the 'support' of the body."[1] Ann Gabhart's statement that "fascinated

Untitled, New York, 1979-80.
Black and white photograph.
5 1/4 x 5 1/8 in.

*Untitled, from
Space Squared,*
Providence
1975-76.
Black and white
photograph.
5 1/4 x 5 1/8 i

Courtesy Betty
and George
Woodman.

by the sensuous and tactile qualities of objects, she always saw them in relation to the soft aloofness of flesh"[2] stands as a corollary to Krauss's emphasis on the objective language of visual form. In her photographs, Woodman sets the body first against the material surfaces of the world that surrounds it and then against the geometry that contains it. In *Space Squared* (1975–76), for example, space becomes both metaphor and fact of the body at its limits, as Woodman pushes herself against the confines of the glass case that encloses her. The material and the formal come together to comprise the external reality either inscribed onto Woodman's body or animated through association with her presence.

The examination of limits in Woodman's work finds its structure largely through the principle of analogy. In a photograph taken in 1980, a year after her graduation from the Rhode Island School of Design, Woodman stands in front of a dilapidated wall, facing away from the camera. She wears a vintage dress decorated with a leaf pattern, its back cut away to expose her flesh. Against her back she holds a fish skeleton that serves as a visual analogue to her spine, the design of the dress, and a horizontal band of wall where the plaster and paint have chipped away to reveal the surface's infrastructure. In this work's companion image, Woodman renders the connection between herself and the wall even more explicit, positioning the skeleton just above the horizontal band as, eyes half-closed, she dreamily leans into the architectural support of her surroundings.

Together these photographs establish a dynamic of interior to exterior—the skeleton of the wall to its plaster and paint, or the human skeleton to the flesh. This chain of associations; spine, skeleton, dress, wall, is established through a succinct series of analogies that, on a psychological level, creates a contiguity between Woodman and the world around her. With analogy, two things are brought together through a visual similarity; contiguity entails an actual physical contact, a border or meeting point between the two. Woodman's contiguity relates the individuation of the body to the seamlessness of its environment, the internal world of subjectivity to an external field that absorbs its uniqueness, so that, at a certain point, it becomes impossible definitively to separate self from other.

In Jacques Lacan's formulation of the Imaginary order, the mirror phase—the moment when the infant first recognizes her own image as such—marks the passage from an undifferentiated extension of the self in the world to the production of meaning through differentiation between subject and object. However, because this moment takes place before the infant has mastered her own physical functioning, the infant's apprehension of herself as an independent subject is based on a fundamental misrecognition. In a triangular fashion, the mirrored image, perceived as both autonomous and coherent, actually becomes an object of desire, a longing that splits the subject into two competing halves—the self as uncoordinated and indistinguishable and the self as victorious possessor of the image. The construction of identity established in the mirror phase contains a fundamental paradox: the image is equated with the subject's autonomy, yet the subject's existence as an image allows it to be apprehended as an object in the field of an other's vision. This implicit contradiction is often concretized either in the image of the infant propped upright before the mirror in its mother's arms or in an imaging of the mirror as a metaphor for the mother's eyes. However formulated, the desire for autonomy, which both motivates the ego and accounts for its fundamental rivalry, must be read through this initial tension between interdependence and independence.

As self-portrait, the photographic image reinscribes the salutary fiction of a unified ego (the photograph, like the mirror's plane, functions as the mechanism that enables self-representation). The self as photographic subject denotes the victorious possessor of this Imaginary unity, and the photographer symbolizes the self that lurks just beyond the fringes of representability. In *Camera Lucida,* Roland Barthes asserts that, unlike other art forms, the photograph can never function as an agent of transcendence because it inevitably bears the indexical trace of its lost object. "The Photograph," he states, "is violent: not because it shows violent things, but because on each occasion *it fills the sight by force,* and because in it nothing can be refused or transformed."[3] However, this intractable insistence is generated after the fact, from the vantage point of a viewer who was not present at the moment of the photograph's execution. For the photographer staging her own representation, the photograph may well offer the illusion of transformation or transcendence in its ability to wrest a static moment from the entropy of everyday life. Rather than a memento mori, the indexical imprint of the subject could be viewed as a narcissistic projection perhaps even more fundamental than the expressionistic brushstroke of an abstract painter. Hence, one might find an Imaginary moment of pleasure in self-objectification through the evocation of the ego's original identification with its own ideal, an experience of "peculiar satisfaction deriving from the integration of an original organic disarray"[4] that can be likened to the pleasure of seeing one's image consolidated and framed within photographic space.

Yet while there may be a fleeting identification with oneself as an image, the underlying structure of internalized mediation renders this moment highly unstable. Describing Woodman's work, curator Matthew Teitelbaum states that, "It is as if, by making herself a subject to be looked at, she makes herself disappear. Indeed, many of her photographs convey a tension between bodily presence and bodily absence. In works from the *Angel* series (1977) for example, or from the *Self-Deceit* series (1978), she often reaches out of the picture frame, spins out of focus, hides behind an object, or twists her body away from the viewer."[5] The fragility of self-recognition necessitates an endless restaging of the subject's autonomy. The tension and strength of Woodman's work lies in her ability to return again and again to this

precise point of instability, to simultaneously create and explode the fragile membrane that protects one's identity from being absorbed by its surroundings.

In "Mimicry and Legendary Psychasthenia," Roger Caillois examines the mechanism used by certain insects to produce a mimetic camouflage that blends their bodies into the environment that surrounds them. Caillois shows that such mimicry cannot be simply understood as a protective measure. Indeed, it can even lead to cannibalistic self-destruction as in the case of the phyllia who, browsing among themselves, actually mistake each other for leaves. Instead, Caillois locates a common root between biological and magical instances of mimicry and eventually links them to psychasthenia, a psychic disorder in which the individual is no longer able to distinguish between its interior and its environment. For Caillois, mimicry is "accurately defined as *an incantation fixed at its culminating point* and having caught the sorcerer in his own trap. . . . The search for the similar would seem to be a means, if not an intermediate stage. Indeed, the end would appear to be *assimilation to the surrounding*."[6] This "temptation by space," this giving over of oneself to the field of one's surroundings thus stands as the extreme but ultimate counterbalance to the narcissistic unity of the ego.

The mirror image affords a momentary haven of identification that prefigures the functioning of metaphor—to provide a stopping point of meaning that opposes the endless sliding of the signifier along a metonymic chain. Mimicry too functions as a metaphor and is similarly appealing in its seamlessness. In the act of self-portraiture, the camera's clicking shutter resounds like an incantation. But the "I am, I am, I am" of throwing images of oneself into the world can at any moment revert into its opposite, into the "I am not" of having given oneself over to a circulation in space that one no longer controls.

This process of simultaneous violation and abandonment of the self can be seen in a pair of photographs, taken in Rome during Woodman's academic year abroad. Both works are set against an old plaster wall on which broad arches of dripping color have been painted. In both, Woodman has streaked paint on her naked body to create an obvious link between herself and her surroundings. This connection is reinforced through Woodman's poses, which associate the curves of her body with the painted forms. In one work, Woodman twists backward in the lower left corner of the frame to face the viewer, creating a strong diagonal line with the arches behind her. The photograph's shallow depth of field brings the painted wall into focus, leaving the foreground—Woodman's face and forearm—in blurred shadow. More than the record of an individual, the distorted face seems like a mask of pain, its mouth open and its eyes empty and glazed. In black and white, the dark paint suggests blood. Woodman appears a wounded victim, the exterior of her body writhing, while its internal fluids splatter against the wall. But this destruction has no apparent agent. The violence seems to be a product of the image itself, its force suspended in the stasis of a moment caught endlessly between autonomy and immolation.

The physical vulnerability of Woodman's body to the space around it that is established in her individual photographs is thus echoed by the psychic vulnerability of allowing oneself to be constituted as an image. While the physical world contains environments as well as objects to confront, the formal realm speaks both to the composition within a frame and to the entire mechanism in photography through which an animate thing is transformed into an image. Krauss describes the action whereby a three-dimensional object is transcribed onto a two-dimensional surface as "giving oneself to the paper." But not only is the body submitted to a flattened surface, one's subjectivity is also imperiled in this movement from flesh to image.

A photograph from 1977–78, which makes use of Woodman's common trope of juxtaposing her body to the texture of its surroundings, provides perhaps the most striking illustration of this process. Shot in Rome, the image shows a paint-chipped wall divided horizontally in half, white on top and dark on bottom. With her hands pressed tightly to the wall and her face tilting outward toward the viewer, Woodman stands naked in the middle of the frame, trapped between the background and the picture plane. Across her groin—right at the point where the lower half of the wall begins—Woodman's body is smeared with a dark substance that resembles dirt or human excrement. The pressure of the body's pose seems in some way linked to the appearance of the dark substance on her flanks. The image invokes a single impulse that forces Woodman to the visual limits of the frame at the same time that it destroys the limit between the body's internal contents and its external shell.

For all the penetration of limits, Woodman's photographs ultimately lead the viewer to a perimeter that cannot be traversed. As a genre, the self-portrait seems to promise self-knowledge and mastery of one's image in the world. But if Woodman's photographs initially aim at knowing the self, they attest finally to the limits of such knowledge—or rather, to the knowledge that the self, no matter how often approached, is never fully captured by its representations. A picture from the series *I Stopped Playing the Piano* (1977), entitled *I Could No Longer Play I Could Not Play by Instinct,* makes this revelation startlingly clear. Woodman, chest bared and face cropped from the frame, wields a knife while a string of photo-booth self-portraits drips from her breast like blood. Echoing the self-consciousness of its title, the photograph presents the quest for self-knowledge as an act of mutilation that results not in the capturing of a "true" self but in the production of a never-ending chain of images.

NOTES:

I would like to thank Betty and George Woodman for supporting my interest in their daughter's work. I am also grateful to Rosalind Krauss and Mary Kelly for their comments on an earlier version of this essay, which appeared under the same title in *Documents,* no. 3 (Summer 1993).

1. Rosalind Krauss, "Problem Sets," in *Francesca Woodman: Photographic Work,* ed. Ann Gabhart (Wellesley, Mass.: Wellesley College Museum, 1986), 47.
2. Ann Gabhart, "Francesca Woodman 1958–1981," in *Francesca Woodman: Photographic Work,* 54.
3. Roland Barthes, *Camera Lucida,* trans. Richard Howard (New York: Farrar, Straus and Giroux, 1984), 91.
4. Jacques Lacan, *Ecrits* (Paris: Seuil, 1966), 21.
5. Matthew Teitelbaum, "Absent Bodies," exhib. brochure (Boston: Institute of Contemporary Art, 1992).
6. Roger Caillois, "Mimicry and Legendary Psychasthenia," trans. John Shepley, *October* 31 (Winter 1984).

On the Board, 1993.
Molded cement (wall object). 41 x 46 cm.
Courtesy of the artist.
Photo: Romulo Fialdini.

Anna Maria Maiolino: The Doing Hand

Paulo Venancio Filho

All of these objects bear the imprint of the hand. It is the hand that does: shapes, compacts, pinches, kneads, stretches. The doing hand; it is the mold. In general, everything that the hand accomplishes in everyday life tends to disappear without our being aware of it—even at the very moment in which we are acting. It acts, and we forget that which it touches, picks up, grasps, pushes, among so many other actions. In some way, these clay objects by Anna Maria Maiolino may very well represent the sum total of the daily actions that the hand performs obviously. They are concrete witnesses of the routine doings that customarily dissipate without leaving a record. In each of them, the time and action necessary for performance are present. They literally deserve the generic name that designates the art object: work.

In modern industrial society, repetition is associated with the social division of work and alienation. Repetitive work dominates individuals, rendering them unable to total their meaning. Their actions always remain disarticulated fragments. This universal situation tends to impregnate daily life too, making it more and more programmed and mechanical. Thus, we are frequently unaware of the hands and their actions. They seem to have acquired an independence that places them, in the ultimate instance, beyond consciousness. They become mere operative and specialized instruments. For example, we react with indignant surprise when we break something, as though it were an act of the hands' irresponsibility. Breaking something is no longer part of daily life. It is a lamentable failure in our chain of operations.

In some way, Anna Maria Maiolino's clay objects inversely imply the energy that erupts in the unmotivated act of breaking. Actions characterized by force, perhaps even excessive for routine acts, are vested in the compaction, in the substantiation of a series of repeated gestures in which the actions break with the equalized intensities of everyday routine. These compact forms result from the repetition of simple gestures that, though executed by one person, the artist, bear the presence of many, of the collective. They remind one of elementary and archaic tasks, extremely meaningful and very remote from today: the preparation of the constructive element and food—inaugural tasks and labors.

These products mark the instauration of a world, the separation between nature and culture. They arise from the possibilities of one and the same gesture, of one and the same operation, which can be readily transmitted, like the sounds of a language just beginning. Herein we find the original meaning of repetition. We could be in the presence of an anthropological experience or, rather, an experimental anthropological act, were it possible to relive those fundamental moments, not with the faculty of the intellect in its full measure but with simple

441

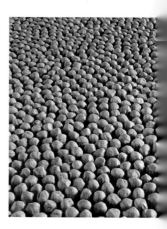

manual gestures, in the initial apprehension of matter and its meaningful transformation. Moments of amazement, of fulfillment and communication, of the construction of the artifact that distinguishes and humanizes us. An initial concept of the form of matter arises, a *clay concept,* concrete and tactile, instituted by ourselves and therefore distinct from nature. And also a form of language, an object language, *codicilli,*[1] material units of communication, of an interchange of meanings.

While these objects remind us also of the form of the constructive element, of food and of language, they identify the first desires for stability and fixation as well. They project an established collective, a community. Thus, they are not organic objects but, rather, vital objects. Repeated and produced to answer the appeal of many, of all without exception, of those of today and of those to come.

The community appeal that they anticipate implies the distribution of the object, in itself also a form of pedagogy. They transmit an immediate, incorporated knowledge. They are molds for actions vital to the community, offerings. Fundamentally collective, they transparently reveal themselves through a task that arouses one's tactile sense, to feel things with the hand: firmness, texture, roundness, weight, volume. Molded by the hand, the formless turns into a stabilized form. Another relation to the body appears at this instant. Perhaps the metaphor of the Creation from clay is appropriate here. In some ways these objects are also generated by the body—they owe their existence to the body. They are generated *in* the body.

A first glance might give the mistaken impression of a minimalist sensibility. Indeed, repetition is one of the structural procedures of minimalism. Both these works and minimalism intend to occupy real, rather than illusory, space. Certainly, these objects do not possess the industrial or urban scale that characterizes minimalism. On the contrary, they seem to belong to a preurban, traditional, community space, where manual work is dominant and the machine is absent. This suggests a culturally oriented reading, circumscribing the work within the peripheral and underdeveloped Third World. Indeed, this is the local situation of this work. But is this its perspective? The crisis of modern universality produced by pop art seems to have made the legitimacy and reality of autochthonous cultural values the order of the day, as if they perceived the emancipatory power of the modern project as a form of domination. To return to the preindustrial world and its forms of living and working would indicate a desire for liberation and the relativizing of universal values. I believe that nothing could be further from Maiolino's work. The search for preindustrial and premodern experiences harbors no utopian intent to disqualify contemporary life, but rather aims to show its unilateralness. Here lies the contemporaneity of these clay objects, apparently so archaic.

Many, 1995.
Molded clay.
Installation at
the Béguinage o.
Kortrijk
(Belgium).
Courtesy Kanaal
Art Foundation,
Kortrijk.

The experience and thought that they incorporate do not belong to a specific, localized culture; they express common, everyday, universal values. They are objects of an "intimate minimalism," in which the scale of the body and its actions still outweighs the urban scale of the metropolis and the modern means of communication. What count in Maiolino's world of objects are the contact, the proximity, the state of togetherness. Nothing in this contradicts the urban world; rather, it reveals one of its scales, just as the minimal reveals another.

In Maiolino's work, the state of togetherness is manifested through gesture. As in minimalism, her objects reveal a certain inexpressiveness, but one effected through contention or, more precisely, through concentration. These clay objects are not characterized by gesticulation in expansion. On the contrary, they are nuclei made compact by the accumulated force of the gesture, by the effort to contain expansion and dispersion: the gesture concentrated. One finds this in the work of Lucio Fontana. In his *Concetto spaziale*, Fontana too tried to break with illusory space: the pinpoint concentration of the incision in the canvas. Maiolino seeks a similar yet opposite way, not through the slashing and revealed gesture but through concentration, through successively introjecting the gesture into matter. The space, in this way, appears saturated to the maximum and exhausted: space saturated with space; gravid with space.

Now, as they appear, arranged on a flat surface, a table, Maiolino's objects show her community-spirited vocation even more, that of sharing. One could apply Pirandello's beautiful title, in modified form, which the artist gave to one of her works: "table for one, none, one hundred thousand."

Translated from the Portuguese by Esther Stearns d'Utra e Silva

NOTE:
1. Anthropologist André Leroi-Gourhan identifies the appearance of language with the making of the first utensils.

*ttle Rolls in
e Horizontal,
93.
lded plaster
all object).
x 130 cm.
irtesy of the
tist.
oto: Romulo
aldini.*

Installation at Chisenhale Gallery, London, 1993.
Courtesy of the artist and Micheline Szwajcer Gallery, Antwerp.

Ann Veronica Janssens: Images in Places

Marie-Ange Brayer

I mages are structured like a threshold."[1] We might extrapolate this quote from Georges Didi-Huberman referring to Ann Veronica Janssens's work, in which images are reabsorbed at the thresholds of perception between object, architecture, and space. These three terms are closely related. An object never exists on its own. Nor is there any kind of autonomous architecture; nor is there space as substratum. Rather, there is a working resonance, or responsiveness, among these three elements. The imposition of an object in space, which is peculiar to sculpture, disappears here in favor of a perceptive construction of the place and an activation of its formative conditions of both visibility and invisibility. In this regard, the processes of displaying things converge with those that make them vanish. And this is what happens when Janssens covers the baseboards of a room with mirrors or runs a false wooden molding across a ceiling. The work becomes part and parcel of the place, diffracting it and very slightly shifting its perception off center. At the same time, seeing is the equivalent of a physical understanding of architectonic space.

In 1990, at the Villa Gillet in Lyons, Janssens installed glass surfaces between the mirrors in one room. The glass, transparent but made opaque by the wall, distorted the analogical reflection of the mirrors and their metaphorical echo between interior and exterior. Outside the villa, she filled in half the stairway leading to this mansion with piles of stone blocks. The only partly passable stairway was thus transformed into parasitic architecture. Its progression became a plateau of perception, a horizontal platform leading one's gaze off into the surrounding space. By working with surfaces inside the villa, where the opacity of the walls reflected the windows, and by defining a volume of space outside, which fit into the concavity of the stairway, Janssens shifted the parameters of the place.

All of her works swerve, meaningfully, to the edge, but an edge that is not a limit or delimitation—rather an easily crossed threshold of perception, an opening toward a dialectic between the opaque and the transparent, interior and exterior, and the center and its edges. Janssens frequently resorts to materials such as glass, which stratifies space and alters and amplifies visibility, and aluminum foil, which diffracts and reflects space. These two materials develop a dialectic between interior and exterior, inflecting the perceptual parameters of space. She also uses gravity and the physical placement of blocks of concrete and bricks. Here, the piling constructs a place both fragmentary and empirical while rebalancing the verticality of the architecture with a horizontal expanse of perception. The architecture is reduced to nonfunctional subfoundations, which "lower" the perception of space to ground level.

In most of her works, the concrete blocks circumscribe a void. They convey the echo of the place in which they are put while setting up a constructive tension. In 1988, Janssens obstructed the space of the Galerie Inexistent in Antwerp by piling up concrete blocks, which the visitor could step over. The installation was at once obstacle and passage. Through the physical concretion of the blocks, one became aware of a new spatial materiality. At the exhibition "Intention and Rational Form," in Mol, Belgium, in 1987, a low wall of concrete blocks echoed the perimeter of the room at a three-foot distance. The viewer walked along beside this waist-high wall, jutting out over an empty central space. This division of space, expressing the emptiness in the midst of the architecture through the intermediate device of the low wall, gave rise to a circuit that referred the visitor to an ambiguous space, neither interior nor exterior. At the De Lege Ruimte Gallery in Bruges, in 1988, concrete blocks, again loosely arranged, formed a *U* at the gallery entrance, holding the space hostage and luring the visitor into a dead end. At the "Le Choix des femmes" ("Women's Choice") exhibition in Dijon in 1990, a low concrete wall faced a wall punctuated with windows, indicating the exterior lumi-

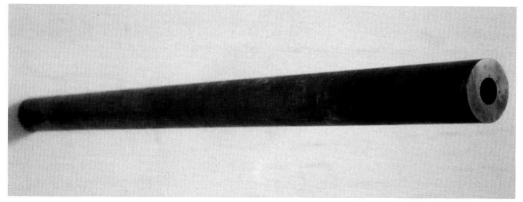

Installation at Chisenhale Gallery, London, 1993. Detail. Courtesy of the artist and Micheline Szwajcer Gallery, Antwerp.

nosity by way of its opaque finiteness. The piles of concrete blocks established a spacing between the place and its perception—an interval or junction between the within and the without. Just as at the Dhondt-Dhaenens Museum in Deurle in 1992, the concrete blocks are not, in effect, just blocks. As an unstructured mishmash, they serve no architectonic function. They remain fundamentally *materials* that give rise to a *construction* of space, which, in turn, does not comply with the rules of architecture. Moreover, the blocks construct an outline or plan rather than a volume, paradoxically expressing void rather than solid. They may form a whole, but they are never anything more than an assembly of elements. Piled up in two or three layers, the blocks stratify the perception of space. Just like the piles of sheets of glass, they play on the edge of the structure. Their porous matter, receptive to the exterior, also refers to the receptiveness of the glass: both materials are at once sensors and receivers. They are non-objects that merely designate a function of space and absorb or refract the luminosity.

At the Casa Frollo in Venice, in 1988, twenty-five sheets of glass were laid one on top of the other against a window sill, opposite the shimmering surface of the canal. The phosphorescence of the glass sheets transformed the perspectival intersecting plane of the window into pure phenomenality—a crystallization of light broken into a horizontal spread of permeable spaces. These sheets were neither planes nor volume but laminated thickness, a dimension of light, a "voluminosity" of light where interior and exterior merged. Each work thus has a transitive function, which makes the perception slide from a space on the edge of visibility,

446

intercepting a diffraction and reabsorbing light and shadow. In 1991, in a display case, two sheets of glass, cut in the middle, were placed on top of one another to create a concave volume filled with light. The resulting visual distortion fragmented and destabilized the space. These systems, in which space and light are presented almost in "liquid form," culminated in the cubic glass structures of 1992, where the combination of water, oil, and methanol crystallized, within a transparent cube, in an opaque spherical form, floating in watery space.

Above all, Janssens's work forms a field of perception, a perceptual formation without inscription or foundation. These cubes are "an implication of the void as a 'process,' otherwise put, as something that clearly upsets the volume."[2] Space becomes strained at the edges of a sheet of glass or a cube. It is also constructed as an aggregate. The bricks or concrete blocks are piled up empirically without forming a unitary volume (which would make them space-proof). Instead, a porosity is created between the material and the space, a structural permeability that incorporates in its process-oriented form the viewer's perception; one invariably sees oneself called into question. The object presented is thus never factual. It is never "fashioned," which would delimit it and hamper its dialectical relationship with the surrounding space. Instead of a volume, Janssens proposes surface layerings, stratifications of thickness or depth, and laminar cross sections of light. Against the solid she sets form as a hollow, intercalary space, the formation-in-progress of a new field of perception, proposals for surveying space or taking perceptual measurements of the place. As such, her works deploy other procedures for qualifying space, other processes involving the subjective stages of perception and seeing.

Some of Janssens's works may call to mind the formal, geometrically oriented propositions of Robert Morris or Larry Bell, through the recurrence of the cube, for example; they may even call to mind Carl Andre in their use of the horizontal, but they are independent of the minimalist legacy in the sense that Janssens's work never *occupies* space and is never *included* in it. Rather, it questions the formative conditions of space, works with it, and reformulates its conditions of visibility in a balancing movement between appearance and disappearance.

Mallarmé wrote: "Nothing will have taken place save the place."[3] In May 1995, in the Box exhibition space run by the Expositions du Palais des Beaux-Arts in Brussels, when Janssens filled the display case facing the street with light. On the ground, between a white box six feet high and thirteen feet long, made by Richard Venlet, and the wall of glass, some two feet from this box, she placed mirrors that intercepted the light outside and diffused it inside the white-painted construction. Once again, she was operating on the edge, in the interstice, lending a new operational quality to this intercalary space, where the mirrors functioned as light-transmitting agents, thus diffracting the unitary perception of the box in space. This reabsorption of the work in space attests to the indexical presence of all of Janssens's works. The mirrors are put there not as objects but as conveyors of a reconversion of the place's conditions of visibility. At the Creux d'Enfer contemporary art center in Thiers, France, she covered part of the rough stone wall of one room with a square of aluminum foil. This aluminum surface was actually molded in the raw material of the wall, giving it a particular iridescence, at once physically tangible and intangible in its shiny, epidermislike detachment. Janssens's work is not a supplement of factual presence but rather the constitution of a thinner-than-thin visibility, which calls into question or offsets the perception of the place. The aluminum foil here worked as a tenuous arrangement for making space present, which in some way enabled absence to take place. At issue is getting the eye to travel about in a nonformalist space, one not occupied by a form but traversed by a perceptive formulation of the place. The reflectiveness of these works, in the actual as well as the figurative sense, prohibits associations with geometric ideals because they interact with the tectonics of space.

This construction of form in space recurs in the work produced for the São Paulo Biennial in 1994. Here Janssens salvaged bricks, which she covered with aluminum foil, to construct a house with incomplete walls. A strip of adhesive paper affixed three feet from the ceiling announced in Portuguese: "Leisure and survival." The salvaged bricks heightened the impression of a precarious dwelling with shaky foundations, unfailingly calling to mind the never-ending rebuilding and destruction of the local *favelas*. A pile of bricks, left just so, which were not used for the construction of this house, was set against a wall. The aluminum house was presented in a strange temporal frame: were these the ruins of something destroyed, traces of a landslide or alternatively of a building under construction, where the work had suddenly stopped? If the aluminum-covered bricks lent a certain unreal quality to the construction, they also transformed the architectonics into an system of seeing at once absorbing and reflecting space and light. The bricks in the crumpled foil were so many small nuclei, exploded and banked up with light, diffracting in space. The house was totally open to the surrounding space. Likewise, this foundationless house circumscribed an empty space, developing an interplay between interior and exterior, also indicated in the dichotomy between "leisure" and "survival" on the adhesive paper running around the picture rail. Possibly the void, and the gutting or hollowing out, gnaws away at the walls of this house, rendering all volumes lifeless and decrepit because here form is always a method for constructing space. Whereas "minimalist research has to do with the factual research of sculpture, in such a way that architecture would be a habitable sculpture" and "architecture is taken into account not for its monumental value, but in its existence as a limit,"[4] Janssens posits an act of spatial construction that turns the work into a procedural form, and hence one that is never completed.

This incompletion takes on another dimension in Janssens's acoustic works. The first of these was made for "Zoersel 93" in Belgium, where in the gardens you could hear a sequence of birdsong. At the Kanaal Art Foundation in Kortrijk, Belgium, Janssens filled a room with explosive sound effects. The visitor did not enter the room but picked up the violent detonations from outside. This occupation by sound produced a physical grasp of the space, whose limits exploded in a virtual way, under the almost tactile thrust of the sound. This work united the tactile with the acoustic. The acoustic upheavals gave rise to a foundationless work, not inscribed in space but rather unfolded on several perceptual levels. In the old Tobacco Warehouses in Tourcoing, France, Janssens came up against imposing architecture: a complex structure of smallish girders, once designed for drying tobacco, divided the space into cubic modules. The visitor coming upon the exhibition was drawn in by a soundtrack, mainly made up of human breathing, which spatialized the sound in the exhibition space. The exhalations and puffing of the mouth lent the place a disquieting organic dimension. Drawn in and up by this puffing and blowing, toward the timberwork, visitors lost their own points of reference in their grasp of the space. In this way, the process-oriented form of Janssens's works is freed from the visible and becomes a purely perceptual configuration that links the visible to the acoustic, the acoustic to the tactile, and the tactile to the invisible in a never-ending permutation of the perceptual conditions of the place.

Translated from the French by Simon Pleasance and Fronza Woods

NOTES:
1. Georges Didi-Huberman, *Ce que nous voyons, ce qui nous regarde* (Paris: Minuit, 1992), 192.
2. Ibid., 98.
3. Stéphane Mallarmé, *Un coup de dés jamais n'abolira le hasard* (Paris: Gallimard), 173.
4. Germano Celant, "La scultura, un'archittetura non abitabile," *Rassegna* (December 1988): 17.

1. Installation Initiatief d'Amis, 1986, Vooruit Ghent.

2. Installation Villa Pino Casagrande, 198 Rome. Courtesy Espace 251 Nord.

3. Aquarium, 199 One Five Gallery Antwerp.

4. Corps Noir, 1995. Courtesy Marie-Puck Broodthaers Gallery. Photo: Manfred Jade.

5. Prototype, 1995. Courtesy Marie-Puck Broodthaers Gallery. Photo: Manfred Jade.

6. Belle de Jour 1994. Musée d'Art Moderne, Brussel. Photo: Manfred Jade.

7-9. Box, 1994. Installation, Brussels. Courtesy Michelil Szwajcer Gallery, Antwerp. Photo: Paul Degobert.

2

3

4

5

6

7

8

9

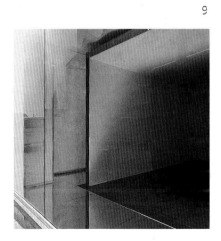

Something about How a Tuerlinckx Machine Traverses the Exhibition Machine

Frank Vande Veire

> I want to comment on limits, also on those between nothing and much, between nothing and everything.
> —Joëlle Tuerlinckx

S tories are nice. They begin, unwind themselves, and end, however "open" that end may be. Life however, is no novel and suffers from a literally unimaginable long-windedness and confusion. Little of what we think, feel, say, or do leads to something. Most of it is lost in the abyss of time. If one were to follow someone—even someone who "knew what he had to do," someone with a so-called consistent life, with a successful career, etc.—from birth till death, in everything he did, even in his inner "stream of consciousness," his life would leave one with the impression of terrible chaos. Even if one can point out a number of lines in someone's life that show a certain regularity or a thoroughgoing development of something, next to them one finds immense quantities of things in such a state of uncertainty that the person's motives and objectives remain totally opaque. And even though each us has known (scarce) moments when the trifling caboodle that is life all of a sudden seems to fall into place, we must admit that, in comparison with the "ordinary" course of events, such experiences seem unreal and to a large extent obscure. Freud's question "What does woman want?" was in fact a trick used to postpone asking that even more unfathomable question: "What does man want?"

This is not just any old question one can ask about that strange species called mankind. This question *is* mankind. But, since he is the question, he never dwells upon it, because if he did, he would have to admit that he does not know the answer. Yet if he wishes to be considered as being more or less human by himself as well as by others, he must always look like someone who does know. So he always has some kind of alibi up his sleeve (some noble aim, some "interesting" activity) that he uses to hide, from the world and from himself, that he in fact wants *nothing*. Man wants absolutely nothing, but this does not prevent him from *wanting* and even wanting all kinds of everything. And when he is completely at a loss, he would rather want *nothing* than not want—according to Nietzsche, this would increasingly happen to us—and compared with this nothingness everything else will turn pale.

Man does a lot and one must admit that, in doing so, most of the time he obtains no results at all. He opens and closes a curtain; switches a light on and immediately turns it off again; scrawls on paper, tears it to shreds, crumbles it, forms it into a ball; counts the pieces of dust on a windowsill; spills water on a tabletop . . . Through these superfluous activities, which normally are considered not even worth mentioning, man betrays the fact that he really wants nothing. We often notice this in lapses, in activities with a repetitive, even "compulsive" nature, or in activities that are somehow stopped halfway. Although usually involuntary, such actions reveal a strictly established pattern. They clearly have no aim whatsoever but do not, therefore, create chaos—or, better still, they cause chaos but, in one and the same movement, create order, as if wishing to avert the "nothingness" with which they are nevertheless playing. Shreds of paper will be used to compose strict geometric structures, for instance.

Imagine now that one is not just someone whose hand, with which one does not know what to do, scribbles on a notepad during a boring meeting. Suddenly one says very decidedly: I will bring this hand, which does not know what to do with itself and which everyone is carefully ignoring as if it were something obscene, I will bring this hand to the foreground. I will allow this hand that is fleeing from the nothingness that haunts it, yet can only speak about that nothingness, to stand in full daylight. I will mobilize it deliberately and shamelessly exhibit its nonresults. I will write, draw, outline, and project the "story" of this storyless hand.

It is very hard to discover what Joëlle Tuerlinckx is doing because—paradoxically—she is very consciously doing what she does not know. Or better still: she is attentively busy *ignoring* what she is doing. Why? Because she does not want to do this or that but wants to show us the general significance of "doing": what one does when one is doing (anything at all). In order to become everyone and no one she must, for a moment, be unaware where she is heading; she must empty her deeds, rid them of those specific motives or objectives with which they might be ascribed. She must act *sans histoire,* without a story that might justify or explain her behavior. She therefore strives after some kind of "historical amnesia." This amnesia is not pure oblivion, nor is it the tabula rasa from which an absolutely autonomous and "original" creation might emerge; this amnesia is her attempt at disappearing as an individual and, through this disappearance, creating the space for a "storehouse" in which "the sum of all constructive and destructive gestures of the entire humanity" is stacked.

I am not referring to the storehouse of all human achievements but that of the *un*achieved, the fruitless: the reservoir of deeds that have remained in a state of uncertainty and therefore have remained unnoticed—gestures without a story, through which a person rebels, in a speechless, somewhat stupid manner, against the demand to produce anything whatsoever and through which a person remains faithful to his "nothingness," without any belief or conviction. It seems therefore, as if Tuerlinckx "constructs" nothing that does not immediately bend itself back to this "nothingness" and that therefore contains no moment of destruction. Her constellations of "little things," which literally never get of the ground, reflect a well-meant attempt to create order yet simultaneously provide a vision of a landscape following a catastrophe. It seems as if everything still has to begin, still has to find its place. At the same time, everything is no more than a trace, a memory.

Inscribed in Tuerlinckx's constellations is the immense deficit in the economy of life. This deficit is never turned into profit. The loss itself in fact refuses to disappear and is endlessly slowed down. Tuerlinckx presents us with the result of activities that have interrupted themselves, have gotten stuck in themselves, as if the inevitably unsuccessful refusal, the hesitation, the unwillingness to do anything whatsoever that lives in all of us is the only thing to which they owe their existence. Here the inertia of someone or rather of "something" is at work, the force of a kind of machine the most striking feature of which is that it *cannot do nothing.* Yet on the borderline of this nothingness, everything is possible, or, better still, everything appears as pure possibility. All artistic media are present at the

Les Archives de la
Galerie, 1991.
Galerie des
Archives, Paris.
Courtesy of the
artist.

embryo stage in the manner in which Tuerlinckx brings a whole range of utterly ordinary activities to a halt within themselves and transforms them into empty gesture.

Or can all of this be considered as a commemoration? Something is being "drawn" or "painted," but with adhesive tape, confetti, balls of paper, etc.; here and there, things stand upright, yet they do not deserve to be called "sculptures"; projections are being made, but no image or film can be seen, theater curtains open and close . . . various different media are briefly indicated without being actually used. All that appears are "extracts," "samples" of them, as if each artistic activity is reflected in a kind of parodic miniature of itself before it is actually exercised. Because we find ourselves at a zero point of art, all modernist procedures are reviewed in miniaturized form: pure line, pure color, primary material, objet trouvé. Tuerlinckx crosses or steps through a space as if she were a memory machine that memorized and virtualized all imaginable artistic gestures.

Tuerlinckx is not just trying to escape from existing exhibition requirements through explicit opposition or by means of that ironic distance of which insiders to contemporary art are so fond. On the contrary, she "embraces" these requirements. She wants to know "what the walls have to say"; what is going on generally in museum and exhibition spaces. She likes to slide into the story that slumbers in each space, even though it does its very best to look "neutral," which then inevitably awakens certain expectations for each work that is given a place there. Of course, she does not simply fulfill these expectations, nor does she turn fully against them. She does something much more estranging. She signifies, even oversignifies, the question raised by the (physical and institutional) space. She does not take possession of the space but repeats it time and again, lets its structure enter into all articulations of the work itself.

In display cases, we can see balls of paper or photographs of her work or of the building's windows and roof, the entrance hall, the office, the lighting, the exhibition poster, the invitation, etc. Slide and film projectors and episcopes throw empty light surfaces onto the wall or project a deformed enlargement of the near-nothingness of a minuscule layer of paint applied to a slide. The touching, slightly clumsy care with which worthless objects such as balls of paper, rags, confetti, and other items are arranged in unsteady formations or depots—as if to form mini-exhibitions—time and again reflects the pure and empty act of displaying. Adhesive tape or lines of paper shreds mark the shape of walls and windows and, like the carpets and plastic floor cloths, outline spaces where something can be seen, even if it is often no more than the spaces themselves. "Rien n'aura eu lieu que le lieu" ("Nothing will have taken place, except the place"). According to Tuerlinckx, "art" apparently has nothing better to do than introduce a minimal shift in the always impure, busy, talkative void of the exhibition space, a shift that nevertheless changes everything.

Each separate element or "ensemble" reflects, in its own manner, the whole happening that the exhibition is or would like to be. Each part comprises the whole. Such a consequent and obstinate tautology leaves nothing unaffected. Because the exhibitive act is not just considered as an obvious given but is foregrounded on each occasion, whatever is exhibited becomes rarefied. When Tuerlinckx shows us a box wrapped in gold paper or a cube made of styrofoam, they are not minimalist objects confronting us with the absolute evidence of their presence. These objects are more like allegories of dreamed presences; more particularly they allegorize the desire of art institutions to present "real presences," to give them to the specta-

tors as a "present." Tuerlinckx is not reticent about this desire but, on the other hand, does not go out of her way to place her "artistic personality" in the balance. She takes this longing upon herself, accepts it as hers, deciphers it, and hands it back to the institutional space: she sows the space with signs of its desire to make some space available for the "real thing." The space seems to say the same thing wherever we look: "Attention! Here it is being shown, here it has been selected, shaped, grown, kneaded, recomposed . . . for you."

Exactly this ironic overidentification with the rhetoric of space—ironic, without being facetious or distant—prevents the rhetoric from being *filled in*. Stripped of its substance, it no longer yields any effect and can only repeat itself in a void, like a machine that can only reproduce itself. Within the rhythm of this reproduction, which yields no product worthy of the name, Tuerlinckx opens up the void that sets the "exhibition machine" in motion, a void that it ignores time and again because of its longing to make space for the "arts."

Tuerlinckx's relationship with the exhibition machine is of the same tender and lucid nature as her relationship with all human activity. She is only interested in the latter to the extent that it is interrupted and loses itself in a gesture that yields nothing but simultaneously, being afraid of this nothingness, slides over it to weave a pattern, structure, or constellation across it. Similarly, the artist only affirms the data of an exhibition if the act of exhibiting can suspend itself for a moment, i.e., when that curious demand for something like art and

Liquid Vision, 1995. Installation at the Béguinage o Kortrijk (Belgium) Studio images i Aachen. Courtesy of the artist.

the longing to show art are reflected back upon themselves. Such a reflection only discloses the irreparable want from which this demand and this longing arise and upon which they inevitably remain focused. This want can never be uncovered just like that; it can only be endlessly bypassed by all kinds of things that seem to owe their existence merely to a suspension of the process of their disappearance.

"We need art in order not to go to ground because of the truth"—i.e., we need art in order to learn to accept or even in order to learn to enjoy. But what obscure enjoyment is this? That the thing that we wish to see reappear time and again is *nothing* and that, therefore, what we do actually see is always too much. Tuerlinckx does not annihilate this "surplus"—this is what we live from—but by emphasizing it, by an overt strategy of proliferation and acceleration, she allows the commotion to silence itself so that it can manifest itself as the echo of an unheard void.

The little balls arranged meticulously on squares of a kitchen towel only attract our attention because this towel—the stage on which the balls are presented—has a hole that no mending job will ever be able to hide. They tell us about nothing but that tear from which they try to divert our attention with their pretty colors, though, on closer examination, each carries a trace of it in the shape of a small hole . . .

Translated from the Flemish by Catherine Thys

Plates

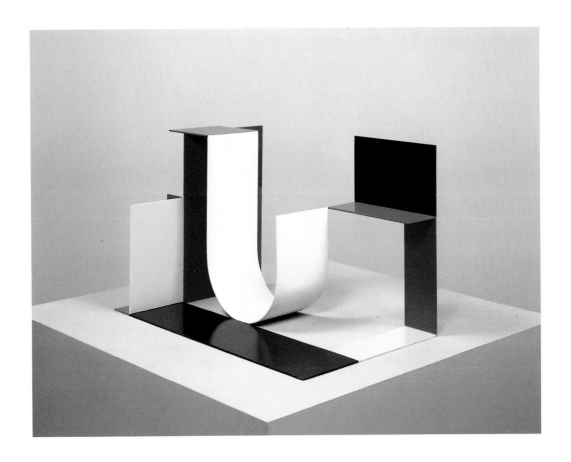

KATARZYNA KOBRO, *Space Composition 4*, 1929.
Painted steel. 40 x 64 x 40 cm.
Kröller-Müller Museum, Otterlo, The Netherlands.

ANN VERONICA JANSSENS,
Morocco Series, 1993.
Color photograph.
Courtesy of the artist.

ANN VERONICA JANSSENS,
Sans titre, 1995.
Bricks, aluminum paper, and tape.
176 x 510 x 320 cm.
Courtesy Galerie Micheline Szwajcer, Antwerp.

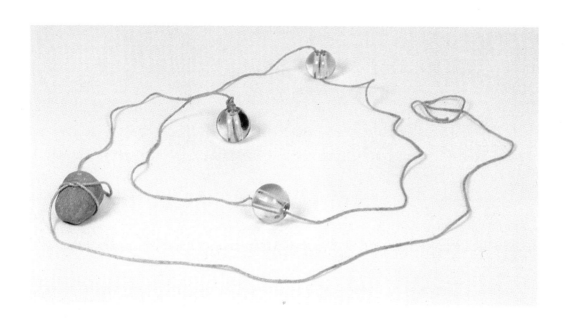

ANN VERONICA JANSSENS, *Sans titre*, 1993.
Glass and stone. Variable dimensions.
Courtesy Galerie Micheline Szwajcer, Antwerp.

FRANCESCA WOODMAN, Four untitled black and white photographs
from *The House* series (1975-76).
5 1/4 x 5 1/4 in. each.
Courtesy of Betty and George Woodman.

Next pages: JOËLLE TUERLINCKX, artist page, 1995.

avril 1993,Palais des Beaux-Arts,Bxl(B)

septembre 1995,Gal.des Beaux-Arts,Bxl(B)

mars 1994,Musée des Beaux-Arts,Cha

novembre 1994,Witte de With,Rotterdam(N)

mai 1995,APP.BXL,Bruxelles(B)

mai 1995,APP.BXL,Bruxelles(B)

novembre 1994,Witte de With,Rotterdam(N)

septembre 1995,Galerie des Beaux-Arts,Bxl(B)

mars 1994,Musée des Beaux-Arts,Charleroi(B)

mars 1995,Opus Operandi,Gand(B)

mai 1995,APP.BXL,Bruxel

mars 1994,Musée des Beaux-Arts,Charleroi(B)

mai 1995,APP.BXL,Bruxelles(B)

mars 1994,Musée des Beaux-Arts,Charleroi(B)

septembre 1995,Galerie des Beaux-Arts,Bxl(B)

septembre 1993,Goethe

avril 1993,ANTICHAMBRES,Palais des Beaux-Arts,Bxl(B)

septembre 1993,Goethe Institut,Bxl(B)

novembre 1994,Witte de With,Rotterdam(N)

mars 19

septembre 1995,Galerie des Beaux-Arts,Bxl(B)

novembre 1994,Witte de With,Rotterdam(N)

mars 1995,Opus Operandi,Gand(B)

novembre 1994,Witte de With,Rotterdam(N)

mars 1995,Opus Operandi,Gand(B)

mars 1995,Opus Operandi,Gand(B)

septembre 1995,Galerie des Beaux-Arts,Bxl(B)

995,Opus Operandi,Gand(B)

avril 1993,ANTICHAMBRES,Palais des Beaux-Arts,Bxl(B)

mars 1994,Musée des Beaux-Arts,Charleroi(B)

de With,Rotterdam(N)

mars 1995,Opus Operandi,Gand(B)

mai 1995,APP.BXL,Bruxelles(B)

avril 1993,ANTICHAMBRES,Palais des Beaux-Arts,Bxl(B)

novembre 1994,Witte de With,Rotterdam(N)

94,Witte de With,Rotterdam(N)

mai 1995,APP.BXL,Bruxelles(B)

nov.1994,Witte de With,Rotterdam(N)

mars 1995,Opus Operandi,Gand(B)

mars 1995,Opus Operandi,Gand(B)

mai 1995,APP.BXL,Bruxelles(B)

nov.1994,Witte de With,Rotterdam(N)

mai 1995,APP.BXL,Bruxelles(B)

and(B)

novembre 1994,Witte de With,Rotterdam(N)

mars 1995,Opus Operandi,Gand(B)

novembre 1994,Witte de With,Rotterdam(N)

mars 1995,Opus Operandi,Gand(B)

SOPHIE TAEUBER-ARP, *Collage à éléments d'objets*, 1938.
Collage. 45.7 x 34.8 cm. Stiftung Hans Arp und Sophie Taeuber-Arp e.V.,
Rolandseck, Germany. Photo: Fotostudio Wolfgang Morell.

SOPHIE TAEUBER-ARP, *Mouvements de lignes en couleur*, 1940. Pencil on paper.
35.9 x 28 cm.
Stiftung Hans Arp und Sophie Taeuber-Arp e.V., Rolandseck, Germany.
Photo: Fotostudio Wolfgang Morell.

SOPHIE TAEUBER-ARP, *Mouvements de lignes*, 1940.
Pencil on paper.
34.6 x 26.3 cm.
Stiftung Hans Arp und Sophie Taeuber-Arp e.V., Rolandseck, Germany.
Photo: Fotostudio Wolfgang Morell.

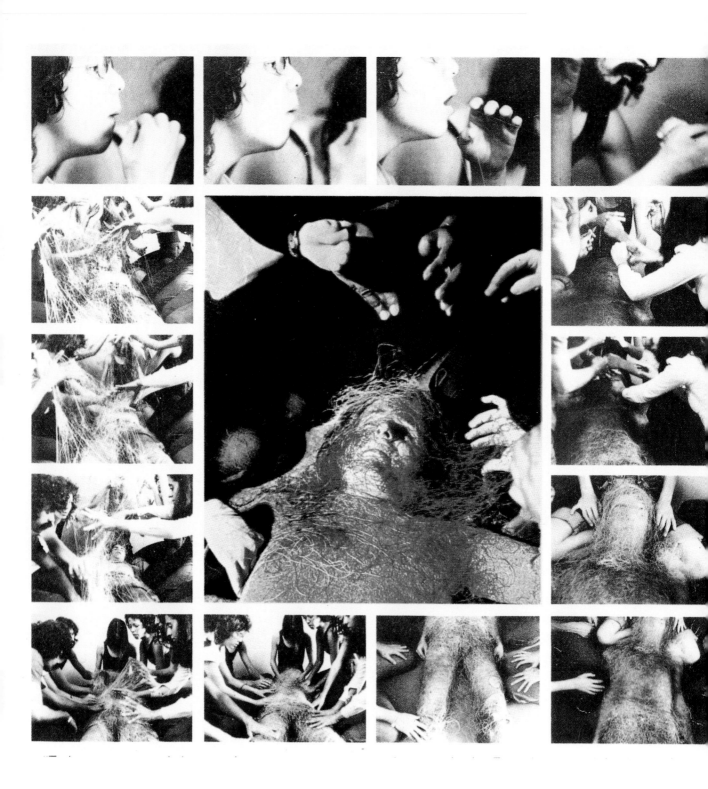

LYGIA CLARK, *Baba Antropofágica (Cannibalistic Dribble)*, Paris, 1973.
Photo: Hubert Josse.

LYGIA CLARK, *Bicho (Animal, Beast)*, 1962.
Aluminum hinged plates. Private collection.
Photo: Clay Perry.

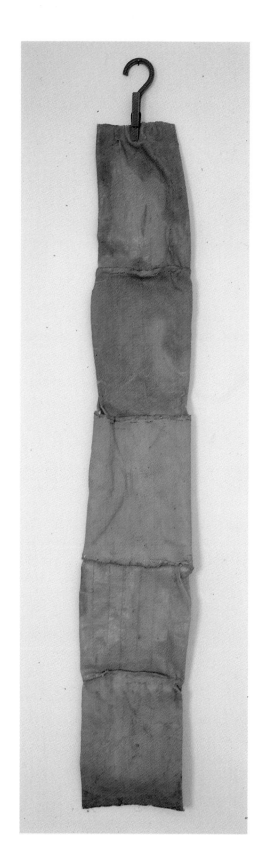

Right: Eva Hesse, *Top Spot*, 1965.
Flexible metal cord, elastic cord, metal
hardware, paint, plastic ball, and porcelain
socket on Masonite.
68.8 x 53.9 cm.
The Estate of Eva Hesse.
Courtesy Robert Miller Gallery, New York.
Photo: Peter Bellamy.

Eva Hesse, *Untitled*, 1968.
Rubberized cheesecloth and clothespin.
76.2 x 22.9 cm.
The Estate of Eva Hesse.
Courtesy Robert Miller Gallery, New York.

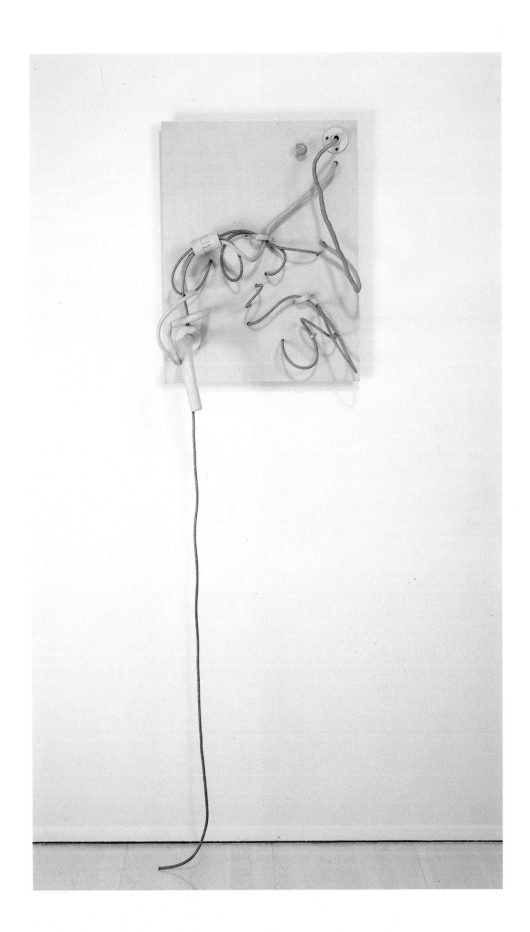

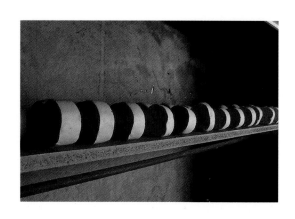

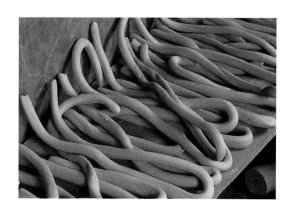

ANNA MARIA MAIOLINA, *Many*, 1995.
Molded clay. Installation at the Béguinage of Kortrijk (Belgium).
Courtesy Kanaal Art Foundation, Kortrijk.
Photo: Rien van den Eshof

OF THEE + ME

My hands work
I weave with the threads of hope
in my shriek together dwell pleasure
pain
the call of the children
my paradigm is Antigone in her fraternal love
compassion accompanies me
my sex is an abstraction
a vacuum
I feel the walls of my hollow in the presence of the other
multiplying in spirals the ecstasy
my hands work
they wash
they cook
they knead bread
I mold clay
and with my eyes I read philosophy
I like poetry
frightened am I by technology
politics
the dominion of intolerance
greed frightens me
after all, why such haste?
and thou my companion
why dost thou emphasize the differences so much?
for I am in thee
and thou art me

Anna Maria Maiolino, 1995

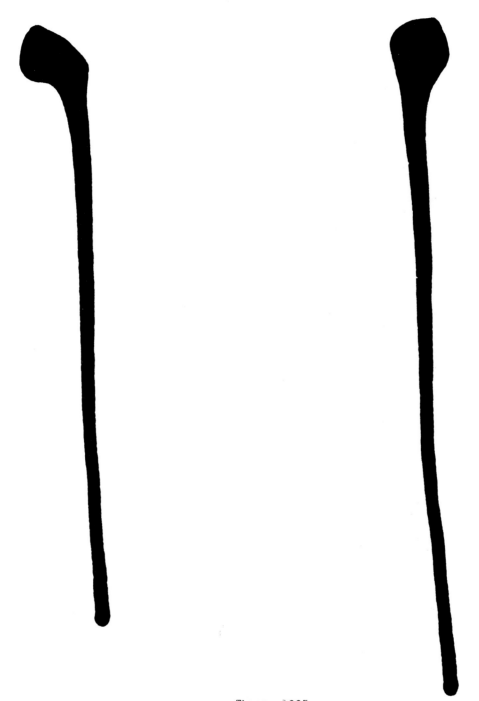

These, 1995.
Ink on paper. 32 x 21 cm.
Courtesy of the artist.

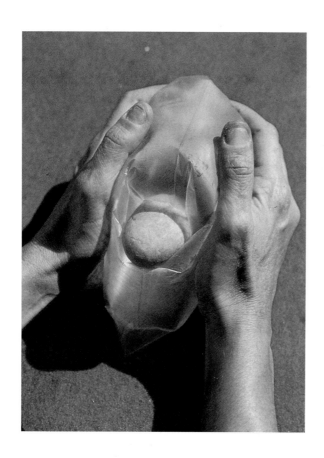

LYGIA CLARK, *Air and Stone*, 1966.
Inflated plastic bag and
pebble. Multiple.

JOËLLE TUERLINCKX, *Les Archives de la Galerie*, 1991.
Galerie des Archives, Paris.
Courtesy of the artist.

sequence 3 du video
"A WONDERFUL JOURNEY
AROUND ZERO"

Biographical Notes on the Artists and Authors

Yve-Alain Bois

Yve-Alain Bois is currently the Joseph Pulitzer, Jr., Professor of Modern Art at Harvard University and an editor of the journal *October*. He has published numerous essays on the art of this century, some of which are reprinted in *Painting as Model* (MIT Press, 1990). Bois co-curated the Piet Mondrian retrospective that was shown in 1994–95 at the Gemeentemuseum, the Hague, the National Gallery of Art, Washington, D.C., and the Museum of Modern Art, New York. He is currently working on a book about noncomposition in twentieth-century art and one on Matisse. Together with Rosalind Krauss, he is organizing an exhibition devoted to the notion of "formlessness" to be held in 1996 at the Centre Georges Pompidou in Paris. His recent writings include prefaces for the exhibition catalogues *Ad Reinhardt* (Museum of Modern Art, New York, 1991); *Ellsworth Kelly: The Years in France, 1948–1954* (National Gallery of Art, Washington, 1992); *Henri Matisse: 1904–1917* (Centre Georges Pompidou, 1993); and *Brice Marden* (Kunsthalle Bern, 1993).

Louise Bourgeois

Louise Bourgeois was born in 1911 in Paris. As a child she worked in her family's tapestry restoration workshop. In 1935 she was accepted at the Ecole des Beaux-Arts but soon chose to study at the less academic Parisian academies (Ranson, Julien, la Grande Chaumière) and in the studios of artists such as Fernand Léger. In 1938 she married American art historian Robert Goldwater and moved to New York City. From 1945 to 1962 Bourgeois exhibited her work at the Whitney Museum of American Art. During this period she also began working in Stanley Hayter's printmaking studio. Bourgeois was included in Lucy Lippard's 1966 exhibition "Eccentric Abstraction"; since then the artist has been involved with the feminist movement and political activities. In 1977 she received an honorary doctor of fine arts degree from Yale University. Bourgeois has also been Officier de l'Ordre des Arts et des Lettres and received the Skowhegan Medal for Sculpture and the Distinguished Artist Award for Lifetime Achievement from the College Art Association. Her first major museum retrospective was held at the Museum of Modern Art in New York in 1982. In 1993 she represented the U.S. at the 45th Venice Biennale. She continues to live in Manhattan and to work with Jerry Gorovoy.

Marie-Ange Brayer

Born in Belgium in 1964, Marie-Ange Brayer is an art critic and author of numerous essays on the work of contemporary artists, including James Coleman, Rodney Graham, Hermann Pitz, and Lothar Baumgarten. She is editorial director of the aesthetic and contemporary art journal *Exposé* (Orléans). She was previously custodian of the Society of the Exhibitions of the Palais des Beaux-Arts in Brussels and is currently a resident in the history of art at the Villa Médicis, Academy of France in Rome, where she is preparing a publication on cartography in contemporary art. She is director of the collection "Singularités," dedicated to contemporary artists, at Editions de la Lettre Volée in Brussels.

Guy Brett

Guy Brett was born in 1942 and lives in London. He was art critic for the *Times* (London) from 1964 to 1975. His books include *Kinetic Art* (Studio Vista/Reinholt, 1968), *Through Our Own Eyes: Popular Art and Modern History* (New Society, 1986), *Transcontinental: Nine Latin American Artists* (Verso, 1990), and *Exploding Galaxies: The Art of David Medalla* (Kala Press, 1995). He is the author of several studies of Lygia Clark's work.

Marianne Brouwer

Marianne Brouwer, an art historian with a degree from the Sorbonne, has worked as a writer and an art critic. Since 1981 she has been curator of sculpture at the Kröller-Müller Museum, Otterlo, Holland. Her recent activities include curating and organizing the Louise Bourgeois retrospective (Kunstverein Frankfurt, among others); the Matt Mullican retrospective (Magasins, Grenoble); the first historical retrospective of Pino Pascali (Musée d'Art Contemporain, Paris); and "Palimpsests," works by Jo Baer. She has written catalogues on the work of Pino Pascali, Gordon Matta-Clark, and Robert Smithson. Brouwer is cofounder of the New Music Festival, Arnhem, and the New Music Podium Circuit, Gelderland. She recently curated "Heart of Darkness" for the Kröller-Müller Museum.

Benjamin H. D. Buchloh

Benjamin H. D. Buchloh teaches twentieth-century and contemporary art at Barnard College, Columbia University. His most recent publications include essays on Allan Sekula, Hans Haacke, and Marcel Broodthaers. He is currently preparing a collection of his essays to be published by MIT Press in 1996 and a monograph of the work of Gerhard Richter.

Christine Buci-Glucksmann

Christine Buci-Glucksmann is professor in aesthetics and contemporary art at the University of Paris VIII, conducting a seminar titled "Aesthetic and Anti-aesthetic in Contemporary Arts." She is the author of *La raison baroque. De Baudelaire à Benjamin* (Galilée, 1984; translated into English, Italian, and Japanese); *La folie de voir. De l'esthétique baroque* (Galilée, 1986; translated into Japanese); *Le tragique de l'ombre. Shakespeare et le maniérisme* (Galilée, 1990); *Raoul Ruiz* (Dis Voir, 1991); and *L'enjeu du beau* (Galilée, 1992). She has worked on numerous exhibition catalogues with galleries and museums, including ones on the work of Richard Serra, Dan Graham, Janis Kounellis, and Antonio Tapies.

Claude Cahun

Born Lucy Schwob in 1894 in Nantes, France, Claude Cahun adopted her more sexually ambiguous name in 1918. Moving from Nantes to Paris with her stepsister and lifelong partner Suzanne Malherbe, Cahun was actively involved in a number of literary and artistic circles, including those of Sylvia Beach and Adrienne Monnier, as well as those of the surrealists. In 1930, Cahun's book *Aveux non avenus* was published, featuring poems, prose, and photomontages. A member of the Association des Ecrivains et Artistes Révolutionnaires (AEAR), an antifascist organization, Cahun was politically active on the Left throughout the 1930s. Moving to the Isle of Jersey in 1938, Cahun participated in the Resistance during the Nazi occupation until she was captured and condemned to death; the liberation of the island in 1945 spared her this fate. In failing health, she continued to live on Jersey until her death in 1954.

Edwin Carels

Edwin Carels, born in 1964 in Kortrijk, Belgium, teaches film history at St. Lucas High School of the Visual Arts in Brussels and also conducts seminars at the Film Museum in Antwerp and at Stuc in Louvain. As a freelance critic of film, video, and animated film, he is under engagement to the BRTN public broadcasting radio station and writes for the media review As; the magazine for architecture, urbanism, and the visual arts Archis; and the newspaper *De Morgen*, among others.

Emily Carr
Emily Carr (1871–1945) is Canada's most renowned female artist. A native of the West Coast, Carr sought a distinctly Canadian modernist style. Unlike her contemporaries the Group of Seven in Ontario, Carr's vision of the landscape included the peoples of the First Nations. She journeyed throughout British Columbia, documenting the native villages in which she sojourned and later the forests, leaving a record of the encroachment of cities on the wilderness and the abuses of logging practices such as clear-cutting. In her later years, Carr turned to writing and earned a Governor General's Award for Literature for her autobiographically based books.

Rina Carvajal
Rina Carvajal is an independent curator and writer from Venezuela who is currently living and working in New York. She is former curator of contemporary art at the Museum of Fine Arts and assistant director of the Museum of Contemporary Art, both in Caracas; museum educator at the Metropolitan Museum of Art, New York; and visiting scholar at McGill University, Montreal. Carvajal is a contributing author for numerous catalogues and anthologies on twentieth-century art in Latin America and the author of *Uno, dos, tres, quatro* (Museum of Fine Arts, Caracas) and *Guillermo Kuitca* (Witte de With).

Theresa Cha
Theresa Hak Kyung Cha was born in 1951 in Pusan, South Korea. She emigrated to the United States with her family in 1962 and attended the University of California, Berkeley, from 1968 through 1978. Before her early death in 1982, Cha produced a large body of innovative work, including performance, video, film, artist's books, concrete poetry, audio works, slide pieces, sculpture, and collage. Her work has been exhibited at the University Art Museum, Berkeley; Other Books and So, Amsterdam; Living Art Museum, Reykjavik; the New Museum for Contemporary Art, New York; the Kitchen, New York; and Mills College Art Gallery, Oakland. In 1992 the Whitney Museum of American Art presented a full retrospective of Cha's work.

Lygia Clark
Lygia Clark was born in Belo Horizonte, Brazil, in 1920 and died in Rio de Janeiro in 1988. With Hélio Oiticica, she was a central figure in the neoconcrete group, founded in 1959, and in the Brazilian avant-garde. She lived in Paris from 1948 to 1950, studying with Fernand Léger, and from 1968 to 1977. After her early reliefs and articulated metal sculptures, Clark created objects that have no meaning without the living support of the participant's body.

Laura Cottingham
Laura Cottingham is a critic who lives in New York and teaches at the Cooper Union for the Advancement of Science and Art. She is the author of *How Many "Bad" Feminists Does It Take to Change a Lightbulb?* (1994) and numerous other critical essays on the relationship between visual culture and feminism. In 1996 she will present her first curatorial project as part of the "Now-Here" exhibition at the Louisiana Museum of Modern Art, Humlebæk, Denmark. She is currently working on *Not for Sale*, a video history of the feminist art movement in the United States during the 1970s.

Hanne Darboven
Hanne Darboven was born in 1941 in Munich and raised in Hamburg. After a brief career as a pianist, she studied art at the Hochschule für Bildende Kunst in Hamburg. In 1965 she made the first of many extended visits to New York and began a sys-tem of daily writing that continues to shape her work today. In 1969 Darboven returned to Hamburg, where she has continued to live and work, making regular visits to New York. Darboven's work was first shown in 1967 in solo exhibitions in Düsseldorf, Turin, Brussels, Milan, and London; her New York debut was a solo show at Leo Castelli Gallery in 1973. Her numerous solo exhibitions include Stedelijk Museum, Amsterdam; Rheinisches Landesmuseum, Bonn; Musée d'Art Moderne de la Ville de Paris; Kunsthalle Hamburg; Renaissance Society/University of Chicago; Goldis Paley Gallery/Moore College of Art, Philadelphia; and Leo Castelli Gallery, New York. Since 1967 she has participated in group exhibitions at the Art Institute of Chicago, the Museum of Modern Art, New York, the Montréal Museum of Fine Arts, and the Solomon R. Guggenheim Museum, New York, and in major international exhibits including Biennale Nürnberg (1971), Biennale of Sydney (1979), Biennale de Paris (1971), Documenta (1972–1982), Venice Biennale (1982), and Bienal São Paulo (1972). Darboven is represented by the Leo Castelli Gallery in New York.

Leen De Backer
Leen De Backer was born in 1958 in Antwerp, Belgium. She is an art historian and curator of the Museum of Contemporary Art, Antwerp (MUHKA). She administers the museum collection and, in addition to contributions on current museum exhibitions, curated a show on Nadine Tasseel in 1994.

Lieven De Cauter
Lieven De Cauter was born in 1959 in Tielt, Belgium. He studied philosophy and art history at the University of Leuven. He has published two books, *Het hiernamaals van de kunst* (The Hereafter of Art, 1991) and *Archeologie van de kick* (Archeology of Kicks, 1995). He is now preparing a book on Walter Benjamin.

Paul De Vylder
Paul De Vylder was born in 1942 in Belgium. He studied art at the academies of Antwerp, St.-Niklaas, and Ljubljana and art history and archaeology at the State University of Ghent. De Vylder teaches semiotics at the Royal Academy of Fine Arts, Ghent. His artistic projects include *Discipline* (1980); *Quarantaine* (1981–82); *Dr. Joseph Goebbels* (1982–83); *Gringo total* (1982–83); *Gjölbaschi I* (1983); *Gjölbaschi II* (1985–86); *La morte di Cesare* (1986); *Rebus rebis* (1986–88); *Cappella famosa* (1989–90); *Hieroglyphica* (1991–94); *Machinae* (1993–96). His publications include *The Non-entity "Art" and What to Do about It?* (1988), *Ut Rebus Rebis: The Sp.speaker with the Sp.split Tongue* (1988), *The Panoptic Gaze* (1990), *The Monkey's Labyrinth* (1992), *Babel Revisited* (1992), *The "Brisure," Nine Metaphors about the Art of the Eighties* (1993), *The Hilton System* (1993), and *Desymbolized Bodies* (1995).

M. Catherine de Zegher
Born in 1955 in Groningen, the Netherlands, M. Catherine de Zegher studied art history and archaeology at the State University of Ghent, Belgium. From 1977 to 1985 she worked as an archaeologist, doing inventories and restorations of historic monuments. In 1985 she became a cofounder of the Kanaal Art Foundation, a center of contemporay art, opting for self-willed, uncompromising projects with an international emanation (Cildo Meireles, Tadashi Kawamata, Everlyn Nicodemus, Gabriel Orozco). In 1992 she co-curated (with Paul Vandenbroeck) the exhibition "America, Bride of the Sun: 500 Years of South America and the Low Countries," and in 1995 she became visiting curator at the Institute of Contemporary Art, Boston. Mother of three children, she lives and works in Belgium and the United States.

Christophe Domino
Born in 1958, Christophe Domino is a freelance art writer and essayist based in Paris. He has published books on the collection of the Musée National d'Art Moderne (Centre Georges Pompidou) and has contributed to many publications (including *Artstudio* and museum catalogues). He also writes criticism for magazines (*Beaux Arts Magazine* and *Art Press* in France, *Atelier* in Japan) and lectures in art schools and at the Sorbonne University. He is interested in the conditions of knowledge and discourse on art and in the espiteme of art conceptions.

Lili Dujourie
Born in 1941 in Belgium, Lili Dujourie has been exhibiting her video and sculptural work since 1968. Since her first solo exhibition in 1970 at X-One Gallery, Antwerp, she has had others in the Hague, Düsseldorf, Ghent (Gewad), Liège (Galerie L'A), London (Lisson Gallery), Rotterdam ('t Venster), Amsterdam (De Appel), and New York (Louver Gallery). In 1989–90 her work was shown in a major exhibition touring from the Bönner Kunstverein (Bonn) to Le Magasin, CAC (Grenoble) and the Kröller-Müller Museum (Otterlo). She has participated in many group exhibitions, including "Inzicht—Overzicht: Present Art in Belgium" (Museum Hedendaagse Kunst, Ghent, 1979); "Camere incantate" (Palazzo Reale, Milan, 1979); "De tijd—Le temps" (Palais des Beaux Arts, Brussels, 1985); at the Stedelijk Van Abbemuseum (Eindhoven, 1985); "Falls the Shadow" (Hayward Gallery, London, 1986); "Sonsbeek 86" (International Sculpture Exhibition, Arnhem, 1986); "Initiatief 86" (St.-Peter's Abbey, Ghent, 1986); the 1986 Venice Biennale; "A Distant View" (Museum of Contemporary Art, New York, 1986); "L'art en Belgique, Flandre et Wallonie au XXe Siècle, un point de vue" (Musée d'Art Moderne de la Ville de Paris, 1989); "Carnegie International" (Carnegie Museum of Art, Pittsburgh); "L'art en Belgique depuis 1980" (Museum van Moderne Kunst, Brussels, 1993); and "Cocido y crudo" (Museo Nacional, Madrid, 1994).

Jean Fisher
Jean Fisher is an artist and freelance writer on issues of contemporary art. She currently teaches at the Slade School of Art, University College, London, and the Jan van Eyck Academy, Maastricht, the Netherlands. She is the editor of the journal *Third Text*.

Ellen Gallagher
Born in Providence, Rhode Island, in 1965 to an Irish mother and an African American father, Ellen Gallagher attended a Quaker school in Providence, then Oberlin College. She left college in 1984 and spent the next several years sailing and working as a deckhand in Maine and throughout the Caribbean. From 1988 to 1992 she attended the School of the Museum of Fine Arts in Boston. While living in Boston, she was active in the Dark Room, a collective of African American poets and artists based in Cambridge. Gallagher had a one-person show at the Mario Diacono Gallery in Boston in 1994 and was included in the 1995 Whitney Biennial. She is currently a fellow at the Fine Arts Work Center in Provincetown, Massachussetts.

Gego
Gego (Gertruda Goldschmidt) was born in 1912 in Hamburg, Germany; she died in Caracas, Venezuela, in 1994. Completing her studies in architecture and engineering at the Technical University at Stuttgart in 1938, she emigrated to Venezuela in 1939. From 1959 to 1977 she taught in Caracas as part of the Faculty of Art and Design, Universidad Central de Venezuela and at the Escuela de Artes Plásticas Christóbal Rojas and the Instituto de Diseño (Fundación Neumann-Ince), of which she was cofounder. Gego had more than twenty-six one-person shows in both America and Europe during her lifetime and produced numerous monumental structures to be integrated into architecture. Her works are included in important public and private collections throughout the world.

Isabelle Graw
Isabelle Graw was born 1962 in Hamburg, Germany. She currently lives and works in Cologne. Graw is editor and publisher of *Texte zur Kunst* and author of numerous articles and publications.

Serge Guilbaut
Serge Guilbaut was born in Valence, Drôme, France, in 1943. He received his master's degree in 1972 at the University of Bordeaux and his Ph.D. at University of California, Los Angeles, in 1979. He currently teaches at the University of British Columbia in Canada. His publications include *How New York Stole the Idea of Modern Art: Abstract Expressionism, Freedom and the Cold War* (1983), *Reconstructing Modernism* (1990), and numerous articles in French and English.

Mona Hatoum
Mona Hatoum was born to a Palestinian family in Beirut (1952) and since 1975 has lived and worked in London. After studying at the Byam Shaw School of Art at the Slade University London, she worked mainly in live performance and video. Since 1989 she has created installations that have been included in "The British Art Show" (1990) and in major international exhibitions such as "The Interrupted Life" (New Museum of Contemporary Art, New York, 1991) and "Pour la suite du monde" (Musée d'Art Contemporain de Montréal, 1992). In 1994 she participated in "Sense and Sensibility" (Museum of Modern Art, New York), "Cocido y crudo" (Centro de Arte Reina Sofia, Madrid) and the fifth Havana Biennial. In 1995 her work was included in "ARS 95" (Helsinki), "Identity and Alterity" (Venice Biennale), and "Rites of Passage" (Tate Gallery, London). Hatoum has had a one-person exhibition at Chapter Art Centre, Cardiff (1992), the Arnolfini Gallery, Bristol (1993), the Centre Pompidou, Paris (1994), and the Kanaal Art Foundation, Béguinage, Kortrijk (1995). She has been nominated for the 1995 Turner Prize.

Nathalie Hervieux
Born in 1966 in Normandy, France, Nathalie Hervieux received the National Certificate of Visual Arts and settled in Paris, where in 1991 she was selected for the Master of the National Superior School of Fine Arts. Since 1990 she has had a dozen exhibitions in France and elsewhere in Europe (Paris, Amiens, Caen, Reims, Milan, Berlin, Bad-Homburg, Copenhagen, Kortrijk). She was laureate of the 5th Biennial of Young French Photography. Her photographs are included in numerous collections, including that of the Bibliothèque National. She currently works and lives in Paris and in a village on the Baie de Somme.

Eva Hesse
Eva Hesse was born in Hamburg, Germany, in 1936 and in 1938 was expatriated to Amsterdam on a children's train with her sister. Hesse was placed in an orphanage until being reunited with her parents and brought to the United States. She studied art at several institutions, including the Cooper Union and Yale University. While married to sculptor Tom Doyle she returned to Germany; she began her mature work in the factory that served as Doyle's studio. Back in New York, by 1966 she was actively showing in galleries and museums. During the last few years of her life, as she struggled against a

477

brain tumor, Hesse created sculpture in plastics and latex. She died in May 1970 in New York.

Susan Hiller

Susan Hiller was born in the United States in 1940. She pursued a Ph.D. in anthropology and conducted field research in Central America, until she experienced what she has described as a "kind of crisis of conscience" that led her turn away from a career in anthropology. At the end of the 1960s Hiller moved to Europe and traveled extensively before settling in London, where she had her first solo exhibition in 1973. Hiller has worked in painting, sculpture, video, photography, installation, and artist's books. She has had one-person exhibitions at the Serpentine Gallery, London (1976), the Museum of Modern Art, Oxford (1978), the Institute of Contemporary Arts, London (1986), Matts Gallery, London (1980, 1991), and the Freud Museum, London (1994), as well as at numerous venues across Europe and the United States. In 1996 a major survey of her work will be held at Tate Gallery, Liverpool. Hiller is the coauthor of *Dreams: Visions of the Night* (London, Paris, and New York, 1976; revised 1991), which examines the relationships between art and dreams, and is the compiler of *The Myth of Primitivism* (London and New York, 1991), an anthology of texts by artists, critics, and anthropologists.

Hannah Höch

Most famous for her participation in Berlin dada, Hannah Höch (1889–1978) was a prolific painter, photomontagist, collagist, and draftsperson throughout her carreer. She exhibited widely during the Weimar period and was included in major shows such as "Dada-Messe" and "Film und Foto" but earned her living working part-time at Ullstein Verlag. During the Nazi years she went into internal emigration, after 1939 living in relative isolation in Heiligensee outside Berlin. She began exhibiting again after the war and in 1976 had a retrospective at the Musée d'Art Moderne in Paris and the Nationalgalerie in Berlin.

bell hooks

Distinguished Professor of English at the City University of New York, bell hooks is a cultural critic and feminist theorist. Her most recent books include *Outlaw Culture: Resisting Representations, Black Looks: Race and Representation*, and *Talking Back: Thinking Feminist: Thinking Black*.

Rosi Huhn

Rosi Huhn is a German art historian and critic who has lived in Paris since 1982. In addition to essays about Picasso's Guernica and the World's Fair of 1937, she works extensively on contemporary art. She produced a film on Jochen Gerz in 1994. Among her recent publications are "Passages vers une barbarie positive" (on Gerz, Bracha Lichtenberg Ettinger, Christian Boltansky), in *Passages d'après Walter Benjamin* (Mainz: Schmidt, 1992); "Lichtenberg-Ettinger's aesthetischem Konzept der Matrix und Metramorphose," in *Denkräume* (Berlin: Reiner, 1993); "Moving Omissions and Hollow Spots into the Field of Vision," in *Matrix-Borderlines* (Oxford University Press, 1993); and "Des femmes artistes contemporaines," in *Féminisme, art et histoire de l'art* (Ecole Nationale Supérieure des Beaux-Arts, 1994).

Ann Veronica Janssens

Ann Veronica Janssens, born in 1956 in Folkstone, England, is an arist living and working in Brussels. Her work has been shown in solo exhibitions at the Museum of Modern Art, Brussels (1987), Villa Gillet, FRAC Rhônes-Alpes (1989), the Espace d'Art Contemporain, Lausanne (1994), and the Micheline Szwajcer Gallery, Antwerp (1990–95) and in group shows in Antwerp, Brussels, Kortrijk, Bordeaux, Amsterdam, Kassel, Rome, and Venice.

Katarzyna Kobro

Katarzyna Kobro was born in Moscow in 1898 and died of cancer in Lodz in 1951. In 1917 she began studying sculpture in Moscow, where she befriended numerous members of the Soviet avant-garde and met Wladyslaw Strzeminski. In 1920, she moved to Smolensk with Strzeminski, whom she married, and became a member of Unovis, the group led by Malevich. In 1922, she and Strzeminski left Russia for Poland, and by 1924 they were both key members of the Polish avant-garde: cofounders of the group Blok in 1924, then members of the group Praesens from 1926 to 1929 and, after they quit the latter, cofounders of the group "a.r.," which remained active until 1936. Kobro reached her mature style in 1925 and in 1931 published her major theoretical work, *Composition of Space—Calculation of Spatio-Temporal Rhythm*, which she coauthored with Strzeminski. That same year she moved to Lodz, where she taught at the Industrial School for Women and where she and Strzeminski lived until the end of their lives (although they seperated in 1945). Her last known abstract sculpture dates from 1933, and most of her work was destroyed by the Nazis during the war. After the war, while seriously ill, she realized several small deco bronze nudes related to the work of Archipenko and to her own earlier cubist studies.

Rosalind E. Krauss

Rosalind Krauss is Meyer Schapiro Professor of Art and Theory at Columbia University and a founding editor of *October* magazine. Her most recent books are *The Optical Unconscious* (MIT Press, 1993) and *Cindy Sherman* (Rizzoli, 1993). She served as curator for the Guggenheim Museum's retrospective "Robert Morris: The Mind/Body Problem" (1994) and is currently preparing "L'Informe: Modernism Against the Grain" for the Centre Georges Pompidou, Paris.

Yayoi Kusama

Yayoi Kusama was born in Matsumoto City, Nagoya Prefecture, Japan, in 1929. She had her first solo show in Japan in 1952 and six solo shows in the following three years; in 1955 Kusama was selected to represent Japan at the "18th Biennial International Watercolor Exhibition" at the Brooklyn Museum in New York. In 1957, on the occasion of her first American solo show (Seattle), Kusama traveled to the United States, eventually making her residence in New York. Often associated with neodada and No art in the United States, with Group Zero and Nul in Europe, and with Obsessional Art in Japan, her work had international exposure throughout the 1960s. Toward the end of that decade, as her focus on the publicity surrounding her activities—by then including happenings, film, design, and publishing as well as gallery art—increased, the critical climate for her work in New York grew hostile. In 1972 Kusama moved back to Japan. She has lived in a private mental hospital there since 1977, where she continues to work in a variety of media.

Miwon Kwon

Miwon Kwon is a writer living in New York. She is a doctoral candidate in architectural history and theory at Princeton University and is coeditor/copublisher of the journal *Documents*. Kwon also teaches in the museum of fine arts program in Visual Art at Vermont College.

Maud Lavin
Born in Canton, Ohio, in 1954, Maud Lavin is the author of *Cut with the Kitchen Knife: The Weimar Photomontages of Hannah Höch* (Yale University Press, 1993) and the coauthor of *Montage and Modern Life* (Institute of Contemporary Art, Boston, and MIT Press, 1992). Currently she is working on a book to be published by Farrar, Straus and Giroux titled *Clean, New York: The Politics of Graphic Design from John Heartfield to the Internet*. Her essays on women, culture, and politics have appeared in *The New York Times Book Review, The Nation, Art in America, New German Critique, New Woman, Harper's Bazaar*, and other publications.

Bracha Lichtenberg Ettinger
Bracha Lichtenberg Ettinger is an artist and psychoanalyst, born in Israel and working in Paris and Tel Aviv. She has had solo exhibitions at the Israel Museum, Jerusalem (1995); La Cité du Livre, Aix en Provence (1995); Kanaal Art Fondation, Kortrijk, Belgium (1994); Leeds Metropolitan University Gallery, Leeds (1994); the Museum of Modern Art, Oxford (1993); the Russian Museum of Ethnography, St. Petersburg (1993); Le Nouveau Musée, Villeurbanne (1992); Centre Culturel, Herblay (1992); the Goethe Institut, Paris (1990); Musée des Beaux Arts, Calais (1988); and Centre Georges Pompidou, Paris (1987). Her group exhibitions include "Kabinet" (Stedelijk Museum, Amsterdam, 1996); "Face à l'histoire" (Centre Georges Pompidou, Paris, 1996); "Reminiscences and Obsession" (Artists' House, Jerusalem, 1994–95); "Quelles hystéries?" (L'Ecole des Beaux Arts, Renne, 1994); "Public and Private" (Stills, Edinburgh, 1993); "Routes of Wandering" (Israel Museum, Jerusalem, 1992); "Israeli Art Now" (Tel Aviv Museum of Art, 1991); and "Feminine Presence" (Tel Aviv Museum of Art, 1991). Some of her recent publications are "Matrix and Metramorphosis," *Differences* 4, no. 3 (Indiana University Press, 1992); "The Becoming Threshold of Matrixial Borderlines," in Robertson et al., eds., *Travellers' Tales* (Routledge, 1994); *Time Is the Breath of the Spirit*, with Emmanuel Levinas (Museum of Modern Art, Oxford, 1993); *A Threshold Where We Are Afraid*, with Edmond Jabès (Museum of Modern Art, Oxford, 1993); *Matrix. Halal(a)—Lapsus: Notes on Painting 1985–1992* (Museum of Modern Art, Oxford, 1993); "The Almost-Missed Encounters as Eroticized Aerials of the Psyche," *Third Text*, nos. 28–29 (Kala, 1994); *The Matrixial Gaze* (Department of Fine Arts, University of Leeds, 1995); "Woman as Objet a between Phantasy and Art," *Journal of Philosophy and the Visual Arts*, no. 6 (1995), "Metramorphic Borderlinks and Matrixial Borderspace," in J. Welchman, ed., *Rethinking Borders* (Macmillan, 1995).

Anna Maria Maiolino
Anna Maria Maiolino, a naturalized Brazilian, was born in Italy in 1942. She currently lives and works in Rio de Janeiro. She studied at the National School of Fine Arts, Caracas, Venezuela; National School of Fine Arts, Rio de Janeiro; and Pratt Graphics Center, New York. Her group shows include "Opinion 1966" (Museum of Modern Art, Rio de Janeiro); "New Brazilian Objectivity" (Museum of Modern Art, Rio de Janeiro, 1967); "8th Biennial of São Paulo" (1967); "0th Biennial of Young Artists" (Paris, 1973); "16th Biennial of São Paulo" (1991); "America, Bride of the Sun: 500 Years Latin America and the Low Countries" (Antwerp, 1992); "Segni d'arte" (Venice, 1993); "Brasil século XX—22nd Biennial of São Paulo" (1994); "Inside the Visible: Begin the Beguine in Flanders" (Kanaal Art Foundation, Kortrijk, Belgium, 1995); and "2nd Clay Biennial of America, Caracas" (1995). Her

works are part of the collections of the Museum of Modern Art, Rio de Janeiro; the Museum of Contemporary Art, São Paulo; the National Museum of Havana, Cuba; and the Gilberto Chateaubriand Collection, among others.

Agnes Martin
Agnes Martin was born in 1912 in Maklin, Saskatchewan, Canada. She received her bachelor of science from Columbia University in 1942 and taught art at the University of New Mexico in Taos and Albuquerque. In 1951 she returned to Columbia to enter the master of arts program. She had her first solo exhibition in 1958 at the Betty Parsons Gallery. Martin has since exhibited internationally and was elected member of the American Academy and Institute of Arts and Letters in 1989.

Judith Mastai
Judith Mastai is director of the Vancouver Art Forum Society, publishers of *Collapse: the view from here*, a new journal of visual arts and culture with a distinctly Canadian point of view. Formerly head of public program at the Vancouver Art Gallery for seven years, Mastai has worked as an independent educator, critic, and curator for a variety of galleries, universities, and publications in Canada and abroad.

Ana Mendieta
Ana Mendieta was born in Havana, Cuba, in 1948. In 1961 she moved to Iowa and received her bachelor of arts from the University of Iowa in 1969. She moved to New York City in 1978 and received a Visual Artist Grant from the National Endowment for the Arts and a Guggenheim Fellowship in Sculpture. She received an American Academy Fellowship to study in Rome, where she lived until her death in New York in 1985.

Laurie J. Monahan
Laurie J. Monahan is a doctoral candidate at Harvard University, where she is writing a dissertation on André Masson and surrealism in the 1930s. Most recently she has published on the role of myth and violence in Matisse's work of the 1930s for the exhibition catalogue *Matisse* (Brisbane, Melbourne, and Sidney, 1995). Other publications include an essay on the American pavilion at the 1964 Venice Biennale in the anthology *Reconstructing Modernism: Art in New York, Paris and Montreal, 1945–1964* (MIT Press, 1989).

Avis Newman
Avis Newman was born in London in 1946 and currently lives in London. Recent solo exhibitions have been held at Gallery Akumatory 2, Posnan (1985); Lisson Gallery, London and the Renaissance Society of Chicago (1987–88); Arnolfini Gallery, Bristol (1990); Douglas Hyde Gallery, Dublin, and De Appel Foundation, Amsterdam (1993); Saatchi Gallery, London (1994–95); Casa Masaccio, San Giovanni Valdarno, Florence (1995); Kanaal Art Foundation, Kortrijk (1994); Ikon Gallery, Birmingham (1995); and Camden Arts Centre (1996). Avis Newman was also included in recent group exhibitions in Sidney, Venice, Philadelphia, Ohio, Ghent, California, Winnipeg, Paris, London, and Bruges.

Michael Newman
Michael Newman writes on art and philosophy and is head of Theoretical Studies and Art History at the Slade School of Fine Art, University College, London. He is no relation to Avis Newman.

Desa Philippi
Desa Philippi was born in Hamburg in 1960. She studied art history at London University and the University of Leeds. Her writings on contemporary art have appeared in numerous catalogues and journals, including *Third Text, Artforum, October,* and *Parachute*. A freelance writer based in London, she is currently working on a novel titled *Modern Alarms*.

Griselda Pollock
Griselda Pollock is professor of the Critical and Social Histories of Art and director of the Centre for Cultural Studies at the University of Leeds. She is the author of *Old Mistresses: Women, Art & Ideology* (with Roszika Parker), *Vision and Difference: Dealing with Degas* (ed. with Richard Kendall), and *Avant-Garde Gambits: Gender and the Colour of Art History.* Forthcoming texts include *Differencing the Gogh, Avant-Gardes and Partisans Reviewed* (with Fred Orton), and *Generations and Geographies in the Visual Arts: Feminist Readings.* Mother of two children, she lives in Leeds, England.

Carol Rama
(Olga) Carol Rama was born in Turin in 1918, where she resides today. Her first solo exhibition was in Turin in 1945. Since then she has exhibited her work continuously in Italy. She was included in the Venice Biennale in 1948, 1950, 1956, and 1993.

Lawrence Rinder
Lawrence Rinder is curator of twentieth-century art at the University Art Museum and Pacific Film Archive of the University of California at Berkeley. Among the exhibitions he has organized are "In a Different Light," "Louise Bourgeois Drawings," and "Where There Is Where There: The Prints of John Cage." As curator of the MATRIX program, he has presented exhibitions by artists including Nayland Blake, Matthew Heckert, Richard Tuttle, Kiki Smith, Sophie Calle, Dieter Roth, and Cecilia Vicuña. Other exhibitions he has organized include "Theresa Hak Kyung Cha: Other Things Seen, Other Things Heard" at the Whitney Museum of American Art, "Tim Rollins + K.O.S." at the Walker Art Center, and "Self-Evidence" at Los Angeles Contemporary Exhibitions.

J. F. Rodenbeck
J. F. Rodenbeck is an art historian and writer physically resident in New York. Her work focuses on issues of trauma, representation, and the public sphere, with specific address to event structures of the late 1950s and early 1960s. She leads a double life on the Internet.

Martha Rosler
Martha Rosler was born in Brooklyn, New York, and spent the 1970s in California. She currently lives in Brooklyn. She studied painting at the Brooklyn Museum Art School, but her work and choice of media changed under the influence of her participation in antiwar and feminist activism. One of the first artists actively to pursue the aesthetic possibilities of video, Rosler finished her first tape, *Budding Gourmet,* in 1974, followed by *Semiotics of the Kitchen* (1975). *Her Vital Statistics of a Citizen, Simply Obtained* (1977) was based on a performance first presented at the University of California, San Diego in 1974. Along with video, performance and photography were Rosler's dominant media before 1980, when her interest in performance began to transform into an interest in installation works. Rosler continues to work in video, photography, and installation. Throughout her career, her work has offered a critical analysis of society, politics, and the media. She has been widely exhibited, most recently at the San Francisco Museum

of Modern Art, Centre d'Art Contemporain, Geneva, and the 1995 Johannesburg Biennale. Her writings include "The Private and Public: Feminist Art in California," *Artforum,* September 1977; *Service: A Trilogy on Colonization* (New York: Printed Matter, 1978); "Lookers, Buyers, Dealers, and Makers: Thoughts on Audience," *Exposure,* Spring 1979; *3 Works,* ed. Benjamin Buchloh (Halifax: Press of the Nova Scotia College of Art and Design, 1981); *If You Lived Here: The City in Art, Theory, and Social Activism,* ed. Brian Wallis (Seattle: Bay Press, 1991); and "In the Place of the Public: Observations of a Frequent Flyer," *Assemblage,* 1995.

Charlotte Salomon
Charlotte Salomon, born in Germany in 1917 and exiled to France in 1939, was killed in 1943 in Birkenau. During her exile in France she created her life history in images, Life or Theatre? The work consists of more than eight hundred watercolors overlaid by written texts and tunes that captured the dramatic events of her own life and of the European Jews during the Holocaust.

Sônia Salzstein
Sônia Salzstein is an art historian living in São Paulo, where she was born in 1955. Throughout the 1980s she worked as a curator of galleries and museums. In these institutions she developed several projects on both research and programming exhibitions on Brazilian modern and contemporary art. From 1989 to 1992 she created and directed a center of contemporary art at the cultural secretariat of the state of São Paulo, involving mainly young artists. Her latest articles have focused on the works of Carlos Fajardo, Waltercio Caldas, Lygia Clark, and Hélio Oiticica, among others. She is a doctoral candidate in aesthetics in the Department of Philosophy at the University of São Paulo and is currently preparing her thesis on the idea of modernity in Brazilian art. The thesis includes— as a possible interpretative model for Brazilian art—a special chapter on baroque artists living in the colony of Minas Gerais during the eighteenth century.

Mira Schendel
Mira Schendel was born in Zurich in 1919. Early she moved with her family to Milan, where she studied philosophy. She began her self-taught career after arriving in Brazil in 1949, working first in Porto Alegre. Throughout the 1950s, in São Paulo, she produced a vast number of drawings and paintings that already showed her affinity for a very reduced vocabulary of forms. During the sixties she began experimenting with unconventional materials and working her drawings in a "sculpturelike" manner, suspending them in space: the best-known are the *Droguinhas* and the *Objetos Gráficos*. At the same time, the work included lyrical and enigmatic sentences or just words and letters taken at random and thin lines freed from any formal rigidity. During the last decades of her life (she died in 1988) she sought to reconcile two paradoxical claims. On the one hand, her work was at odds with the purist demands of an essentialist perception, aiming for the basic structures of vision, performing the harmonic fitting of the object and the subject; on the other hand, the work evoked the material and social conditions that serve as a substratum to vision.

Lynn Silverman
Lynn Silverman was born in 1952 in Syracuse, New York. In 1975, after graduating from Pratt Institute in Brooklyn with a bachelor of fine arts in photography, she emigrated to Sydney, Australia. Horizons was produced during her six years in Australia. After a brief period back in the United States, she

emigrated to Britain in 1983. In 1992 she was awarded a master's in fine art from Goldsmith's College, London. Silverman has regularly mounted one-person exhibitions and has participated in group shows. Her work is in the collections of the National Gallery of Victoria, Melbourne; Australian National Gallery, Canberra; Visual Arts Board, Australia Council of the Arts, Sydney; Art Gallery of New South Wales, Sydney; and Department of Education and Science, London. Her publications include *Furniture Fictions* (Cornerhouse Publications, 1989) and *1:1* (Angel Row Gallery with Camerawork and Derby University, 1993). She currently lives in Derby and lectures in fine art at the University of Humberside.

Nancy Spero
Nancy Spero was born in 1926 in Cleveland, Ohio. She received a bachelor of fine art from the School of the Art Institute of Chicago in 1949; in 1949–50 she attended the Ecole des Beaux-Arts, Paris, and the atelier of André L'Hote, Paris. In 1951 she married artist Leon Golub and subsequently had three sons. In 1956–57 she lived in Florence, Italy; in 1959–64 in Paris; and from 1964 to the present in New York City. Spero's work in the 1950s involved painting on paper and canvas; later works included *The Paris Black Paintings* (1959–64); *War Series* (1966–69); *Artaud Paintings* (1969–70); *Codex Artaud* (1971–72); *Licit Exp., Torture in Chile, The Hours of the Night* (1973–74); *Torture of Women* (1974–76); *Notes in Time on Women* (1976–79); *The First Language* (1979–81); *To the Revolution, Sky Goddess/Egyptian Acrobat,* and *Totems* (1980s). Since 1988 she has executed numerous site-specific wall printing installations as well as works on paper and silk. She participated in the "Inside the Visible: Begin the Beguine in Flanders" project at the Kanaal Art Foundation, Kortrijk.

Jana Sterbak
Jana Sterbak was born in Prague in 1955. In the second half of the 1960s she moved to Canada, where she received a bachelor of fine arts from Concordia University, Montreal. Since the beginning of the 1980s her work has been shown extensively throughout Canada, the United States, and Europe, notably at the New Museum of Contemporary Art, New York (1990); the National Gallery of Canada, Ottawa (1991); the Museum of Modern Art, New York (1992); the Louisiana Museum, Humlebæk, Denmark (1993); the Musée d'Art Contemporain de Montréal and the Musée des Beaux-Arts de Nantes (1994); and the Kanaal Art Foundation, Kortrijk, Belgium. In 1995–96, a major exhibition of her work was presented at the Musée d'Art Moderne de Saint-Etienne and Fundació Tàpies, Barcelona, and at the Serpentine Gallery, London. Her work is represented in numerous public collections, among them the National Gallery of Canada, Ottawa; the Walker Art Center, Minneapolis; Musée des Beaux-Arts de Nantes; Musée d'Art Contemporain de Montréal; Fonds National d'Art Contemporain, Paris; San Diego Art Museum; and Musée de Québec. Jana Sterbak lives and works in Montreal and Paris.

Margaret Sundell
Margaret Sundell was born in New York City in 1965. She is a Ph.D. candidate in art history at Columbia University and a founding editor of the journal *Documents*.

Sophie Taeuber-Arp
Sophie Taeuber-Arp was born in Davos, Switzerland, in 1889. After studying textile design at the St. Gall School of Arts and Crafts, she worked at the Swiss branch of the Wiener Werkstätte, which Josef Hoffmann had set up in Zurich. She also studied dance with von Laban. From 1916 to 1929 she taught textile design at the Zurich School of Arts and Crafts. In 1921 she married Jean Arp, whom she had known since 1916. Both were closely involved in the activities of the Cabaret Voltaire and the dada group. In 1931 she became a member of Abstraction-Création but resigned in 1934 in protest at the group's exclusion of all figurative art. She founded the art periodical *Plastique* in 1936. Taeuber-Arp died in Zurich in 1943.

Nadine Tasseel
Photographer Nadine Tasseel was born in 1953 in Sint-Niklaas, Belgium. She studied painting at the academy in Antwerp and later specialized in photography. She has had shows in several Belgian cities (including the Kanaal Art Foundation, Kortrijk) and abroad (in Rotterdam and Reims).

Ana Torfs
Ana Torfs, born 1963, is a communication scientist. She studied at the University of Leuven (1981–86) and the High Institute for Visual Arts, film-video division, at Sint-Lukas, Brussels (1986–90). Her work has been selected for several festivals in Belgium and abroad; she received the Prix de Jeune Créateur at the 1995 International Video festival in Geneva.

Joëlle Tuerlinckx
Joëlle Tuerlinckx, born in 1958, is an artist living and working in Brussels. Her work has been shown in solo exhibitions at the Centre d'Art Contemporain, Lausanne (1990), Witte de With, Rotterdam (1994), and Opus Operandi, Ghent (1995), and in group exhibitions in Brussels, Toulouse, Paris, Aachen, and Kortrijk.

Ernst van Alphen
Ernst van Alphen, born in the Netherlands in 1958, teaches comparative literature at the University of Leiden and is a member of the Amsterdam School of Cultural Analysis. He is the author of Francis Bacon and the Loss of Self (1993) and of the forthcoming *Caught by History: Holocaust Effects in Contemporary Art and Theory*.

Frank Vande Veire
Frank Vande Veire was born in Belgium in 1958 and now lives in Amsterdam. He studied philosophy and cultural antrhopology at the University of Leuven. He works in the field of philosophical aesthetics and art and literary criticism and has published in several magazines. He teaches in the Advanced Studies Program for Fine Arts in Rotterdam and is working on a book entitled *Atopos: An Introduction in Modern Aesthetics*.

Paulo Venancio Filho
Paulo Venancio Filho is art critic and professor of art history at the Federal University of Rio de Janeiro. He has a master's degree from that university's School of Communication and a bachelor's degree in philosophy. He is the author of *Marcel Duchamp: A beleza da indiferença* (Marcel Duchamp: The Beauty of Indifference) and articles on modern and contemporary Brazilian artists published in Brazilian and foreign newspapers, magazines, and catalogues.

Lea Vergine
Lea Vergine was born in Naples in 1938 and currently lives in Milan, where she writes for *Corriere della Sera* and *Il Manifesto* (Rome). Her publications include *Body Art and Similia* (1974), *Practica Politica* (1976), and *L'altra metà dell'avanguardia 1910–1940* (1980–82). She was one of the curators of the 1990 Venice Biennale.

Cecilia Vicuña

Born in 1948, Cecilia Vicuña is a Chilean artist and poet. She is the author of many books, most recently *Unravelling Words & Weaving of Water* (Graywolf Press, 1992). She has worked in nature and on city streets since 1966. Her work has been exhibited at the Museum of Modern Art in New York, the Royal Museum in Antwerp, the Museum of Fine Arts in Santiago, and the University Art Museum in Berkeley. Currently a retrospective exhibition of her work is being circulated by the Kanaal Art Foundation, Kortrijk, Belgium, which will also publish a book devoted to her work: *Knot-Thing*. Vicuña lives and works in New York and Chile.

Maria Helena Vieira da Silva

Maria Helena Vieira da Silva, born in 1908 in Lisbon, Portugal, moved to Paris in 1928. She married Arpad Szenes in 1930 and in 1956 became a French citizen. In 1932 she met Jeanne Bucher, director of her first permanent gallery. Vieira da Silva lived in Brazil from 1940 to 1946. From 1945 on she successively exhibited at Marian Willard, New York; the 1953 Biennial of São Paulo; and the 1955 Biennial of Caracas. In 1958 she had a retrospective at Kestner-Gesellschaft. She was nominated for the Guggenheim Prize and the fourth Carnegie Prize. In 1959 and 1964 she participated in Documenta, Kassel. Other exhibitions include Knoedler Gallery, New York (1961); Philips Collection, Washington, D.C.; Grand Prix, Biennial of São Paulo (1962); Grand Prix, National Art (1966); and retrospectives in Paris, Rotterdam, Oslo, Bali, and Lisbon (1969–70). She also had retrospectives at the Museum of Modern Art, Paris (1977) and the Gulbenkian Foundation, Lisbon, and Grand Palais, Paris (1988). Vieira da Silva died in Paris in 1992.

Carrie Mae Weems

Carrie Mae Weems was born in Portland, Oregon, in 1953. She attended the California Institute of the Arts in Valencia and later obtained graduate degrees at the University of California at San Diego (M.F.A.) and the University of California at Berkeley (M.A. in folklore). Her lecturing, teaching, and photographic work focuses primarily on issues of African American representation in photography, literature, and cultural history. For the past fifteen years she has shown extensively in alternative galleries. She was also included in the 1991 Whitney Biennial and in the recent exhibition "Black Male: Representations of Masculinity in Contemporary American Art," curated by Thelma Golden for the Whitney Museum of American Art and the Armand Hammer Museum of Art in West Los Angeles. A book of Weems's photographs and texts, *Then What? Photographs and Folklore*, was published by CEPA Gallery in 1990. She currently resides in Northhampton, Massachusetts, and teaches at Hampshire College.

Judith Wilson

Judith Wilson is an assistant professor of art history and director of undergraduate studies in African and African-American studies at Yale University. A member of the international council for Third Text and of the editorial board of the College Art Association's Art Journal, she was an associate editor of *Ms.* magazine from 1975 to 1978 and an art reviewer for the *Village Voice* during 1979 and 1980. Since 1979 she has written extensively about the work of African American artists for a variety of exhibition catalogues and journals. Wilson holds a Ph.D. and a master's degree in art history from Yale and a bachelor of arts in literature from Bennington College.

William S. Wilson

William S. Wilson was born in Baltimore, Maryland, in 1932. Educated in philosophy at the University of Virginia, he received a Ph.D. in English literature from Yale University. He has published a novel, a book of short stories (*Why Don't I Write Like Franz Kafka*), and essays on visual artists such as Paul Cezanne, Ray Johnson, Robert Morris, Mel Bochner, John Willenbecher, and Alison Knowles. He is the son of the late assemblage artist May Wilson and the father of two daughters and a son.

Francesca Woodman

Francesca Woodman was born in 1958 in Denver, Colorado. She received her early schooling in Denver and in Florence. She attended Rhode Island School of Design in Providence from 1975 to 1979 and spent the 1977–78 school year in Rome on the RISD Rome honors program. She moved to New York in 1979, and in 1981 she published *Some Disordered Interior Geometrics* (Philadelphia: Synapse Press). She committed suicide on January 19, 1981, at the age of twenty-two.

Louise Bourgeois

Gardner, Paul. *Louise Bourgeois*. New York: Universe, 1994.

Kotik, Charlotta, Terrie Sultan, and Christian Leigh. *Louise Bourgeois: The Locus of Memory, Works 1982–1993*. Exhibition catalogue. New York: H. N. Abrams, in association with the Brooklyn Museum, 1994.

Kuspit, Donald. *Bourgeois: An Interview with Louise Bourgeois*. New York: Vintage Books, 1988.

Louise Bourgeois. Exhibition catalogue. Frankfurt: Frankfurter Kunstverein, 1989.

Louise Bourgeois, Works on Paper. Exhibition catalogue. Amsterdam: Museum Overholland, 1988.

Pincus-Witten, Robert. *Bourgeois Truth*. Exhibition catalogue. New York: Robert Miller Gallery, 1982.

Storr, Robert. Introduction to *Louise Bourgeois Drawings*. New York: Robert Miller Gallery, 1988.

Wye, Deborah. *Louise Bourgeois*. Exhibition catalogue. New York: Museum of Modern Art, 1982.

Wye, Deborah. *The Prints of Louise Bourgeois*. New York: Museum of Modern Art, 1994.

Claude Cahun

Cahun, Claude. *Aveux non avenus*. Paris: Editions du Carrefour, 1930.

Cahun, Claude. *Les paris sont ouverts*. Paris: José Corti, 1934.

Lasalle, Honor, and Abigail Solomon-Godeau. "Surrealist Confession: Claude Cahun's Photomontages." *Afterimage* 19, no. 8 (March 1992): 10–13.

Leperlier, François. *Claude Cahun: L'écart et la métamorphose*. Paris: Jean-Michel Place, 1992.

Lichtenstein, Therese. "A Mutable Mirror: Claude Cahun." *Artforum*, no. 8 (April 1992): 64–67.

Place, Jean-Michel. *Claude Cahun, photographe*. Exhibition catalogue. Paris: Musée d'Art Moderne de la Ville de Paris, 23 June–17 September 1995.

Emily Carr

Appelhof, Ruth S. *The Expressionist Landscape: North American Painting, 1920–1947*. Birmingham, Alabama: Birmingham Museum of Art, 1988.

Carr, Emily. *Klee Wyck*. Toronto: Oxford University Press, 1941.

Crosby, Marcia. "Construction of the Imaginary Indian." In Stan Douglas, ed., *Vancouver Anthology*. Vancouver: Talonbooks, 1991.

Shadbolt, Doris. *Emily Carr*. Vancouver: Douglas & McIntyre; Seattle: University of Washington Press, 1990.

Thom, Ian M. *Emily Carr in France*. Vancouver: Vancouver Art Gallery, 1991.

Theresa Hak Kyung Cha

Hanhardt, John. "Theresa Hak Kyung Cha: Exilee." *The New American Film and Video Series*, no. 76 (program note). New York: Whitney Museum of American Art, 1995.

Kim, Elaine H., and Norma Alarcon, eds. *Writing Self, Writing Nation: Essays on Theresa Hak Kyung Cha's Dictee*. Berkeley: Third Woman Press, 1994.

Lew, Walter K. *Excerpts from ΔIKTH DIKTE for DICTEE* (1982). Seoul: Yeul Eum Sa, 1992.

Martin, Stephen-Paul. "Theresa Cha: Creating a Feminine Voice." In *Open Form and the Feminine Imagination: The Politics of Reading in Twentieth Century Innovative Writing*. Washington, D.C.: Maisonneuve Press, 1988.

Rinder, Lawrence. "Theresa Cha: Other Things Seen, Other Things Heard." *New American Film and Video Series*, no. 69 (program note). New York: Whitney Museum of American Art, 1992–93.

Stephens, Michael. "Korea: Theresa Hak Kyung Cha." In *The Drammaturgy of Style: Voice in Short Fiction*. Carbondale: Southern Illinois University Press, 1986.

Wolf, Susan. "Theresa Cha: Recalling Telling Retelling." *Afterimage*, Summer 1986.

Lygia Clark

Brett, Guy. "Lygia Clark: In Search of the Body." *Art in America*, July 1994.

Clark, Lygia. *Nostalgia of the Body*. Intro. by Yve-Alain Bois. October, no. 69 (Summer 1994).

Gullar, Ferreira, Mario Pedrosa, and Lygia Clark. *Lygia Clark*. Rio de Janeiro: Funarte, 1980.

Lygia Clark e Hélio Oiticica. Exhibition catalogue. Rio de Janeiro and São Paulo: Funarte, 1986.

Milliet, Maria Alice. *Lygia Clark: Obra-Trajeto*. São Paulo: Editora da Universidade de São Paulo, 1992.

Signals (London) 1, no. 7 (1965). Lygia Clark special issue. Rpt. London: Insitute of International Visual Arts, 1995.

Hanne Darboven

Darboven, Hanne. *Primitive Time/Clock Time*. Exhibition catalogue. Philadelphia: Goldie Paley Gallery, Moore College of Art and Design, 1990.

Grande, John K. "Hanne Darboven, Writing Time." *Espace*, no. 17 (Fall 1991).

Graw, Isabelle. "Marking Time: Time and Writing in the Work of Hanne Darboven." *Artscribe International*, January/February 1990.

Lippard, Lucy R. "Hanne Darboven: Deep in Numbers." *Artforum*, October 1973.

Pohlen, Annette. "Hanne Darboven's Time: The Content of Consciousness." *Artforum*, April 1983.

Lili Dujourie

Bos, S. *Lili Dujouri*. In *FRAC pays de la Loire, Abbaye Royale de Fontevraud*. Exhibition catalogue. Meymac: Centre d'Art Contemporain, Abbaye Saint-André, 1987-88, pp. 7-12.

Bos, S. "Topics and Atopy." *De Appel*, no. 2 (1989-90): 16-19.

Cassiman, B. *L'envers de l'endroit*. In *Lili Dujouri*. Exhibition catalogue. Grenoble: Centre National d'Art Contemporain, 1990, pp. 13-25.

Cooke, L. *Mantissa*. In *Passageworks*. Exhibition catalogue. Malmö: Rooseum, 1993, p. 30.

De Decker, A. "Het Kunstwerk als zelfportret van de kunstenaar." In *Inzicht/Overzicht*. Ghent: Museum van Hedendaagse Kunst, 1979, pp. 7-11.

de Duve, T. In *Lili Dujouri, Bernd Lohaus, Jan Vercruysse, Didier Vermeiren, Marthe Wéry*. Exhibition catalogue. Tournai: Ancienne Imprimerie l'Avenir, 1979.

Newman, M. "Fallen Haloes." In Artscribe International, no. 58 (June-July 1986): 54-57.

Ellen Gallagher

Duffy, Robert W. "Art of the 90s." *St.Louis Post-Dispatch*, April 2, 1995.

Lloyd, Ann Wilson. "Ellen Gallagher at Mario Diacono." *Art in America*, April 1995.

McQuaid, Cale. "Modern Mettle." *Boston Phoenix*, March 17, 1995.

Smith, Roberta. "Artists Select," Part I. *New York Times*, January 7, 1994.

Stapen, Nancy. "Paintings Probe the Imagery of Racism." *Boston Globe*, November 3, 1994.

Termin, Christine. "Exploring Identity Internationally." *Boston Globe*, January 19, 1994.

Gego

Blanco, Lourdes. "Gego libre y abstracta." *El Diario de Caracas*, September 24, 1994.

Blanco, Lourdes. *Gego: Reticulárea*. Caracas: Ediciones Galeria Conkright, 1969.

Figarella, Mariana. *Gego: dibujos sin papel*. Caracas: Ediciones

Museo de Bellas Artes, 1984.
Ossott, Hanni. *Gego*. Caracas: Ediciones Museo de Arte Contemporáneo, 1977.
Traba, Marta. *Gego*. Exhibition catalogue. Caracas: Editiones Museo de Arte Contemporáneo, 1977.
Traba, Marta. "Gego: Caracas tres mil." In *Mirar en Caracas*. Caracas: Mèonte Avila Editores, 1974.

Mona Hatoum
Disserted Space. Exhibition catalogue. Cardiff: Chapter, 1992.
Four Rooms. Group exhibition catalogue. London: Serpentine Gallery, 1993.
Mona Hatoum. Exhibition catalogue. Bristol: Arnolfini Gallery, 1993.
Mona Hatoum. Exhibition catalogue. Paris: Musée National d'Art Moderne, Centre Georges Pompidou, 1994.
Rites of Passage. Group exhibition catalogue. London: Tate Gallery, 1995.
Sense and Sensibility. Group exhibition catalogue. New York: Museum of Modern Art, 1994.

Nathalie Hervieux
Domino, Christophe. *L'entre-image*. Caen: FRAC Basse-Normandie, 1996.
Domino, Christophe. *Rivages contemporains*. Caen: FRAC Basse-Normandie, 1993.
Durand, Régis. *Catalogue des Acquisitions 1992–93*. Bobigny: FDAC, 1993, pp. 44–45.
Lemagny, Jean-Claude. *Corps transparents*. Exhibition catalogue. Reims: Le Mai de la Photo, 1994, pp. 6–8 .
Lemagny, Jean-Claude. *La matière de l'ombre, la fiction*. Exhibition catalogue. Paris: Nathan/Bibliothèque Nationale de France, 1994, pp. 52–53.
Müller-Pohle, Andreas. *Photography European Award '92*. Göttingen: Deutsch Leasing Support for the Arts, 1992, pp. 36–39.

Eva Hesse
Cooper, Helen A. *Eva Hesse: A Retrospective*. New Haven: Yale University Art Gallery, 1992.
David, Catherine. *Eva Hesse*. Valence: IVAM; Paris: Editions du Jeu de Paume, 1992.
Kozloff, Max. *Eva Hesse Paintings 1960–1964*. New York: Robert Miller Gallery, 1992.
Lippard, Lucy R. *Eva Hesse*. New York: New York University Press and Da Capo Press, 1992.
Reinhardt, Brigitte, ed. *Eva Hesse: Drawing in Space*. Ulm: Ulmer Museum, 1994.
Wilson, William. "Eva Hesse: Alone and/or Only With." *Artspace* 16, no. 5 (September–October 1992).

Susan Hiller
Coxhead, David, and Susan Hiller. *Dreams: Visions of the Night*. London: Thames & Hudson; New York: Avon; Paris: Editions du Seuil; Amsterdam: de Haan; Frankfurt: Umschau Verlag; Tokyo: Heibonsha Ltd., 1976, 1989, 1991.
Einzig, Barbara, ed. *Thinking about Art: Conversations with Susan Hiller*. Preface by Lucy Lippard. Manchester: Manchester University Press, 1995–96.
Fisher, Jean. *The Revenants of Time*. London: Matt's Gallery; Sheffield: Mappin Gallery; Glasgow, Third Eye Centre, 1990.
Hiller, Susan. *After the Freud Museum*. London: Books Work Press, 1995.
Hiller, Susan, comp. and intro. *The Myth of Primitivism*. New York and London: Routledge, 1991.
Warner, Maria, Stuart Morgan, Guy Brett, and Susan Hiller. *Susan Hiller 1976–'96*. Liverpool: Tate Gallery Publications, 1996.

Hannah Höch
Adriani, Götz, ed. *Hannah Höch*. Cologne: DuMont Buchverlag, 1980.
Bergius, Hanne. *Das Lachen Dadas: Die berliner Dadaisten und ihre Aktionen*. Giessen: Anabas, 1989.
Berlinische Galerie. *Hannah Höch 1989–1978, ihr Werk, ihr Leben, ihre Freunde*. Berlin: Argon Verlag, 1989.
Dech, Jula, and Ellen Maurer. *Dada zwischen Reden zu Hannah Höch*. Berlin: Orlanda-Frauenverlag, 1991.
Lavin, Maud. *Cut with the Kitchen Knife: The Weimar Photomontages of Hannah Höch*. New Haven: Yale University Press, 1993.
Theater-Schulz, Cornelia, ed. *Hannah Höch: Eine Lebenscollage*. 2 vols. Berlin: Berlinische Galerie, 1989.

Ann Veronica Janssens
Brayer, Marie-Ange. "Ann Veronica Janssens, l'espacement du regard." *Art Press* 175 (1992).
De Decker, Anny. "Ann Veronica Janssens." *Artefactum*, 1991.
Jacquet, Jean Paul. "Ann Veronica Janssens." *Blocnotes*, no. 8 (1995).
van den Abeele, Lieven. "Ann Veronica Janssens." *Forum International*, no. 15 (1992).

Katarzyna Kobro
Gresty, Hilary, and Jeremy Lewison, eds. *Constructivism in Poland 1923 to 1936*. Exhibition catalogue. Cambridge: Kettle's Yard Gallery, 1984.
Grzechca, Ursula. "Kobro und die konstruktivistische Bewegung." Doctoral dissertation, Wilhems Universität, Münster, 1986.
Stanislawski, Ryszard, ed. *Constructivism in Poland 1923–1936: BLOK, Praesens, a.r.* Exhibition catalogue. Essen: Museum Polkwang; Otterlo: Rijksmuseum Kröller-Müller, 1973.
Stanislawski, Ryszard, Ursula Grzechca-Mohr, and Jaromir Jedlinski, eds. *Katarzyna Kobro 1898–1951*. Exhibition catalogue. Cologne: Edition Wienand, 1991.
Zogrodzki, Janusz. *Katarzyna Kobro i kompozycia przestrzena*. Warsaw: Panstwowe Wydawnictwo Naukowe, 1984.

Yayoi Kusama
Adams, Brooks. "Proliferating Obsessions." *Art in America* 78, no. 4 (April 1990): 228ff.
Bhupendra, Karia, ed., with an essay by Alexandra Munroe. *Yayoi Kusama: A Retrospective*. New York: Center for International Contemporary Art, 1989.
Japon des Avant Gardes 1910–1970. Paris: Centre Georges Pompidou, 1986.
Kusama, Yayoi. *Kusama Yayoi: driving image = Yayoi Kusama*. Tokyo: Parco shuppan, 1986.
Munroe, Alexandra, ed. *Japanese Art After 1945: Scream Against the Sky*. New York: Abrams, in association with the Guggenheim Museum and the San Francisco Museum of Modern Art, 1994.
Read, Herbert, Udo Kultermann, Gordon Brown, and Yusuke Nakahara. *Obsession: Yayoi Kusama*. Exhibition catalogue. Tokyo: Fuji Television Gallery, 1982.

Bracha Lichtenberg Ettinger
Ducker, Carolyn. "Translating the Matrix." Versus Occasional Paper no. 1, in *Versus* (Leeds), no. 3 (1994).
Huhn, Rosi. *Bracha Lichtenberg Ettinger et la folie de la raison*. In French and German. Paris: Goethe Institut, 1990.
Huhn, Rosi. "Das Problem der Entsorgung in Kunst und Kultur als Passage zum 'Positiven Barbarentum.'" In French and German. In *Passagen nach Walter Benjamin*. Mainz: Verlag Hermann Schmidt, 1992.
Lyotard, Jean-François, Christine Buci-Glucksmann, and Griselda Pollock. In exhibition catalogue *Bracha Lichtenberg Ettinger: Halala-Autistwork*. In English, Hebrew, and French. Jerusalem: Israel Museum, 1995.
Pollock, Griselda. "Introduction to the Work of Bracha Lichtenberg Ettinger." In *Third Text* (London), nos. 28–29 (1994).
Shapira, Sarit. In exhibition catalogue *Routes of Wandering*. In English and Hebrew. Jerusalem: Israel Museum, 1991, pp. 33, 173, 139, 202–208, 155–156.

Anna Maria Maiolino
Herkenhoff, Paulo. "Maiolino, between Piso and Flanders." In *America, Bride of the Sun: 500 Years Latin America and the Low*

Countries. Antwerp: Royal Museum of Fine Arts/Flemish Community and Administration of External Relations, 1992.

Moraes, Frederico. *Chronology of Visual Arts in Rio de Janeiro 1816–1994*. Rio de Janeiro: Top-Books, 1995.

Piccinini, Daisy Valle Machado, coordinator. *The Object of Art: Brazil in the 60's*. São Paulo: Alvaro Penteado Foundation, 1978.

Pontual, Roberto. *Between Two Centuries: Brazilian Art in the 20th Century in Gilberto Chateaubriand Collection*. Rio de Janeiro: J.B., 1987.

Pontual, Roberto. *Contemporary Art: Gilberto Chateaubriand Collection*. Rio de Janeiro: J.B., 1987.

Zanini, Walter. *General History of Art in Brazil*. São Paulo: Walter Moreira Sales Institute and Djalma Guimarâes Foundation, 1983.

Agnes Martin

Haskell, Barbara, with essays by Anna Chave and Rosalind Krauss. *Agnes Martin*. New York: Whitney Museum of American Art, 1992.

Ana Mendieta

Ana Mendieta: A Retrospective. Exhibition catalogue. New York: New Museum of Contemporary Art, 1987.

Broude, Norma, and Mary Garrard, eds. *The Power of Feminist Art: The American Movement of the 1970s. History and Impact*. New York: Abrams, 1994.

Chadwick, Whitney. *Women, Art, and Society*. London: Thames and Hudson, 1990.

Fusco, Coco. "Traces of Ana Mendieta: 1988–1993." In *English Is Broken Here: Notes on Cultural Fusion in the Americas*. New York: The New Press, 1995, pp. 121–125.

Galligan, Gregory. "Ana Mendieta: A Retrospective." *Arts Magazine*, April 1988, pp. 49–51.

Katz, Robert. *Naked by the Window: The Fatal Marriage of Carl Andre and Ana Mendieta*. New York: Atlantic Monthly Press, 1990.

Lippard, Lucy. *Overlay: Contemporary Art and the Art of Prehistory*. New York: Pantheon Books, 1983.

Mendieta, Rachel. "Ana Mendieta: Self-Portrait of a Goddess." *Review: Latin American Literature and Arts*, January–June 1988, p. 39.

Spero, Nancy. "Tracing Ana Mendieta." *Artforum*, April 1992, pp. 75–77.

Avis Newman

Barker, Barry, and Jon Thompson. *Falls the Shadow: Recent British and European Art*. Exhibition catalogue. London: Arts Council of Great Britain, 1986.

Bickers, Patricia, and John Hutchinson. *Vicious Circle*. Dublin: Douglas Hyde Gallery, De Appel Foundation, 1993.

Ferguson, Bruce, Sandy Nairne, and Jean Fisher. *The Impossible Self*. Exhibition catalogue. London: Arts Council of Great Britain, 1988.

Fisher, Jean. *Avis Newman*. Exhibition catalogue. London: Lisson Gallery; Chicago: Renaissance Society, 1987.

Kent, Sara. *Worlds in a Box*. Exhibition catalogue. London: Arts Council of Great Britain, 1994–'95.

Newman, Michael. *The Analytical Theatre: New Art from Britain*. Exhibition catalogue. New York: Independent Curators Incorporated, 1987.

Thompson, Jon, Alexander Moffat, and Marjorie Allthorpe-Guylton. *British Art Show: Old Allegiances and New Directions, 1979–1984*. London: Arts Council of Great Britain, 1984.

Carol Rama

Bonito Oliva, Achille, et al. *Carol Rama*. 1994.

Fossati, Paolo, ed. *Carol Rama*. Umberto Allemandi, 1989.

Sanguineti, Edoardo. *Carol Rama: Luogo e segni*. Venice: Galleria il Capricorno, 1994.

Vergine, Lea, ed. *Carol Rama*. Exhibition catalogue. Milan: Mazzotta, 1985.

Martha Rosler

Buchloh, Benjamin H.D. "Appropriation and Montage in Contemporary Art." *Artforum*, September 1982. Reprinted in *Open Letter*, Summer-Fall 1983.

Carmichael, Virginia. "Martha Rosler's Unknown Secrets." In *Framing History: The Rosenberg Story and the Cold War*. Minneapolis: University of Minnesota Press, 1993.

Mellencamp, Patricia. "Avant-Garde TV: Simulation and Surveillance." In René Payant, ed., *Vidéo*. Montreal: Artextes, 1986.

Owens, Craig. "The Discourse of Others: Feminism and Postmodernism." In Hal Foster, ed., *The Anti-Aesthetic: Essays on Postmodernism and Culture*. Port Townsend, Washington: Bay Press, 1983.

Public Information: Desire, Disaster, Document. Exhib. cat. San Francisco: Museum of Modern Art, 1994. Essays by Robert R. Riley ("Leave Proof: Media and Public Information"), Abigail Solomon-Godeau ("Inside/Out"), and John S. Weber ("Martha Rosler").

Sekula, Allan. "Dismantling Modernism, Reinventing Documentary (Notes on the Politics of Representation)." *Massachusetts Review*, Winter 1979.

Taubin, Amy. "And What Is a Fact, Anyway? (On a Tape by Martha Rosler.)" *Millenium Film Journal*, no. 4/5 (Summer/Fall 1979).

Williams, Val. "The Myth and the Media: Photography and the Vietnam War, 1968-1992." In *Warworks: Women, Photography and the Iconography of War*. London: Virago, 1994.

Charlotte Salomon

Elbaum, Dalia. "Analyse esthétique de l'oeuvre de Charlotte Salomon." In *Charlotte Salomon: Leben oder Theater ?* Exhibition catalogue. Brussels: Consistoire Central Israélite, 1982.

Lowenthal-Felstiner, Mary. "Taking Her Life/History: The Autobiography of Charlotte Salomon." In B. Brodzki and C. Schenk, *Life/Lines: Theorizing Women's Autobiography*. Ithaca: Cornell University Press, 1988, pp. 320–337.

Lowenthal-Felstiner, Mary. *To Paint Her Life: Charlotte Salomon in the Nazi Era*. New York: Harper Collins, 1994.

Reichenfeld, Katja. "Leben ? oder Theater ? Regie: Charlotte Salomon." *Jong Holland*, 1991.

Schwarz, Gary. "Life or Theater ? The Autobiography of Charlotte Salomon." *Art News*, 1981, pp. 168–171.

Van Alphen, Ernst. "Salomon's Work." *Journal of Narrative and Life History* 3, nos. 2–3 (1993): 239–254.

Mira Schendel

Brett, Guy. "A Radical Leap." In Dawn Ades, org., *Art in Latin America: The Modern Era 1820–1980*. New Haven: Yale University Press, 1989.

de Campos, Haroldo. *Mira Schendel*. Rio de Janiero: Museo de Arte Moderna, 1966.

Herkenhoff, Paulo. "Brazil: Origins and Breakthroughs of Contemporary Art." In Lori Ledis and Robert Flam, *Art from Brazil in New York*. New York: American Cultural Institute, Ledisflam Inc., and Galery Lelong, 1995.

Iriarte, Maria Elvira. "Mira Schendel." *Art Nexus* (Bogota), June 1993, pp. 83–87.

Naves, Rodrigo. "Conseitos sensiveis." In *Mira Schendel*. São Paulo: Paulo Figueiredo Galeria de Arte, 1985.

Tassinari, Alberto. "Mais ou menos frutas." In *Folhelim*. São Paulo: Folha de São Paulo, September 23, 1984.

Lynn Silverman

Fisher, Jean. "Reveries on 1:1." *Portfolio*, no. 20, pp. 48–49.

Furniture Fictions. Manchester: Cornerhouse, 1989.

Isherwood, Sue. "Lynn Silverman, Locating Ourselves: A Meeting with Sue Isherwood." In *Viewfindings*, ed. Liz Wells. West Country Books (Available Light), pp. 85–93.

Morris, Meaghan. "Two Types of Photography Criticism Located in Relation to Lynn Silverman's Series." In *The Pirate's Fiancée: Feminism, Reading, Postmodernism*. London: Verso, 1988.

Nancy Spero

Blazwick, Iwona, ed. *Nancy Spero*. London: Phaidon Press, 1986.

Golub, Leon, and Nancy Spero. *War and Memory*. Exhibition catalogue. Paris: American Center; Cambridge: MIT List Visual Arts Center, 1995.

Harris, Susan, and Sune Nordgren. *Nancy Spero*. Exhibition catalogue. Malmö, 1994.

Nahas, Dominique, Jo Anna Isaak, Robert Storr, and Leon Golub. *Nancy Spero: Works Since 1950*. Exhibition catalogue. Syracuse: Everson Museum of Art, 1987.

Reinhardt, Brigitte, Robert Storr, Noemi Smolik, Achille Bonito Oliva, and Klaus Vierneisel, with interview excerpt of Nancy Spero and Jon Bird. *Nancy Spero: Women Breathing*. Published in conjunction with exhibition. Ulm: Ulmer Museum, 1986.

Storr, Robert. *Nancy Spero: Rebirth of Venus*, ed. Edith de Ak. Kyoto: Art Random, Kyoto Shoin, International Co., 1989.

Jana Sterbak

Ferguson, Bruce. *Jana Sterbak*. New York: New Museum of Contemporary Art, 1990.

Kalinovska, Milena. "Jana Sterbak in Conversation with Milena Kalinovska." In *Jana Sterbak: States of Being/Corps à Corps*. Ottawa: National Gallery of Canada, 1991, pp. 46–53.

Martinez, Rosa. "Dressed for Intensity." In *I Want You to Feel the Way I Do*. Barcelona: Fundació La Caixa, 1993, pp. 28–29.

Murray, Irena Zantovská. "Domesticity and Diremption: Poetics of Space in the Work of Jana Sterbak." In *Velleitas, Jana Sterbak*. Barcelona: Fundació Antoni Tàpies, 1995, pp. 23–38.

Nemiroff, Diana. "States of Being." In *Jana Sterbak: States of Being/Corps à Corps*. Ottawa: National Gallery of Canada, 1991, pp. 14–43.

Noble, Richard. "Jana Sterbak: The Dialectic of Creation and Containment." In *Velleitas, Jana Sterbak*. Barcelona: Fundació Antoni Tàpies, 1995, pp. 51–70.

Storsve, Jonas. "I Long for the Land That Is Not." In *Jana Sterbak*. Copenhagen: Louisiana Museum of Modern Art, 1993, pp. 17–25.

Sophie Taeuber-Arp

Lancher, Carolyn. *Sophie Taeuber-Arp*. Exhibition catalogue. New York: Museum of Modern Art, 1981.

Schmidt, Georg, ed. *Sophie Taeuber-Arp*. Basel: Holbein Verlag, 1948.

Sophie Taeuber-Arp. Exhibition catalogue. Paris: Musée d'Art Moderne de la Ville de Paris; Lausanne: Musée Cantonal des Beaux-Arts, 1989.

Staber, Margit. *Sophie Taeuber-Arp*. Lausanne: Editions Rencontre, 1970.

Nadine Tasseel

De Backer, Leen, and Lieven De Cauter. "The Mannerism of Nadine Tasseel." In *Tableau Vivant, Nature Morte (& vice versa)*. Exhibition catalogue. Antwerp: Museum of Contemporary Art, 1994, pp. 19–21.

Eelbode, Erik. "Messages des ombres noires—Nadine Tasseel—Vanitas en une matière stylisée." *Art et Culture*, no. 9 (May 1993).

Ana Torfs

Asselberghs, Herman. "Akarova-Baugniet, Being Modern." *Andere Sinema* (Belgium) 110 (1992).

Asselberghs, Herman. "Video as a Borderline Case, on 'Il Combattimento'." *Etcetera* (Belgium) 99 (1993).

Ernie, Tee. "Filming Anne Teresa De Keersmaeker, from Greenaway to Torfs and Persijn." In *Skrien* (Netherlands) 190 (1993).

Le prix de la jeune peinture belge. Exhibition catalogue. Fonds Mercator Paribas, 1994.

Prat, T., T. Raspail, and G. Rey, eds. *La Biennale d'Art Contemporain de Lyon*. Exhibition catalogue. Paris: Réunion des Musées Nationaux, 1995.

Joëlle Tuerlinckx

Brianconi, I., J. P. Deridder, S. Eyberg, J. Tuerlinckx, and C. Vandamme. *Anti Chambres*. Exhibition catalogue. Brussels: Exhibitions of the Palais des Beaux-Arts.

Crabeels, Cel, Johanna Roderburg, Andreas Sansoni, and Joëlle Tuerlinckx. Exhibition catalogue. Ludwig Forum für Internationale Kunst.

Kremer, Mark, and Joëlle Tuerlinckx. *Witte de With Cahier 3*. Rotterdam. Pp. 149–153, 155–161 .

Luyckx, F. *Photographies Joëlle Tuerlinckx*. Sint-Lukas, December 1995.

Tuerlinckx, Joëlle. *Witte de With Cahier 2*. Rotterdam.

Cecilia Vicuña

Bercht, Fatima. "Document in Wool." In *America, Bride of the Sun*, exhibition catalogue. Antwerp: Royal Museum of Fine Arts, 1992.

de Zegher, Catherine. "Cecilia Vicuña's Ouvrage: Knot a Not, Notes as Knots," In Griselda Pollock, ed., *Generations and Geographies*. London: Thames and Hudson, 1996.

Kuoni, Carin. "Nuchterheit und Idealismus: EXIT ART." *Kunstforum* 118 (1992).

Lippard, Lucy R. "Cecilia Vicuña, hilando la fibra comun." *Arte Internacional* (Museum of Modern Art, Bogota), no. 18 (1994).

Lippard, Lucy R. *Mixed Blessings: New Art in a Multicultural America*. New York: Pantheon, 1990.

Rinder, Larry. *El Ando Futuro*. Exhibition catalogue. Berkeley: University Art Museum, Matrix Series, 1993.

Witzling, Mara R. "Cecilia Vicuña." In Mara R. Witzling, ed., *Voicing Today's Visions:Writings by Contemporary Women Artists*. New York: Universe Publishing, 1994.

Maria Helena Vieira da Silva

Butor, Michel. *Vieira da Silva. Peintures*. Paris: L'Autre Musée, La Différence, 1983.

Claude, Esteban. Preface to *La conscience et l'étoilement*. Exhibition catalogue. Paris: Musée National d'Art Moderne, 1969.

Laude, Jean. "Vieira da Silva." *Cimaise* (Paris), no. 145 (1978).

Roy, Claude. *Vieira da Silva*. Paris: Ars Mundi, 1988.

Seuphor, Michel. "Promenade autour de Vieira da Silva." *Cahiers d'Art*, no. 2 (1949).

Solier, René de. *Vieira da Silva*. Le Musée de Poche. Paris: Georges Fall, 1956.

Weelen, Guy, and Jacques Lassaigne. *Vieira da Silva*. Paris: Cercle d'Art, 1987.

Carrie Mae Weems

Golden, Thelma. *Representations of Masculinity in Contemporary Art*. New York: Whitney Museum of American Art, 1994.

Johnson, Ken. "Generation Saga." *Art in America*, June 1991, pp. 49–51.

Jones, Kellie. "In Their Own Image." *Artforum*, November 1990, pp. 132–138.

Squires, Carol. "Domestic Blitz: The Modern Cleans House." *Artforum*, October 1991, pp. 88–91.

Wallis, Brian, ed. *Blasted Allegories: An Anthology of Writings by Contemporary Artists*. New York: New Museum of Contemporary Art; Cambridge: MIT Press, 1988.

Willis, Deborah. *Black Photographers 1940–1988: A Bio-Bibliography*. New York: Gardner Press, 1988.

Francesca Woodman

Antomarini, Brunella. "Francesca Woodman." *Parkett*, no. 15 (January 1988).

Brenson, Michael. "Francesca Woodman: Photographic Work." *New York Times*, March 7, 1986.

Gabhart, Ann. "Francesca Woodman, 1958–1981." In *Francesca Woodman, Photographic Work*, exhibition catalogue. Wellesley, Massachusetts: Wellesley College Museum, 1986.

Haus, Mary Ellen. "Francesca Woodman." *Art News* 85, no. 1 (April 1986).

Kenny, Lorraine. "Problem Sets: The Cannonization of Franceska Woodman." *Afterimage* 14, no. 4 (November 1986).

Krauss, Rosalind. "Problem Sets." In *Francesca Woodman, Photographic Work*, exhibition catalogue. Wellesley, Massachusetts: Wellesley College Museum, 1986.

Solomon-Godeau, Abigail. "Just like A Woman." In *Francesca Woodman, Photographic Work*, exhibition catalogue. Wellesley, Massachusetts: Wellesley College Museum, 1986.

Checklist to the Exhibition

Dimensions are in inches or centimeters; height precedes width precedes depth.

Louise Bourgeois

Persistent Antagonism, 1946–48
painted wood
67 1/2 x 12 x 12 in.
Collection Frances and Thomas Dittmer, New York

Paddle Woman, 1947
bronze
57 3/4 x 16 1/4 x 12 in.
Courtesy Robert Miller Gallery, New York

The Tomb of a Young Person, 1947–49
bronze
46 x 12 x12 in.
Courtesy Robert Miller Gallery, New York

Portrait of C.Y., 1947–49
painted wood with nails
169.5 x 30.4 x 30.4 cm.
Courtesy Robert Miller Gallery, New York

Pillar, 1947–49
bronze and stainless steel
156.2 x 30.4 x 30.4 cm.
Courtesy Robert Miller Gallery, New York

Depression Woman, 1949–50
bronze, white patina
189.9 x 30.4 x 30.4 cm.
Courtesy Robert Miller Gallery, New York

Friendly Evidence, 1950
bronze,
177.8 x 30.4 x 30.4 cm.
Courtesy Robert Miller Gallery, New York

Memling Dawn, 1951
painted wood
67 1/4 x 9 x 7 in.
Collection Frances and Thomas Dittmer, New York

*Spiral Woman,*1951–52
wood and steel
127 x 30.4 x 30.4 cm.
Courtesy Robert Miller Gallery, New York

Claude Cahun

Self-Portrait, 1919
gelatin silver print
23.8 x 18 cm.
Private Collection, Paris

Self-Portrait, 1925
vintage gelatin silver print
20 x 16 in.
Collection Leslie Tonkonow, New York

Self-Portrait, 1929
gelatin silver print on carte-postal stock
5 3/8 x 3 1/2 in. (framed 21 1/8 x 18 in.)
Private Collection, New York

Aveux non avenus VI, 1929–30
photomontage
6 x 4 in. (framed 19 1/2 x 15 1/2 in.)
Collection Helen Kornblum,

St. Louis, Missouri
L'humanité (Poupée), 1936
gelatin silver print
21.2 x 16.2 cm. (framed 27.2 x 23.4 cm.)
Sackner Archive of Concrete and Visual Poetry, Miami Beach, Florida

Emily Carr

Vanquished, 1930
oil on canvas
92 x 129 cm. (framed 105.5 x 142.9 cm.)
Vancouver Art Gallery, Emily Carr Trust

Forest, British Columbia, 1932
oil on canvas
130 x 86.8 cm.
(framed 148.3 x 104.5 cm.)
Vancouver Art Gallery, Emily Carr Trust

Theresa Hak Kyung Cha

Passages Paysages, 1978
three-channel videotape
10 min
University Art Museum, University of California at Berkeley; Gift of the Theresa Hak Kyung Cha Memorial Foundation

Lygia Clark

Linear Egg, 1958
nitro-cellulose paint on wood
ø 13 in.
Collection David Medalla, London

Bichos, 1960
aluminium; two pieces
ø 60 cm.; 20 x 40 x 40 cm.
Collection Gilberto Chateaubriand, Rio de Janeiro

Rubber Grubs, 1964-65
black rubber; four pieces
from 60 x 40 cm. to 70 x 100 cm. each
Family of Lygia Clark, Rio de Janeiro

Respire comigo (Breath with Me), 1966
rubber; two pieces
ø 20 cm.
Museo de Arte Moderna do Rio de Janeiro

Diálogos das Mãos (Dialogue of the Hands), 1966
elastic tape; two pieces
various dimensions
Museo de Arte Moderna do Rio de Janeiro

Pedra e Ar (Stone and Air), 1966
stone and plastic bag
irregular size approx. 15 x 15 x 15 cm.
Museo de Arte Moderna do Rio de Janeiro

Concha e Água (Water and Shells), 1966
two plastic bags, shells and rubber strings
various dimensions
Museo de Arte Moderna do Rio de Janeiro

Capacetes Sensoriais (Sensorial Helmets), 1967

wire, fiber, aromatic herbs, shells; six pieces
various dimensions
Museo de Arte Moderna do Rio de Janeiro

Máscara Abismo (Abyss Masks), 1968
net of cotton and stone
various dimesions
Museo de Arte Moderna do Rio de Janeiro

Glove and Ball, c. 1966-68
four pairs of gloves (leather, latex) and five balls
various dimensions
Museu de Arte Moderna do Rio de Janeiro

documentary video on Lygia Clark
Museu de Arte Moderna do Rio de Janeiro

Hanne Darboven

Letter and Indices to 24 Songs, 1974
16 drawings
pen and ink on vellum
16 1/2 x 11 1/2 in. each
The LeWitt Collection
Courtesy the Wadsworth Atheneum, Hartford, Connecticut

Lili Dujourie

Hommage à (I, II, IV), 1972
black and white video
16 mm film transferred to video
30 min.
Courtesy of the artist

Ellen Gallagher

Untitled, 1995
oil, graphite, and paper on canvas
84 x 71 3/4 in.
Whitney Museum of American Art, New York, gift of Charlene Engelhard

Untitled, 1995
oil, pencil, paper on canvas
84 x 72 in.
Collection Charlene Engelhard, Boston

Gego

Reticulárea cuadrada, 1971–76
mixed media
70 x 100 x 130 cm.
Collection Patricia Phelps de Cisneros, Caracas

Reticulárea, 1973-76
nylon and light steel
66 x 59 cm.
Collection Patricia Phelps de Cisneros, Caracas

Dibujo sin papel no. 11, 1978
galvanized steel net and enamel
37.9 x 40.5 x 2.5 cm.
Fundación Gego, Caracas

Dibujo sin papel no. 2, 1979
bronze, steel and metallic thread
59 x 56 x 3.5 cm.
Fundación Gego, Caracas

487

Didujo sin papel no. 6, 1979
iron, steel, thread and metallic screws
41 x 34.6 cm.
Fundación Gego, Caracas

Dibujo sin papel no. 18, 1979
steel and metallic thread
35.7 x 37 cm.
Fundación Gego, Caracas

Dibujo sin papel no. 5A, 1983
galvanized net, iron and wire
47.5 x 40 x 8 cm.
Fundación Gego, Caracas

Dibujo sin papel no. 7, 1983
iron and enameled wire
ø 31 cm.
Fundación Gego, Caracas

Bicho no.87/3, 1987
mixed media
51 x 22,5 x 10 cm.
Collection Patricia Phelps de Cisneros,
Caracas

Mona Hatoum

Recollection, 1995
site-specific installation with hair
Courtesy of the artist

Nathalie Hervieux

La première chambre de Babel, 1993
series of 23 plates
50 x 60 cm. each
Collection of the artist

Eva Hesse

Untitled, 1966
paint and cord over papier-maché on wood
19 x 19 x 10.2 cm.
The LeWitt Collection
Courtesy the Wadsworth Atheneum,
Hartford, Connecticut

Washer Table, 1967
rubber washers, wood, and metal
21 x 125.7 x 125.7 cm.
The LeWitt Collection
Courtesy the Wadsworth Atheneum,
Hartford, Connecticut

Susan Hiller

Élan, 1982
13 c-type photographs with colored ink,
blockmounted, 30 x 20 in. each
stereo soundtrack, 11 min.
overall dimensions 304.8 x 233 cm.
Courtesy Gimpel Fils, London

Hannah Höch

*Spaziergang . . . lehrreich, befreiend,
klärend*, 1919
collage on paper
12 5/8 x 10 7/8 in.
Private Collection, Des Moines, Iowa

Druckschnitt Filetgrund, c.1925
collage
approx. 19 x 20 cm.
Germanisches National Museum,
Nürnberg

Die Sängerin, 1926
photomontage
28.5 x 29 cm.
Courtesy Galerie Berinson, Berlin
Negerplastik (Negro Sculpture)
from the series *Aus einem ethnographi-
schen Museum (From an Ethnographic
Museum)*, 1929
26 x 17.5 cm.
Private Collection on laon to the
Scottish National Gallery of Modern
Art, Edinburgh

Ann Veronica Janssens

Untitled, 1994
bricks, tin foil
176 x 510 x 320 cm.
Courtesy of the artist and Micheline
Scwajzer Gallery, Antwerp.

Katarzyna Kobro

Spatial Composition, c. 1928
painted steel
60.4 x 47.9 x 25.5 cm.
Muzeum Sztuki, Lodz (Poland)

Spatial Composition 3, 1928
painted steel
40 x 64 x 40 cm.
Muzeum Sztuki, Lodz (Poland)

Spatial Composition 4, 1929
painted steel
40 x 64 x 40 cm.
Muzeum Sztuki, Lodz (Poland)

Spatial Composition 6, 1931
welded steel, painted
64 x 25 x 15 cm.
Muzeum Sztuki, Lodz (Poland)

Yayoi Kusama

Bronze Coat, c. 1962
mixed media
106.7 x 88.9 x 7.6 cm.
Collection Richard Castellane, Esq.,
Hubbardsville, New York

The Hat, c. 1962
27.9 x 76.2 x 38.1 cm.
Collection Richard Castellane, Esq.,
Hubbardsville, New York

Silver Coat, c. 1962
mixed media
106.7 x 88.9 x 7.6 cm.
Collection Richard Castellane, Esq.,
Hubbardsville, New York

Bracha Lichtenberg Ettinger

Matrixial Borderline, 1990–91
India ink, pencil, pastel, and photocopy
on paper; plexiglass
polyptych, 4 panels with 25 elements
160 x 35 cm. each
Courtesy of the artist

Autistwork no. 1, 1993
oil and photocopy on paper mounted on
canvas
32.5 x 28 cm. (framed 43.5 x 37.5 cm.)
Courtesy of the artist

Autistwork no. 3, 1993
oil and photocopy on paper mounted on
canvas
31 x 27 cm. (framed 40.5 x 36.7 cm.)
Courtesy of the artist

Autistwork no. 4, 1993–94
oil and photocopy on paper mounted on
canvas
43 x 26.7 cm. (framed 52.5 x 36.3 cm.)
The Israel Museum, Jerusalem

Autistwork no. 5, 1993-94
oil and photocopy on paper mounted on
canvas
42.4 x 26.4 cm. (framed 52.6 x 36.7 cm.)
Collection Christine Buci-Glucksmann,
Paris

Autistwork no. 9, 1993–94
oil and photocopy on paper mounted on
canvas
28.4 x 25.5 cm. (framed 38.5 x 35 cm.)
Courtesy of the artist

Anna Maria Maiolino

Equalities/Differences, 1995
site-specific installation with ceramist clay
Courtesy of the artist.

Agnes Martin

Desert, 1964
oil and pencil on canvas
72 x 71 7/8 in.
Collection Richard and Roselyne Swig,
San Francisco

Ana Mendieta

Silueta Works in Mexico, 1973–77
color photograph documenting
earth/body work with sand, "Incantation
a Olokun-Yemaya"; Oaxaca (Mexico)
13 1/4 x 20 in.
Private Collection, New York
Courtesy the Estate of Ana Mendieta
and Galerie Lelong, New York

Silueta Works in Mexico, 1973–77
color photograph documenting earth/body
work with earth; Culipan Monastery
(Mexico)
20 x 13 1/4 in.
Private Collection, New York
Courtesy the Estate of Ana Mendieta
and Galerie Lelong, New York

Silueta Works in Mexico, 1973–77
color photograph documenting earth/body
work with sand, water, flowers;
Salina Cruz (Mexico)
13 1/4 x 20 in.
Private Collection, New York
Courtesy the Estate of Ana Mendieta
and Galerie Lelong, New York

Silueta Works in Mexico, 1973–77
color photograph documenting earth/body
work with pigment at pre-Columbian ruin
site; Monte Albán, Oaxaca (Mexico)
20 x 13 1/4 in.
Private Collection, New York
Courtesy the Estate of Ana Mendieta
and Galerie Lelong, New York

Silueta Works in Iowa, 1976–78
color photograph documenting earth/body
work with water, moss, mud; Iowa
20 x 13 1/4 in.
Courtesy the Estate of Ana Mendieta
and Galerie Lelong, New York

Silueta Works in Iowa, 1976–78
color photograph documenting earth/body
work with tree and flowers; Iowa
13 1/4 x 20 in.
Courtesy the Estate of Ana Mendieta
and Galerie Lelong, New York

Silueta Works in Iowa, 1976–78
color photograph documenting
earth/body work with carved earth at
riverbank; Old Man's Creek, Iowa
13 1/4 x 20 in.
Courtesy the Estate of Ana Mendieta
and Galerie Lelong, New York

video of Ana Mendieta's performances,
1973-80
Courtesy the Estate of Ana Mendieta
and Galerie Lelong, New York

Avis Newman

Webs (Backlight) IV, 1994–95
acrylic, graphite, and pigment on linen
254 x 254 cm.
Courtesy Lisson Gallery, London

Carol Rama

Gli scopini (Opera no. 7), 1937
watercolor on paper
17.5 x 25 cm. (framed 55 x 70.5 cm.)
Private Collection, Turin

Opera no. 9, 1938
watercolor on paper
50 x 34 cm. (framed 90 x 77 cm.)
Private Collection, Turin

Opera no. 27, 1939
watercolor on paper
44.5 x 26 cm. (framed 67 x 44.5 cm.)
Collection Anna Garis, Turin

Opera no. 18 (Dentiere), 1939
watercolor on paper
34.5 x 29 cm. (framed 88 x 68 cm.)
Collection Andrea and Paolo Accornero,
Turin

Le palette, 1940
watercolor on paper
13.7 x 25.8 cm.
(framed 36.5 x 44.5 cm.)
Private Collection, Turin

Opera no. 34, 1940
watercolor on paper
50 x 33.5 cm.
(framed 92 x 71 cm.)
Collection Andrea and Paolo Accornero,
Turin

Appassionata, 1940
watercolor on paper
41.5 x 30.5 cm.
(framed 68.5 x 59.5 cm.)
Galleria Civica d'Arte Moderna e
Contemporanea, Turin

Appassionata, 1940
watercolor on paper
23 x 33 cm.
(framed 51.5 x 59.5 cm.)
Galleria Civica d'Arte Moderna e
Contemporanea, Turin

Opera no. 54, 1941
watercolor on paper
48 x 33 cm.
(framed 82 x 66.5 cm.)
Collection Andrea and Paolo Accornero,
Turin

Martha Rosler

Balloons
from the series *Bringing the War Home*,
1967-72
photomontage
13 1/4 x 10 1/4 in.
Courtesy of the artist and Jay Gorney
Modern Art, New York

Cleaning the Drapes
from the series *Bringing the War Home*,
1967-72
photomontage
14 x 10 1/4 in.
Courtesy of the artist and Jay Gorney
Modern Art, New York

House Beautiful/Giacometti
from the series *Bringing the War Home*,
1967-72
photomontage
9 1/4 x 12 1/8 in.
Courtesy of the artist and Jay Gorney
Modern Art, New York

Patio View
from the series *Bringing the War Home*,
1967-72
photomontage
11 3/4 x 9 3/8 in.
Courtesy of the artist and Jay Gorney
Modern Art, New York

Red Stripe Kitchen
from the series *Bringing the War Home*,
1967-72
photomontage
11 x 14 in.
Courtesy of the artist and Jay Gorney
Modern Art, New York

Roadside Ambush
from the series *Bringing the War Home*,
1967-72
photomontage
14 x 17 5/8 in.
Courtesy of the artist and Jay Gorney
Modern Art, New York

Tron (Amputee)
from the series *Bringing the War Home*,
1967-72
photomontage
11 x 14 in.
Courtesy of the artist and Jay Gorney
Modern Art, New York

Semiotics of the Kitchen, 1975
black and white video
6:09 min.
Electronic Arts Intermix, New York

*Vital Statistics of a Citizen Simply
Obtained*, 1977
color video
39:20 min.
Electronic Arts Intermix, New York

Charlotte Salomon

Prelude, 1940-42
from *Leben? oder Theatre? (Life? or
Theater?)*
51 gouaches, 47 transparencies
32 x 25 cm.; 25 x 32.5 cm.
Jewish Historical Museum, Amsterdam

Mira Schendel

Trenzinho (Little Train), 1964
paper strip with rope
23 x 47 x 5 cm.
Collection Ada Schendel Bento, Rio de
Janeiro

Droghuinas, 1965
knotted rice paper
ø 30 cm.
Collection Guy Brett, London

Untitled, 1968
Objetos gráphicos
ink on paper between acrylic plates
100 x 100 cm.
Collection Konrad Gromholt,
Hovikodden, Norway

Untitled, 1968
Objetos gráphicos
ink on paper between acrylic plates
100 x 100 cm.
Courtesy Henie-Onstad Art Center,
Hovikodden, Norway

Lynn Silverman

Untitled (94.47.12), 1994
black and white photograph
36 x 47 3/4 in.
Courtesy of the artist

Untitled (95.4.12), 1995
black and white photograph
36 x 47 3/4 in.
Courtesy of the artist

Nancy Spero

Codex Artaud VI, 1971
typewriter and painted collage on paper
22 1/2 x 127 in.
Courtesy Jack Tilton Gallery, New York,
and P.P.O.W., New York

Codex Artaud VIII, 1971
typewriter and painted collage on paper
21 x 103.5 in.
Courtesy Jack Tilton Gallery, New York,
and P.P.O.W., New York

Bodycount, 1974
handprinting and drawing on paper
112 x 21 in.
Courtesy Jack Tilton Gallery, New York,
and P.P.O.W., New York

Stalks I, 1974
handprinting and painted collage on
paper

94 1/2 x 21 in.
Courtesy Jack Tilton Gallery, New York,
and P.P.O.W., New York

Jana Sterbak

Condition, 1995
black and white video in collaboration
with Ana Torfs
7 min.
Courtesy of the artists and Kanaal Art
Foundation, Kortrijk (Belgium)

Sophie Taeuber-Arp

Echelonnement, 1934
oil on canvas
65 x 50 cm.
Stiftung Hans Arp und Sophie Taeuber-
Arp e.V., Rolandseck (Germany)

Composition dans un cercle blanc,
(Composition in a White Circle), 1936
relief, painted wood
ø 49 cm. x 4 cm. high
Stiftung Hans Arp und Sophie Taeuber-
Arp e.V., Rolandseck (Germany)

Relief circulaire en trois coupes
(Circular Reliëf in Three Layers), 1936
painted wood
ø 60 cm. x 6 cm. high
Stiftung Hans Arp und Sophie Taeuber-
Arp e.V., Rolandseck (Germany)

Envol, 1937
relief, painted wood
ø 60 cm. x 3 cm. high
Stiftung Hans Arp und Sophie Taeuber-
Arp e.V., Rolandseck (Germany)

Collage à éléments d'objets, 1938
collage
45.7 x 34.8 cm.
Stiftung Hans Arp und Sophie Taeuber-
Arp e.V., Rolandseck, (Germany)

Mouvements de ligne, 1940
pencil on paper
34.6 x 26.3 cm.
Stiftung Hans Arp und Sophie Taeuber-
Arp e.V., Rolandseck (Germany)

Mouvements de ligne en couleur, 1940
pencil on paper
35.9 x 28 cm.
Stiftung Hans Arp und Sophie Taeuber-
Arp e.V., Rolandseck (Germany)

Mouvements de ligne en couleur, 1940
pencil on paper
26.5 x 34.8 cm.
Private Collection

Mouvements de ligne en couleur, 1940
pencil on paper
26.5 x 34.8 cm.
Private Collection

Nadine Tasseel

Untitled (Self-Portraits), 1992
black and white photographs on
barite-papers
56.5 x 48; 50 x 50 cm.
(framed 61 x 48 cm.)
Courtesy of the artist

Ana Torfs

Condition, 1995
black and white video
in collaboration with Jana Sterbak
7 min.
Courtesy of the artists and Kanaal Art
Foundation, Kortrijk (Belgium)

Joëlle Tuerlinckx

Liquid Vision, 1994
site-specific installation
table, cloth, buckets, water, slide projector
Courtesy of the artist

Cecilia Vicuña

Winay Rutusqua
Tejer en Tiempo Quebrado, 1996
(Weaving in Broken Time)
site-specific installation
Courtesy of the artist

Precarious Objects, 1977–80
mixed-media
Courtesy of the artist

Maria Helena Vieira da Silva

Composition, 1936
oil on canvas
81 x 100 cm. (framed 84 x 103.5 cm.)
Fundação Calouste Gulbenkian, Centro
de Arte Moderna José de Azeredo
Perdigão, Lisbon

Normandie, 1949
gouache on canvas
40 x 47 cm. (framed 43 x 50 cm.)
Courtesy Galerie Jeanne-Bucher, Paris

Carrie Mae Weems

The Apple of Adam's Eye, 1993
folding screen
Australian lacewood frame with pigment
and silk embroidery on sateen
73 x 81 x 1 3/4 in.
Courtesy of the artist and P.P.O.W.,
New York

From the Very Beginning, 1995
leather, wood, and audio component
3–5 narrative/music boxes
13 3/4 x 5 3/4 x 5 3/4 each
Courtesy of the artist and P.P.O.W.,
New York

Francesca Woodman

Space², *Providence*, 1975–76
Italy, Rome, 1977–78
Providence, 1975-76
Space², *Providence*, 1975–76
House #3
Polkadots
Italy, Rome, 1977–78
Italy, Antella, 1978
New York, 1979–80

gelatin silver prints
printed on 8 x 10 in. paper
Courtesy George & Betty Woodman,
New York

Index